A HISTORY OF
THE ANGLO-AMERICAN COMMON LAW OF CONTRACT

Recent Titles in
Contributions in Legal Studies

Truman's Court: A Study in Judicial Restraint
Frances Howell Rudko

The Gladsome Light of Jurisprudence: Learning the Law in England and the United States in the 18th and 19th Centuries
Michael H. Hoeflich, editor and compiler

James Madison on the Constitution and the Bill of Rights
Robert J. Morgan

Lawyers, Courts, and Professionalism: The Agenda for Reform
Rudolph J. Gerber

John Marshall's Achievement: Law, Politics, and Constitutional Interpretations
Thomas C. Shevory, editor

Affirmative Action and Principles of Justice
Kathanne W. Greene

Unfounded Fears: Myths and Realities of a Constitutional Convention
Paul J. Weber and Barbara Perry

Protecting Constitutional Freedoms: A Role for Federal Courts
Daan Braveman

The Employment Relationship in Anglo-American Law: A Historical Perspective
Marc Linder

The Aristocracy of the Long Robe
J.M. Sosin

Equal Separation: Understanding the Religion Clauses of the First Amendment
Paul J. Weber, editor

Common Law in Southern Africa: Conflict of Laws and Torts Precedents
Peter B Kutner

A HISTORY OF THE ANGLO-AMERICAN COMMON LAW OF CONTRACT

Kevin M. Teeven

Contributions in Legal Studies, Number 59
Paul L. Murphy, Series Editor

Greenwood Press
New York • Westport, Connecticut • London

Library of Congress Cataloging-in-Publication Data

Teeven, Kevin M.
A history of the Anglo-American common law of contract / Kevin M. Teeven.
p. cm. — (Contributions in legal studies, ISSN 0147–1074 ; no. 59)
Includes bibliographical references.
ISBN 0–313–26151–2 (lib. bdg. : alk. paper)
1. Contracts—United States—History. 2. Contracts—Great Britain—History. I. Title. II. Series.
KF801.T43 1990
346.73′02′09—dc20
[347.306209] 90–2931

British Library Cataloguing in Publication Data is available.

Library of Congress Catalog Card Number: 90-2931
ISBN: 0-313-26151-2
ISSN: 0147-1074

First published in 1990

Greenwood Press, 88 Post Road West, Westport, CT 06881
An imprint of Greenwood Publishing Group, Inc.

Printed in the United States of America

The paper used in this book complies with the Permanent Paper Standard issued by the National Information Standards Organization (Z39.48-1984).

10 9 8 7 6 5 4 3 2 1

To Edward and Geraldine Teeven

CONTENTS

INTRODUCTION

When I set out on this project, my objectives were twofold: one, to provide a study of the development of the common law of contract, and to a much lesser degree, of commercial law, which would run straight through from Plantagenet days to the present, and, secondly, to make available an accurate history which is of interest to legal historians and is also readable generally by American and English lawyers and law students. On the first score, although much has been written both about the English story up to the first half of the nineteenth century and about American developments, particularly during the nineteenth century, my intent is to provide a comparatively detailed analysis of the full sweep of the evolution of the common law of contract from Henry II's reign (d. 1189) to the 800th anniversary of Henry II's death in the American present. As to the second objective, it had struck me that as a consequence of the spare writing style of many legal histories, especially regarding the archaic aspects of the events prior to the nineteenth century, there is typically inadequate background provided to enable the great majority of the legal profession to fully follow the analysis. I have striven for both technical accuracy and sufficient explication so that the result is understandable, albeit with some effort, by those common law lawyers and students motivated to learn about the history of the common law of contract, a microcosm of the development of the common law itself.

In writing a general legal history today, one must contend with the great diversity of interpretations and methodologies employed by modern legal historians. There are several approaches employed by legal historians in explaining the development of the common law. One view is that the common law possesses internal intellectual demands for legal reasoning which guide the direction the law takes; some modern American writers refer to this phenomenon as the autonomous nature of the law. A second view is that the common law is a reflection of social and economic forces and is thus responsive in the particular to the conditions of the day. Still another view is that the law can play an ideological role wherein the powerful repress the oppressed and also persuade them that their conditions are just under the guise of emotive slogans such as freedom of contract and rugged individualism.

Because of these varying viewpoints, there is bound to be disagreement since hard choices must be made. The approach employed in this study is that it is not all one way or the other: the common law primarily has an autonomous intellectual nature but that autonomy has been overridden during pivotal periods in response to dramatic social and economic changes, e.g., the transition from feudalism to capitalism and the industrial age pressures for a general welfare state. Indeed, in both the common law and Continental civil law, the two legal systems created in post-Roman Europe, Weber points out two fundamental instances of the relative autonomy of both systems from economic forces: one, the high rationality of civil law came from medieval university interest in Roman law rather than from later capitalistic developments, and, two, England developed a highly capitalistic economy earlier than on the Continent without taking on the high degree of rationality found on the Continent (*see* 1954 Rheinstein ed., p. 318). Even when external pressures ineluctably force change in a historical system like the common law, the common law requires that modifications be justified by reference to its intellectual system in order to rationalize overcoming doctrinal obstacles through such devices as analogy, implication and sheer fiction.

Thus the law has an intellectual as well as a social and economic history. Social and economic history cannot, however, provide an explanation of how a new rule developed. It is not an explanation to simply say that change occurred because of either social conditions or mercantile necessity; rather the legal historian must analyze how lawyers and judges accomplished the doctrinal modifications within the confines of the intellectual system. Since the 1950s, there has been a trend among some legal and social historians to develop organizing theories which sometimes precede the evidence and in the process either overlook doctrine not supporting their thesis or assume the very matters which lawyers studying the historical development of their discipline investigate and analyze.

As a final comment on the autonomous and contextual aspects of the development of the common law, a point should be made about the degree of each influence on the growth of the common law over the various phases of the 800–year time span covered in this book. Generally speaking, prior to the mid-sixteenth century, the common law was more independent of social and economic forces than it was later. The medieval period was concerned with retention of the status quo and had not witnessed dramatic changes like those occurring during the Tudor era. Furthermore, the role and interest of the royal courts was much narrower earlier; what accommodation was necessary in contract law during the Middle Ages in responding to changing conditions was more commonly accomplished by local and mercantile courts and by Equity. Then when common law courts began to usurp these competing courts' jurisdiction during the Tudor economic boom and during the constitutional struggles of the seventeenth century, external conditions would from time to time force common law rationalization of accommodating doctrinal modification. From the eighteenth century onward, the pressure for common law responsiveness would further increase due to a more pronounced upsurge in commerce and due to the emergence of industry. The decrease in the autonomy of the common law in the modern period is reflected in this study; whereas the pre-Renaissance period was more impervious to manipulation of doctrine in response to external forces than it would be during the subsequent modern period.

This history of the common law of contract is somewhat unique in breaking down the chapter-by-chapter coverage along chronological rather than topical lines. This approach was selected because it allows a glimpse at the state of the law for the lawyers and parties involved in a given epoch and it also assists in reflecting the felt needs of an era when an issue arose. An additional reason for the chronological approach is that it facilitates the transition from analysis of earlier English developments to later American ones. There has been an attempt to place the development of a topic which overlaps more than one period in the chapter where the principle firmly took root; one of the major exceptions to this rule of thumb is the doctrine of consideration since it will be a recurring issue in chapters from the sixteenth century onward. A few other topics' full evolution do not neatly fall in a single period covered by a chapter, and in those cases the discussion of a topic, which is placed in a given chapter, may overlap prior periods in tracing its early development and may also overlap later periods in following subsequent elaboration; an example of such overlap occurs in the discussion of warranties in the chapter on the English eighteenth century.

The focus of this study shifts from the English to American developments after the American Revolution, though in fact the nineteenth century story is really a mix of American and English developments because of the continued influence of the then advanced English commercial law. Subsequent to the onset of the American industrial revolution, the emphasis becomes more exclusively American; there is, however, the inclusion of comparisons with English approaches and also analysis of points of departure on each side of the Atlantic during the past century.

Finally, there are many individuals whose support and encouragement aided me in continuing over the long haul of completing this work. First and foremost, I want to express my sincere gratitude to Mrs. Mary Lu Reither for her tireless and cheerful assistance during the past couple of years in typing the manuscript and revisions thereto; in particular, she had to endure the frustration of working from transatlantic transmittals of drafts during one of those years when I was doing research in England. At the risk of inadvertently overlooking someone, I also want to express my appreciation to the following individuals: Fred Fry, Jewel Gray, Richard I. Hartman, Jonathan Miller and Luigi Solivetti. My appreciation is also extended to the following institutions: Bradley University, the British Library, London House Trust, the University of Illinois Law Library and the University of London's Institute of Advanced Legal Studies.

Kevin M. Teeven

A HISTORY OF THE ANGLO-AMERICAN COMMON LAW OF CONTRACT

CHAPTER 1

EARLY ACTIONS (1200–1400)

The tortuous route taken in shaping a law of contract by evading the impediments of the ancient remedies, yet paying partial obeisance to them, has left its scars on the contract law of today. Indeed, many of the rules of present day contract can only be explained by looking to their historical origins. By 1400, the end of the period covered in this chapter, a modern theory of contract law still had not developed, but the groundwork had been laid.

During the Middle Ages, property was not "owned" in the modern sense and so could not be freely contracted for. The economy of that time was not influenced to any significant degree by market forces, and experience shows that a market economy often plays a decisive role in the actionability of forward-looking contractual relations.[1] In circumstances where an economy is not directed by market forces and where a society delineates a person's rights based on the status one was born into, there is little need of, nor opportunity for, either freedom of contract or a flexible contractual device for planning. In the main, these early contractual relations did not involve obligations to be performed in the future but rather concerned present exchanges of feudal obligations without any money changing hands. The contract law of the Middle Ages was concerned with security and retention of the status quo rather than with novel trade agreements.

Judicial Administration

Although there were a variety of courts hearing contract disputes during the thirteenth and fourteenth centuries, hindsight shows that the royal courts were to become the most important since it was there that the ultimate development of a modern law of contract occurred. Glanvill mentions two royal courts in the twelfth century: the court of the king in the exchequer and the court of the king in the eyres. The court in the eyres went out on the circuit at least every seven years and dealt with enforcement of the financial rights of the crown and additionally with disputes of private subjects, called "common pleas". The eyres were feared by the populace because of the financial demands made and were too infrequent to be a dependable mechanism in adjudicating common pleas. Due to the irregularity of eyres, common pleas were also heard by local courts and before the person of the king (*coram rege*) when the king travelled across the countryside or before the "Bench" in Westminster whenever he was on the continent. It was expensive, not to mention inconvenient, to follow the King's Bench around if one was involved in a case before it; consequently, the barons received a concession in the Great Charter of 1215 that there would be a court for common pleas and that the court would be held at a "fixed place".[2] In time that fixed place became Westminster Hall, and it continued to be the venue into the nineteenth century. During the latter part of the reign of Henry III (1216–1272), the hearing of common pleas by writ was regularized before a court later called Common Pleas.

There were other courts doing contract work during the Middle Ages, and the practices in these courts would influence the law applied in the royal courts. A brief look will be given to the most important classes of courts handling contract matters: local courts, mercantile courts, the Court of Chancery and church courts. Starting with local courts, actions in the local county and borough courts, some of pre-Conquest origin, were often more flexible than the constraints placed on royal courts by the requirement of a writ from Chancery. Two important contractual actions at the local level were informal covenant and debt. The royal courts adopted the local informal covenant during Glanvill's day during the last quarter of the twelfth century, but it became ritualistic in Common Pleas in the fourteenth century with the requirement of a seal. Royal courts were familiar with local court rules because of the right of a party to remove a case to the royal courts and because writs of error from local court proceedings went to the royal courts. The influence of local courts' practices on the royal courts can be seen in the appearance of similar actions in the royal courts subsequent to their appearance in county courts and in city courts. County court covenant actions were just mentioned, and county debt and trespass actions will be discussed later. Borough and city courts, like the London Mayor's Court, provided consumer protection against shoddy workmanship by those engaged in "common callings", as smiths and surgeons, before similar trespassory actions appeared in the royal courts.[3]

During the heyday of county courts in the thirteenth century, they were an integral part of a unified English judicial system wherein there was considerable similarity between the practices of the local courts and the common law courts.[4] But then a decline of the county courts began in the fourteenth century. One reason for the decline was the way the 1278 Statute of Gloucester's 40 shilling rule was misconstrued to force Debt actions over 40 shillings into the royal courts even though the explicit statutory language only applied to trespass.[5] A second reason for the decline was the bias and corruption at the local level prompting Chancery writs of prohibition and writs of error. And a third reason for the decline was the right of removal by either party as a matter of course by the end of the fourteenth century. Royal court intrusion was partially due to concern about bias in favor of the local lord but it was also a blatant expropriation of business by the royal courts.[6]

Turning to mercantile courts, the piepowder courts applied European-wide mercantile custom, known as law merchant, to disputes between merchants on-the-spot at the international trade fairs. At these proceedings, merchants attending would declare what the relevant law merchant was; this practice would later be adopted by common law courts, first by using special merchant jury verdicts and later by judicial notice of mercantile custom. Law merchant stressed flexible informality, and, in contrast to the exchange-oriented common law, mercantile courts heard important transactions in a money economy and they recognized a variety of devices for transmitting credit. The thirteenth century model for law merchant came from Italian traders who resuscitated Roman commercial law rediscoverd as a result of trade with the Byzantine Empire. International trade fairs reached their zenith in England around the year 1300; then, as English merchants took over the buying and selling of such staple goods as wool by the mid-fourteenth century, the trade fairs fell off and with it went the dominance of Italian merchants. Thereafter royal courts of the Staple and of Admiralty replaced the piepowder courts. By the sixteenth century, courts of the Staple were in decline since wool was now made into cloth in England, rather than being sold to Flemish weavers at the staple ports, and the cloth was sold by "merchant adventurers" on the Continent. The court of Admiralty experienced an upsurge in importance in the sixteenth century, however, thanks to Tudor emphasis on the royal navy. Furthermore, there was a complementary renewal of interest in Roman law during the Renaissance. Admiralty would then lose out to its competitive common law adversary in the seventeenth century. The success of the mercantile courts was a part of the reason that the competitive King's Bench allowed the action of Assumpsit to grow during the sixteenth century in order to claim some of the expanding commercial business for itself.[7] The law merchant would not be completely absorbed into the common law, however, until the eighteenth century under Lord Mansfield.

The Court of Chancery was headed by the Chancellor, whose office also issued writs enabling common law courts to hear cases. The Court of Chancery became active in the fourteenth century both in hearing grievances falling through the cracks of a now limited common law writ system and in ameliorating some of the hardships of the common law. The inadequacies inherent in the common law courts' writ system, restrictive pleading and process, wager of law and embryonic trial by jury made Chancery a busy court by the fifteenth century. Again, the competitive sixteenth century King's Bench encouraged the use of Assumpsit to corral some of this business.[8] There will be further analysis of Chancery's contract work and its influence on the common law in the ensuing chapters.

Church courts administered the Roman-based canon law (*lex ecclesiastica*); they had been prohibited from hearing temporal debts by the twelfth century, though they did handle debts indirectly by punishing the defaultor's sin of a breach of faith under the action of *fidei laesio*. *Fidei laesio* reached its zenith around 1500 and then declined to extinction during the next half century of anti-clericism. Statistics indicate that this business was being taken over by the action of Assumpsit before the King's Bench, and a study of King's Bench pleading forms suggests a borrowing from *fidei laesio*.[9]

Returning now to the royal courts' contract work, since common pleas could not come before the royal courts unless a writ was issued, a study of the writ system, which developed between the time of Henry II (1154–1189) and Edward I (1272–1307), is a study of the framework within which the common law operated into the nineteenth century.[10] The usual forum for pleas that the king had no interest in was in the local courts, and so the special permission of a writ was required in order to bring a common plea before a royal court. At first the royal courts were an extraordinary forum to apply to. Permission to appear there was a royal favor granted by the king in the form of a writ. The requirement of the writ for such extraordinary business made sense in the era of Glanvill (d. 1190), but it was to have an unwelcome effect on the development of the common law in later eras. By the middle of the thirteenth century, the Court of Common Pleas was regularly hearing private disputes and had control of royal court jurisdiction over the personal actions of Debt, Detinue, Covenant and Account, and entry could only be gained with a writ issued by the Chancellor. The writ system provided order to common law actions for the next seven centuries. During the thirteenth century, Bracton, the greatest Medieval legal writer, had said: "there will be as many formulas for writs as there are kinds of actions".[11] A new writ could thus be invented for new wrongs.[12] However, the inventiveness of the Chancery clerks was soon halted by the jealous barons, who perceived the expanding jurisdiction of the royal courts to be an erosion of their own feudal judicial power.

In a continuation of their losing battle against the demise of feudalism, and as a continuation of the tactics used in the Great Charters, the barons, in what was later called the "Mad Parliament,"[13] demanded some changes in exchange for a loosening of the purse strings for Henry III's expensive wars on the continent, which changes are known as the Provisions of Oxford (1258). Among other provisions, this Statute prohibited Chancery from creating any new writs. Although this Statute did not result in an immediate termination of novel writs out of Chancery, it became accepted practice by the end of the thirteenth century that the Chancery clerks would issue a writ only if the plaintiff's cause of action fit within one of the existing writ formulae in the Register of Writs. Plaintiffs were forced to engage in fictions and the twisting of reality in their complaints in order to fit within an existing formula that would allow the issuance of a writ; perversion of archaic mechanisms was necessary to solve more modern problems. Maitland said that by the death of Edward I "the forms are given, the cause of action must be deduced therefrom."[14]

With this background, an analysis of Medieval contract law can begin. In order for a modern law of contract to develop, it had to grow within the parameters of the writ system and the property-based nature of most early actions. The two primary writs available to contract litigants in the thirteenth century were Covenant and Debt.[15] The contrivances which the plaintiff and the courts engaged in during the next three centuries is a necessary part of the story of the evolution of contract law and is an historical explanation for certain features of contract law today.

The personal actions of Covenant, Debt, Detinue and Account were *praecipe* writs, a *praecipe* writ being a demand for a right.[16] The sheriff was to deliver it to the defendant and to order him to satisfy the plaintiff's claim; if the defendant failed to comply, the defendant was summoned to court. The study in this chapter will begin with these old writs before proceeding to the emergence of Assumpsit for misfeasance. These writs' lives were in the Middle Ages, but the ways in which they were circumvented by trespass actions has left traces in the law today.[17]

Personal Actions[18]

The writ of Covenant is one of the oldest actions in the king's court and older still in the local courts. It was once thought that the writ began to protect lessees for years of land, but it's now clear that it was used for a variety of subject matter by the early thirteenth century.[19] Yet many of the early cases did deal with land and were loosely based on breach of a promissory obligation. The writ of Covenant (*conventio*) was directed to the Court of Common Pleas and meant simply agreement. It is the closest that the old writs came to the modern meaning of contract; it was the action for the breach of an executory promise to do something in the future. The remedy in Covenant was at first specific performance but was later converted to damages.

During the thirteenth century there was an acceptance of Covenant actions in the royal courts without a sealed deed—provided the plaintiff could otherwise prove the transaction, as by producing "suit" through the testimony of reliable witnesses. The question arises why unsealed covenants were no longer accepted in the royal courts by the early fourteenth century. The argument that the effectiveness of good suit broke down doesn't seem convincing since it continued to function in Debt. Moreover, the explanation that the royal courts were trying to limit their caseload seems to miss the mark when there were so few Covenant actions coming to the royal courts.[20] Two other explanations seem more plausible. One is that by at least 1280, pleaders acknowledged that a change had occurred for land leases since a sealed covenant was required there; this theory continues that since most covenant cases involved land leases, the requirement was casually transmuted to apply to any covenant by the turn of the fourteenth century.[21] The alternative theory is that the sealed covenant requirement came to the royal courts via the circuitous route of Chancery *justicies* writs; *justicies* writs sent sealed covenant actions to the county courts, when the county courts had the capacity to hear them, and then some of those same actions would end up being removed from the county courts to Common Pleas. This theory holds that since these removed covenants were sealed, the royal courts became accustomed to viewing the seal as an evidentiary requirement.[22] Whichever explanation ultimately proves correct—keeping in mind there is often more than one reason for a change in the common law—it was a fact that the unsealed covenant cases in the royal courts were drying up by the beginning of the fourteenth century. Nevertheless there were still a sprinkling of unsealed covenant cases as late as 1321 and perhaps 1330; there are indications that these are trespass cases dressed up as covenants in order to avoid the requirement of showing force in trespass actions. After 1330, however, these unsealed covenant actions were not attempted in the royal courts,[23] no matter how inconvenient; formal covenants now went to Common Pleas and informal covenants went to the local courts. So in the 1321 *Case of the Waltham Carrier,* the plaintiff complained that you cannot be required to put a simple covenant for a load of hay in writing. But Herle, J. responded: "And for a cartload of hay we shall not undo the law. Covenant is nothing other than the assent of the parties, which lies in specialty."[24]

The local courts did not demand a sealed instrument even into the latter part of the fifteenth century.[25] Thus the populace did have a remedy for informal agreements in the Middle Ages, assuming the parties lived in a jurisdiction with an effective local court, which was not always the case. Those impotent local courts had been one of the historical reasons for plaintiffs seeking to obtain royal relief, but Covenant was not an effective remedy in the royal courts due to Covenant's excessively formal requirements. In those few local courts that remained effective into the late medieval period, informal covenant was still actionable, but the fall of the value of money ended what remained since even Covenant actions over 40 shillings were now forced to the royal courts where a sealed specialty was required. The formalistic requirements of Covenant ultimately developed into an archaic ritual which had to be religiously adhered to in order to obtain relief. Additional limitations under Covenant included its unavailability for promises to pay money or to deliver goods, and it couldn't be used for a poor or a tardy performance. This inflexibility made it an unpopular and infrequently used writ. Instead of using Covenant, the plaintiff tried to use the writ of Debt when possible. Indeed, when there was seemingly a covenant to pay a definite sum or chattels, it was deemed a grant and the obligation could only be brought in Debt.[26]

The second group of personal actions are under the action of Debt, which became available as a matter of course even earlier than Covenant. Debt actions were referred to as "debt-detinue" by Glanvill because initially there was no differentiation between an action of Debt or an action of Detinue. In Debt the plaintiff was not enforcing a promise but was demanding restitution of the very thing belonging to the plaintiff which the defendant was wrongfully withholding, whether it be money or chattels. In the twelfth century there was no difference between a plaintiff demanding of the defendant 20 shillings or a bushel of wheat. The first sign of a difference appears in the thirteenth century when it became an established rule that Debt would lie for money and unascertained goods and Detinue would lie for the return of a specific chattel.[27] Debt actions fell under Debt *sur obligation* and Debt *sur contract*.

The action Debt *sur obligation* represented the greatest number of cases appearing in the Medieval plea rolls. The plaintiff using this form of action was required to produce a sealed document, referred to as a conditional (or conditioned) bond, in order to sustain his burden of proof. The conditional bond was the most common type of document under this action. Since the existence of a debt meant there was a present obligation arising from a grant and a covenant was to be performed in the future, it would seem logical that Debt could not be used for a promise to pay money in the future; nevertheless, conditioned bonds were used for that purpose. It was the form of agreement used by business-like individuals because it was the easiest to enforce in the royal courts. When the plaintiff proffered the bond to the jury, the question of proof was excluded since the bond was dispositive of the issue of the defendant's obligation. Parole evidence of payment was excluded, as was evidence later on that there was no consideration to support the obligation; only fundamental defenses, as forgery or illiteracy, were allowed.

The common conditional bond was executed in twice the amount of the obligation, the bond being subject to defeasance if the obligation was satisfied; however, if it was not satisfied, then plaintiff could pray for the penal amount, though by at least the eighteenth century the courts would only allow recovery for the amount of the obligation.[28] The defendant could not plead that he had already paid the obligation unless he could produce a sealed acquittance. Thus if he paid and failed to obtain an acquittance, he would be required to pay twice—a harsh, but predictable, result. Later it was ruled that if the plaintiff had accepted a lesser performance in settlement of the obligation, he would have the right to sue for the differential, unless he had received the obligation earlier than the due date or received something different, as a cow instead of a horse.[29]

At this juncture, it might be asked whether Covenant doesn't also fulfill the objectives of the conditional bond. The answer is in the negative for several reasons: for one, the formalities of the writing required under Debt *sur obligation* were not as stringent as under Covenant; secondly, through the use of the bond, the creditor had the opportunity to fix the amount of the liability in advance—a forerunner of liquidated damages; and, thirdly, a statute[30] was passed in 1352 extending the rigorous process of *capias,* and thereby giving the possibility of arrest, already available in Trespass, to Debt but not to Covenant.[31]

Before leaving Debt *sur obligation,* there is a somewhat related creditor's device which bears mentioning. In addition to the parties being able to document their rights and protect themselves against future contractual difficulties through the conditional bond, it was also possible for the parties to take their agreement before the court at inception for enrollment. Under this technique, known as a recognizance, the court would enter the acknowledgement on the records, which acted as a judgment enforceable by the writ of Debt.[32]

Hence there were safe, sure ways to recover for a broken obligation in the Medieval period, but these were not the normal everyday modes of entering into agreements. Debt *sur obligation,* recognizance, and similar formal obligations did not provide relief for either the merchant's or the common man's informal executory promises. The progress of the law toward enforcing informal promises is the focus of the remainder of this chapter and the next.

The most important action on an informal obligation before the seventeenth century was Debt *sur contract.* Debt *sur contract* was a very old writ possessing a number of archaic features which did not make it an ideal answer to the dilemma of finding a remedy for breach of an informal agreement. Among other limitations, Debt could not be brought if the price was not fixed at the time the contract was made, and it could not be brought if the goods were not in existence at the time the contract was made. Each debt was created not by agreement, as in Covenant, but by the defendant receiving a sum certain benefit, known as the *quid pro quo*. For example, the purchaser of a tun of wine was obligated, not because he had agreed to pay for the wine, but because he had received the wine. Therefore if the defendant had merely agreed to the transaction but had not yet received the wine, he was not obligated in Debt *sur contract,* though he would have been in Debt *sur obligation* if there had been a bond; thus executory agreements were not enforceable under Debt *sur contract.*[33] Likewise, if the defendant had acted as a guarantor for a third party purchaser receiving the wine, the defendant was not obligated because the defendant had not received the benefit (or *quid pro quo*). Debt, to the common law lawyer, was a granting of something to the plaintiff-creditor; this thing could be claimed by the plaintiff, not because of any promise made by the defendant, but because the transaction entitled the plaintiff to it. The influential archaic notion of the plaintiff's proprietary interest in what the defendant possessed is seen.[34] In modern legal theory a contract is an agreement to do something in the future, but in Debt the plaintiff was suing for the thing transferred to the debtor.

Two of Debt *sur contract's* characteristics, wager of law and *quid pro quo,* bear analysis because of their impact on the later action of Assumpsit. Local courts first used the action of Debt and its attendant proof of wager of law. In Medieval England wager of law was the normal mode of proof in an action of Debt. It had long been recognized that the defendant had an ancient right to wage his law; however, wager of law was unavailable if there was a sealed instrument—the seal being a Norman contribution. Anglo-Saxon wager of law favored the defendant, but by the fifteenth century defendants were choosing trial by jury more than wager perhaps because of social pressure on the honest defendant and because of the fear of the interference of Equity.[35] Wager of law was an ancient proof that developed in Anglo-Saxon days when alternative proofs such as the ordeal of fire or water were also appearing;[36] those old proofs involved an appeal to the supernatural. Debt's proof involved two steps: first there was a judgment that he must prove his case by oath—the defendant was required "to wage his law"; then on the appointed day, the defendant was to appear with his eleven oath-helpers, or compurgators, to "make his law". The oath-helpers were not called on as witnesses to the transaction, but merely to state that the defendant was a credible person.[37] The implication was that if the defendant perjured himself, he was imperilling his soul. There was not even a procedure for punishing the defendant for perjury. Hence an unscrupulous defendant could follow the ritual of wager of law, perjure himself and thus avoid liability. Wager undoubtedly made more sense when the defendant was required to make his oath in the presence of his local community before a local court or a royal court sitting during an eyre. However, once those trials were removed many miles to Westminster Hall, it was not possible for the defendant to bring eleven local compurgators with him; and consequently a tradition was begun of hiring professional oath-helpers, called "knights of the post", who hung around Westminster and probably didn't even know the defendant, much less have any knowledge about the defendant's reputation for veracity.[38] Nevertheless, it should be pointed out that some writers view wager, for all its faults, to have been a superior truth-seeking device to the nascent state of trial by jury up through the fifteenth century.[39]

If wager of law was such an irrational mode of proof, why did it continue in Debt after the appearance of trial by jury in the twelfth and thirteenth centuries for land law, criminal law, trespass and even Covenant?[40] Maitland's response was that Debt evolved during an earlier period than trial by jury, and the procedure of that earlier era stayed with the writ.[41] An alternative view is that wager of law, rather than trial by jury, replaced Debt's earlier mode of proof of trial by battle since a jury of the "men of the country" would have no knowledge of a private informal transaction.[42] Debt had existed in the local courts since Anglo-Saxon days, and when the royal courts began to visit the local communities on eyres in the twelfth and thirteenth centuries, it was looked upon as an ancient right of due process for the defendant to be able to continue to wage his law. Since the royal courts accepted it in the eyres, it was consistently followed at Westminster, even though it made little sense outside the local community.[43]

Keep in mind that wager was the mode of proof in Debt *sur contract* and not Debt *sur obligation.* In the latter action the sealed specialty was proof of the debt, and so there was no need to resort to wager. Under the same logic, if a fact was notorious to the community, as the existence of a rental relationship or of an employment relationship, wager was excluded in Debt *sur contract* and another mode of proof would be used. Furthermore, executors of the defendant were deemed unable to wage the law of the deceased defendant, since no one could wage in another's stead, and thus estates were effectively not liable until the seventeenth century.[44]

Primitive wager of law caused a serious retardation of the development of contract law.[45] It would take until the early seventeenth century to cut wager's stranglehold on Debt *sur contract,* and it would take until the nineteenth century for wager to be officially terminated. In fact much of the story of the development of the common law of contract is the twisted path it took through trespass, where trial by jury was available, in order to avoid the shortcomings of wager.

The other characteristic of Debt *sur contract* requiring analysis is *quid pro quo,* a doctrine recognized since about 1400. It was necessary to show that the defendant had received some benefit (the *quid*) in return for which (*pro quo*) the defendant was obligated in Debt. If there was no exchange of property, there was no liability; there was no recognition of the intangible right to enforce a promise to do something in the future, unless the promise was evidenced by a seal. The transaction was not binding until one of the parties had performed his side of the agreement, though executory sales of goods became enforceable under a fictional passing of property notion in the fifteenth century.[46] In a guaranty contract, even if the contract was executed, the creditor could not proceed against the surety because the surety had not received a *quid pro quo* even though the debtor had. *Quid pro quo* was an evidentiary requirement, and hence if the plaintiff had a sealed specialty, *quid pro quo* was not required. In the sixteenth century the notion of *quid pro quo* would have some tenuous and indirect influence on the development of the doctrine of consideration. But before turning to the trespassory influences on contract and consideration, there are the two additional personal actions of Detinue and Account to discuss.

In the thirteenth and fourteenth centuries the earlier mentioned careless pleading of Debt and Detinue ceased. Debt now concerned a matter of obligation, but Detinue supposed property in the plaintiff. There were several instances where Detinue would be used. One by the fifteenth century was an action brought by a buyer for goods bought. Here the buyer had to be imaginative in order to fulfill the Detinue requirement that there be property in himself. The buyer fulfilled this by arguing that "property" passed to the buyer at the sale, and in effect there had been a kind of constructive delivery of the goods with the seller holding them as a bailee for safekeeping.[47] Another use of Detinue was on a true bailment. A third use of Detinue was against persons other than bailees; the action was not based on any transaction but rather on the fact that ascertainable goods were in the defendant's hands, as when the defendant was a finder of lost property.[48]

Detinue, like Debt, allowed wager of law. Just as ways were to be found to avoid wager in Debt *sur contract,* so also they were found to avoid it in Detinue. In the fifteenth and sixteenth centuries the plaintiff, in consensual and nonconsensual fact situations, would allege a fictitious loss, a finding and a subsequent conversion to the defendant. This pernicious use of conversion allowed a trespassory action to be brought in place of Detinue, and as a result the mode of proof in trespass of trial by jury was used. This new action, which gradually replaced Detinue, was Trover, a form of Trespass on the Case.[49]

The final personal action to discuss is Account. Account was a *praecipe* writ ordering the sheriff to tell defendants like agents and trustees to render an account of the plaintiff's money that the defendant had in his hands under some capacity. The accounting would be before two auditors appointed by the court; the parties involved were the claimant-creditor, the accountant-debtor and the auditors. If a balance was found to be due to the plaintiff, it was a debt which laid the foundation for a Debt action. In the thirteenth century a defendant would be committed to jail until the debt was paid. By the fourteenth century, the plaintiff's sole remedy was Debt. Wager was excluded in this Debt action due to the fact-finding that had already taken place during the accounting. The early Account cases were feudal-era actions against manorial bailiffs as a means of auditing their management of property. Other common defendants became trustees, agents and partners. The partnership form was not widely used in Medieval England. Mercantile partnership disputes heard in the royal courts used the customs of law merchant in an Account action, and Coke indicates that was still the practice in the early seventeenth century.[50] Ultimately the jurisdiction over Account-type actions was superceded by the equitable jurisdiction of the Chancellor.

By the mid-fourteenth century, there was a growing realization that the common law personal actions of Covenant and Debt were ineffective remedies for the money-credit economy beginning to replace feudalism. The Court of Common Pleas and the King's Bench slowly began to fashion a solution under the trespass writ. At this time these two courts were not the primary source of justice for contract breach since the greatest volume of contract actions were brought in the local courts, but it was in the royal courts where the modern remedy of Assumpsit blossomed.

In summary, as the county courts began to decay in the fourteenth century, plaintiffs forced into Common Pleas found the relief given there flawed because of the lack of an adequate common law remedy for the breach of an informal executory contract. This situation would become even more aggravated with the fall of the value of money during the ensuing two centuries. Of course parties with the experience and wherewithal to be represented by counsel could protect themselves by the formality of a conditioned bond or a covenant, though Covenant did not protect against the misfeasance of defective contract performance. The appropriate cause of action for breach of an informal agreement was Debt *sur contract,* but Debt *sur contract* could not provide a remedy for an executory agreement because of the *quid pro quo* requirement; and, even when sales contracts were covered under the passing of property fiction in the fifteenth century, the plaintiff's claim would be answered by the device unduly favorable to defendants of wager of law. In the local courts, where such agreements had formerly been heard and enforced, wager was effective because of the local knowledge of the defendant's reputation for veracity and because local courts often would not allow defendant to wage if he was not believed. However, the misuse of wager of law at Westminster Hall was a notorious obstacle to just decisions in Debt actions. The action of Debt *sur contract* had other limitations besides the obstacles of wager and *quid pro quo*. Debt had a fixed sum requirement, and so, if there was an agreement for lodging without the price and number of days being specified, Debt would not lie even after the benefit had been received. Debt also did not lie until the entire amount was due; thus if land rent or rent on a lease for years was not paid, Debt could not be brought until the period had run, and this was also the rule for the conditioned bond.

Trespass in the Royal Courts

The unavailability of a satisfactory remedy in the Court of Common Pleas for the breach of an informal executory agreement provided an opening for the King's Bench, which had no jurisdiction over Debt, to obtain some jurisdiction in contract by developing a contractual remedy to fill the gap. The remedy that would be developed by the King's Bench was Assumpsit, an action whose origins were in the King's Bench action of trespass (*transgression* or wrong). Assumpsit would not be fully developed until the sixteenth century and would not take over the field until 1602 in *Slade's Case*.[51] This chapter deals with the early use of trespassory relief for contract misfeasance during the fourteenth century.

The beginning of the writ of trespass is in the latter part of the twelfth century, but its genesis is hazy and several suggestions have been put forth. At the onset of the discussion, it should be emphasized that the civil wrongs appearing in the royal courts in the thirteenth century were being heard contemporaneously in the local courts. One theory is that it was developed as a gap-filler to cover those wrongs against the possessor of land which were not covered by the assize of *novel disseisin*.[52] Another view is that trespass was an offspring of the early king's court's jurisdiction over criminal wrongs, trespass providing a remedy for misdemeanors and a compensatory remedy for the victims of crimes.[53] Both of these theories place the birth of trespass in roughly the same era, and both see it as an offspring of the early king's court's jurisdiction over acts of illegal physical force. Both also point to a parent which utilized an early form of trial by jury.

The common law developed from two kinds of recognized legal claims: the demand for a right (*praecipe*) and the complaint of a wrong (trespass).[54] The *praecipe* writ formula was established first, by about 1150, and would cover writs for land and the personal actions of Debt, Detinue, Covenant and Account. The *praecipe* writ did not look to compensation but rather to the restoration of the plaintiff's rights. The trespass writ used the *ostensurus quare* formula wherein the defendant was summoned to show why (*ostensurus quare*) he did whatever he did. In *praecipe* the defendant could put matters right short of a court proceeding by recognizing the plaintiff's demand for a right and yielding up the thing claimed, but in *ostensurus quare* the defendant had committed an irreparable wrong for which compensation must be assessed.[55] This probably stemmed from the quasi-criminal origins of trespass.

The mode of trial in trespass was trial by jury. The right to trial by jury had become invariable by the 1284 Statute of Wales,[56] though there was a subsequent unsuccessful threat that wager of law would invade the trial procedure of trespass on the case due to the indirect, non-criminal nature of the wrong in case.[57] It appears that even earlier than the Statute, trespass had borrowed trial by jury either from the royal assize or from the royal court's criminal procedure.[58] The mode of trial in criminal cases had been the barbaric ordeal of water until it was banned by the Lateran Council of 1215; the royal justices were then forced to grope around for a replacement mode of proof and ultimately settled on the Norman practice of asking the men of the country to tell the truth of the matter in trial by jury. It is feasible, however, that the royal court's adoption of trial by jury in criminal cases was borrowed from the royal assize, which predates 1215.[59]

Since Medieval law was based on writs rather than fundamental theories of liability, no recovery was possible if a dispute did not fall within the scope of a writ system that had become frozen by the end of Edward I's reign in 1307.[60] The growth of the common law from the early fourteenth century to the mid-nineteenth century involved the use of evasory fictions in order to develop modern actions under the flexible writ of trespass, "that fertile mother of actions".[61] A part of the reason for the flexibility of trespass was the ambiguous parameters of the "special" non-forcible wrongs falling under this writ. By the eighteenth century, almost all litigation at common law, in tort or in contract, was being conducted in the *ostensurus quare* actions of trespass and case. The tort of trespass began as an action for a tortious wrong but would develop by fiction and analogy into an action for breach of contract.

Civil wrongs (trespasses), the closest thing to torts today were varied, as crimes were varied, and as a consequence there was no single rule for the writ of trespass but a group of separate wrongs.[62] Trespass was a variable writ lacking any specific form, and it was this flexibility which allowed trespass to be stretched to cover fact situations lacking *contra pacem* by the fourteenth century. In time, trespass would be allowed to extend as long as it did not invade a field covered by another writ.[63] The requirement of *vi et armis et contra pacem regis* (with force and arms and against the king's peace) for entry into the royal courts was an obstacle to the royal courts hearing other types of civil wrongs. These civil wrongs, which were not forcible, were left to the jurisdiction of the local courts, but inventive plaintiffs, who for a variety of reasons wanted royal jurisdiction, began to make disingenuous pleas to Chancery in order to obtain a writ for non-forcible wrongs masquerading as forcible wrongs. This began the process toward the identification of a separate trespass action known as trespass on the case. But before exploring the extensions of trespass on the case, some understanding of the origins of actions on the case is necessary.[64]

In the early thirteenth century the jurisdiction of the royal courts included felonies and trespasses when there was a breach of the king's peace (*contra pacem regis*), as a wrong against a member of the king's retinue. Later, by the mid-thirteenth century, wrongs formerly brought in the local courts, because they were non-violent or did not directly affect the king, were permitted in the royal courts. Since trespasses were remedied in local courts, without the need to allege force, why did plaintiffs bother to seek justice in the royal courts? There are a number of possible explanations. A prime one is the stringent process and execution procedures available in the royal courts, such as *capias*, outlawry and imprisonment of the defendant until the judgment to the plaintiff and the fine to the king were satisfied. Other reasons may have been: the seemingly consistent justice in the royal courts, the opportunity to avoid any local prejudice by bringing the case to a neutral forum, an allegation of breach of the king's peace precluded the defendant from waging his law, the possibility of a fine if the defendant was found guilty, and the spite of subjecting the defendant to the burden of travelling to Westminster. Later, in the sixteenth century, plaintiffs would find that they had no choice but to go to the royal courts because of the 40 shilling rule.

Due to the increasing flow of non-*contra pacem regis* cases into the royal courts, there was a statutory attempt in 1278 to return these cases to their traditional place in the local courts.[65] Nevertheless plaintiffs, keen on royal jurisdiction, found that royal courts would still accept actions on non-forcible wrongs if a fictitious forcible wrong was alleged *contra pacem* and *vi et armis*. Unless plaintiffs were disingenuous, Chancery clerks would refuse to issue a writ because of the inelasticity of the writ system by the early fourteenth century. Hence the plea rolls pay witness to fact situations lurking behind writ language. Examples of the unconvincing forcible wrong verbiage in the writs include: a smith who with force and arms killed the plaintiff's horse, a surgeon charged with battery for what was probably malpractice, a road accident injuring a plaintiff by "force and arm assaulted," and in 1317 purchased wine being deficient because of the defendant's use of "force and arms, to wit with swords and bows and arrows."[66]

Then during the last third of the fourteenth century, Chancery consciously began to accommodate plaintiffs by sealing trespass writs, in the local court form, without the allegation *vi et armis* or *contra pacem,* and the common law courts upheld these writs. The reason for the royal courts' change of heart has not been fully explained. One possible explanation is that the royal courts were filling a gap in non-forcible trespass relief created by the decline of county courts in the fourteenth century. Honesty in the plaintiff's complaint and in the writ was permitted in the landmark 1372 decision known as *The Farrier's Case.*[67] It seems that the smith had negligently driven a nail into the horse's foot, and the horse died. Earlier this case would have been trumped up as an intentional act of force, but the new-found permissiveness of the court allowed the plaintiff to honestly state that the horse was lawfully in the defendant's custody and that he had failed to exercise due care. Although *The Farrier's Case* was in effect a tort malpractice case and not based on breach of a promise, it is important both because it was an important inroad for the use of a trespassory action on a non-forcible wrong and because it was the first open recognition of the writ of trespass on the case in the royal courts. Thereafter trespass was perceived to consist of two distinctly separate categories: "general" (or "common") and "on the case" (or "special"). Due to the quasi-criminal nature of general trespass (*vi et armis et contra pacem*), it included the stringent criminal law process of *capias,* which could result in the imprisonment of the defendant;[68] however, actions on the case did not have *capias* until 1504,[69] which could explain the clear separation of general and special trespass in the fifteenth century. Indeed, the royal courts may have ceased demanding the fiction of *vi et armis* in non-forcible wrongs, as in *The Farrier's Case,* in order to spare the non-violent defendant the extremes of *capias* process.

The emergence of trespass on the case occurred in the midst of a feudal power struggle between the barons and the king. The barons put pressure on the king in the thirteenth century to cease expanding his judicial power, which had been increasing at the expense of baronial power since the days of Henry II (1154–1189). One baronial device was the Provisions of Oxford (1258), which forbade the creation of new writs and as a consequence caused the writ system to become inflexible to newer wrongs. Subsequently, Edward I (1272–1307), a strong-willed monarch, was active in legislation directed at the increase of the crown's power. One statute he caused to be passed, and which must be dealt with in discussing the origins of trespass on the case, was the Statute of Westminster II (1285) and in particular the section referred to as *in consimili casu.*[70] On its face the Statute can be read to state that if there is no existing remedy for the plaintiff, then the Chancery clerk may fashion a new writ "in like case", so that no man may depart without a remedy. The Statute provided:

> And whensoever from henceforth it shall fortune in the Chancery, and that in one case a writ is found, and in like case (*in consimili casu*) falling under like law, and requiring like remedy, is found none, the clerks of the Chancery shall agree in making the writ.

The old theory espoused by Coke, and popularized by Blackstone, was that trespass on the case was developed under the powers of the *in consimili casu* clause to fill the gap.[71] The modern view is that the Statute played no part since Medieval courts followed a policy of emphasizing a statutory origin of an action but the writs, declarations and Year Books made no reference to the Statute.[72] The appearance of trespass on the case was not readily apparent until nearly a century later, and the disingenuous pleas in the interim would not have been needed had the Statute effected what Coke claimed. Another facet of the older theory was that trespass on the case grew out of the older trespass *vi et armis.* The modern view of this second part of the old theory is that, though trespass on the case did not openly appear until the 1370s, remedies for non-forcible wrongs, whether disingenuous or not, were being allowed as early as the origin of trespass *vi et armis.* Trespass had originally simply meant a wrong, whether a "common" forcible trespass (*vi et armis*) or a "special" non-forcible trespass.

Even before *The Farrier's Case,* there had been several non-forcible trespass decisions without the use of *vi et armis* verbiage. Perhaps the best known such case is the "sea-walls case" of 1344.[73] The defendant was a riparian owner who failed to keep up his part of the sea-wall, resulting in flood damage to the plaintiff. The writ made no reference to *vi et armis,* which might cause one to conclude that this is the first trespass on the case decision, but there was something else that probably explains its presence in a royal court. The riparian owner's duty was a duty from time immemorial and was enforceable by indictment, and thus quasi-criminal, which might point to the royal interest in the case. A thread that runs through these early trespass on the case decisions was the view that a wrong should be punished, e.g., contempt of the king by violation of a statute or default of a quasi-public duty.[74]

By hindsight it is possible to identify the early actions "on the case", but the plea roll clerks did not use the terminology "trespass on the case" until the sixteenth century, though the writers of the Year Books were using it much earlier. In the official plea roll records these pre-sixteenth century actions are identified by the *quare cum* or *quod cum* language in the commencement of the writ.[75] *Cum* is translated as "whereas"; the "*cum* clause" would then continue with the special facts which create the duty, as the duty to repair the sea-wall, and that clause would be followed by a description of the wrong and the damage. The *cum* clause had to be varied for each case, thus giving rise to the expression "on the case".[76]

Now attention is turned to trespassory actions with contractual overtones. These actions would blossom under the sub-species of trespass on the case known as Assumpsit for misfeasance. Assumpsit means literally an undertaking. Misfeasance was the tortious act of doing something badly, and it was perhaps predictable to see that the early Assumpsit cases would be more tortious than contractual, though these earliest cases do have a contractual flavor to them in that they were professional negligence cases. The first known case of Assumpsit for misfeasance in the royal courts is the surprisingly early *Humber Ferry Case* (1348).[77] The ferryman accepted the plaintiff's mare for passage across the Humber River, and he so overloaded the ferry that the mare died. Covenant was inappropriate since that action concerned the failure to do what one had undertaken, but here the ferryman was not being sued because he left the mare behind but rather because he performed badly. So Covenant was not appropriate for the consequential damages, and the court allowed the trespassory action, which was in essence like an action of Assumpsit for misfeasance.

The *Humber Ferry Case* would be more important had it been brought by writ rather than by bill. The King's Bench had the authority to hear any case where it happened to be geographically located outside Westminster while travelling with the royal household by an informal bill, akin to the informal local court plaint, without the need for a formal writ requiring Chancery approval. It happened that the King's Bench was fortuitously located in York at the time the *Humber Ferry Case* was ripe for hearing. Therefore this case is not one of Chancery changing course, and it could well be that the King's Bench was adhering to the local law, which undoubtedly would have given relief to the plaintiff here. In the local law, as in the law today, there was not the formality to make it matter whether the remedy was in tort or in contract. Nonetheless, the *Humber Ferry Case* was the first case of a royal court finding liability on an undertaking to do something and having done it badly.

Since the ferryman was subject to status-based customary duties, much like the riparian owner, is this an Assumpsit case at all? The Year Book report uses the French word *emprist* to describe the defendant's undertaking; *emprist* is a word later used as the French translation of the Latin word Assumpsit. It fits the requirement of Assumpsit for misfeasance: a consensual relationship between two individuals, one of whom by misconduct causes damage to the other.[78] Keep in mind that Assumpsit was not a separate form of action in the fourteenth century but was merely a stereotyped word that appeared in a trespass on the case writ to identify the fact that there was an undertaking.

The next Assumpsit for misfeasance case was in Westminster in 1369. The defendant was a veterinary surgeon, and the undertaking was described by the term *manucepit,* which translates "he took in his hand to heal".[79] Unfortunately the horse died due to the veterinarian's negligence. The plaintiff counted of negligent treatment, and the writ did not include *contra pacem.* The defense was raised that it should be a Covenant action or general trespass (*vi et armis*). The reply came, "We cannot have [covenant] without a deed. . . it is right to maintain this special writ according to the case rather than to abate it, for we can have no other writ." Further the plaintiff replied that *vi et armis* could not be used "because the horse was not slain by force." Judgment was for the plaintiff. Then during the 1370s the writ language became more standardized. The term for undertaking became *assumpsit,* and *assumpsit* replaced *manucepit* for surgeons and *emprist* for customary occupations to become the stereotyped word to label an undertaking.[80] These fourteenth century cases of professional negligence based on an undertaking involved individuals with the status of being engaged in "common callings" of that era, e.g., ferrymen, smiths, surgeons, innkeepers, common carriers, etc.[81]

Another strand of misfeasance liability for the poor performance of a promise was an "action on the case in the nature of a deceit" for the breach of a warranty of quality. The seller of shoddy goods was guilty of a misfeasance and punishable both by local authority and by a suit for damages, just as the ferryman was liable both under customary law and for damages for failure to keep the mare safe. Trespass actions were allowed in the royal courts, after the requirement of a royal interest was dropped in the 1370s, despite the objection that there was a breach of a promise sounding in Covenant; the bad performance of the warranty relied on was said to be a deceitful wrong.[82] Two early actions on the case allowed for breach of a warranty of quality were in 1383 and 1387, both dealing with horses warranted to be sound.[83] The seller's special undertaking of quality goods was amenable to a tort theory since the undertaking and the delivery of defective goods were akin to a deceit. As will be discussed in the next chapter, in the fifteenth century this idea would be applied to what was normally a covenant, were it not for a deceitful breach of a fiduciary duty or a disablement.

Conclusion

The royal courts of the thirteenth century provided relief for the breach of important consensual relationships. Propertied interests could adhere to the formalities of conditioned bond and covenant in the knowledge that the royal courts enforced these devices, but the stiffening of the writ system closed the doors on the opportunity for the development of new writs to answer the increasing demand for a more workable law for informal, consensual transactions. Solutions were found by fictions and by sheer circumvention of archaic remedies. The ways in which this evasion took place have left traces on the law of contract today.

With the breakdown of county courts, the traditional forum for informal agreements, plaintiffs turned to Common Pleas for assistance. The possibility of Common Pleas' use of the logical remedy of Debt *sur contract* as a solution was compromised by wager of law, however, and no alternative seemed available due to the narrow rigidity of the writ system. Notwithstanding the Register of Writs, gap-filling hardship relief for contract misfeasance was provided, through the competitive imagination of the justices of the King's Bench, by using the more flexible tort writ of trespass. But what a circuitous path the development of informal contract relief would take and what tortured doctrine would evolve by travelling via tort law to live the lie of conforming to the formulary system.

Starting in the final third of the fourteenth century, the trespassory action of Assumpsit for the misfeasance of improper performance of customary obligations, based on status and then on an undertaking, suggested a possible avenue for plaintiffs searching for a flexible contract remedy, but the possibilities under this action were limited at best. There was still no adequate contract remedy by the year 1400 for the failure to perform an informal promise. It would be nearly two hundred years subsequent to the appearance of Assumpsit for misfeasance before a modern theory of contract would develop.

Notes

1. *See* MAX WEBER ON LAW IN ECONOMY AND SOCIETY 114–115 (Cambridge, Mass., M. Rheinstein ed. 1954). The idea of contract obligation was alien to primitive law; it only knew an obligation arising *ex delicto*. *Id.* at 110.

2. *See* R. VAN CAENEGEM, ROYAL WRITS IN ENGLAND FROM THE NORMAN CONQUEST TO GLANVILL, 77 SELDEN SOCIETY 29–31 (London: 1959); *see also* G. SAYLES, THE COURT IN KING'S BENCH IN LAW AND HISTORY 8–10 (Selden Society Lecture) (London: 1959). Henry II (1154–1189), England's greatest Medieval King, completely overhauled the administration of justice in England. Rannulf Glanvill was the Justiciar of Henry II and in effect regent during his absences. Glanvill is traditionally said to author TRACTATUS DE LEGIBUS ANGLIAE (commonly called GLANVILL). Magna Carta, 16 John, c.17 (1215).

3. A. KIRALFY, THE ACTION ON THE CASE 8 (London: 1951) (e.g., 1300 London action for surgeon's undertaking to cure first appeared in "case"

at Westminster in 1369 and 1375; and 1345 London form for innkeeper's liability first appeared at Westminster in 1369.).

4. R. PALMER, THE COUNTY COURTS OF MEDIEVAL ENGLAND, 1150–1350 141, 147, 292, 296–301 (Princeton: 1982).

5. Statute of Gloucester, 6 Edw. I, c. 8 (1278); S. MILSOM, HISTORICAL FOUNDATIONS OF THE COMMON LAW 244–245 (London: 2d ed. 1981) (Although statute did not set a ceiling on county court plaints in trespass or Debt, it was so interpreted by the 15th century.); R. PALMER, *supra* note 4, at 235–262, 251–252, 288 (40sh. rule applied to Debt by 1290.).

6. R. PALMER, *supra* note 4, at 119–120, 240, 249, 284, 288, 302–306.

7. Baker, *The Merchant and the Common Law Before 1700,* 38 CAMBRIDGE L. J. 295, 297, 308, 313, 318 (1979); T. PLUCKNETT, A CONCISE HISTORY OF THE ENGLISH COMMON LAW 660–665 (Boston: 5th ed. 1956); J. CLAPHAM, A CONCISE ECONOMIC HISTORY OF BRITAIN 140–142, 152–157 (Cambridge: 1949). The old local courts, piepowder and other obsolescent courts were not formally abolished until 1977. Administration of Justice Act, c. 38, s. 23, sch. 4 (1977).

8. Barbour, *The History of Contract in Early English Equity* in IV OXFORD STUDIES IN SOCIAL AND LEGAL HISTORY 55, 130, 163–168 (P. Vinogradoff ed., Oxford 1914); *see* Y.B. 21 Hen. VII, M. f. 41, pl. 66 (1506), *reprinted in* C. FIFOOT, HISTORY AND SOURCES OF THE COMMON LAW 353 (London: 1949).

9. Helmholz, *Assumpsit and Fidei Laesio,* 91 L. Q. REV. 406, 422, 426–429 (1975) (Argues *fidei laesio* came directly to the common law from the church courts rather than by "indirect reception" through Chancery as Barbour had suggested. *Id.* at 430–431.).

10. F. MAITLAND, THE FORMS OF ACTION AT COMMON LAW 1 (originally in EQUITY (1909), published separately in 1936).

11. 4 H. BRACTON, ON THE LAWS AND CUSTOMS OF ENGLAND 286 (fo. 413b) (tr. S. Thorne, ed. G. Woodbine, Cambridge, Mass., 1977) (hereinafter cited as BRACTON). Henry of Bratton, known as Bracton, was a Justice of the King's Bench during the reign of Henry III. He wrote the greatest of the Medieval law books, and his overall grasp of the system would not be equalled until Blackstone in the eighteenth century. *See* Seipp, *Bracton, the Year Books, and the "Transformation of Elementary Legal Ideas" in the Early Common Law,* 7 LAW & HIST. REV. 175, 177–178, 199 (1989) (The canonist Bracton knew Roman law and incorporated it in his work, but the year book writers succeeding him improperly employed Roman terminology since they were only trained in the common law.).

12. F. MAITLAND, *supra* note 10, at 6.

13. Parliament developed out of the King's Council during the first half of the thirteenth century. The first statutes were passed by Parliament in 1320s. *See* G. SAYLES, THE KING'S PARLIAMENT OF ENGLAND 49–50, 103–105 (London: 1975).

14. F. MAITLAND, *supra* note 10, at 6.

15. One must be wary of thinking of "contract" in the Middle Ages as being the same as we think of contract today since the common law lawyer's definition was different. The Year Books used "contract" to mean an informal agreement

where a duty arose from the receipt of *quid pro quo* and gave rise to an action of Debt for a sum certain. Medieval lawyers were thinking about transactions which transferred property or generated a "debt". Consensual transactions to perform in the future were only partially covered by the limited action of Covenant. The use of the term contract in the modern sense of an agreement to perform in the future did not come into general use until the seventeenth century after Assumpsit, and its required consideration, had supplanted Covenant (and Debt).

16. Debt, Detinue and Account have characteristics of "real" actions since *praecipe* was used in an action brought for the benefit the defendant received wherein the plaintiff demanded what he "owns" and not what he is "owed". F. MAITLAND, *supra* note 10, at 38; Ames, *History of Parol Contracts Prior to Assumpsit* in 3 SELECT ESSAYS IN ANGLO-AMERICAN LEGAL HISTORY 304, 304–5, 319 (Boston: 1909). *Cf.* A. SIMPSON, A HISTORY OF THE COMMON LAW OF CONTRACT 75–80 (Oxford: 1975).

17. S. MILSOM, *supra* note 5, at 244.

18. Actions at common law can be divided into real, personal and mixed actions. Bracton said there was no real action for chattels. Real actions were for claiming title to real property and were a claim for the property itself. Whereas personal actions dealt with obligations for money damages, and included such actions as Covenant and Debt. Maitland said Bracton made "An important remark for it is the foundation of all of our talk about real and personal property." F. MAITLAND, *supra* note 10, at 48.

19. C. FIFOOT, HISTORY AND SOURCES OF THE COMMON LAW: TORT AND CONTRACT 255–256 (London: 1949) (citing Bracton, fo. 34); *cf.* F. MAITLAND, *supra* note 10, at 47. According to the Statute of Wales, 12 Edw. I, c.xi (1284), there were as many covenants as there were types of agreements.

20. Ibbetson, *Words and Deeds: The Action of Covenant in the Reign of Edward I*, 4 LAW AND HIST. REV. 71, 79 (1986).

21. *Id.* at 82–87 (The pleading manual, EXCEPCIONES CONTRA BREVIA (1280), was probably a Roman law transplant. *Id.* at 83.).

22. R. PALMER, *supra* note 4, at 198–211; Palmer, *Covenants, Justicies Writs, and Reasonable Showings*, 31 AM. J. LEG. HIST. 97, 98, 116 (1987). Norman king's word was indisputable and so any document with his seal was indisputable; this concept filtered down to nobility using their own seals to mark an instrument as incontestable.

23. Ibbetson, *supra* note 20, at 92–93 (Cites 1321 eyre case against surgeon promising to cure wounded hand but failing to do so.); *see* 2 F. POLLOCK and F. MAITLAND, THE HISTORY OF ENGLISH LAW (BEFORE THE TIME OF EDWARD I) 219–220 (Cambridge: 2d ed. 1911) (hereinafter cited as POLLOCK and MAITLAND).

24. *Case of the Waltham Carrier*, London Eyre (1321) (86 SELDEN SOCIETY 286), *reprinted in* J. BAKER and S. MILSOM, SOURCES OF ENGLISH LEGAL HISTORY 285, 286 (London: 1986) (hereinafter cited as BAKER and MILSOM).

25. *Anon*, 22 Edw. IV, f.1, pl. 6 (1482).

26. Ames, *The History of Assumpsit* (pt. 2), 2 HARV. L. REV. 53, 56 (1888) (no actions of Covenant on a sum certain before 17th century).

27. GLANVILL, x.14 (ca. 1180); F. MAITLAND, *supra* note 10, at 48.

28. *See* S. MILSOM, *supra* note 5, at 250–251 (penal sum secured performance); *see also* A. SIMPSON, *supra* note 16, at 90–95, 118–122.

29. *See* Pinnel's Case, 5 Co. Rep. 117a (1602), *reprinted in* BAKER and MILSOM, *supra* note 24, at 259.

30. Stat. 25 Edw. III, s. 5, c.17 (1352) (covered Debt, Detinue and Replevin).

31. Milsom, *Reason in the Development of the Common Law,* 81 L. Q. REV. 496, 502–503 (1965); S. MILSOM, *supra* note 5, at 252.

32. Statute of Merchants, 1283, 11 Edw. I, *reprinted in* C. FIFOOT, *supra* note 19, at 239 (also called Statute of Acton Burnell). One can't help seeing similarities in modern confession of judgment clauses.

33. *See* Ames, *supra* note 16, at 306n. Debt was available on a wide variety of demands for money, e.g., informal loans, contracts of sale, sale of land, rent due on lease for years, arrearage on an account.

34. 2 POLLOCK & MAITLAND, *supra* note 23, at 205 (though recovery of a chattel is not considered proprietary to a modern lawyer); *cf.* A. SIMPSON, *supra* note 16, at 75–80 (Withholding something to which the creditor is entitled is a misfeasance not a nonfeasance.).

35. Milsom, *Sales of Goods in the Fifteenth Century,* 77 L.Q. REV. 257, 266 (1961) (Ways to oust wager. *Id.* at 261–262.).

36. King Ethelred's Code of Wantage (978–1008), *reprinted in* A. HARDING, THE LAW COURTS OF MEDIEVAL ENGLAND 129 (London: 1973). Compurgation was a Germanic practice from at least the 5th century. J. THAYER, A PRELIMINARY TREATISE ON EVIDENCE AT COMMON LAW 25 (London: 1898).

37. J. THAYER, *supra* note 36, at 25–28 (Wager was most popular mode of trial.); see A. SIMPSON, *supra* note 16, at 138.

38. S. MILSOM, *supra* note 5, at 254–255; J. BAKER, AN INTRODUCTION TO ENGLISH LEGAL HISTORY 64–65 (London: 2d ed. 1979) ("professional perjurers").

39. A. SIMPSON, *supra* note 16, at 138–140. (During Age of Faith fear of hell would have been deterrence to perjury by defendant or compurgators.); S. MILSOM, *supra* note 5, at 354 (Wager was not absurd for private agreements, given the weaknesses of embryonic trial by jury); J. BAKER, *supra* note 38, at 288 (wager protected against unscrupulous claims when no evidence to put to jury); *cf.* McGovern, *Contract in Medieval England: Wager of Law and the Effect of Death,* 54 IA. L. REV. 19, 26 (1968; perhaps courts wouldn't allow wager if belief that defendant owed money). Later Star Chamber rebuked plaintiff for failing to use Assumpsit, thus avoiding wager, by refusing to punish a man for false wager. *Anon,* B.L. MS. Lansdowne 1076, f.122v (1587), *reprinted in* BAKER & MILSOM, *supra* note 24, at 220.

40. Trial by jury was proposed as the mode of proof in Debt *sur contract* in the Statute of Wales (1284), but, unlike Covenant, it was rejected because these informal agreements under Debt were frequently private and would not be known to the parties' countrymen, making it merely the plaintiff's word against the defendant's. S. MILSOM, *supra* note 5, at 248.

41. F. MAITLAND, *supra* note 10, at 38–40. The inference was that the later action of trespass took on the more modern trial by jury, by then available.

42. McGovern, *supra* note 39, at 20–21.

43. S. MILSOM, *supra* note 5, at 245. The Norman kings considered wager of law a lowly Anglo-Saxon tradition, perhaps appropriate for private disputes but considered inferior to the Norman custom of relying on the knowledge of the countrymen of the vicinity for public wrongs, as crimes, and later for trespasses. Jurors were expected to use their personal knowledge of a transaction in resolving a dispute as witnesses rather than judges of fact. *See* F. MAITLAND, *supra* note 10, at 17–18. Wager had been also experimented with on sealed deeds in the eyres, but it was abandoned—perhaps because of the ongoing common law view that mere words were inferior to deeds.

44. Y.B. Trin. 41 Edw. III, f. 13, pl. 3 (1368). This immunity was restricted to cases where the debtor could have waged his law if alive.

45. Milsom, *Law and Fact in Legal Development,* 17 U. TORONTO L.J. 1, 4 (1967) (Defendant would plead the general issue and wage, and thus for centuries contract law didn't grow since this procedure barred questions of law being raised by special verdicts. *Id.* at 14–17.).

46. By the fifteenth century an executory bargain and sale of goods was enforceable because of the use of the fiction that "property" had passed to the defendant without delivery. The fiction allowed an executory "consensual" transaction to fulfill the "real" character of *quid pro quo.* C. FIFOOT, *supra* note 19, at 227–228; Doige's Case, Hen. VI, f.34, pl. 4 (1442), *reprinted in* BAKER & MILSOM, *supra* note 24, at 391. (Dictum: "If I buy a horse from you, now the property in the horse is in me, and for this you shall have a writ of Debt for the money and I shall have Detinue for the horse on this bargain.")

47. Milsom, *supra* note 35, at 273–276.

48. S. MILSOM, *supra* note 5, at 271–273 (exploited when no true bailment).

49. A. KIRALFY, *supra* note 3, at 109–114; Milsom, *Not Doing is No Trespass: A View of the Boundaries of Case,* 1954 CAMBRIDGE L.J. 105, 113–116.

50. *See* Baker, *supra* note 7, at 301. Wager wasn't allowed in an accounting before 2 auditors, but it was before 1 auditor.

51. Slade's Case, 4 Co. Rep. 91a, 76 Eng. Rep. 1072, 1074 (1602).

52. Woodbine, *The Origin of the Action of Trespass*, 33 YALE L.J. 799 (1924).

53. F. MAITLAND, *supra* note 10, at 48, 53.

54. S. MILSOM, *supra* note 5, at 243.

55. *See* S. MILSOM, *supra* note 5, at 243–244 (The ways in which the old *praecipe* writs were circumvented in order to use *ostensurus quare* with its attendant trial by jury have left traces in the law yet today.).

56. Statute of Wales, 12 Edw. I. ch.xi (1284) (Ch.x provided that Covenant "be decided by jury of the countryside".). *See* M. WEBER, *supra* note 1, at 224 (Irrationality of primitive procedure cast off under influence of rational authority of a prince or priesthood.).

57. Y.B. Hil. 48 Edw. III, pl. 11, f.6b (1374).

58. A. KIRALFY, *supra* note 3, at 3 (Breach of peace element of trespass was quasi-criminal and called for same mode of trial as criminal law.).

59. *See* F. MAITLAND, *supra* note 10, at 38–40; cf. McGovern, *supra* note 39, at 20–21.

60. *See* S. MILSOM, *supra* note 5, at 38–40; cf. McGovern, *supra* note 39, at 20–21.

61. *See* F. MAITLAND, *supra* note 10, at 48, 53–57.

62. S. MILSOM, *supra* note 5, at 299–300.

63. *See* A. KIRALFY, *supra* note 3, at 2 (non-forcible trespass actions appeared by 14th century). There was a long-standing prohibition on the overlapping of remedies, and so trespass was not available to plaintiff if another action, as Debt, was available, but this changed dramatically in the sixteenth century.

64. On the origins of trespass and case, *see generally* Milsom, *Trespass From Henry III to Edward III,* 74 L.Q. REV. (3 parts) 195, 407, 561 (1958).

65. Statute of Gloucester, 6 Edw. I, c.8 (1278) (sheriffs were to hear trespass in county courts as was the custom). Other instances of attempts to limit the incidence of less important private wrongs in the royal courts included the requirement of a seal in Covenant and Gloucester's 40 shilling rule. Milsom (pts. 1 & 3), *supra* note 64, at 224, 576, 589. There was baronial opposition to royal takeover of local control. An increased central court involvement may have been daunting to a society incapable of swift travel.

66. Milsom (pts. 1 & 3), *supra* note 64, at 215, 220–223, 567, 571, 586; *see also* S. MILSOM, *supra* note 5, at 288–295.

67. *The Farrier's Case,* Y.B. Trin. 46 Edw. III, pl. 19, f.19 (1372), *reprinted in* BAKER and MILSOM, *supra* note 24, at 341. As late as 1366 an action alleging a negligent carriage of wheat in breach of an *assumpsit* to transport still included allegation of an assault on plaintiff "with swords, bows, and arrows." Rogerstun v. Northcotes, C.P. 40/423, m.134d (1366), *reprinted in* 103 SELDEN SOCIETY 423 (1987). *See* Milsom (pt. 3), *supra* note 64, at 589 (even genuine breaches of the peace had come to be seen as private wrongs).

68. In *capias,* if the defendant was contumacious, the defendant could be ordered seized by the sheriff; and, if the defendant couldn't be found, he could be subjected to outlawry, which in effect banished him from England. *Capias* and outlawry, already available in trespass, were extended to Debt and Detinue in Stat. 25 Edw. III, st. 5, c.17 (1352) but not to trespass on the case until 1504.

69. Stat. 19 Hen. VII, c.9 (1504).

70. Statute of Westminster II, 13 Edw. I, c.24 (1285).

71. 2 E. COKE, INSTITUTES OF THE LAWS OF ENGLAND 407 (London: 1644); *accord* 3 W. BLACKSTONE, COMMENTARIES ON THE LAWS OF ENGLAND 51 (1768) (Statute accounts for great variety of trespass on case writs.); *cp.* F. MAITLAND, *supra* note 10, at 51–52 (Chancery could vary old writs but couldn't invent new rights, though trespass on case "regarded" as exception.).

72. Plucknett, *Case and the Statute of Westminster II,* 31 COLUM. L. REV. 778, 782–785, 798 (1931).

73. Bernardeston v. Heighlynge, Y.B. 16 Edw. III, Rolls Series, p. 235, pl. 6 (1342); on error in K.B. 27/338, m. 41d (Mich. 1344), *reprinted in* BAKER and MILSOM, *supra* note 24, at 338 (Plaintiff lost profit from 200 acres of meadow being flooded.).

74. *See* A. KIRALFY, *supra* note 3, at 32–44.

75. *Id.* at 5. The plea rolls were the official Latin record kept by the clerks of the courts preserving the pleadings and the judgments. The year books, in Law French, were an early form of law report and provided insight into the oral arguments; these reports were originally prepared by law students at the inns of court for pedagogical purposes.

76. *See* A. SIMPSON, *supra* note 16, at 201–202; *see also* Milsom (pt. 2), *supra* note 64, at 407–408, 414–416. Bracton used the word "case": "Some writs are formed on specified cases. . . ." 4 BRACTON, *supra* note 11, at 285 (fo. 413b). "Case" also appeared in 1284 Statute of Wales, ch. 6 and 1285 Statute of Westminster II, ch. 50.

77. *Humber Ferry Case* (a/k/a Bukton v. Tounesende), Y.B. 22 Lib. Ass., pl. 41, f.94 (1348), *reprinted in* BAKER and MILSOM, *supra* note 24, at 358. *See* S. MILSOM, *supra* note 5, at 316–317.

78. *See* S. MILSOM, *supra* note 5, at 316–317; *see also* A. KIRALFY, *supra* note 3, at 39.

79. Waldon v. Mareschal, Y.B., Mich. 43 Edw. III, f.33, pl. 38 (1369), *reprinted in* BAKER and MILSOM, *supra* note 24, at 359. See Broadmeadow v. Rushender, K.B. 27/414, m.37d (1364), *reprinted in* 103 SELDEN SOCIETY 422 (1987) (Non-*contra pacem* trespass action against a surgeon for negligent treatment of woman resulting in loss of hand in breach of "promise" to cure, but jury verdict was for defendant). *Waldon v. Mareschal* added something to the story that the earlier discussed *Farrier's Case* did not since *The Farrier's Case* was based on the wrong of the improper shodding of a horse but *Waldon v. Mareschal* was based on the improper performance of the *undertaking* to cure.

80. *See* A. KIRALFY, *supra* note 3, at 39.

81. *See* A. SIMPSON, *supra* note 16, at 229–234 (No general principle for these varied common callings and no liability in negligence unless a relationship between parties.).

82. Actions on false warranties of quality were allowed in mercantile courts and in local courts in 13th century. Since local courts didn't require writs, these actions appeared as either actions on informal covenants or in trespass, the latter often including deceit language. See Milsom, *supra* note 35, at 278. Before the last quarter of the 14th century, the false warranty was a wrong to a city like London, but it was not a wrong to the king, and so a private victim could not go to a royal court. S. MILSOM, *supra* note 5, at 321.

83. *Anon,* Trin. 7 Ric. II (1383) in FITZ, LEY 41; Garrok v. Heytesbury, Y.B. Trin. 11 Ric. II, p. 4, pl.2 (1387), *reprinted in* BAKER and MILSOM, *supra* note 24, at 507 (Buyer counted that seller knew horse was infirm. Buyer later objected that if defense of facts sounding in Covenant prevailed, he would be without a remedy since there was no sealed warranty.).

CHAPTER 2

INNOVATION FOR INFORMALITY (1400–1602)

The changes in the common law of contract during the fifteenth and sixteenth centuries reflected the European social and economic transition from Medieval to Modern times as traditional ideas were revised under the spell of Reformation and Renaissance thought.[1] Resistance to change relaxed once the dynastic wars had ended, and courts became willing to make adjustments in the law in order to accommodate new circumstances. The explorations in the Americas vastly increased the silver supply, and with it the previous two centuries-long stability in prices was shattered as prices skyrocketed sixfold during the Tudor century.[2] As a result of the expanded money economy, a new class emerged seeking profits from commerce rather than land. Already by the fifteenth century, capitalist clothiers were buying wool and selling abroad what was made by jobbing workers, who were no longer villeins. Artisans were no longer their own distributors of finished products at the village level, and they were no longer protected against rising prices since the guild system was decaying. The brisk demand for wool from clothiers brought a commercialization of land as agricultural land was enclosed for grazing. Progress quickened for those above the bottom rungs of the economic scale with the rise in trade under Tudor stability.[3] The crown became wedded to commercial interests as national and international markets developed. The sixteenth century Reformation favored commercial classes, and the court system was secularized as contract work was taken from ecclesiastical courts. Producers and merchants looked to the courts for assistance in assuring that goods and services contracted-for were provided according to the terms agreed upon.[4] These changes brought on a need for fundamental revisions in the law so that contract law could take on the role of facilitating business planning.[5]

Before the Tudor period mercantile cases were not often heard in the common law courts, but by then the staple courts were in decay and common law judges like Coke began actively competing with the remaining mercantile courts for the expanding commercial business. In order to accommodate this growing commercial business, the common law of contract had to be revised since the old law designed for simultaneous exchanges, or at least partially executed transactions, and transactions documented by a sealed deed did not reflect the merchants' needs for enforcement of informal, executory agreements. The traditional writs of Covenant and Debt were ineffectual in handling these informal transactions. In order to circumvent the rigidity of the writ system, lawyers and judges exploited openings in tort law as a means of reforming contract law. Tort procedures aided in overcoming the barrier to progress presented by the general issue in both wager of law and trial by jury. The general issue masked the detailed facts needed for legal analysis; however, the specific pleading of facts in actions on the case would help to pry open the general issue.[6]

Until the money economy was significant enough to catch the attention of the property-oriented royal courts, there was no pressing need for a flexible common law remedy for informal transactions. Informality was accommodated in those local courts retaining their vitality, in Chancery where not much weight was put on a seal, and in mercantile courts where informal mercantile custom was enforced. Autonomous common law doctrine did not permit an action for failure to perform an informal, executory promise because there was neither a *quid pro quo* nor a seal, and trespass covered misfeasance but not nonfeasance. However, starting in the latter part of the fifteenth century, common law courts rationalized contextual alterations in doctrine in order to both accommodate the needs of capitalism and to compete with other courts for the increasing mercantile business.

As was discussed in the first chapter, by the fifteenth century, plaintiffs using actions on the case in the royal courts were successful in establishing that a promise performed badly was an actionable tortious wrong. The difficult step analyzed in this chapter is the extension of this theory of misfeasance for performing a promise badly to that of nonfeasance liability for not performing at all. As with misfeasance liability, liability for nonfeasance would begin with liability on status-based obligations and then would extend to general promissory liability. Then once nonfeasance liability was in place, the parameters of Assumpsit were established before all the royal courts approved the change, that had the greatest impact from the standpoint of volume of cases, of Assumpsit replacing Debt.

Assumpsit for Nonfeasance

The step from allowing the action of Assumpsit for misfeasance to allowing Assumpsit for nonfeasance was a giant one for the formulary system and for trespass itself. During the Middle Ages the writ of Covenant was the recognized remedy for failure to perform, but it had become an unpopular remedy due to the archaic ritual tied to its use. The inadequacy of Covenant presented a problem because the common law courts traditionally prohibited the availability of more than one action for a given wrong. Nevertheless the prohibition on overlapping remedies would be met head on by beginning to allow Assumpsit for nonfeasance to supplant the ineffectual remedy of Covenant. There was a frequent Medieval incantation invoked when early attempts were made to allow the nonfeasance action: "This sounds in covenant; not doing is no trespass"[7]—that is, there must be some active wrongdoing, or it is not a trespass.

There was no need for the royal courts to change so long as important contracts of more than 40 shillings were evidenced by a sealed covenant or a bond, but there were new demands on the royal courts once there was a rise both in the incidence of informal mercantile transactions and in the number of everyday transactions exceeding 40 shillings because of the drop in the value in money in the sixteenth century. There was a crisis for informal contract actions by the sixteenth century since traditional havens for these actions were drying up. Church, borough and mercantile courts were on the decline, and county courts had already declined. Those few county courts that had not decayed significantly were hamstrung by the 40 shilling rule with the fall in the value of money. The problem was particularly acute for the workhorse Debt since, though wager worked well enough in the local courts, it was a disaster in distant Westminster where hired oath-helpers were used.[8] The need for innovative relief for informal agreements was apparent, and the King's Bench was especially keen to increase its business.

In tracing this innovation, attention is turned back to 1400, by which time the royal courts recognized liability for misfeasance, as a carpenter building badly, but there was no recognition of liability for mere nonfeasance, e.g., a carpenter not building at all. The courts recognized no action for nonfeasance because a trespassory action had to be for an active wrongdoing and because there was a taboo on overlapping a trespass remedy with Covenant's availability for nonfeasance. The fine line between allowing a misfeasance action but not a nonfeasance action was difficult to justify since in both promissory situations the defendant committed a wrong and the plaintiff suffered an injury. This line was gingerly crossed during the fifteenth century as a number of royal court decisions began allowing recovery for certain types of nonfeasance.

The Ordinance and Statute of Labourers (1349–1351)[9] influenced the recognition of an early form of liability for nonfeasance by the fifteenth century. As the feudal system fell into decay, and men fled serfdom to find jobs off the manor that were made vacant by the Black Death of 1348–49, the barons obtained this legislation providing criminal actions against workmen who refused to adhere to their employment contracts. The Plague was a watershed event in social and economic history since it caused the death of approximately 25% of the population. As a result, labor was in short supply, wages doubled and serfs had alternatives to bondage.[10] In an expanded interpretation of the Statute, the royal courts decided that a trespass action could be brought for failing to perform one's statutory duty to work[11]—in-effect liability for a special type of the nonfeasance of not fulfilling a status-based duty. There were objections that the civil liability claimed under the Statute for failure to work should be brought under the writ of Covenant but to no avail.

There were employment-related cases, analogous to those decided under the Statute, which bear mentioning in pointing out another explanation for these early cases. In the *Humber Ferry Case*[12] of 1348 the ferryman was found liable for the death of a mare during a crossing in the first case of misfeasance liability based on an undertaking. It appeared that Covenant covered this situation, but it would have been an unsatisfactory remedy for recovery of the loss of the mare because there was no sealed document. It was not a pure nonfeasance case since there was an entrustment of the mare to the ferryman, suggesting the work had begun. In 1400 in *Watton v. Brinth,*[13] a carpenter had undertaken to build a house and was sued for failure to do so, but the court held no liability. Could it be that there was no liability because the property was not entrusted to the defendant?[14]

Common law liability of an independent contractor for nonfeasance is first seen in the futuristic Common Pleas' decision of *Watkin's Case* (1425).[15] The defendant undertook (*"emprist"*, French for *assumpsit*) to construct a mill by an appointed date and then failed to do the work at all. The plaintiff brought a writ of Trespass. The defendant objected that the case sounded in Covenant, but this was not the type of transaction customarily documented by the aristocratic seal. A majority of the Court voted in favor of allowing the writ of Trespass to stand. Martin, J. dissented from the majority view and made his oft-quoted statement: "If this action can be held up on these facts, then for every broken covenant in the world one shall have an action of trespass." Chief Judge Babington, speaking for the majority, raised several hypotheticals to show that nonfeasance could cause actual damage: damage to furniture and lumber if a roof was not repaired, flood damage caused by failure to repair a ditch, and the injury suffered by a client if his lawyer failed to plead. One view is that this 1425 case was an aberration until 1505, but there must have been some reason for hope in plaintiffs since there were a number of suits in line with *Watkin's Case* brought in the fifteenth century.[16] The *Watkin's* decision may not have been paid much heed because of the age-old concern raised in the dissent. Although *Watkin's Case* is a trespass action, there is a revisionist view that Assumpsit was accepted as sounding in contract for a nonfeasance by 1425; however, the accepted view of Assumpsit's development is that it was viewed as a tort and evolved into a contract action in the sixteenth century.[17]

Two earlier lines of nonfeasance authority should not be viewed as precedents for *Watkin's Case*. First, in the riparian seawalls trespass action of 1344, where the riparian landowner was found liable for failure to repair a seawall, there is an elementary difference in that the riparian owner owed a status-based duty of independent origin created by custom rather than by agreement. Secondly, the Statute of Labourers would not apply to *Watkin's Case* because the carpenter was an independent contractor and his undertaking was not for permanent employment.[18]

In early nonfeasance cases like *Watkin's Case*, the plaintiff's lawyer attempted to differentiate his client's nonfeasance case from the applicability of Covenant by his emphasis of the facts in the pleadings. The plaintiff alleged damages not only for the breach of the undertaking but also for the irremediable loss caused by the defendant not performing on time. Now that the time had transpired, the *praecipe* writ of Covenant, which would order the defendant to perform, could not be obeyed according to the tenor of the original agreement. The plaintiff argued that he had suffered an irremediable loss due to such consequences as loss of credit, expenses of delay, lost profits, etc. He thus argued in the new trespassory action of Assumpsit that only money damages in tort would satisfy the plaintiff.[19]

Nearly concurrent with the appearance of this early form of liability for pure nonfeasance in the early fifteenth century, there was another form of nonfeasance case being allowed in the royal courts on an action of trespass on the case for deceit.[20] As discussed in the first chapter, by the 1380s there had been deceit actions allowed in connection with warranty actions in misfeasance.[21] By the fifteenth century deceit actions were being used to help extend Assumpsit beyond physical damage cases to cases of breach of fiduciary duties and disablement.[22] Many of the early deceit cases in the royal courts were for a deceit committed against the court, e.g., for bringing a felony action in a non-royal court in 1305 or for submitting a forged document in evidence. Another group of early deceit cases was against lawyers for colluding with their client's opponent and also cases of taking fees from both sides of a transaction, known as "ambidextry." Thus many of the thirteenth and fourteenth century deceit cases involved such public offenses as warranty actions stemming from the violation of municipal regulations and deceits against a royal court.[23]

In 1433, *Somerton's Case*[24] held that a lawyer was liable under the action of trespass on the case for deceit. In that case, the plaintiff hired the defendant to be an agent for the purchase of a manor, but the agent wrongfully disclosed his agency to a third party and collusively obtained the property for the third party. Although the failure to obtain the manor was a nonfeasance, there was also the misfeasance of collusion. Babington, C.J. saw no overlap because there was "more than a covenant broken . . . if he betrays his counsel. . . . now here is a deceit." The court ruled that it was the *assumpsit* which made these disclosures to the third person wrongful and liability was found.

At this juncture the legal historian encounters another jump in judicial reasoning from the instance of deception of a trusting client to the "deceit" of breach of an ordinary contract, no fiduciary relationship existing. The deceit notion from the established precedents provided an opportunity for the court, by the use of analogy, to glide into the field of nonfeasance. The instigating case was the famous *Doige's Case.*[25] Here the plaintiff had a land sales agreement with the defendant, but the defendant sold the land to a third party, thus disabling herself from selling to the plaintiff. The plaintiff had paid in advance and was now going to lose his payment in addition to the advantages lost as a result of the contract breach. The principle in *Somerton* was extended in *Doige* from the liability of an agent to the liability of an ordinary seller. Actually, *Doige* does not involve a deceit at all since there is merely a wrongful breach of a contract, but an analogy to deceit was used in order to find a precedent for liability separate from Covenant—this tactic continued through the next century. Deceit would remain in the plaintiff's pleadings long after disablement was of no concern.[26] A defense raised in *Doige* was that the *praecipe* Covenant was the appropriate cause of action. Justice Newton pointed out the inadequacy of Covenant here and thus the gap in the law in the case of a disablement like in *Doige's Case:* "To what purpose would he have a writ of covenant, even if he had a sealed deed, when the defendant cannot carry out his covenant."[27]

One might be lead to the conclusion that the royal court came up with deceit as a means of overcoming the lack of a sealed instrument, but consider what had been going on in the City of London Court for some years prior to *Doige*. Although London allowed an action of informal covenant, it would be of no use in a disablement case, and so the local court allowed an action of deceit in order to provide restitution to the plaintiff for the advance payment. Hence London used deceit as the logical remedy and not because there was no sealed document. If the royal courts borrowed from London, the use of deceit may be looked upon as the logical choice of the plaintiff and not as an unnatural choice in avoiding the formal requirements of Covenant.[28] This logical use of deceit in the London court causes one to wonder whether the use of deceit in *Doige* was influenced by earlier royal cases, such as *Somerton* and the warranty cases, or by London's use of deceit. Perhaps the answer is that one should not fall into the trap of looking for a single source of a new rule but rather one should be aware that several sources may have converged in the formulation of the new rule; the judicial hypotheticals in *Doige* suggest a variety of influences. This should also be kept in mind in regard to other steps in the long development of Assumpsit for pure nonfeasance.

Doige created a rule that deceit liability existed when the selling defendant disabled himself by conveying to a third party. An anomaly resulted in the common law courts: there was now liability if the seller conveyed to a third party, but the seller was not liable if he held onto the property and merely refused to adhere to the informal sales agreement. However, there was a remedy in Chancery and in the local courts where specific performance was available for the second situation. The logic of the common law court's bifurcated approach to this nonfeasance problem was criticized by lawyers of the time. *Doige* pushed the door ajar for the entry of the logical conclusion that there should also be seller's liability for mere failure to comply with the informal agreement, liability for pure nonfeasance; this would happen around the turn of the sixteenth century.

Liability for deceitful disablement provided the middle step between liability for misfeasance and liability for pure nonfeasance. The disablement liability of *Doige* is not referred to as simply nonfeasance because there was also a wrongful conveyance to a third party, thus disabling the seller from keeping his agreement. Pure nonfeasance indicates that the defendant merely refuses to honor his informal undertaking, without any presence of disablement.

The first royal court dictum supporting the actionability of pure nonfeasance came from King's Bench Chief Justice Fyneux in 1499 at Gray's Inn:

> Note, that if one makes a covenant to build me a house by a certain day, and he does nothing about it, I shall have *Action sur mon cas* (action on my case) on this nonfeasance as much as if he had been guilty of a misfeasance, for I am damaged by this. . . . and I will not need to sue out a Subpoena[29] (in Chancery).

In 1505 the Court of Common Pleas adopted Fyneux's view in *Orwell v. Mortoft.*[30] *Orwell* is usually referred to as the first pure nonfeasance decision that caught on. In *Orwell* the buyer had paid for a load of barley, and he sued the seller for not delivering. Common Pleas Chief Justice Frowyk said the defendant was liable whether or not there was the disabling act of wrongfully conveying to a third party. The Court allowed Assumpsit for nonfeasance to act as a remedy for an informal covenant.[31] Frowyk established, however, an additional requirement to avoid overlapping with the writ of Covenant:

> If I covenant with a carpenter to make me a house, and pay him 20 pounds to make the house by a certain day, and he does not make the house by the day, I shall have an action on my case because of the payment of my money: and yet it sounds only in covenant, and without payment of the money in this case there is no remedy.[32]

This requirement of the payment of money was the formality Frowyk required in place of the sealed deed. Vestiges of this requirement would be a part of the story of the development of the doctrine of consideration as Assumpsit for nonfeasance and consideration developed during the sixteenth century.

The reported statements of a majority of the justices in *Orwell* was followed by both the King's Bench and the Court of Common Pleas. Assumpsit would lie in place of Covenant for the enforcement of an informal promise as long as the plaintiff had paid money. *Orwell* did not raise much of a stir because common law Covenant had plainly been an inadequate remedy when the defendant failed to perform his promised act, but when attempts were soon made to just as forthrightly replace Debt (the writ for not paying money) with Assumpsit, Common Pleas would strongly resist it both because Debt had been a largely effective remedy and because the action of Debt was their jurisdiction exclusively. During the remainder of the sixteenth century Assumpsit for nonfeasance would gradually become a more frequently used cause of action, the doctrine of consideration would take shape, and the battle lines would be drawn between the King's Bench and Common Pleas on the question of Assumpsit replacing Debt.

Before leaving the fifteenth century, the influence of Chancery's contract jurisdiction during that century, as reflected in Fyneux's 1499 remark that the plaintiff need not look to Chancery, needs to be evaluated.[33] A century before Assumpsit became contractual, Chancery had given relief by the enforcement of informal promises to individuals, some of humble origin caught by economic changes.[34] Chancery provided a forum for instances of harshness and to fill gaps in the common law of contract. These gaps included the lack of a remedy against a surety, the lack of a theory of *quantum meruit* and the general unenforceability of executory, parol contracts.[35] The clerical Chancellors generally followed canon law principles and procedures[36] and applied the civilian notion that if there was a *causa*, a good motive or reason, for the promise, then it ought to be enforced, notwithstanding the fact that the promise was of a non-commercial nature,[37] e.g., a potentially gratuitous promise of a surety or one in consideration of marriage.[38]

What began as gap-filling activities by Chancery proved a fertile area for the expansion of its contract work to the degree that it developed an extensive contract jurisdiction by the mid-fifteenth century.[39] By then the Chancellor, unfettered by formal requirements, enforced parol promises deliberately given.[40] Thus in 1468 the Chancellor said a nonfeasance was actionable because the petitioner was "damaged by the non-performance, he shall have a remedy here."[41] During the fifteenth century Chancery also developed jurisdiction for enforcement of informal contracts for sales of land on the theory that a bargain and sale passed a "use" to the purchaser.[42]

This expansion by Chancery was unwelcome competition for the King's Bench's emerging contract jurisdiction and prompted King's Bench Justice Fairfax to urge pleaders to fashion declarations that could be heard in the King's Bench, "and then the subpoena will not be used as often as it now is."[43] Common law judges and lawyers were familiar with the clerical Chancellor's contract work,[44] and they tried to coopt the Chancery practice of providing a remedy for the breach of faith of not performing an informal promise by borrowing from Chancery and devising their own nonfeasance remedy.[45] The common law would so completely take over the field that, by the latter part of the sixteenth century, Coke would blatantly declare the law "altered" and if a party could obtain relief in Chancery, then Assumpsit was available.[46] The Chancellor's contract activity would ebb once there was an adequate remedy at law,[47] but he would continue to issue injunctions against harsh common law orders, which intervention would create a crisis between the courts during the second decade of the seventeenth century. The increased use of Assumpsit to curtail the threat posed by Chancery would set the King's Bench on a course of contract law work which would find them infringing on Common Pleas' Debt jurisdiction during the second half of the sixteenth century. But that is getting ahead of the story and so attention will now be returned to the use of Assumpsit for nonfeasance during the first few decades after *Orwell v. Mortoft.*

During a great part of the sixteenth century, Assumpsit for nonfeasance was used primarily for hardship cases where no other remedy was available, and Debt still carried the contract load. The hardship in these informal executory agreements would frequently be that the action of Debt was not available because there was no *quid pro quo,* and Covenant was not available because there was no sealed document; in addition, the fall in the value of 40 shillings precluded any remedies for informal agreements still available in the local courts. As the century wore on, the incidence of these hardship cases increased, and the royal courts began to fill the gap with more regularity[48] until it became a remedy available as a matter of course in the King's Bench in the second half of the sixteenth century. The statistics bear this out: in 1501 there were only six Assumpsit for nonfeasance entries in the Trinity term plea rolls of the Court of Common Pleas,[49] and even as late as 1572 the Trinity term of Common Pleas had 503 Debt *sur contract* actions but only 3 Assumpsit actions.[50] Whereas, in Hilary term of 1573 in the King's Bench, there were 72 Assumpsit actions and 186 Debt actions, wager being possible in only 14 of the Debt actions.[51]

Statistics also show an increase in royal court Assumpsit work because of a transfer of ecclesiastical *fidei laesio* business from the church courts to the common law courts during the anti-clerical first half of the sixteenth century.[52] *Fidei laesio* reached its zenith in about 1500, began to decline by the 1520s and was gone by 1550; whereas, Assumpsit was rare in 1500, was occasional in 1530 and appeared with some regularity by 1550.[53] *Fidei laesio* was a church court action for the enforcement of a sworn promise. There is a marked similarity in the pleading language and the kinds of obligations enforced between the older action of *fidei laesio* and the younger Assumpsit for nonfeasance. It may be that the pleading language of *fidei laesio* was fitted to the reliance-based logic of Assumpsit.[54]

During the sixteenth century, actions for nonfeasance spread, especially in the King's Bench. The trespassory nature of Assumpsit was easier for the King's Bench to accommodate than it was for Common Pleas because the civil side of the King's Bench jurisdiction was basically in trespass, but Common Pleas had authority to hear not only trespass but also the personal actions, which included Debt. Common Pleas was compelled not only to deal with the trespassory nature of Assumpsit but to accommodate Assumpsit with such actions as Covenant and its mainstay, Debt. Whereas, the King's Bench, with no authority to hear actions under the writ of Debt, had none of Common Pleas' accommodation pangs and was furthermore eager to obtain some of the Debt business. A major concern of Common Pleas was the denial of due process in an Assumpsit case to a defendant who was not allowed the ancient right of wager of law available in an action of Debt. So while Common Pleas moved slowly, using Assumpsit mainly as a gap-filler when Covenant or Debt were inappropriate, the King's Bench moved full speed ahead allowing Assumpsit to overlap Debt and creating new remedies when needed.

Although the King's Bench did not have jurisdiction to hear Debt actions, it allowed the disingenuous use of the "bill of Middlesex" to obtain such jurisdiction. If a defendant was in the custody of the jailer of one particular jail known as Marshalsea, a royal prison in the County of Middlesex where Westminster was also located, the King's Bench could hear common pleas, including Debt, by bill (an informal complaint) rather than by writ. The plaintiff would bring a bill of Middlesex for trespass, which would result in the defendant's arrest, and then the plaintiff would file a true bill for debt. If the defendant was not within the sheriff's jurisdiction in Middlesex, the court would issue a writ of *latitat,* meaning he lurks (in another county). Then the sheriff of the other county would arrest the defendant. This device in effect turned the King's Bench into a court of common pleas and greatly expanded the volume of Assumpsit cases.[55]

In 1521 the King's Bench extended Assumpsit to provide a remedy against a surety, a case which was not actionable in Debt due to the lack of a *quid pro quo* in the surety. The case of *Cleymond v. Vincent*[56] was symptomatic of the over-eagerness of the King's Bench to expand Assumpsit's coverage. *Cleymond* also was the first action allowed against the deceased debtor's estate, and it was the first case to use Assumpsit to enforce a gratuitous promise (and a parol one to top it off). It would be well over a century before all of the repercussions of *Cleymond* were sorted out.[57]

Then in 1532 the King's Bench dispensed with the need for the ruse of a bill of Middlesex and allowed Assumpsit to be used in lieu of Debt in *Pykeryng v. Thurgoode*.[58] There were several similar decisions in the decade prior but this was the first reported case, and it seemed to resolve any lingering uncertainty. Although Debt was available here, the plaintiff successfully distinguished the damages suffered by emphasizing that the loss suffered by the breach of the undertaking was not just for the value of the malt but for the damages of paying a higher price elsewhere. Common Pleas resisted Assumpsit in lieu of Debt, except for hardship cases, until after *Slade's Case* (1602).[59]

Pykeryng v. Thurgoode packed a double-barreled punch in that it permitted Assumpsit where Debt lay and it was a pure nonfeasance case. *Pykeryng* is one of the last cases in the King's Bench to concern itself about the old prohibition of nonfeasance. Justice Spelman answered the objection to the use of the trespassory action of Assumpsit for a case lacking a misfeasance, over the dissent of Portman, J., by emphasizing that Assumpsit was an action for the breach of a promise, which had caused consequential damage, and it was therefore a tort. The objection to nonfeasance being actionable was never totally stamped out in the sixteenth century. The objection to nonfeasance was avoided by alleging varying factors which appeared to take it out of pure nonfeasance, e.g., deceit, payment in advance, and loss of credit. The factors alleged were not consistent from case to case, and so there was no one theory of Assumpsit before the mid-sixteenth century but a variety of different causes of action.[60]

Indebitatus Assumpsit and Consideration

Plaintiffs bringing informal contract actions saw advantages in fitting their claim under Assumpsit rather than Debt. Debt had the disadvantages of wager, the lack of a remedy against executors, the narrowness of *quid pro quo* and the requirement of a sum certain.[61] Whereas,

Assumpsit permitted simpler pleading,[62] trial by jury and the discretion of the jury in granting damages for consequential damages;[63] however, Assumpsit could not be brought if there was an older formed writ in the Register covering a given transaction.[64] The formulary writs in the Register had aided lawyers and judges in systematizing the common law, and the consequent prohibition on overlap was not going to be easily ignored.[65] Not to be daunted, plaintiffs' lawyers experimented with pleadings to avoid overlap, as the defendant promising to pay a preexisting debt in consideration of the plaintiff's forbearance from suing in Debt or a simple promise to pay a preexisting debt;[66] the latter approach would become the more common device by the mid-sixteenth century.

The allegation of a simple promise in addition to the debt was set out in differing fashions in the first two cases of their kind: *Whitehed v. Elderton* (1530)[67] and *Pykeryng v. Thurgoode* (1532).[68] In *Pykeryng v. Thurgoode* the plaintiff alleged that the defendant bargained and sold him malt, and that the defendant then promised and assumed to deliver it. The plaintiff won on the breach of the promise, but since the promise was not clearly separated from the debt in the plaintiff's declaration, Portman, J. dissented on the grounds of overlap because the defendant's promise was merely his half of the contractual debt.[69] Portman's objection seemed to be taken seriously because the plaintiff in *Marler v. Wilmer* (1539)[70] more clearly separated the debt and the promise by using the *indebitatus assumpsit* form pioneered in *Whitehed v. Elderton,* wherein the precedent debt (*indebitatus*) had been stated followed by the defendant's subsequent promise (*assumpsit*): "John, being indebted to William in the sum of 10 pounds, promised to pay William 10 pounds." This became the accepted form in the 1540s.[71]

After it was established that the separate promise in the new *indebitatus assumpsit* form avoided the objection of overlap with Debt, the King's Bench eroded the sanctity of the Register further by not requiring the subsequent promise to be proved.[72] The Court of Common Pleas continued to require proof of the subsequent promise while opposing this disruption of the writ system and the incursion of the King's Bench into the domain of Common Pleas' exclusive Debt jurisdiction. By the 1580s the subsequent promise for forbearance was becoming fictional, to the point that the promise no longer need be subsequent.[73] Although the pleading remained the same in both courts, now the King's Bench only required proof of the bargain, but Common Pleas still required proof of the promise.[74] Out of this came the notion that there could be an implied promise to pay in consideration of the debt.[75] Attorney Coke would forthrightly declare in 1587: "... by the common law one could not have an action on the case if he could have another action, but now this old law is altered...."[76] By this time the King's Bench rejected the prohibition on Assumpsit overlapping Debt's jurisdiction, but Common Pleas would not completely acquiesce with that view until *Slade's Case*

(1602). This subversion of the Register would result in Assumpsit wresting away Debt's contract jurisdiction in the seventeenth century. But, again, the chronology of the story of Assumpsit's development requires that attention be returned to the period when *indebitatus assumpsit* was first being employed. As the success of *indebitatus assumpsit* increased the common law courts' Assumpsit caseload, there was a concern voiced that the parameters of Assumpsit needed to be defined. The test of actionability that evolved was the doctrine of consideration, and it would become the essential feature of the common law of contract.

How did the doctrine of consideration develop? When Assumpsit was used early on in the fifteenth century as an extraordinary remedy for hardship cases not covered by the traditional contract writs of Debt and Covenant and also for disputes arising in new economic conditions, as to provide a remedy to a buyer against a seller who refused to deliver in a rising market, there was no such doctrine.[77] Then during the first three decades of the sixteenth century, as the procedural advantages of Assumpsit were exploited in the King's Bench to cover Covenant and common debt transactions, concerns were raised about the parameters of Assumpsit since, unlike the traditional contract writs, Assumpsit's reach was not clearly defined. As the courts grappled with when Assumpsit was permissible, determinations of the circumstances in which Assumpsit could be brought were pieced together as a system of principles ultimately called the doctrine of consideration. This doctrine was rationalized under a single head before the end of the sixteenth century in such cases as *Stone v. Wythipol* (1589), wherein attorney Coke argued "every consideration that doth charge the defendant in an *assumpsit* must be to the benefit of the defendant or charge of the plaintiff, and no case can be put out of this rule."[78] Of Coke's conclusion, a legal historian asks: what was the origin of the doctrine and how did it evolve to that point?

The origin of consideration is one of the great controversies of the history of contract law with nearly as many views as there are writers on the subject.[79] It is a mistake to assume that there was a single source for the doctrine that set the parameters of what was originally a hardship remedy. The doctrine would surface as an amalgamation of various delictual and consensual concepts that had been floating around for several generations. Having said that, the origins found in these various notions will be probed.

One important source of consideration was in the context of liability based on a reliance remedy—the plaintiff could recover if he relied on the defendant's promise to his loss.[80] The Student of the common law informed the Doctor of the civil law of this reliance remedy:

> if he to whom the promise is made have a *charge by reason of the promise, which he hath also performed*, then in that case he shall have an action for

> that thing that was promised, though he that made the promise have no worldly profit by it. (Emphasis supplied).[81]

Reliance was also the basis of recovery pointed to in the dictum of a nonfeasance case roughly dated sometime in the decade before 1537:

> if I am bound in an obligation of 40 pounds to pay 20 pounds by a certain day and I deliver the 20 pounds to a stranger and he promises to deliver before the day, and he does not pay this before the day, so that I have forfeited my obligation, there for the nonfeasance I shall have an action on the case, for he has done wrong (tort) to me.[82]

Emphasis on the delictual side of Assumpsit continued once a subsequent undertaking was alleged in order to avoid overlap. Nonfeasance was made actionable by a deceit ploy in cases where the plaintiff could say that he was induced to forbear from suing at the due date because of the defendant's subsequent promise.[83] However, except for the survival of liability when there was a loss of an actual prepayment,[84] the use of the deceit ploy was a procedural fiction by the 1540s when "consideration" was only an experimental term in plaintiffs' declarations.[85] In addition to the tortious nature of Assumpsit as a source of consideration, the common law borrowed from other sources; for, in justifying when Assumpsit was actionable, the courts were not making a conscious attempt to shape a coherent doctrine for this hardship remedy. Two of the other prominent influences were the Roman *causa* and a long standing notion of reciprocity.

In civilian terms *causa* was the reason or motive for the promise, without which the promise was unenforceable. Common law Assumpsit declarations sometimes included the term *causa* by 1540, though the meaning of *causa* in the common law may have included aspects of both motive and recompense.[86] Furthermore, the *causa* in some of the early decisions may have been the plaintiff's reliance on the defendant's promise.[87] An important influence from Chancery related to *causa* was the requirement of equitable consideration to raise a use, the requirement of consideration in the law of uses appearing a generation earlier than it did in Assumpsit.[88] Indeed, once consideration appeared in Assumpsit declarations, analogies were drawn to its application in uses[89] so that there seemed a convergence of consideration in uses and in Assumpsit until the issue of enforceability of promises based on love and affection broke them apart.

By the 1540s a recognizable doctrine of consideration had yet to surface, but the foundations were being laid. The procedural device of the subsequent promise in the Assumpsit declaration, employed to avoid overlap with Debt, would prompt the doctrine to begin to come into focus. For how could the plaintiff justify the enforcement of the subsequent promise? The subsequent promise could clearly not be enforced independently in Covenant because there was no deed. One possibility already mentioned was to base it on a forbearance, but there was also another approach on the horizon that contained hints of reciprocity. After objections raised in *Marler v. Wilmer* (1539), pleaders seemed to deem it necessary to show some linkage between the bargain and the subsequent promise or there would be no *causa* for the promise and it would hence be *nudum pactum*.[90] The obvious linkage would be to allege the precedent bargain, but that would have been defective since it would have exhibited an overlap with Debt. Experiments with acceptable linkage phrasing between the recital of the obligation and the *assumpsit* clause were soon devised.[91]

Pleading phraseologies drafted to provide the needed linkage were in the form of either a *quid pro quo* clause or an *in consideration* clause or a combination of the two. The first case found thus far with a consideration clause is *Harvy v. Stone* (1539) wherein an impending marriage was the consideration.[92] The mere inclusion of the term "consideration" in the declaration by no means meant that the doctrine had arrived; and, between the consideration clause and the *quid pro quo* clause, the latter was more common until the 1560s. The *quid pro quo* clause was found particularly in actions to recover the price of goods: the *quid* was the goods *pro quo* (for which) the subsequent undertaking was given.[93] The *quid pro quo* of Debt should not be confused with the pleading verbiage used here in relation to the subsequent promise.[94] The fact that the consideration clause did ultimately eclipse the *quid pro quo* clause may have been because of the perceived advantage of consideration encompassing both the reciprocity of *quid pro quo* and the motive of *causa*.[95]

By the mid-sixteenth century the delictual idea of deceit was being subsumed within the contractual notion of reciprocity.[96] The questions of how this transition occurred and how this emerging contractual doctrine was deformed as a result of Assumpsit's trespassory background[97] is still lurking in the haze of the King's Bench plea rolls. Although true reliance in its original sense would continue to be a basis of recovery, the detriment suffered by the deceit was becoming a facet of contractual consideration.[98] Earlier in the sixteenth century detriment had meant the loss suffered because of the defendant's deceitful breach of the undertaking, but now damage need not be proved, and the detriment became the charge or obligation incurred by the plaintiff in making a promise in order to induce the defendant's undertaking. The indiscriminate use of the word "detriment" had obscured its meaning.[99]

By the 1560s consideration was being required and discussed, as in *Isack v. Barbour* (1563), where the King's Bench held for the defendant because "no consideration is alleged by reason of which (she) promised and undertook to pay".[100] The first case of a defendant objecting to the alleged consideration was argued between 1561 and 1563.[101] As the discussions ensued, an important issue bringing the doctrine into focus was what constituted sufficient consideration. Insufficiency never seemed to be found on the basis of the value of the benefits being unequal or inadequate since the parties were deemed the best arbiters of their own interest.[102] Defendants' insufficiency arguments were taken seriously, however, when the consideration was based on love and affection or its cousin past consideration. Was motive enough in these cases or must there be reciprocity? While *causa*, or motive, was still an aspect of consideration, love and affection was sufficient consideration.[103] But there were objections raised in *Sharington v. Strotton* in 1565 to affection raising a use or enforcing a promise: "... the cause is not sufficient. And nothing is done or given from the one side, for you were my brother before and will be so afterwards, and you are of my acquaintance before and will be so afterwards."[104] Then in *Hunt v. Bate* (1568)[105] the love and affection of friends was disallowed as sufficient consideration, and love and affection within the family was disallowed later.[106] These love and affection cases are a source of the rule that past consideration is insufficient:[107] the love and affection that existed before the promise was not something new flowing to the promisor in exchange for his promise.

Except for love and affection as consideration for marriage, the rules on love and affection in the law of uses and Assumpsit had now diverged. Love and affection continued to be sufficient consideration in the law of uses for family land settlements,[108] but reciprocity was now required in Assumpsit. If the notion of *causa* had remained in consideration, it is easy enough to see how a sufficient motive could be found for making a promise in consideration of love and affection or past consideration, but once reciprocity of the bargain took over the field, past consideration was insufficient.[109] Reciprocity runs deep in the common law,[110] and it is perhaps not surprising that during a commercial era the courts would prefer the reciprocity of the bargain over enforcement of any promise found to have a reasonable motive.[111]

The rule that love and affection was insufficient to ground an Assumpsit action involved an analysis in terms of the timing of the consideration and the promise—if the consideration was prior to the promise it was insufficient. If timing was to be a significant test, then could not mere promises simultaneously given in exchange for each other be sufficient consideration? More fundamental to consideration, could such mutual promises bind each other even though there had been nothing done in the way of reliance or receipt of *quid pro quo?* Didn't the plaintiff need to allege performance on his part? In a modern sense one would say it was a totally executory contract,[112] though to contemporaries the terms of the mutual promises might have allowed a promise to be revoked before a breach[113] or might not have made the defendant's promise dependent on the plaintiff's promise.[114] Notwithstanding the misgivings about the lack of the plaintiff's performance, arguments for the enforcement of mutual promises in Assumpsit began appearing in the second half of the sixteenth century.

There was a judicial resistance to the enforcement of mutual promises in the first cases because of the lack of reciprocity or *quid pro quo.*[115] Indeed, there seemed a contemporary sense that good consideration was synonymous with *quid pro quo.*[116] Then, suddenly all seemed resolved in 1589, when it was announced in a laconic note reporting the ruling in *Strangborough v. Warner* that there was sufficient consideration because the promises were reciprocal: 'Note, that a promise against a promise will maintain an action upon the case, as in consideration that you give to me 10 pounds on such day, I promise to give you 10 pounds such a day after."[117] The bargain now was irrevocable from the moment mutual promises were exchanged in consideration for each other. Put in terms of the duality of consideration by the late sixteenth century, there was a mutual benefit and detriment to the parties.[118]

The claim that the advent of enforceability of mutual promises is the dawn of a modern consensual view of contract must be treated cautiously since it was largely restricted in the sixteenth century to exceptional cases of conditional promises, gambling contracts and as a pleading device to avoid overlap with Debt since there was no *quid pro quo* in mutual promises.[119] The adoption of the enforceability of mutual promises made it a part of the story of Special Assumpsit. The allowance of mutual promises helped distinguish Special Assumpsit from *indebitatus assumpsit* and Debt, the latter two requiring a "benefit" to the defendant.[120]

By the 1580s consideration was the recognized doctrine for determining when a promise could be enforced in Assumpsit. The doctrine had begun in common money claims, as contracts for goods, and it became applicable to all types of contracts.[121] Since liability had long been recognized in such common contracts in Debt, once it was clear that the *indebitatus assumpsit* pleading form could be used to avoid overlap with Debt, consideration was largely presumed for those common contracts (over a century later called common counts) by the third quarter of the sixteenth century. The real debates about the meaning of what constituted consideration and its sufficiency were found in mutual promises and in extraordinary cases, such as love and affection, where there had formerly been no liability under any writ, old or new.[122]

In a formularly system like the common law, a plaintiff who wanted to use Assumpsit had to invent a difference in his declaration between his case and those that would have fallen under the older contract writs of Debt and Covenant.[123] Finding the difference required the creation of consideration; this was the price paid for a modern law of contracts.[124]

Consideration became the test for determining whether the necessary circumstances were present to maintain an action of Assumpsit. It was the term identifying the set of rules as to when contractual liability exists in Assumpsit.[125] It was the test selected by the common law courts among several possible alternatives. It should not be overlooked that there were moral underpinnings for the doctrine of consideration based on the ancient truths that bargains should bind both parties and that the promisor should be held to promises relied on.[126]

Slade's Case

During the sixteenth century, Common Pleas dealt with Assumpsit for nonfeasance in a more conservative way than the King's Bench. By the latter half of the sixteenth century, Common Pleas allowed Assumpsit where Debt would lie if there was something in addition to or collateral to the debt, as for example, special damages.[127] By that period the King's Bench was dropping its demands for these additional or collateral factors. Since Debt was only for the liquidated sum and not for additional factors, Common Pleas would allow Assumpsit if payments were in installments or at a certain place or if there was forbearance in suing by the plaintiff in order to give the defendant some more time.[128] Any special loss past the liquidated debt, as a consequential business loss or a loss of credit or a changed market price, was recoverable in the tortious action of Assumpsit.[129] Common Pleas was adamantly opposed, however, to the King's Bench's brazen allowance of Assumpsit in place of Debt when additional factors were not truly present.

Common Pleas made known their opposition to the King's Bench handling of Assumpsit by raising a number of objections: First, by allowing Assumpsit to overlap Debt, the King's Bench was subverting the consistency and systemization of the writ system, which had generally promoted justice for over 300 years. Second, the King's Bench was trying to avoid Debt's wager of law, which was a violation of the defendant's due process.[130] Third, an action of Assumpsit should not be allowed unless an express undertaking was proved over and above the existence of the actual transaction (the King's Bench had been presuming such a promise). Fourth, the damages in Assumpsit for a breach should only be for an irremediable wrong in tort (consequential damages) and not for the enforcement of a duty in contract (the value of the debt itself).[131] Fifth, the general form of pleading allowed by the King's Bench, known as *indebitatus,* merely announced that there was a debt without providing any details and thus caught the defendant by surprise. Sixth, the King's Bench was allowing an action against the executor for a debt, which was not allowed in the action of Debt. Seventh, there was opposition to the disingenuous pleadings and the use of fictions by the King's Bench in order to come up with additional factors to take an action out of Debt.[132] And, eighth, since the time of the Magna Carta of 1215, Common Pleas had sole jurisdiction over Debt, and the King's Bench was violating that ancient law by allowing Assumpsit to do the work of Debt.

The friction between the King's Bench and Common Pleas over the issue of allowing Assumpsit in lieu of Debt came to a head during the period of 1585 to 1602. Until 1585 Common Pleas had no control over the King's Bench since appeals from the King's Bench were taken to the infrequent Elizabethan parliaments. In 1585 a Statute changed that by creating a new court known as the Exchequer Chamber.[133] The membership of this Court consisted of the justices of Common Pleas and the Barons of the Exchequer. This new Exchequer Chamber had the authority to review decisions of the King's Bench, and now Common Pleas was in a position to do something about the King's Bench's improper use of Assumpsit. The issue did not arise until 1592. Perhaps Chief Justice Wray of the King's Bench caused the delay because he had a change of heart and discouraged the extension of Assumpsit, but after Wray's death in 1591 and the accession of the aggressive Sir John Popham as Chief Justice, the issue arose. The new Exchequer Chamber reversed a King's Bench decision in 1595 and another in 1596. Both appeals were from decisions rendered by Popham in which the plaintiff pleaded the *assumpsit,* or undertaking, as the debt itself without any additional factor alleged. The King's Bench continued to allow Assumpsit in lieu of Debt, seemingly ignoring the reversals.[134] Then in 1595 the conflicting positions of Common Pleas and the King's Bench came to a head in *Slade v. Morley (Slade's Case).*[135]

The showdown in *Slade's Case* had been coming for nearly a century. Ever since the fall in value of money, the 40 shilling rule had been forcing everyday agreements, formerly heard in the local courts, into the royal courts. Common Pleas' ancient contract actions of Covenant and Debt, designed for significant, formal transactions, were ineffective in the adjudicating of both the everyday, informal transactions of the common man and the informal mercantile transaction. The King's Bench, which had no jurisdiction over these ancient contract actions except by the surreptitious use of the bill of Middlesex, had the most to gain by promoting Assumpsit in order to expand its trespassory business. But why was the King's Bench making these incursions? The court fees cannot be the only explanation for the deadlock because the King's Bench was by then freely permitting the bill of Middlesex which resulted in that Court hearing many Debt actions.[136] Another factor was probably the monopoly the serjeants-at-law had in Common Pleas. The serjeants were the senior branch and considered the upper-crust of the legal profession. They charged higher fees than the barristers appearing in the King's Bench, and only they could appear in Common Pleas. No doubt the justices of Common Pleas, former serjeants themselves, tried to protect the vested interests of these influential advocates.[137]

Economic self-interest does not seem to be the real answer. The reason for the conflict between the royal courts arguably lies largely in an intellectual conflict over what the law was and whether the organizing function of the three hundred year old writ system and the prohibition on overlapping remedies should continue. Common Pleas represented the *status quo,* and the King's Bench was the activist court ready to right the ills of the archaic rules, particularly the shortcomings of Debt.[138] The Medieval action of Debt was an outmoded remedy for the modern mercantile era; for, again, Debt's faults included: the farce that wager had become as the custom developed of defendants buying supportive testimony at Westminster, the narrowness of *quid pro quo* with its sum certain requirement and its inability to cover third party transactions, its lack of reciprocal remedies in land sales and personal services agreements, its lack of a remedy against the deceased debtor's executor and its pleading and damages shortcomings.

The legality of replacing Debt with Assumpsit was squarely met in the decision of *Slade v. Morley.*[139] The plaintiff, John Slade, filed a bill of Middlesex in Assumpsit against Humfrey Morley alleging that, at the request of the defendant, the plaintiff had "bargained and sold" to the defendant certain growing crops. The bill went on to say that the defendant had faithfully promised to pay sixteen pounds, but that the defendant, intending to deceive the plaintiff, did not pay, to the plaintiff's damage of forty pounds. The case was heard out on the circuit, and, as was the custom, the jury would give their verdict, but final judgment would be made back at Westminster. The special verdict of the jury said: "The said Humfrey Morley did buy the wheat and rye growing . . . from the said John Slade for 16 pounds to be paid . . . but there was no undertaking or promise between the said John Slade and the said Humfrey Morley besides the bargain aforesaid." Two justices on the circuit heard the case: one from the King's Bench and other from Common Pleas. The two justices on circuit caused the jury to render an uncommon special verdict in order to squarely raise the issue of whether Assumpsit could be used in lieu of Debt.[140] The King's Bench referred the case to the *old* informal Exchequer Chamber,[141] as Coke wrote, "for the honour of the law, and for the quiet of the subject."[142] Why didn't Common Pleas push home its advantage by insisting upon the appeal before the new Statutory Exchequer Chamber where there was a strong majority supporting its viewpoint? Perhaps Common Pleas' own conservatism made those justices uneasy about a Parliamentary attempt to affect the ancient judge-made common law.[143]

There were five reported arguments of *Slade's Case* between 1597 and 1602, and the best lawyers of the day argued it, including Coke for the plaintiff and Bacon for the defendant. In the second argument during the Michelmas Term of 1598 at Serjeants' Inn, the plaintiff's lawyers pounded home the fundamental objection to Debt of wager of law.[144] During the fourth argument on May 13, 1602 at Serjeants' Inn, Bacon, for the defendant, argued that Assumpsit lacked the form required for it to be in the ancient Register of Writs, that wager is a better truth-seeking device for a private agreement, which a jury would not have independent information about, and that Debt on a bargain is an executed property right unlike the trespassory and executory nature of Assumpsit.[145]

Out of the lawyerly debates in *Slade's Case*, two issues emerged: (1) can a promise be inferred from entry into a bargain? Or, as Popham, C.J. put it, does every contract executory import in itself an *assumpsit*?[146] (2) Can Assumpsit and Debt be used for the same transaction? (A subcategory of this second issue is the question of the right of the defendant to wage his law.)[147] First, does every executory contract imply an *assumpsit*? The term "executory" has caused some difficulty for historians.[148] The word "executory" causes confusion for modern lawyers since Popham's use of the word has nothing to do with its modern meaning. The contract was executory to a modern lawyer in that it had not been performed by either party—the wheat was not delivered by Slade nor paid for by Morley. However, to contemporaries of *Slade's Case*, the word contract did not mean agreement; it meant a situation where Debt lies, as for a bargain and sale of goods. Popham emphasized that the debt was executory to indicate that the debt was not paid and that, if there had been a Debt judgment thereon, the plaintiff could not sue in Assumpsit. The consideration was not viewed as executory since there was a completed bargain and sale, the consideration being the contract of sale itself and not the defendant's promise.[149] And how was the consideration not considered executory when there had been no delivery of the goods to the defendant-buyer? It was accomplished by the outrageous fiction, first recognized in fifteenth century Debt actions, that "property" in specific goods could pass to the buyer by virtue of the bargain and sale alone, without any actual delivery of the goods.[150] Had sellers not convinced the courts to recognize this fiction, these non-delivery cases (executory in a modern sense) would have failed in Debt actions for lack of a *quid pro quo*, but the fiction passed the benefit of the "property" thus supplying the *quid pro quo*. *Slade's Case* has been wrongly credited with deciding that mutual promises were enforceable, but this was not true because the passing of property fiction supplied the *quid pro quo* for the sale of goods facts of *Slade's Case*.[151] The requirement of *quid pro quo* was under attack by the fifteenth century, as lawyers thought other contracts besides sales of goods should be enforceable without performance by either party; however, the passing of property fiction preserved the dogma of the proprietary doctrine of *quid pro quo,* based on an exchange rather than a promise, arresting the possibility of growth in contract law for contracts other than sales of goods.[152]

Now what about the question of whether a contract imports in itself an *assumpsit.* The resolution in *Slade's Case* was in the affirmative, that the contract itself implied a simultaneous undertaking to perform without the defendant's express words "I promise". Thus the fictional subsequent promise of the defendant need not be alleged because, as the plaintiff's attorney Coke argued in the first Exchequer Chamber arguments in 1597, "Would you have every plain man use the proper words 'I assume' or 'I take upon myself'? It is unnecessary." When a layman does what amounts to an undertaking, then the law will treat it as an undertaking.[153] The justices were giving a new interpretation to the old exchange transaction covered by Debt, in pursuance of the presumed intention of the parties, by finding an implied promise in the transaction formerly only sounding as a grant.[154] Whenever Debt *sur contract* would lie on an unpaid debt (thus executory to contemporaries), an *assumpsit* would be implied. So Popham in delivering the judgment in *Slade's Case* said: "Every contract executory imports in itself an assumpsit."

The second issue, of Assumpsit overlapping Debt, was a seventy year old question on which the King's Bench and Common Pleas could not agree.[155] The King's Bench did not have a good legal argument for allowing overlap other than that the obvious failure to follow the Register of Writs was longstanding error and should not be the law.[156] Popham said, "Although it be error, yet the long use and multitude of precedents must draw it into the law, for *communis error facit ius* (error of the community makes it law)."[157] Common Pleas Justice Walmsley said, "Nevertheless, it is what the books say." To which Popham retorted: "The books are against law." The plaintiff also argued that the ills of wager of law, with its history of paid oath-helpers and rampant perjury, must be ended.[158] In response, the defendant's counsel argued the Common Pleas' position that the sanctity of the three hundred year old writ system required the continued prohibition on overlapping remedies. The defendant further argued that the Englishman's birthright of wager was more effective than trial by jury when the agreement was private, particularly since the parties were barred from testifying.[159] By the late sixteenth century courts were making attempts to exercise control over wager by allowing it only after satisfying themselves that there was a just defense.[160] Nevertheless *Slade's Case* held that Assumpsit could overlap Debt. This spelled the end of Debt *sur contract,* the most frequently used action for hundreds of years, as a viable action.

The resolution of *Slade's Case* was obtained by an extraordinary show of hands of the participants of the informal Exchequer Chamber, resulting in a 6 to 5 majority vote in favor of the plaintiff.[161] The membership of the Statutory Exchequer Chamber was still 5 to 2 opposed, and yet Common Pleas would mysteriously acquiesce to the King's Bench view within a few years, as will be seen in the next chapter. The majority vote was not followed by any public declaration of the judges' rationale. This lack of judicial guidance allowed Coke's disingenuous, plaintiff-oriented report of the case to lead subsequent lawyers to misunderstand the ramifications of *Slade's Case*; for, there was no Bracton or Maitland to set him straight. For centuries subsequent to *Slade,* most lawyers only knew it for what Coke's Report said it did, namely, a clear judgment of all the judges of England replacing Debt with Assumpsit. In the main, Coke's Report merely reflected his arguments as counsel for the plaintiff, John Slade, while avoiding most of his nemesis Bacon's compelling defenses. He did not acknowledge that the plaintiff's principal argument was based on the "error of the community," and he claimed that *Slade* decided questions that were simply not discussed or decided, as will be analyzed in the next chapter.

Although *Slade* did not do all that was attributed to it, the decision did have far-reaching implications. Lawyers of the day were aware there had been a deliberate judicial alteration of the law.[162] As a practical matter, *Slade's Case* ended the use of Debt *sur contract,* when it entailed the use of wager of law, and replaced it with the more flexible Assumpsit and its attendant trial by jury, though wager would not be officially abolished until 1833.[163] Assumpsit did not replace those actions which did not have wager of law, such as Debt *sur obligation* and Covenant; thus the traditional dichotomy of sealed and unsealed obligations was retained. The result of *Slade's Case* was the fusion of the two traditional strands of contract actions for, one, breaching a promise (or covenant) to perform an act, which was absorbed into the common law earlier in *Orwell v. Mortoft,* and, two, for breaching a promise to pay money in *Slade's Case.* The law of informal contracts was now unified under the single form of action of Assumpsit. The modern theory of promissory liability under a single head dates from *Slade's Case* or shortly thereafter, when both common law courts accepted its resolution.

Even though Common Pleas would acquiesce to the King's Bench lead in *Slade's Case,* there would continue to be influential voices raised against this radical step. In 1670 Chief Justice Vaughn objected to the use of Assumpsit for damages, which would include special loss and the value of the whole debt; he was opposed to the confusion of Covenant and Debt, and he denied the validity of *Slade's Case.*[164] In 1760 Lord Mansfield voiced his objections to the use of Assumpsit to effectuate specific performance.[165] In 1672 Chief Justice Hale expressed concern about the perjury in jury trials in Assumpsit actions. He claimed that perjury was so common that men could not safely speak together without a promise springing from it and that *Slade's Case* caused this harmful result.[166] The pendulum would swing too far in favor of the plaintiff as a result of *Slade's Case*, just as wager of law had held it too much on the defendant's side, and so Parliament would try to bring the pendulum to the middle by the unfortunate Statute of Frauds (1677),[167] discussed in the next chapter.

Conclusion

The conservative obeisance to the narrow confines of the Medieval writ system, which had not been designed for a modern money economy, created hardships and stultified doctrinal growth. The only way out was for an activist court to find a window of flexibility in the system. By use of analogy and sheer refusal to adhere to outmoded doctrine, the King's Bench led Common Pleas, the home of the traditional common law of contract, toward a modern law of contract.

The step-by-step stretching of precedent to obtain flexible contractual relief from a tort action began in contract misfeasance cases. During the fourteenth century the first signs of expansion from the tortious nature of trespass can be seen in cases involving the breach of a customary duty. Another early strand of development originated in actions of trespass on the case for deceit, wherein actions were allowed first for public offenses and then for quasi-public offenses of breach of fiduciary duties; then in the fifteenth century, analogies were drawn to the deceitful breach of a fiduciary duty in allowing recovery for the disablement caused by an ordinary seller. The determination that the deceit of disablement was a basis of liability was extended by later courts crossing the line between tort and contract to allow recovery for the pure nonfeasance of simply refusing to honor one's promise. Once the constraints of the writ system had been overcome and Assumpsit was employed as a contractual action, the parameters established for the use of the new procedural device of *indebitatus assumpsit* consisted of a new set of constraints which came to be labelled as the doctrine of consideration. Consideration was the price contract law paid in obtaining a flexible remedy from a trespassory source.

During the period covered by this chapter (1400–1602), the pure nonfeasance cases in Assumpsit represented a small number of cases. The courts were using the action primarily for hardship cases. The breakthrough signalling the replacement of the old contract writs with Assumpsit as a general contract action for the enforcement of informal promises was *Slade's Case*. The next chapter deals with how the ramifications of *Slade's Case* were worked out during the seventeenth century.

Notes

1. *See* S. THORNE, SIR EDWARD COKE (1552–1952), SELDEN SOCIETY LECTURE 3, 4 (1952). Other social and political changes included: dis-

solution of monasteries, growing and now mobile population, rise of the gentry and peace for the first time in 100 years.

2. J. CLAPHAM, A CONCISE ECONOMIC HISTORY OF BRITAIN 186–187 (Cambridge: 1949) (Henry VIII also debased coinage in 1540s.).

3. *See Id.* at 146, 158, 197–198, 208–212, 225.

4. *But cf.* Baker, *English Law and the Renaissance,* 44 CAMBRIDGE LAW J. 46, 47–50 (1985) (True, more actions for greater amounts of money were brought, but the procedural and jurisdictional changes emanate from intellectual causes prompted by the greater professionalism of the courts and of the inns of court rather than from economic and social forces.).

5. *Cf.* S. STOLJAR, A HISTORY OF CONTRACT AT COMMON LAW 34 (Canberra: 1975) (Increase in detinue actions in late fifteenth century may have been because buyers were ensuring future supplies at agreed prices to keep within planned costs in rising market.).

6. Milsom, *Law and Fact in Legal Development,* 17 U. OF TORONTO L. J. 1, 1–17 (1967).

7. Milsom, *Not Doing Is No Trespass: A View of the Boundaries of Case,* 1954 CAMBRIDGE L.J. 105, 108.

8. *Cf.* S. MILSOM, HISTORICAL FOUNDATIONS OF THE COMMON LAW 244–246 (London: 2d ed. 1981).

9. Stat. 25 Edw. III, st. 2, c.1. The Statute provided: "If any reaper, mower or other workman or servant, of whatever state or condition he may be, retained in any man's service, do depart from the same service without reasonable cause or license before the term agreed, he shall have pain of imprisonment."

10. *See* T. PLUCKNETT, A CONCISE HISTORY OF THE ENGLISH COMMON LAW 32 (Boston: 5th ed. 1956); *see also* J. CLAPHAM, *supra* note 2, at 116–119 (Labor enjoyed happy position in 15th century since wages outstripped food prices.).

11. Thelnetham v. Penne, 88 SELDEN SOCIETY 7 (1378); Y.B. Mich. 28 Edw. III, f.21, pl. 18 (1354); Y.B. Mich. 29 Edw. III, f.27 (1355).

12. Humber Ferry Case, Y.B. 22 Lib. Ass., pl. 41, f.94 (1348), *reprinted in* T. PLUCKNETT, *supra* note 10, at 470.

13. Watton v. Brinth, Y.B. 2 Hen. IV, f.3, pl.3 (1400), *reprinted in* C. FIFOOT, HISTORY AND SOURCES OF THE COMMON LAW: TORT AND CONTRACT 340 (London: 1949) (One justice wrongly thought Statute of Labourers might apply.). *See* Teeven, *Proving Fifteenth Century Promises,* 24 OSGOODE HALL L.J. 121, 134 (1986) (courts reluctant to allow embryonic trial by jury to consider such an informal promise).

14. *See* A. SIMPSON, A HISTORY OF THE COMMON LAW OF CONTRACT 210–211, 221–222 (Oxford: 1975).

15. Watkin's Case, Y.B. Hil., 3 Hen. VI, pl.33, f.36v (1425), reprinted in C. FIFOOT, *supra* note 13, at 341.

16. In 1436 there was a case quite similar to *Watkin's Case* which also held for the plaintiff. *Anon,* Y.B. 14 Hen. VI, f.18, pl.58 (1436); see A. KIRALFY, THE ACTION ON THE CASE 149–150 (London: 1951) (writs for failures to repair, to cut timber, and to plough and suits brought for failure to build and to dig); *and* Milsom, *Sale of Goods in the Fifteenth Century,* 77 L.Q. REV. 257, 277 (1961) (action brought for non-delivery of goods against a coal merchant and

against a fishmonger); *cf.* Ames, *The History of Assumpsit,* 3 SELECT ESSAYS IN ANGLO-AMERICAN LEGAL HISTORY 259, 269–271 (Boston: 1909) (*Watkin's* and 1436 case were made without precedent and had no following.).

17. *Cf.* McGovern, *The Enforcement of Informal Contracts in the Later Middle Ages,* 59 CALIF. L. REV. 1145, 1169–1172 (1971). The points McGovern made in support of his view that nonfeasance was accepted much earlier were: (1) he emphasized the two similar failure to build cases decided in 1425 (*Watkin's Case*) and 1436 and also a 1443 case of a surgeon found liable for a failure to perform a covenant to attend a patient (Y.B. Pasch. 21 Hen. VI, f.55, pl.12 (1443)); and, (2) he distinguished the deceit logic of *Doige's Case* (1442) from *Somerton's Case* (1433) because land contracts were so valuable and thus *sui generis.* However, McGovern failed to recognize that the majority in the largely ignored *Watkin's Case* emphasized the tortious nature of the damages caused by a failure to build the roof, such as damages to furniture; and, he likewise ignored the tort implications of negligent malpractice and of reliance of the patient when a surgeon fails to attend after promising to do so. Furthermore, he failed to take into account that Assumpsit was primarily used as a gap-filler in all the cases cited. *See also* Hamburger, *The Development of Nineteenth-Century Consensus Theory of Contract,* 7 LAW & HIST. REV. 241, 294 n. 35 (1989) (McGovern's thesis is questionable since his evidence is susceptible to a variety of interpretations.)

18. Bernardeston v. Heighlynge (1344), *reprinted in* J. BAKER and S. MILSOM, SOURCES OF ENGLISH LEGAL HISTORY 338 (London: 1986) (hereinafter cited as BAKER and MILSOM); S. MILSOM, *supra* note 8, at 327. On the independent contractor point, see Rolfe's statement to that effect in *Watkin's Case.*

19. *See* S. MILSOM, *supra* note 8, at 326.

20. Legal historians have disagreed on the origins of deceit. Fifoot thought there was originally an action of deceit on the case separate from trespass. C. FIFOOT, *supra* note 13, at 333. The accepted theory espoused by Milsom is that a deceit grew out of trespass rather than having a separate origin. Milsom, *supra* note 7, at 107–108 (Assumpsit did not owe its inheritance to trespass *vi et armis.*).

21. *See* J. BAKER, AN INTRODUCTION TO ENGLISH LEGAL HISTORY 278, 294 (London: 2d ed. 1979).

22. *Somerton's Case,* Y.B. Trin. 11 Hen. VI, pl.26, f.55 (1433); *Doige's Case,* Y.B. Trin. 20 Hen. VI, pl. 4, f.34 (1442).

23. A. KIRALFY, *supra* note 16, at 79–81, 83–85, 87 (Borough custom enforced warranties of quality for sales of food and animals.). The cases against lawyers were based on Statute of Westminster I, c. 29 (1275). These public misfeasance origins are a natural extension of trespass' roots in criminal law. The public basis of deceit was also present in the genesis of the related Assumpsit for misfeasance.

24. *Somerton's Case,* Y.B. Trin. 11 Hen. VI, pl.26, f.55 (1433), *reprinted in* C. FIFOOT, *supra* note 13, at 343. There had been an earlier case of a non-lawyer breaching his fiduciary duty in *Anon,* Y.B. Mich. 3 Hen. IV, pl.12, f.3 (1401).

25. Shipton v. Dogge (*Doige's Case*), Y.B. Trin. 20 Hen. VI, pl.4, f.34 (1442), *reprinted in* C. FIFOOT, *supra* note 13, at 347. (Ayscough, J. said there's no liability in deceit if she hadn't sold to third person.). Two of the justices were

against holding defendant liable because disablement was really not any different than merely "not doing."

26. By the sixteenth century the pleadings in a pure nonfeasance case would include fictional deceit language as a matter of formality in order to overcome the, by then anachronistic, objection of nonfeasance; the deceit language suggested a misfeasance.

27. *See* A. SIMPSON, *supra* note 14, at 595 (Chancellor couldn't decree specific performance upon passing of a use since vendor no longer possessed land.). And detinue was not available against a vendor of land.

28. S. MILSOM, *supra* note 8, at 329–332 (Lawyers of time couldn't see novel path being followed.).

29. A. FITZHERBERT, LA GRAUNDE ABRIDGEMENT, *Accion Sur Le Cas*, pl.45 (Trin. 14 Hen. VII) (1577). This 1499 report was not published until 1506. Y.B. Mich. 21 Hen. VII, f.41, pl.66 (1506), *reprinted in* C. FIFOOT, *supra* note 13, at 353. *See* 94 SELDEN SOCIETY 267 (1977) (Marginal note indicates report was of a speech of Fyneux at Gray's Inn.). *Cf.* A. SIMPSON, *supra* note 14, at 260–262 (Assumpsit was gap-filler here since Statute of Labourers didn't apply to independent contractor.).

30. Orwell v. Mortoft, Y.B. Mich. 20 Hen. VII, f.8, pl.18 (C.P. 1505), *reprinted in* BAKER and MILSOM, *supra* note 18, at 408.

31. In *Orwell v. Mortoft* the justices expressly declared Assumpsit could not overlap Debt; and, since the facts were arguably under Debt, the plaintiff's pleader imaginatively alleged the seller was holding the barley for him as bailee, which took it out of Debt. Assumpsit filled a gap here since Detinue was not available for unascertained goods.

32. Orwell v. Mortoft, Keil 69 (1505), *reprinted in* BAKER and MILSOM, *supra* note 18, at 410n. But there is no explicit statement in the record that the carpenter was paid. The transition from granting damages for restitution to granting them for future losses will be covered in the next chapter.

33. *Cf.* Barton, *The Early History of Consideration*, 85 L.Q. REV. 372, 377 (1969) (Fyneux's remark may have been due to fear that Chancery would take over the field of commercial law.). *See also* Baker, *Introduction* in THE REPORTS OF SIR JOHN SPELMAN, 94 SELDEN SOC. 23, 267 (J. Baker ed. 1977) (It was another example of doctrine of conscience being accepted by common law.). Fyneux, C.J.K.B., saw his role as somewhat similar to Chancery, observing that half of his office involved the exercise of discretion. *Id.* at 41. Indeed, the judicial green light to the use of trespass on the case for hardship cases falling through the cracks of the writ system was a case of the common law doing equity.

34. Barbour, *Some Aspects of Fifteenth Century Chancery*, 3 HARV. L. REV. 834, 848–849 (1918) (Chancery used contract theory without needing to approach it through tort.).

35. C. FIFOOT, *supra* note 13, at 302.

36. Barbour, *The History of Contract in Early English Equity* in IV OXFORD STUDIES IN SOCIAL AND LEGAL HISTORY 163–168 (P. Vinogradoff ed. 1914).

37. T. PLUCKNETT, *supra* note 10, at 649–652.

38. *Cf.* Barbour, *supra* note 36, at 105–106, 132–135 (promises for gifts and past promises enforced); *but cf.* Barton, *supra* note 33, at 380–381 (Questions

Barbour here because, though sureties and marriage gifts enforced, promises to make gifts were not generally enforced by Chancery and promises on past services not said to be enforceable in DOCTOR AND STUDENT.).

39. Barbour, *supra* note 36, at 71–118, 150–168. Barbour's early twentieth century plunge into the Public Records Office archives is still the classic research done on Chancery's fifteenth century contract jurisdiction.

40. C. FIFOOT, *supra* note 13, at 304.

41. *Anon,* Y.B. Pasch. 8 Edw. IV, f.4, pl.11 (1468) (And the Chancellor said that petitioner need not go to the church courts under breach of faith or to the common law in Covenant.).

42. A. SIMPSON, *supra* note 14, at 595.

43. Y.B. Pasch. 21 Edw. IV, 23, pl.6 (1482). *See* Barbour, *supra* note 36, at 98–106, 163–168 (in Equity no deed or definite sum required, executors liable and assignments permitted).

44. Barton, *supra* note 33, at 377 (Justices were called to assist the Chancellor with difficult cases and common lawyers practiced there.).

45. Barbour, *supra* note 36, at 62, 98–100, 163–168; *but cf.* Helmholz, *Assumpsit and Fidei Laesio,* 91 L. Q. REV. 406, (1975) (Disagrees with Barbour's conclusion that canon law's *fidei laesio* entered common law indirectly via Chancery. Helmholz sees a direct common law reception from the church courts.). The truth is there was probably a borrowing from both because of common lawyers' knowledge of Chancery forms and the pleading similarities with the ecclesiastical *fidei laesio* (the latter coupled with Helmholz's statistics). *See also* Baker, *supra* note 3, at 46, 50 (Established intellectual view of law in inns of court prior to the Renaissance kept the law English and precluded wholesale reception of Roman law during Renaissance.).

46. *Anon,* Harv. Law Sch. MS. 116, f.401v. (1587), cited in J. BAKER, *supra* note 21, at 284–285. Chancery's relief based on reason and conscience would again be an inspiration for common law change during the eighteenth century.

47. *Cf.* J. BAKER, *supra* note 21, at 89.

48. S. MILSOM, *supra* note 8, at 332–333, 346–347, (Third party transactions, as guaranty contracts, may be the best example.).

49. S. MILSOM, *supra* note 8, at 332–333 (A 1557 K.B. roll shows 45 nonfeasance entries, and, in one term of 1564, C.P. had nearly 1,000 Debt actions but a little over 20 in nonfeasance.).

50. A. KIRALFY, *supra* note 16, at 189 (Appendix A).

51. D. IBBETSON, THE DEVELOPMENT OF THE ACTION OF ASSUMPSIT, 1540–1620 (Cambridge University Ph.D. dissertation 1980) (Appendix 2) 396 *et seq.* (Yet in 1600 K.B. had 48 Assumpsit cases and 472 Debt cases, with wager possible in 69.). Perhaps the drop in K.B. figures in 1600 reflects an insecurity and hesitancy on the part of the King's Bench in the midst of the 1597–1602 *Slade's Case* discussions.

52. Helmholz, *Assumpsit and Fidei Laesio,* 91 L.Q. REV. 406, 426–428 (1975).

53. *Id.* at 426–428. The Reformation emasculated the church courts, thereby causing a transfer of promissory claims to the common law courts. Witness how much more anti-clerical St. Germain's Dialogue II (1530) of DOCTOR AND STUDENT was from Dialogue I (1523). *See* ST. GERMAIN'S DOCTOR AND

STUDENT, 91 SELDEN SOCIETY (J. Barton ed. 1974) (hereinafter cited as DOCTOR AND STUDENT).

54. Assumpsit's emphasis on prepayment and consequential damages is reliance-based logic; the reliance stated in the declaration by the term *fidelitur* (commonly used in *fidei laesio*), and the defendant's breach of the plaintiff's trust was emphasized by pleading deceit. This use of *fidelitur* and deceit may be the tort adaptation of *fidei laesio*. Helmholz, *supra* note 52, at 418–421; S. MILSOM, *supra* note 8, at 336–338.

55. J. BAKER, *supra* note 21, at 38–40 (By late Elizabethan days, there were thousands of *latitats* per year in K.B.).

56. Cleymond v. Vincent, Y.B. 12 Hen. VIII, f.11, pl.3 (1521). Contemporaries thought *Cleymond* meant that an action of case would lie against an executor if Debt was available during testator's lifetime. Fitzherbert thought it was bad law. Y.B. Trin. 27 Hen. VIII, 23, pl.21 (1535). *See* Jordan's Case, Y.B. Mich. 27 Hen. VIII, f.24, pl.3 (1535) (Guarantor liable in Assumpsit. Court divided on whether there was a *quid pro quo* for Debt.). *Jordan's Case* made it clear that Assumpsit would lie for services. *And see also* Norwood v. Read, Plowden 180 (1558) (Executor liable, though Plowden doubted the correctness of decision.). On the proof problems generated by *Cleymond, see* Teeven, *Problems of Proof and Early English Contract Law,* 15 CAMBRIAN L. REV. 52, 64 (1984).

57. Statute of Frauds (1677) would require signed writing for guaranty contract and promises of executor's. Even *Slade's Case* (1602) could not resolve the question of executor's liability. *See* Pinchon's Case, 9 Co. Rep. 86b (1612).

58. Pykeryng v. Thurgoode, B.M. MS. Hargrave 388 (K.B. 1532), *reprinted in* A. SIMPSON, *supra* note 14, at 628. *See also* Edwards v. Burre, Dal. 104 (1573). Just as the distinction between misfeasance and nonfeasance had become untenable, so also it was concluded that if breaching a promise to perform an act was actionable in Assumpsit in lieu of Covenant in *Orwell v. Mortoft,* then Assumpsit ought to be available in lieu of Debt for breach of a promise to pay money.

59. Slade v. Morley, 4 Co. Rep. 91a, 76 Eng. Rep. 1072 (1602).

60. J. BAKER, *supra* note 21, at 279–280 (Liability in nonfeasance was being founded on substantive principles of reciprocity and reliance.).

61. J. BAKER, *supra* note 21, at 282.

62. Manwood v. Burston, 2 Leo. 203 (1586) ("In an action upon the Case . . . the plaintiff needs not to show any certainty of the contract or other circumstances how or in what manner the debt did accrue or begin."). *See* C. FIFOOT, *supra* note 13, at 368 (Litigants could avoid the errors of extended pleading.). There were many egregious results caused by pleading technicalities, e.g., in Pinnel's Case, 5 Co. Rep. 117a (1602), the defendant would have won and only had to pay 5 pounds instead of the penal sum of 16 pounds if his lawyer had pleaded correctly.

63. Ibbetson, *Assumpsit and Debt in the Early Sixteenth Century: The Origins of the Indebitatus Count,* 41 CAMBRIDGE L.J. 142, 146, 148–149 (1982).

64. Y.B. Mich. 21 Hen. VII, f.30, pl.5 (1504) ("one may never have action on the case where one can have another action at law.").

65. A. SIMPSON, *supra* note 14, at 283–284. Witness Dodderidge's strong support of the integrity of the Register a century later in 1602 in *Slade's Case, infra.*

66. J. BAKER, *supra* note 21, at 284 (A third device was for merchants to account together (*insimul computassent*), the suit being in Assumpsit for the total acknowledged.). *See* Helmholz, *supra* note 52, at 420–421 (Requirement of an express promise in *fidei laesio* in the church courts influenced Assumpsit's express promise. Both used pleading language *fidelitur promisit.*). *Cf.* Lücke, *Slade's Case and the Origin of the Common Counts*, (pt. 3), 82 L.Q. REV. 81, 83 (1966), (Debt required strict simultaneousness of consent, but Assumpsit did not, and in fact the separation was emphasized to distinguish it from Debt.).

67. Whitehed v. Elderton, K.B. 27/1076, m.64 (1530), discussed in Ibbetson, *supra* note 63, at 142, 150–151.

68. Pykeryng v. Thurgoode, Spelman, ACCION SUR LE CASE 5 (1532), *reprinted in* A. SIMPSON, *supra* note 14, at 628. This case is well known because of its extension of the nonfeasance theory espoused in *Orwell v. Mortoft* and because King's Bench resolved that Assumpsit could be brought where Debt was available.

69. *See* Ibbetson, *supra* note 63, at 149 (Since the plaintiff had to pay a higher market price upon the defendant's default, consequential damages might have been a preferable way to distinguish Debt, but that argument is probably not good until later than this case.). Another possibility would have been to sue under a reliance theory because of the plaintiff's prepayment, but then the market change might not have been recoverable.

70. Marler v. Wilmer, K.B. 27/1111, m.64 (1539), discussed in Ibbetson, *supra* note 63, at 143–144, 151. The promise in *Marler* was subsequent in fact because the debtor-defendant made the promise to the deceased creditor's son.

71. Ibbetson, *supra* note 63, at 151n. (Ibbetson found 13 declarations in the *Whitehed* style in 1544 but none in the *Pykeryng* form.). *Cf.* Milsom, *supra* note 7, at 111–112 (Subsequent promise took case out of sphere of Debt because of the deceit of not paying after promising to do so in exchange for the plaintiff's forbearance from suing.). In the 1540s the need for linkage between the subsequent promise and the antecedent debt will fuel discussions leading to the emergence of the doctrine of consideration.

72. Lord Grey's Case, Bodl. MS. Rawl., C.112, f.292 (1567), *reprinted in* A. SIMPSON, *supra* note 14, at 633; Edwards v. Burre, Dal. 104 (1573) (Judge told jury, if loan found, to find for the plaintiff since a debt is an *assumpsit* in law.).

73. J. BAKER, *supra* note 21, at 284 (K.B. permitted a nominal forbearance of one day by Elizabethan times; C.P. opposed this.); Ibbetson, *Sixteenth Century Contract Law: Slade's Case in Context*, 4 OXFORD JOURNAL OF LEGAL STUDIES 295, 297 (1984).

74. Ibbetson, *supra* note 73, at 297–299 (The difference in the two courts wasn't on the pleadings but on the jury instructions. K.B. judge would direct jury to not worry about the express promise so long as there was a bargain; whereas, a C.P. judge would require proof of the promise.). *See* Sheffield v. Rise, Moo 367, pl. 505 (1594) (pleadings).

75. *Anon*, Dal. 84 (K.B. 1572).

76. *Anon*, Harv. Law Sch. MS. 116, f.401v (1587).

77. S. STOLJAR, *supra* note 5, at 37–38 (Consideration appeared as Assumpsit adapted to actions on informal promises to pay for services performed in reliance on the defendant's promise.).

78. Stone v. Wythipol, Cro. Eliz. 126 (1589).

79. F. POLLOCK, PRINCIPLES OF CONTRACT 149 (London: 1876) (descended from Roman *causa*); O. HOLMES, JR., THE COMMON LAW 253–259, 267–271 (Boston: 1881) (originated in Debt's *quid pro quo*); Salmond, *The History of Contract,* 3 L.Q. REV. 166, 172–178 (1887) (Modified Roman *causa* of Chancery in the law of uses was borrowed by common law.); J. AMES, LECTURES ON LEGAL HISTORY 129–130, 142–148 (Cambridge, Mass. 1913) (from the detriment in action on the case for deceit); Barbour, *supra* note 36, at 59–65, 166–168 (In competing with Chancery, the common law borrowed Chancery's use of canon law *causa*); C. FIFOOT, *supra* note 13, at 398–399 (from reciprocity of the bargain); T. PLUCKNETT, *supra* note 10, at 650–651 (loss to promisee in Assumpsit due to deceit); S. STOLJAR, *supra* note 5, at 37–38 (explained the motive that induced the promisee to rely); A. SIMPSON, *supra* note 14, at 316–332 (from equitable consideration in the law of uses); S. MILSOM, *supra* note 8, at 357–360 (in Assumpsit conceived as a trespassory reliance remedy); Baker, *Origins of the "Doctrine" of Consideration, 1535–1585* in ON THE LAWS AND CUSTOMS OF ENGLAND: ESSAYS IN HONOR OF SAMUEL E. THORNE 336–342 (M. Arnold ed. 1981) (Motive or reciprocity provided linkage between bargain and subsequent undertaking.); Ibbetson, *supra* note 63, at 153 (from the principle of mutuality). The word "origin" itself causes confusion. For some writers the origin is at the time the word "consideration" began to appear in declarations in the 1540s, which was at a time that Assumpsit was becoming more contractual. Other writers look to the test for liability in Assumpsit in nonfeasance cases of a decade or so before and after 1500 when Assumpsit was more tortious in nature.

80. S. MILSOM, *supra* note 8, at 357; *cf.* Baker, *supra* note 79, at 357 (There were fictional and substantive uses of reliance.). *See also* S. STOLJAR, *supra* note 5, at 37–38 (Advance of Assumpsit occurred in providing buyer with a remedy in a rising market when the seller refused to deliver goods and to cover acts performed in reliance on defendant's promise.).

81. DOCTOR AND STUDENT, *supra* note 53, at 230; *see* S. MILSOM, *supra* note 8, at 358–359 (In the Student's example, there was no *quid pro quo* passing to a third party, who was akin to a guarantor, and hence there was no remedy outside a reliance theory.); *cf.* Barton, *supra* note 33, at 372, 384–385 (Student is speaking of Debt and not Assumpsit.).

82. John Style's Case, B.M. MS. Hargrave 388, f.215b (1527?), *reprinted in* A. SIMPSON, *supra* note 14, at 630; see 94 SELDEN SOCIETY 270n (Baker dated the case sometime between 1526 and 1536.) *John Style's Case* involved failure to return sealed deed to owner with seal still affixed; only action on the case would provide a remedy since return of unsealed deed was of no value.

83. Milsom, *supra* note 7, at 112–113 (From a tort perspective, the plaintiff was arguing he was deceived from suing by the defendant's undertaking; from a "contract" perspective, the undertaking was made in consideration of the plaintiff's forbearance from bringing a Debt action.).

84. This basis of liability continued throughout the sixteenth century in the tradition of three famous nonfeasance cases: *Doige's Case,* Trin. 20 Hen. VI, f.34, pl.4 (1442); Orwell v. Mortoft, Keil 69, 77, 72, Eng. Rep. 229, 239 (1505); and Pykeryng v. Thurgoode, B.M. MS. Hargrave 388 (1532), *reprinted in* A. SIMP-

SON, *supra* note 14, at 628–629 (consequential loss without deceit is relied on). *See also* Sukley v. Wyte, Libr. Congr. MS. Gell at f.13 (1543), *reprinted in* A. SIMPSON, *supra* note 14, at 631–632 (first reported nonfeasance case without a prepayment had inconclusive outcome but was discussed in terms of reciprocity).

85. Baker, *supra* note 79, at 356–357.

86. Marler v. Wilmer, K.B. 27/1111, m.64 (1539), unreported case found by Ibbetson in the K.B. plea rolls. Ibbetson, *supra* note 63, at 154–155 (Ibbetson sees *causa* used here to mean more recompense than motive); *cf.* DOCTOR AND STUDENT, *supra* note 53, at 228–230 (Common law and civilian positions seem quite similar here.). *See also* Helmholz, *supra* note 52, at 406, 416 (Consideration pleaded in early Assumpsit was similar to inducement of ecclesiastical *fidei laesio.*).

87. *Cf.* S. MILSOM, *supra* note 8, at 357 (If use of reliance was influenced by church courts, then the issue might have been viewed with *causa* in mind.); *see also* Barbour, *supra* note 36, at 166 (Chancery enforced promise if promisor had led promisee to alter his position. Then there was a moral duty to fulfill the promise.).

88. A. SIMPSON, *supra* note 14, at 316–332, 372–374 (Note, that the common law had jurisdiction over uses earlier pursuant to Statute 1 Rich. III, c.1 (1483).); *see* DOCTOR AND STUDENT, *supra* note 53, at 124–125 ("consideration" raised a use); *see also* F. POLLOCK, PRINCIPLES OF CONTRACT 134 (P. Winfield, 12th ed. 1946) (St. Germain's use of word consideration may have contributed to use by lawyers.).

89. Sharington v. Strotton, Plowden 298 (1566); Hunt v. Bate, Dyer 272a (1568).

90. Marler v. Wilmer, K.B. 27/1109, m.74 (1539) (Proceedings ended without a ruling on the defendant's objection of no *causa.*); see Baker, *supra* note 79, at 339–340 (No ruling in *Marler* but it can hardly be coincidence that within year linking phrases invented.); *cf.* Ibbetson, *supra* note 63, at 156 (More than motive, recompense was needed.). *See also* F. POLLOCK, *supra* note 79, at 149–150 (*Nudum pactum's* ancient meaning of an agreement not made by specialty under Covenant or not falling within Debt's categories was transformed around 1500 to mean what it does now.).

91. The following discussion of pleading phraseology in linking the debt and the subsequent undertaking is inspired by Baker's report of his plea rolls research. *See* Baker, *supra* note 79, at 340–341 (Baker searched King's Bench plea rolls from 1535–1550, this Court being the innovator.).

92. Harvy v. Stone, K.B. 27/1112, m.65 (1539) (A fictional shilling was thrown in for good measure.); *see* Baker, *supra* note 79, at 341 (Baker found 32 instances of consideration clauses in the 1540s K.B. rolls.). Marriage was often tied to the term "consideration", first in uses and then in Assumpsit. Marriage is the one instance today of love and affection being consideration for a bargain. The term "consideration" was used in a defense of an accord in 1536. Hewton v. Forster, 27/1099, m.76 (K.B. 1536).

93. Baker, *supra* note 79, at 340; *cf.* S. MILSOM, *supra* note 8, at 359 (If the goods are put up as consideration, there is overlap with Debt since they are also *quid pro quo.*).

94. Ibbetson, *supra* note 63, at 156; Baker, *supra* note 79, at 355 (Unlike

Debt, Assumpsit presumed reciprocal actions.); *cf.* Barton, *Introduction* in DOCTOR AND STUDENT, *supra* note 53, at lvii (Contemporaries didn't see great gulf between consideration and Debt's *quid pro quo* that modern writers do.).

95. Baker, *supra* note 79, at 340–341. *See Id.* at 352–356 (Notion of bargain, or *quid pro quo,* would ultimately oust the vaguer notion of causa.).

96. S. MILSOM, *supra* note 8, at 358 (As consideration became contractual, courts looked to reciprocity of Debt's *quid pro quo.*); Ibbetson, *supra* note 63, at 153 (Grafted onto delictual idea of liability for nonfeasance was contractual idea of mutuality—that promisor should be bound if something received in exchange for his promise); Barton, *supra* note 33, at 386 (English lawyers had acquired strong prejudice in favor of mutuality.); *cf.* MAX WEBER ON LAW IN ECONOMY AND SOCIETY 120 (Cambridge, Mass., M. Rheinstein ed. 1954) (Sees consideration as continuation of notion in more primitive societies of a contract consisting of a reciprocal exchange of property.).

97. S. MILSOM, *supra* note 8, at 358.

98. Ibbetson, *supra* note 63, at 153n. This transformed detriment theory facilitated new forms of liability, where Debt would not lie, as when the benefit went to a third person but there was a detriment to the plaintiff: "this will support an action on the case, for although it is not beneficial to Baxter, it is chargeable to Read." Baxter v. Read, 2 Dyer 272b (1584). And likewise in cases against sureties. Lücke, (pt. 1), *supra* note 66, at 422, 431.

99. C. FIFOOT, *supra* note 13, at 396–397.

100. Isack v. Barbour, K.B. 27/1207, m.55 (1563); *see* Baker, *supra* note 79, at 341, 353.

101. Lucy v. Walwyn, K.B. 27/1198, m.183; Gell MS., f.154v–163v (1561–1563), *reprinted in* BAKER AND MILSOM, *supra* note 18, at 485 (deceitful breach of fiduciary duty in this executory contract in which it appears court held for plaintiff); *see* Baker, *supra* note 79, at 346–349.

102. Andrew v. Boughey, 1 Dyer 75a (1552); *see* C. FIFOOT, *supra* note 13, at 402; *cf.* F. POLLOCK, *supra* note 79, at 153–154 (Citing Hobbes, Pollock sees adequacy rule as distinguishing mark of English jurisprudence: just value is measured by appetite of contractors.). But in 18th century, Chancery began to refuse specific performance if consideration was inadequate, though Chancery would not rescind on that basis. Underwood v. Hitchcox, 26 Eng. Rep. 1031 (Ch. 1749); Gwynee v. Heaton, 28 Eng. Rep. 949 (Ch. 1778) ("inequality so strong gross and manifest").

103. Lord Grey's Case, Bodl., MS. Rawl., C.112, F.292 (1567), *reprinted in* A. SIMPSON, *supra* note 14, at 633 (In Assumpsit, Dyer, C.J. accepted averred 2 shilling fiction as not traversable since K.B.'s practice for too long. He added "the benefit of my friend is to my benefit and case also."); Sharington v. Strotton, Plow. 298, 75 Eng. Rep. 454 (1564–1566) (case under law of uses); *see* Barbour, *supra* note 36, at 166–167 (The Chancellor didn't require detriment or benefit, he didn't enforce all promises, but enforced promises of some "general interest", as due to reliance or the purpose of promise.).

104. Sharington v. Strotton, Plow. 298, 302, 75 Eng. Rep. 454, 460 (1564–1566) (An evidentiary objection was that continuing affection doesn't provide "fresh proof" of the contract to the jury). Lord Mansfield would emphasize this evidentiary aspect of consideration's history in the eighteenth century.

105. Hunt v. Bate, Dyer 272, 73 Eng. Rep. 605 (1568) (defendant promised payment to plaintiff-friend because of past favor).

106. Harford v. Gardiner, 2 Leo. 30, 74 Eng. Rep. 332 (1588).

107. Baker, *supra* note 79, at 344; *cp.* S. MILSOM, *supra* note 8, at 359 (Past consideration rule that consideration must move from plaintiff follows from earlier requirement that plaintiff must rely.). *See also* C. FIFOOT, *supra* note 13, at 403 (Promising what plaintiff already obligated to do was insufficient consideration but the consideration was sufficient if plaintiff gave up what he had right to do, as by forbearance.).

108. A. SIMPSON, *supra* note 14, at 434–436; *see* Cruz, *Assumpsit, Consideration and Third Party Rights,* 7 J. of LEG. HIST. 53, 55–58 (1986) (marriage settlement device essential for landed ruling class to perpetuate themselves).

109. Baker, *supra* note 79, at 343, 352–356.

110. *Cf.* C. FIFOOT, *supra* note 13, at 226–227 (In Glanvill and Bracton's days, sellers and buyers were seen linked by reciprocal duties—the transaction binding not by agreement but by delivery of the thing or by payment.). Note reciprocity in early Assumpsit case where a carpenter was liable because he'd been paid or could bring Debt. Y.B. Hil. 3 Hen. VI, f.36, pl.33 (1425). *See also* Barton, *supra* note 33, at 382 (In mid-fifteenth century Chancery used term *quid pro quo* to mean that if defendant got what he bargained for, it was reasonable he pay for it.).

111. C. FIFOOT, *supra* note 13, at 398–399 (In selecting between a promise or a bargain as basis of contract liability, courts opted for the material inducement expected by commercial enterprises seeking a reliable court-administered sanction. Gratuitous promises were irrelevant to commerce and anyway were associated with Covenant.); *but cf.* A. SIMPSON, *supra* note 14, at 487–488 (disagrees with Fifoot because many gratuitous promises enforced in 16th century and because contract law includes moral ideas). *See also* Cohen, *The Basis of Contract,* 46 HARV. L. REV. 553, 573 (1933) (Most "would shudder at the idea of being bound by every promise, no matter how foolish, without any chance of letting increased wisdom undo past foolishness.").

112. Since the fifteenth century, in the exceptional case of mutual promises for sales of goods, contracts had been actionable in Debt *sur contract* without any tangible benefit passing to the defendant. This was rationalized by the fiction that "property" passed to the buyer without delivery, which property provided the *quid pro quo* in the defendant. C. FIFOOT *supra* note 13, at 227–228; Lücke (pt. 2), *supra* note 66, at 543. *See* Milsom, *supra* note 16, at 283–284 (Fiction may have arrested the development of contract law toward enforcement of executory contract since it diverted argument that *quid pro quo* requirement should end.). *See also* A. SIMPSON, *supra* note 14, at 595 (Sales and marriage gifts of land enforced in 15th century Chancery on theory that bargain and sale passed a "use" to purchaser.).

113. A. SIMPSON, *supra* note 14, at 461–462, 466–468 (16th century cases don't concern themselves about when promise is binding, but rather look at when breach is actionable. The former is now determined by offer and acceptance. *Id.* at 466.); *but cf.* Baker, *supra* note 79, at 350 (There was no counter-promise. Simpson's cited cases cover a later period, after 1595.).

114. Dependency issue later solved in Pordage v. Cole, 1 Wms. Saund. 319 (1669).

115. Baker, *supra* note 79, at 346–350, cites 3 early attempts to enforce mutual promises: Lucy v. Walwyn, K.B. 27/1198, m.183, Gell MS., f.154v–163v (1561–1563) (Defendant promised to obtain lease but instead obtained it for himself; there was protest of no *quid pro quo*, but court held for plaintiff.); West v. Stowell, 2 Leo. 154, 74 Eng. Rep. 437 (C.P. 1577) (Bet between bystander and contestant in archery match resulted in a suit when contestant lost. Manwood, J. saw no performance between parties and hence no *quid pro quo*, unlike a bet between the competitors shooting. Case had inconclusive outcome.); and Butterye v. Goodman, C.U.L. MS. Ii.5. 38, f.85v–87 (1583) (Plaintiff sued brother of a woman who plaintiff agreed both to marry if she was found worth 1,500 pounds and to pay 200 pounds to defendant. Majority of court said plaintiff's promise to marry and to pay 200 pounds was not consideration since defendant had no reciprocal remedy.). These cases would have been easier for the plaintiffs if the promises had not been conditional, and the third party aspects of *West* and *Butterye* did not aid plaintiffs, but the deceit in *Lucy* surely assisted the plaintiff.

116. Barton, *supra* note 33, at 385–386; Brett's Case, Cro. Eliz. 755 (1600), *reprinted in* C. FIFOOT, *supra* note 13, at 421, 422 (sufficient consideration requires a *quid pro quo*); *but see* C. FIFOOT, *supra* note 13, at 395 (By 1600 *Brett's Case* was anachronism in light of enforceability of mutual promises.).

117. Strangborough v. Warner, 4 Leo. 3, 74 Eng. Rep. 686 (1589).

118. Kirby v. Coles, Cro. Eliz. 137 (1589) (Mutual bargain indicates agreement with mutual benefits.); Wichals v. Johns, Cro. Eliz. 703 (1599) (mutual promises provide mutual benefits); *cf.* S. STOLJAR, *supra* note 5, at 51–54 (Mutual promises reveal the synallagmatic character of agreement.); *cf.* A. SIMPSON, *supra* note 14, at 461–462 (What had motivated the promise was a counterpromise.).

119. Lücke (pt. 2), *supra* note 66, at 540–542 (By not pleading plaintiff's performance, it wouldn't appear there was a *quid pro quo*.).

120. C. FIFOOT, *supra* note 13, at 400; *cf.* Simpson, *Slade's Case in the History of Contract*, 74 L.Q. REV. 381, 391–392 (1958) (Mutual promises as consideration for each other is not part of story of *Slade's Case*.).

121. Baker, *supra* note 79, at 337, 341; S. STOLJAR, *supra* note 5, at 37–38; Lücke (pt. 3), *supra* note 66, at 96.

122. Baker, *supra* note 79, at 341–342.

123. Milsom, *Reason in the Development of the Common Law*, 81 L.Q. REV. 496 (1965) (Supercession of older forms with more flexible ones was means of change at common law.).

124. *See* Milsom, *supra* note 7, at 117 (better than anything Covenant and Debt could have given us).

125. S. MILSOM, *supra* note 8, at 360.

126. *See* Baker, *supra* note 79, at 358.

127. Edwards v. Burre, Dal 104 (1573).

128. *See* Baker, *New Light on Slade's Case* (pt. 2), 29 CAMBRIDGE LAW JOURNAL 213, 219–220 (1971).

129. *Id.*

130. First known use of term "due process" was in 1354 in Statute, 25 Edw. III, ch. 3: "That no man of what estate or condition that he be, shall be put out

of land or tenement, nor taken nor imprisoned, nor disinherited, nor put to death, without being brought in answer by due process of the law."

131. *See* Milsom, *supra* note 7, at 110–111.

132. *See* Baker, *supra* note 128, at 220. Much of King's Bench's jurisdiction created by invading domain of Common Pleas through use of fictions.

133. Stat. 27 Eliz. I, c.8 (1585): "An Act for Redress of erroneous Judgments in the Court commonly called the King's Bench."

134. Baker (pt. 2), *supra* note 128, at 223.

135. Slade's Case, 4 Co. Rep. 91a, 76 Eng. Rep. 1072 (1602).

136. Baker (pt. 2), *supra* note 128, at 215–216 (more symptomatic of an intellectual conflict between the old and new learning).

137. *See* A. SIMPSON, *supra* note 14, at 293 (New statutory Exchequer Chamber was staffed by Common Pleas justices and those Barons of the Exchequer who were sergeants-at-law.).

138. S. MILSOM, *supra* note 8, at 339–347. *See* A. SIMPSON, *supra* note 14, at 143, 153–160.

139. Slade v. Morley (*Slade's Case*), 4 Co. Rep. 91a, 76 Eng. Rep. 1072 (1602).

140. S. MILSOM, *supra* note 8, at 352.

141. Baker (pt. 2), *supra* note 128, at 224–225. The old informal Exchequer Chamber was a traditional informal conference of justices of King's Bench, Common Pleas and Barons of the Exchequer, who met irregularly to discuss an issue on which there was disagreement.

142. *Slade's Case,* 4 Co. Rep. 92b (1602). Coke conveniently glossed over the forum's identity, and so some historians thought the case was heard by the Statutory Exchequer Chamber. Baker (pt. 2), *supra* note 128, at 224–225.

143. "The customary laws of England . . . doth far exceed our written laws, namely our statutes . . . that when our parliament have altered or changed any fundamental points of the common law, those alterations have been found by experience to be so inconvenient . . . that the common law hath in effect been restored again." J. DAVIES, LE PRIMER REPORT DES CASES EN IRELAND, preface (1615).

144. Yet, defendants, with the option in a Debt action of wager or a jury, were swinging toward electing a jury. One reason may have been fear of interference by Chancery if wager used. Milsom, *supra* note 16, at 266; Barbour, *supra* note 36, at 99–100 (Chancellor would listen to parol evidence to get to merits of case hidden behind wager. Equity was thus appropriating common law jurisdiction. Equity would even hear a case anew when a plaintiff lost at common law because of wager.).

145. BAKER and MILSOM, *supra* note 18, at 431–436 (reprints arguments).

146. The language "every contract executory imports in itself an assumpsit" first appeared in Norwood v. Read, 1 Plowd. 180 (1558), where the court also answered in the affirmative.

147. Baker (pt. 2), *supra* note 128, at 213, 218–219.

148. Until recent past many writers thought it meant that Slade concerned mutual promises. Baker (pt. 2), *supra* note 128, at 226.

149. Simpson, *supra* note 120, at 390–392.

150. C. FIFOOT, *supra* note 13, at 227–229 citing dictum in *Doige's Case:* "If I buy a horse from you, now the property in the horse is in me, and for this

you shall have a writ of debt for the money and I shall have detinue for the horse on this bargain." Note, that fiction works both ways. Passing of property fiction only applied to Debt *sur contract* actions for sales of goods—probably in response to the demands of emerging merchant class for common law here in what is executory contract (in modern sense).

151. Simpson, *supra* note 120, at 390–392. The enforceability of mutual promises came under Special Assumpsit and not Assumpsit in lieu of Debt.

152. Milsom, *supra* note 16, at 283–284 (as sales of land).

153. Baker (pt. 2), *supra* note 128, at 226–227 (n.56).

154. *See* J. AMES, *supra* note 79, at 152.

155. Pykeryng v. Thurgoode, B.M. MS. Hargrave 388 (1532) was early King's Bench case in opposition to Common Pleas' view.

156. Baker (pt. 2), *supra* note 128, at 227–228; but *cf.* Ibbetson, *supra* note 73, at 307–313 (K.B. position on overlap was legally sound since 2 causes of action needed to cover same *damnum* and same injury, but the *damnum* in Debt and Assumpsit differed since Debt was for a liquidated sum unlike Assumpsit).

157. *See* Baker (pt. 2), *supra* note 128, at 222, 227–228 (that Coke and Popham relied on this argument is proof of strength of opposition's argument) (citing Barkley v. Foster, Pasch. B.M. MS. Harl. 4552, f.110 (1597)).

158. *Cf.* Lücke (pt. 1), *supra* note 66, at 426 citing *Anon*, Gould 51, pl.13 (1587) (false wager of law not punishable as perjury in Star Chamber).

159. The writ system had acted as the organizing mechanism of the common law. Conservative contemporaries' support of wager was vindicated by injustices caused by proof problems in trial by jury in seventeenth century. S. MILSOM, *supra* note 8, at 354; *and see* Teeven, *Seventeenth Century Evidentiary Concerns and the Statute of Frauds*, 9 ADEL. L. REV. 252, 252–258 (1983).

160. A. SIMPSON, *supra* note 14, at 298; Baker (pt. 2), *supra* note 128, at 230. *But cf.* Ibbetson, *supra* note 73, at 312–313 (Ending wager was insignificant because invoking the right to wage was, in the community's eyes, tantamount to admitting liability but refusing to pay.). Arguments against defendants raising the Statute of Frauds defense mirror Ibbetson's argument here. *See* Stephen, *Section Seventeen of the Statute of Frauds*, 1 L.Q. REV. 1, 3–4 (1885).

161. Ibbetson, *supra* note 73, at 303–304.

162. *See* Pinchon's Case, 9 Co. Rep. 866 (1612).

163. Stat. 3 + Wm. IV, c.42, s.13 (1833).

164. Edgcomb v. Dee, Vaughan 89 (1670).

165. Robinson v. Bland, 2 Burr. 1077, 1086 (1760).

166. *Anon* (1672) Treby Rep. (MS. in Middle Temple) 747, cited in J. BAKER, *supra* note 21, at 289.

167. Stat. 29 Car. II, c.3, ss.4, 17 (1677).

CHAPTER 3

CONSOLIDATION OF CHANGE (1602–1689)

Slade's Case was a watershed decision in the development of the common law of contract; its spirit more than its letter became the guiding light for the centuries following. It unified the two major strands of contract actions so that Assumpsit could be brought both in lieu of Debt for a promise to pay money and in lieu of Covenant for a promise to perform an act. During the first half of the seventeenth century, the term "contract" began to be used informally in its modern sense of agreement; now its old usage of describing where Debt lay was transmuted into describing transactions covered by Assumpsit. The emergence of Assumpsit reflects the evolutionary capacity of the common law in keeping pace with the changed economic conditions of a money economy and a rising merchant class in need of a flexible remedy for the breach of an informal promise. The changes accommodating merchants were a part of the royal courts' strategy in laying claim to the increasing commercial business of the mercantile courts. During the early seventeenth century, Coke would employ prohibitions to deny commercial jurisdiction to Admiralty, and Interregnum lawyers would complete the common law takeover by mid-century.

The judiciary's contract discussions during much of the rest of the seventeenth century concerned the ramifications of the new theory set out in *Slade's Case*. This chapter covers the period of the reigns of the Stuarts and the Interregnum when there was an explication and a consolidation of the changes that it was claimed *Slade's Case* had brought. There have been many points historically attributed to *Slade's Case* which are incorrect,[1] and although the decision has been much discussed, there are some uncertainties even today about the decision and its immediate impact. As was stated in the preceding chapter, *Slade's Case* determined that a debt implied an undertaking to pay[2] and that the action of Assumpsit could overlap Debt,[3] the latter being the more momentous aspect of the decision.[4] A sub-point of the decision was that the defendant could be deprived of wager of law and forced to trial by jury in actions brought on informal promises.[5] Much of the confusion regarding the meaning of *Slade* can be laid at the feet of the reporters. The reports of both Moore and Yelverton are useless in determining the judicial reasoning of the case.[6] The reasoning in Coke's Report,[7] published in 1604, was until comparatively recently considered the definitive text on *Slade's Case*.[8] For centuries Coke's Report was what most lawyers knew about *Slade's Case*. Coke declared *Slade's Case* to be the decision of all of the English judges, but the obvious disagreement among the judges rebuts that statement.[9] In fact, *Slade's Case* was not accepted immediately by the new statutory Exchequer Chamber or by Common Pleas.

Since the King's Bench had only avoided a reversal in *Slade* by the strategic selection of the old, informal Exchequer Chamber as a forum for the discussion of *Slade's Case*, there had still not been an acquiescence registered by the statutory Exchequer Chamber or by Common Pleas.[10] In a decision contemporaneous with the concluding year of arguments in *Slade's Case*, the statutory Exchequer Chamber, per Walmsley, J. of Common Pleas and Anderson, Chief Justice of Common Pleas, attacked the use of Assumpsit in place of Debt: "There ought to be no accions of the case but grounded upon some fraud."[11] The first case in which the new Exchequer Chamber upheld the King's Bench was *Prowse v. Tom* (1605).[12] Nevertheless Common Pleas continued to criticize the usurpation of Debt by Assumpsit.[13]

Then mysteriously in 1612, what Coke's Report of *Slade's Case* had declared to have occurred, did in fact come to pass in *The Case of the Marshalsea*,[14] when Common Pleas declared the matter to be resolved that Assumpsit could overlap Debt. It was surely no coincidence to Common Pleas' change of position that Anderson, the primary intellectual opponent of Assumpsit's overlap of Debt and a protector of Common Pleas' Debt jurisdiction, was now deceased[15] and that Coke was by then the Chief Justice of Common Pleas. Still, why Common Pleas and the Exchequer Chamber acquiesced to the King's Bench view of the availability of Assumpsit for Debt is, as Baker wrote, a bit of a mystery.[16] One suggestion was given by Tanfield, J. in a statutory Exchequer Chamber case: "There is no reason there should be a difference betwixt the Courts; it would be a scandall to the common law, that they differed in opinion."[17] Whatever the reason for the capitulation of the other royal courts, the confusion surrounding *Slade's Case* in the succeeding two centuries, rather than the decision in *Slade's Case* itself, generated much of the stimulus for the further development of contract law and also for the creation of quasi-contract.[18] Once the royal courts were in concert in accepting the ruling in *Slade's Case*, much of the rest of the seventeenth century judicial discussions about contract law would deal with the ramifications of *Slade's Case*, first, in the context of the parameters of Debt and, secondly, regarding the defenses to the enforcement of a promise supported by consideration. Analysis of these two issues are the subject of this chapter.

Slade's Case and the Parameters of Debt

Since *Slade's Case* involved the replacement of Debt *sur contract* with Assumpsit, the extension of the logic in *Slade's Case* was constrained by the historical parameters of Debt on informal promises. The principal issues concerned the liability of executors, the doctrine of consideration as it applied to past consideration and accords and the form of pleading required.

The liability of an executor for a contractual debt of his testator was expressly reserved in *Slade's Case*,[19] and naturally was soon to come to the forefront. The King's Bench had been holding executors liable for much of the sixteenth century.[20] It appears that Common Pleas had allowed it when Mountague, C.J.C.P., brought the practice from the King's Bench, but by the late 1590s, under Anderson as Chief Justice, the action against an executor wasn't allowed unless there were special damages, and the statutory Exchequer Chamber reversed deviating King's Bench decisions through 1601.[21] The issue came to a head in *Pinchon's Case*[22] in 1612 before all the judges of England. The executor raised two long standing defenses: first, that allowing an Assumpsit action violated the rules of Debt and its attendant wager of law and, secondly, that a personal action dies with the debtor.

The defendant's incantation of wager was yet another reiteration of the argument that the executor wouldn't usually know anything about informal contractual debts of his testator made in private and hence was not in a position to invoke his due process right of swearing in wager. This defense would not work on a sealed instrument because the jury could compare seals and so the testator himself could not have waged.[23] As was mentioned earlier, there is disagreement today about the value of wager of law by the early 1600s and about the effect of the right of wager on the increased use of Assumpsit in place of Debt. The lack of agreement among scholars dampens one's enthusiasm for dwelling long on the point once the demise of wager in contractual debt was a near *fait accompli* after *Slade's Case*; although, as a footnote, it does appear that the defendant's argument was stale[24] and wager's use arguably outdated.[25] The Exchequer Chamber's holding on the wager issue was that it was obsolete because if the testator was alive, even he could not wage his law in Assumpsit as a result of *Slade's Case*. Furthermore, the court followed the fiduciary principle suggested earlier in *Norwood v. Read*

(1558) that the executor held the testator's property for, among other things, the claims of creditors, which did not deny the executor his birthright of wager but rather "justice and right is advanced, for as much as the creditor shall be paid his just and true debt."[26]

The Court also rejected the executor's second objection that a "personal action of Trespass on the Case *moritur cum persona*" (dies with the person). The rule that personal actions were "annexed to the person" of the tortfeasor was an ancient rule of tort law,[27] but in the interim decisions had begun to differentiate Assumpsit from violent types of trespass. *Cleymond v. Vincent* (1520) was such a case, and it was the first reported case holding an executor liable. In *Cleymond,* Fyneux, C.J. said:

> For if someone beats me and dies, my action is gone—or, if I die, my executors shall have no action—because the party cannot be punished when he is dead. In this case, however, the plaintiff can have what he would have had if the party had been alive, namely, the price of his goods. . . .[28]

Coke indicated that the *Pinchon* decision applied the same logic, that an Assumpsit action, "although it is termed Trespass", is not so delictual in nature so as to be:

> annexed to the persons of the parties that it shall die with the persons; for then, if he to whom the promise is made dies, his executor should not have any action; which no man will affirm.[29] And an action *sur Assumpsit* upon good consideration, without specialty, to do a thing is no more personal, i.e. annexed to the person, than a covenant by specialty to do the same thing.[30]

Just as Coke's report of *Slade's Case* is not as forthright as it could have been, his report in *Pinchon's Case* does not clarify that, as with *Slade's Case* for living debtors, the decision covered only Assumpsit actions on contractual debts of deceased debtors.[31] An executor's liability on other promises (covenants) came four years later in *Sanders v. Easterby.*[32] So in the first quarter of the seventeenth century contractual obligations became passively transmissible by death (active transmission by way of assignment would not be permitted until the nineteenth century). Thus the inability to recover from an executor, one of the major disadvantages of Debt and its attendant wager of law, was surmounted on the heels of *Slade's Case*. The ruling in *Pinchon's Case* was a well recognized rule in the seventeenth century[33] and is still the law today.

Concurrent with the royal courts' discussions of executors' liability, issues related to the doctrine of consideration arose. It should probably cause no surprise that the aftershock of such a fundamental change as *Slade's Case* would prompt questions about the basic test for actionability under Assumpsit. A root question that was not seriously entertained, however, was whether *Slade's Case* could have been a catalyst for the abolition of the doctrinal impediment of consideration.[34] *Slade's Case* probably presented the best opportunity in the history of contract for consideration to be removed; but, instead of this happening, there was some fine tuning of the doctrine in regard to past consideration and accords.

The continued use of the *indebitatus assumpsit* pleading form after *Slade's Case* raised a recurring concern that the consideration for the subsequent promise was past consideration. Pleading a subsequent promise was no longer necessary after *Slade's Case* defeated the Debt overlap objection, but the *indebitatus* form continued due to its generalized pleading advantages. In order to see how this past consideration problem arose, a review of the development of the past consideration rule is necessary. Before the doctrine of consideration appeared, it was clear that the action of Debt was not available for a past benefit that a plaintiff had provided to a defendant.[35] This notion first appeared in an action on the case in a deceit action in 1490, wherein a plaintiff was barred from recovering on breach of a warranty because the warranty was given after the sale.[36] Then in the harsh, precedent-setting Assumpsit action of *Hunt v. Bate*[37] in 1568 the plaintiff paid the bail for the defendant's imprisoned servant so that "the business of the master should not go undone." The defendant later said he would reimburse his friend, the plaintiff. The plaintiff brought an Assumpsit action for failure to pay, and the court held for the defendant because "the master never requested the plaintiff to do it, on behalf of his servant, but he did it of his own head."[38] The rule that consideration must move from the plaintiff in reliance on the defendant's request follows from the past consideration rule: the defendant's request is needed before the plaintiff relies.[39] In order to avoid the argument that the precedent bargain was past consideration for the subsequent promise, it became a common practice for the plaintiff to insert a "special instance and request" by the defendant previous in time to the consideration provided by the plaintiff. Furthermore, in *Hunt v. Bate*, the parties' friendship could not act as the consideration since it existed prior to the promise. Then the *Hunt v. Bate* case was followed later in the sixteenth century by *Greenleaf v. Barker* (1590),[40] wherein Barker owed Greenleaf 5 pounds on November 1. Barker, the plaintiff, alleged that Greenleaf made an *assumpsit* to pay 20 shillings if Barker would pay the 5 pound debt by November 3. On a writ of error, the King's Bench held that there was no consideration for Greenleaf's *assumpsit* to pay 20 shillings since Barker promised no more than his pre-existing duty. This is the law today.[41] This type of case can potentially cut across the rule regarding accords,[42] *infra*, but they are by no means synonymous.

A final point of confusion was whether the prohibition on past consideration also precluded executed consideration. After some confusion,

Lampleigh v. Brathwait (1615) settled the law for good by making a distinction between past and executed consideration. In *Lampleigh* the defendant, a felon, requested the plaintiff to obtain a pardon from the King. After the plaintiff exerted himself diligently, though to no avail, the defendant promised him 100 pounds. The plaintiff later sued the defendant, who pleaded *non assumpsit,* and the court held for the plaintiff because the act of the plaintiff was requested by the defendant, as in *Hunt v. Bate,* and because it was based on a business transaction rather than merely out of friendship: "the execution of the act must pursue the request, for it is like a case of a commission for this purpose."[43] The defendant's request, the plaintiff's act and the defendant's subsequent promise of payment might be described as elements of a single transaction.

Returning to the continued use of *indebitatus assumpsit* after *Slade's Case,* didn't the subsequent promise make the consideration past?[44] The issue was raised in *Hodge v. Vavisour* in 1617, but it was overruled because the debt "always continues". It was a quibble to distinguish it from the past consideration rule.[45] The quirk of *indebitatus assumpsit's* subsequent promise, devised to avoid overlap with Debt, conflicting with the past consideration rule was rationalized away. The court was not going to set the clock back at this late date by entertaining the defendant's argument that the "... promise is grounded upon a consideration that is past, and so no good to raise a promise. And here he may have debt for his goods."[46] In fact, now that liability was recognized as existing in the common debts covered by *indebitatus assumpsit,* consideration was normally not at issue during the seventeenth and eighteenth centuries; so, what law did develop about consideration, arose in the more individualized circumstances discussed in Special Assumpsit actions.

The second consideration-related question, prompted by Assumpsit's intrusion into the sphere of Debt, concerned the enforceability of accords. An accord is an agreement that the obligor will do something different than he was originally obliged to do in exchange for the obligee not enforcing the original claim. There are two issues to consider. First, does an accord require consideration? And, secondly, is an executory accord enforceable?

Just as with the past consideration rule, the genesis of the accord rule was in the older competing action of Debt.[47] In a 1495 Debt action, Brian, C.J. stated the rule in accords that payment of a lesser sum in full satisfaction does not discharge the obligation: "This action is brought for 20 pounds, and the concord is that he shall pay only 10 pounds, which appears to be no satisfaction for the 20 pounds; for payment of 10 pounds cannot be payment of 20 pounds. But if it were a horse, which horse is paid according to the concord, that is a good satisfaction; for it does not appear whether the horse is worth more or less than the sum in demand."[48] To Brian it was simply that the part payment of 10 clearly cannot equal the whole of 20. Although this was not then a unanimous view,[49] it was accepted as the law in the sixteenth century.[50] The famous *Pinnel's Case* (1602)[51] was merely a reiteration of this well accepted Debt rule; for, *Pinnel* was an action of Debt on a bond rather than an Assumpsit action. The rationale for the rule that part payment did not discharge the liquidated[52] debt was that Debt was based on a duty, and not on a promise, and part performance would not discharge that duty.[53] Liability in Debt rested on the transaction and not on any promise; the debtor was charged because he received the property rights in money or goods, and that charge had to be discharged by a return through payment.[54] However, if the accord required the debtor to do something other than pay a lesser sum, as a novelty, it was enforceable:

> For it shall be intended that a horse, hawk or robe, etc. might be more beneficial to the plaintiff than the money in respect of some circumstances, or otherwise the plaintiff would not have accepted of it in satisfaction. But when the whole sum is due, by no intendment the acceptance of parcel can be a satisfaction to the plaintiff.[55]

In Pinnel the alleged novelty was paying early.[56]

As long as Debt's accord rule was confined to Debt actions, where consideration was not required, it was seen as a rule inherent in the nature of Debt, but then there was an attempt to translate the Debt rule into consideration-bound Assumpsit. *Richards v. Bartlet* (1584)[57] was the first Assumpsit case relating Debt's accord rule to the requirement of consideration. The defendant pleaded an accord agreement for the plaintiff to accept three shillings on each pound due. The court rejected the defense, "for no new profit but damage comes to the plaintiff by this new agreement, and the defendant is not put to any labour or charge by it."[58]

There have been many critics of the consideration requirement in accords and some disagreement among critics about why consideration was required.[59] A compelling criticism challenges why the consideration requirement, relevant to the formation and enforcement of the contract, is relevant to the discharge of a contract.[60] Nonetheless, the sixteenth century view was that although the plaintiff may have obviously been content to accept a lesser amount, the court required the defendant to also prove a bargain, and the payment of a lesser amount did not qualify.[61] Perhaps those contemporaneous cases that had treated cash-in-hand as sufficient consideration for a new promise by the creditor[62] ought to have been employed since the "bird-in-the-hand" was obviously perceived as a sufficient benefit to the creditor when he agreed to the accord. Moreover, Assumpsit was based on a promise rather than on a duty like Debt, and if the creditor elected to accept a changed promise, should it not be enforceable? This logic could not outweigh the influence on this Assumpsit defense of the well entrenched alternative action on informal promises of Debt *sur contract*, and as a consequence, consideration became essential in place of Debt's novelty for the defendant to avoid liability on the original, undisputed[63] claim.

Assuming there was consideration for the accord, was the creditor bound by an executory accord? In Debt actions it was inevitable that an executory accord would be ineffectual because of the need for actual receipt of the benefit (*quid pro quo*); hence there had to be an accord *and* satisfaction.[64] Although the earlier Assumpsit case of *Richards v. Bartlet* had also been inclined toward this aspect of Debt's accord and satisfaction rule in *dictum*,[65] once mutual promises and executory debts became commonly enforceable in Assumpsit, it seemed logical that executory accords ought to have been enforceable too.[66] The courts seemed disposed toward an executory accord for a while;[67] however, as the seventeenth century wore on, they altered their course and began following *Richards v. Bartlet's* inclination toward a requirement of satisfaction because of confusion with the logic in Debt and the common law trap of a reluctance to throw out the "old books".[68]

There have been several suggestions, besides the "old books" one, for why Assumpsit adopted the satisfaction requirement of Debt. One was that an accord had to be fully satisfied to bar a later suit by the plaintiff[69] because an accord was intended as a bar and not as a basis for enforcing a claim like one on an executory contract.[70] Another suggestion is that an accord usually entails a concession to the debtor, and so performance of the accord, and not merely the debtor's promise to satisfy, is the inducement for the concession.[71] Continuing this logic, a creditor would not be interested in granting a concession if he could not enforce the original claim if the debtor did not live up to his promise.[72] The historical reasons for the rules related to accord and satisfaction might be clear, but this doesn't make the rule any more palatable as a matter of policy or morality. Subject to some exceptions,[73] the rule in *Pinnel's Case* is still the law today in the United States and in England.[74]

Contemporaneous with the judicial discussions concerning executor's liability and consideration matters, the common law courts were rethinking the plaintiff's pleading requirements in Assumpsit when suing on a contract debt. One of the disadvantages of Debt had been its archaically strict pleading rules. The formless character of actions on the case permitted plaintiffs' lawyers to employ a generalized declaration of the contractual debt, and the flexibility of the action was exploited by averment of a subsequent promise in order to avoid overlap with Debt. During the decade following *Slade's Case* the common law courts were actively seeking resolution of two pleading questions: 1. How generalized could the declaration in Assumpsit be? 2. Was the allegation of a subsequent promise necessary? The answers to these questions are important to the history of contract law since the *indebitatus assumpsit* form would facilitate the further development of contract law.

During the last quarter of the sixteenth century plaintiffs began counting that the defendant, being indebted (*indebitatus*), undertook to pay (*assumpsit solvere*).[75] The *indebitatus* was the simple declaration of the existence of an antecedent debt, and the *assumpsit* was the subsequent promise. This form of declaration, called a "general" *indebitatus assumpsit*, was imprecise since it failed to include information as to how, when or where the debt was incurred. During the 1580s both the King's Bench and Common Pleas were allowing plaintiffs to declare in the general *indebitatus assumpsit* form, but by the mid–1590s Common Pleas began to reject all forms of *indebitatus* declarations on contract debts.[76]

Why had the common law courts been willing to demand less specificity in Assumpsit than in Debt? Besides the differences in the traditional forms of the two writs, it is important to look at the difference in the transactions which the plaintiff was suing on. In Debt the cause of the action was the transaction itself, but in Assumpsit the cause of the action was the subsequent promise and the antecedent debt was the consideration. In a 1592 case it was reported:

> the action is not merely founded upon the debt but upon the promise, and the debts are but inducements to it, but if it were to recover the debts themselves in an action of debt, there ought to be made a certainty thereof, to wit when and how it comes.[77]

The determination of how the debt arose in a general *indebitatus assumpsit* action would be left to the jury looking at the totality of the evidence.[78]

By the mid–1590s the Court of Common Pleas was ready for a showdown with the King's Bench on its use of Assumpsit in lieu of Debt, which of course came in *Slade's Case*. It has been claimed that *Slade's Case* declared general *indebitatus assumpsit* declarations to be improper, but did it? There is disagreement on this point. First of all, it is clear that the plaintiff in *Slade's Case* did not employ a general *indebitatus assumpsit*, rather the plaintiff brought an Assumpsit action and specially pleaded the particulars of the antecedent debt. Then how can one argue that *Slade's Case* ended general declarations? Support is found in *Moore's* report[79] of *Slade's Case* and Coke's recollections in the *Case of the Marshalsea* (1612)[80] of what was decided in *Slade's Case*; both reports categorically declared that *Slade's Case* outlawed the general *indebitatus assumpsit* declaration. Some scholars have accepted what the two reports said at face value.[81] Others have questioned the reliability of the two reports since there seemed to be no arguments on the point over the five years of discussing the issues in *Slade*, and there is no corroboration in any of the other reports of *Slade's Case*.[82] Regarding the latter point, although Coke's report of the *Case of the Marshalsea* refers to his own report of *Slade's Case* as dealing with the propriety of the general declaration, in fact his report of *Slade's Case* did not cover it. Another indicator of whether *Slade's Case* resolved the matter would be if the King's Bench ceased approving the general declaration after *Slade*. The last reported case seems to be a 1601 decision, but the plea rolls indicate that one was approved as late as 1605.[83] Assuming Moore's and Coke's reports are correct in reporting that *Slade's Case* declared the general declaration to be improper, and it is not easy to ignore the fact that both reports state it so, lawyers of the day may have waited for a follow-up case holding on the merits since it would have been *dictum* in *Slade's Case*.

Whether or not *Slade's Case* held that the general *indebitatus assumpsit* declaration was improper, all agree that *Woodford v. Deacon* (1608)[84] squarely rejected the general declaration. This case was heard in the Exchequer Chamber on a writ of error from the King's Bench wherein the plaintiff used a general *indebitatus assumpsit* declaration. All the judges agreed the general declaration was defective because it "doth not shew for what cause the debt grew: viz. for rent, or by specialty, or by record; and if by any of those means, a general *assumpsit* lies not." *Woodford v. Deacon* cited a similar holding in the King's Bench earlier that year in *Buckingham v. Costendine*.[85] The judges were intent on containing Assumpsit in lieu of Debt to the confines of informal contractual debt in *Slade's Case* and to not allow its expansion to other uses of Debt.[86] A general *indebitatus assumpsit* was unacceptable because it was not possible to determine how the debt arose from the mere declaration of an antecedent debt. It was hoped that, by barring the general declaration, it would confound plaintiffs' lawyers eager to bring Assumpsit actions not within the spirit of *Slade's Case*. What was it about actions for rent, on a covenant, on a court record, etc. that caused them to not be actionable within the context of *Slade's Case*? A prominent feature of all these ineligible obligations was that the defendant could not wage his law.[87] Other reasons given were that the excluded obligations were "real" actions[88] and of a "higher nature".[89]

Another objection to the general declaration raised in 1612 was that a defendant did not receive adequate notice of the genesis of the debt in order to prepare his defense: "the action would not lie for the inconvenience which might follow. For the defendant should be driven to be ready to give an answer to the plaintiff to the generality."[90] In a case four years later, there was a concern that the defendant might be surprised at the trial: "the defendant, does not know which instructions to give to his counsel for his defence, because it is not ascertained what the plaintiff will put in evidence against him."[91]

After *Woodford v. Deacon* (1608) plaintiffs' lawyers experimented with new language in their declarations in order to satisfy the concerns of the judges without a significant loss of the earlier advantages of pleading in *indebitatus assumpsit.*[92] Of immediate concern was the use of a general declaration in *insimul computaverunt,* wherein the plaintiff was suing on an accounting between the parties of a balance due on a number of outstanding debts.[93] Did the recent prohibition on the general declaration necessitate a full description of every debt included in the accounting? The courts recognized how unmanageable a requirement of too much specificity would be here and so permitted a general declaration.[94] As one judge put it: "the law avoids prolixity of the declaration, which would be infinite, if all petit debts were named."[95]

How general could the plaintiff's declaration still be? Guidance was provided in the two 1608 cases prohibiting the general *indebitatus assumpsit* declaration. In *Woodford v. Deacon* the Exchequer Chamber indicated an *indebitatus assumpsit* would be permitted, without the need for a statement of the particulars of the genesis of the debt, if it briefly stated the type of contract debt, as for goods sold.[96] And in *Buckingham v. Costendine,* the King's Bench had said that only if the declaration showed that "the debt was by reason of wares sold or upon a loan, or for such like cause, would it appear to the Court to be matter whereupon to ground an *assumpsit.*"[97] So the declaration would be good if it assured that the cause was not a transaction like a sealed deed that would be outside the scope of *Slade's Case.*

In *Bellinger v. Gardiner* (1614)[98] the Exchequer Chamber unanimously approved an *indebitatus assumpsit* declaration in the form suggested by *Woodford v. Deacon.* In *Bellinger v. Gardiner* the defendant had objected to the uncertainty of a declaration that he was indebted "for various merchandise," but the Chamber held that the declaration was good, though Chief Baron Tanfield said, "if he had said 'for various thing' I think it would not have been good." There were subsequent objections to the degree of generality approved in *Bellinger v. Gardiner* since it did not require the specificity that the declaration in *Slade's Case* itself had in fact included regarding the genesis of the debt.[99] However, the common law courts had concluded that the spirit of *Slade's* pro plaintiff posture mandated that plaintiffs not be tied to any more particularity in pleading than was practical at the onset of the action. The end result of the attacks on the general *indebitatus assumpsit* count was that generality was retained except for the requirement of a statement that the claim was on an informal contractual debt. Special pleading would still be required in the action of "Special Assumpsit" in order to plead the special circumstances not fitting within the common contractual transactions that were traditionally covered by Debt and were now within the scope of *Slade's Case.*[100]

A review of the two reasons given for defendants opposing the general *indebitatus assumpsit* count of, one, identifying a contractual debt and, two, surprise suggests that the judges were ultimately influenced by the argument that the type of debt incurred must be specified but largely overlooked the argument that adequate information was needed about how the debt arose in order to prepare a defense.[101] This modified form of *indebitatus assumpsit* was well accepted by the end of the seventeenth century. It would become the basis for the evolution of a series of standardized counts on debts in the eighteenth century, known as "common" or "indebitatus" counts, for goods sold, money lent, work done, etc.[102] These will be discussed in the next chapter.

As was stated above, there were two pleading questions to be resolved after *Slade's Case*. The first, just discussed, concerned the degree of specificity required, and the second was whether the allegation of a subsequent promise was necessary. The use of the subsequent promise in Assumpsit had originated before the mid-sixteenth century in order to avoid overlap with Debt.[103] The plaintiff argued there was no overlap because his action was based on the wrong of the defendant's breach of his subsequent promise rather than on the debt transaction itself. This manner of pleading was permitted in Common Pleas and the King's Bench, and by the 1560s the King's Bench wasn't even requiring that the subsequent promise be proved.[104]

In *Slade's Case* there was no subsequent promise in the special verdict, which found: "that between the plaintiff and the defendant there was no other promise or assumption, but only the said bargain". Indeed, there was no ruling in *Slade* either supporting or opposing the subsequent promise.[105] Nonetheless, *Slade's Case* did show by example that a subsequent promise need not be alleged to avoid overlap. There was, however, a situation where the allegation of a subsequent promise was still needed, and that was when a creditor wanted to sue a debtor on more than one contract in a single action. If there was no single promise to pay all the debts, a separate declaration had to be filed for each debt; so plaintiffs began to allege a subsequent promise to pay all the debts, and the Exchequer Chamber allowed the plea in 1610.[106]

After taking this exceptional circumstance into account, why did plaintiffs continue to plead subsequent promises once *Slade's Case* had removed the taboo on overlap? One explanation is that lawyers misunderstood *Slade*. Again, Coke's recollection of *Slade's Case* in the *Case of the Marshalsea* is misleading on the point.[107] *Slade's Case* may have been misunderstood to mean that there was an implied subsequent promise that followed from the existence of the debt.[108] As a practical matter, plaintiffs' lawyers were using the allegation of a subsequent promise as a device to avoid the earlier parameters of Assumpsit prior to *Slade* in a way reminiscent of how a subsequent promise was alleged in the sixteenth century to avoid Assumpsit's overlap with Debt, e.g., a single action on several debts and later amazingly on a quasi-contract.[109]

By perhaps the second half of the seventeenth century, and certainly by the eighteenth century, the subsequent promise need not be proved.[110] In *Slade's Case* the promise was implied in the contract itself, but in *indebitatus assumpsit* the alleged promise was subsequent, and it was imaginary since the demand for proof was diminishing. This imaginary subsequent promise would be the springboard for extensions of the application of Assumpsit to cases of implied contract and, as will be seen in the next chapter, to quasi-contract; for, if the subsequent *assumpsit* could be implied, couldn't the contract itself be implied?[111]

Slade's Case had held that there was a promise to pay implied in a contract debt for a sum certain. The next step was to imply from the conduct of the parties a promise to pay a reasonable sum for a benefit provided. This happened first in cases of common callings, as an innkeeper in 1609 recovered the value of goods and services rendered to a guest who hadn't agreed on a price.[112] Actually recovery had sometimes been permitted in the late sixteenth century in Assumpsit without any objection of overlap with Debt because it was not based on a sum certain obligation.[113] Within, the next twenty years, liability for the amount he deserves (*quantum meruit*) was extended from common callings to regular merchants and to non-merchants and became a commonplace action in the seventeenth century.[114] Later in the seventeenth century, contracts implied in fact would be labelled either *quantum meruit,* the amount he deserves for work done, or *quantum valebant,* the amount he deserves for goods supplied.[115]

Although *quantum meruit's* genesis was different than *indebitatus assumpsit,* since *quantum meruit* was not based on a sum certain debt but rather was a species of express Assumpsit to pay a reasonable sum, after *Slade's Case* the difference was blurred, and a type of a generalized *indebitatus assumpsit* count was employed.[116] Was *quantum meruit* to be classified as an application of *indebitatus assumpsit* or a distinct species of Assumpsit? There was some confusion on this, but by the late seventeenth century the opinion seemed to be that it was distinct since it was not a sum certain.[117] *Quantum meruit* would develop into its own common count, but it would later fall into disuse as the *indebitatus* (common) counts became available in *quantum meruit* after decisions surprisingly allowed Debt on a *quantum meruit.*[118] This merger of *quantum meruit* under the *indebitatus* counts would ultimately erase the legal effect of the distinction between express contracts and contracts implied-in-fact.[119]

The judicial support for promises implied-in-fact set the stage for the incredible jump of allowing the contractual action of Assumpsit to include non-contractual quasi-contractual obligations implied-in-law. This extension caused Blackstone and others to confuse the two; Blackstone placed both contracts implied-in-fact and those implied-in-law under the classification "implied contract".[120] Part of the confusion today is due to the use of *quantum meruit* both in implied-in-fact and in quasi-contract applications.[121] Quasi-contract will be discussed in the next chapter.

Now, as a postscript to the discussion of how Assumpsit in lieu of Debt was defined by the parameters of Debt, attention is diverted to an analysis of the difference between the damages recoverable in Assumpsit and those in Debt. The recovery in Debt was based on the theory of restitution. The plaintiff brought a Debt action for the recuperation of a liquidated sum certain owed him; he sued for the recovery of the debt itself.[122] It would be unjust for the defendant to not be required to disgorge the benefit, or *quid pro quo,* that the plaintiff had bestowed on him. On the other hand, recovery under a trespassory action on the case was not restricted by what was given up by the plaintiff; rather damages were at-large for an unliquidated sum.[123]

Assumpsit, as a type of action on the case, had its genesis in trespassory reliance. By about 1500 damages in Assumpsit for nonfeasance were for the damages suffered as a consequence of relying on the defendant's promise to perform. The reliance might have been by prepayment, by a loss of credit or by entering into a transaction with a third party.[124] These were damages based on tort theory. If Assumpsit was going to be contractual, it needed to redress not just damages caused by reliance but also the value of the promised performance, which it did begin to do in the sixteenth century. The influence of the competing church courts[125] and Chancery may have been felt; both of these courts did all in their power to encourage the defendant's performance,[126] which was in effect a variant on protecting the value of the promised performance.

During the first half of the sixteenth century, arguments about the contractual nature of damages in Assumpsit were raised. In DOCTOR AND STUDENT the Student said, "if he to whom the promise is made have a charge by reason of the promise, which he hath also performed, then in that case he shall have an action for that thing that was promised."[127] This is a description of a cause of action based on reliance entitling the plaintiff to performance rather than restitution.[128] In a 1528 case the jury was directed to measure the damages in a way that the plaintiff would be put in the position he would have been in if the promise had been carried out.[129] Similar positions had been supported by Frowycke, C.J. in *Orwell v. Mortoft* (1505),[130] and the damages recovered seem to have been based on that principle in *Pykeryng v. Thurgoode* (1532).[131] These arguments for the value of the performance based on the loss of the plaintiff's expectation, rather than reliance damages or restitution, were especially important in cases where changes in market values were present.[132] The development of protection of the expectation interest in Assumpsit notwithstanding, it should be recognized that prior to the sixteenth century there was some protection of the expectation interest, in the event of a drop in market value, through specific performance in Chancery at least by the fifteenth century and even earlier in Detinue for the recovery of ascertainable goods.

The transition from reliance damages to expectation damages was largely hidden behind the general issue in trial by jury in the sixteenth century,[133] but in those cases where it wasn't obscured, the new contractual view of damages in Assumpsit resembled the Writ of Covenant's remedy of compensation for the wrong of breaching the promise. The wrong was breach of the promise and not the defendant's deceitful promise that had induced the plaintiff to give up the *quid pro quo.* If the wrong had been the deceitful promise, the plaintiff would only be entitled to restitution of the *quid pro quo* that he parted with on the strength of the deceitful promise. Thus in *Slade's Case* the declaration was that the defendant deceived the plaintiff by not paying, and the proper measure of damages would be the value of the performance. There were obvious advantages to the plaintiff in recovery based on a loss of his expectations rather than restitution in Debt. The damages were normally going to be greater in Assumpsit since it took into account market fluctuations and future profits. If the obligation was payable in installments, the action of Debt could not be brought until all the installments were due because only recuperation of the whole sum was permitted, but in Assumpsit the plaintiff could sue on the default of any installment since the action was based on breach of the promise to pay.[134] Furthermore, the Assumpsit award had the advantage of the near absolute discretion vested in the jury, and, unlike Debt, the jury need not find the exact sum certain pleaded.[135] There would be an elaboration of the rules of contract damages through the nineteenth century with the development of greater controls on the jury, but fundamentally the compensatory principle was established and is recognizable as the underpinnings of the modern rules of contract damages. Subsequent developments in damages rules will be covered in later chapters.

Finally, in musing on the changed roles of Assumpsit and Debt during the first generation of the seventeenth century, it would be remiss to not highlight the influence of Sir Edward Coke. It is surely no mere coincidence that these rapid changes were occurring during his judicial tenure in the common law courts. He was Chief Justice of the Court of Common Pleas from 1606–1613; and then Chief Justice of the King's Bench from 1613–1616. He was removed from the Bench in 1616 because of his heated opposition to the Court of Chancery's encroachment on common law jurisdiction and its practice of effectively reversing common law court decisions through the issuance of injunctions against enforcement of common law judgments the Chancellor disagreed with.[136]

Coke was in tune with the commercial upsurge that England was experiencing and was sympathetic to the needs of merchants for the predictable and effective enforcement of contracts. He was also well aware of the expanded jurisdiction that these commercial cases would provide for the common law courts.[137] It was apparent that the only predictably enforceable contractual action in the common law courts was Debt *sur obligation*,[138] but the conditional bond's formality was not the custom of merchants nor was it used by the common man. Further, with the disadvantages of Debt *sur contract* on informal contracts, Coke saw that Assumpsit was the only viable cure and set about insuring its success, thereby benefitting creditors and increasing the commercial business of common law courts.

Coke was a bridge between Medieval and modern law. He had an unhistorical and disingenuous knack for extracting modern rules from obsolescent doctrine, and he used that facility to promote extensions of *Slade's Case* under the guise of simply following the rulings of *Slade*. Indeed, as to *Slade's Case* alone, he incorrectly stated in his report of the *Case of the Marshalsea*, among other things, that the decision in *Slade* had been unanimous and that the general *indebitatus assumpsit* was declared invalid.[139] Thorne commented that when Coke wrote "for it is an ancient maxim" or listed an inordinate number of authorities, then be prepared for Coke's enunciation of a new rule.[140] His impact on the common law of contract was immense[141] due to his judicial leadership and activism and perhaps more importantly due to his widely read works[142] written during a pivotal period in the history of contract law.

Defenses to Enforcement of Promise Supported by Consideration

Thus far analysis of the defenses to an Assumpsit action on an informal contract has been confined to the defenses of lack of either consideration or a promise (*non assumpsit*). These were the primary defenses throughout the seventeenth century because, as it was put in *Golding's Case*,[143] "In every action upon the case upon a promise there are three things considerable: consideration, promise and breach of promise". Indeed in Sheppard's ACTIONS UPON THE CASE (1663),[144] a reader will search in vain to find references to such modern contract rules as quasi-contract, offer and acceptance and lack of consent. The explanation for the lack of a greater elaboration of the law of Assumpsit was that the legal questions which should have been asked and discussed were hidden behind either the general issue in trial by jury[145] or the doctrine of consideration, the latter then vaguely seen as the circumstances in which the court ought to hold the defendant's promise binding.[146] Although insufficient consideration and *non assumpsit* were the prime defenses raised in seventeenth century Assumpsit actions, Sheppard isolated defenses to a promise supported by consideration known by the time of the Restoration; among those requirements, recognizable today, were that the promise must be "lawful", "clear and certain" and made by one who was not "disabled".[147] Since the Statute of Frauds (1677) was passed subsequent to Sheppard's book, an additional seventeenth century defense to consider is the degree of formality required in an enforceable contract. A majority of the cases cited in Sheppard's 1663 work, republished in 1675, were seventeenth-century cases. As a result of the deterioration of the inns of court, his work became an important contract text to a generation of Restoration lawyers. The Interregnum was a period of attempted legislative reform of the law and was not a time of growth in the common law. Due to the instability of the Civil War years, Sheppard's description of Assumpsit was very similar to the nature of the action at Chief Justice Coke's resignation nearly a half century before.[148]

In the seventeenth century the defense that a contract was not lawful involved mainly restraints on contracts and usury.[149] As to restraints on contracts, the most common example was a restriction on carrying on one's trade. The Medieval position was that there was a religious and communal duty to work, which was reinforced by the guild system and by such statutes as the Statute of Laborers.[150] Medieval law did not concern itself with freedom of contract; the concern was for reinforcing the *status quo* of the established community order. As a consequence, an owner could not obtain full value for the sale of a business or business property if the seller could set up shop next door.[151] By the time of Coke there was a reaction against the guild system's restriction on contract, and the guilds themselves were now perceived as a restraint of trade.[152] In *Rogers v. Parrey* (1614),[153] which involved a 21 year restriction on the business use of property as a part of a lease, Coke upheld the restriction since it was reasonable and only a partial restraint, certain as to time and place. The Exchequer Chamber case of *Broad v. Jollyfe* (1621)[154] took the next logical step and upheld a covenant not to compete against the seller himself in a case where the consideration for the purchase of business stock was set at an inflated price. The rationale in *Broad v. Jollyfe* emphasized it was a voluntary restraint supported by consideration and, following Coke's lead, was only a partial restraint. These two decisions culminated in *Mitchel v. Reynolds* (1711),[155] the beginning of the modern rule. In the settled commercial era following the Glorious Revolution, mercantilists were pressing for eradication of restrictions on free trade, and in *Mitchel v. Reynolds* Lord Parker adapted common law controls to the new economic order of diminishing customary restraints and the advent of free trade. The lessor was bound to his covenant not to open a competing bakery in the parish during a 5 year lease. The ruling in *Mitchel v. Reynolds* provided that a voluntary, partial restraint, limited to a particular place and supported by consideration, was valid if it was reasonable in not preventing the defendant from having a livelihood and was not harmful to the public either because of being deprived of the defendant's skills or because of monopolistic tendencies.

Some restraints on contracting were found unenforceable due to violations of public policy; the lead here was often taken by Chancery. Conditioned bonds with restraints of trade were found unenforceable not only because consideration was not required for a sealed bond but also because the penalty was recoverable without proof of actual damage[156]—more on this point later in this chapter. And contracts restraining marriage were also violative of public policy.[157]

The other major illegality issue was usury. Canon law opposed charging any interest for the use of money because it was seen both as double payment and as setting a sinful, unnatural price, and Medieval law followed the ecclesiastical prohibition.[158] Exceptions were permitted, however, if the additional charge might not be certain of recovery due to a risk[159] or if there was a penalty for consequential damages caused by late payment. The latter reason made the conditioned bond a blatant exception to the usury prohibition.[160] Expanding trade in the sixteenth century caused merchants to realize the productive uses of borrowed money, and if the law was not ready to approve of interest, then it would just have to be implemented by various types of subterfuge.[161] As Tudor society became more secularized and the Reformation lessened the influence of canon law, merchants obtained some statutory relief from punishment for interest not in excess of 10%.[162] Notwithstanding these statutes' seeming toleration of a modest amount of interest, attempts to recover interest in the common law courts met with moral opposition until the seventeenth century since the statutes were construed to protect the creditor from punishment but did not provide a remedy for recovery of the interest.

Plaintiffs were more likely to succeed in common law actions if they could establish that there was a risk and it was therefore uncertain whether the capital sum plus interest would be recoverable; hence annuities and investments at interest were permitted.[163] Although the Statute of Usury of 1623[164] tolerated a maximum interest rate of 8%, it was still not clear in conscience that interest could be recovered in an Assumpsit action until well into the seventeenth century.[165] By this time the necessity of interest charges in the burgeoning English credit economy were undeniable.[166]

Before leaving unlawful conditions in contracts, mention should be made of two attendant rules that the courts had to iron out: one, what were the consequences for the contract if a condition was found unlawful and, secondly, could the remaining lawful portion of the contract be enforced? As to the consequences, in *Bridge v. Cage* (1606)[167] a promise to pay money to a sheriff in consideration of the sheriff doing what he had a duty to do was found quasi-extortion, unlawful and void. Sheppard agreed that unlawfulness made a contract void.[168] But could there be a distinction drawn if one condition of the contract was unlawful and the rest was untainted and lawful? In *Smith v. Colshill* (1595)[169] the partial illegality was due to a statutory rule, and the court rejected the possibility of severability. Then in *Henry Pigot's Case* (1611),[170] in the discussion of a contract condition which was unlawful under common law principles, a majority of the judges thought severability should apply. This resultant conflict was resolved in *Norton v. Syms* (1614)[171] where severability was recognized for common law illegality but not for statutory illegality: "A statute is a strict law; but the common law doth divide according to common reason, and having made that void that is against law, lets the rest stand." This difference was rejected in the eighteenth century and severability was potentially available for both types of illegality.[172]

The second of the defenses to an Assumpsit action mentioned above was that the contract be clear and certain. The requirement is associated with the need to plead to the issue in trial by jury by averring the promise with certainty. Debt, Assumpsit's contract predecessor, had technical rules requiring a fixed and certain sum. Thus if a tailor had not set the price before doing the work, he would fail in Debt, but if the amount was fixed independently by law or for an essential subject matter with a market value, as food or drink, then the sum need not be specified even in Debt.[173] Assumpsit permitted market values or a reasonableness standard to be read into a promise, but a promise to pay money within a "short time" was defective.[174] The inability of the tailor to recover in Debt for his services, when the custom often was to not raise the issue of price during negotiations, was a hardship cured by *quantum meruit*[175] without any compromise of the certainty requirement, assuming market values were available.

The third defense mentioned above was that a person could be disabled from contracting, as because of infancy or lunacy. In 1663 Sheppard wrote, "An Infant under 21 years old, though but a day, will not bee bound by any Contract or Assumpsit of his."[176] The rule for infants is much older,[177] and it was also the rule for lunatics and drunks, though there was some intervening confusion.[178] In light of the underlying policy of providing relief to infants, agreements with infants were rationalized to be lacking in consideration. Capacity, analyzed as a separate element of an enforceable contract today, was still wrapped up in the bundle of concepts called consideration in the seventeenth century. In *Stone v. Withipol* (1589)[179] the plaintiff pointed to his forbearance to sue as consideration, but the court concluded there was no enforceable action for the plaintiff to forbear from suing on since the defendant was under age. The position that an infant's contract was void was modified in the seventeenth century. In 1661 an infant, but not the adult he contracted with, was permitted to elect whether he wanted to enforce the contract. This does not square with the notion that reciprocal enforceability of mutual promises constituted the consideration and probably can only be justified because of the special status of infants.[180] Then in 1697 consideration was found for a former infant's ratification of a contract made during his minority. It was ruled that, "where the defendant under age borrowed money of the plaintiff and afterwards at full age promised to pay it, this is a good consideration for the promise and the defendant shall be charged".[181] In contrast, a contract with a married woman was still found to be void in 1719; thus her later ratification as a widow in exchange for the creditor's forbearance was ineffective because, "forbearance, where originally there is no cause of action, is no consideration to raise an assumpsit."[182]

Infants were consistently bound, however, to a contract for necessaries due to the enrichment received.[183] A 1431 case justified the rule "because these things he must of necessity have;"[184] and, in a 1478 case, "because the law intends that he cannot live without food, drink and clothing, and consequently the law wills that he pay the money due to him in this case."[185] Yet, in 1619 a contract connected to an infant's trade was unenforceable even though his trade profits maintained him.[186] And there was a policy against holding infants to penal bonds for necessaries.[187] There have been suggestions that the basis of an infant's liability for necessaries is quasi-contractual.[188] This view is reinforced in the cases finding liability based on the enrichment received by the infant and by the rule that damages were based on the reasonable value of the necessaries rather than the contractual amount.

The fourth defense mentioned above was that the contract was unenforceable because it lacked the requisite formality. Assumpsit was essentially formless,[189] and that characteristic would create difficulties in the post-*Slade* era, which Parliament would attempt to cure by passage of the Statute of Frauds (1677).[190] Before analyzing the formality required by that Statute, a brief discussion of the formal contractual instruments in general use during the seventeenth century is in order. Throughout the period, sealed conditioned bonds were by far the most common formal contract for important transactions,[191] and their use was widespread even after Assumpsit was being regularly used in place of Debt *sur contract*. Blackstone cited the regularity of its use in the mid-eighteenth century and called it the "shortest and surest" remedy.[192] The action of Assumpsit had not yet taken over the whole of the field of contract.

Throughout the history of the common law of contracts there was always a clear distinction between a sealed and unsealed (or parol) contracts, the latter being either oral or an unsealed writing.[193] A sealed obligation was never required to have consideration; its validity was based on the mere fact of its formal execution.[194] Assumpsit, and its attendant requirement of consideration, never usurped the use of Debt *sur obligation* on conditioned bonds in part because Assumpsit had evolved to avoid the hardship of wager, and wager was not available in defending against a sealed bond.[195] Furthermore, as Gilbert wrote around 1720, consideration was not required since it would be "down right madness to trifle with the solemnity of law and pretend after sealing that nothing seriously designed."[196] England has retained the use of the sealed instrument without the requirement of consideration, while American jurisdictions have in the main abolished its use.[197]

Although the conditioned bond remained popular during the seventeenth and eighteenth centuries, it was under attack because the forfeiture, for the obligor's failure to meet the condition, of typically twice the contract amount was beginning to be perceived for what it was: penal rather than compensatory. The bond forced performance and effectively dissuaded the obligor from electing to breach and pay damages for the actual loss. This type of bond had been a common way of raising capital in the sixteenth century, and it was no doubt a reasonable demand of a creditor then since capital was insecure[198] during that embryonic phase of English capitalism. In addition to securing performance, the enforcement of the bond in Debt *sur obligation* provided advantages to the plaintiff over Covenant and Assumpsit in terms of pleading, proof and damages.[199] The penal nature of conditioned bonds was first questioned by the Court of Chancery and only later did the common law courts follow suit, whether motivated by the desire to stem the flow of business to Chancery or in recognition of changed economic circumstances. By the mid-sixteenth century, Chancery stayed the execution on a penalty at common law[200] in exceptional cases of harshness, such as when a signed but unsealed acquittance existed and when there was a minor default like a payment slightly tardy.[201] There is evidence that by the latter part of the sixteenth century Chancery was issuing stays routinely in money bond cases.[202] This practice may have been curtailed by the attacks on the exercise of prerogative in Chancery during the Commonwealth,[203] but it is clear that during the Restoration there was either a revival or a continuation of the Chancery practice of providing relief as a matter of course on a conditioned bond if it violated the compensatory principle.[204]

The common law ultimately adopted Chancery's treatment of conditioned bonds,[205] but when did this happen? It was one of the inconsistencies of the common law that its courts were so much slower than Chancery here when the common law had been observing the compensatory principle in Assumpsit since the sixteenth century.[206] It has been suggested that the common law was following Chancery's denial of the penalty on at least money bonds as a matter of course by the 1670's since any defendant held to the penalty at common law could immediately run to Chancery for relief.[207] It seems unlikely there was a reception of Chancery wisdom that early for a number of reasons: there is scanty or no common law authority, infamous delays in Chancery in the recent past did not commend it to hopes of speedy action[208] and Parliament still saw the need to intervene and prohibit the recovery of the penalty on the bond by passing statutes in 1696–1697 and 1705.[209] The common law acquiescence came earlier in the case of a money bond, where the penalty would be more evident; and, even in Chancery, the forfeiture on the bond was allowed for the performance of acts other than payment of money if the actual loss was difficult to quantify.[210]

During the eighteenth century the conditioned bond was still popular for reasons other than damages, some of which were mentioned above; and, even under the statutes, the debtor was compelled to pay in a timely fashion or still be subjected to a judgment which included the penalty. However, in the eighteenth century the penalty in the judgment was seen as security for payment of the judgment, and the defendant would not be required to pay on the judgment in excess of the compensation damages.[211] By the late eighteenth century the judgment itself was limited to the compensation figure, to the exclusion of the penalty.[212] These developments naturally led to a demarcation being fashioned between acceptable liquidated damages and prohibited penalties.[213]

The popularity of the conditioned bond waned as the opportunities to recover the penalty lessened; and, as trial by jury took on a modern appearance in the eighteenth century,[214] it became the practise to employ contracts with less formality enforceable in Assumpsit. Thus Assumpsit, once a fledgling contract action for hardship cases in the early sixteenth century, triumphed and, as a practical matter, took over the entire field of contract, formal and informal, when the remainder of transactions not already claimed by *Slade's Case* came its way. This final victory had at least begun by the Restoration and was one of the factors creating pressure for more formality in agreements covered by Assumpsit. The unhappy answer to these concerns about the relaxation of contract formality was the passage of the Statute of Frauds in 1677.[215]

Assumpsit's triumph spelled trouble for defendants no longer able to effectively defend against baseless oral claims by wager. The advantage had shifted to the plaintiff, who could now prevail without being required to produce evidence of an agreement in the form of a *quid pro quo* or a sealed deed. Seventeenth century trial by jury, with its embryonic rules of evidence, was not equipped to handle a private, executory agreement such as *Slade's Case*. This was particularly true when the only witnesses to the agreement were often the parties themselves, and they were barred from testifying.[216]

In order for trial by jury to be an effective fact-finding body, there must be control over what evidence lay jurors consider, but in the seventeenth century, rules of evidence were barely visible. Such fundamental rules as cross-examination, the best evidence rule and impeachment of witness were non-existent; other rules were barely appearing, e.g., hearsay, the parole evidence rule, judicial notice and presumptions.[217] One apparent reason for the paucity of exclusionary rules was the hopelessness of controlling jurors, who were permitted to consider evidence independently obtained outside the courtroom often through hearsay.[218] A modern law of evidence could not develop until jurors acted as passive fact-finders relying solely on the evidence submitted at the trial so that the judge could control all the evidence considered by the jurors.[219] In order to protect the defendant from the weaknesses of trial by jury, Parliament created a jury control device of its own in the form of the Statute of Frauds. The jury would not be trusted to consider an Assumpsit action brought on specified categories of contracts, even if supported by consideration, unless there was a writing signed by the defendant and sufficient to justify the jury finding for the plaintiff.

Thayer labelled the Statute of Frauds a "very un-English piece of Legislation" because it was so comprehensive and far reaching, and he questioned whether such a wide reaching Act would have been passed if trial by jury was on the footing it enjoyed by the nineteenth century.[220] In earlier times Parliament had not made it a practice to interfere with the common law, but this Act was passed on the heels of the Commonwealth experience of Parliamentary experimentation in solving problems formerly outside the sphere of statutory intervention.[221] There had never been such a sweeping legislative intrusion upon the common law of contract—nor would there be anything to equal or exceed it until the twentieth century.

Parliament was not alone in its concern for unscrupulous plaintiffs taking advantage of the inability of trial by jury to cope with the flood of alleged private, executory promises now heard in the common law courts as a matter of course after *Slade's Case*. The common law judges were openly concerned; witness Chief Justice Hale's[222] remarks in 1672:

> For it had become a great grievance, two men could hardly talk together but a promise is sprung. It were well if a law were made that no promise should bind, unless there were some signal ceremony, or that wager did lie upon a promise.... And *Slade's Case*... has done more hurt than ever it did or will do good.[223]

The common law judges had the opportunity to influence the nature of the "signal ceremony" required by the Statute since they testified before the Parliamentary drafting committee.[224]

Parliament fell upon six categories of oral contracts then enforceable under Assumpsit which were perceived to be particularly difficult for juries to handle.[225] A unifying factor for the inclusion of promises of executors, marriage contracts and guaranty contracts was that they were all third party beneficiary contracts. There was uncertainty about the enforceability of such contracts in the sixteenth century, even if partially executed, because there would be no benefit (*quid pro quo*) in the defendant as evidence of the agreement.[226] The group consisting of land contracts,[227] sales of goods over ten pounds[228] and contracts of more than one year[229] are arguably in the Statute because these contracts typically involved valuable transactions.

The Statute has been criticized as a reactionary Restoration measure whereby Parliament tried to return contract law to a pre-Assumpsit formality, and cut off the equitable effect of the jury, and simply substitute the mercantile signature for the aristocratic seal—or at least for the *quid pro quo*.[230] Within nine years, part performance was found to be an exception to the Statute,[231] which is not surprising since the evidentiary crisis precipitated by *Slade's Case* related to purely executory agreements. Over the years a convoluted assortment of exceptions to the Statute were carved out by later courts that were no longer enthusiastic about the Statute under changed conditions.[232] There have been many attacks levelled at the Statute over the years,[233] and some common law jurisdictions, including England, have repealed portions of it,[234] but these criticisms have primarily to do with the failure of later Parliaments, more removed from the activism of the Commonwealth, to undo what was no longer a sensible rule.[235]

The ancient dichotomy of contracts being either sealed or unsealed was partially modified by the Statute of Frauds in that a distinction was made between oral agreements and unsealed written agreements. Now certain unsealed writings, which had formerly been merely testimonial evidence, were looked upon as constitutive.[236] The unsealed writing was not, however, raised to the level of a sealed writing because consideration was still required. It is arguable that Parliament missed the chance, that Mansfield would try to grasp a century too late, of not requiring consideration for an unsealed writing.[237]

Before unsealed writings were given a special status under the Statute of Frauds, sealed writings were considered of a higher nature and hence could not be controverted or varied by a parol agreement, whether it was an unsealed writing or oral.[238] Since the jury could not go behind sealed writings, there was no need for a parole evidence rule; but there was a concern that the writing required by the Statute of Frauds, and indeed the Statute itself, would be rendered meaningless if the jury could look to extrinsic evidence. So once the status of certain unsealed writings was raised a notch by the Statute of Frauds, it was soon determined that oral evidence could not be introduced to controvert or vary those writings either, and soon the idea that the writing was the constitutive thing was extended from unsealed writings under the Statute to all writings.[239] By the late seventeenth century, a modern parol evidence rule for contracts had taken shape.[240]

Holt, C.J. applied the new parol evidence rule strictly;[241] whereas Chancery, sitting without a jury, was slower to adopt the rule.[242] However, by the mid-eighteenth century, Chancery was also applying the rule though with greater flexibility than Holt.[243] This flexibility spilled over into the common law and allowed for the admissibility of extrinsic evidence in some instances. As Lord Mansfield would later point out, when evidence was introduced to establish a defense and not to show that the agreement was different than the writing, there was no parol evidence rule problem.[244] In the same manner, a party could show a contract to be unenforceable due to mistake, fraud or illegality.[245] But what if the introduction of parol evidence was due to an ambiguity? The exhumation of Bacon's Maxim 25 in the 1760s, over 160 years after it was written,[246] resulted in the courts' application of a confused differentiation of ambiguities into curable latent ones and those incurably patent.[247] The confusion about the parol evidence rule and the resultant criticism are still with us today.[248] One fundamental misunderstanding about the rule is that, just as with the Statute of Frauds, the parol evidence rule is a rule of substantive law rather than a rule of evidence since extrinsic evidence is excluded as a matter of form and not because of its untrustworthiness.[249]

Conclusion

Slade's Case provided the impetus for the modernization of contract theory, and Coke's disingenuous reports aided extensions of *Slade's Case* not licensed by the actual decision. The heritage of *Slade's Case* as a replacement for Debt *sur contract* would leave its imprint on contract law as lawyers and judges translated Debt's contract theory into recovery on express and implied contracts in Assumpsit. After Coke left the Bench, much of the rest of the reigns of the Stuarts and the Civil War involved digestion of the significant changes made. The depression of the 1620s and the instability of the Interregnum was not the right climate for advances in the law, but that period did see Coke's revered common law gaining precedence over the prerogative Court of Admiralty, which had been encouraged by the Tudors, and Equity, which had received similar support from the Stuarts. During the Restoration, writers and judges like Sheppard and Hale tried to lend more coherency to Assumpsit, but Assumpsit did not escape the regressive tendencies of the Restoration when there was a reaction against Assumpsit's informality. The result was the passage of the Statute of Frauds and the development of the parol evidence rule, but contract law would never return to its former formality. Important steps had now been taken toward a modern theory of contract law, and yet there was very little elaboration of the law of contract. Much of the lack of specific principles was due to the way the doctrine of consideration and the general issue shrouded detailed analysis. This elaboration would begin during the next century under Mansfield and would accelerate during the nineteenth century.

Notes

1. *See* Simpson, *Slade's Case in the History of Contract*, 74 L.Q. REV. 381, 391–392 (1958) (*Slade* was not authority for mutual promises since *Slade* involved an existing indebtedness with a *quid pro quo.*). Other points that *Slade* did not decide include: it didn't declare *indebitatus assumpsit* invalid; it didn't enable Assumpsit to apply to quasi contract; it didn't make Assumpsit applicable to executors; and it didn't declare Assumpsit to be a formed writ in Register of Writs.

2. Proof of a subsequent promise would no longer be needed in Common Pleas in order for Assumpsit to be brought on a contractual debt. Ibbetson, *Sixteenth Century Contract Law: Slade's Case in Context*, 4 OXFORD J. LEG. STUDIES 315–316 (1984) (liability found in *Slade* without need for a fictional subsequent promise).

3. *Cf.* Baker, *New Light on Slade's Case* (pt. 2), 1971 CAMBRIDGE L.J. 213, 235–236 (Yet it was debatable whether *Slade* settled this point immediately.). There's a minor disagreement over whether the objection was to 2 forms of action on the same cause of action or 2 causes of action on the same facts. *Id.* at 219 (the former); A. SIMPSON, A HISTORY OF THE COMMON LAW OF CONTRACT 285n (1975) (the latter).

4. Simpson, *supra* note 1, at 392; Ibbetson, *supra* note 2, at 295. *But see* next note.

5. Ibbetson, *supra* note 2, at 295. *But see* S. STOLJAR, A HISTORY OF CONTRACT AT COMMON LAW 78 (Canberra: 1975) (Real contention concerned jury replacing wager rather than overlap.); *see also* Baker, Book Review, 21 AM. J. LEG. HIST. 335, 339–340 (1977) (reviewing A. SIMPSON *supra* and S. STOLJAR *supra*) (leans toward Stoljar since otherwise there would have been a similar conflict earlier over Assumpsit's use in lieu of Covenant). The overlap issue with Covenant may have been deliberately ignored due to hardships Covenant brought on.

6. Moore 667; Yelverton 21; *see* Baker (pt. 1), *supra* note 3, at 53.

7. *Slade's Case*, 4 Co. Rep. 91a, 76 Eng. Rep. 1072 (1602).

8. Besides the 3 published reports, Baker studied a dozen unpublished reports in 4 English archives in shedding new light on *Slade*. Baker (pt. 1), *supra* note 3, at 52.

9. Baker (pts. 2), *supra* note 3, at 231; *accord* Ibbetson, *supra* note 2, at 303–304. In Baker's view, judicial support for plaintiff's position was so shaky that plaintiff would have lost if complaint had not emphasized delictual nature of claim ("deceive and defraud"). Baker, *supra* note 3, at 235. Questions were still

raised about the propriety of *Slade* during next 2 centuries, e.g., Edgcomb v. Dee Vaughan 89, 101 (1670) (per Vaughan, C.J.: "illegal resolution of *Slade's Case* . . . is a false gloss to turn actions of Debt into actions on the case; for contracts of debt are reciprocal grants".).

10. The informal vote was 6 to 5 for plaintiff. The statutory Exchequer Chamber was still 5–2 opposed. Wright v. Swanerton, Harv. L. sch. MS. 2069, f.20v (1604) (Walmsley, J. of Common Pleas, said *Slade* was resolved by majority opinion without reasons given and Assumpsit only available when no other action available.). *See* Ibbetson, *supra* note 2, at 303–304. *See* Baker, *The Dark Age of English Legal History* in LEGAL HISTORY STUDIES 1972 (D. Jenkins ed. 1975). *Cf.* Baker (pt. 2), *supra* note 3, at 231.

11. Duppa v. Jones, B.M. MS. Lans. 1074, F.413 (Trin. 1602), cited by Baker (pt. 2), *supra* note 3, at 231 (Baker queries whether this was to divert attention from the implied promise struggle they lost and return the focus to the tortious nature of Assumpsit.).

12. Ibbetson, *supra* note 2, at 304, cites Prowse v. Tom, K.B. 27/1374, m. 168 (Trin. 1605) and also Massey v. Webster, K.B. 27/1347, m.521 (1605). Anderson, C.J. C.P., was near death by time of *Prowse* and didn't sit. *Id.* at 304–305.

13. *Id.* at 304.

14. The Case of Marshalsea (Hall v. Stanley), 10 Co. Rep. 68b (C.P. 1612).

15. Ibbetson, *supra* note 2, at 305.

16. Baker (pt. 2), *supra* note 3, at 230–231. *Cf.* A. SIMPSON, *supra* note 3, at 296–297 (Baker's view rests on fact that no manuscript survives of a final opinion of all of judges, but there is arguably a shift in judges' view as arguments ran on over more than 5 years).

17. Kercher's Case, Godb. 176 (1611). *Cf.* Baker (pt. 2), *supra* note 3, at 236 (Perhaps dormant text may solve riddle of why Common Pleas finally followed *Slade's Case*.). Since then Ibbetson, *supra* note 2, has added some information regarding changes in makeup of Common Pleas, but no clear answer has yet been found.

18. *See* Baker (pt. 2), *supra* note 3, at 236.

19. *Id.* at 66–67 (Yelverton at 21 claimed *Slade's Case* covered executors, but Baker's research makes it clear issue was reserved).

20. Oliver v. Cleymond, Y.B. 12 Hen. VIII, f.11, pl.13 (1521) and Norwood v. Read, 1 Plowden 180 (1558) (defendant argued existing law that executor could only be assured of claims under seal). After Plowden's report of *Norwood,* he indicated that the decision was questioned by "many wise and learned men in our law."

21. Baker (pt. 2), *supra* note 3, at 233.

22. Pinchon's Case (Pinchon v. Legate), 9 Co. Rep. 86b (1612), *reprinted in* C. FIFOOT, HISTORY AND SOURCES OF THE COMMON LAW: TORT AND CONTRACT 373, 374 (London: 1949).

23. S. MILSOM, HISTORICAL FOUNDATIONS OF THE COMMON LAW 257, 354 (London: 2d ed. 1981). *See also* C. FIFOOT, *supra* note 22, at 360. An executor could be held liable if he opted for trial by jury. Fish v. Richardson, Yelv. 55, 56 (1604). An executor was chargeable under the writs of

Covenant or Debt *sur obligation* since the established mode of proof was trial by jury.

24. C. FIFOOT, *supra* note 22, at 358.

25. Ibbetson, *supra* note 2, at 312–313.

26. *See* Norwood v. Read, 1 Plow. 180 (1558). *And see* S. STOLJAR, *supra* note 5, at 90–92.

27. Y.B. Hil. 11 Hen. IV, pl. 20 f.46 (1410). *Cf.* A. SIMPSON, *supra* note 3, at 565 (Rule may have come from the criminal element in trespass since the tortfeasor's liability for punishment due to a violent act, such as a battery, should be personal to him (or "annexed to his person") and not be passively transmissible to his heir.).

28. Cleymond v. Vyncent, Y.B. Mich 12 Hen. VIII, f.11, pl. 3 (K.B. 1520), *reprinted in* J. BAKER and S. MILSOM, SOURCES OF ENGLISH LEGAL HISTORY (PRIVATE LAW TO 1750) 446 (London: 1986) (hereinafter cited as BAKER and MILSOM).

29. Executors had been given the statutory right to sue on trespasses to the testator's property in 1330 (Stat. 4 Edw. III, c.7) and actions on the case were allowed in Russell and Prat's Case, 4 Leon 44 (1589). *Pinchon's Case* ruled that there should be reciprocity.

30. Pinchon's Case, 9 Co. Rep. 866 (1612).

31. A. SIMPSON, *supra* note 3, at 572–573 (cites Cro. Jac. 293, a report of the case expressly excluding other types of promises of the testator from the scope of the decision). Simpson also points to another report of the case (2 Brown 137) reiterating another exclusion supposedly found in *Slade's Case*: that the general *indebitatus assumpsit* action was not to be used in actions of contractual debt. *Id.* at 571–572.

32. Sanders v. Easterby, Cro. Jac. 417 (1616). *See also* Small v. Boyer, 3 Bulstr. 248 (1616); Beresford v. Woodruff, Cro. Jac. 404 (1617); Fawcett v. Charter Cro. Jac. 662 (1623). The continual raising of the issue indicates there was a lingering resistance to holding an executor liable for promises of the testator other than to pay a sum certain. A. SIMPSON, *supra* note 3, at 572–573. If you will, these cases of actions against a deceased debtor accomplished what Orwell v. Mortoft, Y.B. Mich. 20 Hen. VII, f.8, pl. 18 (1505) and Pykeryng v. Thurgoode, B.M. MS. Hargrave 388 (1533) had accomplished in actions against living debtors.

33. The liability of an executor for contract debts was clearly gospel in the mid-seventeenth century: "If a man promise to pay money . . . and hee dye before it bee performed, the Executor or Administrator shall be charged with it." W. SHEPPARD, ACTIONS UPON THE CASE FOR DEEDS, viz. CONTRACTS, ASSUMPSITS, DECEIPTS, etc. 32 (London: 1663) (imperfectly listing citations to *Norwood v. Read* and *Pinchon's Case*). *See* Baker (pt. 2), *supra* note 3, at 233–234 (By time *Pinchon's Case* was decided, Common Pleas had already acquiesced to the logic of *Slade's Case* and minimal opposition was raised.).

34. Since *Slade's Case* did not require an allegation of a subsequent promise, then there was no longer any need for the original linkage that consideration provided between that promise and the prior debt. The consideration test might then have been replaced by a more flexible one like *causa* or perhaps, as Mansfield later tried, a moral obligation. *Cf.* S. STOLJAR, *supra* note 5, at 82 (Since *Slade's*

Case dispensed with the need for forbearance-assumpsit, the *indebitatus* count could have dispensed with any reference to consideration.). *See* Barbour, *The History of Contract in Early English Equity* in IV OXFORD STUDIES IN SOCIAL AND LEGAL HISTORY 166 (P. Vinogradoff ed., Oxford 1914) (Chancery asked whether the promissor made such a promise as in reason and conscience he ought to perform.).

35. Lücke, *Slade's Case and the Origin of the Common Counts* (pts. 1–3) (pt. 1), 81 L.Q. REV. 422, 434–435 (1965). In DOCTOR AND STUDENT, the Doctor asked: "But what hold they if a promise be made for a thing past, as I promise thee forty pounds for that thou hast builded me such a house; lieth an action there?" The Student responded: "They suppose nay; but he shall be bound in conscience to perform it after his intent, as is before said." ST. GERMAIN, DOCTOR AND STUDENT, Dial. II, c.24 (1523, Dial. I; 1530, Dial. II), *reprinted in* 91 SELDEN SOC. 231 (hereinafter cited as DOCTOR AND STUDENT).

36. Y.B. Trin. 5 Hen. VII, f.41v, pl. 7 (1490) ("If one sells a thing and afterwards at another place the seller warrants it, this warranty is void, because it was not made *sur le bargain,* and the buyer shall not have an action of deceit."); *see* S. MILSOM, *supra* note 23, at 359.

37. Hunt v. Bate, Dyer 272 (C.P. 1568), *reprinted in* BAKER and MILSOM, *supra* note 28, at 494. Perhaps the Student was referring to the harshness of the past consideration rule when he referred *supra* (n.35) to the debtor being "bound in conscience to perform it after his intent."

38. Hunt v. Bate, Dyer 272 (C.P. 1568). Part and parcel of *Hunt v. Bate's* rationale was the point that friendship will not provide consideration for a promise. Indeed, the continuing nature of friendship, which existed prior to the promise, makes it like past consideration; the rule that love and affection is not sufficient consideration is a precursor of past consideration rule. *See also* Andrew v. Boughey, Dyer, f.76a (1553) (A warranty of goodness of wax was void since it was made a month after the contract was entered into, citing Y.B. Trin. 5 Hen. VII, f.41v, pl.7 (1490).).

39. S. MILSOM, *supra* note 23, at 359; *cp.* Baker, *Origins of the "Doctrine" of Consideration, 1535–1585* in ON THE LAWS AND CUSTOMS OF ENGLAND 344 (Chapel Hill: 1981) (Insufficiency of love and affection is a source of past consideration rule.).

40. Greenleaf v. Barker, Cro. Eliz. 193 (1590), *reprinted in* C. FIFOOT, *supra* note 22, at 418 (Cites as authority Sidenham v. Worlington, 2 Leon. 224 (1585)); *Sidenham* had specifically approved *Hunt v. Bate.*

41. Stilk v. Myrick, 2 Camp. 317 (1809) (ship captain's promise to pay rest of crew more after two sailors deserted was unenforceable); *Stilk* settled the law in favor of *Greenleaf v. Barker* after some contrary intervening cases. C. FIFOOT, *supra* note 22, at 404.

42. *Greenleaf v. Barker* is not an accord case. A *Greenleaf*-type case and accord cases can both involve questions of consideration. In an accord case the question is whether creditor received consideration for his promise to accept an alternate performance. In a past consideration case, such as *Greenleaf,* the question is whether creditor received anything more than he already had a right to, or put in the alternative, whether the debtor undertook to do anything more than he was already compelled to do. *See* A. SIMPSON, *supra* note 3, at 453 on how St.

Germain's Student links past consideration and accord and satisfaction; *see also* C. FIFOOT, *supra* note 22, at 413 (n.74), 414 (n.75), *and* S. STOLJAR, *supra* note 5, at 121.

43. Lampleigh v. Brathwait, Hob. 105 (1616). Earlier confusion in Docket v. Voyel, Cro. Eliz. 885 (1602) (The terms past and executed are synonyms.).

44. *See* Baker (pt. 2), *supra* note 3, at 218; *see also* Lücke (pt. 1), *supra* note 35, at 435.

45. Hodge v. Vavisour, 3 Bulstr. 222, 1 Rolle Rep. 413 (1617), *reprinted in* BAKER and MILSOM, *supra* note 28, at 504. *Cf.* Simpson, *supra* note 1, at 391 (implied promise and bargain were alleged to have arisen at same moment and so consideration was not past). *See* 8 W. HOLDSWORTH, A HISTORY OF ENGLISH LAW 16 (1926).

46. *Hodge v. Vavisour* (1617), *reprinted in* BAKER and MILSOM, *supra* note 28, at 504. And yet in this post-*Slade* period, 1 Rolle Rep. still adds after its *Hodge* report a query whether the consideration is good because "consideration to forbear for a little while is no good." *Id.* at 505.

47. Y.B. Mich. 33 Hen. VI, f.48, pl. 32 (1455); Y.B. Mich. 10 Hen. VII, f.4, pl. 4 (1495).

48. Y.B. Mich. 10 Hen. VII, f.4, pl. 4 (1495) (Brian added that a novelty would make the accord enforceable.)

49. In same case that Brian stated his view, Fyneux, J. thought part payment or a novelty, as a horse, would discharge the original liability. And in an earlier cited case, Danvers, J. thought that payment of a lesser amount might be a good *quid pro quo,* but Moyle, J. had a view similar to what was to be Brian's later. Y.B. Mich. 33 Hen. VI, f.48, pl. 32 (1455).

50. *Anon,* Dal. 49, pl. 13 (1563) (Common Pleas held that 20 pounds plus a sealed acquittance was enough to discharge a 100 pound obligation.). Not many questions were raised about rule of law here because legal issues were hidden behind wager or general issue in trial by jury. In a 1588 case (*Anon,* 4 Leon. 81 C.P. 1588) there was a rare legal discussion about an accord as an offshoot of the court's inquiry about whether a poor man should be permitted to wage. The raising of the novelty of early payment also opened the door to legal discussions about accords in the 1563 case and in *Pinnel's Case.* S. MILSOM, *supra* note 23, at 256.

51. Pinnel's Case, 5 Co. Rep. 117a (C.P. 1602), *reprinted in* C. FIFOOT, *supra* note 22, at 422 (resolved by whole Court of Common Pleas).

52. An accord to discharge an unliquidated claim was not governed by *Pinnel's* Debt rule since it was not a sum certain. Hence the amount could be less than what the plaintiff might have recovered in damages. Adams v. Tapling, 4 Mod. 88, 89 (1692). But the accord here also must be executed. Andrews v. Boughey, 1 Dy. 75a (1552).

53. C. FIFOOT, *supra* note 22, at 413.

54. S. MILSOM, *supra* note 23, at 260. Debt was based on a duty to pay for a property interest that had already passed; the defendant would in effect be ordered to yield up plaintiff's property.

55. *Pinnel's Case,* 5 Co. Rep. 117a (C.P. 1602). *See* C. FIFOOT, ENGLISH LAW AND ITS BACKGROUND 103 (London: 1932) (The result is absurd that if a creditor takes a horse or a canary there is an accord and satisfaction, but if

he takes less money it is a *nudum pactum.*). It is all the more absurd in the modern era of interchangeable, mass-produced goods.

56. The rule of *Pinnel's Case* was *obiter dictum*—the defendant lost on a rule of pleading in that he failed to aver early payment.

57. Richards v. Bartlet, 1 Leon 19 (1584), *reprinted in* C. FIFOOT, *supra* note 22, at 414. The case name attached to Assumpsit's accord rule would more appropriately be "The rule in *Richards v. Bartlet*" rather than the later Debt case of *Pinnel.*

58. Richards v. Bartlet, 1 Leon. 19 (1584), *reprinted in* C. FIFOOT, *supra* note 22, at 414, 415.

59. Ames wrote, "The rule is older than the doctrine of consideration and is simply a bit of formal logic of medieval lawyers." J. AMES, LECTURES ON LEGAL HISTORY 329 (Cambridge, Mass: 1913). Fifoot disagreed with Ames by pointing to Brian's logical argument in 1495 *supra* and because the development of Debt's accord rule in the mid-sixteenth century was influenced by the contemporaneous development of bargain and benefit. C. FIFOOT, *supra* note 22, at 412–413; *accord* S. STOLJAR, *supra* note 5, at 120–121.

60. C. FIFOOT, *supra* note 22, at 414. However, even before consideration was a doctrine, defendants raising the accord defense mentioned the "consideration" for the accord. Hewton v. Forster, 27/1099, m.76 (K.B. 1536).

61. S. STOLJAR, *supra* note 5, at 121.

62. Reynolds v. Pinhowe, Cro. Eliz. 429 (1595) (prompt payment avoids the cost of suit); Hubbard v. Farrer, 1 Viner Abr. 306, pl. 17 (1635) (good consideration for creditor to have money in his purse). *Accord* Lord Blackburn, all but dissenting, in Foakes v. Beer, 9 App. Cas. 605, 622 (H.L. 1884) *and* (ENGLISH) LAW REVISION COMMITTEE, SIXTH INTERIM REPORT, CMND. No. 5449, at para. 33–35, 50, pp. 19–21 (1937) (may be more beneficial to creditor to accept prompt payment of part).

63. If there was a true dispute, and hence not a liquidated amount, an account stated based on a compromise figure was enforceable. Milward v. Ingram, 1 Mod. 205, 2 Mod. 43 (1675).

64. Peytoe's Case, 9 Co. Rep. 776 (1611). *Cf.* 8 W. HOLDSWORTH, *supra* note 45, at 85, citing Y.B. Pasch. 11 Hen. VI, pl. 30 (1432) (Novation was not enforceable in medieval law since creditor could not recover from the new debtor, who had not received a *quid pro quo* from the creditor.).

65. Richards v. Bartlet, 1 Leo. 19 (1584) (Court stated if there had been sufficient consideration, accord would have been unenforceable because defendant's promise had not been performed.).

66. 8 W. HOLDSWORTH, *supra* note 45, at 83; C. FIFOOT, *supra* note 22, at 414. *See also* Corbin, *New Contract By a Debtor to Pay His Pre-existing Debt,* 27 YALE L.J. 535, 538 (1917) (If there is sufficient consideration, then an executory accord should be enforceable.).

67. Goring v. Goring, Yelv. 11 (1601) (accord to pay 150 pounds in seven installments instead of original 205 pounds was enforceable); Case v. Barber, Sir T. Raymond 450 (1682), *reprinted in* C. FIFOOT, *supra* note 22, at 426 (Court said, despite *Peytoe's* case, an executory accord was "of late" enforceable but statement was *dictum* since there was only part payment without a novelty and it didn't comply with Statute of Frauds.).

68. Allen v. Harris, 1 Ld Raym. 122 (1696) ("And the books are so numerous, that an accord ought to be executed, that it is now impossible to overthrow all the books. But if it had been a new point it might be worthy of consideration.").

69. Lynn v. Bruce, 2 H. Bl. 317 (1794).

70. S. STOLJAR, *supra* note 5, at 124. If this point is to be consistent with the question of the need for consideration in an accord, then a defense should be treated differently and consideration should not be required for the accord defense *per se, supra*. In fact this was the rule for unliquidated claims, *supra*.

71. 2 T. STREET, THE FOUNDATIONS OF LEGAL LIABILITY 93 (Long Island: 1906).

72. *Cf.* (ENGLISH) LAW REVISION COMMITTEE, SIXTH INTERIM REPORT, CMND. No. 5449, at para. 33–35, 50 (1937) (Recommended abolition of *Pinnel* rule, with the proviso that the original obligation revives if the accord is not performed.).

73. Creditors' compositions stood up against the objection of a single creditor in order to bar one creditor from committing a fraud on the others. Butler v. Rhodes, 1 Esp. 236 (1794). Promissory reliance has aided modern debtors.

74. The House of Lords reluctantly affirmed the rule in *Pinnel's Case* in 1884 over Blackburn, J's opposition. Foakes v. Beer, 9 App. Cas. 605 (1884). *See* 15 S. WILLISTON, A TREATISE ON THE LAW OF CONTRACTS, sect. 1837–1847 (3d ed. 1972 & Supp. 1986); G. CHESHIRE, C. FIFOOT and M. FURMSTON, LAW OF CONTRACT 88–90 (London: 11th ed. 1986) (hereinafter cited as CHESHIRE and FIFOOT).

75. Hughes v. Rowbotham, Popham 30 (K.B. 1592) has a representative example of such a declaration.

76. Lücke (pt. 2), *supra* note 35, at 548–560.

77. Hughes v. Rowbotham, Popham 30 (K.B. 1592).

78. S. MILSOM, *supra* note 23, at 354; S. STOLJAR, *supra* note 5, at 106.

79. Morgan v. Slade, Moore 667, 668 (1602) ("every contract executory implies an assumpsit to pay the money at the agreed day. But this is not the case with an *indebitatus assumpsit solvere*, for there the cause does not appear.")

80. Case of the Marshalsea, 10 Co. Rep. 68b, 77a, 77 Eng. Rep. 1027, 1042 (C.P. 1612) (Coke, now C.J.C.P., was a participating lawyer in the *Slade* arguments and he recalled that then Chief Justice Popham observed that all justices "are *unanimously* resolved: 1. that the general declaration in an action upon the case ... without showing the cause of the debt, is insufficient." (emphasis supplied)).

81. Lücke (pts. 1), *supra* note 35, at 557–558, *and see* Lücke (pt. 3), 82 L.Q. REV. 81, 85–86 (1966) (This shows that *indebitatus assumpsit* was identified with the general declaration of the debt.); cf. A. SIMPSON, *supra* note 3, at 308 ("but it is curious that both Moore and Coke seem to have thought that the issue was at least raised in *Slade's Case*." *Id.* at 86.).

82. Baker (pt. 2), *supra* note 3, at 214; *accord* S. MILSOM, *supra* note 23, at 354 and Ibbetson, *supra* note 2, at 295. *See also* Baker, Book Review, 21 AM. J. LEG. HIST. 335, 340–341 (1977) (Moore's laconic final sentence seems to be his own comment rather than a minute of something decided.). Baker and Ibbetson, Baker's former Ph.D. student, hold to the premise that a ruling wasn't made unless a manuscript is found indicating that it was, notwithstanding an accepted change in the law shortly after a particular point in time.

83. D. IBBETSON, THE DEVELOPMENT OF THE ACTION OF ASSUMPSIT, 1540–1620 160 (Cambridge University Ph.D. dissertation 1980) (available in Cambridge University Library) (citing Morgan v. Glanvill, K.B. 27/1390, m. 537v. (1605)). *See* Lücke (pt. 3), *supra* note 35, at 87.

84. Woodford v. Deacon, Cro. Jac. 206, pl.2 (1608), *reprinted in* BAKER and MILSOM, *supra* note 28, at 464. The plaintiff's declaration in *Woodford v. Deacon,* and most declarations thereafter, set out the debt as the consideration unlike the declaration in *Slade,* wherein the sale was the consideration (and unlike Coke's report of *Slade* that the consideration was the seller's promise to deliver the goods themselves).

85. Buckingham v. Costendine, Cro. Jac. 213 (K.B. 1608) ("for it might be by obligation, or recognizance or lease in which case such a general declaration is not good.").

86. A. SIMPSON, *supra* note 3, at 299–300 (Assumpsit not permitted: on Debt on a bond, in lieu of Debt for rent, as an alternative to Debt *sur obligation,* and also in lieu of Covenant on a specialty.). *See* D. IBBETSON, *supra* note 83, at 169, citing Yale MS. GR 29.2, f.127 (1572) (Corporation could not bring Assumpsit since it could only contract by deed.).

87. J. AMES, *supra* note 59, at 153, 168; A. SIMPSON, *supra* note 3 at 308. There were exceptions to the rule of thumb that Assumpsit was unavailable on a Debt if wager was unavailable, *e.g.,* a case of where an infant defendant was barred from waging in Debt and yet could be sued in Assumpsit for necessaries. D. IBBETSON, *supra* note 83, at 172.

88. Bellinger v. Gardiner, 1 Rolle Rep. 24, pl. 1 (1614), *reprinted in* BAKER and MILSOM, *supra* note 28 at 434 (A real contract cannot be changed into a promise in Assumpsit, for "it might be he was indebted for rent—which is real (and not) personal." *Id.* at 465).

89. Specialty is of a "higher nature" than an informal, contractual debt since it is conclusive proof; rent on a lease was of a higher nature since it concerned land. *See* Ames, *Specialty Contracts and Equitable Defences,* 9 HARV. L. REV. 49 (1895) and Sharington v. Strotton, Plow. 298, 308 (1565) (sealed deed of higher nature).

90. Baker of Gray's Inne v. Occould, Godb. 186, pl. 268 (C.P. 1612).

91. Barker v. Barker, Palmer 171 (K.B. 1621). *See* Lücke (pt. 3), *supra* note 35, at 86–87, 90–91.

92. Lücke (pt. 3), *supra* note 35, at 88–91 (Plaintiffs' lawyers preferred to avoid special pleading because of the convenience of pleading generally.); *but cf.* Simpson, *supra* note 1, at 393–394 (Didn't see advantage after *Slade* of keeping distinction between Special *Assumpsit* and *indebitatus assumpsit* for general pleading alone.).

93. Lücke (pt. 3), *supra* note 35, at 88–90. *See* Milsom, *Account Stated in the Action of Debt,* 82 L.Q. REV. 534 (1966).

94. Lücke (pt. 3), *supra* note 35, at 88–90 citing Dalby v. Cooke, Cro. Jac. 234, pl. 4 (1609) and Brinsley v. Partridge, Hob. 88, pl. 118 (1611).

95. Holmes v. Chenie, Hetley 106 (C.P. 1628).

96. Woodford v. Deacon, Cro. Jac. 206, pl. 2 (1608) (Then it would be "good enough for the generality thereof").

97. Buckingham v. Costendine, Cro. Jac. 213 (K.B. 1608).

98. Bellinger v. Gardiner, 1 Rolle Rep. 24, pl. 1 (1614), *reprinted in* BAKER and MILSOM, *supra* note 28, at 464. A. SIMPSON, *supra* note 3, at 311 states that the earliest case approving the new form was Rock v. Rock, Yelv. 175 (1609).

99. Thorne v. Fuller, 1 Rolle Rep. 379, pl. 37 (1616).

100. *E.g.*, breach of a covenant to perform an act; breach of warranty (was already clear there's a contract); guaranty contract and promise for a promise (both lack a *quid pro quo* in the defendant). *Cf.* Simpson, *supra* note 1, at 391–392 (Although *Slade's Case* was specially pleaded, it has no relevance to Special Assumpsit for mutual promises; it is affiliated with *indebitatus* claims, and that means there must be *quid pro quo* which was supplied by passage of property fiction.).

101. A. SIMPSON, *supra* note 3, at 312. *See also* Lücke (pt. 3), *supra* note 35, at 90–91.

102. Lücke (pt. 3), *supra* note 35, at 91; C. FIFOOT, *supra* note 22, at 368–369.

103. *See* Ibbetson, *Assumpsit and Debt in the Early Sixteenth Century: The Origins of the Indebitatus Count,* 41 CAMBRIDGE L.J. 142, 148–151 (1982) (There were early examples in the 1530s and it was on the increase by the 1540s.).

104. Ibbetson, *supra* note 2, at 296–297.

105. Baker (pt. 2), *supra* note 3, at 234.

106. Ibbetson, *supra* note 2, at 315–316, (If an accounting on all the debts, a single *insimul computassent* count in Assumpsit was good.). *See also* Lücke (pt. 3), *supra* note 35, at 91–93 (Proof of subsequent promise probably required for several decades.).

107. Ibbetson, *supra* note 2, at 316–317.

108. Lücke (pt. 3), *supra* note 35, at 93.

109. Ibbetson, *supra* note 2, at 315–317. *Cf.* Lücke (pt. 3), *supra* note 35, at 93 (Seventeenth century saw repetition of adoption of generalized declaration and subsequent promise not needing to be proved.).

110. Lücke (pt. 3), *supra* note 35, at 93 (In the absence of an actual subsequent promise, there was no justification in a general declaration, but this original reason for the general declaration became obscured in time.).

111. J. BAKER, AN INTRODUCTION TO ENGLISH LEGAL HISTORY 306–307 (London: 2d ed. 1979); T. PLUCKNETT, A CONCISE HISTORY OF THE COMMON LAW 648 (London: 5th ed. 1956). *See* Lücke (pt. 3), *supra* note 35, at 93–95 on how implication of subsequent promise facilitated uniform pleading and on the role of the professional pleader in this period.

112. Warbrook v. Griffin, 2 Brown. 254 (1609) ("it is an implied promise of every part, that is, of the part of the innkeeper that he will preserve the goods of his guest, and of the part of the guest that he will pay all duties and charges which he caused in the house"). This was extended to common carriers the next year and then to physicians. Rogers v. Head, Cro. Jac. 262 (1610); (Shepherd v. Edwards, Cro. Jac. 370 (1616). *See also* dictum in Six Carpenters Case, 8 Co. Rep. 146 (1610).

113. Mery v. Lewes, 2 Leo. 53 (K.B. 1587). *But see* Young v. Ashburnham, 3 Leo. 161 (1587) (Innkeeper could not bring Debt against guest since no sum certain and could not bring *indebitatus assumpsit* since no express promise.). *See* A. SIMPSON, *supra* note 3 at 497 (King's Bench and Common Pleas seemed to

both be allowing the action here in Assumpsit by 1600.). *See also* S. MILSOM, *supra* note 23, at 355 (*quantum meruit* never within the scope of Debt).

114. Hall v. Walland, Cro. Jac. 618 (1621) (reasonable sum for procuring a lease); Rolte v. Sharp, Cro. Car. 77 (1627) (Exchequer Chamber action brought by a tailor in *Assumpsit tantum quantum meruit* for the making of a gown and petticoat.). *See* C. FIFOOT, *supra* note 22, at 361; *and see* S. STOLJAR, *supra* note 5, at 109–110. *See also* W. SHEPPARD, *supra* note 33, at 2 (for work done and for innkeepers).

115. Boult v. Harris, 3 Keble 469 (1676).

116. S. STOLJAR, *supra* note 5, at 110 (Hybrid styles of pleas developed mixing *indebitatus assumpsit* and *quantum meruit*.); C. FIFOOT, *supra* note 22, at 361–362 (Alternative pleas were common of *indebitatus assumpsit* for a fixed sum and *quantum meruit* for a reasonable sum.).

117. C. FIFOOT, *supra* note 22, at 361–363.

118. *Id.* at 360 (a strange decision); *but cf.* A. SIMPSON, *supra* note 3, at 66 (nothing surprising due to influence of *Assumpsit* and dicta in later cases). *See also* A. SIMPSON, *supra* note 3, at 498–499 (Once Debt was available on uncertain sum, then *indebitatus assumpsit* was available, and its inherent advantages preferred.); *accord* P. WINFIELD, THE PROVINCE OF THE LAW OF TORT 157–160 (Cambridge: 1931).

119. The distinction between express and implied-in-fact contracts is not based on legal effect but on way mutual assent is manifested. The continued use of the terms express and implied contracts to divide contract law is probably due to the continued influence of Blackstone. *See* 3 W. BLACKSTONE, COMMENTARIES ON THE LAWS OF ENGLAND, ch. 9, 153 (1768).

120. 3 W. BLACKSTONE, *supra* note 119, at 158–162. *See also* W. SHEPPARD, *supra* note 33, at 2, who refers to implied-in-fact recovery by worker or innkeeper as "implied by law".

121. P. WINFIELD, *supra* note 118, at 157–160. Winfield did masterly job of describing the nineteenth century, and later, use in England of *quantum meruit* for (1) a reasonable sum in an implied-in-fact application and (2) in quasi-contract, per Planche v. Colburn, 8 Bing. 14 (1831), when aggrieved has been disabled from completing performance by other party and elects to sue for value of work done.

122. *Cf.* Washington, *Damages in Contract at Common Law* (pt. 1), 47 L. Q. REV. 345, 367 (1931) (Until first decade of sixteenth century, real consequential damages awarded in Debt for the detention of payment, but as Assumpsit grew the detention figure lessened.). Detention damages were becoming a standardized amount by the end of the sixteenth century. D. IBBETSON, *supra* note 83, at 361–362. *See also* J. BAKER, *supra* note 111, at 267 (Debt on loan looks like action to enforce contract since debtor has duty to return the loan amount.); *and see* Robinson v. Bland, 2 Burr. 1077, 1086 (1760).

123. Milsom, *Not Doing Is No Trespass,* 1954 CAMBRIDGE L.J. 105, 109–111. As Assumpsit began to be used widely in place of Debt, Assumpsit was allowed on an uncertain sum. Floyd v. Irish, Sheppard 71 (K.B. 1587).

124. S. MILSOM, *supra* note 23, at 338, 349. By the mid-sixteenth century in *indebitatus assumpsit* the plaintiff complained of damages because of forbear-

ance in suing in reliance on the defendant's subsequent promise to pay. Milsom, *supra* note 123, at 112.

125. S. MILSOM, *supra* note 23, at 337–338. The trust the plaintiff placed in the defendant could have been influenced by church court *fidei laesio*. Helmholz, *Assumpsit and Fidei Laesio*, 91 L.Q. REV. 406, 408, 421 (1975).

126. Helmholz, *supra* note 125, at 406 (Under canon law one was obliged to complete his promise under pain of excommunication.). By fifteenth century Chancery was compelling conscientious behavior of performance by specific performance of land and marriage contracts and by threat of imprisonment for other promises. Barbour, *supra* note 34, at 88, 122–128. *See* S. MILSOM, *supra* note 23, at 90–91.

127. DOCTOR AND STUDENT, *supra* note 35, at 228, 230.

128. S. MILSOM, *supra* note 23, at 358.

129. William Strate's Case, Spelman 295 (1528).

130. Orwell v. Mortoft, Keil 69 (1505), *reprinted in* BAKER and MILSOM, *supra* note 28, at 406, 410 ("and even though the plaintiff could have an action of debt for the barley, he is nevertheless not thereby satisfied for being damaged".).

131. Pykeryng v. Thurgoode, K.B. 27/1073 (1532), *reprinted in* BAKER and MILSOM, *supra* note 28, at 411, 413 (Recovery was for more than what the price plus normal costs would have been.).

132. Fuller and Perdue provided terminology for this type of damage: "expectation interest" (plaintiff is awarded "value of expectancy which the promise created"). They argued that the salutory objective of protecting the reliance interest in a contract required that the expectation interest in an executory contract be protected. Fuller and Perdue, *The Reliance Interest in Contract Damages* (pt. 1), 46 YALE L.J. 52, 54, 62 (1936). There is a penal quality to enforcing expectation interest, as there was in the ecclesiastical *fidei laesio* proceeding for the good of the defendant's soul. S. MILSOM, *supra* note 23, at 337. *See Slade's Case*, 4 Co. Rep. 91a, 94b (1602) ("that the plaintiff in this Action on the Case in Assumpsit should not recover only Damages for the *Special Loss* (if any be) which he had, but also for the whole Debt." (emphasis supplied)).

133. S. MILSOM, *supra* note 23, at 338.

134. A. SIMPSON, *supra* note 3, at 18, 66–69, 583–584. There were also instances in Debt where the plaintiff would receive nothing if he failed to prove the exact same sum due as in his pleading. *Id.* at 62–63. But there were less difficulties for the plaintiff in Assumpsit when the jury verdict wasn't the same. *See* Washington (pt. 1), *supra* note 122, at 350 (The courts generally did not tamper with the jury verdict due to the ineffectiveness of attaint.).

135. Washington (pt. 1), *supra* note 122, at 346–351, 362 (Later, new trials permitted in mid-seventeenth century on question of proper jury award.); *see also* Ibbetson, *supra* note 103, at 146 *and* D. IBBETSON, *supra* note 83, at 353–359 (Study of 1568 and 1588 King's Bench rolls showed that greater variations in judicial increases for costs in Debt *sur obligation* to get award closer to the sum due on the sealed bond than in *Assumpsit* where add-on for costs are more constant.). On a divergence between the pleading and the verdict in Debt, *see Anon*, Mich., 3 Hen. VI, f.4, pl. 4 (1424) (No judgment for plaintiff when plea was for 20 pounds and jury found 40 pounds due.) *and* Blackwell v. Sleggein,

Moo. 49 (K.B. 1562) (No judgment for plaintiff when claim was for 20 pounds and verdict for 13 pounds "because it cannot be intended the same contract".); *see also* 3 W. BLACKSTONE, *supra* note 119, at 154 (If proof varies from claim, it cannot be looked at as same contract, and so plaintiff recovers nothing.).

136. *See* C. BOWEN, THE LION AND THE THRONE (THE LIFE AND TIMES OF SIR EDWARD COKE, 1552–1634) 307–336 (London: 1957); *see generally* Baker, *The Common Lawyers and the Chancery: 1616,* 4 IRISH JURIST 368 (New Series, 1969); Coke was dismissed from office by King James I in 1616 as a result of the jurisdictional squabble with Lord Chancellor Ellesmere. Glanvill's Case, Moo. 1131, 72 Eng. Rep. 939 (1616). Coke went on to a brilliant career in Parliament. *See* LORD NOTTINGHAM'S "MANUAL OF CHANCERY PRACTICE" AND "PROLEGOMENA OF CHANCERY AND EQUITY" 12–15 (ed. D. Yale, Cambridge: 1965).

137. T. PLUCKNETT, *supra* note 111, at 662–664 (Coke succeeded in crippling the Court of Admiralty and capturing its mercantile law jurisdiction through fictions and prohibitions. He allowed mercantile custom to be established before juries of merchants). *See also* 4 W. HOLDSWORTH *supra* note 45, at 153–154, 491–493 (Coke's writings on supremacy of common law later influenced Interregnum politicians and resulted in expansion of commercial jurisdiction for common law courts and Chancery so that England, unlike the Continent, included the law merchant as simply a branch of the common law.).

138. *Cf.* D. IBBETSON, *supra* note 83, at Appendix 2 (Survey includes a table of King's Bench plea rolls of cases in Assumpsit and Debt. In Pasch. term of 1578, there were 75 Assumpsit cases and 208 Debt cases, of which wager was possible in 13 cases. In Mich. term, 1600 there were 48 Assumpsit cases and 208 Debt cases, wager being possible in 69 cases.).

139. *See* Baker, *supra* note 3, at 234 (On Coke and *Slade's Case*: "First, we must lay aside Coke's 'resolutions', in so far as they appear from their relationship with independent manuscript reports to be the heads of his own arguments".).

140. S. THORNE, SIR EDWARD COKE (1552–1952) 7, 13 (Selden Society Lecture, 1952).

141. *Id.* at 17–18 ("Indeed, when I consider all the judges England has had, I can think of no other whose absence would have had more serious effect on the course of English law than that of Edward Coke"). *See also* 5 W. HOLDSWORTH, *supra* note 45, at 491–493.

142. E. COKE, REPORTS (1600–1616); E. COKE, INSTITUTES OF THE LAW OF ENGLAND (4 Parts), especially Part I: A COMMENTARY UPON LITTLETON (1628). *See* C. BOWEN, *supra* note 136, at 436–452.

143. Golding's Case, 2 Leo. 71 (1586).

144. W. SHEPPARD, *supra* note 33. Sheppard's work, though redundant and piecemeal, was a serious attempt to summarize the action of Assumpsit; 240 of its 387 pages were devoted to contract and Assumpsit.

145. Milsom, *Law and Fact in Legal Development,* 17 U. TORONTO L.J. 1, 10–17 (1967) (The legal questions about the facts needed for development of law were not raised with either blank denial or with submission to jury on general issue.)

146. S. MILSOM, *supra* note 23, at 357. The variety of elements perceived as aspects of consideration would prompt Sheppard in 1663 to describe a contract

involving a party under a disability to be a contract "without any valuable consideration". W. SHEPPARD, *supra* note 33, at 26.

147. W. SHEPPARD, *supra* note 33, at 26, 84. *See* A. SIMPSON, *supra* note 3, at 506–557 for a use of Sheppard's book in a way similar to the one herein for analyzing 17th Century Assumpsit defenses.

148. *See* Black, *The Courts and Judges of Westminster Hall During the Great Rebellion, 1640–1660,* 7 J. LEGAL HIST. 23, 24–32 (1986) (Uncertainty about which judges had authority, inns barely functioning and lawyers scarce—civil suits dropped 60–70% in 1640s.). *Also* N. MATTHEWS, WILLIAM SHEPPARD, CROMWELL'S LAW REFORMER 233–234; 240–241 (Cambridge: 1984) (Hale's Commission proposed 20-man appellate body, 18 of whom would be non-lawyers). The intervening social and political instability didn't lend itself to the development of the law as had occurred during the stability of the Elizabethan and Jacobean periods. Restoration lawyers like Hale and Sheppard, viewed the common law as an age old law continuing from the period before the Interregnum. *Cf.* SELECTED ESSAYS OF F.W. MAITLAND 113 (H. Cam ed., Cambridge: 1957); *and see* T. PLUCKNETT, *supra* note 111, at 54–55 on the Restoration.

149. *See generally* A. SIMPSON, *supra* note 3, at 110–117, 518–525, 585 and 8 W. HOLDSWORTH, *supra* note 45, at 53–62.

150. Statute of Labourers, 25 Edw. III, st. 2, c. 1 (1349–1351) attempted to stem the exit of workers from feudal manors caused by labor shortages after the Plague. *See* John Dyer's Case, 2 Hen. V, f.5, pl. 26 (1414) (unsuccessful attempt to hold defendant on a bond to not work as a dyer in a town for 6 months). The idea of duty to work is seen as late as 1602 in a case of a defendant binding himself to not work in two towns for four years, wherein Anderson, C.J. sided with the defendant because a man "might as well bind himself that he would not go to Church." Colgate v. Bacheler, Cro. Eliz. 872 (1602).

151. 8 W. HOLDSWORTH, *supra* note 45, at 58.

152. S. THORNE, *supra* note 140, at 10–11 (Guild system had once regulated economic activity, ensuring quality and fair dealing, but the widening markets and the shifting populations made them combinations in restraint of trade.).

153. Rogers v. Parrey, 2 Bulstr. 136, Cro. Jac. 326 (1614) (Lessee sublet premises for use by a joiner in violation of the restrictive covenant.). This is one of the earliest known action of Assumpsit to enforce such a restriction. *And see* Ipswich Tailor's Case, 11 Co. Rep. 53a, 77 Eng. Rep. 1218 (1614) (guild restriction on exercising a trade unenforceable).

154. Broad v. Jollyfe, Cro. Jac. 596, 2 Rolle Rep. 201 (1621).

155. Mitchel v. Reynolds, 1 P. Wms. 181, 24 Eng. Rep. 647 (1711) (lessor had given bond).

156. *Anon,* March 77 (1614); Barrow v. Wood, March 191 (1642); Hunlocke v. Blacklowe, 2 Wm. Saund. 156 (1670). Another public policy argument against the penalty in a conditioned bond was usury, *infra.*

157. *Anon,* Owen 34 (1588) (A widow lost a bet with her son that she would not remarry, and her son's hardnosed action to collect in Chancery turned on the public policy prohibition on restraints to marriage.). *See* Long v. Dennis, 4 Burr. 2055 (1767) per Mansfield: "conditions in restraint of marriage are odious

. . . they are contrary to sound policy." A gambling contract was not a violation of public policy at common law.

158. A. SIMPSON, *supra* note 3, at 510–511; 8 W. HOLDSWORTH, *supra* note 45, at 101–102 (citing Glanvill and Bracton). The Church was also concerned about the poor man being taken advantage of by sharp practices. *Id.* at 107.

159. A. SIMPSON, *supra* note 3, at 510–511, 514–516 (Contracts for gambling, insurance, investments and annuities were examples of enforceable risk contracts.).

160. *See* Burton's Case, 5 Co. Rep. 69a (1591) (creditor could collect the penalty since he was not certain to receive the penalty if payment was on time). *See also* LORD NOTTINGHAM'S CHANCERY CASES, 79 SELDEN SOCIETY 9 (D. Yale ed. 1961) (hereinafter cited as NOTTINGHAM'S CASES) (The use of the conditioned bond to evade the canon law prohibition on usury no doubt delayed the Chancery and common law courts from questioning the fairness of the penalty.).

161. 8 W. HOLDSWORTH, *supra* note 45, at 103–107 (Subterfuges included a triple contract, sale and resale, rent charges, etc.)

162. Statute of Usury of 1571 (Acte Against Usurie), 13 Eliz. I, c.8, extended by 39 Eliz. I, c.18 (1597). Statute of 1571 doesn't make usury lawful but does provide that there would be no punishment if the interest charged was less than 10%. It reintroduced similar Statute of 1545, 37 Hen. VIII, c.9 (1545).

163. A. SIMPSON, *supra* note 3, at 516–517; 8 W. HOLDSWORTH, *supra* note 45, at 103–106; *See* 1 J. ASHLEY, AN INTRODUCTION TO ENGLISH ECONOMIC HISTORY AND THEORY 405–411, 440–447 (London: 1893).

164. Statute of Usury of 1623, 21 Jac. I, c.17 (1623). *See* Stat. 12 Car. II, c.13 (1660) (rate reduced to 6%).

165. A year before the 1623 statute the judges discussed the tug between the law of God and trade practices in Sanderson v. Warner, Palmer 291, 2 Rolle Rep. 239 (1622). *See* Harris v. Richards, Cro. Car. 273, 79 Eng. Rep. 838 (1632) (It is lawful consideration to pay interest not in excess of what law permitted.). *Cf.* Wilson v. Dove, 3 Keb. 183 (1673) (Vaughan, C.J. dissented because As- couldn't be brought to recover interest even at the permitted rate.).

166. *Cf.* 8 W. HOLDSWORTH, *supra* note 45, at 112–113; *and see Id.* at 108, quoting BACON, ESSAY ON USURY: "two things are to be reconciled: the one that the tooth of usurie be grinded, that it bite not too much; the other that there be open a meanes to invite moneyed men to lend to the merchants for the continuing and quickening of trade."

167. Bridge v. Cage, Cro. Jac. 103, 79 Eng. Rep. 89 (1606) (Warburton, J. drew analogy to uncollectible usury.).

168. W. SHEPPARD, *supra* note 33, at 86–87.

169. Smith v. Colshill, 2 And. 56 and 108 (1595).

170. Henry Pigot's Case, 11 Co. Rep. 27a (1611).

171. Norton v. Syms, Moo. 856, Hob. 14 (K.B. 1614).

172. Collins v. Blantern, 2 Wils. 351 (1767) (Wilmot, C.J. said, "I think there is no difference between things made void by Act of Parliament, and things made void by the common law.").

173. *Anon*, 12 Edw. IV, f.8, pl. 22 (1482). *See* C. FIFOOT, *supra* note 22, at

230 (A verdict in Debt for more or less than the amount claimed would fail since this isn't same contract as was made.).

174. Tolhurst v. Brickenden, Cro. Jac. 250, 1 Rolle Rep. 5 (1610).

175. *See* A. SIMPSON, *supra* note 3, at 65 (Skilled artificer made bargains in situations where freedom of contract prevailed).

176. W. SHEPPARD, *supra* note 33, at 27.

177. Y.B. Pasch. 2 Hen. IV, f.18, pl. 7 (1400) (a valid covenant could be made at age 12); Y.B. Hil. 21 Hen. VI, f.31 pl. 18 (1442) (voidable at option of infant); Y.B. Pasch. 1 Hen. VII, pl. 2, p. 15 (1485).

178. Coke thought the contracts of lunatics and drunks should be enforceable. E. COKE, A COMMENTARY UPON LITTLETON 247a (1628). But it is unlikely that he was correct since it was not the rule in Bracton's day; Fitzherbert disagreed; and it was certainly not the law in the eighteenth century. 8 W. HOLDSWORTH, *supra* note 45, at 52–53.

179. Stone v. Withipol, 1 Leo. 113, Cro. Eliz. 126 (1589), *reprinted in* BAKER and MILSOM, *supra* note 28, at 498 (Coke, as attorney for the infant's executor argued: "For the plaintiff is not at any charge for which the defendant can have any benefit, for it is but the forbearance of the payment of the debt which she was not compellable to pay.").

180. Forrester's Case, 1 Sid. 41 (1661).

181. Ball v. Hesketh, Comberbatch 381 (1697). Consideration is arguably based on a moral obligation here.

182. Loyd v. Lee, 1 Strange 94 (1719). But why did a married woman lack capacity at common law? One idea was that personal property, as a chose-in-action, could not be owned by a married woman. 3 W. HOLDSWORTH, *supra* note 45, at 528; *but cf.* A. SIMPSON, *supra* note 13, at 545 (scanty authority to support Holdsworth). A second suggestion was that she did not have her own will but depended on the will of her husband. A. SIMPSON, *supra* note 3, at 546–547 (citing Jordan's Case, Mich., 27 Hen. VIII, f.24 pl. 3 (1536)).

183. W. SHEPPARD, *supra* note 33, at 27 ("And yet his Contract for necessary meat, drink, apparel, physick, schooling, and the like necessaries is as good and binding as another mans Contract is.").

184. Y.B. Mich. 10 Hen. VI, f.14, pl. 46 (1431). The decision confuses necessity and benefit together. *See* Mansfield's comments later in Zouch v. Parsons, 3 Burr. 1801 (1765) (policy protects right to obtain necessaries for their benefit.).

185. Y.B. Pasch. 18 Edw. IV, pl. 7, f.1, at f.2 (1478).

186. Hill v. Whittingham, Cro. Jac. 494, 1 Rolle Ab. 729 (1619).

187. Randal's Case, Godbolt 219 (1602); Hutchin's Case, Dyer 104b (1619).

188. 8 W. HOLDSWORTH, *supra* note 45, at 51 (Form of the action was often Assumpsit on a *quantum meruit*, which gave rise to the modern idea of quasi-contract for necessaries.); *see also* A. SIMPSON, *supra* note 3, at 543–544.

189. W. SHEPPARD, *supra* note 33, at 84.

190. Statute of Frauds, 29 Car. 2, c. 3 (1677).

191. Searches of common law plea rolls in late sixteenth show that there was still a continued preference for the conditioned bond. A. KIRALFY, THE ACTION ON THE CASE, Appendix A (London: 1951); D. IBBETSON, *supra* note 83, at 396 *et seq. See* 3 W. BLACKSTONE, *supra* note 119, at 154. The

reports are filled with actions on conditioned bonds in the seventeenth and eighteenth centuries.

192. 3 W. BLACKSTONE, *supra* note 119, at 153–154 ("Express contracts include three distinct species, debts, covenants and promises." As to debts he cites the regular use of Debt on specialties but indicates that Debt *sur contract* rare because of wager and the requirement that plaintiff prove the exact sum claimed.). There were advantages of proof and damages with a sealed instrument since the jury was not permitted to look behind the instrument.

193. W. SHEPPARD, *supra* note 33, at 18. *Cf. Pinnel's Case,* 5 Co. Rep. 117a (1602) (dictum indicates that a sealed acquittance to take less money than the amount due in the money bond was effective without a novelty).

194. Sharington v. Strotton, Plow. 298, 308 (1565); *see* Ames, *supra* note 89, at 49–50.

195. S. MILSOM, *supra* note 23, at 356. There could be hardship since jury couldn't go behind document to see if actual loss was less than penalty and there was no relief if bond or acquittance lost.

196. G. GILBERT, OF CONTRACT, Brit. Lib. MS Hargrave 265, ff. 75–77 (ca. 1720); *cf.* W. SHEPPARD, *supra* note 33, at 18 (A sealed deed "is under another Consideration, and may in many cases differ from a Parol contract".).

197. Early inclinations toward using the seal in America were snuffed out in the nineteenth century. The only consistent usage of a formal instrument without consideration in the U.S. today is the negotiable instrument.

198. NOTTINGHAM'S CASES, *supra* note 160, at 18 (Equitable intervention followed increased security of capital, and by the eighteenth century penal bonds not used extensively to raise commercial credit.). *See* Williston, *The History of the Law of Business Corporations Before 1800,* in 3 SELECT ESSAYS IN ANGLO-AMERICAN LEGAL HISTORY 195 (Boston: 1909) (The corporation was growing in importance in generating financing in the eighteenth century, but it couldn't engage in important business transactions without a sealed deed. *Id.* at 203, 210–211.).

199. S. STOLJAR, *supra* note 5, at 84–85 (In Debt *sur obligation* the jury did not have the discretion to lower damages set.); creditors preferred advantages of fixing the penalty and placing onus on defendant to show performance to avoid penalty rather than in Covenant and Assumpsit where *plaintiff* had to show breach of covenant. Ames, *supra* note 89, at 49–50 (The bond's validity was due to the mere fact of its formal execution.).

200. Henderson, *Relief From Bonds in the English Chancery: Mid-Sixteenth Century,* 18 AM. J. LEG. HIST. 298, 299–304 (1974), (study of Chancery records from their inception in 1543–1544 to 1568 and isolated years thereafter).

201. *Id.* at 299–303 (also the harshness of the penalty being outrageously disproportionate to underlying debt and the inability to repair a river bank because of flood); *see also* 4 E. COKE, INSTITUTES, *supra* note 142, at 84 (debtor's servant robbed while on the way to pay).

202. Henderson, *supra* note 200, at 299, 304–306 (found cases by 1560s and clearly so by 1590s). *But cf.* A. SIMPSON, *supra* note 3, at 119–121 (At the Restoration Chancery began to give relief as a matter of course.). Simpson relied on Yale's study of Nottingham's Chancery cases from 1673–1682, which found Chancery staying the penalty as a matter of course by then. *See* NOTTING-

HAM'S CASES, *supra* note 160, at 7–30. Simpson may not have been aware of Henderson's study when his book went to press.

203. *See* LORD NOTTINGHAM'S "MANUAL OF CHANCERY PRACTICE" AND "PROLEGOMENA OF CHANCERY AND EQUITY" 7–8 (ed. D. Yale, Cambridge: 1965) (hereinafter cited as PROLEGOMENA) (Coke championed the common law over royal prerogative, and his position won out during Commonwealth; consequently, Chancery, tainted with political associations to Star Chamber, was in jeopardy but survived since by then it was an integral part of machinery of the law.). *See* Henderson, *supra* note 200, at 298 (proper records of decrees not kept in Chancery until 1543); *see also* T. PLUCKNETT, *supra* note 111, at 692 (By the Restoration, Chancery was following precedent) *and* N. MATTHEWS, *supra* note 148 at 113–115 (Major Commonwealth reform was restricting Equity to relief unavailable at common law.)

204. NOTTINGHAM'S CASES, *supra* note 160, at 15, 20 (evidence of it in earlier Stuart period, but clearly common practice by the Restoration); A. SIMPSON, *supra* note 3, at 119–120, 120 (Chancery was not prepared to accept the penalty on the bond unless it fulfilled a compensatory function.). The equivalent of compensatory damages could be obtained by specific performance in Chancery since at least the fifteenth century.

205. There was a fundamental difference in the way the two courts viewed their roles when a contract broke down. Chancery tried to obtain performance, but the common law courts provided damages for breach; in the former approach compensation would give the equivalent of performance, and in the latter the common law would simply enforce the damages agreement (equivalency being irrelevant). In the eighteenth century it would be settled that no specific relief would be given in Equity if money damages were adequate at-law.

206. Perhaps the lag was due to the earlier allowance of the penalty during Coke's time, when there was a greater concern for security. Later merchant juries declared this past custom, thus freezing the old practice, despite the changes in economic conditions.

207. A. SIMPSON, *supra* note 3, at 121–122, citing PROLEGOMENA, *supra* note 203, at 203 (Nottingham said in his Prolegomena that the common law courts were refusing to enforce the penalty so that the defendant would not bring suit in Chancery).

208. PROLEGOMENA, *supra* note 203, at 15. (There were inordinate delays from Coke's time through the Commonwealth; it was claimed that the backlog was 23,000 cases of 5 to 30 years standing during the Commonwealth. Although these figures are not for the Restoration, and assuming Nottingham improved Chancery's reputation, how long did it take to catch up and how soon was the reputation for delay eradicated?). *See also* Langbein, *Fact Finding in the English Court of Chancery: A Rebuttal,* 83 YALE L.J. 1620, 1628–1629 (1974) (At least from the sixteenth century, the one man Chancery was undermanned, with jurisdiction and volume exceeding its resources, causing delays.).

209. Stat. 8 and 9 Wm. III, c.11 (1696–1697) (Plaintiff could assign the breaches of covenants, the jury would assess the damages for injuries suffered, judgment could include the penalty as security for the damages, but the plaintiff's recovery was limited to the assessed damages.); Stat. 4 and 5 Anne, c.3 (Debtor on a money bond could avoid penalty by making payment by the date of the

action, and payment without a sealed acquittance could be pleaded.). Indeed, there was ongoing disagreement about the meaning of the statutes through much of the eighteenth century. 12 W. HOLDSWORTH, *supra* note 45, at 519–520. *See also Pinnel's Case,* 4 Co. Rep. 117a (1602) (money bond could be discharged by an informal accord and satisfaction).

210. *See* Blake v. East India Co., 2 Ch. Cas. 198 (1674) *and* East India Co. v. Maniston, 2 Ch. Cas. 218 (1676). Both of these Chancery cases concerned unlawful trading by East India Co. traders, and Chancery allowed the penalties since it was not possible to determine what damages might arise to the Company. *See also* Fletcher v. Dyche, 2 T.R. 32, 36, 37, 100 Eng. Rep. 18, 20–21 (1787) (case at-law).

211. Goodwin v. Crowle, 1 Cowp. 357, 359, 98 Eng. Rep. 1128 (1775), (Judgment was to stand as security for satisfaction of damages sustained but penalty was not recoverable.). The notion of what "security" meant in the context of the conditioned bond changed after the 1697 statute from the Tudor need for security of performance of the contract to security for payment of the *judgment.* On the former view, *see* PROLEGOMENA, *supra* note 203, at 275 (penal bond to secure performance of covenants).

212. Roles v. Rosewell, 5 T.R. 538, 101 Eng. Rep. 302 (1794).

213. Fletcher v. Dyche, 2 T.R. 32, 36, 37, 100 Eng. Rep. 18, 20–21 (1787). (If sum fixed in contract in circumstances where difficult to determine damages, it was not viewed as a penalty and could be recovered as liquidated damages.).

214. *See* J. THAYER, A PRELIMINARY TREATISE ON EVIDENCE AT COMMON LAW 180, 429, 489 (1898) (late seventeenth century was early period for anything like a modern law of evidence); *see also* Langbein, *The Criminal Trial Before the Lawyers,* 45 U. CHI. L. REV. 263, 306 (1978) (formation of rules of evidence in mid-eighteenth century).

215. An Act for Prevention of Frauds and Perjuries, 29 Car. II, c.3 (1677). Nottingham prepared the first draft, and since Chancery not so directly concerned with problems created by *Slade,* this draft in the main required an unsealed writing for land contract and it limited damages on parole agreements. Hening, *The Original Drafts of the Statute of Frauds and Their Authors,* 61 U. PA. L. REV. 283, 285, 289 (1913).

216. Dymoke's Case, Savile 34, pl. 81 (1582). Spouses of the parties were also excluded. G. GILBERT, THE LAW OF EVIDENCE 252 (ca. 1726). But only interested witnesses were permitted to testify until the mid-seventeenth century. 2 J. WIGMORE, EVIDENCE IN TRIALS AT COMMON LAW sect. 575 (rev. ed. 1979, Supp. 1986). The parties were excluded until Evidence Act of 1851.

217. *See* Teeven, *Seventeenth Century Evidentiary Concerns and the Statute of Frauds,* 9 ADEL. L. REV 252, 254–257 (1983). *Cf.* S. MILSOM, *supra* note 23, at 58–59 (Improper admission of oral evidence could not be appealed since no record of it on plea rolls.). Control of jury verdicts by attaint had become ineffectual. Bushel's Case, Vaughan 135 (1670). Motion for new trial not fully developed until eighteenth century. T. PLUCKNETT, *supra* note 111, at 56; *cf.* 3 W. BLACKSTONE, *supra* note 119, at 375.

218. M. HALE, THE HISTORY OF THE COMMON LAW 292–294 (C. Runnington 4th ed., London: 1779) (Hale cited with approval that a juror may

personally know of facts not raised at trial because he is of the vicinity.); Rabel, *The Statute of Frauds and Comparative Legal History*, 63 L.Q. REV. 174 (1947).

219. J. THAYER, *supra* note 214, at 195–198, 266–270 (Law of evidence developed as a means of controlling the jury); *but cf.* Langbein, *supra* note 214, at 306–314 (Law of evidence in criminal trials developed as judicial reaction to lawyers' attempts to take control of trial by jury in the eighteenth century.).

220. J. THAYER, *supra* note 214, at 180, 429–431.

221. *Cf.* R. Robinson, *Anticipations Under the Commonwealth of Changes in the Law* in 1 SELECT ESSAYS IN ANGLO-AMERICAN LEGAL HISTORY, 467, 470–473, 485–490 (Cambridge: 1907) (Commonwealth recommendations had included: (1) registration of transfers of property and (2) Hale's Law Reform Commission may have planned for a requirement akin to the Statute of Frauds.). *See* MAX WEBER ON LAW IN ECONOMY AND SOCIETY 230–231 (Cambridge, Mass. M. Rheistein ed. 1954) (English Puritans sought more rational procedures through codes since bourgeoisie interested in clear, systematized procedures.).

222. Maitland said of Matthew Hale (d. 1676): he was perhaps "the last of the great record-searching judges, [who] sketched a map of English law which Blackstone was to colour." F. MAITLAND, *supra* note 148, at 113. *Cf.* 6 W. HOLDSWORTH, *supra* note 45, at 594–595 (Hale had a modern point of view and was the greatest common law lawyer since Coke and a better lawyer and historian.). Francis North, principal draftsman of later drafts of the Statute of Frauds, said Hale was chief in fixing the Statute and that North had simply done the urging of Hale's ideas in Parliament. 1 R. NORTH, LIVES OF THE NORTHS 141 (1826). Hale had become accustomed to legislative intrusion while sitting on the Law Reform Commission during the Commonwealth.

223. *Anon,* Treby's Reports, MT MS., p. 747 (1672), *reprinted in* BAKER and MILSOM, *supra* note 28, at 444. *Cf. Anon,* Treby's Reports MT MS., p. 775 (1672), *reprinted in* BAKER and MILSOM, *supra* note 28, at 444n ("It were well that some solemnity, as the delivery of a piece of money or something like livery of seisin, were requisite to the making of every promise. It was the wisdom of the law to require a solemnity in contracts (as well as marriages), which if not observed the party should have liberty to wage his law.").

224. Hening, *supra* note 215, at 297–311.

225. The categories of contracts included in the Statute were typically executory and had usually been unenforceable prior to Assumpsit, unless a sealed deed was produced—the most glaring exception being a sale of goods in Debt *sur contract* under the passage of property fiction, though there the defendant could at least protect himself by wager of law.

226. *Cf.* A. SIMPSON, *supra* note 3, at 156–160. Until 1830, if a testator named no residuary legatee, the executor could retain the balance after paying all debts; so the executor had an interest in promising individually to pay estate debts. *See* Stat. 11 Geo. IV and 1 Will. IV, c.40 (1830).

227. This transaction had a tradition of formality from the time of the ritual of livery of seisin, but this broke down as oral land contracts were enforced under Assumpsit, e.g., Doige's Case, 20 Hen. VI, pl. 4, f.34 (1442), and as land spread to the emerging middle class where the ancient ceremony was lost.

228. We may never know if it was sheer coincidence that this 10 pound barrier

would have barred the plaintiff from recovery on the 16 pound contract in *Slade's Case*.

229. Contract for personal services would have been the main contract impacted here. The normal employment contract term under the Statute of Labourers was one year. Statute of Labourers, 23; Edw. III, ss. 1 and 2 (1349–1351). Scots law required service contracts of more than one year to be in writing. A. SIMPSON, *supra* note 3, at 612. *Cf.* Smith v. Westhall, 1 Ld. Raym. 316 (1697) (Per Holt: "The design of the statute (of Frauds) was, not to trust to the memory of witnesses for a longer time than one year.). *See* Shop Books Act, 7 Jac., I, c.12 (1610) (Merchant could not dredge up accounts book to place in evidence on debt of non-merchant made more than one year before.).

230. *See* A. SIMPSON, *supra* note 3, at 610. *See also* 1 S. GREENLEAF, A TREATISE ON THE LAW OF EVIDENCE, sect. 262 (14th ed., Boston: 1883) (suggests Statute revives Roman writing requirements). *And see* 2 F. POLLOCK and F. MAITLAND, A HISTORY OF ENGLISH LAW 207–208 (Cambridge: 2d ed. 1911) (North's alternative to section 17 is same as Glanvill exceptions.).

231. Butcher v. Stapley, 1 Vern. 363, 1 Eq. Cas. Abr. 21 (1686) (in Chancery); approved by House of Lords in Wankford v. Fotherby, 2 Vern. 322, 2 Freeman 201 (1694).

232. One full 800 page volume of Corbin's eleven volume set on contract law was devoted to the Statute. 2 A. CORBIN, A COMPREHENSIVE TREATISE ON THE RULES OF CONTRACT LAW (St. Paul: 1950). *See* Corbin, *The Uniform Commercial Code—Sales; Should It Be Enacted?*, 59 YALE L.J. 821, 829 (1950) (Due to myriad of exceptions, the belief in the uniformity and certainty of the Statute is a "magnificent illusion".). For example of how extreme exceptions could be, *see* Bailey v. Sweeting, 9 C.B. (N.S.) 843, 142 Eng. Rep. 332 (1861) (Repudiation letter may satisfy writing requirements of Statute.).

233. *E.g.*, protects frauds, contrary to trading habits, poorly drafted; common law is only body of law requiring writing for commercial contract. *See generally* Teeven, *supra* note 216, at 265–266.

234. Law Reform Act of 1954, 2 + 3 Eliz. II, c.34 (1954). Land contracts and guaranty contracts are two categories still requiring writing in England. Besides England, other jurisdictions repealing all but land and guaranty contracts are Manitoba, British Columbia, New Zealand, New South Wales and Queensland; South Australia made no exception for guaranty; Western Australia has retained sect. 17 (goods). Repeal recommendations have been proposed by legislative committees in California, New York, Alberta and Ontario.

235. Maitland portrays eighteenth century parliaments as complacent, adverse to drastic legislation and "loth to admit that the common law was capable of amendment." F. MAITLAND, *supra* note 148, at 113–114.

236. 9 J. WIGMORE, *supra* note 216, at sect. 2426, p. 90–91. *See also* J. THAYER, *supra* note 214, at 390–393 (a substantive requirement of form and the ground of the action). The writing required by the Statute is not the contract itself, as is the case with a sealed deed, but it is more than mere evidence since the specified categories of agreements cannot be enforced without a writing.

237. Pillans v. Van Mierop, 3 Burr. 1663 (1765) (per Mansfield); cf. A. SIMPSON, *supra* note 3, at 619–620 (missed opportunity).

238. F. BACON, A COLLECTION OF SOME PRINCIPAL RULES AND

MAXIMES OF THE COMMON LAWES OF ENGLAND 91 (London: 1635) (Regula 23 (often called Maxim 25): A patent ambiguity may not be averred because "the law will not couple and mingle matters of specialty, which is of a higher account, with matter of averment, which is of inferior account in law."). *Cf.* Sharington v. Strotton, Plow. 298, 308 (1565) (sealed deed of a higher nature).

239. 9 J. WIGMORE, *supra* note 216, at 89–91.

240. There were older cases concerned with the exclusion of parol evidence from sealed documents: The Lord Cheyney's Case, 5 Co. Rep. 68, Moo. 727 (1591) (a will with two sons named John), which case may have influenced Bacon, who wrote his Maxims 4 years later; Countess of Rutland's Case, 5 Co. Rep. 25 (1604) (rule as to a covenant's declaration of the uses of fines). The parol evidence rule seems to have caught on by the early part of the eighteenth century since it appeared in LILLY'S PRACTICAL REGISTER 48 (1719), as quoted in 5 C. VINER, A GENERAL ABRIDGMENT OF LAW AND EQUITY 515–516 (1742) (If an agreement made by parol to do anything be afterwards reduced into writing, action must be brought on the writing because of its greater certainty, citing a 1681 case.).

241. Falkland v. Bertie, 2 Vern. 333, 337 (1696), per Holt (parol intent of testator excluded and uncertainty about proof necessitated Statute of Frauds); Holt's dissent in Cole v. Rawlinson, 1 Salk 234 (1702) (Holt was opposed to looking to testator's intent past the will since lawyers would then not know how to draft and men's rights would be precarious.).

242. Strode v. Russell, 2 Vern. 621 (1708) ("We will consider how far it shall be allowed and how far not, after it is read; and this is not like the case of evidence to jurors, who are easily biased by it, which this Court is not.").

243. Ulrich v. Litchfield, 2 Atk. 372 (1742) (Chancellor Hardwicke criticized Chancery's earlier practice of largely ignoring the parol evidence rule.); *but cf.* Goodinge v. Goodinge, 1 Ves. 231 (1749) (Hardwicke criticized Holt in being too strict in refusing parol evidence.).

244. Pole v. Harrobin, 9 East 416n., 103 Eng. Rep. 632n. (1782) (Party may show circumstances to vitiate entire deal).

245. Baker v. Paine, 1 Ves. 456 (1750) (Hardwicke: "How can a mistake in an agreement be proved but by parol evidence?"); Collins v. Blantern, 2 Wils. 347 (1767) (illegality). Exceptions also made in Hampshire v. Pierce, 2 Ves. 216 (1750) (ambiguity) and Elkins v. Maclisk, Ambler 184 (1753), per Hardwicke (mercantile practice admitted in construing a power of attorney).

246. F. BACON, *supra* note 238, at 91. Bacon's Maxim 25 was republished in 1761 in *Theory of Evidence* (probably by Bathurst) and was included in part 6 of F. BULLER, AN INTRODUCTION TO THE LAW RELATIVE TO TRIALS AT NISI PRIUS 221 (1771) (part 6 entitled *Of Evidence in General*).

247. J. THAYER, *supra* note 214, at 471–473 (Bacon intended the Maxim as a rule of pleading, but Buller uses it as a rule of evidence. The rule has been used in an unthinking fashion.); *cf.* Patch v. White, 117 U.S. 211, 224 (1886) (Dissent: "a mere mistake is not a latent ambiguity. Where there is no latent ambiguity, there no extrinsic evidence may be received".).

248. J. THAYER, *supra* note 214, at 390 (the rule "is, perhaps, the most difficult branch of the law of evidence. The chief reason is that most of the questions brought under this head are out of place".); 9 J. WIGMORE, *supra*

note 216, at 4 ("the so-called parol evidence rule is attended with confusion and obscurity which make it the most discouraging subject in the whole field of evidence"); ENGLISH LAW COMMISSION (Working Paper No. 70, 1976) (Parol evidence rule no longer serves a useful purpose since it "is a technical rule of uncertain ambit, which, at best, adds to the complexities of litigation without affecting the outcome and, at worst, prevents the courts from getting at the truth".).

249. J. THAYER, *supra* note 214, at 325, 328, 390–391; 9 J. WIGMORE, *supra* note 216, at 4–5.

CHAPTER 4

MERCANTILE AND EQUITABLE IDEAS ABSORBED (1689–1789)

This chapter covers the 100 year period from Holt's appointment in 1689 as Chief Justice of the King's Bench after the Glorious Revolution to Mansfield's resignation from that same position in 1789. At no time since Coke did the abilities and inclinations of chief justices matter so much as the common law courts were called on to adapt the common law to the appearance on the docket of novel commercial transactions generated by the most dynamic capitalist economy in the world in the eighteenth century. Britain became the greatest trading nation in the first half of the eighteenth century and was the first to embark on an industrial revolution by mid-century. By the end of the period covered in this chapter, well over half the country's workforce was in non-agricultural pursuits and nearly half of its GNP came from industry.

The installation of the commercially-minded Dutchman, William of Orange, on the throne with Mary in 1689 by forces aligned with commercial interests meant peace with the Dutch and the advent of a commercial upsurge. Indeed the entire period covered in this chapter was marked by stability and royal support for commerce and industry. Former restrictions on trade and industry were removed and many monopolies were ended in the interest of free trade, which was now perceived as beneficial to the nation-state. This new policy opened up new markets and caused an electrifying economic boom from 1692 to 1695 during which the number of private companies increased tenfold. By the early eighteenth century, a nascent industrial revolution was emerging as water and steam power were emphasized and new techniques for pooling business capital resulted in the formation of larger business firms on an unprecedented scale.[1] During the eighteenth century, the transition from Tudor mercantile capitalism to industrial capitalism would be completed.

As a result of the Revolution of 1688, Parliament, and commercial interests supported by the Whigs, had the upper hand over crown prerogative. Judges were to serve on good behavior rather than at the whim of the crown, and law was now seen as man-made rather than immutable. By the mid-eighteenth century, Lockean views of unrestricted property rights and faith in reason were guiding principles in fashioning a commercial law for the burgeoning economy. The common law courts were now the forum for adjudication of commercial transactions as a result of the triumph of the revered common law over Equity and the remaining mercantile courts by the third quarter of the seventeenth century, and practices in those declining courts began to be absorbed by the common law. The development of effective controls over a modern trial by jury system by the eighteenth century began the process of the discussion of the legal meaning of facts and the creation of predictable rules.

Whig commercial interests influenced Holt's appointment to the Bench; however, his traditional common law perspective caused him to grant only grudging accommodation for mercantile usage. Mansfield would usher in a more flexible law of contract that was less dependent on ancient forms, and he would institute a commercial law by the absorption of law merchant and equity into the common law. In the process the law would begin to transform from a static property-based law into one based on consent; indeed, feudal obligations formerly owed by tenants of land had been replaced by rights of ownership, and with that change came the freedom to choose what to do with property. The personal relationship of superiors and inferiors based on a reciprocal exchange of service for land was replaced by a relationship between equals, governed by contract rather than status, wherein the medium of exchange was cash.

Holt's Conservative View of Commercial Law

With the possible exception of Hale, Sir John Holt was arguably the finest common law thinker to sit on the Bench since Bracton. His common law training and reverence for the orderliness of the writ system made him conservative, and his modest origins caused him to be pedantic to prove both his orthodoxy and his commitment to the social order of the post-Revolutionary period. Although he appreciated the importance of trade to the economy of England, his background as a barrister made him feel an aloof superiority to merchants. Notwithstanding his reservations, he did more to bring commercial law into the common law than any chief justice from Coke's resignation to Mansfield's accession to the King's Bench.

The decline of the trade fairs and the wool trade caused the administration of the law merchant to pass from the courts pepoudrous and the courts of the staple to the Admiralty Court by the mid-sixteenth century. Coke instituted the common law courts' assault on the Admiralty Court's commercial law jurisdiction,[2] and the common law lawyers of the Commonwealth finished the process, so that most commercial law matters had passed to the common law courts and Chancery by the Restoration. Merchants now had no alternative but to apply to common law courts, which were ill-suited to adjudicate their transactions. Unlike mayors of the staple and judges of Admiralty, common law judges and juries were not selected because of their knowledge of law merchant. Coke carved out a potentially large mercantile business for the common law courts; but Holt, by no means an innovator and not given to Coke's overreaching in the absence of precedent, did not exploit Coke's lead. Holt's concern for the symmetry of the common law made for guarded extensions of the common law in accommodating commercial interests. Indeed, he discouraged merchants from any structuring of their transactions in a way novel to the common law. Yet, Holt declared that the common law had jurisdiction in all matters, including commercial law.[3]

Although Holt was willing to permit a wider consideration of the usage of merchants,[4] he continued Coke's practice of requiring that those usages remain as facts to be proved before a jury of laymen for their consideration rather than allowing them to develop into general principles of law for the certainty of future cases sought by merchant.[5] So in each case a plaintiff had to plead and prove *secundum usum et consuetudinem mercatorum* (according to the use and custom of merchants) for the purpose of explaining the terms of a contract.[6] The facts of the case at hand and the accepted mercantile usage were indistinguishable in a general verdict and so no law grew out of it. The usage of merchants would not be assimilated as generalized principles of law[7] until Mansfield was Chief Justice.

One pressing concern of merchants, precipitating a face-off between them and Holt, was the slowness of the common law courts in adopting the mercantile practice of assignment (negotiation) of bills of exchange and promissory notes, such transfers being an essential characteristic of commercial promises to pay money in a modern credit economy. One of the reasons Holt resisted the negotiation of commercial paper was the ancient prohibition on assignment of contract rights. Straight assignments were not permitted until the nineteenth century because a contract obligation was seen as a personal one owed to a specific creditor and not to a possibly cruel assignee, to whom the debtor did not consent to be bound,[8] in an era when sanctions against breaching debtors were severe. Coke opposed assignments because "it would be the cause of contentions, suits and other inconveniences."[9] Fomenting lawsuits and interfering in others' lawsuits was punishable by the tort of maintenance. The prohibition on assignments did not apply if the debtor consented to the assignment, as in a novation[10]—lack of the debtor's consent was the original reason for the prohibition on assignments. By the fourteenth century, inventive merchants found a way around the prohibition through the use of a power of attorney, whereby the creditor appointed his transferee as his attorney with the power to enforce the claim in the creditor's name and retain whatever was recovered; however, by the fifteenth century this circumvention was refused on grounds of maintenance, unless executed for the benefit of the transferor's creditor.[11] Due to the injustices caused by this common law opposition, as early as the fifteenth century Chancery was enforcing assignments of debts as it would any other property. Blackstone said, "our courts of equity, considering that in a commercial country . . . will protect the assignment of a chose in action."[12] Goaded on by the competition of Chancery, the common law courts came full circle in the late eighteenth century and recognized assignments if the assignee sued in the assignor's name,[13] and, finally, in the nineteenth century assignments were recognized in England by statute.[14] Most nineteenth century American jurisdictions also passed statutes permitting an assignee to sue in his own name. As a consequence, the personal, relational aspect of proprietary contractual relations was dealt a serious blow. The feudal approach was being converted into property in the modern sense as contracts went the way of all property in becoming freely alienable. The cash nexus permitted an infinite variety of human relationships.

Returning now to assignment in Holt's era, given that assignments were prohibited at common law, Holt resisted, and even resented, merchants pressing for the common law to adapt to the mercantile practice of negotiation of bills of exchange and promissory notes. (There is a sloppiness in the cases of this period in that the terms negotiation and negotiability were used interchangeably; the proper term is negotiation since these cases concern the transferability of bills and notes and not the insulation of a holder from contract defenses, the latter feature not appearing until Mansfield's day.). The tradition of the common law was to adhere to the static proprietary writ system, set up for the benefit of landed wealth, and not to accommodate an emerging commercial class. Any ground given to commerce was done so reluctantly, and inevitably it had to be rationalized to fit within the old formulary system. Therefore, Holt opposed the promissory note because "it amounted to the setting up of a new sort of specialty, unknown to the common law, and invented in Lombard-Street."[15] Answers to questions about commercial practices had to be provided by analogies to common law rules, thus a question regarding a bill of exchange was solved by drawing an analogy to a conveyance of land.[16] And, shouldn't a bill of exchange be analogous to a non-assignable common law contract? At least as to bills of exchange, there were precedents before Holt's judgeship permitting assignment according to the custom of merchants, and so Holt grudgingly allowed it to continue but qualified it by refusing the same privilege to bills payable to bearer.[17]

The major test on the issue of the negotiation of a promissory note arose in *Clerke v. Martin* (1702).[18] Holt was adamantly opposed and was obviously agitated with the "obstinacy" of merchants in continuing to use these notes "since he had always expressed his opinion against them." He urged that instead of pleading an action on the case according to the custom of merchants that they should bring a general *indebitatus assumpsit* for money lent.[19] Holt reiterated his opposition to the negotiation of promissory notes two years later, denouncing them as "an invention of the goldsmiths in Lombard-Street; who had a mind to make a law to bind all those that did deal with them . . . to turn a piece of paper, which is in law but evidence of a parol contract, into a specialty."[20] Holt was treating the custom of merchants as a static set of practices, much like he viewed the immutable common law; perhaps, as a Restoration lawyer, Holt was refusing to allow any mercantile practices that arose after 1640.[21]

Influential London merchants saw that Holt was not going to change, and, since unlike former times they did not have the option to resort to a mercantile court for enforcement of promissory notes, they applied to Parliament for relief. Parliament, in a classic example of mercantilism in action, passed a statute during Queen Anne's reign in 1705 providing for the assignability of promissory notes in the same manner as bills of exchange.[22] Holt then tried to narrow the applicability of the statute in the last year of his life.[23]

Turning to the traditional common law of contract realm, Holt's conservatism opposed attempted extensions of *indebitatus assumpsit*, that device so accommodating to the growth of contract law, to cover certain non-contractual money obligations formerly actionable either in Debt or in tort. Since the contractual action of *indebitatus assumpsit* could not be brought on these obligations, which were in no sense contractual, they were called contracts implied-in-law or quasi-contract.[24] Holt wanted the use of Assumpsit to be kept within the orderly framework of the forms of action by only allowing it for genuine agreements pursuant to *Slade's Case*, and he thought allowing *indebitatus assumpsit* on quasi-contracts would bring chaos to the system. Plaintiffs' attorneys did not share Holt's qualms, and during the last quarter of the seventeenth century they were manipulating the fictitious subsequent promise of *indebitatus assumpsit* in order to bring non-contractual obligations based on custom within the ambit of the action. It was conceivable that any non-contractual debts could be covered by *indebitatus assumpsit* if a fictitious subsequent promise could be attributed to it. Holt thought it wrong to stretch *indebitatus assumpsit* past debts covered by wager of law: "it is mischievous to extend it further than *Slade's Case*: for an *indebitatus* is laid generally, and the defendant can't tell how to make his defence, but debt is laid more particularly."[25] Holt, in opposition to the inroads already approved, said: "I think it hath been carried too far and I will retrench them."[26] However, precedents had been set before Holt came onto the Bench, such as for money due on a government levy and for when a disputed official wrongfully kept funds.[27] It was too late for his purist logic to set the clock back by relying on the antiquated defendant's surprise argument, which had failed a century earlier when *indebitatus assumpsit* was usurping contractual Debt.

Therefore, despite Holt's formidable intellectual influence on his fellow justices, he found himself the lone dissenter in the well known early contract implied-in-law case of *Shuttleworth v. Garnett* (1689),[28] which involved a plaintiff suing in *indebitatus assumpsit* for a customary charge due on a land tenure. The plaintiff's attorneys argued, "Where money is due, the law doth imply a contract." But Holt said, "It doth not follow that an *indebitatus* lies because debt lies; where wager of law doth not lie, there an *indebitatus* don't lie . . ." By 1705 the sheer weight of the authorities against Holt forced him to guardedly accept the precedents set and he said as much in *Lamine v. Dorrell.*[29] The advantages of the promissory action of Assumpsit were obtained for the recovery of sums due under circumstances that were quasi-contractual and in no way promissory. Mansfield would conceptualize these disparate implied-in-law contract decisions by emphasizing the common theme of unjust enrichment running through all of them.

Notwithstanding Holt's conservatism, he was sympathetic to certain changes in the old law and was not above rationalizing it, when questions of morality seemed more compelling. This is exhibited by his adjustments to the past consideration rule in cases involving the special defenses of minority and statute of limitations. He did not look kindly on such special defenses when there had been an unquestioned promise to pay money. In *Ball v. Hesketh* (1697),[30] Holt "Ruled, that where the defendant under age borrowed money of the plaintiff, and afterwards at full age promised to pay it him, this is a good consideration for the promise, and the defendant shall be charged." An infant's promise had formerly been deemed void,[31] but Holt made it voidable to allow ratification. In *Hylings v. Hastings* (1699)[32] the debtor's promise to pay, after the running of a statute of limitations, revived the original debt on the grounds of waiver. Holt further modified the doctrine of consideration, in light of commercial needs, as it applied to a promise obviously made in connection with a promissory note by ruling "that it was not necessary for the plaintiff to prove, upon what consideration the note of (the maker) was given, the defendant having admitted it to have been given upon good consideration by his promise."[33] Holt's modifications of the doctrine of consideration for moral and commercial reasons caused some to wonder how sacrosanct the consideration requirement really was if it was clear a promise had been made; these cases would later be invoked by Mansfield in his frontal assault on consideration.

Holt's death in office in 1709 had a liberalizing effect on commercial law since his successors were more sympathetic to mercantile needs, and, once freed of Holt's intellectual domination, they rendered decisions to accommodate commerce.[34] These successors prior to Mansfield, however, were of mediocre abilities and were too often mired in the daily intricacies of common law pleadings and forms to distill coherent principles from the patchwork of commercial law cases.[35] The one shining exception was the gifted Hardwicke, but his tenure on the King's Bench was short since he was appointed Lord Chancellor (1737–1756). When the opportunity arose, Chancellor Hardwicke would independently inquire of commercial usage and incorporate it in his decree,[36] but Chancery's commercial jurisdiction was not as extensive as in the seventeenth century, though it was active in cases of partnership and accounts and had taken over bankruptcy.[37]

Another eighteenth century figure worthy of note in the post-Holt period was William Blackstone, the common law's first law professor, who was delivering his lectures on the common law prior to Mansfield's arrival on the Bench. Blackstone gave his Vinerian[38] lectures at Oxford in 1753, and they were published first in syllabus form in 1756 and then in his updated COMMENTARIES in four volumes (1765–1769). Although Hale had planned a similar project, Blackstone's global view of the common law was the first since Bracton. His objective was to educate the lay sons of the gentry about the structure of the legal system and in the process to provide a defense of the status quo of landed wealth after the Glorious Revolution. Since he opposed colonial independence, it is ironic that his impact on the common law was greater in America than in England.

Since Blackstone's students had no background in the common law, many having no intention of becoming lawyers, he had to take a broad view of the system, avoiding immersion in the ancient detail. He found guidance in his search for general principles from the civilian writers, who, unlike common law lawyers, did not engage in a case by case search for specific precedents. Blackstone has been criticized for not being a well prepared common law lawyer himself, but he turned this shortcoming to his advantage since his removal from the intricacies of the common law practitioner gave him a better perspective on the overall system.[39] He deduced general principles of law from the detail in the year books, reports and abridgements. Law books before Blackstone consisted of discussions of separate cases without any attempt to distill general rules from the cases.

Blackstone's technical expertise was in land law, and this is the emphasis in his lectures. His treatment of contract law was sketchy, covering barely fifty pages of the four volumes, and in that sketch he failed to grasp the sophistication of the common law of contract in his day and in some instances was simply wrong. He was still thinking in the old proprietary ways and characterized a contract as a method of conveying property and so he grouped contracts in terms of the effects of various types of contracts on property rights.[40] In his discussion of consideration he referred to Continental civil law authority, where consideration wasn't recognized, and stated that such questionable elements as blood or affections of relatives and prior moral obligations were good consideration.[41] Furthermore, it can generally be said that he ignored the equitable doctrine applicable to contract law. He wrote that contracts could be express or implied. As to express contracts, debts and informal promises were covered by Assumpsit and sealed covenants by the Writ of Covenant. As to implied contracts, he made the error of joining contracts implied-in-fact and contracts implied-in-law as belonging under the same head: "which class extends to all presumptive undertakings or *assumpsits*."[42] Blackstone may have incorrectly lumped together contracts based on an implied agreement, as *quantum meruit*, and quasi-contractual liability independent of agreement because he became confused by the availability of Assumpsit for both.[43] His treatment of the quasi-contractual obligation of money had and received incorporated Mansfield's ruling in *Moses v. Macferlan* (1760),[44] but he misinterpreted the case since Mansfield expressly repudiated the requirement of an implied promise as a basis for quasi-contractual liability.[45] Because of the wide circulation of Blackstone's opus, his error was perpetuated into the twentieth century, retarding the growth of unjust enrichment. As an example, there were no independent rules of capacity for quasi-contract developed even though contractual capacity is inappropriate to unjust enrichment[46] since it is the unjust enrichment and not a promise that determines liability.

The flaws in Blackstone's treatment of contract law notwithstanding, he made an important contribution in pulling together the fragmented caselaw and drawing general principles from them. It was surely not humanly possible to summarize the whole of the common law without erring in fields a writer would inevitably be less informed about. His big picture of the common law would aid the eventual development of a coherent system of substantive principles, transmuting the law from one of formulary procedures into a body of substantive rules.[47]

The Common Counts and Quasi-Contract

During the century after *Slade's Case*, a series of stylized declarations evolved out of *indebitatus assumpsit* known as the "common counts".[48] Generalized pleading was advantageous to the plaintiff because it avoided the pitfalls of the intricate pleading rules. Although one of the results of *Slade* was that the *indebitatus assumpsit* form was not necessary to avoid overlap with Debt, the *indebitatus* form continued because of its advantage of general pleading. Within a decade of *Slade*, the courts approved a revived form of *indebitatus assumpsit* that simply provided a brief statement of the type of contract sued on, as for goods bargained and sold, in order to assure it fit under Assumpsit.[49] The generalized nature of *indebitatus assumpsit* presumed that the facts would come out before a jury looking at the totality of the evidence. By the late seventeenth century there had been a reinvention of the sixteenth century King's Bench's practice of allowing an *indebitatus assumpsit* without requiring proof of the subsequent promise—all that need be shown was that it was a case for Assumpsit and of course not on a sealed deed.[50] The approved generalized pleading in *indebitatus assumpsit* evolved into the common counts by the early eighteenth century[51] and were widely used in England and America until the mid-nineteenth century.

There were ultimately eight common counts[52] permitting the plaintiff to get his case to the jury without special pleading. They were for: goods sold and delivered,[53] work done, money lent, money paid by plaintiff to the use of defendant, money had and received to plaintiff's use; money, due on account stated,[54] goods bargained and sold,[55] and money due as interest. There were shortcomings to the common counts in that the lack of specificity could catch the defendant by surprise; and, since the common counts were an extension of *indebitatus assumpsit*, a plaintiff could not employ them for unliquidated damages, as for a non-Debt situation like breach of contract covered by Special Assumpsit.[56] Even if it seemed clear enough that *indebitatus assumpsit* applied, it was not always so clear which common count applied; consequently, alternative pleading declaring the circumstances in a myriad of versions became rife.[57]

One of the most common combinations of counts was to declare on an *indebitatus* count for a fixed sum and on a count of *quantum meruit* for a reasonable sum—in case the alleged sum certain could not be proved. As was discussed in the last chapter, *quantum meruit* for an uncertain sum had an origin separate from *indebitatus assumpsit* and so developed its own common count as a separate species of Assumpsit. By about the second half of the eighteenth century, the joinder of a *quantum meruit* common count and an *indebitatus* common count was no longer necessary since Debt, and thus *indebitatus*, had become available on a *quantum meruit*, but lawyers cling to old forms, and so that pleading practice continued into the nineteenth century.[58] Eventually *quantum meruit* was phased out as a pleading form, but it has survived as a substantive doctrine. And, as to alternative pleading in general, the subtleties that arose in the use of the common counts created pleading nightmares nearly as pernicious as the old manner of pleading, which the common counts were intended to cure. In the mid-nineteenth century there would be extensive judicial and legislative reforms of this pleading system in England and in the United States.[59]

In addition to the contractual common counts, there were two quasi-contractual common counts, "money paid by plaintiff to the use of defendant"[60] and "money had and received to the plaintiff's use," the latter being the principal one and the one addressed hereafter. Quasi-contractual liability was permitted to appear under the contractual action of Assumpsit thanks to *indebitatus assumpsit's* subsequent promise becoming fictitious during the latter part of the seventeenth century. When the fictitious subsequent promise was applied to a contractual debt, it was after all a needless repetition of the promise implicitly present in the debt itself. Imaginative plaintiffs' lawyers tried bringing non-contractual debts under *indebitatus assumpsit* since there was no need to prove the subsequent promise, and the courts permitted this extension.[61] During the Restoration *indebitatus* was allowed to cover customary charges due by operation of law and then for the recovery of money received by the defendant; in the second case, the money received was an unjust enrichment. Assumpsit was supposed to cover only duties to pay based on a promise, but *indebitatus assumpsit's* subsequent promise, which had already assisted the development of contract law, now afforded non-contractual liability in quasi-contract. These quasi-contractual claims fell under the common count of money had and received to the plaintiff's use by around 1700. They were not contracts at all but rather were constructive obligations, contracts implied-in-law; there was no assent or consideration required for their enforcement. Since obligation had traditionally been classified as sounding either in tort or in contract, it is perhaps understandable why, of the two, the contract category would be selected for the duties to pay money included under money had and received.[62] No one before Mansfield would be confident enough to take a broad view and declare what in fact was happening, and what Holt had resisted: the creation of a third category of common law obligation based on unjust enrichment. Attention will not be turned to the birth and subsequent development of quasi-contract up to the end of Mansfield's tenure.

The first *indebitatus assumpsit* case on customary duties, traditionally covered by Debt, of *City of London v. Goree* (1676) used the Roman term quasi-contract: "this is a duty that ariseth *ex quasi contractu* and not *ex delicto,* though it was originally but a charge upon the subject (goods), for, it being agreed that Debt lieth *a fortiori* and *indebitatus.*"[63] The jury found a customary duty but no express promise; nonetheless, the court found *indebitatus assumpsit* to lie. In *Shuttleworth v. Garnett* (1689)[64] liability was found on a customary charge in the face of Holt's dissent and the objection: "that no *Indebitatus Assumpsit* lieth where the cause of action is grounded on a custom."

The more fertile branch of quasi-contract cases came under the principle of unjust enrichment. A multitude of cases appeared in the reports of the eighteenth and nineteenth centuries based on the equitable principle that one person shall not unjustly enrich himself at the expense of another. This principle has its roots in the common law action of Account. In the Middle Ages, agents, such as bailiffs administering real property, were said to have a duty to account to the owner. By the fourteenth century this duty was extended to constructive agents and receivers who had no agency or contractual relationship with the rightful owner.[65] In the sixteenth century this strain of cases lended support to Account applying against a defendant who was mistakenly paid money on an alleged debt.[66] Debt was soon found to lay where Account lay on these quasi-contractual cases for a sum certain,[67] as for money received due to a mistake or on a void contract, and the train chugged on when *indebitatus assumpsit* was permitted to cover any quasi-contractual cases that Debt did on the *indebitatus assumpsit* count of money "had and received to the use of the plaintiff."[68] Account's formal "received" phraseology[69] was adopted in this quasi-contractual *indebitatus assumpsit* count. The plaintiff pleaded that, due to the mistake, the funds were said to have been "had and received" by the defendant "to the use of the plaintiff".

During the Restoration the boundaries of the *indebitatus assumpsit* money had and received count were pushed outside the parameters of Account to cover money had and received by a defendant, who was a usurper of office, for the use of the plaintiff, the rightful office holder. In *Woodward v. Aston* (1676)[70] a usurper of the office of clerk of the court was sued for fees received, and the court allowed the action without any discussion of the use of *indebitatus assumpsit* outside of Account's purview. In the next year a similar disputed office case arose,[71] but here the defendant had the wits to object that there was no privity and no contract; nevertheless, there was the terse judicial response that Account would lie. These two usurpation of office cases were cited in *Howard v. Wood* (1680),[72] a case involving a question of who had the right to a stewardship and the attendant profits due the steward. The plaintiff prevailed, and Scroggs, C.J. said:

> Whether *indebitatus assumpsit* lies against a man who receives profits of an office, claiming a right. If this were now an original case, we are agreed

> it would by no means lie... But because judgments have been upon it... we are therefore willing to go the same way, and are of an opinion that it is better to comply with things once used, that are not of very pernicious consequence.

And, it was also reported that it was "resolved by the whole court that the action lay, for it is an expeditious remedy, and facilitates the recovery of just rights."[73] It was not the first time the force of precedent perpetuated a known error, especially when the court was disposed toward its positive contribution.

Next came the question of the had and received count's availability in lieu of the tort of trover. Account was unavailable here, but a way was found for *indebitatus assumpsit* to do the job, and this time it was with Holt's acquiescence. The wrongful detention of funds in the disputed offices cases opened the door to this possibility. In *Lamine v. Dorrell* (1705)[74] the defendant was sued under a had and received count for the proceeds of sale of a decedent's debentures, which were obtained by the defendant employing a subterfuge in order to be named administrator. The defendant objected that trover was the proper action, but Holt held for the plaintiff. Holt regretfully accepted that *indebitatus assumpsit*'s had and received count was available in the disputed office cases, and, if those cases were law, he saw no reason why it would not also be for a conversion and sale where the plaintiff waived the tort and in effect consented to the sale. The plaintiff preferred Assumpsit over tort because of the advantages of general pleading and the possibility the judgment in Assumpsit might be enforceable against an executor. However, the difference between a sale and a tort was too great to allow *indebitatus assumpsit* in lieu of trover if the defendant converted the plaintiff's property but then held onto it or consumed it since he received no money for the count to apply to.[75] Likewise a plaintiff could not use *indebitatus assumpsit* if the defendant received no money from the tort.

By the time Mansfield took up the cause of quasi-contract in the famous case of *Moses v. Macferlan* (1760),[76] nearly a century had elapsed since the first had and received cases had exceeded the limits of Account. With this hodgepodge of cases as a background, Mansfield, in his inimitable way, took a broad brush to paint the general principle that natural justice required an unjustly enriched defendant to refund money received. In *Moses v. Macferlan* the plaintiff brought a money had and received count for money paid to the defendant, under the compulsion of a local court order,[77] in violation of an agreement they had.[78] The defendant's first objection was Holt's earlier view that Assumpsit would only lie where wager on a Debt did, but Mansfield said that though *Slade's Case* allowed Assumpsit in lieu of Debt, that it did not restrict Assumpsit to Debt—a recognition of the success of quasi-contract since the Restoration. Mansfield saw the equities in favor of the plaintiff and ruled for him: "If the defendant be under an obligation, from the ties of natural justice, to refund, the law implies a debt and gives this action, founded in the equity of the plaintiff's case, as it were upon a contract." Notice, no promise, express or implied, was required for liability here despite the defendant's objection that there was no express or implied contract.

Instead of limiting his decision to the facts of the case, Mansfield gave examples of when he thought this equitable principle ought to apply. He said it should apply when in fairness the defendant ought to refund the money, and so he said there was no refund obligation when there were payments on a Holt-type debt barred by a statute of limitations or contracted during infancy.[79] However, a refund would be ordered:

> for money paid by mistake; or upon a consideration which happens to fail; or for money got through imposition (express or implied); or extortion, or oppression; or an undue advantage taken of the plaintiff's situation, contrary to laws made for the protection of persons under those circumstances. In one word, the gist of this kind of action is that the defendant, upon the circumstances of the case, is obliged by the ties of natural justice and equity to refund the money.

The scope of Mansfield's doctrine seemed so expansive that it might eclipse the older writs and turn the whole of contract law into a body of equitable principles administered under Assumpsit. Mansfield was politic enough to realize that resistance by lawyers trained in the common law would set in against his civilian ideas if his reforms went too far. Hence he tried to restrict it and said, "I am a great friend to the action for money 'had and received', and therefore I'm not for stretching, lest I should endanger it."[80] Mansfield's quasi-contract principle would survive his adjustments of consideration, his other major attempt at contract reform, because, unlike consideration, quasi-contract was for the exceptional case and did not invade the territory of any established action.[81]

It took Mansfield's civil law training to isolate a general principle, as opposed to the common law search for a past precedent, and thereby find the strand running through the earlier cases that natural justice requires a refund when the defendant takes unfair advantage of the plaintiff. Mansfield, not drawn to common law technicalities, rested his doctrine on natural justice, which was no less rational than the use of the fictitious promise.[82] *Indebitatus assumpsit's* had and received count was essentially an equitable cause of action, and its growth placed the common law in competition with Chancery, to the extent it was employed outside the scope of Debt and Account.[83] As in Equity, the had and received count was flexible and need not be allowed if the conditions were not oppressive. Actually, quasi-contract belonged more to the sphere of Chancery's trust law jurisdiction than to contract law, and the refund obligation under the had and received count would more appropriately be labelled a constructive trust rather than a contract implied-in-law.

Although quasi-contract cases proliferated in the eighteenth and nineteenth centuries, it was more than a century after *Moses v. Macferlan* before Ames became the first scholar to isolate "The equitable principle which lies at the foundation of the great bulk of quasi-contracts, namely, that one person shall not unjustly enrich himself at the expense of another."[84] In the twentieth century, while England has reverted to the fictitious promise in quasi-contract,[85] the United States has been more influenced by the Mansfieldian view. Scholars in the United States have employed the term "restitution" to cover various types of equitable relief in addition to the money refund cases of quasi-contract.[86] That later development will be analyzed in the penultimate chapter.

Mansfield Embraces Law Merchant

William Murray, later Lord Mansfield, was born in Scotland and, like Holt earlier, was initially an outsider to the English establishment. Mansfield was a product of the rational age of Voltaire, and he brought that viewpoint to the King's Bench when he became Chief Justice in 1756 after a successful Parliamentary career.[87] He valued rational analysis of the merits of an issue over pedantic adherence to procedure and precedent. He had a modern perspective and was intent on a practical adaptation of the law to the times. His opposition to the general verdict forced discussion of legal issues and facilitated a process of elaboration of specific contract rules that would continue in the nineteenth century. The refinement of appellate procedures also facilitated discussion of questions of law. For the certainty of contract law in a commercial age, Mansfield fashioned comprehensive principles from the isolated cases that were spread throughout the reports and abridgements. Fictions were either abandoned, if they were no longer functional, or restricted to their original purpose.[88] Assumpsit was expressed as a contractual action, as opposed to Blackstone's continuation of the dated proprietary view. He saw that the scope of a contract should be determined by the intent of the parties and not by the quirks of a form of action.

Mansfield found it necessary to reform procedural law in the furtherance of his objectives. He contained some of the irrational pedanticism of common law lawyers, who had acquired excessive latitude in the courtroom during the period of the mediocre judiciary succeeding Holt. He ended the harassment of jurors and witnesses and stamped out dilatory practices causing shameless delays; however, these abuses would resurface after Mansfield's resignation. He regularized the functions of counsel during the trial and shaped the format of the trial still used today. At the pleading stage, Mansfield would refuse technical objections to pleadings which had nothing to do with the merits of the case.[89] In his application of the law of evidence, he did not emphasize the need for written evidence to the degree of his predecessors and he extended the use of expert witnesses. *Indebitatus assumpsit* was encouraged over Special Assumpsit since the detailed pleading of the latter encouraged scholastic objections. Dwelling on technicalities would have had a deterrent effect on the law functioning for the promotion of certainty and speedy relief. The intent of the parties rather than the forms of action was emphasized; Mansfield signalled a movement toward a consensual theory of contract.[90]

Although he had no great reverence for stare decisis, he saw the value of adhering to clear precedent for the promotion of commercial certainty; and, for the same reason, he discouraged the use of the general verdict so that the basis of the decision would be known. There were no clear precedents for many of the new types of commercial contracts entering the King's Bench for the first time. The appearance of these novel disputes was the result of the expanded contract jurisdiction of the common law courts and the developments in the boom in trading and the onset of the British industrial revolution. When the established common law contract doctrine did not fit, Mansfield was not inclined to make awkward adaptations of the ancient law to these new disputes, and so he turned to a variety of sources in making contract law relevant to current commercial practices. He borrowed from the civil law, Chancery and the customs of merchants in honing a practical set of commercial rules. He was probably more familiar with the civil law than any chief justice before or since because he had been educated in the civil law at Oxford, had qualified for law practice in Scotland and was widely read in Continental writers on contract law such as Pothier.[91] Civil law commercial law rules were more advanced than those of the common law; it was fortuitous that Mansfield should be on the Bench to take advantage of the civilian mercantile work to modernize the common law.

The quantity of commercial cases appearing in the common law courts were no longer infrequent; for, Britain had become the greatest trading nation in the World, and the alternative courts to the common law courts had largely dried up. In the interest of the political and economic welfare of the now influential merchant class, and indeed of the nation, the British government pursued a mercantile policy of promoting commerce and industry. Mansfield was in tune with this policy from his days as the Solicitor General arguing as an advocate of the Crown's mercantile policies, and he continued this policy once he was appointed Chief Justice. It was in the realm of commercial law that Mansfield would make his greatest contribution to the law.[92] He had an immense influence on the law of contract and on branches of commercial law that would later become independent of common law contract, to varying degrees, e.g., negotiable instruments, insurance and sales of goods.

Unlike Holt, Mansfield adjusted the common law in order to accommodate the needs of merchants, and the principal way of achieving this was by the absorption of commercial practices into the law as rules of law and as judicially noticed custom. Indeed, mercantile usages were not assimilated into the common law itself until Mansfield accomplished it[93] since Holt had allowed the jury to consider mercantile usage only as a fact to weigh in arriving at a general verdict. Mansfield opposed the general verdict because it established no legal doctrine to provide guidance to judges and merchants in the future.[94] Mansfield created a special corp of merchant jurors at Guildhall to declare what the mercantile usage, or law merchant, was in a given case,[95] and Mansfield sought out merchants privately to learn further about commercial practices. Thus the special jury solved the immediate problem, and Mansfield gave doctrinal significance to the custom found by incorporating it into the judgment for use in future cases and thereby made eighteenth-century usage a part of the common law. He sought the principles behind the custom both in order to rationalize them in his judgments and in order to construct generalized principles for future decisions and thereby avoid the drift into unpredictable decisions based on natural justice alone. He found these principles in the civil law and in the *jus gentium* (the law of nations) found in the law merchant.[96]

Once a custom was incorporated in a judicial opinion, judicial notice was taken of it thereafter, and it would be read into later contracts before the court as a means of clarifying and supplementing them.[97] The parties could elect to vary the trade custom by the express terms of a subsequent contract[98] since the law of commerce applied to a segment of society able to protect itself. Unlike Holt's approach, after the court accepted a mercantile usage as custom, a special jury would not be permitted to reconsider what the usage was. Clear rules of commercial law began as Mansfield formulated rules formerly hidden behind the defendant's general plea of *non assumpsit.* Elaboration of contract rules occurred as greater control was exerted over juries through Mansfield's use of special juries and of jury instructions to ordinary juries. Juries were instructed on the applicable uniform rules rather than it being left generally to the juries as questions of fact.[99]

Mansfield's unprecedented attempts to distinguish between law and fact and between those customs assimilated into the law and those not caused confusion even for himself. In *Buller v. Harrison* (1777)[100] Mansfield allowed a new trial because he should have separated the law from the facts in a jury instruction rather than leaving the question open. In *Grant v. Vaughan* (1764)[101] Mansfield mistakenly left to a special jury of merchants the settled question of whether a note payable to bearer was negotiable. The jury found that it was not, but the verdict was set aside, "for it is a question of law 'whether a bill or note is negotiable or not.' It appears in the books, 'that these notes are, by law, negotiable'". Reconsideration of custom after it was accepted by the court would have bred uncertainty inimical to business planning. Mansfield purposely referred cases to the full court at Westminster, which he could have ruled on alone out on the circuit, "to prevent other disputes by making the rules of the law and the ground upon which they were established certain and notorious."[102]

One branch of commercial law of particular concern to merchants was the conservative view of the common law to bills and notes. Merchants used bills and notes to extend credit and for safe transmittal of funds when contracts were transacted in distant locales, and they were eager to have the common law assist its transferability by treating bills and notes as akin to cash by recognizing the notion of negotiability. Holt had tried to treat bills of exchange, both foreign and inland, and promissory notes as distinct devices, each with its own applicable rules; and, he had only recognized the right to negotiate bills and notes by force of precedent in the case of bills and by statute for notes. Up to the time of Mansfield, bills and notes were not deemed like cash by the courts, but within two years of becoming Chief Justice, Mansfield had undercut Holt's barriers. In *Heylyn v. Adamson* (1758) Mansfield declared that bills and notes should be treated the same: "The law is exactly the same, and fully settled, upon the analogy of promissory notes to bills of exchange. . . . When it (note) is indorsed, the resemblance begins."[103] And, in *Miller v. Race* (1758)[104] the concept of negotiability was first brought into the common law in an action involving the ownership rights in stolen notes transferred to the plaintiff, an innocent purchaser for valuable consideration. The defendant attempted to analogize the plaintiff's position to one possessing stolen goods, but Mansfield said notes are:

> treated as money, as cash in the ordinary course and transaction of business, by the general consent of mankind, which gives them the credit and currency of money to all intents and purposes. They are as much money as guineas themselves are

Unlike stolen goods, once the stolen notes had "passed in currency" to a bona fide purchaser, that purchaser would prevail over the victim of the theft. Mansfield pointed to two strains of authority for his holding in *Miller v. Race.* First, there was mercantile custom: "upon the general course of business, and from the consequences to trade and commerce: which would be much incommoded by a contrary determination." And, secondly, there were Chancery cases involving estates and bankruptcy from an earlier part of the century treating notes as akin to cash.[105] Mansfield then used the same logic in *Grant v. Vaughan* (1764)[106] to hold in favor of a bona fide holder of lost bearer paper over the loser of the note. Blackstone was aware of *Grant v. Vaughan,* and though he noted that bills and notes were assignable, he failed to grasp that holders were insulated from contract defenses.[107]

Any lingering doubts about negotiability were dispelled in *Peacock v. Rhodes* (1781),[108] a case involving a bill of exchange stolen from a blank endorsee. A stranger named "William Brown" transferred the bill to the plaintiff, who in turn sued the drawer. The defendant argued first that there were precedents for the negotiability of notes, but not for bills, and, secondly, that a prudent trader would not take a bill unless he knew the transferor. To the first defense Mansfield responded:

> The holder of a bill of exchange, or promissory note, is not to be considered in the light of an assignee of the payee. An assignee must take the thing assigned, subject to all the equity to which the original party was subject. If this rule applied to bills and promissory notes, it would stop their currency. The law is settled, that a holder, coming fairly by a bill or note, has nothing to do with the transaction between the original parties.

To the second defense, Mansfield acknowledged there were grounds for suspicion but it had been found here to be "received in the course of trade." Mansfield's logic and language stood as the common law of negotiable instruments for over a century and would be the basis of the statutes passed in England and the United States when negotiable instruments became again separate from the common law.

Mansfield's Reform of Contract Doctrine

Mansfield's commercial bias can also be seen in his attempt to recast contract law. His principal contributions to the common law of contract were his adjustments in connection with consideration, express warranty and dependency of promises. Mansfield's attempts to reform the doctrine of consideration were the most spectacular of the lot but in the end the least long lasting. He viewed consideration as an impediment to the enforcement of obvious promises, and so he made a frontal challenge of the doctrine. He conducted a two-pronged attack, arguing first that commercial contracts and written contracts generally did not need consideration and, secondly, that a moral consideration alone would fulfill the consideration requirement. More than two centuries after the appearance of consideration, the doctrine was still not clearly defined or understood; it was simply accepted as dogma that a parol promise (oral or unsealed writing) must be supported by consideration. A rational man like Mansfield was not inclined to accept dogma when it restrained the growth of contract law. Furthermore, his civil law education made him sympathetic to equitable solutions.

Mansfield instituted his assault on consideration in *Pillans v. Van Mierop* (1765),[109] wherein there was a past consideration objection to a commercial undertaking to honor a bill of exchange.[110] Holt's modification of the past consideration rule in the cases of a waiver of a statute of limitations and an adult's ratification of a contract made during minority opened the door for Mansfield's rationalization of the function of the doctrine of consideration. Mansfield declared that the usage of merchants did not require consideration and that in other contracts consideration was not required if the contract was evidenced by a writing. The three other justices agreed with Mansfield that a commercial contract did not need consideration: "A nudum pactum does not exist, in the usage and law of merchants." As a matter of common sense, would a merchant enter into a contract without an anticipation of a benefit?

As an alternative reason for not requiring consideration, Mansfield imaginatively argued that the Statute of Frauds, passed subsequent to the appearance of consideration, implicitly allowed an unsealed writing to be enforced without consideration:

> I take it, that the ancient notion about the want of consideration was for the sake of evidence only: for when it is reduced into writing, as in covenants, specialties, bonds, etc. there was no objection to the want of consideration. And the Statute of Frauds proceeded upon the same principle.

Although the Statute of Frauds did not do this, it did make certain categories of unsealed writings constitutive; and Mansfield, rejecting the magic of the seal, wanted to elevate all promises evidenced by a writing to the status of the sealed contract. Mansfield and Wilmot, J. even doubted there were any cases in the reports of an unsealed writing being a nudum pactum.[111] They were urging that consideration should be only one of several ways of proving a contract, and, if proved, no outmoded doctrine should stand in the way of enforcement.[112]

The *Pillans v. Van Mierop* ruling stood for 13 years until the House of Lords took a contrary position in *Rann v. Hughes* (1778).[113] In *Rann v. Hughes* the House of Lords reviewed a King's Bench decision for the plaintiff on a consideration issue of whether an administrator's separate written promise to pay an estate debt was enforceable when the estate had insufficient assets. After some vacillation in the sixteenth and seventeenth centuries, the courts had been holding in favor of the creditor even if there were insufficient estate assets. However, there were still doubts about this view because, if the consideration for the administrator's promise was the estate creditor's forbearance from suing, what was the benefit to the administrator if there were no estate assets? In *Rann v. Hughes* the House of Lords concluded that this was not sufficient consideration. In anticipation of such a ruling, the plaintiff argued alternatively that the defendant should be liable without consideration simply because there was a writing. The plaintiff was arguing that, notwithstanding insufficient estate assets, the defendant should be liable on an unsealed writing since the Statute of Frauds impliedly provided for liability, even in the absence of consideration, by its reference to a "special promise to answer damages out of his own estate."[114]

The plaintiff's attorney in *Rann v. Hughes* argued against the farcical distinction of consideration being required for an unsealed writing but not for a sealed writing:

> In reason, there is little or no difference between a contract which is deliberately reduced into writing and signed by the parties without seal, and a contract under the same circumstances, to which a party at the time of signing it puts a seal or his finger on cold wax.

Remember that the status of an unsealed writing had been lifted to that of a constitutive nature by the passage of the Statute of Frauds and all writings had been further boosted by the development of the parol evidence rule. However, it was too late to rationalize the anachronistic seal in the face of several centuries of precedents. Skynner, speaking for a unanimous House of Lords in *Rann v. Hughes*, ruled against the plaintiff:

> All contracts are by the laws of England distinguished into agreements by specialty and agreements by parol; nor is there any such third class as some of the counsel have endeavoured to maintain as contracts in writing. If they be merely written and not specialties they are parol, and a consideration must be proved.

Lord Skynner did not stop there; he went on to declare *Pillans v. Van Mierop* erroneous in its ruling that there was no need for consideration when there was a writing. He said the Statute of Frauds was "merely negative" to protect certain debtors[115] and not to charge them with new liabilities, and so consideration was required on top of the Statute's writing requirement. The rule that consideration is required for parol agreements, whether written or oral, but is not required for the more ancient sealed agreement is still the law in England today.

Mansfield's revolutionary attempt to equate an unsealed writing with consideration, the long standing test of actionability in Assumpsit, went too far for a tradition-bound system. Mansfield's emphasis on the evidentiary function of consideration ignored other reasons for the evolution of consideration, such as, reciprocity, motive and the procedural aspects of *indebitatus assumpsit*. In *Rann v. Hughes* the House of Lords reiterated that consideration was essential in parol contracts, but the Lords made no attempt to define this nebulous, universal requirement. The Lords disposed of Mansfield's writing point in *Pillans v. Van Mierop*, but they did not address his point that the usage of merchants did not require consideration. Conceivably, Mansfield could have continued to push the mercantile usage point, but he seemed to conclude there was too much resistance to a fundamental change, and so he retreated to a compromise position in his mission of tempering the ill effects of consideration. Thereafter, he admitted that consideration was required, but he liberalized it by including within its sphere the flexibility of promissory liability supported by a moral obligation.[116]

Unlike Mansfield's view that an unsealed contract should be the equivalent of a sealed one, there was some caselaw authority for his stand that a moral obligation constituted sufficient consideration. Holt's exceptions to the past consideration rule for a waiver of a statute of limitations and an adult's ratification of a promise made during infancy were precedents for Mansfield to latch onto. Mansfield's moral obligation cases had two common ingredients: one, the consideration for the promise was grounded in conscience and, two, the promise was enforceable in Chancery when specific relief was available. Mansfield, who had earlier practised law before Chancellor Hardwicke, did much to bring Chancery practices into the common law courts, and he would unashamedly cite Chancery practice and precedent as his authority when there was none at-law. The decision of *Trueman v. Fenton* (1777)[117] involved a debtor's waiver of bankruptcy, and, of Mansfield's moral obligation cases, it was the most obvious descendant of Holt's statute of limitations waiver case. Mansfield thought that the debtor was guilty of fraud or gross dishonesty in purchasing a large quantity of linen from the plaintiff "on the eve of bankruptcy" (5 weeks before filing) and that the creditor had been reasonable in taking the waiver for a lesser amount. In ruling for the creditor, Mansfield cited Chancery precedents and said, "all the debts of a bankrupt are due in conscience, notwithstanding he has obtained his certificate."

The other line of Mansfield's moral obligation cases did not come from Holt but was a direct response to his stunning setback in *Rann v. Hughes*. In *Hawkes v. Saunders* (1782)[118] he set about distinguishing estates with sufficient assets, wherein there were promises of executors to pay estate obligations, from the *Rann v. Hughes* case of an estate with insufficient assets. Mansfield disagreed that consideration could only be grounded on a benefit or a loss and said, "Where a man is under a moral obligation, which no Court of Law or Equity can enforce, and promises, the honesty and rectitude of the thing is a consideration." Although he then cited Holt's precedents, this case is more removed from Holt than the bankruptcy waiver case because the estate case did not involve a debt due at common law but later barred by such a positive law as a statute of limitations.

Buller, J., Mansfield's disciple, emphasized the equitable nature of the obligation in *Hawkes v. Saunders:* "The true rule is, that wherever a defendant is under a moral obligation, or is liable in conscience and equity to pay, that is a sufficient consideration." In Buller's unpublished, handwritten opinion in *Hawkes v. Saunders,* he cited *Moses v. Macferlan* in employing quasi-contract logic, rather than Mansfield's moral obligation, in support of the holding and stated that it wasn't an action on an express promise, where consideration was needed, but instead was an obligation to pay under the ties of natural justice. The difference in approach of Mansfield and Buller here reflects Mansfield's overall attempt to reform obligations related to contract under the two equitable lines of moral obligation and quasi-contract.[119]

Mansfield's verbiage about a moral obligation being sufficient consideration was more sweeping than the facts of the cases he actually decided, but there is little doubt he envisioned applications of the moral obligation logic extending outside Holt's precedents. If Mansfield's statements were taken literally, Lord Denman, C.J. would later complain, they "would annihilate the necessity for any consideration at all, inasmuch as the mere fact of giving a promise creates a moral obligation to perform it."[120] Denman objected to the early nineteenth century decisions which did take Mansfield's dicta seriously by enforcing promises to pay moral obligations which at no prior time would have been considered an enforceable debt. Hence a promise of an adult stepchild to pay his stepfather for maintenance provided during his childhood was enforceable in an 1803 English decision because "the plaintiff having done an act beneficial for the defendant in his infancy, it is a good consideration for the defendant's promise after he came of age."[121] This holding fit neither under the old consideration rule that there must first be a request of the debtor before the benefit is provided[122] nor under Holt's exceptions for when the prior debt was barred by positive law. In the United States, however, an 1825 Massachusetts decision was that a father's promise to pay the plaintiff's expenses in caring for his ill son earlier was unenforceable because it was only an obligation "of conscience" and not a later promise removing an impediment created by positive law like a statute of limitations would be.[123]

In the absence of chief justices of Mansfield's perspective and ability, the common law retreated in the nineteenth century when there was a reaction to Mansfield's civilian attempt to rationalize consideration by judges trained solely in the common law. In *Eastwood v. Kenyon* (1840)[124] Denman, C.J. adopted an 1802 reporters' case note,[125] which note argued that, "however general the expressions used by Lord Mansfield may at first sight appear," a careful reading of Mansfield's actual decisions showed that he did not go outside Holt's exceptions. Denman agreed with the earlier reporters' note that:

> an express promise can only revive a precedent good consideration, which might have been enforced at law through the medium of an implied promise, had it not been suspended by some positive rule of law; but can give no original cause of action, if the obligation, on which it is founded, never could have been enforced at law, though not barred by any legal maxim or statute provision.

By this ruling Denman contained Mansfield's attempt to blow consideration wide open and declared: "In holding this declaration bad because it states no consideration but a past benefit not conferred at the request of the defendant, we conceive that we are justified by the old common law of England." Denman's rejection of moral consideration reflected the nineteenth century view that market bargains had no place for amorphous moral obligations; however, had Mansfield's suggestion that consideration should not be required for merchants' bargains been pressed, it might have received a more receptive hearing during that later instrumental period. It has also been suggested that an increased strictness in pleading, which was put into effect six years prior to *Eastwood v. Kenyon,* caused lawyers to study and become more aware of the historical and procedural bases of consideration, thereby forcing the retreat from Mansfield's revisionism.[126] This refusal to accept Mansfield's liberalizing moral obligation as sufficient consideration is still the law in England and the United States.

The second area of Mansfield's contract work for discussion here involved his recognition of express warranty as a contract principle. Within a generation or so of his resignation, spin-offs of his contribution here would result in the development of modern rules for misrepresentation and the recognition of an implied warranty of quality; those later developments will also be covered here. The "action on the case in the nature of deceit" was discussed earlier in the chapter two connection with the breakdown of opposition to nonfeasance actions in the fifteenth century. This action continued to develop separately and is the foundation of both modern actions on contract warranties and the tort of deceit for fraudulent misrepresentation. This 400 year story is included in this chapter because of the importance of related contractual theory developed during the eighteenth century and slightly later.

The first tort actions of deceit on the case were in the last quarter of the fourteenth century for the breach of express warranties which defendants knew to be false.[127] Covenant was unavailable because of informality, and Debt *sur contract* was unavailable because there was no fixed sum. The tortious character of this false warranty, viewed as a wrong and not as a breach of an undertaking, would always stay with this old form of deceit on the case.[128] Since it was a tort action for the reliance damages of entering into the contract, it had no effect on the enforceability of the contract, even if there was fraud. One exceptional subject matter under this action, where no express warranty was needed, was the retail sale of victuals, such as food for consumption; and, by at least the late fifteenth century, no knowledge of falsehood (scienter) was required here.

The exceptional treatment of victuals was a lingering example of protection of status prevalent in the Middle Ages, but outside that area, sales of unfit goods were not a deceit unless there was an express warranty, and this lack of actionability was reinforced in the early sixteenth century with the emergence of the doctrine of *caveat emptor*. There was strict municipal regulation of market practices and relief in local courts during the Middle Ages, but the increasingly transient nature of transactions between distant parties emasculated local control. Nineteenth century merchants, and their lawyers, would disingenuously claim that *caveat emptor* was the ancient law, but in fact it arose as a Tudor mercantile rule in support of trade concurrent with the breakdown of the customary protection of purchasers.

Caveat emptor was an indigenous development unique to the common law—there was no such rule in the civil law or law merchant. The term was first used when Fitzherbert wrote about the purchase of a horse in 1534: "if he be tame and have been rydden upon, then *caveat emptor*".[129] *Caveat emptor* may have first appeared in the common law courts in response to the upsurge of itinerant merchants where buyers had to be aware that the seller would not be around to answer complaints.[130] The impersonality of developing market forces was breaking down local customary protection based on status. The forty shilling rule forced more of these cases before less sympathetic common law judges. In the influential *caveat emptor* case of *Chandelor v. Lopus* (1604),[131] a goldsmith "affirmed" it to be a precious bezoar stone, but the court held that, excepting victuals, there was no liability unless there was an express warranty. As the defendant's attorney argued, "if there is no warranty... an action on the case does not lie, even though he is deceived: for *caveat emptor*". There was a concern that a distinction be drawn between puffery, "for everyone in selling his wares will affirm that his wares are good," and a binding promise of quality, the difference being a jury question. Popham, C.J. added: "This case is a dangerous case, and may be the cause of a multitude of actions if it be understood that a bare affirmation by the seller causes the action."

By Tudor days, actions on the case for deceit were approved on an express warranty without the seller's knowledge of the falsehood of the warranty of quality goods.[132] Although tort in name, the action was becoming contractual in nature since the question now was whether the defendant was deceived out of his bargain rather than whether the defendant was dishonest. Liability was now absolute, or contractual, and not dependent on the defendant's fault of a knowing falsehood. Then, by at least the late Tudor period, a defendant could be liable in deceit for a knowingly false affirmation of quality (a statement short of a warranty) in a sale of defective goods.[133] This is not our modern tort of deceit for fraud since it only covered the narrow case of an affirmation of quality inducing the reliance damages of entering into a contract for sale of goods. So before the end of the Tudor period, *caveat emptor* notwithstanding, there was liability under the tortious action of case in the nature of deceit for inducing a sale by a knowing false affirmation or by an express warranty, scienter or not, and that is how the law remained until the time of Holt.

Holt extended warranty liability without scienter from the case of an express warranty of quality to an implied warranty of title. Actually the buyer's fundamental expectation that the seller was in title was protected as early as the fourteenth century without an express warranty if there was scienter. Scienter seemed to be a near formality by the seventeenth century so that the theory was becoming essentially contractual.[134] Holt announced a contractual approach by allowing actions of case on an implied warranty of title based on the seller's bare, false affirmation that the goods in his possession were his, without any allegation of scienter in the declaration.[135] This was a warranty implied-in-fact and sounding in tort. The distinction between an affirmation and a warranty had begun to break down.

The change from tort logic to contract logic is seen in the shift in Holt's emphasis from the wrong of the seller's knowing falsehood to the right the buyer acquired by placing faith in the seller's assertion. In a case of a sale of lottery tickets the seller pleaded he bought them in good faith and sold them to the plaintiff in good faith, but Holt said the seller's possession of the lottery tickets sold amounted to a warranty of title—the seller's lack of fault was irrelevant. This is similar to the budding contract logic in the earlier express warranty cases where the scienter requirement was dropped. Holt's implied title decisions helped lessen the resistance to the recognition of implied warranties, though it would not be until the early nineteenth century before implied warranty applied past victuals or title. Through the time of the writings of Blackstone, there was still no contract action for breach of express or implied warranties of quality and no theory of fraud independent of a sales contract.[136]

Plaintiffs had an interest in turning the deceit action on an express warranty into a contract action in Assumpsit because of the pleading[137] and damages advantages. The damages in deceit would return the plaintiff to his position before relying on the representation, but the contract damages in Assumpsit would cover the loss of the bargain. Furthermore, in fairness to an innocent defendant, in Assumpsit enforcement of the contract could be avoided if it was established there was a fraud defense. Mansfield saw little difference between breach of warranty sounding in tort and one in contract. After all, hadn't the tort action of deceit on a warranty been available only for the reliance of the plaintiff entering into a contract with the defendant and hadn't the deceit action on a warranty become contractual at least in theory once scienter was dropped? Therefore in *Stuart v. Wilkins* (1778)[138] Mansfield declared that an express warranty of quality was enforceable in Assumpsit in a case of a horse warranted sound but soon found diseased. Predictably, Mansfield added: "A warranty extends to all faults known and unknown to seller." Mansfield, and courts have ever since, treated the promise to pay the debt and the collateral warranty obligation as almost separate transactions because of the historic use of the action of Debt on the obligation to pay and the tort of deceit on the warranty. The legal analysis of warranty as a contract term separate from consideration opened up the bundle of elements called consideration to analysis as individual contract terms;[139] formerly, a defense to an Assumpsit action on the grounds of breach of warranty or fraud was only raised indirectly by an attack on the sufficiency of the consideration.

Stuart v. Wilkins took over the warranty business heretofore falling under the old deceit action on the case and prompted a reappraisal of that tort action within 11 years in *Pasley v. Freeman.*[140] In that case the plaintiff brought a deceit action for the defendant's knowing false representation of a third person's credit.[141] The plaintiff advanced credit in reliance on the defendant's representation and the third person went bankrupt. Gross, J. dissented from a judgment for the plaintiff because the misrepresentations did not induce the plaintiff to enter into a contract with the defendant, the historic basis for the old deceit action, nor did the defendant have any personal interest in the credit extended to the third person. A majority of the court departed from the four hundred year old rule by expanding the actionable reliance to other circumstances besides entering into a contract with the defendant.[142] Ashhurst, J. said, "the gist of the action is the injury done to the plaintiff, and not whether the defendant was or was not to gain by it." *Pasley v. Freeman* originated the new tort, still existing today, of deceit for frauds wholly independent of contract transactions. The common law had finally plugged a gap in the common law long filled by local courts and Chancery.

In order for this new form of deceit to apply, Buller, J. emphasized in *Pasley v. Freeman* that the defendant must know it was false and there must be the intent to cause injury.[143] The new requirements of intent to deceive in fraud and intent to make a warranty in contract left misrepresentations short of fraud to fall through the cracks without any clear rule of liability until quite recently.[144] The emphasis in this new form of deceit on a misrepresentation made with the intent to mislead, and which as a consequence caused damage, seemed to be the only justification for holding the defendant liable since he had no benefit from the misrepresentation.[145] Ashhurst, J. said the malice was more "diabolical" because the defendant had nothing to gain from the lie. Recovery was now allowed for moral fraud.

Then in the early nineteenth century, buyers of defective goods succeeded in wringing further concessions before nineteenth century courts, favorably disposed to merchandisers, halted the changes. Plaintiffs picked up a strand suggested by Mansfield's dictum in *Stuart v. Wilkins:* "Selling for a sound price without warranty may be a ground for assumpsit, but, in such a case, it ought to be laid that the defendant knew of the unsoundness." Mansfield's remark was a harbinger of recognition of the implied warranty of merchantability less than 40 years later. Mansfield had flirted with the notion of an implied warranty of quality in holding a brewer to an obligation to sell quality beer in 1781 and in implying a warranty of seaworthiness in a marine insurance contract the next year. There was a widespread recognition of an implied duty of quality in the eighteenth century under statutes, mercantile custom and local court rulings; and, as a consequence, it has been argued that the King's Bench saw little need to develop a full-fledged implied warranty of quality.[146]

Sound price was not the equivalent of implied warranty because scienter is not required in implied warranty, and under the adequacy rule the price paid would not normally be at issue in a warranty action. An attempt in England to obtain recognition of an implied warranty of quality in *Parkinson v. Lee* (1802)[147] failed in a case of a latent defect in a strong reaffirmation of *caveat emptor*. Grose, J. said, "It is the fault of the buyer that he did not insist on a warranty." And, in the New York case of *Seixas v. Woods* (1804)[148] the old bezoar stone *caveat emptor* case was cited by the court in support of the seller's position when the buyer had an opportunity to inspect.

Despite these strong reiterations of support for *caveat emptor*, an opening was found for buyers when there was no opportunity to inspect the goods. In 1815 two similar English cases arose where a buyer, after looking at a seller's merchantable sample, agreed to a purchase without the opportunity to inspect the actual goods purchased, which later proved defective.[149] Both cases held *caveat emptor* should not apply when there was no opportunity to inspect, and that in this limited circumstance, there was an implied warranty of merchantability implied in law. When no inspection was possible, "the intention of both parties must be taken to be, that it shall be saleable in the market."[150] There was no need to show a misrepresentation in this purely contractual approach. Within 14 years, it was ruled that a manufacturer selling copper, for the particular purpose of sheathing a ship, was held to an implied warranty of fitness for a particular purpose. There was an objection that there was an opportunity to inspect, but, since the defect was latent, the court held that the seller of manufactured goods should be treated differently than the seller of a horse with a latent defect since a manufacturer could guard against this defect by using proper materials in manufacture.[151] Thus appeared the first, albeit limited, exceptions to *caveat emptor*, and, throughout the nineteenth century, this implied warranty of merchantability applied only to sales of goods. The zenith of *caveat emptor* would occur, however, in the nineteenth century,[152] and so these early developments in implied warranty would be narrowly applied and not extended until toward the end of that century.

When there was a breach of warranty or fraud, what avenues of relief did a buyer have available? Before *Stuart v. Wilkins* and *Pasley v. Freeman,* recovery for breach of warranty and fraud were both covered by the same tort action of case for deceit, but, as a result of these two cases, the old deceit action was replaced by a contract action in Assumpsit for breach of warranty and a new tort action on the case for deceit when there was fraud. At common law, the relief for breach of warranty was now contract damages, and if a party to the contract was guilty of a fraud[153] amounting to a total failure of performance, then a rescission could be obtained if restoration was possible. In order to obtain tort damages for fraud, a separate action of deceit had to be brought; however, since the first half of the seventeenth century, the common law did permit the quasi-contractual action of money had and received for recovery of any payments made because of the fraud. By the sixteenth century, before the common law courts adopted rescission from Chancery, Chancery granted rescission for fraud, and the plaintiff could then bring a deceit action on the case for damages; or, if the fraud was not related to a contract, Chancery could grant restitution.[154] If fraud normally caused the failure of a term affecting the whole of the contract so that rescission could be obtained, could the same be said of breach of warranty or was it merely a basis for recovery of damages? The answer to that is wrapped up in the story which follows about whether contract covenants were dependent or independent, conditional or not.

Mansfield's third area of reform of common law contract for discussion here concerns dependency of covenants. The issue of dependency concerns the order and manner of performance.[155] First, in an executory contract, must plaintiff aver performance? For example, which must precede in a contract of conveyance, the conveyance or the payment? The rules of independency and dependency originated by the late Middle Ages in the action of Covenant, then the realm of executory contract. The rule in Covenant was that covenants were independent thus allowing the plaintiff to bring his action without performing his side.[156] This general rule did not apply if conditional verbiage in the covenant made defendant's performance dependent, as the defendant agreed to pay wages *pro* (for) services of a year. Then as mutual promises became enforceable in Assumpsit, the general rule of independence was applied to this new form of executory contract, despite the fact that a promise for a promise was more similar to the exceptional *pro* approach. Covenant's rule of independence was then inappropriately transferred to sales contracts as they became executory, resulting in the treatment of a sale as two independent obligations, as in Covenant, rather than as the exchange it was. Thus in Covenant and Assumpsit, a plaintiff's declaration would stand up if he averred only his readiness to perform. This caused confusion about performatory order in executory contracts, not to mention the injustices of holding a defendant when the plaintiff was not in a position to perform. A possible flexibility in applying Covenant's rules of independency or not was suggested in *Pordage v. Cole* (1669), a case better known for the reporter Serjeant Williams' notes to the case than the case itself.[157] The plaintiff sued on an executory covenant of conveyance, and the defense was that the word *pro* made the conveyance dependent: "a condition precedent which ought to be performed before the action brought." The plaintiff was undoubtedly reluctant to part with his deed in reliance on the defendant's credit. The court ignored the technical word *pro* and applied the general rule of independent covenants because the defendant had a reciprocal remedy against the plaintiff. The rationale was unsatisfactory, but the decision suggested that technicalities would be overlooked in interpreting these cases.

Holt suggested a solution to the failure of the rules of dependence and independence to reflect the concurrent nature of a sales exchange. His suggestion was the use of tender: "If either party would sue upon this agreement, the plaintiff for not paying, or the defendant for not transferring, the one must aver and prove a transfer or a tender, and the other a payment or a tender, though there be mutual promises."[158] Simultaneous tenders fitted the concurrent nature of a sales exchange.

Mansfield consolidated these developments toward concurrency by putting any doubts to rest in the famous case of *Kingston v. Preston* (1773).[159] In this case the agreement required the buyer to provide security for future payments on the purchase of a business, but the buyer sued for the transfer of ownership without providing the security. The seller defended that transfer was dependent on the buyer providing security, but the buyer took the traditional position that covenants were independent. Holt and other judges had already suggested the concurrency solution to this problem, but Mansfield is usually credited with bringing concurrent conditions into the law—although his actual holding in *Kingston v. Preston* was that providing security was a "condition precedent" or a dependent condition.[160] He emphasized the equitable nature of the dependency doctrine as a rule to avoid forfeiture: "it would be the greatest injustice if the plaintiff (buyer) should prevail: the essence of the agreement was, that the defendant should not trust to the personal security of plaintiff." Mansfield did give his considerable support to concurrency and did clearly delineate three kinds of covenants: (1) "mutual and independent," (2) "conditions and dependent" and (3) "mutual conditions to be performed at the same time." Besides the consolidating contribution of *Kingston v. Preston,* Mansfield emphasized that the type of dependency comes from the meaning of the parties, from the "intent of the transaction." Mansfield elaborated on concurrency eight years later saying "when it is not certain [who] is to do the first act," one party could show his readiness and initiate simultaneous performance by demanding the other's response, as by submitting a draft of a deed for the buyer's approval.[161] Later, Kenyon, C.J. said "readiness and willingness" on the part of a buyer, as plaintiff, required the plaintiff to aver he was "ready to pay for it."[162]

The discussion of conditions thus far has concerned executory contracts. Did the same rules apply to a contract which the plaintiff partially performed but broke a term of his obligation in the process? What kind of a performance must the plaintiff give in order to hold the defendant to the contract? This is of particular interest when the broken term is a warranty. In the pivotal decision of *Boone v. Eyre* (1777) the plaintiff conveyed his West Indian plantation, but the buyer refused to make remaining annuity payments because the conveyance was to include a stock of slaves that the plaintiff did not possess at the time of conveyance.[163] Mansfield held for the plaintiff because the covenant regarding the slaves went to a "part" and not the "whole of the consideration". He said, "where they go only to a part, where a breach may be paid for in damages, there the defendant has a remedy on his covenant, and shall not plead it as a condition precedent." This decision was consistent with *Kingston v. Preston* where Mansfield said the buyer's failure to give security went to the "essence" of the agreement and was hence a condition precedent. When the plaintiff's performance was incomplete, but a substantial benefit was given, the condition would be construed as independent to achieve justice. This view was a harbinger of the nineteenth century substantial performance rule.

The flip-side of *Boone v. Eyre* emerged in *Duke of St. Albans v. Shore* (1789),[164] where between the time of contracting and date for conveyance of a farm the seller cut 1,500 valuable trees. The defendant showed that the cutting caused a serious diminution in value. Loughborough, J. said *Boone v. Eyre* applied to the question of "whether the covenant of the plaintiff goes to the whole of the consideration." The court held for the defendant that the covenant was dependent and that the change in "the nature of" the land went to the whole of the consideration. The equitable solution was that, although the buyer's covenant was characterized as independent in *Boone v. Eyre,* it would be dependent if the inadequacy of the seller's performance went to the "whole". From the above caselaw on dependency, Serjeant Williams, in a 1798 note to a belated report of *Pordage v. Cole,* deduced five principles concerning when covenants were dependent or independent.[165] Despite the fact that Williams misapplied *Boone v. Eyre* and that two of the rules were inconsistent, his was the only serious attempt to synthesize the "technical" decisions, and it stood as an influential guide during the nineteenth century in the United States and England. His vague rendering of the principle in *Boone v. Eyre* resulted in breaches that went to the "whole" being called breaches of conditions and breaches that went to "part" were called breaches of terms.[166]

The ruling in *Duke of St. Albans v. Shore* raised a novel question that had implications for breach of warranty cases. If a dependent obligation was performed by a seller, what type of performance did the seller need to give to bind the defendant? Until dependency was recognized in cases such as *Kingston v. Preston,* an objection directed to the seller's inadequate performance as a grounds for repudiation was not possible.[167] With the onset of dependency in the eighteenth century, the failure of a condition permitted repudiation; however, as long as a warranty was considered collateral, it did not have the status of a condition, and the buyer's remedy was money damages rather than repudiation.[168] In nineteenth century England, if the breach of the warranty caused a total failure of consideration, then repudiation was permitted since it was deemed a failure of a condition;[169] otherwise it was the breach of a term and only money damages were recoverable.[170] American law avoided this confusion by allowing the buyer to repudiate contracts when there was a breach of an express or implied warranty of quality without worrying about whether it was a term or a condition.

Conclusion

Over the course of the century covered by this chapter the common law of contract moved from a disjointed array of caselaw, still drawn to the old common law learning, riddled with technicalities and out of touch with the realities of modern trade and industry, to a more cohesive and responsive body of law. Mansfield was the pivotal figure in providing enlightened leadership for an acceleration of the transition during the final third of this chapter's period. Although the tradition of common law judges like Holt was not to mould isolated decisions into the general principles desired for business planning, Mansfield did this and also took the unorthodox step of seeking inspiration outside the hodgepodge of fragmented common law decisions by grafting concepts to the common law of contract from Equity, civil law and law merchant. There was a rational incorporation of mercantile usage as formulary obstructions were removed and custom became law. New rules were devised for the emerging law of sales; contractual warranties were developed; transferability of certain contract rights were permitted and the concept of dependency of promises was recognized. The increase in freedom and informality in contract design was evidence of the elimination of remaining traces of status in the law as contract was becoming a tool of creative change for growing self-determination in a commercial and industrial economy. In the process, courts were becoming referees of the wills of the parties as a consensual theory of contract emerged.

Holt, the consummate common law lawyer, began the process in a halting, piecemeal fashion, as commercial interests pressed for modernization, and Mansfield followed with sweeping reforms. Mansfield employed equitable ideas, to an extent not duplicated until the twentieth century, to fashion principles of unjust enrichment, concurrent conditions and moral consideration. But that is not to say that Mansfield was acting as a chancellor; rather he was moulding these equitable notions into common law principles. His attempts to rationalize consideration opened the doctrine up to analysis of issues formerly behind the doctrine, starting with contract warranty. This process of isolating the principles bundled within the doctrine of consideration and elaborating them as separate rules would expand during the nineteenth century. The ideas and techniques instigated by Mansfield would be carried forward to a greater extent in the United States than in England. There would be a greater opportunity for experimentation with his innovations amidst the ferment of various American jurisdictions which were more inclined toward informality and were less stifled by *stare decisis* than England's solitary jurisdiction.

Notes

1. J. CLAPHAM, A CONCISE ECONOMIC HISTORY OF BRITAIN 225–229, 233, 246, 270, 282, 290–291 (Cambridge: 1949) (The population doubled from 1500 to 1750 and again from 1750–1821. *Id.* at 185–186. Prices were stable throughout 18th century. *Id.* at 188.).

2. Admiralty courts thrived under Tudor mercantile policies and had extensive jurisdiction over maritime matters and contracts made abroad. Coke was

jealous of this expanding jurisdiction and used prohibitions against it on the basis that admiralty had no jurisdiction over contracts made on land, whether at home or abroad. 1 W. HOLDSWORTH, A HISTORY OF ENGLISH LAW 544–556 (London: 7th ed. 1956).

3. Shermoulin v. Sands, 1 Ld. Raym. 271, 272, 91 Eng. Rep. 1078, 1079 (1697) ("the common law is the over-ruling jurisdiction in this realm").

4. Since the 16th century, King's Bench had considered merchant usage. Dolphyn v. Barne, K.B. 27/1116, m.35d. (1540), cited in Baker, *The Law Merchant and the Common Law Before 1700,* 38 CAMBRIDGE L.J. 295, 308–309 (1979).

5. *Cf.* Baker, *supra* note 4, at 298–299 (Custom dating from time immemorial was absorbed into common law as custom of the realm before Holt's time, but shifting local usage was only used to explain a contract.).

6. Holt struggled with practice of giving jury full rein. In Bank of England v. Newman, Ld. Raym. 442, 91 Eng. Rep. 1193 (1699) Holt granted new trial since transferor of bearer paper not liable without endorsement but second jury again found for transferee.

7. Once a long standing usage was judicially noticed as custom and adopted as law, the rule would be certain and need not be retried in later cases.

8. J. AMES, LECTURES ON LEGAL HISTORY 210–213 (Cambridge, Mass. 1913).

9. Lampet's Case, 10 Co. Rep. 47 (1612); *cf.* J. AMES, *supra* note 8, at 211 (Coke gave wrong reason for prohibition since it's older than maintenance—real reason is personal relation cannot be assigned without consent of obligor. *Id.* at 211–212.).

10. J. AMES, *supra* note 8, at 212 (Novation was unknown before assumpsit on mutual promises. Assignment could be without consent by act of sovereignty, as bankruptcy.).

11. *Id.* at 213 (assignment to a purchaser or donee void until Holt's time); South and Marel's Case, 3 Leon. 234 (1590) (assignment to creditor allowed).

12. Barbour, *The History of Contract in Early English Equity* in IV OXFORD STUDIES IN SOCIAL AND LEGAL HISTORY 107–109 (Oxford: 1914, P. Vinogradoff ed.) (fifteenth century). Chancery continued the practice. 2 W. BLACKSTONE, COMMENTARIES * 442; Carteret v. Paschal, 3 P. Wms. 198, 199, 24 Eng. Rep. 1028, 1029 (Ch. 1733) (assignment allowed without consideration); Fashon v. Atwood, 2 Ch. Ca. 6, 36, 22 Eng. Rep. 819, 835 (Ch. 1679) (assignee protected when assignor died).

13. Winch v. Keely, 1 Term. Rep. 619, 99 Eng. Rep. 1284 (K.B. 1787).

14. Judicature Act of 1873, 36 & 37 Vic., c.66, s.25(6).

15. Clerke v. Martin, 2 Ld. Raym. 757, 96 Eng. Rep. 6 (K.B. 1702). Regular private bankers emerged between the 1640s and 1675 from the goldsmiths. The Bank of England was founded in 1694.

16. Hawkins v. Cardy, 1 Ld. Raym. 360, 31 Eng. Rep. 1137 (K.B. 1698).

17. Hodges v. Steward, 12 Mod. 36, 88 Eng. Rep. 1148 (K.B. 1692). Holt admitted that foreign bills and inland bills had for some time been assignable. Buller v. Crips, 6 Mod. 29, 87 Eng. Rep. 793 (K.B. 1704). In a foreign bill one of the parties is not English. And, as to the old requirement that the law merchant only apply to merchants, Holt said anyone drawing a bill would be covered.

18. Clerke v. Martin, 2 Ld. Raym. 757, 92 Eng. Rep. 6 (1702).

19. *Indebitatus assumpsit* would not have been helpful to transferees of note because of prohibition on assignments. The need for easy transferability of commercial paper according to mercantile custom was irrelevant to a common law mind familiar with the face-to-face transfer of property interests.

20. Buller v. Crips, 6 Mod. 29, 87 Eng. Rep. 793 (K.B. 1704). In *Buller v. Crips* Holt justified approval of bills of exchange because they were for reasons of safety and hindered exportation of money from realm. Dicta in the case suggested that Lord Treby, C.B., had earlier supported notes "as a mighty conveniency for trade" but now doubted it because of Holt's arguments.

21. At a later discussion in *Buller v. Crips,* Holt said he had talked to 2 prominent merchants who said promissory notes had been used frequently for 30 years and it was "pretended" that "mighty ill consequences" would "ensue by obstructing this course." Holt responded: "why do not dealors use that way (bills of exchange) which is legal?" He then suggested a typical common law subterfuge to make promissory note look like bill of exchange. Buller v. Crips, 6 Mod. 29, 30, 87 Eng. Rep. 793, 794 (K.B. 1704). Cranch found evidence of inland bills of exchange and promissory notes being accepted by the common law by late 1640s. Cranch, *Promissory Notes Before and After Lord Holt,* in 3 SELECT ESSAYS IN ANGLO-AMERICAN LEGAL HISTORY 72, 84–89, 91–94 (Boston: 1909).

22. Stat. 3 & 4 Anne, c.9 (1705).

23. Garnet v. Clarke, 11 Mod. 226, 88 Eng. Rep. 1005 (1709) (Note to pay on one's own account is under Statute of Anne, but note to pay on another's account is not.).

24. *See* Starke v. Cheeseman, 1 Ld. Raym. 538, 91 Eng. Rep. 1259 (1704) ("the notion of promises in law was a metaphysical notion.").

25. Shuttleworth v. Garnett, Comb. 151, 90 Eng. Rep. 398, 399 (1689).

26. *Anon,* Holt 35 (1695).

27. City of London v. Goree, 2 Lev. 174 (1676); Woodward v. Aston, 1 Mod. 95 (1676).

28. Shuttleworth v. Garnett, 1 Show. K.B. 35, pl. 34 (1689), *reprinted in* J. BAKER and S. MILSOM, SOURCES OF ENGLISH LEGAL HISTORY 480 (London: 1986) (hereinafter cited as BAKER and MILSOM). The defendant's attorney argued: "this fine don't arise by contract of the party, but by custom out of the land." Trial by jury was the mode of proof in Debt cases on customary land fines.

29. Lamine v. Dorrell, 2 Ld. Raym. 1216, 92 Eng. Rep. 303 (K.B. 1705).

30. Ball v. Hesketh, Comb. 381, 90 Eng. Rep. 541 (1697).

31. Stone v. Wythipol, Cro. Eliz. 126 (1589), *reprinted in* BAKER and MILSOM, *supra* note 28, at 498. A promise of a married woman was still considered void. Loyd v. Lee, 1 Strange 94, 93 Eng. Rep. 406 (1719).

32. Hylings v. Hastings, 1 Ld. Raym. 389, 421 (1699). A 6 year statute of limitations was inaugurated for actions on the case in 1623. Stat. 21 Jac. I, c.16, s.3.

33. Meredith v. Chute, 2 Ld. Raym. 759, 760, 92 Eng. Rep. 7 (1702).

34. Bromley v. Frazier, 1 Strange 441 (K.B. 1720) (foreign bill of exchange allowed against endorser so that bills might pass like money for commercial convenience); Morice v. Lee, 8 Mod. 362, 88 Eng. Rep. 258 (1725) (Stat. 3 & 4 Anne, c.9 to be construed "as a remedial law, to be extended in construction as

far as in reason we can."); Rawlinson v. Stone, 3 Wils. 1, 95 Eng. Rep. 899 (K.B. 1746) (Denison, J., found, on his inquiry of merchants, that endorsement of note to payee's administrator was established commercial custom.).

35. C. FIFOOT, HISTORY AND SOURCES OF THE COMMON LAW: TORT AND CONTRACT 22–26 (London: 1949).

36. Kruger v. Wilcox, Amb. 252, 27 Eng. Rep. 168 (Ch. 1755).

37. Chancery's developed discovery procedures made it a superior forum on an accounting. 3 W. BLACKSTONE, *supra* note 12, at 363. First bankruptcy statute did not provide for a discharge and it was under common law jurisdiction. Stat. 13 Eliz., c.7 (1571). Stat. 4 Anne, c.17 (1705) provided for bankrupt's discharge. Stat. 5 Geo. II, c.30, s.24 (1732) gave Chancery control of bankruptcy.

38. Charles Viner (d.1756), the great abridger of cases, bequeathed funds for establishment of first academic post for teaching of the common law at Oxford. The COMMENTARIES derived from those lectures was an important influence in ending the old learning that Viner was a part of. H. Finch's LAW, OR A DISCOURSE THEREOF (1627) was a precursor in rejecting abridgement in favor of systematic analysis.

39. C. FIFOOT, LORD MANSFIELD 25–26 (Oxford: 1936).

40. 2 W. BLACKSTONE, *supra* note 12, at 442–470 (The principal contract section is Chapter 30, entitled: "Of Title by Gift, Grant and Contract.").

41. *Id.* at 443–445 (On prior moral obligations, he refers to Holt's decision regarding waiver of a statute of limitations.). He varied his discussion of consideration from his lectures to his Commentaries to reflect Mansfield's early consideration discussions, though he exhibits some misunderstanding. *See* C. FIFOOT, *supra* note 39, at 127–128.

42. 3 W. BLACKSTONE, *supra* note 12, at 161.

43. Blackstone may have become confused by reading Sheppard who broke down Assumpsit into "express" and "implied" contracts. Sheppard said the latter was "implied by law" and then proceeded to give an implied-in-fact example of a traveller's duty to pay an innkeeper. *See* W. SHEPPARD, ACTIONS UPON THE CASE 2 (London: 1663).

44. Moses v. Macferlan, 2 Burr. 1005, 97 Eng. Rep. 676 (1760), discussed *infra.*

45. Moses v. Macferlan, 2 Burr. 1005, 97 Eng. Rep. 676, 678 (1760) (Per Mansfield: "this action [is] founded in the equity of the plaintiff's case, as it were upon a contract ('quasi ex contractu' . . .)."); *cf.* 3 W. BLACKSTONE, *supra* note 12, at 162 ("money had and received for the use of the owner . . . implies that the person so receiving promised and undertook to account for it to the true proprietor."); *see* Birks and McLeod, *The Implied Contract Theory of Quasi-Contract: Civilian Opinion Current in the Century Before Blackstone,* 6 OXFORD J. LEGAL STUDIES 46, 50 (1986) (Blackstone should have said implied *assumpsit* was by the accident of Assumpsit taking over all of Debt.).

46. Birks and McLeod, *supra* note 45, at 52–53; Bristow v. Eastman, 1 Peake 291, 170 Eng. Rep. 160 (1794) (capacity required).

47. Milsom, *The Nature of Blackstone's Achievements,* 1 OXFORD J. LEGAL STUDIES 1, 8 (1981).

48. Common counts go by a variety of synonyms: *indebitatus* counts, money counts or standard counts.

49. Woodford v. Deacon, Cro. Jac. (1608).

50. Hibbert v. Courthope, Carth. 276, 90 Eng. Rep. 764 (1694); Hayward v. Davenport, Comb. 426, 90 Eng. Rep. 569 (1697) (no subsequent promise need be proved if debt proved to jury); Lücke, *Slade's Case and the Origins of the Common Counts* (pt. 3), 82 L.Q. REV. 81, 93–94 (1966); S. STOLJAR, A HISTORY OF CONTRACT AT COMMON LAW 106–107 (Canberra: 1975); *cf.* A. SIMPSON, A HISTORY OF THE COMMON LAW OF CONTRACT 579 (Oxford: 1975) (Greater control over jury by about 1700 may have reduced need for special pleading.).

51. Hibbert v. Courthope, Carth. 276 (1694) (plaintiff need only show it wasn't debt on specialty); Hayes v. Warren, 2 Strange 933, 93 Eng. Rep. 950 (1731) (Common counts are every day's experience.).

52. The first six common counts listed are found in H. STEPHEN, A TREATISE ON THE PRINCIPLES OF PLEADINGS IN CIVIL ACTIONS 393 (2d ed. London, 1827); the remaining two appear in E. BULLEN and S. LEAKE, PRECEDENTS OF PLEADINGS IN ACTIONS IN THE SUPERIOR COURTS OF COMMON LAW 35 (3d ed. London, 1868).

53. For sales contract executed on the plaintiff-seller's side.

54. Unlike action of Account, account stated was voluntary accounting by parties of amount due and defendant agreed to pay arrearage. There was no need to detail genesis of debts in count since agreement reduced them to a sum certain. Homes v. Savill, Cro. Car. 116 (1628).

55. For sales contract which was executory in the modern sense since goods had not been delivered. It lay because of old Debt fiction of a passing of property to buyer-defendant at the time of agreement.

56. *Anon*, Comb. 341 (1695), *reprinted in* BAKER and MILSOM, *supra* note 28, at 468 (Holt said: "Away with your *indebitatus*, 'tis but a bargain.").

57. *See* H. STEPHEN, *supra* note 52, at 312, where a suggested declaration form combines 6 common counts.

58. 1 J. CHITTY, A TREATISE ON THE PARTIES TO ACTIONS, THE FORMS OF ACTION, AND ON PLEADING 200 (4th ed. Phila., 1825).

59. *See* Hepburn, *The Historical Development of Code Pleading in America and England,* in 2 SELECT ESSAYS IN ANGLO-AMERICAN LEGAL HISTORY 643 (Boston: 1908).

60. The other quasi-contractual common count, "for money paid by the plaintiff to the use of the defendant," arose later. It had both a contractual and a quasi-contractual use. In its contractual context, it was an *indebitatus assumpsit* action for money paid out on defendant's behalf and at defendant's request. Its quasi-contractual function, without the requirement of defendant's request or consideration, did not appear until 1799 when it provided reimbursement to a plaintiff, who paid under some compulsion, for the defendant's use. Exall v. Partridge, 8 T.R. 308, 101 Eng. Rep. 1405 (1799) (The plaintiff paid defendant-lessee's rent in order for plaintiff to recover his own property located on premeses and distrained by landlord for non-payment of rent.). And in the next year this common count was used to borrow from Equity the concept of contribution among joint obligors, by implying that one obligor had paid a joint obligor's share at the latter's request. Cowell v. Edwards, 2 Bos. & P. 268, 126 Eng. Rep. 1275 (1800).

61. *Cf.* Lücke (pt. 3), *supra* note 50, at 93 (Subsequent promise was desirable procedurally since it created uniformity of pleading making it possible to use *indebitatus assumpsit* in all Debt cases.).

62. *See* Ames, *The History of Assumpsit—Implied Assumpsit,* 2 HARV. L. REV. 53, 64 (1888). Nevertheless, the action seems more akin to tort since it is a duty imposed in law.

63. City of London v. Goree, 3 Keb. 677 (1676), *reprinted in* BAKER and MILSOM, *supra* note 28, at 477.

64. Shuttleworth v. Garnett, 3 Mod. 240 (1689).

65. *See* J. BAKER, AN INTRODUCTION TO ENGLISH LEGAL HISTORY 301 (London: 2d ed. 1979).

66. Hewer v. Bartholomew, Cro. Eliz. 614 (1598); Framson v. Delamere, Cro. Eliz. 458 (1595).

67. Lincoln v. Topliff, Cro. Eliz. 644 (1597); Shaw v. Norwood, Moo. 667 (K.B. 1600). Account's imprisonment of defendant during audit had fallen into disrepute.

68. Beckingham and Lambert v. Vaughan, 1 Rolle Rep. 391, p. 11, Moo. 854, *reprinted in* BAKER and MILSOM, *supra* note 28, at 465 (K.B. 1616).

69. *See* 1379 Account case where defendant "received ten marks of money" from the plaintiff to apply for the plaintiff's benefit. Hastynges v. Beverley, C.P. 40/474, m.274 (1379), *reprinted in* BAKER and MILSOM, *supra* note 28, at 292; *see also* C. FIFOOT, *supra* note 35, at 365n.

70. Woodward v. Aston, 2 Mod. 95, 86 Eng. Rep. 961 (1676).

71. Arvis v. Stewkley, 2 Mod. 260 (1677), *reprinted in* BAKER and MILSOM, *supra* note 28, at 466 (comptroller of a port).

72. Howard v. Wood, 2 Show 24 (K.B. 1680), *reprinted in* BAKER and MILSOM, *supra* note 28, at 478, 479.

73. Howard v. Wood, T. Jones 125, *reprinted in* BAKER and MILSOM, *supra* note 28, at 479.

74. Lamine v. Dorrell, 2 Ld. Raym. 1216, 92 Eng. Rep. 303 (1705).

75. Yet later on, a defendant was liable in *indebitatus assumpsit* if he obtained plaintiff's goods by fraud, even though no proceeds passed to defendant, because there was implied-in-fact promise to pay reasonable value of the goods in his possession. Hill v. Perrott, 3 Taunt. 274, 128 Eng. Rep. 109 (1810).

76. Moses v. Macferlan, 2 Burr. 1005, 97 Eng. Rep. 676 (1760).

77. Mansfield picked unfortunate case to announce his doctrine since he was in uncomfortable position of having to finesse what was not a reversal but rather appeared to be an interference with a competent court's decision. In 1797 Kenyon, C.J. cleared the air: "After a recovery by process of law, there must be an end of litigation, otherwise there would be no security for any person." Marriott v. Hampton, 7 T.R. 269 (1797).

78. *Cf.* Oldham, *Eighteenth Century Judges' Notes: How They Explain, Correct and Enhance the Reports,* 31 AM. J. LEG. HIST. 9, 15–16 (1987) (Mansfield's trial notes indicate there was an arbitration agreement which the local court of conscience ignored, and Mansfield was a great friend of arbitration.). Commercial arbitration was common during the Stuart era and was formally recognized by Parliament in Stat. 9 & 10 Wm. III, c.15 (1702). Blackstone may have become confused about quasi-contract by the hold harmless agreement in *Moses v. Mac-*

ferlan by thinking that some sort of implied promise was required in quasi-contract, when in actuality that agreement merely raised equities in favor of refund. Another explanation for Blackstone's misapprehension might have been Mansfield's statement, "the law implies a debt." *See* 3 W. BLACKSTONE, *supra* note 12, at 161.

79. Mansfield further consoled defendant by pointing out that the plaintiff's benefit of pleading generally was counterbalanced by benefits to defendant of not being bound for an amount more than he received and being able to raise equitable defenses and a release without pleading them.

80. Weston v. Downes, 1 Doug. 23, 24, 99 Eng. Rep. 19 (1778). Mansfield wouldn't allow the action to expand in the following cases: Nightingal v. Devisme, 5 Burr. 2589 (1770) (action for stock improperly transferred to bankrupt); Power v. Wells, 2 Cowp. 818 (1778) (special Assumpsit needed for warranty); Lindon v. Hooper, 1 Cowp. 414 (1776) (had and received should not supplant traditional remedies of trespass or replevin).

81. *Cf.* C. FIFOOT, *supra* note 39, at 245. Fifoot saw quasi-contract appearing in mature form in *Moses v. Macferlan. Id.* at 141–143. But Jackson saw *indebitatus* used the way it had been in the past as a remedy available in various specified circumstances. R. JACKSON, THE HISTORY OF QUASI-CONTRACT IN ENGLISH LAW 118–120 (1936).

82. *See* C. FIFOOT, *supra* note 39, at 145–146. *And see* Trueman v. Fenton, 2 Cowp. 544, 98 Eng. Rep. 1232 (1777) (Mansfield on a procedural technicality: "But I never like to entangle justice in matters of form, and to turn parties around upon frivolous objections where I can avoid it.").

83. Clarke v. Shee, 1 Cowp. 197, 98 Eng. Rep. 1041 (1774) ("liberal action in the nature of a bill of equity"). Buller, J's unreported opinion in the moral obligation case of *Hawkes v. Saunders infra* invoked the quasi-contract logic of *Moses*. *See* Oldham, *Reinterpretations of 18th-Century English Contract Theory: The View from Lord Mansfield's Trial Notes,* 76 GEO. L. J. 1949, 1966 (1988).

84. Ames, *supra* note 62, at 66. James Barr Ames, America's greatest legal historian, may have made his finest contribution with this lucid article.

85. Sinclair v. Brougham, App. Cas. 398, 452 (H.L. 1914). There is a trend toward the American view. *See* Denning, *The Recovery of Money,* 65 L.Q. REV. 37 (1949).

86. *See* RESTATEMENT OF THE LAW OF RESTITUTION (1937) (Sect. 1: "A person who has been unjustly enriched at the expense of another is required to make restitution to the other."). Restitution includes quasi-contract and such specific equitable relief as constructive trust, equitable lien, subrogation and equitable accounting.

87. For an outstanding, lawyerly analysis of Mansfield's career, *see generally* C. FIFOOT, LORD MANSFIELD (Oxford: 1936).

88. Fabrigas v. Mostyn, 1 Cowp. 161 (1774) (per Mansfield: "a fiction of law shall never be contradicted so as to defeat the end for which it was invented, but for every other purpose it may be contradicted.").

89. Rex v. Lyme Regis, 1 Doug. 135, 99 Eng. Rep. 89 (1779) (clerical error in mandamus amended); Trueman v. Fenton, 2 Cowp. 544, 98 Eng. Rep. 1232 (1777) (defective pleading overlooked to get to merits of case).

90. *See* C. FIFOOT, *supra* note 39, at 121; Robinson v. Bland, 2 Burr. 1077

(1760) ("The parties had a view to" a particular body of law.); Oldham, *supra* note 83, at 1961 (Mansfield's trial notes show intent was prominent, as in warranty cases. *Id.* at 1961, 1982); *accord* P. ATIYAH, THE RISE AND FALL OF FREEDOM OF CONTRACT 216 (Oxford: 1979) (*Rann v. Hughes* didn't reject the implication in *Pillans v. Van Mierop* that intent is the primary basis of contract liability).

91. M. POTHIER, TRAITE d' OBLIGATION (1761) (translated by W. Evans as A TREATISE ON THE LAW OF OBLIGATIONS, 1806, in 2 vol.). Pothier taught at the University of Orleans. His great work included the academic and practice sides of the civil law.

92. In the twilight of Mansfield's career, Buller, J. declared Mansfield to be "the founder of the commercial law of this country." Lickbarrow v. Mason, 2 T.R. 63, 73, 100 Eng. Rep. 35, 40 (1787).

93. Scrutton, *General Survey of the History of the Law Merchant,* in 3 SELECT ESSAYS IN ANGLO-AMERICAN LEGAL HISTORY 7, 13–14 (Boston: 1909); Baker, *supra* note 4, at 320.

94. Vallejo v. Wheeler, 1 Cowp. 143, 98 Eng. Rep. 1012 (1774) (Per Mansfield: "It is not easy to collect certainty from a general verdict."). In Hankey v. Jones, 2 Cowp. 745, 751, 98 Eng. Rep. 1339, 1343 (1777) Mansfield disagreed with his predecessor Lee, C.J. requiring jury to determine whether frequent drawing of bills made him a trader under bankruptcy law because frequency of drawing is a fact for jury but whether that made him a trader was question of law for court.

95. Stat. 3 Geo. II, c.25 (1730) (party could request special jury on any issue at own expense); Stat. 24 Geo. II, c. 18 (1751) (judge could certify need for special jury).

96. Luke v. Lyde, 2 Burr. 882, 97 Eng. Rep. 614 (1759) (freight to be paid in case of French capture of ship solved by looking to civil law and even Rhodian laws).

97. Pelly v. Royal Exchange Assurance, 1 Burr. 341, 97 Eng. Rep. 342 (1757) (Marine insurance policy covered fire loss of ship's tackle stored on land because storage on land when in port was practice.).

98. Tyrie v. Fletcher, 2 Cowp. 666 (1777) (Per Mansfield: "If the parties do not choose to contract according to the established rule, they are at liberty, as between themselves, to vary it."). This approach is a harbinger of the will theory of contract law. Contract was being opened up as a planning device for traders and industrialists.

99. Baker, Book Review, 43 MOD. L. REV. 467, 469 (1980); Simpson, *The Horwitz Thesis and the History of Contracts,* 46 U. CHI. L. REV. 533, 600 (1979); Oldham, *supra* note 83, at 1958, 1982.

100. Buller v. Harrison, 2 Cowp. 565, 566, 98 Eng. Rep. 1243, 1244 (1777).

101. Grant v. Vaughan, 3 Burr. 1516, 1523, 97 Eng. Rep. 957, 961 (1764) (Yates, J. said: "It was not within the province of the jury, to determine upon the negotiability of this note: it was a question of law, not of fact, 'whether such a bill or note was or was not negotiable.'"); *see also* Edie v. East India Co., 2 Burr. 1216, 1222, 97 Eng. Rep. 797, 800 (1761) (Special jury's finding that blank endorsement made bill non-negotiable was reversed when Mansfield discovered custom settled to the contrary).

102. Luke v. Lyde, 2 Burr. 882, 887, 97 Eng. Rep. 614, 617–618 (1759).

103. Heylyn v. Adamson, 2 Burr. 669, 676, 97 Eng. Rep. 503, 507 (1758).

104. Miller v. Race, 1 Burr. 452, 97 Eng. Rep. 398 (1758) (trover action).

105. Walmsley v. Child, 1 Vez. 341, 343, 27 Eng. Rep. 1070, 1071 (Ch. 1749) (Hardwicke said maker of lost bearer note could demand that payee provide surety before receiving payment because bearer of lost note might appear and no dispute ought to be made of bearer who came by it fairly.).

106. Grant v. Vaughan, 3 Burr. 1516, 97 Eng. Rep. 957 (1764). (2 counts: action upon the case on the bill and money had and received.)

107. 2 W. BLACKSTONE, *supra* note 12, at 468.

108. Peacock v. Rhodes, 2 Doug. 633, 99 Eng. Rep. 402 (1781) (action on special case).

109. Pillans v. Van Mierop, 3 Burr. 1663, 97 Eng. Rep. 1035 (K.B. 1765).

110. It is arguable that no consideration was required in this contract anyway because of rule that consideration is normally not inquired into with negotiable instrument.

111. Wilmot emphasized that Roman law made distinction between written and oral and that Plowden had done same in Sharington v. Strotton, 1 Plow. 298 (1566). This is a misreading of Plowden since he was referring to sealed deeds.

112. *Cf.* 8 W. HOLDSWORTH, *supra* note 2, at 47 (good sense in Mansfield's view that consideration should not be sole test but simply as evidence); and T. PLUCKNETT, A CONCISE HISTORY OF THE COMMON LAW 654 (London: 5th ed. 1956) (Mansfield questioned why consideration should fetter contract law after old problem of proving contracts was solved by Statute of Frauds and by methodical business practices.).

113. Rann v. Hughes, 4 Brown P.C. 27, 2 Eng. Rep. 18 (H.L. 1778).

114. Statute of Frauds, 29 Car. II, c.3, s.4 (1677).

115. Burden of proving writing in addition to consideration reflected distrust of jurors who were not well controlled and could give discretionary damages in absence of sealed bond.

116. Even Lord Skynner acknowledged in *Rann v. Hughes* that, although consideration was required, "It is undoubtedly true that every man is by the law of nature bound to fulfill his engagements."

117. Trueman v. Fenton, 2 Cowp. 544, 98 Eng. Rep. 1232 (1777) (waiver entered into after the filing).

118. Hawkes v. Saunders, 1 Cowp. 289, 98 Eng. Rep. 1091 (1782) (executor's promise to pay legacy). *See* Atkins v. Hill, 1 Cowp. 284, 98 Eng. Rep. 1088 (1775), which was case decided before *Rann v. Hughes* but also involved executor's promise in solvent estate. Mansfield said, "In this case the promise is grounded upon a reasonable and conscientious consideration; namely, that the defendant had assets to discharge the legacy. If so, he was compellable in a Court of Equity, or in the Ecclesiastical Court, to pay it." *See also* Oldham, *supra* note 83, at 1962 (1772 case similar to *Hawkes* found in Mansfield's trial notes.).

119. Oldham, *supra* note 83, at 1966 (Moral obligation and quasi-contract were congenial parts of Mansfield's overall philosophy of moral transactional behavior. *Id.* at 1962–1963.). Atiyah has taken the position that there was no conceptual distinction between contract and quasi-contract at this time, but Buller clearly recognized the distinction between express promises requiring consid-

eration and obligations in equity implying a debt in his handwritten opinion in *Hawkes. See* P. ATIYAH, *supra* note 90, at 184.

120. Eastwood v. Kenyon, 11 Ad. & El. 438, 450, 113 Eng. Rep. 482, 486 (1840).

121. Cooper v. Martin, 4 East 76, 102 Eng. Rep. 759 (1803). *See also* Lee v. Muggeridge, 5 Taunt. 36, 128 Eng. Rep. 599 (1813) (widow promised to pay obligation originally void since incurred during her marriage).

122. Lampleigh v. Brathwait, Hob. 105 (1616), *reprinted in* C. FIFOOT, *supra* note 35, at 423 (Executed or executory consideration is good but past consideration is not.).

123. Mills v. Wyman, 20 Mass. (3 Pick.) 207 (1825). The father had no legal obligation to pay his adult son's expenses here. It's arguable the plaintiff had an unjust enrichment action against the son.

124. Eastwood v. Kenyon, 11 Ad. & El. 438, 113 Eng. Rep. 482 (1840) (Guardian advanced funds for the benefit of a minor ward, and in adulthood the former minor made promise to repay the guardian but promise was found to lack consideration.). This decision is in accord with Mills v. Wyman, 20 Mass. (3 Pick.) 207 (1825).

125. NOTE TO Wennall v. Adney, 3 Bos. & Pul. 247, 127 Eng. Rep. 137, 138 (1802).

126. *See* Holdsworth, *The New Rules of Pleading of the Hilary Term, 1834*, 1 CAMBRIDGE L.J. 259, 273–274 (1923). *Cf.* P. ATIYAN and R. SUMMERS, FORM AND SUBSTANCE IN ANGLO-AMERICAN LAW 242 (Oxford: 1987) (Benthamite formalist view that policy and morals for legislature rather than the courts contributed to demise of moral consideration.).

127. *Anon*, Trin. 7 Ric. II (1383), *reported in* FITZHERBERT, LEY 41; Garrok v. Heytesbury, Trin. 11 Ric. II, p. 4, pl. 2 (1387), *reprinted in* BAKER and MILSOM, *supra* note 28, at 507 (falsely warranted horse sound).

128. *Cf.* S. MILSOM, HISTORICAL FOUNDATIONS OF THE COMMON LAW 363 (London: 2d ed. 1981) (Retention of tortious character may be because first deceit cases in royal courts were cases with crown interest and quasi-criminal nature.).

129. A. FITZHERBERT, BOKE OF HUSBANDRIE sect. 118 (1534); *see also* A. FITZHERBERT, NATURA BREVIUM 94c (1534) (caution to horse buyer: it is "at the other's peril, for his eyes and tastes ought to be his judges").

130. Hamilton, *The Ancient Maxim Caveat Emptor,* 40 YALE L.J. 1133, 1162–1163 (1931). Indeed, Chandelor v. Lopus, Cro. Jac. 4, 79 Eng. Rep. 3 (1603) involved a foreign buyer. The medieval paternalism seen by Hamilton was stronger at local judicial and regulatory levels than at common law since the economic underdog didn't appear much in common law courts until the period of capitalism when 40 shilling rule compromised local protection. *Cf.* Hamburger, *The Development of the Nineteenth Century Consensus Theory of Contract,* 7 LAW & HIST. REV. 241, 267, 313 (n. 157) (1989).

131. Chandelor v. Lopus, Cro. Jac. 4 (1604), *reprinted in* BAKER and MILSOM, *supra* note 28, at 518 (action on the case); *see also* Harvey v. Yonge, Harv. MS. 105 (1602), *reprinted in* A. SIMPSON, *supra* note 50, at 639. *But cf.* Oldham, *supra* note 83, at 1977 (*Chandelor v. Lopus* may not have always been followed in

either London Mayor's Court or, according to Mansfield's trial notes, in mercantile cases before the King's Bench.).

132. Note, Keil. 91, pl. 16 (ca. 1505), *reprinted in* BAKER and MILSOM, *supra* note 28, at 516 (per dictum of Frowyk, C.J.).

133. Dale's Case, Cro. Eliz. 44 (1586); Southern v. How, Cro. Jac. 468 (1618); Frowyk, C.J. suggested it in Keil. 91, pl. 16 *supra*.

134. *See* S. MILSOM, *supra* note 128, at 364.

135. Crosse v. Gardner, Carth. 90, 90 Eng. Rep. 656 (1689) (sale of bullocks); Medina v. Stoughton, 1 Ld. Raym. 593, 91 Eng. Rep. 1297 (1700) (sale of lottery tickets).

136. *See* 2 W. BLACKSTONE, *supra* note 12, at 452.

137. Williamson v. Allison, 2 East. 446, 451, 102 Eng. Rep. 439, 441 (1802) (pleading advantages of money counts).

138. Stuart v. Wilkins, 1 Doug. 18, 99 Eng. Rep. 15 (1778) (Two justices thought ruling reiterated rule at least 20 years old.).

139. J. BAKER, *supra* note 65, at 294–295.

140. Pasley v. Freeman, 3 T.R. 51, 100 Eng. Rep. 450 (1789).

141. Concern that oral guaranty, under Statute of Frauds, could be sued on as misrepresentation of third party's credit, pursuant to *Pasley v. Freeman*, prompted passage of Lord Tenterden's Act in 1828, which required that representation of third party's credit be in writing.

142. Query whether plaintiff's reliance was reasonable in *Pasley v. Freeman* since: defendant was not alleged to be an expert in credit matters, defendant wasn't paid for his advice and plaintiff could have asked for other opinions. On last reason, *see* Bailey v. Merrell, 3 Bulstr. 94 (1616) (not reasonable to rely when carrier had ability to weigh goods instead of relying on other party's figures).

143. Buller's intent point is his own, though he misleadingly attributes it to Holt. Ashhurst, J. said plaintiff correctly averred intent to deceive and defraud.

144. *Cf.* Derry v. Peek, 14 App. Cas. 337 (H.L. 1889) (Careless false statement believed true is not actionable since had to be knowledge or recklessness.).

145. *Cf.* S. STOLJAR, MISTAKE AND MISREPRESENTATION 133 (London: 1968) (Scienter, something lost in warranty, was the justification.).

146. Oldham, *supra* note 83, at 1971–1976, citing Harding v. Enkell, 492 Mansfield's Trial Notebooks 80 (1781); Schoolbred v. Nutt, 495 Mansfield's Trial Notebooks 73 (1782); *see also* Capstack v. Williams, 494 Mansfield's Trial Notebooks 174 (1782).

147. Parkinson v. Lee, 2 East 314, 102 Eng. Rep. 389 (1802). Decision determined who should bear loss when latent defect was caused by third person.

148. Seixas v. Wood, 2 Caine R. 48 (N.Y. 1804) (2–1 vote). *Cf.* G. VERPLANCK, AN ESSAY ON THE DOCTRINE OF CONTRACTS 217 *et seq.* (New York: 1825) (Opposed to both *caveat emptor* and sound price: disclosure should be mandatory if known latent defect.).

149. Gardiner v. Gray, 4 Camp. 144, 171 Eng. Rep. 46 (1815) is the leading case and was followed later that year by Laing v. Fidgeon, 6 Taunt. 108, 128 Eng. Rep. 974 (1815) (irrelevant that the contract price was low). These cases were not like Bailey v. Merrell, 3 Bulstr. 94 (1616) (Carrier barred from relying on other party's weight figures because had opportunity to weigh goods.). *And see* Holcombe v. Hewson, 2 Camp. 391, 170 Eng. Rep. 1194 (1810) (Assumpsit

action on agreement to buy beer would not be allowed if beer wasn't of merchantable quality.).

150. Gardiner v. Gray, 4 Camp. 144, 171 Eng. Rep. 46 (1815). *See* Laing v. Fidgeon, 6 Taunt. 108, 128 Eng. Rep. 974 (1815) ("it resulted from the whole transaction that the article was to be merchantable: the Defendant might have rejected the order, but having accepted it, he ought to furnish a merchantable article."). It was an implied assumpsit.

151. Jones v. Bright, 5 Bing. 531, 130 Eng. Rep. 1167 (1829) (Opportunity to inspect point of Laing v. Fidgeon, 6 Taunt. 108 (1815) distinguished because the defect was latent, and latency point of Parkinson v. Lee, 2 East. 314 (1802) distinguished because defect was not caused by seller in Parkinson.).

152. *Caveat emptor* had a stronger 19th century following in the United States than in England. *See* Hamilton, *supra* note 130, at 1178–1179 (strong in the U.S. due to frontier individualism and resistance of emerging industry to control); *and see* Barnard v. Kellogg, 77 U.S. (10 Wall.) 383 (1870) (*Caveat emptor* universally accepted in U.S., except for South Carolina.).

153. When a seller makes a representation, there is possible dual liability since it could constitute a warranty and also be fraudulent.

154. The practice of appealing to Chancery when there was a fraud was the start of the voidable contract concept. *Cf.* S. MILSOM, *supra* note 128, at 88–89 (in sixteenth century if fraud behind sealed deed). Another early example was Holt's decision on ratification of a former minor's contract. Ball v. Hesketh, Comb. 381 (1697).

155. For a discussion of dependency, *see generally* Stoljar, *Dependent and Independent Promises,* 2 SYDNEY L. REV. 217 (1957).

156. *Anon,* Y.B. 15 Hen. VII, f.10b, pl. 7 (1500).

157. Pordage v. Cole, 1 Wms. Saund. 319, 85 Eng. Rep. 449 (1669) (Debt upon a specialty). Sjt. Williams' 1798 note at 1 Wms. Saund. 320, 85 Eng. Rep. 450n.

158. Callonel v. Briggs, 1 Salk. 112, 91 Eng. Rep. 104 (1703).

159. Kingston v. Preston, 2 Doug. 689, 99 Eng. Rep. 437 (1773).

160. Stoljar, *supra* note 155, at 238.

161. Jones v. Barkley, 2 Doug. 684, 99 Eng. Rep. 434 (1781) (assignment of equity of redemption).

162. Morton v. Lamb, 7 T.R. 125, 129, 101 Eng. Rep. 890, 892 (1797).

163. Boone v. Eyre, 1 H. Bl. 273n., 126 Eng. Rep. 160 (1777). Mansfield recognized contracts for sales of slaves in America as enforceable, but he ordered the discharge of a slave, who was brought to England by his owner and resisted being forced to leave with his owner. Somerset v. Stewart, Lofft 1, 98 Eng. Rep. 499 (1772).

164. Duke of St. Albans v. Shore, 1 H. Bl. 270, 126 Eng. Rep. 158 (1789) (action by duke for penalty in agreement for defendant's failure to purchase).

165. 1 Wms. Saund. 320, 85 Eng. Rep. 450n. Stoljar suggested a pattern in the cases preferable to Sjt. Williams: (1) executory sales were dependent (and concurrent as to performatory order): *Kingston v. Preston;* (2) dependent if judged by the whole performance seller owed: *Duke of St. Albans v. Shore;* (3) Promises are independent when contract executed and no longer executory: *Boone v. Eyre. See* Stoljar, *supra* note 155, at 244.

166. Stoljar, *supra* note 155, at 245–251 (The term versus condition approach obscured the fact that all promissory terms were conditional, some requiring strict fulfillment and others having their effects adjusted. *Id* at 251.).

167. *Id.* at 244.

168. This rule was codified in the English Sale of Goods Act of 1893, sects. 11 and 62. *See* Stoljar, *Conditions, Warranties and Descriptions of Quality in Sales of Goods* (pt. 1), 15 MOD. L. REV. 425, 425–426, 430–431 (1952) (In 16th century express warranty of quality seen as collateral to contract's principal purpose of transfer of title.).

169. Poulton v. Lattimore, 9 B & C 259, 109 Eng. Rep. 96 (1829); Young v. Cole, 3 Bing. 724, 132 Eng. Rep. 589 (1837); Dawson v. Collis, 10 C.B. 523, 530, 138 Eng. Rep. 208, 210 (1851).

170. An unfortunate nineteenth English rule developed that a descriptive statement as to quality about unascertained goods was a condition but a sale of a specific good was a warranty, the latter not permitting rejection or rescission. *See* Stoljar, *Conditions, Warranties and Descriptions of Quality in Sales of Goods* (pt. 2), 16 MOD. L. REV. 174, 184 (1953).

CHAPTER 5

AMERICAN COLONIES TO YOUNG REPUBLIC (1600s–1800)

This chapter concerns American legal development from colonial settlement to 1800. The conclusions drawn here are based on comparatively sparse evidence due to the paucity of archival work done on this period. Although colonial settlement commenced in the modern post-*Slade's Case* period, seventeenth century colonial law was not in that modern mold because of the adaptations needed to the new environment. The story of the first century after settlement is a compressed parallel to the 500 year development of the English common law of contract from a local, status-based law of exchange, which was laden with community regulation, to a modern theory of contract. By the end of the second quarter of the eighteenth century, however, American contract law had evolved to a state roughly parallel with contemporary English law, at least in the colonial commercial centers.

Development of Colonial Legal System

In the early part of the twentieth century some writers presented a "frontier thesis" of colonial legal history. Under that view, a primitive law of equity based on custom and God's law was administered with little reference to the English common law throughout the seventeenth century. This theory goes on that there was a continued absence of the sophisticated formalities of the common law during the first half of the eighteenth century in the more homogeneous colonies, such as Massachusetts, though by then more heterogeneous states like New York had begun to integrate the common law.[1] Goebel provided a generally accepted refutation of the frontier thesis.[2] His conclusion was that seventeenth century New England settlers were former English commoners who were more familiar with the local English manorial and borough law than they were with the common law of Westminster, and they adapted that local English law to their new circumstances. In particular Goebel saw similarities in the Plymouth colony with English borough courts' leet jurisdiction.[3] This pattern varied in an early commercial colony like New York where the influence of law merchant was felt;[4] in the southern colonies, the common law was integrated earlier because the settlers were gentry who were more familiar with the common law.

Seventeenth century colonial law tended to be defensive, emphasizing the security of the colony more than the economic rights of the individual. Thus licensing for such quasi-public occupations as a ferryman or a miller excluded competitors, and better informed persons were restricted in their opportunities to take advantage of the unsophisticated. These monopolistic, anti-entrepreneurial regulations emphasized stability over economic growth.[5] Before the mid-seventeenth century, colonies were promulgating codes as a complete statement of their law. Written rules of conduct were not novel to the early colonists since the religious communities were accustomed to living by the Bible and there was a practice in England of committing customary borough law to writing.[6]

The alternative to a code was a full-blown common law system, but this was not practical since there were not the lawyers available to administer that technical body of law. The lack of a lawyerly class was consistent with the colonists' anti-lawyer sentiment. The Interregnum had fueled resentment against the arcane expertise and unethical behavior of lawyers, and religious leaders in the colonies reflected that attitude; witness Cotton Mather's condemnation of advocates who "bolster out a bad case by quirks of wits, and tricks and quillets of law." Indeed, the early colonial fusion of religious and legal ideas were an inspiration to Interregnum reformers.[7] Colonies passed statutes to restrict the work of lawyers who were "to the greate prejudice and charge of the inhabitants of this colony."[8] The opposition to lawyers and the technicalities of the common law made arbitration, that ancient progenitor of private contract, an appealing forum for adjudication of disputes. Arbitration was especially popular in New York where there was an established Dutch arbitration tradition before the English arrived.[9]

As a consequence of the absence of lawyers, seventeenth century judges were necessarily laymen. County courts and appellate courts were established, and in Massachusetts, appeals of magistrate's cases under 40 shillings were *de novo.*[10] Juries were used early on and were seen as a popular control of seventeenth century judicial abuses and crown prerogative abuses remembered from seventeenth century England. There were ineffective judicial controls of juries in Massachusetts since they could ignore jury instructions without fear of reversal, and settlers refused to compel a juror to a verdict against his Puritan conscience;

however, at least by the end of the century, judges were asserting themselves in New York.[11] Although the records indicate these lay judges were applying English law to the best of their ability,[12] not much law could develop in the seventeenth century with lay judges and uncontrolled juries giving general verdicts. The change would come as lawyers came to the colonies in the early eighteenth century and took control of trials.

As the colonies became more commercial and heterogeneous during the last quarter of the seventeenth century, there was a need for lawyers and licensing statutes were passed.[13] At first these lawyers were planters or merchants who practiced law only on a part-time basis because of the paucity of cases, but by the 1690s there was adequate business for a full-time practice. Once these opportunities became apparent, English lawyers began to move to the colonies. Nicholas Trott came to South Carolina in 1699 and was soon chief justice of its highest court, and in 1712 Massachusetts appointed Chief Justice Lynde, who was that state's first professional lawyer.[14] The attributes of a legal profession were now appearing with trained full-time lawyers and the wider availability of English law books. Since the growing merchant class was particularly in need of legal representation, it is not surprising that the most commonly available law books dealt with contract law.[15] Since the Southern colonies retained closer ties with England, more of their young lawyers studied at the English inns of court; indeed, South Carolina required it for admission.[16] The emerging profession of lawyers trained in the common law set about replacing the English borough law of the seventeenth century with the more sophisticated common law of Westminster Hall.[17] During the first quarter of the eighteenth century, there was a greater inclination to apply the English common law to the increasing amount of litigation generated by a burgeoning, more heterogeneous, population, unified now more by the tradition of the common law than by commonly held religious tenets. Colonial statutes were passed adopting the English common law.[18]

Colonial Integration of English Common Law of Contract

During the eighteenth century, American law became increasingly similar to English law as the upsurge of commerce in the colonies made the two economies more alike. It was only natural that there would be a borrowing from England's legal experience as a trading nation.[19] That is not to say that American law became identical with English law; instead there was an adaptation of the melange of seventeenth century colonial customary law and English borough law to the more sophisticated and formal common law of Westminster Hall.[20] Accordingly, a 1732 Maryland act provided "where the acts and usages of the province are silent the rule of adjudicature is to be according to the laws and statutes and reasonable customs of England, as used and practiced within the province."[21] Although colonial common law did not become identical with the English common law, it became substantially the same before the mid-eighteenth century. This assimilation of the common law by about the 1740s went hand-in-glove with the establishment of a trained lawyerly class, and as commercial interests recognized the need for lawyers, anti-lawyer sentiment receded.[22]

Lawyers began to assert themselves in trials by jury, though there was not as much judicial control of juries as there was in England because trial by jury was seen as a popular protection against judicial and crown abuses.[23] Trial by jury was viewed as a balance against abuses by crown surrogates, and consequently there was opposition to the prerogative of the royalist court of chancery sitting without a jury,[24] though colonists like the Puritans were not against equitable law as such since they assumed all law to be equitable. The latitude of jurors was restricted, however, as the appearance of trained lawyers in trials became commonplace. Lawyers began to dominate *voir dire,* and they injected a greater complexity into the rules of pleading and of evidence.

The increased formality in pleading altered the seventeenth century colonial practice of simply bringing an action on the case without any further characterization.[25] Before the mid-eighteenth century, it had become necessary to follow the English practice of specifying whether the action was *Indebitatus Assumpsit,* Special Assumpsit or Debt.[26] The colonies had reenacted the English experience of first allowing the enforcement of promises under the action of case before evolving into the more sophisticated employment of Assumpsit. By the mid-eighteenth century, Assumpsit was also being used for both contracts implied in fact and in law, and decisions rendered after Blackstone's COMMENTARIES were available in the colonies in the early 1770s perpetuated Blackstone's incorrect lumping together of *quantum meruit,* a contract implied-in-fact, with the quasi-contractual count of money had and received, a contract implied-in-law.[27] In actions for a fixed sum, colonial lawyers followed the English practice of joining in the declaration an *indebitatus assumpsit* count for a fixed sum and a *quantum meruit* count for a reasonable sum, in the event the fixed sum was not provable.[28]

The use of *indebitatus assumpsit* on an informal agreement paralleled the contemporary English practice before the mid-eighteenth century. Formal contracts were also arranged along English lines through the use of sealed covenants and sealed conditional bonds, and, perhaps because of the inadequate control of colonial juries, these sealed promises may have been utilized more frequently in America than in England.[29] Merchant-creditors preferred sealed obligations for several reasons: one, the burden of proof was satisfied by producing the document; two, default judgments were common since there were few viable defenses;[30] three, the ease of proof and the default rate avoided delays; and four, juries had no discretion to alter the damages prescribed. If the penal amount in a conditional bond was in excess of the defendant's just damages, the defendant had the opportunity, also by then available in England, of applying to chancery to have the penalty cancelled or "chancered".[31]

During the second quarter of the eighteenth century, commercial law was developing as an alliance formed between the merchant class and the legal profession;[32] this alliance would further intensify during the nineteenth century. In New York this process gained added momentum with the 1733 appointment of James DeLancey, a representative of commercial interests, as Chief Justice of New York's Supreme Court; he presided until 1760. Mercantile customs were read into contracts, e.g., merchants' custom regarding interest on an account, the custom of indebtedness in the whaling industry and whether a deviation cancelled a marine insurance contract.[33] Specialized vice-admiralty courts, where there was no trial by jury, were set up in nine of the colonies by 1763 to hear the increasing number of trade and maritime cases.[34]

The increase in commercial activity caused the bulk of the legal work performed by the legal profession to be debt collection for merchants.[35] Due to the combination of commercial influence and conservative moral values, creditors were well protected by measures as severe as imprisonment until the debt was paid and there were stringent execution procedures.[36] There was little legislation for debtor relief during the early colonial period, and later attempts in Massachusetts to enact insolvency statutes in 1756 and 1757 were disallowed by the English Privy Council, but New York did enact a diluted bankruptcy statute in 1755.[37]

With the growth in commerce, promissory notes increased because of the shortage of currency. Commercial paper could be payable in commodities, as tobacco, corn and beaver skins, rather than in money. The negotiation of notes and the assignment of contracts was recognized in the seventeenth century, earlier than in common law England, because the colonists brought the customs of the court staple and mayoral courts with them.[38] Commercial paper needed to be drawn according to the custom of merchants, but the drawer need not be a merchant. Then a conservatism set in in the first decade of the eighteenth century with the arrival of English lawyers under the spell of the English Chief Justice Holt. These lawyers caused a retardation of liberal colonial customs; nevertheless, about half of the colonies reiterated the right of negotiation by statute during the first generation of the eighteenth century.[39]

The influence of commercial interests on colonial contract law should not mislead one into concluding that there was a wholesale abandonment of traditional seventeenth century colonial law. This was especially true of the lingering eighteenth century protection of the status of the consumer. The English doctrine of *caveat emptor* did not mesh well with the ethical values of colonial communities; in fact, *caveat emptor* was occasionally rejected in sales disputes before the nineteenth century, as by refusing the defense of the absence of an express warranty in preference for a loose notion of merchantability.[40] The occasional application of this vague notion of an implied warranty of merchantability preceded its adoption in England by fifty years; those few more regularized decisions that a sound price gave rise to an implied warranty were later on in the 1790s and consistently then only in the Carolinas.[41] As to an express warranty of quality, contractual actions for breach thereof were upheld more than a decade before Mansfield did the same.[42] And sellers were found liable in fraud without proof of scienter at the time of the sale if subsequent intent was established.[43]

Continuity of American Contract Law: 1750 to 1800

The original royal charters in the seventeenth century issued the injunction that colonial law was not to be "contrarie or repugnant to the law of England." Although there would be dissenting voices later, this was carried forward soon after the American Revolution when the former colonies passed reception legislation adopting the English common law as the applicable law of these new governments. Was the intervening 150 years of colonial contract law relevant to the story of the common law of the young Republic? One writer has argued that it is pointless to speak of an American law before 1800[44] because law reports were not published before 1789.[45] If the absence of case reports meant there was no recognized and followed judicial law, then one would be forced to conclude that there was no English common law in Bracton's day since year book reports did not commence until several generations later—a proposition which no one champions. Horwitz argued that colonial law is irrelevant due to both the changed socio-economic circumstances precipitated by the Revolution and the subsequent lessening of the jury's power as an alliance formed between the bench and commerce.[46] Under this "transformation" theory, contract law moved from a colonial law, which was ethical and defensive in emphasizing the security of the community, to a nineteenth century law of expansive change for the promotion of economic growth.[47] This view does not take into account the maturity of colonial law and commerce by the 1740s nor does it recognize that by then there had been a curtailment of the power of the jury since an alliance had already been forged between the bench and commerce.[48] A study of the caselaw of the young republic indicates that, to the contrary, judicial reasoning was not being made in a vacuum—advanced colonial commercial law was relevant and applied. Modifications of the common law necessitated by changed circumstances after the Revolution were judicial extensions of the theory embodied in the colonial admixture of customary law and English common law.

Colonial law is the genesis of American law and it was not forgotten at the formation of the Republic. The reception clause in the Massachusetts Constitution of 1780 provided for the continuation of prior laws that had been "adopted, used and approved" during colonial days.[49] This was construed to include the English common law and colonial modifications made because of the Commonwealth's "new state and condition".[50] Colonial laws were still being applied in the caselaw after the Revolution.[51] In 1813 Pennsylvania Chief Justice Tilghman declared:

> Every country has its Common Law. Ours is composed partly of the Common Law of England and partly of our own usages. When our ancestors emigrated from England, they took with them such of the English principles as were convenient for the situation in which they were about to place themselves. It required time and experience to ascertain how much of the English law would be suitable to this country. By degrees, as circumstances demanded, we adopted the English usages, or substituted others better suited to our wants, till at length before the Revolution we had formed a system of our own.[52]

American colonial law was heavily anglicized by the mid-eighteenth century and was not fundamentally different in the early nineteenth century;[53] the patterns set by late colonial days continued into the republican period.[54] Later changes would occur by the elaboration of contract rules and the full development of the will theory in the nineteenth century in the United States and England. The later transformation of the economy and law in the nineteenth century as a result of the pressures of heightened capitalism would occur contemporaneously in the United States and England.[55]

Returning to the transformation argument that, unlike nineteenth century law, colonial contract law was ethical and defensive, the details supporting that conclusion are that colonial contract law did not enforce executory contracts, that expectation damages were not granted in a premarket economy and that contract enforcement was generally based on equitable principles.[56] This argument is probably descriptive of the settlement phase in the seventeenth century, but it is not an apt characterization of the state of colonial law after the upsurge of commerce and the arrival of lawyers in the early eighteenth century. Starting with the executory contract point, the argument runs that the plaintiff could not recover in Assumpsit unless the plaintiff had performed his part and that executory contracts were unenforceable in England and America until the 1790s.[57] Blackstone is cited as authority,[58] but Blackstone's treatment was incorrectly based on a dated view of contract as an exchange of property rather than on the doctrine for promissory liability it had become. In fact there are many examples of the enforcement of executory contracts by the sixteenth century in England and by the late seventeenth century in America.

One of the earliest examples of common law enforcement of executory contracts was on sixteenth century mutual promises in Special Assumpsit, and it was established in 1618 that an executory promise could not be revoked by a promisor.[59] In the United States in 1795 Zephaniah Swift, America's first treatise writer, cited a 1615 English case in support of the established practice of the enforceability of mutual promises so intended.[60] Also by the sixteenth century, sales contracts sued on in Assumpsit in lieu of Debt were enforceable, without the seller's delivery of the goods, through the passing of property fiction.[61] In the colonies, executory contracts were enforced as early as the second half of the seventeenth century.[62] Common instances of colonial enforcement of executory promises can be found in the great volume of actions in Covenant and in Debt on conditional bonds. Furthermore, the argument that colonial executory promises were unenforceable fails to appreciate the effect of the rules governing the dependency of promises since, as Swift noted, the agreement could be enforced without performance if that was the intent.[63] Lastly, passage of the Statute of Frauds was implicit recognition that executory contracts were being enforced; it limited enforceability of certain executory contracts unless there was a writing, and it was not interpreted to bar enforcement of partially executed oral contracts pursuant to the part performance exception.

The second leg of the transformation argument, that there was a primitive, pre-market colonial law of contract based on the exchange of property, is that the rise of the executory contract did not begin until expectation damages for the loss of the bargain were first allowed in the 1790s in England and the United States.[64] The theory is that juries' ethical opposition to speculative contracts caused verdicts to be anti-entrepreneurial and that the need for protection of expectation would have been minimal anyway in a pre-market economy where contracts for future delivery were rare.[65] The argument continues that the prevailing title theory of exchange was not concerned with future monetary return, and so no recovery was given for loss of the bargain.[66] Contrary to these conclusions, the eighteenth century colonial economy was not pre-market in the commercial centers and expectation damages were recoverable. By the first half of the eighteenth century, the English economy was sophisticated with a complex system of shipping, insurance on cargoes and finance, and the American colonies were actively involved in trade with England. By mid-century England's trade with all its colonies exceeded its trade with Europe. The degree of colonial commercial activity is evidenced in the eighteenth century judicial system by the increased volume of commercial cases in the colonial courts, a decreasing percentage of which were heard by juries, and by the establishment of vice-admiralty courts.[67] Influential judges like Mansfield in England and DeLancey in New York were sympathetic to commercial interests.

As to whether expectation damages were awarded, specific performance was a means of protecting the expectation interest, and specific performance was granted by Chancery long before the American Revolution.[68] Likewise the penal bond in conditioned bonds, which were frequently used during the colonial period, secured actual performance and could be drafted to cover more than the exchange value. Moreover, in Assumpsit, loss of the bargain was obtainable since the sixteenth century.[69] In English Assumpsit cases for sales of stock and sales of goods, damages were the difference between the contract price and the market price at the delivery date, and in gambling contracts the plaintiff could recover the amount of the wager and not just the stake.[70] In the first reported American cases awarding expectation damages around 1790, the expectation interest was protected as a matter of long standing practice without any suggestion it was an innovation.[71] Furthermore, the argument that expectation damages were not protected before the Revolution fails to recognize the development of dependency of covenants rules during the seventeenth and eighteenth centuries, which rules would have had no purpose if contract damages were limited to the restitution of the value transferred by the plaintiff.[72]

The fourth leg of the argument for a primitive colonial law of contract is that there was an equitable conception of eighteenth century contract law. Under this theory, because of inadequate judicial controls, juries were free to apply an ethical, customary law of the community.[73] Thus, if consideration was found inadequate, juries would lessen the damages and specific performance would also be refused in Equity. The theory continues that payment of a sound price would give rise to an implied warranty of quality.[74] A fundamental underpinning of this equitable theory of contract is that relief was available when the consideration was inadequate, but a study of the evidence does not bear this conclusion out. After a brief refusal by the English Chancellor Hardwicke to grant specific performance because of inadequacy in the mid-eighteenth century, English and American courts required a gross inequality or conduct suggesting fraud before specific performance was refused. Likewise, there were no cases of courts granting a rescission because of inadequate consideration;[75] if the consideration was inadequate, it was easier for courts to assist by refusing to act, as by not decreeing specific performance, than to take the active role of granting a rescission. And, regarding the attempt to point to the "chancering" of the penalty on conditioned bonds, that has to do with the issue in chancery of excessive damages and not inadequate consideration or jury discretion. As to the jury's role in determining damages in a contract with inadequate consideration, juries naturally did equity in assessment of damages at their discretion, but that unregulated determination of fact should not be confused with what the legal requirements of the doctrine of consideration were. The eighteenth century was not a golden age of equity in the common law but was, for most of it, simply prior to the time that effective jury controls consistently applied.[76] What equitable relief juries did achieve by lessening damages was waning by the mid-eighteenth century in the colonies as the alliance of merchants and the bench began a curtailment of the influence, and even the use, of trial by jury.[77]

Lastly, was there a sound price doctrine in the eighteenth century protecting a buyer of defective goods? There was no such doctrine in England or America before the Revolution, though Mansfield suggested there perhaps could be one if there was scienter. The first sound price cases in the United States were in the 1790s, primarily in the Carolinas, and the authority was civilian-influenced treatises since there was no such prior caselaw.[78] It should be reiterated, however, that, outside private Assumpsit actions, there was some evidence of a continuation of the occasional seventeenth century community regulatory practice of affording relief for the purchase of unfit goods.

As a final thought on the matter of the continuity of American contract law from colonial days to the republican period, it must be acknowledged that, although the legal doctrine was in place for the enforcement of executory contracts and the recovery of expectation damages by the eighteenth century, commercial practices were not as planning-oriented in either the colonies or England as they would become in the nineteenth century when there would be an increased division of labor and a greater vulnerability to market swings. Since market forces were not as strong as they would be later, it is probably true that the paradigmatic mode of exchange in the mid-eighteenth century was a partially executed contract, and there was therefore not a great need then for enforcement of executory contracts or the recovery of expectation damages. It also seems correct to say that juries had wide discretion in determining the amount of damages since there was minimal effective control over damage determinations until the mid-nineteenth century. In addition, the judicial process was no doubt more equitable in outlying rural communities removed from the colonial commercial centers. Evidence was overlooked or ignored, however, in the interest of developing the unitary, contextual construct that continuity was lacking between the law of the colonial and republican periods. The unitary construct emphasizes the dearth of reports of actions on executory contracts for the recovery of expectation damages and overlooks the actual reported cases, albeit not numerous, permitting such actions. The dearth of cases discussing detailed contract principles was due to both the paucity of transactions generated by the economy then and to the lack of control of juries until the late eighteenth century.[79]

As is not infrequently the case in the development of the common law, it was not quite all one way or the other; the story of the development of the common law has a doctrinal and a contextual side. The common law developed as a self-contained intellectual system, and its nature was more autonomous then than it is today. It was not necessary for a particular socio-economic state of affairs to exist before a rule could develop.[80] A principle of law could evolve if the inner logic of the common law of contract either permitted it or ineluctably pushed it along a particular path—whether or not that principle was a reflection of the real world; the survival of the doctrine of consideration, an impediment in commercial cases, is a good example of the doctrinal independence of the common law.

Conclusion

During the seventeenth century settlement phase, colonial contract law consisted of an amalgam of community ethics, English borough law and a generalized notion of common law contract principles under the action of case in a system administered by non-lawyers. As trade increased by about 1700, lawyers began to arrive to represent commercial interests, and thereafter colonial contract law began to become more like the law of Westminster Hall. The colonial legal community was under the influence of Enlightenment ideas and followed Mansfield's lead in injecting greater rationality into the common law. By the second quarter of the eighteenth century an alliance had formed between commercial and legal interests, and a commercial law was taking shape. The post-Revolutionary period was thus not the beginning of a modern commercial law, and indeed the Revolution retarded further development for a generation. Both the alliance and the commercial emphasis would, however, revive and be carried forward throughout much of the nineteenth century. Moreover, although the executory contract was not the paradigmatic transaction at the middle of the eighteenth century, the contract doctrine was in place for the recovery of expectation damages on those few executory contracts appearing in the courts for enforcement. By the 1740s the colonial contract law developed in American commercial centers was closely parallel to that in England, subject to the retention of some adaptations to the new environment. The conditions were in place for the nineteenth century elaboration of contract rules and the implementation of the will theory in the United States and England.

Notes

1. Reinsch, *The English Common Law in the Early American Colonies* in 1 SELECT ESSAYS IN ANGLO-AMERICAN LEGAL HISTORY 367, 380, 390 (1907); R. POUND, SPIRIT OF THE COMMON LAW 112 (1912).

2. Goebel, *King's Law and Local Custom in Seventeenth Century New England,* 31 COLUM. L. REV. 416 (1931); *see also* D. ALLEN, IN ENGLISH WAYS 205–209 (Chapel Hill: 1981) (English local customary practices brought to New England.); *cf.* Van Ness v. Packard, 2 Peters (U.S.) Rep. 137, 144 (1829) (Joseph Story made unsupported claim that common law was in place from time of settlement.).

3. Leet jurisdiction had governmental and judicial functions and employed trial by jury. In the Middle Ages, court leet became the governing body in some boroughs. Although court leet jurisdiction was still widespread in 17th century, it was in decay. 1 W. HOLDSWORTH, A HISTORY OF ENGLISH LAW 134–137 (London: 7th ed. 1956).

4. *See generally* R. MORRIS, SELECT CASES OF THE MAYOR'S COURT OF NEW YORK CITY (1674–1784) (Wash. D.C. 1935) (law merchant of London mayor's court influenced New York's mayor's court).

5. W. NELSON, AMERICANIZATION OF THE COMMON LAW 50–56 (Cambridge, Mass. 1975). The developing colonial system mirrored English law in Medieval period when protection of status was preferred to *caveat emptor.*

6. Goebel, *supra* note 2, at 429–435 (Plymouth code resembled Winchester custumal and Liverpool Town Books.).

7. COLONIAL JUSTICE IN WESTERN MASSACHUSETTS (1639–1702): THE PYNCHON COURT RECORD 199 (ed. J. Smith, 1960) (hereinafter cited as PYNCHON RECORD); Prest, *The English Bar 1550–1700,* in LAWYERS IN EARLY MODERN EUROPE AND AMERICA 73–74 (ed. W. Prest, N.Y. 1981) (Lawyers were guilty of ambidextry, breach of confidentiality and failure to appear at hearings.); N. MATTHEWS, WILLIAM SHEPPARD, CROMWELL'S LAW REFORMER 146, 172–174 (Cambridge: 1984) (Mass. Bay colony, a godly commonwealth based loosely on common law, was an inspiration to Sheppard.)

8. 1658 Virginia Statute (1 Hening 419) cited in READINGS IN THE HISTORY OF THE AMERICAN LEGAL PROFESSION 43 (ed. D. Nolan, Indianapolis: 1980) (hereinafter cited as READINGS IN PROFESSION) (In 1640s Mass. and Va. barred lawyers from taking fees. *Id.* at 31, 42.).

9. R. MORRIS, STUDIES IN THE HISTORY OF AMERICAN LAW 60–61 (Phila. 2d ed. 1959); *see* D. KONIG, LAW AND SOCIETY IN PURITAN MASSACHUSETTS (ESSEX COUNTY, 1629–1692) 108–116 (Chapel Hill: 1979) (Disenchantment with arbitration in Mass. by 1670s because: awards not observed, outsiders discriminated against, and a preference growing for the precision of legal forms.). *See* MAX WEBER ON LAW IN ECONOMY AND SOCIETY 104 (Cambridge, Mass. M. Rheinstein ed. 1954) (The voluntary submission to a verdict by arbitration by kinship groups "is not only the source of all procedural law but also the point of departure to which the oldest contracts of private law can, very broadly speaking, be traced.").

10. W. NELSON, *supra* note 5, at 15–16 (appeals to English Privy Council possible but rare due to obstacles inspired by colonists).

11. *See Id.* at 20–28; *cf.* Rosen, *The Supreme Court of Judicature of Colonial New York: Civil Practice in Transition, 1691–1760,* 5 LAW AND HISTORY REVIEW 213, 244–245 (1987) (Of 29 cases going to jury in 1694–1696, judges interfered in fact finding of 10.).

12. Woodbine, Book Review, 43 YALE L.J. 1036, 1036–1038 (1934) (book review of publication of 1671–1680 Suffolk County, Mass. court records); PYNCHON RECORD (lay magistrates hearing actions in Debt and in action on the case).

13. *See* Day, *Lawyers in Colonial Maryland, 1660–1715,* 17 AM. J. LEG. HIST. 145, 146 (Short-lived 1674 Md. act gave courts discretion to admit "honest and able Attorneys."); *see also* READINGS IN PROFESSION, *supra* note 8, at 43–44 (In 1680 Va. required license from governor to avoid incompetence.).

14. L. FRIEDMAN, A HISTORY OF AMERICAN LAW 85 (N.Y. 1973); Reinsch, *supra* note 1, at 385 (common law authority cited more frequently thereafter). The colonists who settled northern colonies like Massachusetts were commoners and dissidents critical of English system generally and were more anti-lawyer than the gentry who settled the southern colonies for profit.

15. *See* Day, *supra* note 13, at 148–149, 153 (Coke's INSTITUTES most popular); *see also* Eaton, *A Mirror of the Southern Colonial Lawyer,* 8 WM. & MARY Q. 520, 521–526 (1951). W. Blackstone's COMMENTARIES (1765–1769), first published in America in 1771–1772, were for a later generation of lawyers.

16. R. MORRIS, *supra* note 9, at viii (1721 S.C. statute required 5 years study at inns.). The absence of a bifurcated profession in America was in part due to opposition to English barristers' elitism and due to the lack of inns and also presumably because of the London inns' opposition to a second legal center. M. HOEFLICH, THE GLADSOME LIGHT OF JURISPRUDENCE 4 (Westport, Conn. 1988). Surely the dearth of lawyers made it infeasible to have 2 lawyers on each side of a case.

17. *See* Chafee, *Colonial Courts and the Common Law,* in ESSAYS IN THE HISTORY OF EARLY AMERICAN LAW 53, 78–82 (ed. D. Flaherty, Chapel Hill: 1969) (There may have been more observance of common law in seventeenth century than Goebel supposed.).

18. Smith, *New Light on the Doctrine of Judicial Precedent in Early America: 1607–1776* in LEGAL THOUGHT IN THE U.S.A. UNDER CONTEMPORARY PRESSURES 9–39 (ed. J. Hazard, Brussels: 1970); Rhode Island adopted the whole of the common law and statutes in 1700. CHARTER AND ACTS OF RHODE ISLAND (1719) (Riders reprint 45 (1895)); in 1712 South Carolina adopted common law and statutes selected by Trott, C.J.; N.C. followed suit in 1715; N.Y. adopted the common law and also pre–1691 English statutes; D. KONIG, *supra* note 9, at 108 (references to the Bible in petitions being replaced by positive law); Rosen, *supra* note 11, at 222–223 (New York's population grew 1693 to 1756 from 15,000 to 97,000 and civil suits increased twelve-fold.).

19. H. JOHNSON, ESSAYS ON NEW YORK COLONIAL LEGAL HISTORY 193–195 (Westport: 1981); L. FRIEDMAN, AMERICAN LAW 41 (N.Y. 1984).

20. R. MORRIS, *supra* note 9, at 11 (Citing ABRIDGEMENT OF THE LAWS IN FORCE AND USE IN HER MAJESTY'S PLANTATIONS (London: 1704), which indicated a difference.); *see* Poor v. Greene, 5 Binney 554 (1813).

21. Cited in Reinsch, *supra* note 1, at 402–403.

22. L. FRIEDMAN, *supra* note 14 at 81–84; *see* Klein, *The Rise of the New York*

Bar: The Legal Career of W. Livingston, 15 WM. & MARY Q. 334, 335 (1958) (Transformation of colonial law coincided with business expansion.). By the 1760s lawyers were powerful and feared by the Crown's surrogates. McKirdy, *Before the Storm: The Working Lawyer in Pre-Revolutionary Massachusetts,* 11 SUFFOLK U. LAW REV. 46, 47, 59–60 (1976).

23. W. NELSON, *supra* note 5, at 17–22; *cf.* Rosen, *supra* note 11, at 228–230 (decrease in civil jury trials by 1750s because of delays and use of bonds). As in England, parties to contract could not testify.

24. Katz, *The Politics of Law in Colonial America: Controversies Over Chancery Courts and Equity Law in the Eighteenth Century* in COLONIAL AMERICA: ESSAYS IN POLITICS AND SOCIAL DEVELOPMENT 401, 413–414 (ed. S. Katz, Boston: 2d ed. 1976) (First N.Y. chancery court was in 1683; crown-appointed governor acted as chancellor 1711 to Revolution; complaints about delays by 1770s.). Pa. was unique in unifying court at-law and equity.

25. *See* PYNCHON RECORD, *supra* note 7, at 164–165; R. MORRIS, *supra* note 9, at 50 (citing cases from last third of 17th century).

26. *See* W. NELSON, *supra* note 5, at 54–55, 201, citing: Glover v. LeTestue, Quincy 225 (Mass. 1770) (*Indebitatus assumpsit* lay only where Debt lay.), Parton v. Gray, Suffolk Superior Court, (Mass. 1761) (failure to plead precedent debt cause for abatement).

27. *See* Palfrey v. Palfrey (Mass. 1772) *reported in* W. CUSHING, NOTES OF CASES DECIDED IN THE SUPERIOR AND SUPREME JUDICIAL COURTS OF MASSACHUSETTS, 1772–1789 1–2, App. 1–7 (Harv. L. Sch. MS.) (uses quasi-contractual logic in discussing *quantum meruit*); *and see* 3 W. BLACKSTONE, COMMENTARIES* 158, 161–162 (1768) ("that are only implied in law. Which are such as reason and justice dictate").

28. *Cf.* M. HORWITZ, THE TRANSFORMATION OF AMERICAN LAW, 1780–1860, 171–172 (Cambridge, Mass. 1977) (a contradiction in joining an express contract action and an equitable action). Horwitz is erroneous here when *quantum meruit* was used correctly since *quantum meruit* was not an equitable action but was a contract implied-in-fact.

29. *See Id.* at 167–168 (bonds more common in America than England by mid–18th century); *see also* Rosen, *supra* note 11, at 232–235 (18th century increase in bonds and notes).

30. Chadwick v. Fowler, Berkshire Ct. of Common Pleas (Mass. 1766) (plea of mere payment without sealed acquittance not a defense), cited by W. NELSON, *supra* note 5, at 205; Rosen, *supra* note 11, at 228–230 (Defaults increased with use of bonds by 1750.).

31. Brooks v. Blanchard, Middlesex Ct. C.P. (Mass. 1760), cited by W. NELSON, *supra* note 5, at 61, 204.

32. Rosen, *supra* note 11, at 237, 240–242.

33. W. NELSON, *supra* note 5, at 59.

34. L. FRIEDMAN, *supra* note 14, at 45–46 (These pro crown courts sitting without juries were opposed by colonists); *cf.* Rosen, *supra* note 11, at 228–230 (Bench trials increased at common law due to futility of defending against sealed bonds.).

35. McKirdy, *supra* note 22, at 52–53; Eaton, *supra* note 15, at 524–525 (al-

though Patrick Henry's fame was in criminal law, debt collection occupied him more); Rosen, *supra* note 11, at 232.

36. *See* W. NELSON, *supra* note 5, at 41–45 (Mass. measures more stringent than common law remedies).

37. *Id.* at 43–44; *Rosen, supra* note 11, at 234 (1755 N.Y. Act allowed creditor to petition. 1730 Act released debtor after 3 months in prison if no property.).

38. Beutel, *Colonial Sources of the Negotiable Instruments Law of the United States*, 34 ILL. L. REV. 137, 137–142 (1939) (Assignment allowed by statute in Mass. in 1648 and Conn. in 1650, even before negotiation. Assignment, negotiation and negotiability appeared in the colonies well before it did in England. *Id.* at 145.).

39. *Id.* at 149–150.

40. Waddill v. Chamberlayne (Va. 1735), *reported in* 2 VA. COLONIAL DECISIONS B45 (R. Barton ed. 1909) (action on case in nature of a deceit for sale at a high price of slave who seller knew was ill); Baker v. Frobisher, Quincy 4 (Mass. 1762) (Seller had obligation to see that soap was merchantable.); *see* Simpson, *The Horwitz Thesis and the History of Contracts*, 46 U. CHI. L. REV. 533, 583–585 (1979) (though some colonial recognition of *caveat emptor*); *see also* M. HORWITZ, *supra* note 28, at 164–167 (Inadequate consideration would reduce damages.).

41. Simpson, *supra* note 40, at 583–585 (Sound price cases of 1790s seem based on English treatises rather than 1735 Va. and 1762 Mass. cases.).

42. *See* W. NELSON, *supra* note 5, at 195, n.68 (citing 3 Mass. cases between 1764 and 1768 involving warranties in sales and a warranty of a third party's credit).

43. *See Id.* (citing Taylor v. Fowler, Hamp. Superior Ct. (Mass. 1764)).

44. G. GILMORE, THE AGES OF AMERICAN LAW 8 (New Haven: 1977); *but cf.* H. JOHNSON, IMPORTED EIGHTEENTH-CENTURY LAW TREATISES IN AMERICAN LIBRARIES, 1700–1799 (Knoxville: 1978) (catalogue of extensive collections of English law books held by colonial lawyers).

45. E. KIRBY, REPORTS OF CASES ADJUDGED IN THE SUPERIOR COURT OF THE STATE OF CONNECTICUT FROM THE YEAR 1785, TO MAY 1788 (Litchfield: 1789); A. DALLAS, REPORTS OF CASES, RULED AND ADJUDGED IN THE COURTS OF PENNSYLVANIA, BEFORE AND SINCE THE REVOLUTION (Philadelphia: 1790).

46. M. HORWITZ, *supra* note 28, at 30, 266; *see* W. NELSON, *supra* note 5, at 5, 173–174; see also R. POUND, THE FORMATIVE ERA OF AMERICAN LAW 3–8 (Boston: 1938).

47. M. HORWITZ, *supra* note 28, at 173–185; W. NELSON, *supra* note 5, at 3–7; J. HURST, LAW AND THE CONDITIONS OF FREEDOM IN THE NINETEENTH CENTURY UNITED STATES 37 (Madison: 1956); *and see* P. ATIYAH, THE RISE AND FALL OF FREEDOM OF CONTRACT 142, 195, 199–200, 208–213 (Oxford: 1979). The colonial contract law details that Horwitz relies upon were exhumed by Nelson. Nelson's conclusions were based on archival research of Massachusetts courts that were, in the main, not reflective of practices in 18th century colonial commercial centers.

48. Simpson, *supra* note 40, at 542–561; Rosen, *supra* note 11, at 214, 237–247.

49. *See* W. NELSON, *supra* note 5, at 8 (citing Mass. Constitution of 1780,

Part II, ch. 6, art. 6); *see also* Simpson, *supra* note 40, at 542 (Eighteenth century and early nineteenth century contract law are essentially the same.).

50. Sackett v. Sackett, 8 Pick. 309, 316 (Mass. 1829) (Court gave weight to colonial laws. *Id.* at 316–321.).

51. Sackett v. Sackett, 8 Pick. 309, 316–321 (Mass. 1829). Mass. colonial assignment statute remained until at least 1814. 1705 Va. assignment statute continued in force long after Revolution. Beutel, *supra* note 38, at 149–150. Maryland assignee failed to recover in 1790 because he failed to comply with Md. Statute of 1763. Dorsey v. Barnes, 2 Harr. & M. 477 (Md. 1790). 1715 Pa. statute and pre-Revolution caselaw applied in 1789. McCullough v. Houston, 1 Dall. 441, 442–444 (Pa. 1789).

52. Poor v. Greene, 5 Binney 554 (Pa. 1813).

53. *See* Simpson, *supra* note 40, at 541–551, 600–601.

54. *See* Rosen, *supra* note 11, at 214–215 (N.Y. procedures the same before and after Revolution).

55. *Accord* Ferguson, *The Horwitz Thesis and Common Law Discourse in England,* 3 OXFORD J. LEG. STUDIES 34, 37–38 (1983) (There wasn't unique Americanization of the common law but an embourgeoisement of the law in America and England.).

56. For a careful study criticizing these points, *see generally* Simpson, *supra* note 40, (Thesis of primitive 18th century law followed by modern 19th century law after the Revolution not supported by evidence. *Id.* at 542.); *see also* Baker, Book Review, 43 MOD. L. REV. 467, 467–469 (1980).

57. W. NELSON, *supra* note 5, at 55–59 (Delivery of goods created liability. Defendant bound by virtue of consideration given); M. HORWITZ, *supra* note 28, at 161, 169, 173–175.

58. M. HORWITZ, *supra* note 28, at 162; *cf.* W. NELSON, *supra* note 5, at 60 (in the main customary more than promissory liability).

59. West v. Stowell, 2 Leo. 154, 74 Eng. Rep. 437 (1577); Strangborough v. Warner, 4 Leo. 3, 74 Eng. Rep. 686 (1589); Hurford v. Pile, Cro. Jac. 483 (1618).

60. Z. SWIFT, A SYSTEM OF THE LAWS OF THE STATE OF CONNECTICUT 375–376 (Windham: 1795). *But see* W. NELSON, *supra* note 5, at 58, wherein Nelson points to forms published later by T. Parsons, which specified that plaintiff must allege performance in an action of a minister suing for his salary. From this Nelson concludes that if there were such forms, then lawyers surely followed them, and therefore performance was a condition precedent not only for ministers but also for sellers of goods. This conclusion does not stand in the face of Swift's treatise and the caselaw.

61. Slade's Case, 4 Co. Rep. 92b (1602) is an archetypal example. *Cf.* Coggs v. Bernard, 2 Ld. Raym. 909, 919–920, 92 Eng. Rep. 107 (1703) (Dictum that Assumpsit covers either an act performed or a "future agreement.").

62. *See* PYNCHON RECORD, *supra* note 7, at 163–164 (e.g., failure to deliver gun according to bargain, failure to break ground according to bargain, failure to perform arbitration award); *see also* R. MORRIS, *supra* note 9, at 50 (citing cases between 1666 and 1682).

63. Simpson, *supra* note 40, at 547.

64. M. HORWITZ, *supra* note 28, at 171–177.

65. W. NELSON, *supra* note 5, at 55–56 (likewise gambling contracts illegal

in Mass.); M. HORWITZ, *supra* note 28, at 162–163, 169 (In pre-market economy, where a title theory of exchange was appropriate, there was little need for contracts to cover future developments.). Nevertheless, Nelson did recognize that a set customary price did not apply in Special Assumpsit even when the consideration was low. W. NELSON, *supra* n.5, at 61–62.

66. M. HORWITZ, *supra* note 28, at 162–163.

67. Rosen, *supra* note 11, at 232 (Decreased use of jury trial accrued to benefit of commerce. *Id.* at 230–232, 242.); L. FRIEDMAN, *supra* note 14, at 45 (heard without jury). The American shipbuilding industry was a good example of the developed state of the colonial economy: by 1770 1/3 of the British mercantile fleet was "colonial built." J. CLAPHAM, A CONCISE ECONOMIC HISTORY OF BRITAIN 235–236 (Cambridge: 1949) (Britain did not pursue a free trade policy with the colonies. *Id.* at 291.).

68. Fuller and Perdue, *The Reliance Interest in Contract Damages* (pt. 1), 46 YALE L.J. 52, 54 (1936) (Credit economy eliminates distinction between present and future goods. Expectation of future values becomes present property value. *Id.* at 58–59. Juristic development of enforcement of promises preceded economic need for it. *Id.* at 60).

69. Pykeryng v. Thurgoode, Spelman, ACCION SUR LE CASE 5 (1532); William Strate's Case, Spelman 295 (1528); Lucy v. Walwyn (K.B. 1561), discussed in Baker, *supra* note 56, at 468; Brigs Case, Palm. 364 (1623); J. BAKER, AN INTRODUCTION TO ENGLISH LEGAL HISTORY 284 (London, 2d ed. 1979); *but see* M. HORWITZ, *supra* note 28, at 162–163, wherein he relies on Blackstone's treatment of a contract as a transfer of property (an approach abandoned centuries before Blackstone) to conclude that expectation damages were unavailable in the eighteenth century.

70. Gardener v. Pullen & Phillips, 2 Vern. 394, 23 Eng. Rep. 853 (Ch. 1700); Cud v. Rutter, 1 P. Wms. 570, 24 Eng. Rep. 521 (Ch. 1719); Dutch v. Warren, 1 Strange 406, 93 Eng. Rep. 598 (K.B. 1720) (plaintiff forced to take stock, rather than recovery of amount paid, in a falling market in order to get the "benefit" of bargain); Horwitz cites Flureau v. Thornhill, 2 W. Bl. 1078, 96 Eng. Rep. 635 (1776) for proposition that 18th century courts refused to grant expectation damages. M. HORWITZ, *supra* note 28, at 162–163. However, Fuller and Perdue point out that Flureau represents an exception, continuing into this century, which barred expectation damages against a seller of land because of uncertainties about land values and the condition of a title. *See* Fuller and Perdue (pt. 2), *supra* note 68, at 377–378. Specific performance is of course impossible when there's defective title.

71. Marshall v. Campbell, 1 Yeates 35 (Pa. 1791) (cites 1700 English case of *Gardener v. Pullen & Phillips*); Lewis v. Carradan (Pa. 1786), unpublished decision quoted in *Marshall v. Campbell* (*Lewis* held damages based on difference of wheat's value in contract and at delivery.); Graves v. Graves, 1 Va. (1 Wash.) 1 (1790); *see* Simpson, *supra* note 40, at 558–561.

72. *See* Simpson, *supra* note 40, at 547, 552. If a covenant were found to be independent, then a plaintiff could recover damages without having performed, as for lost profits.

73. W. NELSON, *supra* note 5, at 20–29, 60. Horwitz follows Nelson's lead here. M. HORWITZ, *supra* note 28, at 161–172. Nelson's research on Massa-

chusetts courts largely concerns jurisdictions removed from the 18th century colonial commercial centers.

74. M. HORWITZ, *supra* note 28, at 164–168 (There was a "substantive doctrine of consideration".).

75. Simpson, *supra* note 40, at 561–566.

76. *See Id.* at 573–575; *see also* Baker, *supra* note 56, at 469 (mistake to see increased control over jury in the nineteenth century as a shift in doctrine). *See* Hamburger, *The Development of the Nineteenth Century Consensus Theory of Contract,* 7 LAW & HIST. REV. 241, 315–317, N. 171 (1989). (Cities 1663 English case of direction to jury on amount of damages. Also points out that cases of English Chancery overturning for unfairness were actually lack of competency cases, e.g., sailors and expectant heirs.) In 1768 a judge's instruction to the jury to award expectation damages in sale of goods was approved on review. Smee v. Huddleston (C.P. 1768) in J. SAYER, THE LAW OF DAMAGES 49–51 (London: 1770).

77. Rosen, *supra* note 11, at 228–230, 246–247 (In N.Y. in 1690, 87% of civil trials had juries, but that dropped to 53% of trials by 1750 because merchants increased the use of bonds and caused costly delays for defendants in jury trials.). Special statutory merchant juries and arbitration were also employed to avoid trial by jury.

78. Timrod v. Shoolbred, 1 S.C.L. (1 Bay) 324, 326 (S.C. 1793) (citing 1 J. POWELL, ESSAY UPON THE LAW OF CONTRACTS AND AGREEMENTS 150 (London: 1790), (Powell was under civilian influence.); State v. Gaellard, 2 S.C.L. (2 Bay) 11 (1793) (citing 17th century French lawyer Jean Domat); *see* Simpson, *supra* note 40, at 573–574, 580–584. Thus for a brief period after Revolution, contract law was more equitable regarding unfit goods than it had been before in a few states like the Carolinas, but sound price was soon clearly rejected in Seixas v. Woods, 2 Cai. R. 48 (N.Y. S. Ct. 1804).

79. Baker, *supra* note 56, at 468–469. *See* Oldham, *Reinterpretations of 18th-Century English Contract Theory: The View from Lord Mansfield's Trial Notes,* 76 GEO. L. J. 1949, 1979 (1988) (Although executory contracts were "not operative in practice", a consensual theory of contract had taken root earlier.). Throughout American history, there have been significant regional cultural differences reflected in the contract law of different jurisdictions, e.g., varying degree of acceptance of commercial law in rural and urban areas, the positions on slavery in the North and the South and the Carolinas' minority position rejecting *caveat emptor,* etc.

80. Capitalism has not been a decisive factor in the development of the law, as evidenced by the failure of English law to take on the degree of rationality found on the Continent despite similar capitalistic developments. The greater rationality on the Continent seems to come from the medieval intellectual interest in Roman law and thus it developed before capitalism. *See* Hamburger, *supra* note 76, at 243–247. MAX WEBER ON LAW IN ECONOMY AND SOCIETY 318 (M. Rheinstein ed. Cambridge, Mass. 1966).

CHAPTER 6

ELABORATION ACCOMMODATES ENTREPRENEUR (1800–1875)

This chapter covers the period from 1800 to 1875 when there was a further development of eighteenth century English and colonial commercial law. During this period, the courts elaborated the consideration contract into generalized principles to provide the predictability and flexibility business planners needed during an era of dramatic economic growth. Notions of free market, political economy and civilian consensus theory influenced analyses of principles behind the doctrine of consideration, and the result was the final fashioning of the "classical" rules of contract law known today. A value reflected in judicial decisions, which was consonant with the Romantic Age, was the attraction to individualism. Courts, and now legislatures, removed restrictive doctrine in order to provide space for entrepreneurial activities. By the mid-nineteenth century, judicial support for freedom of contract based on the will of the parties would reach its pinnacle. Private contract would become more significant than at any earlier period of legal history as a result of the role played by market orientation.

As late as 1800 there were still no rules of offer and acceptance, mistake, undue influence, or limitations on damages, and pleaders were still laboring under the technicalities of the forms of action. The paucity of specific contract rules, past the requirement that there be a breach of a promise supported by consideration, was due to the lack of discussion of the legal ramifications of facts left to the jury on the general issue of *non assumpsit.* The existence of the doctrine of consideration, the test for promissory liability in Assumpsit, precluded certain independent defenses; instead, the defendant would proffer evidence of a failure of consideration, and the question would be left generally to the jury. Earlier Mansfield had begun the process of elaborating contract law by prying open the lid on consideration, in attempting to rationalize its meaning, and, in managing the jury, he prompted discussions of how the law applied to facts formerly shrouded by the general issue. These facts were then converted into law; this process would continue during the nineteenth century. Juries were brought under control by modern rules of evidence, by judicial notice of mercantile usage, by motions to arrest and for new trial, and by jury instructions. These devices provided the machinery for producing detailed rules of contract law rather than leaving them generally to juries as questions of fact. Consideration was becoming fragmented into a number of sub-doctrines, and the new writers of contract treatises would help carry this subdivision process forward.

In terms of American contract development, not much happened during the first decade or so after the American Revolution because of the post-war depression and the legal elite's concentration of energies on developing the constitutional structure of law. As a consequence, there was a general tendency to borrow from the more advanced English legal and mercantile practices so that, ironically, American law became even more English than before the Revolution. Once creative energies were directed to private law, the issue of the reception of the English common law was belatedly discussed in an atmosphere of a general national Anglophobia. As is not uncommon after a revolution, the victorious young republicans were inclined to reject the solutions inspired by their former colonial masters; in its place there was a new political ideology of republicanism emphasizing the desire for a utopian reformation on the basis of common welfare, morality and earlier precommercial values.

American opinion of the common law depended upon whether one had Coke's view that the common law was above the monarchy or Blackstone's view that law was the will of the ruler. The common law won out[1] probably because of colonial traditions and the lack of a deep understanding of any other system, but, consistent with Americans' natural law ideals, the common law was not adopted if "necessity, convenience or public policy" dictated a deviation.[2] During the nineteenth century, English decisions rendered after the Revolution were looked to for guidance since England's more advanced commercial practices were transformed into law there earlier than the need was felt in the Republic.

The source of the common law for many American lawyers was Blackstone; his generalized overview of the common law made him more influential in the United States than in England because of the lack of the training advantages of the centralized English bar and courts. As discussed earlier, Blackstone's contract coverage was superficial, and yet, in oversimplifying the forms of action by saying that all contracts were either express or implied, he prepared lawyers for changes later in the century. The other eighteenth century English jurist who was more influential in the United States than in England was Mansfield. Later English judges, not as sympathetic to commerce, reacted against his policies, but Mansfield's approach fared better in the United States where influential judges such as Joseph Story were attracted to Mansfield's flexible adaptation of the common law of contract to the needs of commerce.[3]

Blackstone was the first writer to isolate general principles lurking in the confusion of the caselaw, and his example heralded the advent of treatises devoted to contract law. The first such contract work was written in England by John Powell in 1790.[4] His work borrowed heavily from Continental civil law with its advanced commercial law and its tradition of developing general principles. Indeed, for the century after about 1760 there was a significant common law interest in the commercial rules found in Roman and civil law. For the first time in the history of contract law, inspiration for innovation came from writers rather than judges.[5] Mansfieldian flexibility permitted the intrusion of civil law, and, since law merchant was *jus gentium* (the law of nations), courts rationalized the appropriateness of going outside the common law. The first American treatise devoted to contract law was the excellent book popular with lawyers written by Justice Story's son, William, in 1844.[6]

Offer and Acceptance

From the sixteenth century until the early nineteenth century, there was no concern about when a contract was formed—the parties either emerged from face-to-face negotiations with an agreement or they didn't.[7] There was little discussion in the cases about whether a promise was revocable but rather whether a promise was actionable short of reliance.[8] Agreements were treated as unilateral, and actionability was determined in terms of the rules of conditions and consideration.[9] As markets became more geographically extended in the eighteenth century, the use of consideration to determine if a promise was binding presented difficulties as agreements were formed by mail rather than face-to-face. The solution was the addition of the doctrine of offer and acceptance on top of the consideration requirement.

The inspiration for a solution to the problem of formation of agreements emerging other than from a face-to-face discussion was found in civil law. Powell picked up on the civilian Pothier's statement that an offer (*pollicitatio*) was not enforceable until there was a "concurrence of intention" by an acceptance.[10] But since this new type of promise for a promise was not a simultaneous exchange of one promise in consideration for the other promise, there was a consideration problem in transferring the civilian idea to the common law. The earlier offer was unsupported by consideration and the later acceptance was for a past consideration. This was the dilemma for the King's Bench in *Cooke v. Oxley* (1790).[11] Here the parties agreed that the buyer had until 4 P.M. to buy a quantity of tobacco. The buyer seasonably agreed to the purchase at 4 P.M., but the defendant then refused to sell. The justices analyzed the promises, separated in time, as a consideration problem and concluded that there was no agreement because there was not a simultaneous exchange of one promise in consideration for the other at 4 P.M. The court made no reference to the doctrine of offer and acceptance.

In *Kennedy v. Lee* (1817)[12] Chancellor Eldon employed the civilian offer and acceptance in the case of an offer accepted by mail to resolve *Cooke v. Oxley's* demand for simultaneity: "if, within a reasonable time of the acceptance being communicated, no variation has been made by either party in the terms of the offer so made and accepted, the acceptance must be taken as simultaneous with the offer." Eldon had transferred the application of consideration's requirement of simultaneity in mutual promises to a bilateral agreement governed by the doctrine of offer and acceptance. Eldon's approach might have provided a complete solution had there not been a concern that if the offeror normally had the right to notice of assent before being bound, then the offeree ought to have the reciprocal right to know that the offeror had assented. This was a point of concern in *Adams v. Lindsell* (1818),[13] wherein the King's Bench concluded that a specific point in time should be established for when a contract was formed by correspondence or else the communications could go on *ad infinitum*. The court selected the time of sending the acceptance as the effective date and found compliance with consideration's simultaneity requirement for mutual promises, as now translated into the notion of a bilateral "meeting of the minds", through the fiction that the offeror was making an offer "during every instant of time" up to the acceptance.[14] The *Adams v. Lindsell* rule that an acceptance was valid when sent was adopted in the United States[15] and was justified on grounds of necessity, certainty and the intent of the offeror.[16]

Adams v. Lindsell has not been without its critics. Because of the ruling later in the century that a revocation is valid when received, critics of *Adams v. Lindsell* have argued that there is no meeting of the minds if a revocation is in the mail before the acceptance is sent, and hence *Adams v. Lindsell* violates its own reciprocity goal in giving greater weight to the subjective intent of the offeree. Perhaps the advantage given the offeree is explained by the potential reliance of the offeree in making other commitments after accepting at the instigation of the offeror.[17] As a middle ground, it has been suggested that the acceptance ought to be actually received before it is treated as effective as of the date sent.[18] Civil law has answered some of these concerns both by not allowing an offer to be revoked for a statutory period, an approach consideration militates against, and by placing a burden on the offeree to mail properly and assure the acceptance arrives in time.[19]

Adams v. Lindsell answered the need of commercial interests for a rule for when a contract became enforceable when entered into by correspondence. The increase in manufacturing and the use of middlemen brought on the formation of more contracts by correspondence between distant parties; in *Adams v. Lindsell* a wool dealer mailed his offer to a woolen manufacturer. The decision provided predictability to business planners. Now the formation of the contract was an event in itself, altering rights thereafter and making the parties forward looking. Formation of a contract now required compliance with both the doctrine of offer and acceptance and that of consideration. Had *Eastwood v. Kenyon* (1840)[20] not struck down the validity of moral consideration, it is conceivable that the doctrine of offer and acceptance could have in time become the sole test for formation and liability. Since this did not happen, the two doctrines, which were developed for different reasons, have had an uneasy relationship.

The doctrine of offer and acceptance signalled a shift from the unilateral notion of a promise supported by consideration to the bilateral concept of whether, under the consensus or "will theory", the parties had a concurrence of intention.[21] Once a contract was viewed as a bilateral consensus formed by an offer and acceptance, attention was drawn to the anomaly of the modern version of the unilateral contract, and there was a fitful attempt to rationalize it under the doctrine of offer and acceptance. This analysis was made first in reward cases and spread to other cases wherein acceptance, without notice, was inferred from the performance of the consideration.[22] The terms bilateral and unilateral were used in American but not in English cases, and in the United States the labels are disappearing since the bifurcation does not encompass the formation of all contracts.[23]

Classical Contract Law

The first three quarters of the nineteenth century are seen as the "years of contract" or the classical period both because the idea of freedom of agreement was the organizing principle for the period's dynamic burst of growth[24] and because the details of contract law were filled out as known today. The intellectual inspiration for the elaboration of the consideration contract was provided by two eighteenth century theorists, one French and the other Scottish. Pothier's jurisprudential will theory of the voluntary concurrence of intention complemented Adam Smith's political economy since freedom of contract promoted entrepreneurial activity in a free market.[25] The following discussion of nineteenth century contract law is broken down into an analysis of, first, the will theory and, secondly, the influence of market ideas.

Beginning in the eighteenth century and reaching a full-blown state in the nineteenth, a consensual theory of contract was discovered hidden behind the veil of consideration; inspiration was found in natural and civil law. Before the eighteenth century, the consensus of the parties was not much considered—the plaintiff needed simply to show a sealed deed or a *quid pro quo* in Debt or consideration in Assumpsit. Previously in Assumpsit, lawyers spoke of the defendant's promise alone. Indeed, earlier, no doubt partially due to the primitive state of trial by jury, the intent of the parties was deemed not triable.[26] The idea of giving weight to the common intention of the parties comes from natural law and civilian thought. Grotius wrote in 1625 that if a contract arose from a promise and not from what the parties had done, then the obligation was based on the "act of will" of the parties, and natural law would enforce that expressed common "intention concerning something in the future".[27] Pothier, who was more directly influential on the common law, cited the natural lawyer Grotius as a source for his oft-quoted influential statement: "A contract includes a concurrence of intention in two parties, one of whom promises something to the other, who on his part accepts such promise."[28] Blackstone, writing a few years after Pothier, in his own definition of a contract merely added the requirement of consideration to Pothier's remark that, "An agreement by which two parties reciprocally promise and engage, or one of them singly promises and engages to the other to give some particular thing, or to do or abstain from doing some particular act."[29] In adopting the will theory, Blackstone was basing his own definition of contract on an "agreement" rather than providing an abridger's listing of the types of transactions enforceable in Assumpsit.

Although there were earlier caselaw allusions to the common intent of the parties,[30] Mansfield was the first common law judge to generalize the rules of Assumpsit to show the intention of the parties as the essence of contract. Mansfield tried to reconcile consideration with his assumption that the function of contract law was to implement the intention of the parties. If consideration could be established on the basis of moral obligation, then intention could be used as a unifying factor,[31] and the parties' common intention to be bound might become the sole basis of contractual liability, but it never went that far. Mansfield wanted to generalize Assumpsit in order to provide a more predictable remedy, and he found the highest common factor in Assumpsit to be that an agreement based on the intention of the parties was worthy of sanction and should determine the scope of a contract.[32] In *Kingston v. Preston* (1773)[33] he said: "the dependance, or independance, of covenants, was to be collected from the evident sense and meaning of the parties" and from "the intent of the transaction" and in *Tyrie v. Fletcher* (1777)[34]: "If the parties do not choose to contract according to the established rule, they are at liberty, as between themselves, to vary it."

In the United States the legal writings available during the first half of the nineteenth century reflected a shift to the will (or consensual) theory. Circuit Judge Cranch, in an 1804 Appendix to his U.S. Supreme Court reports, wrote: "Every man has a natural right to make such contracts as he pleases . . . and all contracts entered into without fraud or force, are legally and morally obligatory according to their spirit and intent."[35] Evans wrote in his 1806 Appendix to Pothier, republished in Philadelphia in 1826: "As every contract derives its effect from the intention of the parties, that intention, as expressed or inferred, must be the ground and principle of every decision respecting its operation and extent, and the grand object of consideration in every question with regard to its construction".[36] William Story stated in his treatise: "Every contract is founded upon the mutual agreement of the parties." In express and implied contract Story said the law enforces "the agreement intended by the parties."[37] By the early nineteenth century, American courts were following Mansfield's lead in allowing the parties to alter the rules of contract in their agreement so that contract doctrine was becoming a stop-gap for when the parties did not cover a point.[38]

The implication of the ascendancy of the will theory was that contract obligations were now viewed as mutual obligations voluntarily created by the parties and now expressed in the form of an offer and acceptance. The court's role now was to discover the intention of the parties and enforce it when there was a concurrence of their free wills; this was in contrast to the court's former function of enforcing only those promises which conformed to the set transactions covered by the ancient forms of action. Concurrence of intention was becoming a universal guiding principle for all contracts. Later in the century in England, a requirement that the parties "concur in expressing a common intention" became an independent requirement for contract formation heaped on top of the already partially duplicitous functions of the doctrines of consideration and offer and acceptance.[39]

In determining whether there was a concurrence of intention under the will theory, was a subjective or an objective interpretation employed? Under a subjective inquiry the parties' actual or real intention would be sought; whereas, under an objective test, the outward manifestations of apparent intention would be the key. There is controversy about which prevailed during this period. Generally, it is said the predominant approach was a subjective one and that it gave way to an objective analysis during the latter part of the nineteenth century.[40] Having said that, it should be kept in mind that neither test can claim a position of exclusivity before or after 1875.[41] In the law prior to the eighteenth century, it has been suggested that it was an objective standard of finding either a *quid pro quo* or consideration, but there are cases of a subjective approach going back to the sixteenth century; and, as a practical matter, there was much less room for misunderstanding in earlier face-to-face transactions.[42] The issue came to the forefront once the parties' communications were separated by time and distance.

The first modern case using a subjective standard was *Cooke v. Oxley* (1790), discussed above, wherein the seller was deemed to have revoked his offer by his uncommunicated sale to a third person. In the abstract, the actual mental assent of the parties ("meeting of the minds") complemented Pothier's will theory: "We ought to examine what was the common intention of the contracting parties rather than the grammatical sense of the terms."[43] However, in practice, such a result as *Cooke v. Oxley* presented problems in contracts formed by correspondence. Thus in *Adams v. Lindsell* (1818) the court employed a fiction but in reality mixed objective and subjective standards. A subjective standard was applied in finding the offeree's actual intent—when the letter was sent; but, the lack of actual consent on the part of the offeror, since he had sold elsewhere, was overcome by the fiction that the offeror's intent was present "during every instant" his letter was travelling to the offeree. If one casts aside the fiction, the offeror's revocation was governed by an objective standard: revocation was only valid once it was manifested to the offeree. So the legal ramifications of the *Cooke v. Oxley* facts were rejected in a contract formed by mail, but the subjective standard was reinforced. And early nineteenth century American courts followed the *Cooke v. Oxley* lead.[44]

The leading treatise writers of the first half of the nineteenth century supported a subjective theory. Chancellor Kent, citing Pothier and eighteenth century English cases, said that in finding mutual intention, it may be necessary to allow the plain intention to prevail "over the strict letter of the contract," even when the contract is in writing.[45] William Story, cited Mansfield in advocating a subjective theory:

> Whenever such intent can be distinctly ascertained, it will prevail, not only in cases where it is not fully and clearly expressed, but also, even where it contradicts the actual terms of the agreement. The object of the law in laying down the rules of exposition, is to discover the meaning of the parties, and not to impose it, and the expression is, therefore, wholly subservient to the manifest intention.[46]

Nonetheless, this period was not one of pure subjectivity. The mixed aspects of offer and acceptance were just discussed. In addition, the courts strictly applied the parol evidence rule, thus excluding the actual intent of a party. Adequacy of consideration was not inquired into, and so a seller was barred from showing that a sale for a trifle was not intended.[47] During the heyday of *caveat emptor*, if the purchaser did not investigate the objective indicators of quality, he suffered the consequences.[48] And, by mid-century, damages were based on objective measurements in order to provide predictable consequences for entrepreneurs.[49] Indeed, by the mid–1850s the inclination toward a subjective theory was being questioned. Parsons was the first American treatise writer to argue that an objective standard was needed in a market-oriented society in order to provide consistent, uniform principles in interpreting contracts so that men of business knew the effect of words used in contracts.[50]

The notion prevailing during the first half of the nineteenth century, however, was of a subjective concurrence of intention, and it generated the doctrines of mistake, undue influence and a modern version of duress. Before the elaboration of contract in the nineteenth century, such defenses would have been hidden behind the doctrine of consideration and treated as a failure of consideration since consideration excluded promises made without good reason. Thus, although duress was an ancient defense, there were no Assumpsit cases on duress as such before the eighteenth century.[51] Once the courts recognized mistake, duress and undue influence as contract defenses, the will theory and the free market dictated that these defenses be based on a lack of free will rather than on an unfair exchange since the spirit of the market was that voluntary bargains determine value.[52] The inspiration for the doctrine of mistake came from the civilian exponents of the will theory. Pothier wrote: "Error is the greatest defect that can occur in a contract, for agreements can only be formed by the consent of the parties, and there can be no consent when the parties are [in] error respecting the object of the agreement."[53] Kent advocated the same viewpoint prior to the courts' adoption of the doctrine when he wrote that there was no mutual consent if there was an "error or mistake of fact, or in circumstances going to the essence of [the contract]."[54]

Decisions adopting the modern doctrine of mistake began cropping up by at least in the third quarter of the nineteenth century.[55] In the famous, and confusing, English case of *Raffles v. Wichelhaus* (1864)[56] the defendant (buyer) avoided liability on the contract based on his argument of no consensus due to the mutual mistake of the plaintiff having in mind a December shipment of cotton on a ship called "Peerless" and the defendant having in mind an October shipment on a different ship also called "Peerless". It was a rare case both because normally a mistake would concern the subject matter and because neither party knew there were two ships with the same name. The court ignored the plaintiff's argument that the identity of the ship was an immaterial element in the contract. The implication of the decision was that the plaintiff needed to show a consensus as to the December shipment. It is unfortunate that a case of such an exceptional nature became a leading case on mistake when it is arguable that the mistake did not go to Chancellor Kent's "essence" of the contract[57] but simply had the effect of a later shipment for which damages would be recoverable. A preferable case illustrating the doctrine of mistake was the unnoticed Massachusetts case of *Kyle v. Kavanagh* (1869),[58] decided 5 years after *Raffles*, where a contract provided for the sale of land on "Prospect Street" but there were two Prospect Streets in the town on which the seller owned land, the seller meaning one and the buyer the other. The court held for the buyer since "their minds did not agree as to the subject matter of the sale."

Duress, caused by the threat of physical violence, was known at common law at least from the time of Bracton.[59] Prior to the nineteenth century, the test for duress was based on the objective standard of what men of "ordinary firmness" would succumb to.[60] Before the middle of the nineteenth century, courts had expanded the analysis by asking whether there was an actual exercise of free will.[61] Again, W. Story and Parsons followed Pothier's statement that "violence" makes the agreement "defective" because the "consent is imperfect".[62] As a subjective theory became applicable, courts had to look to the nature of the victim, who was no longer presumed to be a person of ordinary firmness, to determine whether he could withstand the pressure.[63] This new approach did have a restrictive impact elsewhere: the nineteenth century emphasis on the free will of entrepreneurs set up an additional barrier to the expansion of earlier glimmerings of a theory of economic duress and left its development to the twentieth century in the United States.[64]

Undue influence developed because duress covered too narrow a range of interference with a victim's free will. Undue influence acted as a gap-filler to protect the weakened who were not in fact incapacitated nor subjected to coercion amounting to duress. The modern view of duress, as seen under the will theory, played a role in that it "exorcised" the objective standard applicable since the days of Bracton and facilitated relief for the weak and submissive.[65] Before the common law took up undue influence, the idea of improper persuasion of the weak had been developed in Chancery largely in the law of wills and other gratuitous transfers.[66] As the common law borrowed from Chancery and from its own notions of duress, the "wrong" in undue influence was the interference with free will rather than that one was totally overpowered. Unlike duress, undue influence was never thought of as emanating from the law of tort or crime—instead, prevailing standards of ethics were applied to those short on legal capacity. Undue influence was said to apply "to every case where influence is acquired and abused, where confidence is reposed and betrayed."[67] This fiduciary principle placed limits on when wrongful persuasion, short of duress, could be a basis for a defense. The two essential elements of the modern doctrine of undue influence were now present: defect in free will, from modern duress, and a fiduciary standard from Equity.[68]

Attention will now be turned to the second half of the classical contract discussion: how classical contract law reflected the market. The following comments will not show how market ideas changed the letter of the largely autonomous common law directly; rather, they are intended to point out the commercial spirit of the times, which reinforced the direction the law would take. The legal system encouraged nineteenth century productivity by the implementation of the ideas of political economy suggested by Adam Smith and his disciples. The political economists argued that the greatest economic benefit would accrue if the forces of supply and demand determined value in a free market of open competition wherein private parties were given freedom to contract for goods and services desired. Competition would solve all market problems. This view was not entirely novel to the common law since notions of anti-monopoly and trade free of government intrusion had been a part of common law theory since Coke's time.[69] In a market economy, unfairness of price was not an issue since bargains set the price, and the market would determine damages in the event of breach. The rise of political economy was roughly contemporaneous with the abstraction of freedom of contract, which had also been influenced by natural lawyers and civilians, and freedom of contract became the organizing principle of an economic system based on private transactions. In contrast to earlier law, in an expanding market, those with market influence predominate in determining which transaction the law should regulate. Those political and economic interests in power promote rational procedures which they perceive as a guarantee of "freedom".[70]

There are competing interpretations of who benefited from the free market and its corollary freedom of contract. One view is that there was only freedom for the commercial class, that wealth was distributed in their favor, and that the oppressor employed the ideology of the legal order to reconcile the oppressed with the system oppressing them.[71] Others take the view that freedom of contract generated choices providing a broad sharing of opportunities and that the increased wealth was in the public interest until modifications were necessary later due to the excesses of full scale industrialization. No matter which approach is adopted, the outrage of slavery continued until near the end of this period.[72]

Under the political economy theory, if courts would afford business planners' autonomy, freedom of contract would encourage the release of creative entrepreneurial energy. In equating contract with the free market, individuals were said to be able to bargain with each other on an equal footing and at arm's length—each being capable of protecting himself. The courts took on a new role of removing contract obstacles and carrying out the will of the parties.[73] There was little concern for settlement of hardship cases because equitable relief would mar certainty in future cases. Hence courts were reluctant to strike down contracts on the ground of public policy since that would have been inconsistent with both the objective of certainty[74] and the presumption of the rugged individual's ability to protect himself. There was a greater tendency toward the abstraction of freedom of contract in the United States than in England because of less static property and the opportunities to develop the vast continent's resources.[75]

Under pure contract abstraction, the particulars of subject matter and the identity of the parties were irrelevant in order to not restrict individuals or the free market in the name of social policy. Although Friedman's treatment of "classical" contract rules as consisting of abstract principles is used here for discussion purposes, it should be recognized that it is too narrow and formalistic to be included in a comprehensive definition since it ignores the extent to which even mid-nineteenth century contracts were regulated by legislatures. The abstraction of freedom of contract facilitated generalized principles providing predictability for abstract economic activities. This abstraction, so beneficial to commercial planners, could be harsh for the weak; cold abstraction stripped contract subject matter of human value and so it could treat the sale of a slave as just another unit of production.

Abstraction enabled contract law to expand its subject matter to supplant a rival branch of law like land law since traditional land law left little room for novel arrangements. Another reason for transfers of land becoming viewed as contracts of disposition was due to Savigny's influence in recognizing that contracts are either obligatory or dispositive.[76] As the forms of action began to lose their grip, modern contract law took on the flexibility to absorb transactions that heretofore would not have fit neatly under any particular common count. In the nineteenth century such fields of law as land law, mercantile law, intangibles and insurance marched into contract's domain, and by the end of the century insurance, negotiable instruments and labor law had departed due to the loss of abstraction brought on by regulation of the particular. The transactions covered by contract changed but the rules of contract law remained the same.[77] Hence, when defendants tried to rebut *caveat emptor* in sales by drawing an analogy to the obligation of full disclosure in insurance law, courts began to distinguish insurance from pure contract law because insurance had become alien to the generality needed by the market economy.[78]

Two doctrines fundamental to the courts' implementation of freedom of contract were the adequacy rule and *caveat emptor*. Adequacy concerns the values of the subject matter exchanged and *caveat emptor* concerns quality. The long recognized common law rule that inadequate consideration did not constitute insufficient consideration,[79] fit neatly with Adam Smith's theory that there was no fixed just price but rather one fixed by private parties on the basis of supply and demand, and courts at-law continued the doctrine that the price fixed by private bargain was conclusive proof of objective market value.[80] In equity there were no cases of rescission for inadequacy. Inadequacy was no basis for refusal of specific performance in England unless it was either shocking or evidence of fraud; and, after some hesitancy, American cases agreed.[81]

At the beginning of the nineteenth century, American and English decisions reaffirmed the strictness of the *caveat emptor* rule announced in the 1603 case of the sale of the supposed precious bezoar stone.[82] The unbargained-for reliance in the absence of an express warranty went unprotected at common law. Furthermore, it was not always easy to pin down whether an express warranty was made.[83] Classical economists approved of *caveat emptor* because, if buyers inspected defective goods and refused to buy them, they soon would not be made. There was strong support for *caveat emptor* in the nineteenth century, to a greater degree in the United States than in England.[84] Despite the dominance of caveat emptor, there was a mild undercurrent of protection for buyers of defective goods provided by a narrow implied warranties of quality and of fitness for a particular purpose. The implied warranty of quality, discussed in chapter four, was only available when there was no opportunity to inspect, and it would therefore make no sense to apply *caveat emptor*.[85] The law had become decidedly pro seller as the earlier environment of a tight clique of London traders, who could be buyers one day and sellers another, gave way to a system of middlemen and distant markets. It has been suggested that in the passage from an agrarian to an industrial society, the tendency toward a legislative laissez-faire is often accompanied by an increased judicial emphasis on *caveat emptor*.[86]

Under the political economy theory, the enhancement of an individual's economic opportunities was said to require a laissez-faire policy, though in fact the emotional support for laissez-faire was not always followed if regulation could be seen to promote a release of creative human energy.[87] There were legislative regulations concerning national banks, loans to railways, mixed ownership of canals, inspection of food and weights, corporate charters, usury, homestead and bankruptcy. As has been discussed, courts were intervening in the market and departing from freedom of contract by inquiring into fraud, mistake, duress, undue influence and implied warranties. Indeed, by courts performing the fundamental function of enforcement of contracts, the courts were deviating from laissez-faire. The most glaring aspect of the courts' intervention in the market was the alleged policy of promoting commercial interests, a so-called policy of "instrumentalism".[88]

There were a variety of reasons why, since Holt's time, the common law was beginning to be perceived as a man-made instrument of will. As a result of the Glorious Revolution of 1688, Parliament, under the influence of commercial interests, became the law-giver in place of the monarchy. Mansfield rationalized and generalized the law, despite technical precedents to the contrary, to provide certainty to commercial interests. The young American democracy created its own Constitution and voluntarily elected the common law in contravention of the Blackstonian idea of the law coming from the sovereign above. Under the ideology of the will theory, the common law was no longer seen as an immutable body of ancient principles. And Bentham was attacking the shortcomings of the common law and urging a codification of the law.

In the United States the common law became a new nation's self conscious instrument of social policy for the release of productive energy through freedom of contract. There was a policy of mercantilism to strengthen the emerging nation's own position[89] and to develop and lay claim to the resources and territory of the continent. There was plenty of interest in taking up the challenge since, as Tocqueville observed in the 1830s, Americans were deeply agitated by commercial passions.[90]

Judges had at their disposal the contract rules needed to implement an instrumental approach even before the eighteenth century. *Caveat emptor* and the adequacy rule were long recognized, as was the right of recovery for loss of the value of a bargain due to breach of an informal, executory contract. What was lacking earlier was a throbbing market economy in need of the support and stability provided by the courts. Once judges saw the benefits to the nation and to commercial interests of an activist posture supportive of the free market, the ideas of will theory and political economy were available to rationalize an instrumental approach. Influential judges like Kent understood and participated in business affairs and encouraged commercial cases to be brought before common law courts rather than such rival forums as arbitration.[91] The informal alliance was further strengthened, both in England[92] and in the United States, between the legal elite and commercial leaders, each sharing similar economic objectives, for an instrumental application of the common law to facilitate unfettered growth.[93] Llewellyn labelled the courts' overtly instrumental manner of ignoring precedents not in conformity with the policy of promoting commerce as the "grand style" of judicial discourse.[94] The decisions were Mansfieldian in being rational and functionally related to the life of commerce.[95]

On constitutional issues brought before the United States Supreme Court, concern for vested property interests did not give way to an instrumental preference for dynamic property in a national context until the 1830s. The "contracts clause" limited the power of states to tamper with vested property and contract rights.[96] This provided predictability for business, but it did not encourage growth. The conflict between protecting static property and dynamic property came to a head in *Charles River Bridge v. Warren Bridge* (1837).[97] In *Charles River Bridge* the

Supreme Court refused to imply an exclusive right to an earlier bridge franchise when the Massachusetts legislature granted a later franchise to build a competing bridge. Now when vested property rights were monopolistic, they would be subservient to policy favoring competitive uses of property.[98] Nevertheless, continued protection of the vested property interest of slavery ground on. Lastly, in *Swift v. Tyson* (1842) Story, C.J. encouraged the national uniformity not provided for in the Constitution but needed by merchants planning in a national market.[99]

Hence federal and state judges, sympathetic business planners' needs for clear rules, century judges continued Mansfield's elaboration of contract rules to further predictability. The goal of certainty necessitated the curtailment of the unpredictability of trial by jury in favor of judge-made law.[100] There were increased discussions of the legal meaning of facts, and cases were no longer submitted to juries on a general issue without detailed jury instructions. Potentially conflicting jury instructions given by each judge, sitting en banc, were replaced by a single instruction in Massachusetts in 1804; Connecticut judges were required to give jury instructions in 1807, and verdicts would be set aside if instructions were not followed. New trials were granted when the rules of evidence, refined in the eighteenth century, were not followed.[101]

Once more effective control of trial by jury was achieved in the United States, there was a greater judicial receptivity to informal contracts, the modus operandi of the hurly-burly of the marketplace. As a result, there were changed attitudes regarding the testimony of interested witnesses and the status of sealed contracts. Before the nineteenth century, parties to contracts and other interested witnesses with a pecuniary interest could not testify because testimony for one's own benefit was deemed suspect. The preclusion of this testimony about private agreements had a significant influence on the passage of the Statute of Frauds (1677) because, if only the parties were present when an informal contract was made, there was no reliable way of proving the agreement before the then primitive form of trial by jury. As confidence increased in the jury system, the disqualification of interested parties was questioned. Since benefit to the witness was the reason for the disqualification, the bar on witnesses with a pecuniary interest fell first in England in 1843, followed by the parties' testimony in 1851. Michigan, Connecticut and New York did likewise, and the remaining states followed suit by the 1860s.[102]

During the first quarter of the nineteenth century, American states still recognized the power of the seal to bind the obligor in the absence of consideration. Assumpsit, with its trial by jury, was never allowed at common law on a contract under seal for fear the jury would go behind the document. Sealed conditional bonds had continued in the eighteenth century, even after the penalty was not recoverable. The decrease in the use of the bond in early nineteenth century America may have been due to the greater confidence creditors had in judicial control of trial by jury; Sedgwick argued against the distinction between sealed and unsealed contracts because of the state of the law of evidence by the 1840s.[103] Furthermore, the aristocratic seal was dysfunctional in the informality of the market—especially when most Americans didn't own a seal. States began to abolish the distinction between sealed and unsealed contracts by the 1830s, and today the only related remnant is the negotiable instrument.[104] Since England retains the seal today, promises of a purely gratuitous or moral nature are enforceable; and, partly because such intended promises were not binding in the United States, the innovation of promissory estoppel would develop.

Right to Damages

Contractors planning for the future needed clear rules for when damages were recoverable and for the extent of any recovery. By the 1850s, the courts refined the law of damages by developing rules for substantial performance, anticipatory repudiation and quantum limitations based on foreseeability. Now that there were more effective techniques for judicial control of the jury, these new damage related rules could be implemented by appropriate evidentiary rules, more detailed jury instructions and, when the rules were not followed, new trial orders.

The necessity of a substantial performance rule arose once dependent covenants were recognized in the eighteenth century. Now it was possible that a substantial performer would recover nothing if his recovery was dependent on his performance being in strict conformity with the details of the contract. In *Boone v. Eyre* (1777),[105] in a partially completed sale of a West Indian plantation along with its slaves, Mansfield said the covenant for the slaves went only to a part of the consideration and was not a condition precedent; so the seller could recover, subject to a damages action for failure to convey the slaves. Refinement of Mansfield's equitable solution occurred in service contracts along separate lines for business and non-business contracts. The substantial performance test arose in the context of the detailed performance of construction contracts. The early decisions were inconsistent in defining the rights of the performer; an 1807 case held a builder could recover for any benefit provided, but an 1810 case refused recovery when a builder deviated from contract specifications.[106] The *Cutler v. Close* decision in 1832 used a substantial performance test as a compromise between the 1807 case favoring the builder and the 1810 case favoring the landowner.[107] In *Cutler v. Close* the plaintiff recovered for a stove installation found "in the main substantial," since it "answer[ed] the purpose intended," less the jury's deduction of 1/7 the price for the "requisite to make it complete". Without substantial performance, a literal application of dependency rules would be unjust to the substantial performer, especially when a significant benefit had flowed to the defendant. Courts would not characterize a covenant as "dependent" if there was substantial performance; the methodology of conditions was made subservient to the test's approximate justice.[108] The application of the rule was unpredictable because of the subjective analysis of the amount of benefit the defendant reasonably expected from the bargain.

Substantial performance provided a just result for business contracts, but there were problems in applying it to employment contracts. *Cutter v. Powell* (1795)[109] announced the strict rule that full completion of the contract term was a condition precedent to recovery. The executor of a deceased sailor could not recover wages for the deceased second mate, who died three weeks before the end of a three month voyage, since he had agreed to work the "entire journey" for a lump sum. An express contract for a fixed sum precluded *quantum meruit* for a reasonable sum for work done; this was the heritage of the action of Debt's requirement that an action be for a specific amount.[110] Why were construction contracts and employment contracts treated differently? The paradox reflects the opposing principles of the strict requirement of complete performance of the contract in *Cutter v. Powell* versus the synallagmatic principle of concern for the parties' actual exchange position in imperfectly performed contracts, as in *Boone v. Eyre* and *Cutler v. Close.* The rules for the two groups of cases developed separately, and when the law became compartmentalized, the conflict was overlooked.[111] An 1828 Massachusetts court explained the difference on the basis that the employee voluntarily left his employment but the breach of a building contract was often unintentional.[112] Another explanation was that construction contracts were too complex for complete satisfaction. Nevertheless, one can't help suspecting a class bias in favor of entrepreneurs.[113]

The second elaboration of the law of damages was the development of anticipatory repudiation to assist the planning of a victim of a contract repudiation made before performance was due. Before the mid-nineteenth century, the victim had the alternatives of accepting the breach and treating it as a mutual rescission, thereby renouncing a claim to damages, or of ignoring the breach and waiting through a period of uncertainty until the due date. Before the leading anticipatory repudiation case of *Hochster v. De La Tour* (1853),[114] it didn't matter that a party indicated in the interim that he would not perform so long as he did in fact perform at the due date.[115] There were earlier exceptional cases where the date of repudiation was the operative date for both termination of the contract and calculation of damages if the repudiator had disabled himself, as a marriage contract where the man married another woman or a sales contract where the goods were sold to a third party. However, Campbell, C.J. in *Hochster v. De La Tour,* denied the validity of these disablement cases because circumstances could change before the performance date, as the first wife might die or the defendant might repurchase the goods.

In *Hochster v. De La Tour* the plaintiff contracted to act as the defendant's courier for three months starting on June 1, but three weeks before employment was to begin the defendant repudiated, and the plaintiff sued two weeks later. The Queen's Bench ruled, first, that the plaintiff could elect to treat the contract as terminated at the date of repudiation so that he could be "at liberty to consider himself absolved from any future performance" and seek employment elsewhere. Secondly, the court made the controversial ruling that the plaintiff could sue before the date for performance, with damages calculated as of the performance date. Campbell said: "If the plaintiff has no remedy for the breach of the contract unless he treats the contract in force, and acts upon it down to the first of June, 1852, it follows that, till then, he must enter into no employment which will interfere with his promise." In permitting the victim's immediate suit, Campbell seems to have been vaguely reflecting the notion in consideration of the simultaneity of the exchange of rights and duties, whether in the original bargain or here in a subsequent discharge short of performance—if there was to be a right to sue on the rescission, it should be contemporaneous with the rescission.[116]

Morally speaking, the defendant should have to pay for the damages caused by the repudiation,[117] but query whether the plaintiff should have the right to sue prior to the date of performance since the premature suit encourages speculative damages, especially in a long term contract, when the court must guess what the market value will be at the due date. There was no doctrinal reason why Campbell could not have granted an immediate discharge but deferred the right to sue until the due date, as Massachusetts did in 1874 in taking a minority position.[118] Nevertheless, the time for suing aside, the change in the old law which now allowed both immediate discharge and damages did cure uncertainties for the plaintiff in not requiring him to remain ready to perform up to the due date in order to collect damages for loss of the bargain. The new rule erased any incentive on an early repudiation in a rising market while at the same time a victim accepting repudiation had an incentive to find a productive alternative under the mitigation principle. The rights of the victim upon anticipatory repudiation announced in *Hochster v. De La Tour* were not applied as a matter of course until the latter part of the nineteenth century in England and a bit later in the United States.[119] The 1893 edition of the Parsons contract treatise, edited by Williston who was a critic of the doctrine, stated that anticipatory repudiation rules only applied to an irreversible disablement.[120] Nonetheless, a majority of American jurisdictions adopted the rule by the early twentieth century.[121]

The third, and most important development in the law of damages, was the placement of limitations on the recovery of arguably remote damages. Before the sixteenth century there was little concern about damages being excessive when relief was sought in Debt for restitution of the *quid pro quo* or for the price of the debt plus incidentals. The issue arose once damages for loss of expectation and reliance were recoverable in Assumpsit.[122] As Assumpsit for nonfeasance evolved as an action distinct from an action for misfeasance, it continued the practice in tort of recovery of the full measure of the damages caused as a consequence of the wrong.[123] From the beginning of open use of Assumpsit for pure nonfeasance, courts applied the compensatory principle of placing the plaintiff in the position he would have been in if the promisor had performed. So if the seller failed to deliver goods in a rising market, the future loss of the bargain was recoverable in the sixteenth century,[124] though these cases were infrequent in that economy.

The allowance of future damages due to market fluctuations was a step past recovery in misfeasance for damages already done. A tort action looks backwards from injury to the cause, but a contract creates new rights from formation onward. Throughout the seventeenth and eighteenth centuries, courts continued to protect the expectation interest in those infrequent cases where it arose by granting damages based on the difference between the contract price and the later ascertainable market price.[125] There was an increased frequency of such cases as commerce heated up in the second half of the eighteenth century, when there was more trading between distant parties, a greater division of labor and a greater need to plan on a subcontractor's promised performance. In a commercial society wealth is largely made up of promises and so society has an interest in expectation damages and in enforcing promises to protect the promisee. By the last third of the eighteenth century, the plaintiff's right to the difference between the contract price and the market value at the due date was limited by the notion that the plaintiff had a right to recover for the loss of opportunity, and so he could not recover the full difference if it was reasonable to mitigate. Thus a seller could recover the difference between the contract price and what he could sell for elsewhere in a declining market.[126]

In the eighteenth century merchants sought more certain rules of damages than the then existing practice of damages being assessed by juries in their largely uncontrolled discretion. It was not that there were no judicial attempts at control, because there were occasional jury instructions on damages,[127] but judicial controls could ultimately be ineffective since new trials were not ordered if a jury did not follow judicial guidance. Chancery began the procedure of ordering new trials at-law when a jury verdict was unjust, and the common law courts, finding their decisions returned by Chancery, adopted the same procedure when a jury verdict was out of line.[128] Once the granting of a new trial became more regularized, during the final third of the eighteenth century, for an incorrect jury instruction or for the failure of a jury to follow either a correct instruction or the evidence,[129] courts began taking greater care in devising jury instructions on damages and limitations thereon.[130]

Although the compensatory principle and jury controls were in place, effective limitations on the remoteness of damages were not fashioned until the mid-nineteenth century. Before taking business risks, entrepreneurs wanted clearer limitations on the extent of liability than was in place during the first half of the nineteenth century. In *Bridge v. Wain* (1816)[131] scarlet cloth supplied by the defendant was not suitable for resale by the plaintiff in China, and the plaintiff was allowed loss of profits for "all the loss" sustained. In *Walton v. Fothergil* (1835)[132] the extent of damages recoverable were also left open-ended: "for such damages as are the necessary and natural consequence." Instead of developing a less expansive general rule of limitation, some courts would seek a specific rule anew in each case from the suggestions of the parties or a witness. In *Startup v. Cortazzi* (1835),[133] the trial judge told the jury that since "neither the witnesses nor the plaintiff had pointed out any precise line, which may mark the proper estimate of damages," they "ought not to give speculative or vindictive damages." And as late as 1847 in *Black v. Baxendale*,[134] when the plaintiff sued for the failure to deliver goods on time for their sale at a Saturday market, the court brushed aside the defendant's objection that he had no notice of the plaintiff's intent and left the problem of remoteness generally to the jury.

Then in 1854 entrepreneurs received workable limitations on remote damages when the Exchequer Court wrested control of the matter from the jury in *Hadley v. Baxendale*.[135] The defendant, a common carrier, caused a delay of five days longer than reasonable in transporting a broken crank shaft, needed in order to reopen the plaintiff's mill; the shaft was to be transported to a manufacturer in another town. The plaintiff sued for damages for resultant expenses and for loss of profits while the mill was shut for the five extra days. Baron Alderson said "in the great multitude of cases not affected by any special circumstances" damages would be assessed according to the clearly "established" principle of loss of the bargain. Alderson then laid down the oft-quoted rule for cases of "special circumstances" where a breach caused consequential damages past the loss of the bargain:

> [The damages] should be such as may fairly and reasonably be considered either arising naturally, i.e., according to the usual course of things, from such breach of contract itself, or such as may reasonably be supposed to have been in the contemplation of both parties, at the time they made the contract, as the probable result of the breach of it.

Alderson's rule contains alternative tests of damages "arising naturally" or those "in the contemplation of both parties". Recovery for damages "arising naturally" added nothing since it was simply a reiteration of the open-ended "necessary and natural consequences" test in *Walton v. Fothergil* (1835) and likewise in William Story's earlier "consequential injury fairly and naturally resulting."[136] If "arising naturally" was applied as a true alternative test, it would emasculate Alderson's innovation of a foreseeability limitation. Under the foreseeability test, consequential damages were too remote unless "special circumstances" were "communicated" to the defendant so that the resulting damages, past the loss of the bargain, were in his "contemplation" when the contract was made. In applying this new foreseeability standard, Alderson concluded that the mill's shutdown was not communicated by the plaintiff by telling the defendant's representative that he was the miller of the mill from which the broken shaft came.[137]

What was the source of this foreseeability standard? The notion of special circumstances being communicated to the defendant was first raised by the defendant, albeit unsuccessfully, in *Black v. Baxendale* (1847), the case of the failure to deliver goods in time for their sale at the Saturday market. Authority for a damages limitation based on the defendant's foresight was found in American sources. In the Exchequer case of *Waters v. Towers* (1853)[138] the plaintiff sued for loss of profits caused by the defendant's failure to fit up machinery in a reasonable time. The defendant cited Kent's COMMENTARIES as authority for the proposition that recovery for loss of profits was too remote if they were not in the "contemplation" of the parties.[139] Again, the defendant was unsuccessful, but later Baron Parke did infer in *Hadley v. Baxendale* that the defendant's knowledge of the consequences was more likely in *Waters* than in *Hadley*.[140] In *Hadley v. Baxendale* the plaintiff turned to another American source supporting the foreseeability limitation by quoting from Sedgwick's superb 1847 damages treatise: "the defendant shall be held liable for those damages only which the both parties may fairly be supposed to have at the time contemplated as likely to result from the nature of the agreement." And Parke quoted Sedgwick's adoption of the French rule: "The debtor is only liable for the damages foreseen, or which might have been foreseen."[141] In the 1760s Pothier wrote that the defendant should not be liable for damage not "foreseen" and "not contemplated at the time of the contract."[142] In addition to citing Pothier and the contemporary French Code as authority, Sedgwick also cited the Louisiana case of *Williams v. Barton* (1839), which court stated that damages were to be in the "contemplation of the parties at the time of the contract."[143]

Hadley v. Baxendale furthered the common law courts' aim of establishing clear rules of damages with definite limits. Now the jury had to be instructed that the defendant's liability for consequential loss was limited to damages foreseen when the contract was made. This abstract standardized rule limiting damages sprouted from the will theory. The civilian "concurrence of intention in two parties"[144] was the inspiration for damages being "in the contemplation of both parties." Civil law's earlier absorption of aspects of law merchant made it an advanced model for the common law translation into jury control devices.[145] In *Hadley* Baron Alderson laid down the rule that when a case was left generally to the jury as to the natural consequences of the breach,[146] a new trial would be granted in order to give a "definite rule to guide" the jury on retrial. The heritage of *Hadley v. Baxendale* is not solely the negative aspect of barring a jury's remote damages verdict since the case erased any doubts about whether consequential damages were recoverable.[147]

There was an unsettled period during the generation after *Hadley v. Baxendale* before it became the leading case on remoteness.[148] Several American decisions soon adopted the *Hadley* rule, the leading case being *Griffen v. Colver* (N.Y. 1858);[149] however, an English court said there must be a contract to bear the consequential damages.[150] *Hadley v. Baxendale's* success as a leading case was assisted both by Sedgwick's promotion of "the rule [laid down] in *Hadley v. Baxendale,*" which of course Sedgwick had originally influenced, and by the fact that opposing counsel in the *Hadley* case thereafter emphasized it as co-editors of SMITH'S LEADING CASES.[151] It became clear in American cases that the "arising naturally" alternative was not going to be permitted as an independent test, and thus foresight of special circumstances was essential for recovery of consequential damages.[152]

Controls on when a jury could award consequential damages now favored the risk-taking entrepreneur, who, if he found it best for his enterprise, could now elect the predictable and limited consequences of breaching.[153] Before *Hadley* the defendant had to put the plaintiff in the same position as if the contract had been performed, but now there was a compromise between the entrepreneur being an insurer and the plaintiff receiving nothing. The defendant in *Hadley* cited Sedgwick: "the object is to discriminate between that portion of the loss which must be borne by the offending party and that which must be borne by the sufferer. The law in fact aims not at the satisfaction but at a division of the loss". Furthermore, the mill owner could have protected himself by keeping a spare shaft.[154] In actual practice, the courts applied the *Hadley* rule in a manner even more favorable to entrepreneurs than that precedent provided.

Baron Alderson had suggested the possibility of a contract provision for consequential loss in *Hadley v. Baxendale:* "had the special circumstances been known, the parties might have specially provided for the breach of contract by special terms as to damages in that case." Before the law was settled on the foreseeability test in the generation following

Hadley, an English court in *British Columbia Saw Mill v. Nettleship* (1868) preferred at least an implied undertaking: "the mere fact of knowledge cannot increase the liability . . . he must know that the person he contracts with reasonably believes that he accepts the contract with the special condition attached to it."[155] Holmes agreed since foreseeability alone should only create liability in tort, but for contractual liability there should be some form of consent, whether the breach was willful or not.[156] Holmes overlooked the fact that the objection of uncertainty is not as strong in contract as it is in tort, especially when the breach is willful, since the criteria for damage assessment are more certain in contract than in tort.[157] Nevertheless, with influential judges, as Holmes in the United States and Blackburn in England, opposing the recovery of consequential damages in the absence of consent, there was a restrictive application of the rule in *Hadley v. Baxendale* during the rest of the nineteenth century.[158] In the twentieth century the resistance to consequential damages lessened as the sympathy for freedom of contract and unbridled business growth waned and business became better able to bear the risk and protect itself with insurance.[159]

Legislative Reform

The expression of popular sovereignty found in the recently adopted Constitution caused Americans to be favorably disposed to legislative creation of an indigenous private law based on the will of the people. There was suspicion of Blackstone's common law because it was thought to encourage Mansfieldian judicial discretion favoring privileged groups.[160] The influences of the consensual theory, the writings of Jeremy Bentham, the appearance of the Code Napoleon (1804–1810) and the ideas of the German Pandectists spurred a movement for codification of American common law. The causes of opposition to the English common law were multitudinous. The disorderly labyrinth of inaccessible caselaw was mysterious and often irrational and caused uncertainty. The incongruity of the separation of law and equity forced a party to suffer expensive delays of going to and fro in search of justice. The arbitrary technicalities and fictions of pleading and the forms of actions had little relationship to reality, and defendants were often caught by surprise when the real facts hidden behind the *indebitatus* counts and the general issue emerged at the trial.

Bentham's critical analysis of the common law was the most important inspiration for codification. His writings[161] portraying the law as man-made helped demystify the law. He railed against his former teacher, Blackstone, who opposed reform of a perceived immutable common law, and he both opposed Mansfield's unpredictable judicial discretion and saw Mansfield's reforms as too slow and fragmented. He held to the positivist view that the Parliament as sovereign was the law-maker. In economics he followed Mill's laissez-faire and in contract law he supported freedom of contract. In pursuit of his utilitarian "happiness to the greatest number," he wanted a clear, rational codification of the entire law in order to make it known and totally free of judicial discretion. He failed to include practicing lawyers in his reform proposals, and lawyers in turn largely ignored him during his lifetime since they viewed him as a mere visionary theoretician, inexperienced in the practicalities of the law. However, by the 1850s, that fertile decade of innovation in contract law, his ideas took hold in the abolition of the forms of actions, pleading simplification, admissibility of interested witnesses' testimony, the end of debtor prisons and, to a greater extent in the United States than in England, the fusion of law and equity. Because of antipathy toward Bentham, later reformers often failed to credit him, though Edward Livingston acknowledged his influence on Livingston's civil code prepared for Louisiana in 1825, which code was in part devised to avoid the prolixity of common law procedure and trial by jury.[162]

In this atmosphere, the American codification movement reached its height from 1820 to 1850—driven by the objectives of making the law rational, certain and uniform. Some reformers such as H. Sedgwick, Sampson and Field wanted a Benthamesque complete codification. A fundamental argument against this was that a complete code would not evolve to meet change if judges were barred from interpreting the law. Joseph Story, a key representative of the proponents of partial codification, wanted only a codification of commercial law to provide the certainty and uniformity merchants needed. The codification movement prompted the appearance of the treatises written by the judges Kent and Story, who defended the scientific character of the common law and provided clear, generalized rules.[163] Story was concerned about the growing lack of uniformity due to the proliferation of caselaw found in 150 volumes by 1821, but his interest in a uniform commercial code did not mean that he was opposed to judicial discretion. His most ambitious decision in support of uniformity and a national commercial law was *Swift v. Tyson.*[164]

The event marking both the apotheoses and the onset of the decline of the codification movement was New York's adoption of David Dudley Field's Code of Civil Procedure in 1848. England and other states soon followed in the abolition of the forms of action, the allowance of simpler pleading and procedures and a single route to justice. The formulary system in existence before the mid-nineteenth century legislation was not nearly as inflexible as medieval law due to judicial innovations during the interim, but courts had gone as far as they could in reforming the forms of action by the innovations of Assumpsit and the common counts. Abolition of the formulary system would have to come from its source in the executive and legislative realm and the same could be said of the division of law and equity. The advent of actions "on the case" on an *assumpsit* in the sixteenth century had begun the reform of the rigidity of the ancient formulary system; and, once the *indebitatus* counts took over, there was a tendency toward uniformity and less technical pleading problems.[165] In the same vein, Mansfield curtailed technical pleading and delays during his tenure, but pedantic common law pleaders reasserted their arcane practices when lesser judges followed in the early nineteenth century.[166] The plaintiff's task of determining whether Special Assumpsit or one of the common counts was the correct form of action was not easy, and so Serjeant Stephen's ingenious system of pleading the case under as many counts as was imaginable was welcomed by English and American lawyers,[167] but fundamental reform was still demanded.

In order to cure the pleading defects in England, a Parliamentary commission was formed in 1830 and Stephen was a member. Under Stephen's conservative influence, blame was laid at the foot of the general issue instead of occult pleading practices. The resulting 1834 Judicial Rules of Hilary Term forced the plaintiff to select just one count—with disastrous consequences. It was now an all or nothing proposition for plaintiffs, and it prompted defendants' highly technical objections and a profusion of nonsuits. These technical arguments forced courts to scrutinize the scope and logic of the forms in a way not done in 200 years because the issues now being dredged up by defendants had been obscured by the use of multiple common counts and by eighteenth century rationalization.[168] This was exemplified by Denman, C.J. looking behind Mansfield's rationalization of moral consideration in *Eastwood v. Kenyon* (1840) in attempting to make sure that Assumpsit's actionability test of consideration was still all the things it had been in the seventeenth century before the appearance of the common counts.[169]

Due to the injustices of the Hilary Rules, England followed New York in abolishing special pleading and the common counts and in instituting fact pleading by the enactment of the Common Law Procedure Acts of 1852 and 1854. Then England went further than New York in sweeping away common law pleading in the Judicature Acts of 1873 and 1875, but it did not follow New York in completely fusing law and equity. By the 1870s, 27 states followed New York's lead in reforming civil procedure, though about one-half did not abolish chancery. Chancery's absence did not create a crisis because of notorious delays there and because the need for chancery to reverse a jury's excess had diminished with improved jury controls.[170] In those states where chancery was abolished, it was welcomed by those codifiers who saw the law based on science rather than discretion.

David Field's codification ambitions went past a code of civil procedure since he also wanted substantive law codified. His objective was dashed in 1885 in the New York legislature, largely due to the opposition of James Carter, president of the New York City Bar Association. Carter picked up on the German professor Savigny's historical school view that law was made up of custom that was constantly evolving; thus Carter argued that a complete civil code would arrest the growth of the law. In particular, Carter feared the adverse affect of a codification of contract law on business.[171]

Returning to Field's code of civil procedure, now in the place of issue pleading, there was now the uniformity and simplicity that merchants wanted in a formless action based on the facts of the contractual transaction.[172] There were liberal rules for joinder of parties and actions so that express and implied contracts could now be joined in the same declaration. The abolition of the ancient formulary system and the fusion of the courts was not supposed to change substantive law, but in fact it created a void for two reasons. First, the old classifications provided by the forms of action to save the law from chaos were gone, and judges had to fill in by continuing to develop general principles. Actually the abolition of the forms was a recognition that considerable progress had already been made in elaborating a general consensual theory of contract, starting with the lead provided by Mansfield. Secondly, common law courts had to provide the relief granted by Chancery before.[173] In the case of contract assignments, the fusion of law and equity meant that an assignee could sue in his own name, as he had been able to in Chancery where the real party in interest could sue in his own name.[174] The new pleading flexibility could more easily accommodate increasingly sophisticated and novel transactions, shaped by the parties' will and not fitting neatly within the parameters of the former common counts, which never totally came out from under the shadow of their precursor Debt.

The irrelevancy of the nature of the transaction and of the subject matter under the new pleading rules complemented classical contract abstraction. Now, rather than contractors being hemmed in by the strictures of the common counts, the parties' common will was enforceable subject only to illegality. The removal of the restrictions of the forms of action promoted freedom of contract.

In addition to reforms in civil procedure, the codification movement, influenced by the notion of freedom of contract, attempted to increase the pool of potential productive contractors by removal of restrictions on married women and insolvent debtors. At common law, a contract made with a married woman was rationalized as lacking in consideration; then once contractual capacity was analyzed as a separate contract element, she was found to lack capacity because she had no will independent of her husband's. In this period of encouragement of growth and entrepreneurial freedom, the lack of a self-determining role for women had to fall.[175] By 1850 a majority of American jurisdictions had given some contractual capacity to married women. In the nineteenth century legislatures began to provide sympathetic relief for favored classes, but it was only in the twentieth century that courts became so inclined. American jurisdictions were earlier than England in granting capacity to married women both because development of the vast resources of the continent would be assisted by making everyone productive and because American women had a greater stake in property less static than in England, where Equity employed trust theory to aid married daughters of the gentry.[176] Under contract abstraction, the identity of the parties should be irrelevant in order to not restrict individuals or the free market. Moreover, in addition to economic reasons, the influence of the period's Women's Movement cannot be ignored.[177]

Legislative humanitarian concerns for certain categories of debtors caused a breach of abstraction by restrictions on creditors' collection rights through such provisions as homestead allowances, ending debtor prisons and bankruptcy relief. Homestead, started in Texas to encourage settlers and not recognized in England, violated freedom of contract in restricting the transfer of a property interest in which there was a market. The imprisonment of a judgment debtor existed under Debt since the fourteenth century and under Assumpsit since the early sixteenth century,[178] and the practice was adopted in colonial America, though sympathies began to change in the early republican period. Pennsylvania barred it in 1776 if a debtor was insolvent, and New York released imprisoned debtors once all property was surrendered under an 1811 act. New Hampshire abolished all debtor prisons in 1840, and by mid-century other states were falling into line.[179] A creditor attacked the 1811 New York statute as a violation of the "contracts clause" in *Sturges v. Crowninshield* (U.S. 1819), but Marshall, C.J. upheld the humanitarian statute because: "Imprisonment is no part of the contract, and simply to release the prisoner does not impair its obligation."[180] The first federal bankruptcy act was passed in 1800 for bankrupt merchants, but it was repealed three years later. Bankruptcy acts followed in 1841 and 1867, the latter being the first to provide that a non-merchant could be forced into it; a permanent bankruptcy act was not passed until 1898. Bankruptcy acts tended to follow in the wake of depressions but were repealed in short order after economic recovery as rugged individualism won out. The first bankruptcy acts were passed to protect creditors against dishonest debtors, but by the mid-nineteenth century there was a policy to free debtors to become productive entrepreneurs contributing to the market.[181]

Conclusion

Due to Assumpsit's essentially formless nature, it had operated as an anomaly within the formulary system for three centuries, but notwithstanding its malleability, Assumpsit was out of step with the complexity of nineteenth century commercial transactions. The details of Assumpsit's scope were hidden from business planners behind the mysteries of consideration and the generality of the common counts and the general issue. Business needed both more flexibility for novel transactions than was afforded by the common counts and less unpredictability than existed under consideration and the general jury verdict. Nineteenth century courts and legislatures responded with greater jury controls and the abolition of the forms of action. As jury controls improved and the forms ended, the legal meaning of facts formerly hidden behind the general issue and the doctrine of consideration were discussed and were converted into law to provide an elaboration of the principles formerly housed within the doctrine of consideration. This elaboration provided clear rules for business to employ in planning for the future. In devising the specific rules in the elaboration process, there was an unprecedented borrowing from ideas external to the intellectual thought of the common law.

Two major sources of inspiration for the needed elaboration came from the more advanced civilian commercial law and from market ideas espoused by the political economists. These two complementary sources provided the guiding principles for judicial enforcement of freely negotiated bargains of rugged individuals meeting in the market. The courts were the principal arbiters of these economic exchanges in the market, though courts were beginning to have to share that oversight role to a limited degree with legislatures. For the first time since the passage of the Statute of Fraud, legislatures dared to make significant intrusions upon the common law by regulating private contracts through, among other measures, abolition of the forms of action and the fusion of law and equity. Courts, and to a degree legislature, removed antiquated barriers standing in the way of entrepreneurial activities. This instrumental approach provided certainty for planning, limits on damages and predictable enforcement of the parties' common will. The belief in the general societal benefit of the abstract freedom of individual contractors pursuing their economic destinies reached its zenith by the mid-nineteenth century. These attitudes would begin to change, however, during the industrial period, as there was a growing realization that abuses of the market were occurring and that the common law courts were not curtailing these excesses. Remedial action would then come from the representatives of the democratic majority.

Notes

1. 11 of the 13 former colonies passed some form of reception statute between 1776 and 1784. E. BROWN, BRITISH STATUTES IN AMERICAN

LAW, 1776–1836 24 (Ann Arbor: 1964) (reception in R.I. in 1798 and Conn. in 1818). Ohio abolished the common law in 1806, but Ohio courts ignored the statute within a decade.

2. *See* Commonwealth v. Hutchison, 1 Mass. 7, 8 (1804).

3. *Cf.* Waterman, *Thomas Jefferson and Blackstone's Commentaries,* 27 ILL. L. REV. 629, 642–6 (1933) (Jefferson was opposed to what he saw as Mansfield's discretionary equity.).

4. J. POWELL, ESSAY UPON THE LAW OF CONTRACTS AND AGREEMENTS (1790). A subsequent book influential in England and the U.S. was J. CHITTY, A PRACTICAL TREATISE ON THE LAW OF CONTRACTS, NOT UNDER SEAL (London: 1826).

5. *See* Hoeflich, *Savigny and His Anglo-American Disciples,* 37 AM. J. COMP. LAW 17, 19–20 (1989); *and see* 1 F. MAITLAND, COLLECTED PAPERS 489 (Fisher ed. 1911) ("When great work has been done, some fertilizing germs have been wafted from abroad."); *see also* Simpson, *Innovation in Nineteenth Century Contract Law,* 91 L.Q. REV. 247, 277–278 (1975).

6. W. STORY, A TREATISE ON THE LAW OF CONTRACTS NOT UNDER SEAL (Boston: 1844) (Story cured Blackstone's error of confusing contracts implied-in-fact with those implied-in-law. *Id.* at 4.). There were American contract writings prior to W. Story, e.g., T. METCALF, *Law of Contracts,* 20–23 AMERICAN JURIST (1838–1841) (These articles were included in Metcalf's PRINCIPLES OF THE LAW OF CONTRACTS (New York: 1867)) and 2 J. KENT, COMMENTARIES ON AMERICAN LAW (New York: 1827). New York Chancellor Kent did for American law what Blackstone had done for the English common law. *And see* T. PARSONS, THE LAW OF CONTRACTS (2 vol.) (Boston: 1853–1855), the best 19th century contract work to follow W. Story.

7. W. SHEPPARD, ACTIONS UPON THE CASE 33 (London: 1663) ("If two speak together about an Agreement, and they in the midst of their discussion break off, and say they will talk further of it tomorrow; this is imperfect, and no Action will arise upon this conference.").

8. Hurford v. Pile, Cro. Jac. 483, 79 Eng. Rep. 412 (1616) (Dodderidge, J. argued that a promise was revocable until acted upon.).

9. *See* A. SIMPSON, A HISTORY OF THE COMMON LAW OF CONTRACT 461–470 (Oxford: 1975).

10. 1 J. POWELL, *supra* note 4, at 334; 1 R. POTHIER, A TREATISE ON THE LAW OF OBLIGATIONS 4 (W. Evans ed., London: 1806) (first published in France 1761–1764). Evans' translation into English was second to an American one. R. POTHIER, A TREATISE ON OBLIGATIONS CONSIDERED IN A MORAL AND LEGAL VIEW (tr. F. Martin, Martin & Ogden ed., Newbern, N.C. 1802).

11. Cooke v. Oxley, 3 T.R. 653, 100 Eng. Rep. 785 (K.B. 1790) (no mailing involved).

12. Kennedy v. Lee, 3 Mer. 441, 36 Eng. Rep. 170 (Ch. 1817) (specific performance).

13. Adams v. Lindsell, 1 B. & A. 681, 106 Eng. Rep. 250 (1818) (offeror at fault in misdirecting offer resulting in delay).

14. *See also* Boston & Maine Ry. v. Bartlett, 3 Cush. 224 (Mass. 1849) (The

fiction of the continuing offer until acceptance "was precisely as if the parties had met at the time of acceptance, and the offer had then been made and accepted and the bargain completed at once". *Id.* at 227.). *And see* Farnsworth, *"Meaning" in the Law of Contracts,* 76 YALE L.J. 939, 945 (1967) (Fiction of making offer during every instant squared contracts formed by correspondence with idea of "meeting of minds".).

15. Mactier v. Frith, 6 Wend. 103, 113–116 (N.Y. 1830) (cited Pothier and *Adams*); Averill v. Hedge, 12 Conn. 423, 433–436 (1838) (cited *Adams* and *Mactier*); W. STORY, *supra* note 6, at 53–55 (cited Barbeyrac's 18th century notes on Grotius that an acceptance by letter was effective when sent. *Id.* at 55n.). There's disagreement about whether consensus theory in offer and acceptance was present in cases for several decades prior to *Adams v. Lindsell.* Hamburger, *The Development of the Nineteenth Century Consensus Theory of Contract,* 7 LAW & HIST. REV. 241, 325–6 (n.240) (1989).

16. 2 J. KENT, COMMENTARIES ON AMERICAN LAW 606–607 (7th ed., N.Y.: 1851) (certainty); Tayloe v. Merchants' Fire Ins. Co., 9 How. (50 U.S.) 390, 400–401, 13 L. Ed. 187 (1850) ("For why make the offer, unless intended that an assent to its terms would bind them?").

17. Nussbaum, *Comparative Aspects of the Anglo-American Offer and Acceptance Doctrine,* 36 COLUM. L. REV. 920, 920–926 (1936); *cf.* Williston, *Mutual Assent in the Formation of Contracts* in CELEBRATION LEGAL ESSAYS 525, 527 (Chicago: 1919) (If effective date of revocation had been determined before 1850, a subjective test would have made it effective when sent.).

18. F. POLLOCK, PRINCIPLES OF CONTRACT 39 (9th ed., London: 1921) (*Adams* reflects common law doctrine that exchange of promises be concluded at some *one* point.).

19. Nussbaum, *supra* note 17, at 226–227; Routledge v. Grant, 4 Bing. 653, 130 Eng. Rep. 920 (1828) (Promise to keep offer open without consideration may be revoked at any time.).

20. Eastwood v. Kenyon, 11 Ad. & E. 438, 113 Eng. Rep. 482 (1840).

21. *See* Simpson, *supra* note 5, at 258–259, 265–266.

22. Williams v. Carwardine, 1 B. & A. 621, 110 Eng. Rep. 590 (1833) (public offer of reward); First National Bank v. Watkins, 154 Mass. 385, 387 (1891); Carlill v. Carbolic Smoke Ball Co., 1 Q.B. 256 (1893) (public offer to any purchaser getting flu after having treatment); *see* Simpson, *supra* note 5, at 261–262.

23. *See* F. POLLOCK, *supra* note 18, at 36–37; *and see* RESTATEMENT (SECOND) OF CONTRACTS sect. 50 (St. Paul: 1981).

24. *See* J. HURST, LAW AND THE CONDITIONS OF FREEDOM IN THE NINETEENTH-CENTURY UNITED STATES 3–13, 18 (Madison: 1956) (1800–1875 were "years of contract in our law".).

25. R. POTHIER, *supra* note 10; A. SMITH, THE WEALTH OF NATIONS (1776). *See* Cox v. Troy, 5 B. & A. 474, 480, 106 Eng. Rep. 1264 (1822) (Best, J. said Pothier's authority was "as high as can be had, next to a decision of a court of justice in this country.").

26. *Anon,* Y.B. 17 Edw. IV 1 (1477) (Per Bryan, C.J.: "The thought of man is not triable for the devil himself knows not the thought of man".); ST. GERMAN'S DOCTOR AND STUDENT (1530), 91 SELDEN SOCIETY 530 (T.

Plucknett and J. Barton eds., London: 1974) ("no accyon can lye agaynste hym upon suche promyses, for yt ys secrete in hys owne conscyence whether he entendyd for to be bounde or naye.").

27. 2 H. GROTIUS, DE JURE BELLI AC PACIS LIBRI TRES 328–330 (1625) (Oceana Pub., Carnegie End., tr. F. Kelsey, Washington: 1964). Natural lawyers fused the Renaissance view of law as secular with Roman commercial law.

28. R. POTHIER, *supra* note 10, at 4 ("An agreement is the consent of two or more persons to form an engagement." *Id.* at 3.).

29. *Id.* at 3–4; 2 W. BLACKSTONE, COMMENTARIES ON THE LAWS OF ENGLAND 442 (Oxford: 1766) (A contract is "an agreement, upon sufficient consideration to do or not to do a particular thing.").

30. Thorp v. Thorp, 12 Mod. 455, 460, 88 Eng. Rep. 1448, 1451 (1701) (Per Holt: meaning is "gathered from words and nature of the agreement".); Russen v. Coleby, 7 Mod. 236, 87 Eng. Rep. 1213 (1733). Early suggestions of modern consensus theory can be seen from 16th century onward, as use of Assumpsit in place of Covenant and references to mutual agreement, but it was in the 18th century that theory took hold. *See* Hamburger, *supra* note 15, at 246–252, 264 (Consensus theory developed gradually from around 1700 rather than view of Simpson, Atiyah and Horwitz that it appeared suddenly around 1800).

31. Atkins v. Hill, 1 Cowp. 284, 98 Eng. Rep. 1088 (1775); Trueman v. Fenton, 2 Cowp. 544, 98 Eng. Rep. 1232 (1777); Hawkes v. Saunders, 1 Cowp. 289, 98 Eng. Rep. 1091 (1782); *see* C. FIFOOT, LORD MANSFIELD 135 (Oxford: 1936); *see also* Baker, *Origins of Consideration* in ON THE LAWS AND CUSTOMS OF ENGLAND 336, 351 (M. Arnold ed., Chapel Hill: 1981) (Mansfield attempted to revive Plowden's sixteenth century notion of "deliberation" or intention to be bound as an aspect of consideration.). *And see* 2 H. GROTIUS, *supra* note 27, at 329 (According to the law of nature and the law of nations, "Nothing is so in harmony with the good faith of mankind as that persons should keep the agreements which they have made with one another.").

32. Barclay v. Lucas, 2 Doug. 321, 99 Eng. Rep. 676 (1783) ("The question turns on the meaning of the parties."); Robinson v. Bland, 2 Burr. 1077, 97 Eng. Rep. 717 (1760) (Bill of exchange drawn in France has English law applied because "The parties had a view to the laws of England."); C. FIFOOT, *supra* note 31, at 121–122, 243.

33. Kingston v. Preston, 2 Doug. 689, 99 Eng. Rep. 437 (1773).

34. Tyrie v. Fletcher, 2 Cowp. 666, 98 Eng. Rep. 1297 (1777).

35. 5 U.S. 367, 423 (1 Cranch, Appendix) (1804).

36. 2 R. POTHIER, A TREATISE ON THE LAW OF OBLIGATIONS 31 (W. Evans ed., Phila. 1826). *See* Haynes v. Haynes, 1 Dr. & Sm. 426, 433, 62 Eng. Rep. 442, 445 (1861) ("in order to constitute an agreement or contract, two things are requisite—1stly, the will; and, 2dly, some act . . . whereby that will is communicated to the other party." This is a sound principle of "universal law."); *see also* Dickinson v. Dodds, 2 Ch. Div. 463, 45 L. J. Ch. 777 (1876) *and* Cundy v. Lindsay, 3 App. Ca. 459, 47 L.J.Q.B. 481 (1878).

37. W. STORY, *supra* note 6, at 4; *see* Kane v. Hood, 13 Pick. 281, 283 (Mass. 1832) ("The intent of the parties is to govern".).

38. Gordon v. Little, 8 S. & R. 533 (Pa. 1822) ("be the common law what it

may, the parties have a right to alter and modify it by special contract, and when they have done so, the question is, what is the construction of the contract?"); *see* L. FRIEDMAN, CONTRACT LAW IN AMERICA 23 (Madison: 1965).

39. F. POLLOCK, PRINCIPLES OF CONTRACT AT LAW AND IN EQUITY 2–5 (London: 1876); Carlill v. Carbolic Smoke Ball Co., 1 Q.B. 256 (1893). The English approach might make more sense in a civilian jurisdiction where consideration is not required. For the American position, *see* 1 S. WILLISTON, A TREATISE ON THE LAW OF CONTRACTS 37–41 (W. Jaeger ed., Mount Kisco, N.Y. 1957) (Common law doesn't require as an independent element a positive intention to create a legal obligation.).

40. On this theory, *see generally* Williston, *Mutual Assent in the Formation of Contracts* in CELEBRATION LEGAL ESSAYS 525 (Chicago: 1919); but cf. P. ATIYAH, THE RISE AND FALL OF FREEDOM OF CONTRACT 459 (Oxford: 1979) (objective approach because of distrust of jury in the face of will theory).

41. *See* 1 A. CORBIN, CORBIN ON CONTRACTS sect. 106, pp. 474–479 (St. Paul: 1963) (Contract cannot be explained exclusively by a subjective or objective theory.); *see also* S. STOLJAR, MISTAKE AND MISREPRESENTATION 8–14 (London: 1968) (normally both objective and subjective factors at work).

42. Williston, *supra* note 17, at 525; Reniger v. Fogossa, 1 Plowd. 1, 75 Eng. Rep. 1 (Exch. 1548); S. STOLJAR, *supra* note 41, at 8.

43. 1 R. POTHIER, *supra* note 10, at 47; *and see* 2 R. POTHIER, *supra* note 36, at 32. Pothier parted from Grotius here. H. GROTIUS, *supra* note 27, at 330–334 (Outward manifestation of intent matters.).

44. Bruce v. Pearson, 3 Johns. 534, 535 (N.Y. Sup. Ct. 1808) (no contract since no meeting of the minds). A possible reason for American courts using a subjective standard was the uncertainty of values in a period prior to a true national market. M. HORWITZ, THE TRANSFORMATION OF AMERICAN LAW, 1780–1860, 200 (Cambridge, Mass. 1977).

45. 2 J. KENT, *supra* note 16, at sect. 554–556. But then on the next page, Kent opposed using parol evidence to vary the writing.

46. W. STORY, *supra* note 6, at 149–150, citing: Backe v. Proctor, 1 Doug. 382, 99 Eng. Rep. 247 (1780) (per Mansfield) and Quackenboss v. Lansing, 6 Johns. 49, 50 (1810) ("covenants are to be construed according to the spirit and intent").

47. Armstrong v. McGhee, Addis. (Pa. C.P. 1795) (Seller argued he hadn't intended to sell horse for trifle, but court refused to go behind his words.).

48. *See* L. FRIEDMAN, A HISTORY OF AMERICAN LAW 276–277 (N.Y. 2d ed. 1985) (objectivity applied to freely-made bargains).

49. J. HURST, *supra* note 24, at 20–22 ("intent" proved by external evidence).

50. 2 T. PARSONS, *supra* note 6, at 3–9; J. HURST, *supra* note 24, at 21–22; *see* M. HORWITZ, *supra* note 44, at 198 (As stable markets began to appear by mid-century, objective measure of value was possible.). *See* Smith v. McGuire, 3 H & N. 554, 157 Eng. Rep. 589 (1858) (objective standard used in basing liability on apparent agency authority).

51. *See* A. SIMPSON, *supra* note 9, at 537 (evidence given on general issue that no consideration). The losses caused by lack of free will would be a fertile

area for development of Mansfield's quasi-contract suggestions: "for money paid by mistake... or extortion; or oppression; or an undue advantage taken of the plaintiff's situation." Moses v. Macferlan, 2 Burr. 1005, 97 Eng. Rep. 676 (1760).

52. *See* L. FRIEDMAN, *supra* note 38, at 99 (lack of assent expanded to mitigate harshness of market); *see also* M. HORWITZ, *supra* note 44, at 263 (Lawyers felt pressure to develop meeting of minds as contract law disengaged from fairness of bargain.); *but cf.* Williston, *supra* note 17, at 532–533 (Equity should base decision on injustice rather than unfair exchange.). Since free market said that exercise of free will requires one to protect himself rather than for court to interfere, there weren't a large number of cases involving lack of assent.

53. 1 R. POTHIER, *supra* note 10, at 11.

54. 2 J. KENT, *supra* note 16, at 606.

55. Raffles v. Wichelhaus, 2 H. & C. 906, 159 Eng. Rep. 375 (1864); Kennedy v. Panama Royal Mail, L.R. 2 Q.B. 580 (1867); Henkel v. Pape, L.R. 6 Ex. 7 (1870); Cundy v. Lindsay, 3 App. Cas. 459 (1878); Kyle v. Kavanagh, 103 Mass. 356 (1869); Wood v. Boynton, 64 Wis. 265, 25 N.W. 42 (1885); Sherwood v. Walker, 66 Mich. 568, 33 N.W. 919 (1887).

56. Raffles v. Wichelhaus, 2 H. & C. 906, 159 Eng. Rep. 375 (1864). *See* G. GILMORE, THE DEATH OF CONTRACT 36, 120–121 (Buyer probably refused deal due to market drop, which may have been due to Lincoln's Civil War sale for export of confiscated cotton.).

57. *See* Sherwood v. Walker, 66 Mich. 568, 33 N.W. 919 (1887) (Contract unenforceable because mistake not merely to quality but to the very nature of contract when cow, mistakenly thought barren by both parties, sold for 1/10 its value.); *and see* Wood v. Boynton, 64 Wis. 265, 25 N.W. 42 (1885) (Contract was enforceable since no mistake as to the nature but only as to quality, when stone worth $700 sold for $1.).

58. Kyle v. Kavanagh, 103 Mass. 356, 359–360 (1869).

59. H. BRACTON, DE LEGIBUS, fo. 16b–17 (d. 1268); Y.B. Mich. 21 Edw. IV, pl. 14, f.13 (1482); Y.B. Pasch. 1 Hen. VII, pl. 2, f.15 (1485); *accord* E. COKE, SECOND INSTITUTE 482–483 (1642) (for fear of loss of life, limp or imprisonment); *and* 1 W. BLACKSTONE, *supra* note 29, at 131–132.

60. 1 W. BLACKSTONE, *supra* note 29, at 131.

61. Skeate v. Beale, 11 Ad. & El. 983, 113 Eng. Rep. 688 (1840); *see* Dawson, *Economic Duress—An Essay in Perspective,* 45 MICH. L. REV. 253, 256 (1947) (victim's burden aggravated by requirement of showing both wrongful act and loss of free will).

62. 1 R. POTHIER, *supra* note 10, at 15–16 (Voidable since ratification was possible. *Id.* at 14.); W. STORY, *supra* note 6, at 57 (Assent "must be freely and voluntarily given".); 1 T. PARSONS, *supra* note 6, at 429 (Duress makes contract void because "consent is the essence of a contract".).

63. Jordan v. Elliott, W.N.C. 56 (Pa. 1882); Parmentier v. Pater, 13 Ore. 121, 125–126 (1885) (Found lack of free assent by person not of ordinary firmness.).

64. Astley v. Reynolds, 2 Stra. 915, 93 Eng. Rep. 939 (K.B. 1732) ("duress of goods" found); *see* Skeate v. Beale, 11 Ad. & El. 983, 113 Eng. Rep. 688 (1840), where free will restricted duress of goods notion. *And see* Hackley v. Headley, 45 Mich. 569, 8 N.W. 511 (1881) (nor duress to threaten contract

breach precipitating economic ruin). Economic duress will be discussed in the last chapter.

65. Dawson, *supra* note 61, at 265. Undue influence was an exceptional instance in the 19th century when inadequate consideration was relevant.

66. Joy v. Bannister (Ch. 1617) in BACON'S REPORTS 33 (Ritchie ed. 1932) (will of 80 year old man to Mrs. Death (!) declared invalid); Clarkson v. Hanway, 2 P. Wms. 203, 24 Eng. Rep. 700 (Ch. 1723) (weak 72 year old easily imposed on—inadequacy relevant); Williams v. Baily, 2 L.R. Eq. 731 (1866) (pressure of husband on wife in separation agreement).

67. Smith v. Kay, 7 H.L.C. 750, 779, 11 Eng. Rep. 299, 310–311 (1859) (House of Lords review of Chancery presumes confidence put in fiduciary, as an attorney.); *and see* Haydock v. Haydock, 34 N.J. Eq. 570, 574 (1881) (fiduciary relationship).

68. *See* Adams v. Irving National Bank, 116 N.Y. 606 (1889).

69. Colgate v. Bacheler, Cro. Eliz. 872, 78 Eng. Rep. 1097 (1602) (contract restraining trade void); Ipswich Tailors Case, 11 Co. Rep. 53a, 77 Eng. Rep. 1218 (1614) (Guild system not allowed to bar entrant to trade. Coke disingenuously said this was and "always has been the common law".); *cf.* Mitchel v. Reynolds, 1 P. Wms. 181, 24 Eng. Rep. 347 (1711) (reasonableness test for restraints).

70. *See* 1 T. PARSONS, *supra* note 6, at 3 ("The law of contracts, in its widest extent may be regarded as including nearly all the law which regulates the relations of human life. Indeed, it may be looked upon as the basis of human society".). *And see* MAX WEBER ON LAW IN ECONOMY AND SOCIETY 100–101, 228–229 (Cambridge, Mass., M. Rheinstein ed. 1954).

71. M. HORWITZ, *supra* note 44, at xvi, 201, 259–260; Tushnet, *Perspectives on the Development of American Law: A Critical Review of Friedman's "A History of American Law,"* 1977 WIS. L. REV. 81, 94.

72. J. HURST, *supra* note 24, at 5–6, 29; P. ATIYAH, *supra* note 40, at 389–390; Ferguson, *The Horwitz Thesis and Common Law Discourse in England,* 3 OXFORD J. LEGAL STUDIES 34, 39 (1983). *Cf.* Simpson, *The Horwitz Thesis and the History of Contracts,* 46 U. CHI. L. REV. 533, 600–601 (1979) (Oppressed lived outside world that contract doctrine impacted.). Slaves' lack of personal freedom, let alone contractual freedom, festered in a semi-autonomous regional realm of racism within Southern society. Grossberg, *Legal History and Social Science: Friedman's History of American Law, The Second Time Around,* 13 LAW AND SOCIAL INQUIRY 359, 377–380 (1988).

73. Williams v. Phelps, 16 Wis. 83, 86 (1862); Printing and Numerical Co. v. Sampson, L.R. 19 Eq. 462, 465 (1875); Diamond Match Co. v. Roeber, 106 N.Y. 473, 13 N.E. 419 (1887).

74. Egerton v. Brownlow, 4 H.L.C.1, 10 Eng. Rep. 359 (1853) (Public policy was refused as basis for overturning a will, or a contract, because vague and uncertain.). *Cf.* Hamburger, *supra* note 15, at 291 (Political economy did little to shape consensus theory other than to contribute skepticism about civilian ideas of equality.).

75. *See* J. HURST, *supra* note 24, at 8–13.

76. L. FRIEDMAN, *supra* note 38, at 18–21 (Parol evidence rule complemented abstraction in providing consistent objective treatment for similar doc-

uments. *Id.* at 95–96); Riesenfeld, *The Influence of German Theory on American Law: The Heritage of Savigny and His Disciples,* 37 AM. J. COMP. LAW 1, 3 (1989). But the use of specific performance for land was exception to notion of land as abstract commodity due to both peculiarities of land and carryover of earlier class-conscious era. *Id.* at 131–132. *But cf.* Summers, *Collective Agreements and the Law of Contracts,* 78 YALE L.J. 525, 566n (1969) (Would modify Friedman's "pure" contract point to recognize there were social values other than freedom of contract injected by courts and legislatures.). It has been argued that Friedman's idea in his HISTORY OF AMERICAN LAW (2d ed. 1985) that the common law of contract is a 'mirror" of society overlooks both the relatively autonomous nature of the law in regard to particular events and the ability of the law to purvey values. Tushnet, *supra* note 71, at 81, 94; Grossberg, *supra* note 72, at 373–374.

77. L. FRIEDMAN, *supra* note 38, at 23–24 (Due to contract's residual character, there was no need to change its structure by codification.).

78. *See* M. HORWITZ, *supra* note 44, at 264.

79. Andrew v. Boughey, 1 Dyer 75a, 73 Eng. Rep. 160 (1552).

80. Haigh v. Brooks, 10 Ad. & El. 309, 113 Eng. Rep. 119 (1839); see W. STORY, *supra* note 6, at 73.

81. Mortimer v. Capper, Bro. C.C. 156, 28 Eng. Rep. 1051 (Ch. 1782); Ward v. Weber, 1 Va. (1 Wash.) 274 (1794); Seymour v. Delancey, 3 Cow. 445 (N.Y. 1824) (N.Y. High Court of Errors reversed Chancellor Kent's refusal to grant specific performance due to inadequacy.); *but cf.* Clitherall v. Ogilvie, 1 S.C. Eq. (1 Des. 250) (S.C. 1792) (specific performance refused due to inadequacy). South Carolina was more equitable in applying adequacy and *caveat emptor* during 19th century.

82. Chandelor v. Lopus, Cro. Jac. 4, 79 Eng. Rep. 3 (1604); Parkinson v. Lee, 2 East 314, 102 Eng. Rep. 389 (1802) (*caveat emptor* when no express warranty and no implied warranty of quality); Seixas v. Woods, 2 Cai. R. 48 (N.Y. 1804) (Kent, J. concurred in 2 to 1 decision, which cited *Chandelor v. Lopus,* in refusing relief when peachum wood sold for more valuable brazilletto wood.).

83. McFarland v. Newman, 9 Watts 55 (Pa. 1839); Hopkins v. Tanqueray, 15 C.B. 130, 139 Eng. Rep. 369 (1854); *but cf.* Smith v. Justice, 13 Wis. 600, 602 (1861) (Court turned seller's statement that horse was "allright" into a warranty.).

84. Wright v. Hart, 18 Wend. 449 (N.Y. 1837) (harsh); Barnard v. Kellogg, 77 U.S. 383, 388 (1870) ("of such universal acceptance" that almost all states use it); Hamilton, *The Ancient Maxim Caveat Emptor,* 40 YALE L.J. 1133, 1176–1181 (1931); W. STORY, *supra* note 6, at 331–333.

85. Laing v. Fidgeon, 6 Taunt. 108, 128 Eng. Rep. 974 (1815); *see* W. STORY, *supra* note 6, at 331–333. Story provided a masterly discussion and bemoaned the "perplexed and unsatisfactory" state of warranty law. If inspection possible, *caveat emptor* applied with a vengeance. *See, e.g.,* Emmerton v. Mathews, 7 H. & N. 586, 158 Eng. Rep. 604 (1862) (no implied warranty for meat). But the Carolinas used notions of sound price to soften *caveat emptor.* Torris v. Long, 1 N.C. (Tayl. 17) 111 (1799).

86. *See* Hamilton, *supra* note 84, at 1173.

87. *See* J. HURST, *supra* note 24, at 7–8.

88. *See Id.* at 23–24 (Modern notion of private property began as legislature

became responsive to property interests.); *see also* M. HORWITZ, *supra* note 44, at 22–30. *Cf.* Paine, *Instrumentalism and Formalism: Dissolving the Dichotomy,* 1978 WIS. L. REV. 997 (The 2 models of legal decision making of instrumentalism and formalism aren't mutually exclusive: rational argument requires both principles (formalism) and reasons referring to consequences (instrumentalism). *And see* Hamburger, *supra* note 15, at 247 (common law wasn't instrument of commercial interests if it would cause open discontinuity in doctrine.).

89. American courts interpreted marine insurance contracts to serve "the solid interests of this growing country" rather than giving full faith and credit to English decisions which were related to England's own "political expediency" as a nation often at war. Vandenheuvel v. United Ins. Co., 2 Cai. Cas. 217, 289 (N.Y. 1805); *see* Ludlow v. Bowne, 1 Johns. 1, 7 (N.Y. 1806); *and see* M. HORWITZ, *supra* note 44, at 27–28.

90. 2 A. DE TOCQUEVILLE, DEMOCRACY IN AMERICA 156–157 (tr. H. Reeve, 1840) (Americans' love of order essential to business). The phenomenal power of abstractions in a democratic society, observed by Tocqueville, surely contributed to the success of the slogan freedom of contract.

91. Dorfman, *Chancellor Kent and the Developing American Economy,* 61 COLUM. L. REV. 1290, 1290–1295 (1961) (Kent was investor, speculator in land, trustee of proposed R.R. and receiver of bank.); M. HORWITZ, *supra* note 44, at 149–154.

92. P. ATIYAH, *supra* note 40, at 369–388; Ferguson, *supra* note 72, at 37–38 (1983) (alliance and instrumentalism not uniquely American).

93. Stocker v. Harris, 3 Mass. 409, 413 (1807); Rice v. Austin, 7 Mass. 197, 206 (1821); *cf.* M. HORWITZ, *supra* note 44, at 16–30, 140–159 (started in 19th century); *see also* J. HURST, *supra* note 24, at 10–11.

94. *See* K. LLEWELLYN, THE COMMON LAW TRADITION: DECIDING APPEALS 36–37 (Boston: 1960).

95. *See* Silva v. Low, 1 Johns. Cas. 184, 190 (N.Y. 1799) (If precedent rigidly followed, common law can't be improved.).

96. U.S. CONST. art I, sect. 10(1); Fletcher v. Peck, 6 Cranch 87 (U.S. 1810) (protection for executed contracts and deeds); Dartmouth College v. Woodward, 4 Wheat. 518 (U.S. 1819) (protection to legislative grant of corporate charter); Bronson v. Kinzie, 1 How. 311 (U.S. 1843) (Illinois statute extending mortgagor's redemption period unconstitutional).

97. Charles River Bridge v. Warren Bridge, 36 U.S. (11 Pet.) 420 (1837).

98. *See* L. FRIEDMAN, *supra* note 38, at 134 (breach of abstraction when use of common resources singled out); *see also* M. HORWITZ, *supra* note 44, at 130 (Monopoly privilege that was necessary to sustain first bridge no longer needed in expanding economy.). Story, J. dissented in *Charles River Bridge* case due to uncertainties for franchise holders.

99. Swift v. Tyson, 16 Pet. 1 (U.S. 1842). Admiralty and maritime jurisdiction was extended under CONST. art. III, sect. 2 to provide uniformity in shipping at sea and on inland waterways. *See* DeLovio v. Boit, 7 Fed. Cas. 418 (No. 3, 776) (C.C.D. Mass. 1815) (marine insurance cases included, per Story).

100. *See* Simpson, *supra* note 72, at 600 (dethronement of jury with reception of civil law elaboration); *and see* W. NELSON, AMERICANIZATION OF THE

COMMON LAW 7 (Cambridge, Mass. 1975) (Consensus of community gone as Mass. became heterogeneous, but business needed certainty.).

101. W. NELSON, *supra* note 100, at 3–4, 8, 167–168; M. HORWITZ, *supra* note 44, at 143.

102. Stat. 6 & 7 Vic., ch.85 (1843) ("Lord Denman's Act"); Mich. Rev. Stat., c.102, s.99 (1846). Parties could testify in Connecticut 2 years before they could in England. Bentham wanted all parties to be required to testify.

103. T. SEDGWICK, A TREATISE ON THE MEASURE OF DAMAGES 48–49n (N.Y. 1847). Equity would go behind the seal to the substance, and after the fusion of the courts, the remaining states followed with legislation.

104. In N.Y. seal was only rebuttable presumption of consideration by 1836. Rev. Stats. N.Y. 1836, vol. II, p. 328; L. FRIEDMAN, *supra* note 38, at 91–92 (Seal had no importance in Wisconsin from Territorial days of 1830s.); L. FRIEDMAN, *supra* note 48, at 278–279 (U.S. literacy rate high).

105. Boone v. Eyre, 2 W. Bl. 1312, 96 Eng. Rep. 767 (1777); *see* Broom v. Davis, cited at 7 East 481n., 103 Eng. Rep. 186n (1794) (Builder could sue for work and owner could counterclaim for breach.); *see also* Hall v. Cazenove, 4 East 477, 102 Eng. Rep. 913 (1804) (*Boone* applied as court looked to "substance of the covenant" and found "primary intention of [charter] parties" was shipment and not that done on time.).

106. Farnsworth v. Garrard, 1 Camp. 38, 170 Eng. Rep. 867 (1807); Ellis v. Hamlen, 3 Taunt. 52, 128 Eng. Rep. 21 (1810).

107. Cutler v. Close, 5 C. & P. 337, 172 Eng. Rep. 1001 (1832); *see* S. STOLJAR, A HISTORY OF CONTRACT AT COMMON LAW 167–168 (Canberra: 1975); *see also* Ellen v. Topp, 6 Exch. 424, 155 Eng. Rep. 609 (1851) (*Boone v. Eyre* must be interpreted to require substantial performance.).

108. *See* Ellen v. Topp, 6 Exch. 424, 155 Eng. Rep. 609 (1851); *see also* 3A A. CORBIN, *supra* note 41, at sect. 660.

109. Cutter v. Powell, 6 T.R. 320, 101 Eng. Rep 573 (1795); *see* W. STORY, *supra* note 6, at 8–9.

110. *See* Y.B. Mich., 10 Hen. VI, f.23, pl.78 (1432); Countess of Plymouth v. Throgmorton, 1 Salk. 65, 91 Eng. Rep. 61 (1688) (Employee got nothing on 1 year contract for £100 when employer died after 9 mo.); Barton, *Contract and Quantum Meruit: The Antecedents of Cutter v. Powell*, 8 J. LEGAL HIST. 48, 48–49 (1987) (Employee could recover for work done if "hired generally".).

111. S. STOLJAR, *supra* note 107, at 176, 197.

112. Hayward v. Leonard, 24 Mass. (7 Pick.) 181 (1828).

113. L. FRIEDMAN, *supra* note 38, at 109–110; M. HORWITZ, *supra* note 44, at 188 (courts aiding capital investment of building trade).

114. Hochster v. De La Tour, 5 El. & Bl. 678, 118 Eng. Rep. 922 (1853).

115. Phillpotts v. Evans, 5 M & W 475, 477, 151 Eng. Rep. 200, 202 (1839) (If there was notice of anticipatory repudiation and a later failure to perform, damages were calculated from due date and not date of notice, citing Leigh v. Paterson, 8 Taunt. 540, 129 Eng. Rep. 493 (1818), a case of a rising market.).

116. In a similar vein, the court in Pinnel's Case, 5 Co. Rep. 117a, 77 Eng. Rep. 237 (1602) fell into the trap of thinking that the requirement of consideration for the formation of a contract should also be present for a discharge by accord.

117. Campbell, C.J. said in *Hochster* there was a breach of a "relation" created by making the contract. *See* Vold, *The Tort Aspects of Anticipatory Repudiation of Contracts*, 41 HARV. L. REV. 340 (1928) (may be a tort). *See also* E. FARNSWORTH, CONTRACTS 629n. (Boston: 1982) (like a breach of good faith—contract value impaired if victim tries to assign after repudiation).

118. Daniels v. Newton, 114 Mass. 530 (1874).

119. F. POLLOCK, PRINCIPLES OF CONTRACT 8 (London: 1876) (makes only oblique reference to *Hochster*); W. STORY, A TREATISE ON THE LAW OF CONTRACTS (5th ed. M. Bigelow, 1874) (cites *Hochster* as merely emerging rule).

120. 2 T. PARSONS, THE LAW OF CONTRACTS 781, 790–791 (S. Williston ed., 8th ed. 1893); *see* Williston, *Repudiation of Contracts* (pts. 1 & 2), 14 HARV. L. REV. 317, 421 (1901).

121. Roehm v. Horst, 178 U.S. 1 (1900) RESTATEMENT OF CONTRACTS sect. 318 (St. Paul: 1932). Reporter Williston capitulated to caselaw and included it in Restatement.

122. For a discussion of the 3 purposes for awarding contract damages, *see* Fuller and Perdue, *The Reliance Interest in Contract Damages* (pt. 1), 46 YALE L.J. 52, 52–54 (1936) (In protecting expectation, the law is not merely healing disturbed status quo, due to reliance or the need for restitution, but is bringing into being a new situation. *Id.* at 56. Expectation is protected in furtherance of policy of promoting reliance. *Id.* at 61–62.).

123. Washington, *Damages in Contract at Common Law* (pt. 1), 47 L.Q. REV. 345, 373 (1931).

124. Orwell v. Mortoft, Y.B. Mich. 20 Hen. VII, f.8, pl.18, Keil. 69 (1505) and Pykeryng v. Thurgoode, K.B. 27/1073, m. 70 (1532), both *reprinted in* J. BAKER and S. MILSOM, SOURCES OF ENGLISH LEGAL HISTORY 406, 408, 411 (London: 1986).

125. Field's Case, 2 Rolle Rep. 133, 81 Eng. Rep. 707 (1619) (award of wager and not just stake); Gardener v. Pullen & Phillips, 2 Vern. 394, 23 Eng. Rep. 853 (Ch. 1700); Cuddee v. Rutter (Ch. 1719) in 5 C. VINER, A GENERAL ABRIDGMENT OF LAW AND EQUITY 538–540 (Contract and Agreement, M.21) (London: 2d ed. 1792), reported also in 24 Eng. Rep. 521 (Damages are difference of contract price and delivery date market value for sale of stock or of corn.); Dutch v. Warren, 1 Stra. 406, 93 Eng. Rep. 598 (K.B. 1720) (Buyer must take stock rather than recovery of payment in falling market.); Smee v. Huddleston (C.P. 1768) in J. SAYER, THE LAW OF DAMAGES 49–51 (London: 1770) (goods); 2 J. POWELL, *supra* note 4, at 232–233 (specific performance for failure to deliver stock); Lewis v. Carradan (Pa. 1786), cited in 1 Yeates 37 (sale of wheat); Groves v. Graves, 1 Va. (1 Wash.) 4 (1790) (securities); Marshall v. Campbell, 1 Yeates 36 (Pa. 1791) (stock); Davis v. Richardson, 1 Bay 105 (S. C. 1793) (securities); *see* T. SEDGWICK, *supra* note 103, at 260–265 (citing 18th century English and American cases).

126. Smee v. Huddleston (C.P. 1768) in J. SAYER, *supra* note 125, at 49–51 (The loss the seller suffered wasn't the value of tea but difference between contract price and amount received at public sale held after defendant's refusal.); Sands v. Taylor, 5 Johns. 395 (N.Y. 1810); Boorman v. Nash, 9 B. & C. 145, 109 Eng. Rep. 54 (1829); Clark v. Marsiglia, 1 Denio 317 (N.Y. Sup. Ct. 1845).

127. Case of William Strete aka Strate (1528) in THE REPORTS OF SIR

JOHN SPELMAN, 94 SELDEN SOC. 295 (J. Baker ed., London: 1978) (Jury instructed to put plaintiff where he'd have been if promise performed.). Damages were limited to the amount in plaintiff's declaration. Osborne's Case, 10 Co. Rep. 130a, 77 Eng. Rep. 1123 (1613).

128. Bright v. Eynon, 1 Burr 390, 394, 97 Eng. Rep. 365 (1757) (Since Equity granting new trials, common law courts of late doing the same.); Huckle v. Money, 2 Wils. 205, 95 Eng. Rep. 768 (1763) (new trial on damages in non-contract case). *See* Markham v. Middleton, 2 Stra. 1259, 93 Eng. Rep. 1167 (1746) (writ of inquiry set aside for smallness of damages).

129. J. SAYER, *supra* note 125, at 200–202 ("as much reason for granting new trial on account of smallness of the damages, as the largeness thereof"); Washington, *Damages in Contract at Common Law* (pt. 2), 48 L.Q. REV. 90, 90–92 (1932) (courts more likely to overturn contract than tort verdicts since contract criteria more certain); Tutton v. Andrews, Barn. 448, 94 Eng. Rep. 998 (1741) (New writ of inquiry due to improper evidence. Dictum that new trial on excessive damages but not when too little.). The plaintiff-oriented common count system, allowing even arguably questionable claims to get to the jury, may have prompted the court to lean toward the defendant when reviewing damages verdicts.

130. Smee v. Huddleston (C.P. 1768) in J. SAYER, *supra* note 125, at 49 (Wilmot, C.J. directed jury to assess damages at difference between contract price and public sale after defendant-buyer's refusal of tender.). Serjeant Sayer's book was the first written on damages. T. Sedgwick wrote the first American treatise on damages in 1847.

131. Bridge v. Wain, 1 Stark 504, 506, 171 Eng. Rep. 543, 544 (1816). For an earlier view, *see* Nurse v. Barns, T. Raym. 77, 83 Eng. Rep. 43 (1664) (Jury allowed to award "all the special loss" of 500 pounds reliance damages on 10 pound lease.). Much of the discussion in the early 19th century centered on whether calculations should be based on market value at the date of breach, the due date or trial date. Shepherd v. Johnson, 2 East. 211, 102 Eng. Rep. 349 (1802) (Plaintiff could have damages based on higher value at due date or trial date.); *see* Shepherd v. Hampton, 16 U.S. (3 Wheat.) 200 (1818) (due date).

132. Walton v. Fothergil, 7 C. & P. 392, 173 Eng. Rep. 174 (1835) (failure to ship brandy).

133. Startup v. Cortazzi, 2 C.M. & R. 165, 150 Eng. Rep. 171 (1835).

134. Black v. Baxendale, 1 Ex. 410, 154 Eng. Rep. 174 (1847).

135. Hadley v. Baxendale, 9 Ex. 341, 156 Eng. Rep. 145 (1854).

136. Walton v. Fothergil, 7 C. & P. 392 (1835); W. STORY, *supra* note 6, at 428; *see* Armstrong v. Percy, 5 Wend. (N.Y.) 535, 538 ("such as naturally arise from the breach".). *See also* Boorman v. Nash, 9 B. & C. 145, 109 Eng. Rep. 54 (1829) (damages that "necessarily resulted" from breach).

137. Alderson's conclusion seems unsympathetic to the plaintiff in light of the case report of evidence at trial that plaintiff told defendant the mill was stopped, to send shaft immediately and to use a special entry if it would hasten it. *But cf.* Victoria Laundry v. Newman Ind., 2 K.B. 528, 537, 1 All Eng. Rep. 997, 1001 (1949) (Alderson must have rejected that evidence at trial or he would "have decided the case the other way around."). Or it could be interpreted that Alderson didn't conclude it was communicated that the mill was stopped because of broken shaft.

138. Waters v. Towers, 8 Ex. 401, 155 Eng. Rep. 1404 (1853).

139. 2 J. KENT, COMMENTARIES ON AMERICAN LAW 480 (N.Y., 4th ed. 1830).

140. Hadley v. Baxendale, 9 Ex. 341, 349 (1854). Parke probably said this because the loss in *Waters* was caused by the unavailability of the machinery the defendant was to fit up. *See* Danzig, *Hadley v. Baxendale: A Study in the Industrialization of the Law,* 4 J. LEGAL STUDIES 249, 264 (1975) (1830 statute limiting carriers' liability for loss of valuables, unless notice, influenced Parke.). *See also* J. BAKER, AN INTRODUCTION TO ENGLISH LEGAL HISTORY 173 (London: 2d ed. 1979) (Parke's emphasis on following precedent helped elevate *stare decisis* in 19th century.).

141. T. SEDGWICK, *supra* note 103, at 64, 67.

142. 1 R. POTHIER, *supra* note 10, at 81.

143. Williams v. Barton, 13 La. R. 404, 410 (1839) (cited La. code); T. SEDGWICK, *supra* note 103, at 64–67, 76.

144. *See* 1 R. POTHIER, *supra* note 10, at 4.

145. *See* Barton, *Contractual Damages and the Rise of Industry,* 7 OXF. J. LEGAL STUDIES 40 (1987) (civilian rather than judicial invention).

146. The report of *Hadley v. Baxendale,* 9 Ex. 341, 345 (1854) said case was left "generally to the jury", but Danzig writes that a *Gloucester Journal* news story reported a "natural consequences" instruction. Danzig, *supra* note 140, at 252. It is arguable that there is no difference between the 2 instructions.

147. Plaintiff in *Hadley* cited consequential damages case of Nurse v. Barn, T. Raym. 77, 83 Eng. Rep. 43 (1664), wherein reliance damage of laying in 500 pounds worth of stock recoverable in reliance on 10 pound lease. *See* Fuller & Perdue (pt. 1), *supra* note 122, at 78 (assumes there was foreseeability in *Nurse*). *And see* Danzig, *supra* note 140, at 250 (judicial invention for industry); *contra* Barton, *supra* note 145, at 58–59 (consequential loss no less serious in pre-industrial period).

148. *Hadley v. Baxendale* was not even mentioned in the 5th edition of W. Story's contract treatise edited by M. Bigelow in 1874.

149. Griffen v. Colver, 16 N.Y. 489 (1858); Shepard v. Milwaukee Gas Co., 15 Wis. 318 (1862); Abbott v. Gatch, 13 Md. 314 (1858).

150. British Columbia Saw Mill Co. v. Nettleship, L.R. 3 C.P. 499 (1868).

151. T. SEDGWICK, A TREATISE ON THE MEASURE OF DAMAGES 78–81 (A. Sedgwick 5th ed., N.Y. 1869) ("affirmation of the doctrine" in his treatise's 1847 edition. *Id.* at 79n.); Danzig, *supra* note 140, at 275.

152. Griffen v. Colver, 16 N.Y. 489 (1858) (and "certain" damages); T. SEDGWICK, *supra* note 151, at 79n (unlike English alternatives). England agrees with U.S. courts today. Victoria Laundry v. Newman Ind. 2 K.B. 528, 537, 1 All Eng. Rep. 997, 1001 (1949) (requires foreseeability either "actual" or "imputed").

153. Washington (pt. 2), *supra* note 129, at 97; J. HURST, *supra* note 24, at 20; *see* Wilson v. Newport Dock Co., 35 L.J. Ex. 97, 103 (1866) (Pollock, C.B. said that Martin, B., who in *Hadley* was concerned with excessive damages, saw case taking into account the "exigencies of commerce".); *cf.* Danzig, *supra* note 140, at 282 (Potential breachor could calculate whether breach would be an efficient move.). Mitigation and limited liability for corporations were other

examples of limitations. *And see* Danzig, *supra* note 140, at 266–267 (*Hadley* judges Martin and Parke had personal connections with defendant.).

154. Washington (pt. 2), *supra* note 129, at 97, 107; T. SEDGWICK, *supra* note 103, at 38; L. FRIEDMAN, *supra* note 38, at 125–128 (Protection from ruinous loss was catalyst for enterprise.).

155. British Columbia Saw Mill Co. v. Nettleship, L.R. 3 C.P. 499, 509 (1868). Although the Uniform Commercial Code allows parties to exclude liability for consequential commercial loss under U.C.C. sect. 2–719(3), a "tacit agreement" test for recovery of consequential damages is rejected. U.C.C. sect. 2–715, Comment 2.

156. O. HOLMES, JR., THE COMMON LAW 301–302 (Boston: 1881).

157. *See* Washington (pt. 1), *supra* note 123, at 364 (New trial after jury verdict is more likely in contract than in tort because contract damages more certain.); *see also* Fuller and Perdue (pt. 2), *supra* note 122, at 374–375 (more likely to avoid "uncertainty" of damages objection if breach willful).

158. Globe Refining Co. v. Landa Cotton Oil Co., 190 U.S. 540, 544–545 (1903) (per Holmes); Elbinger Actien-Gesellschaft v. Armstrong, L.R. 9 Q.B. 473, 478 (1874) (per Blackburn); *see* G. GILMORE, *supra* note 56, at 50.

159. *See* L. FRIEDMAN, *supra* note 38, at 126–127. However, the U.C.C. requires a buyer to mitigate by "covering" by purchasing substitute goods. U.C.C. sect. 2–715(2)(a).

160. *See* Waterman, *supra* note 3, at 644–646 (Jefferson opposed anti-republicanism of Blackstone and Mansfield.).

161. Bentham's writings relevant to contract law include: LEGISLATION (1802), CODIFICATION (1817) and JUDICIAL EVIDENCE (1823). His anonymous A FRAGMENT ON GOVERNMENT (1776) was an attack on his former teacher, Blackstone.

162. Dillon, *Bentham's Influence on the Reforms of the Nineteenth Century* in 1 SELECT ESSAYS IN ANGLO-AMERICAN LEGAL HISTORY 492 (Boston: 1907); Holdsworth, *Bentham's Place in English Legal History,* 28 CALIF. L. REV. 568, 570–579, 583 (1940) (Bentham invented the word "codification".); P. ATIYAH, *supra* note 40, at 324–332; C. COOK, THE AMERICAN CODIFICATION MOVEMENT: A STUDY OF ANTEBELLUM LEGAL REFORM, 74–89 (Westport, Conn., 1981). Interregnum reformers were precursors of Bentham's ideas on: restricting judicial discretion, fusion of law and equity and making the law more understandable. *See* N. MATTHEWS, WILLIAM SHEPPARD, CROMWELL'S LAW REFORMER 125, 149–150, 175–176 (Cambridge: 1984).

163. *See* Waterman, *supra* note 3, at 657 (Kent and J. Story brought in Blackstone's common law.). Kent emphasized uniform practices in commercial centers.

164. Swift v. Tyson, 16 Pet. 1 (U.S. 1842); *see* G. GILMORE, THE AGES OF AMERICAN LAW 34 (New Haven: 1977) (The anticipatory repudiation case of Roehm v. Horst, 178 U.S. 1 (1900) is an example of the unification of commercial law under *Swift.*).

165. J. BAKER, *supra* note 140, at 59–60.

166. Some American courts continued Mansfield's flexibility. *See* Kline v. Husted, 3 Cai. R. 275, 278 (N.Y. 1805) (amendment of pleading allowed when technical objection).

167. H. STEPHEN, A TREATISE ON THE PRINCIPLES OF PLEADING IN CIVIL ACTIONS 312 (London: 2d ed. 1827).

168. Hepburn, *The Historical Development of Code Pleading in America and England* in 2 SELECT ESSAYS IN ANGLO-AMERICAN LEGAL HISTORY 643; Holdsworth, *The New Rules of Pleading of the Hilary Term, 1834,* 1 CAMBRIDGE L.J. 261, 261–272 (1923); C. FIFOOT, *supra* note 31, at 232–241.

169. Eastwood v. Kenyon, 11 Ad. & E. 438, 113 Eng. Rep. 482 (1840); Holdsworth, *supra* note 168, at 273–274. *See* Simpson, *supra* note 5, at 268 (Hilary Rules may have forced mistake to be handled under consideration.).

170. Hepburn, *supra* note 168, at 655–680; M. HORWITZ, *supra* note 44, at 265–266 (a move to formalism); P. ATIYAH, *supra* note 40, at 394.

171. Reimann, *The Historical School Against Codification: Savigny, Carter and the Defeat of the New York Civil Code,* 37 AM. J. COMP. LAW 95, 98–99, 103–104, 114–116 (1989) (Savigny's ideas fit with Darwinist ideas of Carter's day. *Id.* at 108.). Savigny was attracted to Roman law and thought law could only be understood in an historical dimension. Field's ideas for a code of substantive law fared better in California, Georgia, Montana, Idaho and Dakota Territory.

172. Although the common counts were creditor-oriented, since there was a stronger policy to allow the plaintiff's case before the jury than to protect the defendant from surprise, merchants still preferred the new system since it cut down on expenses and delays.

173. Hepburn, *supra* note 168, at 681; C. FIFOOT, HISTORY AND SOURCES OF THE COMMON LAW 370–371 (London: 1949); Williams, *Pleading Reform in Nineteenth Century America: The Joinder of Actions at Common Law and Under the Codes,* 6 JOURNAL OF LEGAL HISTORY 313–315 (1985).

174. 3 T. STREET, THE FOUNDATIONS OF LEGAL LIABILITY 57–58 (1906). Partnerships with common members couldn't sue each other at-law, but now it was allowed since Equity had allowed it. Cole v. Reynolds, 18 N.Y. 74 (1858). *See* L. FRIEDMAN, *supra* note 38, at 118–120 (furthered goal of facilitating transfer of any asset with a market).

175. J. HURST, *supra* note 24, at 14, 24.

176. L. FRIEDMAN, *supra* note 38, at 84; L. FRIEDMAN, *supra* note 48, at 208–211.

177. *See* L. FRIEDMAN, *supra* note 38, at 84–85 (Courts left incapacity of women alone, to preserve abstraction, but gave relief by expanding fraud, mistake and undue influence.); *see also* L. FRIEDMAN, *supra* note 48, at 208–211.

178. A. SIMPSON, *supra* note 9, at 588–590 (Its use in Assumpsit may have contributed to that action's rise.).

179. W. NELSON, *supra* note 100, at 41, 150 (1713 Mass. statute provided for imprisonment, but debtor prisons ended by Mass. Laws of 1855, ch. 444); L. FRIEDMAN, *supra* note 48, at 272.

180. Sturges v. Crowninshield, 4 Wheat. (17 U.S.) 122, 200–201 (1819) ("An excess of inhumanity" not to be "imputed to the illustrious patriots who framed our constitution."). *See* Gold, *John Appleton of Maine and Commercial Law: Freedom, Responsibility and Law in the Nineteenth Century Marketplace,* 4 LAW AND HIST. REV. 55, 56–57 (1986) (There were moral values and ideas of responsible individualism within 19th century judiciary.).

181. L. FRIEDMAN, *supra* note 48, at 269–270, 480; C. WARREN, BANKRUPTCY IN UNITED STATES HISTORY 21–22 (Cambridge, Mass. 1935); J. HURST, *supra* note 24, at 26.

CHAPTER 7

MODERN DOCTRINAL REFORMULATION (1875 onward, I)

This chapter focuses on the adjustments made to classical contract rules from 1875 onward. The final chapter which follows will also cover the period 1875 onward but will focus on the legislative and judicial modifications made to attain some balance between those contractors having leverage in the market and those that do not. The course of American contract law during the modern period continued to be influenced by treatise writers, who were now teachers in the emerging national law schools and members of a newly organized national bar and would later be drafters of codes and restatement. These lawyers continued to answer the ongoing call for reform by pushing for more clarity, uniformity and formality in the law; and, under the spell of market ideas, they would reshape the doctrine of consideration to reflect the market. Reformulation of doctrine would also be influenced by changes in the economy and in legal procedure. The loss of individualism, brought on by the disparity of bargaining power during the industrial revolution, and the fusion of law and equity influenced the development of supplemental equitable grounds for relief based on unjust enrichment and reliance. The differences between American and English law became more pronounced during the last century; this divergence can be attributed in part to the relative ease of modifying the common law in a country of multiple jurisdictions like the United States where the degree of judicial conservatism generated by *stare decisis* is not as great.

Urge to Codify

During the last quarter of the nineteenth century, the established bar responded to the public pressure for law reform by avoiding the issue of social consciousness and instead promoting the distillation of uniform, consistent principles from the complexity of the vast body of caselaw in the various jurisdictions.[1] The emergence of national law schools and treatise writing law professors searching for the true rule of law were manifestations of the legal profession's interest in developing a construct that came to be known as Legal Formalism[2] in order to show the consistency and neutrality of the law and thereby head off uniformity through codification. There was a concern that codification would take away the flexibility of the common law and its capacity to grow. The German Historical School, pioneered by Savigny, was influential here since it preferred constantly evolving custom over codes; furthermore, Savigny thought academics were the appropriate ones to improve legal science rather than legislators.[3]

This return to a sort of early eighteenth century formalism, albeit with greater uniformity, occurred in both England[4] and the United States. The American leader was Dean Langdell, more important as a pedagogical innovator than as a theorist, who found the desired uniformity in leading English contract cases. English law provided a unified paradigm for Langdell since England had an advanced commercial law and the advantage of a single common law jurisdiction. Langdell presented the law of contracts as consisting of universal absolutes wherein the "true rule" could be found in its scientific deductive system[5]—a writer has a penchant for order and categorization in spite of the lack of those characteristics in the pronouncements in the scattered caselaw. Policy and fairness were not considered in the interest of generality. Consistent with this view, the unpredictability of the jury system's softening of the harshness of the common law was curtailed, thus limiting particularized equitable inquiries.[6]

This emphasis on generality was the continuation of a process commenced with Mansfield's concern for certainty in commercial law. And, formalism, a sycophant of commerce, paid homage to the free market and the right of the individual to be free to contract and own property without government interference. Formalism has been criticized for cloaking the status quo with a mathematical accuracy thereby making the law appear apolitical and objective and concealing its diversity; a general principle can obscure the subtleties of a rule's history, its policy and deliberation.[7]

There are several possible explanations for the rise of formalism. The concept of law as a science based on higher principles permitted courts to ignore potentially volatile issues in the post Civil War period when there was a longing for peace and repose.[8] Reconstruction's conservatism paralleled a similar trend during the English Restoration. It has been suggested that formalism is the result of a coalescence of the "higher law" jurisprudence of the antislavery movement with a prevailing intellectual preoccupation with the scientific method. The common law as a science was reinforced by the intellectual influences in vogue of Savigny's emphasis on the law as a legal science and of Darwin's evolutionary theory.[9] Others see a class struggle wherein formalism disguised the disparities in bargaining power to preserve the status quo and deter redistribution of the increasing disparity in wealth.[10] It is also suggested that the rise of secularism caused a lessening of the hold of the equitable considerations in natural law. Still another view is that a lingering Jacksonian distrust of lawyers stimulated the profession to present the law as autonomous, neutral principles untainted by self interest.[11] Finally, one more influence of the legal profession that cannot be ignored was its attempt to retain its position as the American interest group most influential in interpretation of the complexity of the common law and in charting its course.[12]

Formalists, led by Langdell, saw a paradigmatic transaction for their general principles in a sale of goods.[13] The tightness of doctrine in sales, bolstered by the regularity of mercantile usage, would prove an ideal choice for the first partial codification of the common law of contracts in the 1890s, but, before turning to that, there will be a digression to analyze the development of this important field of contract law. The separate identity of a law of sales appeared in the late eighteenth century, but special treatment of sales of tangible personal property were evident much earlier, e.g., Debt's fifteenth century passing of property fiction, *caveat emptor*, *Slade's Case* itself, the common counts, the Statute of Frauds and expectation damages. With the onset of the British industrial revolution in the mid-eighteenth century, law merchant had to adapt to a shift from a usage for transactions among a close-knit clique of London traders, who could be a buyer one day and a seller the next, to long distance transactions between strangers, who were now manufacturers, suppliers, middlemen and purchasers. A pivotal case for the emergence of a law of sales was *Lickbarrow v. Mason* (1787), rendered by Justice Buller, a disciple of the dying Mansfield.[14] Buller used the terminology of common law "property", but only as a label, to provide general principles regarding the rights of sellers and distant buyers, rather than leaving it all generally to the jury. By holding that an unpaid seller could stop goods in transit upon a buyer's insolvency, greater value was given to the manufacturer over the purchaser of goods. Buller decreased buyers' rights by declaring that a buyer had only a defeasible right to the "property" in the goods, which was defeated by insolvency. One can sense a shift from an emphasis on the fifteenth century passing of property fiction to modern notions of transfer of title. This new law of sales was concerned with the distribution process from the manufacturer to the ultimate buyer, and courts interpreted the passing of title and risk of loss during transit in favor of the seller.[15]

Sales law, enunciated in leading English cases and based on common law doctrine and mercantile practices, developed rapidly during the first half of the nineteenth century. Nineteenth century common law judges, who were not steeped in the civil law as Mansfield had been, failed to follow Mansfield's lead of restricting commercial law to mercantile cases but instead merged it with agrarian common law thinking,[16] making it applicable to all buyers and retaining a bias for manufacturers long after the industrial revolution was no longer at an embryonic stage. The common law courts provided further security of title to the mass producer, as credit transactions became common by the 1880s, through recognition of the conditional sales device.[17] This preference for the seller was consistent with earlier common law doctrine, such as *caveat emptor*, but a view favoring the seller had never existed in law merchant.

Just prior to the turn of the twentieth century, advocates of formalism caved in to the push for codification and uniformity in the two safe areas consisting of tight doctrine of negotiable instruments and sales, fields where the rules were highly developed. Diversity in regional commercial law could not be tolerated in a national market generated by the American industrial revolution and its nationwide railroad network. The American Bar Association instigated the creation of the National Conference of Commissioners On Uniform State Laws in 1895, and in the next year there appeared the highly successful Negotiable Instruments Law, which relied heavily both on the English Bills of Exchange Act of 1882 and on California's Field Code of 1872. On the heels of this success, Williston drafted the Uniform Sales Act of 1906, based largely on the English Sales of Goods Act of 1893,[18] in an attempt to preserve the common law by its loose codification. Although the Sales Act did not really attempt to change the common law, it was a watershed event since the legislative process had never intruded upon the common law of contract in such an expansive, forthright manner, with the exceptions of the Statute of Frauds and the more recent abolition of the forms of action. The Uniform Sales Act did, however, highlight a trend in the caselaw[19] by recognizing an improvement of the rights of a buyer, when goods were defective, through the employment of a legal fiction that the implied warranty of merchantability was a condition precedent to the buyer's obligation to accept the goods. This revision was necessary due to new techniques of marketing and financing through middlemen over great distances. Furthermore, thereafter, as to sophisticated manufactured goods, inspection didn't necessarily bar the availability of implied warranty.[20] The crowding of consumers into the market in mass produced goods made it inevitable, from a policy standpoint, that implied warranties be strengthened in contravention of the former law for face-to-face sales of such non-standardized subject matter as horses.[21] *Caveat emptor* was no longer an entirely workable rule since buyers were not relying on their own judgment as much as on the integrity of the seller.[22]

The Uniform Sales Act did not pacify those identified with the movement known as Social Jurisprudence, a lawyerly counterpart to the Progressive Movement, since the Act did not include social and economic considerations. In reaction to these attacks, the established bar formed the American Law Institute in 1923 to restate the law in order "to clarify and simplify the law and to render it more certain."[23] This was once again the law profession's attempt to preserve their common law in the Langdellian mold rather than to reform it. A code heavily laden with reforms would diminish the importance and prestige of a legal profession vested with the role of interpreter of a complex science.[24] The Restatement of the Law of Contracts was published in 1932. Williston, the Restatement's Reporter and the author of the best contracts treatise to that date, was a latter day formalist desirous of retaining general principles, devoid of social or economic influence, and his viewpoint prevailed. Williston's Special Advisor on the Restatement was Corbin, a modern thinker who emphasized factual analysis and approved of judicial flexibility more than Williston; he would later complete an even greater contract treatise[25] and would have a large impact on the Restatement Second. The contrasting approaches of these two contract theorists gave the Restatement First a split personality, simultaneously drawn to past thinking and to the future. This duality was exhibited in a traditional handling of consideration, a mixed approach to the promissory estoppel innovation and a relatively liberal treatment of third party beneficiary, anticipatory repudiation and frustration.[26] The Restatement was almost immediately criticized for overemphasizing the objective standard, for glossing over opposition in both the caselaw and in the opinion of some experts and for preserving the status quo rather than reforming in light of economic and social changes.[27] Nevertheless, it did usher in some innovation, in particular promissory estoppel, and it aided uniformity by apprising judges of majority positions.

This restatement of the whole of contract law, which looked back to nineteenth century doctrine without taking into consideration the actual behavior of modern business contractors, was bound to come under attack. The bulk of the legal profession, judges included,[28] seemed to be out of touch with current mercantile practices. Mercantile usage had first started coming into the common law with Mansfield, though he had intended to keep the law of merchants and non-merchants separate, as it was under the civil law; however, his successors, trained only in the common law, mixed it all together. In the common law tradition, Williston favored unitary principles applicable to all contracts and thus opposed a law of sales for merchants separate from the law for non-merchants. Llewellyn, the heir apparent to Williston's position as the national sales law expert, was in accord with Corbin and Cordozo in failing to see a unity of doctrine necessarily applicable to all contracts.

Llewellyn thought, as Mansfield had, that the law for merchants should conform to business practices and standards. Legal Realists, led by Llewellyn, followed in the Progressive tradition of adjusting the law by legislation and pressed for a drastic revision of not only the Uniform Sales Act but commercial law generally, and their persuasiveness prompted an interest in a uniform commercial code.

The National Conference of Commissioners on Uniform State Laws convened in 1940 both to consider codification of portions of commercial law and to head off a Federal Sales Act proposed the same year. Llewellyn was named Reporter, and he began almost immediately. He drew on ideas he had formulated in the late 1930s and also on the contemporary state of law merchant. The old formalism was now in disrepute, and the restaters of the American Law Institute joined the project in 1942. A Uniform Revised Sales Act was approved in 1943, and that became the basis of Article 2 of the Code.[29] The final draft of the full Uniform Commercial Code was approved in 1952, and Pennsylvania passed it the next year, followed by Massachusetts four years later. The Code replaced seven uniform acts passed around the turn of the century, including the Uniform Sales Act (1906) and the Negotiable Instruments Law (1896).

There were several important innovations in the Code. To begin with, this was the first attempt to draft a comprehensive code of the commercial law, and it was in a precise language rather than the loose common law verbiage of the earlier uniform acts.[30] Good faith and unconscionability were adopted in opposition to an objective standard. The firm offer rule resurrected the notion of a sealed promise; here the Code went a step past the Restatement's recognition of irrevocability of the offer once there was part performance or reliance.[31] The Code abandoned the bilateral/unilateral dichotomy, with the offeror controlling the terms of the offer, since it bore little relation to business practice.[32] There was a deemphasis of who had the "property" at breach.[33] And there was a liberalization of the rules applicable to warranty, indefiniteness, impracticability, the parol evidence rule and the Statute of Frauds.

The U.C.C. was not without its critics. Williston, a defender of the common law, ultimately could not contain his opposition to the Code's use of language novel to the common law since it lacked an established judicial meaning.[34] On the other extreme, there was criticism of the old-fashioned priority on order and uniformity over reform since there was little concern for consumers[35] and the U.C.C. committee overruled such Llewellyn proposals as greater separation of rules for merchants and non-merchants, increased manufacturers' liability for defects, and futuristic interpretation opportunities for activist courts to use in averting the approaching obsolescence of a 1950s Code based on the law merchant of the late 1930s.[36]

U.C.C. Article 2 was of course for sales of goods, but its widespread acceptance by the 1960s prompted analogies to be drawn to the Code in other areas as services, land, franchises and in a Restatement (Second) of Contracts. Suggestions for another restatement began shortly after the U.C.C.'s publication, and work began on a second restatement in 1962. The first draft was published in 1964, and, after 14 tentative drafts, it was adopted in 1979 and published in 1981. Corbin, a supporter of the U.C.C., acted as consultant to the Restatement Second project by providing a critical review of the Restatement First.[37] The major changes from the Restatement First were innovations made by drawing analogies to the U.C.C. and also the increased recognition of reliance and restitution;[38] however, the U.C.C. innovations were not always followed when the prior caselaw failed to support it, especially when freedom of contract was restricted.[39] There have been criticisms of the Restatement Second effort both because it is argued to be a futile effort to preserve a judge-made system of contract law after fifty years of legislation and because it is said to be an illusion that general classical principles can still represent the law of contract without reference to particular facts.[40]

Reevaluation of Doctrine of Consideration and Related Matters

The cumulative effect of nineteenth century market forces and the statutory reforms of abolition of the forms and fusion of the courts would leave its imprint on contract law during the second half of the nineteenth century. Once the formulary system crumbled, judges found it necessary to dwell on principles as a means of retaining the order in the common law previously provided by the forms of action. It was then probably inevitable there would be a reappraisal of the so-called classical contract rules developed by the 1850s.[41] Not even the doctrine of consideration was immune from the process.

By the turn of the twentieth century, consideration's 350 year old duality of a detriment or a benefit was gradually being supplanted in the United States by the single test that consideration be "bargained for". The analysis of the principles behind consideration during the first half of the nineteenth century had caused an elaboration of consideration into independent sub-doctrines; as consideration fragmented, there was an urge to redefine the doctrine more narrowly. And, roughly contemporaneous with this reevaluation of consideration, the abolition of the forms of action and the merger of law and equity brought forth a unitary contract action in place of the alternatives of the various *indebitatus* counts and Special Assumpsit. These forces could lead one to logically conclude that this new action should appropriately have a unitary test of enforceability; this did indeed occur in both the United States and England but with different outcomes.

The impetus in the United States for the modern doctrine of bargain consideration as the sole test came from the writings of Holmes and was carried forward by Williston. In 1881 Holmes adumbrated the new theory when he wrote: "the root of the whole matter is the relation of reciprocal conventional inducement, each for the other, between consideration and promise." Holmes added, "It is hard to see the propriety of erecting any detriment which an instrument may disclose or provide for, into a consideration, unless the parties have dealt with it on that footing."[42] Two decades later Justice Holmes opined: "It is not enough that the promise induces the detriment or that the detriment induces the promise, if the other half is wanting."[43] In his view the benefit or detriment must be bargained for. Furthermore, under Holmes' bargain consideration theory, meaning should depend on the objectivity of the "overt acts" of the parties "according to the form of words" used rather than the "limited slavery" of the "state of the parties' minds".[44]

The influences on Holmes' conclusion that consideration was grounded on an objectively determined bargain seem to have come from his theory that consideration originated in Debt and from contemporaneous ideas floating around regarding community standards, the market and assent. Like St. Germain's sixteenth century work DOCTOR AND STUDENT, Holmes' book on the common law reflected contemporary social thought. Taking first the contemporary notion of community standards, his reciprocity idea may well have been influenced by his association with the Pragmatists, who were rejecting individualism in favor of collective, objective standards shared by the community.[45] There were contemporary collective social actions emerging among farmers, laborers and other urban groups. Holmes had contact with the Pragmatists' idea that meaning and practical effect of words were determined by minds in communication with each other. A bargain was communal; whereas, the alternatives of benefit and detriment were singular, independent effects. Regarding the influence of market ideas, the archetypal nineteenth century transaction was the commercial bargain. Holmes was exposed to the objective standard preferred by free entrepreneurs desirous of the predictable results of not being bound until they struck a bargain and which, once formed, would not be subject to the vagaries of inadequacy objections.[46] As to whether Holmes derived bargain consideration from notions of mutual assent,[47] he wrote in 1881 that "the promise must be made and accepted as the conventional motive or inducement for furnishing the consideration."[48] Just 5 years before Holmes wrote this, the well publicized decision of *Dickinson v. Dodds*[49] used an objective standard in determining the relationship between consideration and assent. In *Dickinson* a bald offer to be held open until Friday at 9 A.M. could be revoked so long as it was communicated to the offeree before acceptance.[50] In discussing objective manifestations of revocation, Holmes dwelt upon "the sufficiency of the consideration and the moment when the contract is made."[51]

In fact, notions of bargain and reciprocity had preceded Holmes by several centuries—Holmes simply put his finger on one of the vital factors in the development of consideration.[52] The idea of bargain was a basis for Debt *sur* contract.[53] Indeed, the idea of reciprocity was an accepted principle of morality in Western Europe during the sixteenth century when consideration developed,[54] and behind early forms of consideration there was the same moral principle that bargains should bind parties.[55] Moreover, during the half century preceding Holmes' declaration, bargain ideas appeared in legal treatises and caselaw.[56]

Holmes cloaked his treatment of consideration with an historical analysis, but his study was neither good legal history nor a correct statement of the law then.[57] Holmes wrote that consideration originated in Debt on unsealed contracts for money payable in the form of the benefit of *quid pro quo* to the promisor and that it then spread to Assumpsit.[58] In Debt the *quid pro quo* was a constituent element of a bargain, only one side of which was remediable in Debt. The binding character of mutual promises or recovery for reliance were foreign to the "real" nature of Debt.[59] Assumpsit was employed to fill those gaps, and consideration set the parameters of this novel action. Consideration was a single label in Assumpsit actions, but not a uniform rule, for both detriment to the promisee and a benefit to the promisor, the latter being an impingement by *indebitatus assumpsit* on the work of Debt.[60] Once Holmes concluded that consideration's genesis was in the bargain of Debt's *quid pro quo*, he had a simple, uniform doctrine mirroring the market economy of his time. Although Cardozo, along with other judges, and Corbin did not follow in the wake of Holmes' aura, Williston enthroned bargain consideration in his influential treatise and in Section 75 of the Restatement (First) of Contracts.

Bargain consideration was not without its detractors. In *Allegheny College v. National Chautauqua Bank* (N.Y. 1927)[61] Cardozo, C.J. presided over a charitable subscription case where a memorial fund was to be set up in the donor's name. Instead of taking the recognized promissory estoppel route for enforcement of charitable gifts, he challenged the idea of bargain consideration. In referring to Holmes' bargain consideration theory, he said: "The half truths of one generation tend at times to perpetuate themselves in the law as the whole truths of another, when constant repetition brings it about that qualifications, taken once for granted, are disregarded or forgotten." Cardozo then proceeded to find that, in accepting a 20% installment on a pledge, the college incurred the detriment of undertaking a duty to perpetuate the donor's name, and that was sufficient consideration in itself to enforce the subscription. No bargained-for exchange had occurred in any market sense; nevertheless, he found consideration for the gratuitous promise in that the motive for the promise was the charity's undertaking of a duty to memorialize the donor. Cardozo also found a benefit to the promisor in "the longing for posthumous remembrance." This self-serving motive was arguably more flexible than mid-nineteenth century consideration doctrine and leaned more toward earlier notions of *causa* or moral consideration.[62] Corbin also proposed a more flexible definition of consideration to take into account the melange of factors historically held sufficient to make a promise enforceable, and he pointed out that just because the Restatement First narrowed the definition of consideration did not mean that courts ceased their finding of a sufficient reason, such as reliance, for enforcing a promise in addition to the reason of an agreed exchange of promise and consideration.[63]

The success of the objective bargain consideration theory in the twentieth century is an unprecedented story of legal commentators effectuating a modification of the pivotal doctrine of consideration in the face of opposition—a feat of which even Mansfield had been incapable. Now, although many other factors were recognized as making a promise enforceable, there was a black letter definition of consideration of one "bargained for and given in exchange for the promise," and the existence of the bargain depended "upon the manifested intention of the parties."[64] Neither of the Restatements use the terminology detriment or benefit at all.

The shift to bargain consideration had little impact on market bargains, but there were hardship cases that went without relief. After the merger of law and equity, judges continued to think common law thoughts, and so with courts of chancery snuffed out, there was no independent authority for the amelioration of the hard cases not fitting the market paradigm. Bargain consideration left no room for detrimental reliance, even though it played an important part in the genesis of the doctrine of consideration. Furthermore, under the objectivism of bargain consideration, there only need be an external adherence to form, and so there was less of an opening for relief to the weaker party since equitable exceptions and fault were divorced from the objective analysis.[65]

One other reevaluation of the consideration doctrine affecting both American and English contract law must be mentioned, and that was the question raised in the English case of *Foakes v. Beer* (1884) about whether the rule in *Pinnel's Case* (1602)[66] should be abandoned. The rule in *Pinnel's Case,* that past consideration was no consideration, had rarely been questioned since the seventeenth century. However, the consideration doctrine had been overhauled in England a generation before *Foakes,*[67] and so it was probably inevitable that there would also be a review of the past consideration rule. As was discussed earlier, the application of the rule in *Pinnel's Case* to Assumpsit cases was flawed both because there was a failure to recognize the difference between the "real" nature of Debt and the consensual nature of Assumpsit[68] and because there was a confusion of the requirements for contract formation with those for contract discharge.[69]

A majority in *Foakes v. Beer* were of the opinion that *Pinnel's Case* had been the accepted rule since its announcement and that it would be unwise to overrule it after 280 years of acceptance. However, research published before the end of the nineteenth century established that *Pinnel* was not immediately accepted,[70] and, in 1846, part payment by negotiable instrument was held sufficient to discharge an obligation.[71] Lord Blackburn was inclined to dissent in *Foakes* on the ground Coke had erred in *Pinnel* because businessmen recognize that prompt payment may be more beneficial than insisting on the whole,[72] but he elected to avoid dissension with his fellow lords and deferred to their ancient books argument.

The failure to reform the past consideration rule in *Foakes* stuck on both sides of the Atlantic despite the supposed nineteenth century obeisance to the freedom of parties to bargain for any desired objective.[73] There have been some attempts, however, to abolish *Foakes* legislatively[74] and to soften its impact in the courts when there is reliance.[75]

Nearly concurrent with the American tilt toward bargain consideration, the English courts were revising their own doctrine of consideration to fit it under a single test. In England the duality of benefit and detriment consideration devolved into only detriment consideration qualifying as sufficient consideration. It was then said that consideration must move from the promisee, who was in privity with the promisor, and as a consequence no actions were permitted by third party beneficiaries. This prohibition on third party beneficiary actions was inconsistent with the sixteenth century view that such parties were not barred since, one, Assumpsit was not thought of as an action between parties but an action on a promise and, secondly, consideration did not need to move from the promisor.[76] But then in *Bourne v. Mason* (1669) a creditor beneficiary could not recover since he was a "stranger to the consideration" and lacked "privity".[77] Lurking in the background was the common law concern about strangers fomenting lawsuits, as earlier reflected in the tort of maintenance and the prohibition on assignments.[78]

At least in *Bourne v. Mason* there was the possibility of an action against the original debtor, but this was not true of a donee beneficiary, a matter raised eight years later in *Dutton v. Poole.*[79] In *Dutton,* despite the argument that the plaintiff was "neither privy nor interested in the consideration," a daughter was successful against her brother on his promise to his father to pay the father's customary duty to the daughter if in exchange the father would refrain from cutting timber to raise her dowry. Later Mansfield reinstated the older sixteenth century rule, while citing *Dutton* with approval, in *Martyn v. Hind* (1776).[80] At the time of *Dutton,* the motives of love and affection and moral obligations, particularly when connected to a family relationship, were relevant to the issue of sufficient consideration.[81] The moral consideration idea was of particular interest to Mansfield as a part of his campaign to reform consideration, as exemplified one year after *Martyn v. Hind* when Mansfield lent support to moral consideration in a case where there was a benefit to the promisor.[82] Then in the nineteenth century, as a conservative common law reaction set in to Mansfield's consideration work, there was an odd swing to requiring detriment consideration exclusively instead of continuing the old dichotomy of benefit or detriment.

Tweddle v. Atkinson (1861) was seen to finally resolve the modern English rule that a third party beneficiary may not sue since consideration must move from the promisee. Here the defendant promised the plaintiff's father that he would pay the plaintiff a marriage portion once the plaintiff married the defendant's daughter. The court held for the defendant since "it is now established that no stranger to the consideration can take advantage of a contract, although made for his benefit."[83] *Tweddle* was perceived as a rejection of the lack of concern about whether the plaintiff was a party to the consideration in *Dutton v. Poole* and *Martyn v. Hind.* Compton, J. thought it would be a "monstrous proposition" if the plaintiff could sue but couldn't be sued.

Formerly, in the actions of Debt and Detinue, a third party beneficiary could sue if a property interest passed through a "trust" created by delivery "to the use" of the beneficiary. This was true whether or not there was either a reciprocal action available or the beneficiary was the promisee. Problems arose, however, when third party beneficiaries employed Assumpsit as a replacement action since now anyone could conceivably sue on a contract, in the absence of the trust theory of Debt, unless consideration could act as a control. So in *Bourne v. Mason* the right to sue turned on whether there was consideration.[84] *Dutton v. Poole* surmounted the consideration hurdle because the motives of love and affection and morality were then still relevant in finding sufficient consideration in family transactions, but once these motives lost out to the forces of reciprocity in the determination of sufficient consideration in the post-Mansfield period, there was confusion in third party beneficiary actions.

The English solution of excluding third party beneficiaries from suing was found in mutual assent, but it had the more pervasive and undesirable side-effect of generating a restrictive redefinition of consideration. In *Williams v. Everett* (1811) there needed to be "a privity between the plaintiff and defendant" and an "assent express or implied [was] necessary."[85] Civilian notions of "concurrence of intention," translated into offer and acceptance, were in the air and were having an effect by the turn of the nineteenth century.[86]

The modern idea of privity came from early nineteenth century offer and acceptance, which identified the parties, and resulted in a contract having an effect only on them.[87] Then in *Price v. Easton* (1833)[88] the third party beneficiary plaintiff lost because one judge said consideration must move "from the plaintiff to the defendant" and another judge said: "No privity is shown between the plaintiff and defendant." In *Price v. Easton* the defendant cited *Bourne v. Mason* as supporting his position and he distinguished *Dutton v. Poole* as based on "privity of blood." The interplay between privity and consideration moving from the promisee has caused some to see the two rules as nearly, if not in actuality, identical.[89]

The rule that third party beneficiaries could not sue because consideration must move from the promisee was soon exploded to apply to all plaintiffs, irrespective of whether they were third party beneficiaries. To be uniform and consistent, any plaintiff's right to sue was soon tied to the detriment side of the old consideration dichotomy—detriment to the promisee being the former alternative identified with the plaintiff-promisee.[90] It is perhaps regrettable that *Tweddle v. Atkinson* did not simply resolve the donee beneficiary's rights to the marriage dowry on the grounds that love and affection was no longer sufficient consideration in a era different than *Dutton v. Poole's* and thereby preserve both the possibility that creditor beneficiaries could show consideration and the flexibility of consideration's historic duality.[91]

The most radical parting of the ways by American jurisdictions and England on the fundamentals of the common law of contract occurred with these changes in consideration doctrine. Why did these two common law countries react differently to the nineteenth century influences of civilian concurrence of intention and the inclination toward a unitary theory after the abolition of the forms? Was late nineteenth century American thought more in tune with the market idea of bargain while in the midst of its later commercial and industrial upsurge? And, did the fact that English courts did not give mutual assent as central a role as American courts cause the development in England of the superfluous requirement of intention to create legal relations?[92]

Although American jurisdictions and England shared similar doctrinal problems regarding consideration and privity during the first half of the nineteenth century, the American treatment of third party beneficiaries became markedly different than England's during the second half of that century.[93] The landmark American case allowing a creditor beneficiary to recover is the well known *Lawrence v. Fox* (N.Y. 1859),[94] decided two years before *Tweddle v. Atkinson.* In *Lawrence* the defendant, Fox, induced Holly to lend him $300, and Fox promised to pay the plaintiff, Lawrence, who was Holly's creditor. The defendant objected that there was no consideration and no privity. The court had little difficulty with the consideration objection responding that the money received by defendant was consideration for defendant's promise to pay plaintiff. There was no need for consideration to move from the promisee since benefit consideration was sufficient consideration.[95]

The privity objection in *Lawrence v. Fox* presented the court with more difficulty because the plaintiff relied heavily on earlier American cases employing a trust theory, but there was no intent for the defendant to receive the money as a trust fund for the plaintiff. The court solved this by drawing an analogy to trust theory implying a promise and a duty to a beneficiary without the requirement of privity. Here the court said the receipt of the consideration and the promise to Holly created a duty and a promise could be implied.[96] The lingering influence of Debt's fifteenth century trust theory for executory transactions, transferred to *indebitatus assumpsit* for money had and received[97] and subsumed in the doctrine of consideration, had an effect on the right of third party beneficiaries in the United States. The *indebitatus* count worked if there was an agreement coupled with delivery of the money to the defendant to act as consideration, but in the early nineteenth century the forces of mutual assent, translated into privity, scuttled these actions in the absence of an express trust. The court in *Lawrence v. Fox* solved this by reasoning that, just as privity was not required for trust cases, privity was not required in contract actions because the right of the beneficiary to bring the action wasn't exclusively for trust cases but was a principle applicable to contract action at-law. After the fusion of law and equity, American courts began to dwell on policy and were willing to draw analogies to fiduciary principles. The failure to completely fuse law and equity in England may have precluded this conclusion there at-law.[98]

Although ideas in *Dutton v. Poole* influenced the majority in the creditor beneficiary case of *Lawrence v. Fox,* the rights of donee beneficiaries were not clearly established until *Seaver v. Ransom* (1918), another New York leading case, adopted the rule in *Dutton v. Poole* in a case of a husband promising his wife to make a gift to her niece.[99] The *Seaver* majority thought it desirable to progressively extend *Lawrence v. Fox* "to do justice rather than apply with technical accuracy strict rules calling for a legal or equitable obligation." The trial court used trust theory to benefit the plaintiff, but for technical trust law reasons that was incorrect. Also, at-law there was no privity, but Pound, J. said, "it is just and practical to permit the person for whose benefit the contract is made to enforce it against one whose duty it is to pay." With that resolved, American jurisdictions, with minor exceptions,[100] generally recognize the right of "intended" third party beneficiaries today.[101]

What was the underlying policy for this departure from the doctrine of privity in the United States? Earlier the faith in the market had contributed to privity's breakdown which helped overcome the reluctance to transfer abstract property rights through the recognition of the rights of third party contract beneficiaries and the allowance of assignments.[102] And by the early twentieth century there was a reaction against privity's notion of the need for each person to protect himself as an awareness grew of the interdependence in society and the impersonality of the market. An equitable aversion to the shortcomings of privity was in the air in New York since it had been rejected two years before *Seaver* in the manufacturer's negligence case of *MacPherson v. Buick Motor Co.*[103]

Continuing now with the American reevaluation of the doctrine of consideration during the period, there are remaining for analysis the theories of frustration and mutuality of obligation, which, whether technically correct or not, were perceived to be related to the doctrine of consideration. Starting with the frustration doctrine, the failure of a basic assumption on which a contract is made is a failure of the parties' bargain expectations and a failure of consideration for the promisor.[104] Although impossibility and impracticability are more like each other than either is like frustration, there is a modern tendency to use the term frustration in identifying these three types of failure of a basic assumption.[105] When the doctrine is broken down, impracticability is an aspect of impossibility in that the purpose is still achievable, but at an unreasonably higher cost; whereas, in frustration of purpose, the contract can be performed at probably no greater cost, but to no purpose. Frustration is the other side of the excuse coin from mistake in that mistake deals with the assumption of facts in existence at the time the contract is made, and frustration concerns the failure of predicted facts. The common law has been less receptive to excuse on account of subsequent events both because a common intention was present at contract formation and because of the general rule requiring the promisor to bear the risk of increased difficulties. Excuse due to impossibility was first permitted in the nineteenth century, but in the early impossibility cases the modern policy of doing what is reasonable and just was hidden behind doctrinaire implied condition logic.[106]

Prior to the seventeenth century, impossibility was an excuse for avoidance of the strict common law liability for performance of a contractual duty in cases of a subsequent illegality, an act of God, the death of a performer, or the death of a bailed animal.[107] Then the English civil war case of *Paradine v. Jane* (1647)[108] strongly reiterated the strict contract liability rule in an action for rent brought against a real property lessee ousted by an invader. The court's statement that the defendant "ought to pay his rent" came from a cited 1537 case,[109] where a penalty was not recoverable for alleged breach of a covenant to repair a river bank damaged by a terrible flood but there was still a duty to repair when the water subsided. The *Paradine* court added that this strict principle could be avoided "because he might have provided against it by his contract," but, without the express exclusion, the lessee must run the risk of either profits or losses. A defense of total impossibility was still available, as an act of God, but it was not impossible to pay the rent.[110]

Paradine v. Jane was not often cited until Serjeant Williams publicized it in the early nineteenth century.[111] The static principle emanating from this conservative real property lease case became a leading contract rule in the nineteenth century in England and the United States; it provided a predictable rule favoring such vested property owners as lessors and sellers. In an 1837 Massachusetts case involving a fire, the court stated: "if he had not intended to incur this risk, he should otherwise have stipulated, in his agreement."[112]

Blackburn, J. provided an inroad to the absolute contracts rule in the famous impossibility case *Taylor v. Caldwell* (1863). There a fire destroyed a music hall the plaintiff had rented before the rental date. Blackburn held the parties had "contemplated" the "continued existence" of the hall as an "implied condition" of their agreement, and the destruction of the hall excused the hall owner from performing.[113] Now an express stipulation regarding the existence of the hall was unnecessary. The sources for what the "parties contemplated", the "continued existence of the thing" and "implied condition" was in the parties' consensus of intention and dependent conditions—concepts not recognized at the time of *Paradine v. Jane.* Moreover during the first half of the nineteenth century, courts adhered to the literal terms of the contract, freely arrived at, notwithstanding unforeseen circumstances. The irrelevancy of what was in the contemplation of the parties had undergone revision, however, just nine years earlier as the civilian concern for what the parties had foreseen was employed in establishing a rule for remoteness of damages.[114] Blackburn cited the civilian Pothier as a source for granting a discharge when the contemplated thing "essential for the fulfillment of the contract" ceased to exist. Analogies were drawn to relief given in earlier common law cases of the perishing of the contract performer and of bailed property and of goods under contract but perishing before the risk passed.[115] Blackburn brought the civilian contemplation of the parties into *Taylor v. Caldwell* through the invention of the fiction of an implied condition. A dissent five years earlier suggested the notion of an implied condition.[116] The genesis of implied condition is in the merger of the two disparate theories of dependent conditions and implied warranties, both having entered the common law during the preceding century.[117] The opportunity for implication of a term, as a warranty, was grafted to the idea of a conditional promise.

Impossibility is a more apt description of the event in *Taylor v. Caldwell* than it is of *Paradine v. Jane* because it was not impossible to pay the rent in *Paradine* but it was impossible to provide the music hall on time in *Taylor.*[118] The rules in *Paradine* and *Taylor* favored property owner over the one who was to pay. These common law rules provided relief to lessors, even when a lessee didn't have access to the property or when the premises burned; and, by the nineteenth century, relief had been given to sellers when the goods were destroyed before the risk of loss had passed.[119] The inequity to payors, among other promisors, would be alleviated by development of the frustration of purpose defense.

The approach in frustration cases was different from impossibility cases; rather than looking to whether it was possible to perform, the question was whether the promisor should be required to perform when the purpose had been frustrated. Thus, even though the other party would still benefit from the contract, it was unenforceable since both parties knew the defendant's purpose for contracting.[120] Focus on frustration of purpose, rather than on the possibility of performance, first appeared in nineteenth century shipping cases involving such events as undue delays and a naval blockade.[121] There was supportive dictum in these cases, and occasionally a discharge was granted either because of a fundamental failure of consideration or because the contract was "wholly frustrated" and the event "put an end to the whole object."[122]

A frustration principle applicable to contracts generally, rather than only to frustration of a shipping adventure, was announced in the leading case of *Krell v. Henry* (1903).[123] The defendant hired a flat to view Edward VII's coronation procession, but it didn't take place as planned due to the King's appendicitis. In the suit brought by the flat owner for the balance due, Vaughan Williams, L.J. asked whether the "Roman law" in *Taylor v. Caldwell,* allowing a discharge for the unforeseen perishing of the thing, could be extended to cases where the "state of things" which were "assumed by the parties to be the foundation or basis of the contract" ceased to exist. Not surprisingly the flat owner argued that an excuse was limited to destruction of the subject matter or an express contract clause regarding the state of things anticipated. However, the court extended excuse by making the test whether the foundation of the contract was prevented by an unforeseen event, that is, "whether the object of the contract was frustrated by the non-happening of the coronation."

Under the modern doctrine of frustration in *Krell v. Henry,* the court dispensed with the fiction of an implied condition in basing excuse on what was reasonable and just. It didn't seem reasonable to expect the defendant to keep a bargain when he was entirely deprived of any benefit. But, how much of an adjustment for fairness should there be? In *Krell* there was effectively an equitable apportionment of the damages, making it easier for the court to excuse the defendant from the balance due, since the defendant withdrew his claim for refund of his downpayment of one-third the contract price. Indeed, dictum in *Krell* suggested what was in fact held in another coronation case in 1904, where the court refused a requested refund because only performance subsequent to the unforeseen event was affected by impossibility or frustration—rights acquired before the event were not to be disturbed.[124] The injustice of this half-way measure, when there was a total frustration of purpose, has been sometimes remedied through the liberal use of restitution for the value of the part performance received.[125]

This restitutionary analysis of benefit conferred by the defendant also prompted, however, an analysis of benefit received. If the defendant could turn the bargain to a different benefit, then perhaps he shouldn't receive a discharge at all.[126] To give an example of the type of analysis made: could the defendant in *Krell* have used the flat for another purpose, say, for a card party? Although this example might be unreasonable, this approach limited the finding of total frustration. In 1944 Traynor, J. did not give relief to a lessee because the leasehold could be used for another purpose, and he added that frustration is "limited to cases of extreme hardship so that businessmen, who must make their arrangements in advance, can rely with certainty on their contracts."[127] Traynor did not base his rejection of the frustration defense on the traditional rule that lessees are never excused, though he acknowledged that lessees had been unsuccessful in the past. It is true that lessees lost in *Paradine v. Jane* and *Taylor v. Caldwell* (*Krell v. Henry* involved a license not a lease), but, at least in the wartime case, Traynor opined that the defense could be available to lessees.

In the United States the development of impossibility and frustration were advanced by their inclusion in the Restatement First.[128] Although the Restatement required a relatively strict objective standard for impossibility, there was a liberalization by including unforeseeable "impracticability". The notion of impracticability had been floating around since the mid-nineteenth century, but in the United States the case of *Mineral Park Land Co. v. Howard* (1916)[129] had a more immediate influence on the restaters' adoption of impracticability. There the defendant agreed to excavate all the gravel and earth needed for bridge work from plaintiff's neighboring land, but due to a rise in the water level, defendant's cost would have increased tenfold. The court excused the defendant because: "A thing is impossible in legal contemplation when it is not practicable; and a thing is impracticable when it can only be done at an excessive and unreasonable cost." Restatement Section 454 adopted the *Mineral Park* language almost verbatim. As in frustration of purpose, the fiction of implied condition was abandoned in favor of the court imposing a just solution when an unanticipated change arose.[130]

The next step was the recognition of impracticability as a full-fledged independent doctrine. Support for impracticability gained some momentum with its recognition in the Uniform Commercial Code. The Code draftsmen rejected the common law fiction of an implied condition in favor of an admixture of trade usage, equitable principles and of civilian concern for foreseeability.[131] As to trade usage, emphasis was laid on commercial standards in determining how much risk the seller had assumed, and provisions could be made to protect a seller's regular customers in the event of a partial failure. Flexible adjustment rules based on equity and good faith were used, rather than the historic absolutist all or nothing approach, so that total impossibility is not required, temporary excuse is possible and subrogation rights are available to the buyer. Nevertheless the traditional preference for the seller is apparent.

Despite the Code's open embrace of commercial impracticability, courts have had difficulty with the unpredictability generated by the doctrine in the face of the general rule that the promisor assumes all risks.[132] This judicial resistance was reflected in the series of sea transport cases precipitated by the 1956 closure of the Suez Canal and in the 1970s oil embargo cases. In the Suez cases the purpose was neither frustrated nor was it impossible since there was an alternative route around the Cape, and in both American and English Suez cases, a less than one-third increase in expense for the longer route was not so drastic as to make it unjust to enforce the contract.[133] The lingering ghost of *Paradine v. Jane* still haunts these attempts at excuse. Nevertheless, twentieth century frustration and impracticability cases, based on equity and social policy, loosened up the absolutist common law posture.

In reviewing the developments in impossibility, precursors of the modern erosion of the absolutist view appeared as early as *Boone v. Eyre* (1777), wherein there was a softening of the demand for full performance by weighing the partially completed exchange position of the parties.[134] But during the first half of the nineteenth century, courts refused to become involved in policy, leaving it to each individual to protect himself against increased, unforeseen difficulties by contract stipulation. Even when the use of implied condition made a crack in the absolute contract armour, it retained the deference to freedom of contract by disingenuously basing the outcome on intent. Then in the twentieth century courts began to openly admit that they were allocating the unreasonable, unanticipated hardship caused without fault on the basis of equitable principles.[135] This was a breakdown of faith in freedom of contract as adjustments based on social policy were made.[136]

The infusion of equitable principles in cases of hardship caused by unforeseen disasters did not erase the stark reality that generally the promisor assumed the risk of losses due to a change in circumstances. This is exemplified by an 1892 Minnesota case[137] where a farmer's contract to supply a seedsman with 591 bushels of beans was broken when he only raised 152 bushels due to an unusual September frost. The court held for the plaintiff-seedsman since the contract did not limit the farmer to obtaining the crop from a particular plot. Likewise a manufacturer would not be excused if unforeseen circumstances precluded promised production before the completion date. Producers were desirous of a contract stipulation which would avoid the hardships of the absolute contract principle by only obligating themselves to the actual "output" produced, but the use of an open-ended term like output triggered mutuality of obligation and indefiniteness objections.

By the last quarter of the nineteenth century there were increased uncertainties in an economy in the midst of an industrial revolution, and business sought more open-ended contract language in order to permit unpredictable subsequent conditions and behavior to dictate the exact details of the relationship. The causes of the increased uncertainty included the use of new production techniques, the tendency toward longer term contract relationships and wide fluctuations in the market. New production techniques created uncertainties as to output; and, the appearance of new products and of purchasers not in the market before, created uncertainties of demand and hence of contract requirements. The rise of the corporate state was a major cause of longer term contracts. A corporation with perpetual life developed ongoing relations, over greater distances than before, with its suppliers, with prized purchasers and with franchisees who were no longer casually related middlemen; furthermore, in the labor sector, ongoing collective bargaining was replacing the former manner of contracting with individual employees. The parties to these, often novel, long-term relationships could not expect all details to be set at contract formation but rather looked to an ongoing integration of future events and behavior as the future unfolded.[138] And, there were wider market fluctuations in the last quarter of the nineteenth century than at any time before in the first truly national market, facilitated by the completed railroad network.[139] The futures contract, a version of the output contract, was invented by agricultural entrepreneurs to spread the risk of these fluctuations over the long term, but this device was initially found illegal because: they were deemed immoral, they didn't add to productivity, and they interfered with accepted rules of supply and demand.[140]

These novel, long-term, open-ended contracts did not conform to classical contract requirements of mutuality of obligation and definiteness. Classical rules had developed for the earlier paradigm of the one-shot, discrete transaction; the franchise arrangement, as an example, replaced former discrete contracts with various middlemen, who had been less controllable than franchisees. Despite initial opposition, commercial needs were met by judicial modification of doctrine.

What were the bases of the requirements of mutuality of obligation and definiteness and how were they overcome? Starting with the oft-cited mutuality case of *Bailey v. Austrian* (1873),[141] the defendant promised to supply plaintiffs with all the pig-iron they might "want" for a given time. Prior to contract expiration, defendant refused to supply more. In the action brought, the court held for the defendant because there was: "'No absolute mutuality of engagement'" on the plaintiffs' part "to want" nor was there any consideration. The market slogan ringing through many of the cases was: "Both parties must be bound or neither is bound."[142] Without this binding reciprocity, there was no bargain. The genesis of mutuality seems to have been before the middle of the nineteenth century,[143] when there was a keen interest in the civilian concurrence of intentions as reflected in the notion in the bilateral contract that would result, that both parties became bound at the moment the offer was accepted.[144]

Mutuality of obligation was criticized for overlooking the difference between bilateral and unilateral contracts and for being an unnecessary overload on the enforcement of an intended agreement supported by consideration.[145] Mutuality was a by-product of the unfortunate offer and acceptance add-on to what was required for the formation of a contract supported by consideration. Mutuality didn't mesh well with unilateral contracts; for instance, an option contract was enforceable without mutuality. Mutuality became a confused doctrine, vaguely seeming to be something over and above consideration.[146] From the perspective of the doctrine of consideration, an output agreement lacks consideration if there is no duty to forbear from producing the product for third persons, but that is cured if defendant promises to sell what's produced exclusively to the plaintiff.[147] Corbin thought that a seller's subsidiary promise in an output agreement to run a factory or farm diligently was not necessary to find sufficient consideration;[148] but, if mutuality of obligation ever had any meaning independent of consideration, Corbin's remark may touch on where it lay since caselaw from the late nineteenth century onwards has emphasized the need for either an implied promise of reasonable efforts or a good faith performance in output and requirements contracts. Although lingering allusions to mutuality of obligation still filter through some judicial opinions, the accepted modern view is there is no added requirement of mutuality of obligation if sufficient consideration is found.[149]

In an 1891 New York requirements case, the court read a standard of reasonableness into the contract because otherwise it would "place one of the parties entirely at the mercy of the other."[150] This was a prelude to the implication of commercial standards of fair dealing and the fiduciary principle of good faith in output and requirement contracts during the next generation.[151] When there was a severe swing in market value in a requirements contract, so that one party was "at the mercy" of the buyer with discretion, the buyer could purchase an amount "in [the] usual course of business" but could not "speculate" on the seller.[152] In the exclusive dealings contract of *Wood v. Lady Duff-Gordon* (1917), the plaintiff's exclusive right to market defendant's services had value because Cardozo said: "a promise is fairly to be implied" to "use reasonable efforts."[153] The implication of a promise avoided the parol evidence rule problem of looking to extrinsic evidence. The case, a watershed decision in a number of ways, included Cardozo's dictum: "The law has outgrown its primitive stage of formalism when the precise word is the sovereign talisman." The concern about mutuality had been overcome in seeming one-sided transactions in order to protect the expectations of the promisee. Courts now saw the indefiniteness in long term commercial contracts as a reflection of the market rather than of the parties failure to agree, and the discretion given to a party was policed through contract interpretation and the implication of business practices and good faith as to subsequent behavior.[154]

In addition to the mutuality problems raised because of the open-ended nature of output, requirements and exclusive dealings contracts, there was an indefiniteness problem when a contract had an open term, e.g., open price or time period. Well before the nineteenth century, the common law had a certainty requirement associated with the need to plead a promise with certainty in trial by jury, but this did not stand in the way of market values and reasonable standards being read into promises in Assumpsit actions.[155] In order for a court to decide on expectation damages, a court must know the scope of the promise—something not so vital in an action for reliance damages.[156] However, once intent to contract was found, a contract was not indefinite if the terms of the promise provided a sufficiently definite, objective basis for the court to determine the damages.[157] Thus Cardozo employed liberal interpretation and implication of terms to sustain intended promises in order to give business needed flexibility. He thought it unfair for a party to use the strict letter of the law to avoid a promise, but he did not uphold a contract in 1923 when the time period and price were to be agreed on later.[158]

The earlier objections to open-ended provisions of indefiniteness and lack of mutuality fit the market theory that no one buys a "guess". Then in the last quarter of the nineteenth century, there was a revision of the earlier business opposition to allowing uncertainty to creep into contract doctrine since business was now interested in greater flexibility in longer term contracts in order to take into account subsequent unforeseeable conditions and behavior.[159]

Thus far the analysis has primarily concerned the reevaluation of the doctrine of consideration. Attention will now be focused on a tangential issue related to a point raised earlier regarding Holmes' bargain theory of consideration. Holmes held that an objective standard should be used in determining whether there was sufficient consideration. Now, as a postscript to consideration-related issues, the question is raised: what was the standard of interpretation applicable in determining contractual intent during this period? The accepted version is that during the second half of the nineteenth century there was a tendency to shift the emphasis from the subjective will of the promisor to an objective standard based on the reasonable expectations aroused in the promisee.[160] Starting in the 1850s writers such as Parsons, and then Langdell, Holmes and later Williston,[161] noted the need of commerce for predictability, and the pressures grew to align the law with the objective expectations of business planners as to formation, meaning and enforceability of a bargain.[162] It seems no coincidence that this tendency toward objectivity occurred after the fusion of law and equity at mid-century since the absence of the independent role of equity in eliminating the harshness of the common law would have removed some subjective unpredictability, and the process was further encouraged by a contemporaneous increase in control of the jury.

It was the promotion of the objective standard during the first quarter of the twentieth century by a writer of the stature of Williston that assured that the objectivity test would not be ignored.[163] Williston picked up where Parsons and Holmes left off in arguing that assent should be determined by the meaning the other party could reasonably expect to attach to external manifestations; thus the expression of mutual assent, and not assent itself, was essential. Williston admitted that there were exceptional instances of subjectivity, as when a party died while an offer was outstanding or in cases of duress and certain other cases in equity, but he thought that more representative cases were those of an offeror being bound to mistaken terms in an accepted offer and cases of a revocation only being valid when received[164]—Williston and Holmes seemed particularly taken by the late nineteenth century caselaw regarding revocation of an offer.[165] Williston cited with approval the strongly objectivist views of Judge Hand, who wrote in 1911 that a contract has "nothing to do with the personal, or individual, intent of the parties. A contract is an obligation attached by the mere force of law to certain acts of the parties, usually words."[166] Williston embraced the parol evidence rule as an ideal complement to the objective standard, a rule that aided in avoiding the subjectivity of the jury. The fusion of law and equity again furthered the objectivist approach because the objective standard was not emphasized as much in equity, and equity had formerly applied the parol evidence rule with more flexibility than did common law courts; Williston acknowledged that equity did not read a contract as written when that was not what the parties intended.[167]

Williston's push for a generalized, uniform standard did not accurately portray the caselaw, and consequently Corbin, a perceptive analyst of the facts in cases, saw support for objectivity exclusively to be a "great illusion" because words have the meaning each person attaches to them.[168] Corbin agreed that the main purpose of contract law is the realization of reasonable expectations induced by the promise, and stated that a finding of consideration is evidence that the expectation of performance was reasonable,[169] but he disagreed with Williston and Hand on how those expectations were to be determined. He saw the role of the courts to be to ascertain the common intention of the parties, or, if none, then what one party knew the other party to understand, if that could be shown. Corbin supported a modified subjective standard since the law of contracts could not be explained exclusively by either a subjective or an objective theory.[170] Therefore Corbin encouraged the notion that there was no parol evidence rule problem when there was a need to interpret the contract in furtherance of the modern policy of determining what the parties intended.[171] Nevertheless, the influence of the elder and then more dominant figure, Williston, prevailed in the Restatement First.

The Restatement First provided that words "are given the meaning which the party making the manifestations should reasonably expect that the other party would give to them."[172] By ignoring the caselaw requiring actual agreement, equitable considerations could be minimized and support was given for increased predictability for the business planner. Criticism was immediately levelled that, in Williston's yearning for a uniform rule, he had focused on exceptional cases, such as the mistaken offer and revocation of an offer, rather than the normal judicial requirement of actual consent.[173]

Corbin's modified subjective theory more accurately reflected the caselaw, but its full effect on other commentators did not come until the drafting of the Restatement Second. Although assent to the Holmesian bargain was still determined in the Restatement Second by "external manifestation rather than the undisclosed mental state,"[174] the standard for the determination of the parties' words now had a subjective flavor to it. The parties' common understanding was to apply, no matter what an objective standard might establish, and a party's understanding would apply if the other party had reason to know that understanding.[175]

New Grounds for Recovery: Restitution and Promissory Estoppel

Benefit and reliance, traditional bases for relief under Assumpsit and in equity, blossomed into the independent grounds for recovery of restitution and detrimental reliance, known by the misnomer of promissory estoppel during this period. These developments caused an erosion of the consensual theory. One of the influences for these changes was that some cases of benefit or reliance, formerly actionable under benefit or detriment consideration, fell through the cracks once a benefit or a detriment had to be bargained for. The emergence of these two doctrines followed the fusion of the courts where courts now of law and equity could both grant relief in transactions formerly falling under Assumpsit and also soften the asperities of the common law when justice demanded. Modern courts could follow procedures more akin to those in chancery since there was no worry about the procedural requirements of the forms of action, and a court need no longer deny relief simply because it was not available in Assumpsit.[176] There was a resultant expansion of the range of liability as equity's ideas about benefits received, fiduciary duties, specific relief and reliance took on a heightened importance in promissory actions. The notions flowing from the equity side were more difficult to fashion into rules because of the case-by-case build-up of working hypotheses deliberately left open and ambiguous for future development; nevertheless, the inclination of common law treatise writers and restaters was to close these ideas in with structured boundaries.[177] Attention is now turned to the development of these two grounds for recovery.

The genesis of restitution was in the bits and pieces in seventeenth and eighteenth century caselaw brought together by Mansfield in *Moses v. Macferlan* (1760).[178] As discussed earlier, Mansfield adopted the equitable notion that a defendant need not make a promise in order to be obliged by the demands of "natural justice" and "equity" to refund money received. Assumpsit was supposed to only cover promissory duties, but the fictitious subsequent promise in *indebitatus assumpsit* allowed Mansfield to supplement common law remedies. Mansfield, in his civilian manner of approaching a specific problem with a legislative mind, went past the facts of *Moses v. Macferlan* to state that the principle should apply when in fairness the defendant ought to refund money.

Mansfield's statement was too expansive to operate as a clear rule without further development, and up until the mid-nineteenth century there was only limited use of Mansfield's dictum in the United States and England. One reason for the resistance to quasi-contract was the common law judges' abhorrence to the use of Mansfield's open-ended and imprecise doctrine to compromise the orderliness of the formulary system. The reaction to Mansfield's general proposition began only eight years after Mansfield's resignation in Lord Kenyon's opinion in *Marriott v. Hampton* (1797).[179] Furthermore, there was a lack of clear thinking about quasi-contract because of a confusion of quasi-contract, a contract implied-in-law, with true consensual relationships implied-in-fact.[180] Quasi-contract has the objective of preventing unjust enrichment, rather then protecting expectation or reliance interests, since it is based on what the defendant ought to do in good conscience and not what the defendant's intentions were in-fact.

Then in the second half of the nineteenth century, the United States and England took separate paths as American courts began to take a more expansive view of unjust enrichment and English courts narrowed the doctrine to specific circumstances. There are several suggestions for why, in contrast to the United States, there was a freezing of quasi-contract, and indeed of contract doctrine generally, in England. One explanation is that there was no enlightened English judge after Mansfield to avert the reversion to the pedantic details of the common law forms. Secondly, especially as to restitution, the English Chancery's independent trust jurisdiction was not fused with the common law courts. Thirdly, by around 1900 there was a resuscitation of the earlier American republican reaction against static precedents that were inconsistent with notions of fairness and equality based on Jeffersonian natural law. A fourth reason is that by around 1900 English judges were becoming more formalist in their adherence to *stare decisis* while American judges were becoming less so; this point of departure between the two systems became more marked by the 1930s. The explanation for the changed attitude of American judges toward precedent seems to be tied to the realist realization that precedents could be found in the immense volume of American caselaw on either side of an issue and fairness required that the policy behind the rule be considered. However, English lawyers fell under the sway of Austin's legal positivism wherein law reform and policy were to be provided by the sovereign legislature and judges were simply to follow the law.[181]

After the abolition of the forms of action and the complete fusion of law and equity in the various American jurisdictions, the way was open to consider the possibility of jettisoning the fictitious implied promise so that unjust enrichment could stand as a third branch of the law independent of contracts and torts. Thus during the second half of the nineteenth century, there were extensions of quasi-contract, an action at-law for money damages, by quoting Mansfield and by drawing analogies to the unjust enrichment principle in equitable restitution—a process continuing today.[182] This process of development of unjust enrichment was largely overlooked until Ames and Keener pointed it out.

In 1888 Ames was the first to isolate the unifying principle of unjust enrichment floating through the caselaw of the seventeenth and eighteenth centuries and traced its development through Mansfield's synthesis.[183] Ames wrote that quasi-contract was essentially equitable since there was neither mutual assent nor consideration but that it was like contract in that there was a positive duty. Keener followed up five years later, in a treatise dedicated to Ames, and carried the study of quasi-contract's development forward from Mansfield's time. Keener abhorred the confused thinking wrought by the fictional promise in *indebitatus assumpsit*, and to avoid confusion, he substituted the term "quasi contract" for "contract implied in law".[184] Ames' and Keener's distillation enabled lawyers and judges to see the common impulse connecting the cases which influenced widespread acceptance of this attractive equitable theory during the succeeding decades. Their writings continued the nineteenth century tradition of legal writers influencing the direction of the common law. The culmination of this process would be the publication of a Restatement of Restitution in 1937.

The Restatement of Restitution[185] used language very similar to Ames' in Section 1: "A person who has been unjustly enriched at the expense of another is required to make restitution to the other." The guiding principle of unjust enrichment was retained; however, unlike Ames and Keener, the new term restitution had a broader sweep since it was not limited to developments under the action at-law of quasi-contract, but, consistent with the fusion of law and equity, also included developments on the equity side under specific restitution.[186] The academic dogma in the Restatement of Restitution encouraged the further development of restitution, as Mansfield had done earlier, and provided a clear framework for extending relief on the basis of unjust enrichment, a ground independent of contract law, in cases where there were no clear precedents in the scattered caselaw.[187]

The Restatement of Restitution's contract-related use of restitution at-law were extensions of the quasi-contractual liability announced by Mansfield in *Moses v. Macferlan,* wherein he said the defendant ought to refund "money paid by mistake," "money got through . . . oppression," and when "undue advantage taken of the plaintiff's situation." Succeeding caselaw granted relief for benefits conferred on indefinite agreements and even benefits conferred during negotiations.[188] Restitution was granted for benefits under agreements made by mistake or obtained by undue influence, duress or fraud.[189] Restitution was available under unenforceable contracts, as for the benefit bargained for and conferred under an agreement not complying with the Statute of Frauds.[190] Indeed, quasi-contract has primarily been used for unwinding benefits conferred in unenforceable contracts.[191] So restitution was also given for contracts discharged due to impossibility and under breached contracts—and even breachors could obtain restitution.[192] Although quasi-contract is not an action for breach of a contractual duty, there is a line of cases allowing restitution to be used as a remedy for breach of contract, as an alternative to contract damages, when it resulted in a termination of the contract, especially when it was unjust to restrict the plaintiff to lower contract damages. Thus in an 1818 Connecticut case, a buyer paid $5,000 down prior to the seller's failure to deliver. The buyer recovered $5,000 restitution despite the seller's argument that contract damages were $2,000 on account of a $3,000 drop in the value of the goods by the delivery date.[193]

Decisions limited quasi-contractual recovery of money at-law to the scope Mansfield had given it, but a court's equitable power to grant specific restitution was less restricted and has become the predominant side of modern restitution. The origins of specific restitution in equity predated the common counts, and when justice could not be obtained once the common counts were in place in the eighteenth century, Chancery heard the injured's bill for "rescission and restitution."[194] Modern instances of equity's specific restitution, some available at least since the early seventeenth century, include constructive trust, equitable lien, subrogation, equitable accounting, contribution and indemnity.[195] Constructive trust began in the last quarter of the seventeenth century in English cases of oral testamentary dispositions and inter vivos trusts of land[196] in violation of the Statute of Frauds and also in cases of fiduciaries engaging in self-dealing. What makes constructive trust the most important specific restitution remedy is its tracing function; for example, a trust could be imposed if a trustee wrongly used trust assets and it could be traced to an acquired asset. American and English courts agreed that a constructive trust could be imposed to deprive a fiduciary of a gain obtained through misuse of his position, but English courts didn't go much past that.[197] During the last quarter of the nineteenth century, American courts began to extend the use of constructive trust to nonfiduciary situations.[198] The principal difficulty was in freeing it from the context of a fiduciary relationship, but by the early twentieth century there were extensions to cover contract cases of mistake, fraud, duress, undue influence and simple breach of contract. This transformation turned constructive trust into a generalized remedial device for specific restitution.[199]

As to other instances of specific restitution at-equity, the restitutional enforcement device known as the equitable lien is an offshoot of constructive trust since the end result of tracing may be a lien on an asset. Subrogation is arguably a form of tracing today. And equitable accounting, unlike other forms of equitable restitution, results in a money decree, which is attractive in reaching profits realized.[200]

So by the 1930s academic writers and restaters had provided clear, generalized principles for courts of law and equity to adopt and extend when there was unjust enrichment. The downside has been that the various extensions of money and specific restitution have been so confused and sprawling that it is difficult to easily discern an organized pattern to it all. This is further complicated by the diverse origins of the remedies, each with its own traditions, means and procedures.[201]

Attention will now be turned to reliance-based promissory estoppel, the other major equitable ground for recovery in promissory transactions emerging during this period. As a starting point, a few comments are in order about the relationship between restitution and promissory estoppel. The issue of fairness is not much relevant to consensual transactions but is an essential factor in restitution and promissory estoppel.[202] Restitution and promissory estoppel are both cases of liability imposed by law in the absence of consent, and in this regard, they have an affinity with tort law.[203] Furthermore, the typical partially completed contract in dispute includes the interrelated aspects of reliance and unjust enrichment. Take the case of a buyer paying $100 for goods which the seller now refuses to deliver—here the buyer has relied and the seller is unjustly enriched.[204] Indeed, the interrelationship is such that it has been pointed out that restitution is normally an instance of reliance since reliance by the plaintiff causes a resultant gain to the defendant.[205] They are not always mirror images, however, and then the restitution interest is more important than reliance because in restitution there are the dual injustices of unjust impoverishment to the plaintiff and unjust gain to the defendant. However, between recovery of the reliance interest and the expectation interest, there is a stronger case for curing the injustice caused by reliance than satisfying mere disappointed expectations.[206] There is a trend in this century toward an increasing protection of the restitution interest and the reliance interest and less emphasis on the expectation interest.[207]

There are several reasons why the emphasis on restitution and reliance might be increasing while expectation is not. As equitable notions of fairness have been emphasized more in the twentieth century, courts have begun analyzing the equities in favor of each party in determining whether to protect any of three basic damage interests of expectation, reliance or restitution; thus, when there is a great disparity between an enormous loss of expectation and much smaller losses of either the restitution or the reliance interests, a court could be reluctant to cause a hardship to the promisor by satisfying expectations.[208] In the opposite circumstance of there being no appreciable change in the market price between the date of contract formation and its due date, there is no real sanction provided by expectation damages. Furthermore, only clear damages will be assessed and the burden of clarity for the expectation interest can be more difficult to sustain than for the restitution or reliance interests.[209]

Although ordinary standards of justice might show a preference for the restitution interest over the reliance interest, restitution doesn't necessarily adequately compensate when there are also reliance facts. An injustice might not be avoided if restitution is not possible or is inadequate or if the unjust enrichment is not calculable as a monetary amount.[210] Likewise, the restitution interest will not adequately compensate if the plaintiff's reliance does not benefit the defendant. And, the granting of restitution alone may not be fair when the legitimate expectation aroused by the promise, and relied on, are greater than the net benefit bestowed.[211]

In light of the recognition of an independent reliance interest protected in the cases, Williston and his fellow restaters constructed a generalized doctrine of "promissory estoppel" in the 1920s from a mishmash of loose groupings of gratuitous promises that became enforceable starting in the third quarter of the nineteenth century; these cases had the common thread of a promisee's justifiable reliance on a promised gift and the hardship of refusing enforcement.[212] Actually these cases were not entirely novel to either Chancery or the common law since reliance on a promise had been a basis for recovery from at least the year 1500.

In fifteenth century Chancery, if a promisor led the promisee to alter his position, there was a moral duty to fulfill his promise since it was in the general interest of the community that such an expectation be fulfilled.[213] In 1500 the breach of a promise relied on was a tortious deceit both at-law and in equity. At-law a new contract category was forming under the action of Assumpsit, separate from the old action of Covenant, for hardship cases of a justifiable reliance on a promise.[214] The Student in DOCTOR AND STUDENT (1530) gave an example of a charitable nature in describing this new remedy for an induced reliance.[215] The induced reliance wasn't the motive for the promise but rather it was the motive inducing the promisee to rely. However, Assumpsit moved from this tort perspective to perform a broader contractual role later in the sixteenth century, as a reciprocal motive of the promisor also became actionable under Assumpsit. This urge for a single test of enforceability in Assumpsit caused a perversion of reliance, as it was forced into the detriment side of consideration; and, as a consequence, detrimental reliance as an independent ground for contract relief on informal promises was lost at-law.[216]

For the next 300 years these reliance notions can be seen in Chancery discussions but they were simmering beneath the surface in contract at common law, until several developments brought the matter back into the open in the United States. At about the middle of the nineteenth century, there was the abolition of both the forms of action and the seal and there was the fusion of law and equity. Once the *indebitatus assumpsit* forms were abolished, questions, formerly hidden behind the forms, were asked about the doctrine of consideration. The fusion of the courts brought into the common law the equitable treatment of injurious reliance and a greater concern for fairness of the result. The continued availability of the seal in England, even today, allowed the enforcement of serious gratuitous promises, but American jurisdictions now had to fashion a replacement contractual theory in order to avoid the injustice of failure to provide relief for justifiable injurious reliance on a gratuitous promise.[217] Courts began to enforce gratuitous promises relied on in certain categories of cases: charitable subscriptions, land conveyances, forbearance from mortgage foreclosure, gratuitous bailees and agents, waivers of defenses, marriage agreements, family gifts, employee benefits and rent reductions. The most influential category in the development of promissory estoppel was to prove to be charitable subscriptions.[218]

The rationales for enforcing nineteenth century gratuitous promises that were relied upon were varied and included: findings of detriment consideration; two-pronged justifications of consideration and reliance; breach of trust coupled with consideration in bailment and agency cases; and pure reliance logic, often tied to the notion of estoppel. Starting with the cases resting partially or entirely on consideration logic, it was often disingenuous to find consideration when the promisee's reliance was not in fact requested by the promisor as the consideration for his promise. Thus the unavoidable conclusion of an Alabama common law court employing strict consideration rules, before the fusion of law and equity, in *Kirksey v. Kirksey* (1845)[219] was that the promise was unenforceable. The court found no consideration for the defendant's promise to provide a place for his widowed sister-in-law if she would "come down and see" him—her coming down to see him was not the motive inducing his promise. That is not to say that some courts were not flexible enough to find a sufficient reason for enforcing a promise other than because there was either a request for the reliance or, as bargain consideration came on, an agreed exchange of promise and consideration. In an 1870 Illinois case, money borrowed by a charity in reliance on a subscription was said to show they had incurred a new liability, even though the funds were applied to a preexisting debt; the court held there was "sufficient consideration".[220] Reliance was not always required to be consciously exchanged for the promise; however, the influence of the new bargain consideration theory would begin to push this type of analysis aside by the early twentieth century.[221]

A common nineteenth century category of cases using consideration logic were actions, often for specific performance, on gratuitous promises to convey land or to forbear from foreclosing.[222] These land cases were often preoccupied with whether the injurious reliance could act, by an analogy to sales, as a part performance exception in equity to the Statute of Frauds, and the courts paid scant attention to analyzing whether consideration was present.[223] Where reliance was relevant, the entrustment of land was an indicator, though taking possession was usually not enough alone in the land cases; however, entrustment of the property was an essential ingredient in showing the reliance needed for a finding of consideration in the gratuitous bailment and gratuitous agency cases. The reliance of entrustment of personal property to a gratuitous bailee had been a basis of recovery from at least the fifteenth century in Chancery.[224] Holt, C.J. emphasized it in *Coggs v. Bernard* (1703), a case of a negligent delivery of a brandy cask by a gratuitous bailee. Holt stuck to common law doctrine in saying that, "a bare being trusted with another man's goods, must be taken to be a sufficient consideration."[225] The dictum of Powell, J. in *Coggs v. Bernard* had a more modern ring to it: "when I have reposed a trust in you, upon your undertaking, if I suffer, when I have so relied upon you, I shall have my action."[226] But Holt's line of logic continued on into the twentieth century in both gratuitous bailment and gratuitous agency.[227]

Turning now to those nineteenth century cases using pure reliance logic as the basis for enforcement of gratuitous promises, these decisions began the process of liberating that compartment of contract law from the shackles of convoluted attempts to rationalize the presence of consideration. The open recognition of pure justifiable reliance as a ground for recovery probably first appeared in charitable subscriptions at least by the early 1860s.[228] In *Thompson v. Board of Supervisors of Mercer County* (1866) defendant was liable on his charitable subscription for a new courthouse due to the reliance of: "liabilities incurred by others in consequence of such subscriptions... should, on general principles, be deemed sufficient to make them obligatory."[229] In *Pryor v. Cain* (1861)[230] defendant was liable on a charitable subscription relied on by other subscribers personally borrowing money and expending their labor to build a church; the court said the defendant was "bound in good faith to fulfill the obligation, the party paying the money or furnishing the labor and materials having a right to rely on such subscription." Not all the nineteenth century cases of pure reliance logic were charitable subscriptions. An example is *Irwin v. Dyke* (1885),[231] a case of a son's reliance on his father's promise to give him the farm. The court said the son's returning to the farm, making modest improvements and paying some on a note were "done in reliance upon the promise, a court of equity will enforce a specific performance of the agreement." There was no requirement of, nor even discussion of, consideration in the above cases; there was a frank admission that no bargain was necessary since promissory liability rested purely and simply on the injustice of injurious reliance on the gratuitous promise. It would have been cleaner if the justification for granting relief would have remained on that basis, but the inclination of the common law to graft established doctrine onto an emerging theory resulted in a confusion of equitable estoppel with this new reliance ground for recovery.

Equitable estoppel had originally been a rule of pleading and evidence estopping a party's denial of his earlier representation of a fact relied on by the other party. This idea of reliance on a representation was translated to cases of reliance on a promise, and the promisor was said to be estopped from a denial of the presence of consideration. In 1921 Williston suggested "the term 'promissory' estoppel or something equivalent should be used to mark the distinction"[232] from equitable estoppel since the term estoppel kept cropping up in the rationales of promissory reliance cases. The inclusion of estoppel in the label to the new reliance action was a misnomer that both Restatements of Contracts refrained from employing. Nevertheless, by at least the 1890s, there was a judicial practice developing of using the terminology promissory estoppel as courts now of law and equity systematized formerly loose equitable practices; and so, what was once a rule of evidence for misrepresentations, was incorporated into the new reliance formula applicable to the formation of contracts.[233] Thus in *Beatty v. Western College of Toledo* (1898), when the donor executed a promissory note for the construction of a "Ladies Boarding Hall", the defense of want of consideration could not stand up when "money has been expended, or liabilities have been incurred, in reliance upon the note.... the donor or maker thereof is, in good conscience bound to pay."[234] That should have been enough, but the court, perhaps uneasy about this new theory, added: "the gift will be upheld upon the ground of estoppel, and not by reason of any valid consideration in the original undertaking."

Occasionally a court would simply mislabel a promissory estoppel case as an equitable estoppel case, as in *Ricketts v. Scothorn* (1898).[235] There a grandfather induced his granddaughter to quit her job and thereby "to alter her position for the worse on the faith of a note" he executed on her behalf in furtherance of his promise that he had "fixed out something that you have not got to work any more." There was no consideration for the grandfather's unconditional promise since he didn't request or bargain for her to quit work in exchange. She recovered against his executor on the basis of what the court labelled as "equitable estoppel," but this was not a case of being estopped from proving a fact but rather, as the court said, "it would be grossly inequitable... to resist payment on the ground that the promise was given without consideration."

It is perhaps understandable why a court shopping around for a precedent for the new theory would alight on equitable estoppel since both equitable estoppel and the promissory reliance remedy did have the similarities of: one, justifiable reliance on the other party's words; two, the wrong of the misrepresentation or the failure to keep the promise;

and, three, the bar to raising a defense otherwise available due to the injustice of injurious reliance.[236] Nonetheless, the dissimilarities between the doctrines caused confusion and erroneous thinking. The contorted translation of equitable estoppel's ideas were not apt since there was no misrepresentation in promissory estoppel and equitable estoppel concerned the past or present while promissory estoppel dealt with the future. Indeed the confusion was such that some courts seemed more likely to grant promissory estoppel when there was a misleading representation,[237] and some modern courts go so far as to require fraud, or at least constructive fraud, before they will apply promissory estoppel.[238]

One issue worthy of mention before leaving equitable estoppel was whether promissory estoppel could be used to enforce an oral promise not complying with the Statute of Frauds. There are two schools of thought on the application of the reliance remedy to a promise falling under the Statute of Frauds: one holding that only equitable estoppel should be available and the other that promissory estoppel is available. The first cases were of the equitable estoppel vintage, and this was in the main the position adopted by the Restatement First.[239] Under this approach, the Statute of Frauds defense would be estopped when any of the three following misrepresentations was made and relied on: that the Statute of Frauds was satisfied or that the Statute wouldn't be raised as a defense or a promise was made that a writing would be signed. Some courts, even today, would not go past this to allow promissory estoppel to subvert the legislative mandate of a writing. This conservative approach has been reinforced by the appearance of the U.C.C. statute of frauds for sales of goods because legislatures had the chance to repeal the Statute of Frauds but instead reaffirmed it, subject to a few exceptions, and the only explicit code exception for reliance relief here was in the case of specially manufactured goods. The specificity in U.C.C. 2–201 is seen by many to have displaced promissory estoppel on a sale of goods not complying with the writing requirement, and consequently promissory estoppel has made little progress here.[240] Under the alternate school of thought, an oral promise directed to contract performance, rather than concerning a misrepresentation regarding compliance with the Statute of Frauds, should be enforced despite failure to comply with the statute if there would otherwise be an injustice caused by the reliance. Indeed, in a 1909 equitable estoppel case, a promise to make a signed writing in compliance with the Statute of Frauds had elements of promissory reliance (promissory estoppel) since a promise, the promise of compliance, was enforced. This notion was extended in cases like *Monarco v. Lo Greco* (1950) to other promises to perform, as in *Monarco* a promise to leave property to a son if he stayed and worked on the farm.[241] The Restatement Second adopted this view and was more liberal than Traynor, J. in *Monarco* in not requiring unconscionability or unjust enrichment.[242]

Now that the development of the ideas behind Restatement First of Contracts Section 90 have been traced through the fitful marriage of pure reliance logic with the principle of estoppel, there will be a brief step backwards to focus on why charitable subscriptions were the most fertile category of cases in the emergence of promissory reliance as a substitute for consideration. Because the rigors of the doctrine of consideration stood in the way of enforcement of solemnly executed charitable subscriptions, whether sealed or not, courts resorted to equitable theories of reliance and estoppel in order to realize public policy objectives.[243] Cardozo said, "public policy and reason will not be overruled to save the symmetry of" consideration, a concept formed without much regard to a sense of justice; and, he added: "conceptions of public policy have shaped" the charitable subscription rulings on "breaches of faith toward the public... and an unwarrantable disappointment of the reasonable expectations of those interested."[244] From a public policy standpoint the courts were initially more sympathetic to charities than to other reliance cases, and consequently they were not as demanding as to the degree of reliance required—thus paying off an old debt or consulting an architect could be enough for a charity but actual entrustment of property would be required in a gratuitous bailment.[245]

The nineteenth century charitable subscription decisions fit the Victorian bourgeois view of private philanthropy for the public welfare as an ideal and as a complement to laissez-faire government.[246] An analysis of the identity of the detrimental reliers in nineteenth century reliance cases shows that they frequently came from protected classes, such as, charities, holders of an equity of redemption, debtors subject to large forfeitures and employees making employment decisions. And, as courts began enforcing charitable subscriptions relied upon as a matter of course by the last quarter of the nineteenth century, a logical question raised was why a regularized application of promissory estoppel should not also be extended to other classes of gratuitous promisees. The drafters of the Restatement First of Contracts saw the merits of that logic and generalized the doctrine in order to open it up to all types of promises.[247]

The modern allowance of hardship relief for the reliance injury of those the law tried to protect was not novel to the common law. Milsom calls the modern development of a contractual reliance remedy "A Pageant in Modern Dress" since there is a striking parallel with the original development of Assumpsit in the late fifteenth century. By about 1500 there was a resort to the essentially trespassory idea of detrimental reliance as Assumpsit acted as a "backdoor" remedy for cases falling through the cracks between Covenant's sealed contract and Debt's *quid pro quo*. The modern reliance remedy returned to what Assumpsit had originally set out to do before the doctrine of consideration entered the picture later in the sixteenth century and Assumpsit took on a broader role. In the nineteenth century promissory estoppel began to fill the gap for hardship cases enforceable neither under sealed promise nor under the increased demand for reciprocity in bargain consideration.[248] Two other parallels between some fifteenth century and nineteenth century reliance cases were the emphasis both on the reliance of the entrustment of property and on the difference between misfeasance and nonfeasance.[249]

One fundamental difference, however, between the early evolution of Assumpsit and promissory estoppel is that Assumpsit and Covenant were seen from the beginning as separate compartments with different rules, but the substitute for consideration of promissory estoppel and the consideration contract continue an uneasy coexistence within the same compartment.[250] The total range of promises enforceable in a contractual sense was expanded to cover those fitting under an emerging doctrine of bargain consideration and to again include those promises inducing injurious reliance which were now covered by promissory estoppel. The emergence of the reformulated doctrine of bargain consideration flushed into the open true reliance cases formerly hidden behind findings of detriment consideration. Hardship cases were going to fall through the cracks unless there was a resolution of the tension between the emphasis on the realization of the shared expectations of bargaining parties, brought on by the will theory, and the exclusion of justifiable reliance from the consideration formula. The notions of will theory and of an individual relying only on himself had to give way to the right to rely in order to avoid injustices in an increasingly impersonal, and yet interdependent, society.[251]

In jurisdictions where bargain consideration was not adopted as the definition of consideration, such as Cardozo's New York, it was possible to enforce a gratuitous promise without the need to resort to promissory estoppel; thus in *Allegheny College v. National Chautauqua Bank* (1927) the inducement or motive for the charitable promise was the detriment of the charity undertaking to memorialize the donor. This line of thinking could logically lead to the conclusion that beginning construction of a building that the donor wanted built would also qualify. Under the Cardozo and Corbin view, there was a symmetry between consideration and promissory estoppel wherein promises were enforceable if they were seriously made in order to protect the promisee's reasonable reliance.[252]

The construction of the reliance doctrine of promissory estoppel "in modern dress" entailed a borrowing from both tort and equity sources. The ideas drawn from tort and equity can be summed up by the statement that a promisor is accountable only for injurious reliance which he should foresee (a tort notion), and that enforcement must be necessary to avoid an injustice.[253] The misrepresentation aspect of equitable estoppel is obviously tortious, but a study of estoppel's origins proves it to be an amalgam of tort and equity notions. From the standpoint of tort, promissory estoppel includes the tortious elements of reliance, foreseeability, a duty imposed by law and the arguably negligent wrong of making a promise that foreseeably could be injuriously relied upon. A reasonable man should not carelessly make a promise when there is a reasonably foreseeable risk that it will induce justifiable reliance and resultant harm.[254] Promissory estoppel employs an objective standard, also present in tort's reasonable man standard, to determine whether a promise was made and whether reliance was foreseeable and reasonable; however, determining whether an injustice has occurred is a subjective question better handled on the equity side. From the equity side, decisions of the new courts of law and equity employed equitable notions of trust, good faith, reliance and simple justice to soften the harshness of the proposition that a rugged individual should rely only on himself and hence should suffer the consequences of being so naive as to rely on a promise unsupported by consideration. Indeed, promissory estoppel is perceived to be of such an equitable nature in some jurisdictions that there is no right to trial by jury.[255] The fusion of the courts facilitated a more regularized infusion of equitable principles into the common law of contracts, and promissory estoppel was one of the techniques devised to do that. The regularization of promissory estoppel received its biggest boost with its inclusion in the Restatement of Contracts.

The draftsmen of the Restatement First could have restricted the promissory estoppel doctrine to the nineteenth century categories of gratuitous promises declaring the rule to be *sui generis* to their narrow circumstances instead of announcing a generalized reliance ground for recovery. Although the thread of "the justifiable reliance of the promisee" was isolated as running through the scattered categories, there was no systematic pattern otherwise due to the many inconsistencies and quirks unique to each category. Ironically, Williston's use of generalized principles to preserve the abstraction of classical contract law and to provide predictability and clarity in order to save the common law from codification made him a major contributor to a revolutionary change in the rules of the common law of contract in the twentieth century. Section 90 was the most significant departure from precedent in the Restatement First, and the 1928 Official Draft admitted as much: "(Section 90) states a broader general rule than has often been laid down."[256] The harshness of bargain consideration was out of step with the modern concern for the reasonable expectations and reliance of the promisee,[257] and Section 90 gave authority for equitable growth outside the peculiarities of the original narrow categories.

The process of tacking on a new ground for recovery on a promise, notwithstanding a contemporary definition of consideration at odds with it, is reminiscent of Mansfield's ultimately unsuccessful attempt to modify the doctrine of consideration by his general principle that a moral obligation constituted sufficient consideration. The parallel doesn't stop there since, although moral consideration was broader than promissory estoppel in not demanding reliance, both doctrines involved obligations grounded in conscience and enforceable at equity.[258] There is the ring of a moral obligation to a rule holding a promisor accountable on the basis of a promise reasonably expected to induce injurious reliance, even when the promisor received no benefit.[259] A century after Mansfield, in the New York case of *Freeman v. Freeman* (1870), the reliance was said to "constitute in equity a consideration for the promise."[260] Just as Mansfield's quasi-contract work cured some problems on the benefit side of the consideration test, his moral obligation theory could have covered detrimental reliance and more.

Restatement Section 90 caught on rapidly during the generation after its 1932 publication and was widely cited as authority for the general principle of promissory estoppel in fact situations far afield from the original loose groupings of nineteenth century gratuitous promises.[261] Promissory estoppel obviated the need to make a wholesale reform of the doctrine of consideration in order to cure the injustices caused by bargain consideration. The wider application of the new doctrine raised new issues, however, such as: whether it should act as a gap-filling substitute for consideration or should it be an alternative remedy; whether it was applicable to commercial promises; what type of damages were recoverable; was it applicable to third party reliance; and whether it should be used in lieu of other contract requirements like offer and acceptance, definiteness and the Statute of Frauds.

Before analyzing the later development of Section 90, there will be a digression to investigate the English view of promissory estoppel. The urge for a reliance remedy in England in the second half of the nineteenth century was not so great since England retained the seal and had not reduced the flexibility of the detriment side of consideration by adoption of the bargain theory of consideration.[262] The limited extent to which English courts have developed a promissory estoppel theory is found in *Central London Property Trust Ltd. v. High Trees House Ltd.* (1947).[263] In that case a landlord and tenant had agreed to a rent reduction on a lease during the war, but after the war the landlord sued for the full amount of future payments, and he also sued for the amount lopped-off of past payments due since the past consideration rule barred enforcement of the modification. Denning, J. acknowledged there was no consideration for the landlord's promise to reduce but said he would be willing to enforce the promise, for the wartime period anyway, because a "promise to accept a smaller sum, if acted upon, is binding."[264] The decision created an exception to the rule in *Pinnel's Case* and in *Foakes v. Beer*, which required consideration for a release from, or a reduction of, a contractual obligation. An analysis of Denning's opinion on the specific facts of *High Trees* shows it to be based on promissory reliance logic rather than equitable estoppel logic because it was the landlord's promise about the future that was relied upon and not his representation of a present fact.[265]

Denning's dictum in *High Trees* suggested that a broader application of promissory reliance might be possible: "I prefer to apply the principle that a promise intended to be binding, intended to be acted on and in fact acted on, is binding so far as its terms properly apply." Several years later an English lower court took Denning at his word by employing reliance logic to uphold a cause of action for the enforcement of a promise; but, perhaps due to the reaction of a conservative legal community against what extensions of *High Trees* might do to the doctrine of consideration, Denning, L.J. himself reversed the lower court, saying, "The principle stated in the *High Trees* case . . . does not create new causes of action where none existed before. It only prevents a party from insisting upon his strict legal rights, when it would be unjust to allow him to enforce them."[266]

So promissory reliance logic was available in England as a defense to suspend an obligation but not as a basis for a cause of action when consideration was lacking. In its narrowest sense, *High Trees* could be read to merely provide a reliance defense in support of a suspensory release from, or at least a reduction of, a contractual obligation. It did lend support to the proposition that a contract discharge was not necessarily governed by the same rules applicable to the formation of a contract. The "anemic" English version of promissory reliance has not been able to move past the welcomed reform of *Foakes v. Beer* because of the reverence for precedent, which that single jurisdiction has, as contrasted with the multiplicity of American jurisdictions where a needed restatement of the law could point a new way.[267] English judicial reasoning was becoming more formal than in the United States by around 1900. Indeed, Langdellian formalism notwithstanding, the American natural law notion of a higher law had been less formal than England's approach from the time of the founding of the Republic. England's formalist tradition began with Bentham's opposition to judge-made law and his positivist idea that law was made by the sovereign Parliament. From this source, conservatives, seeing its advantages for themselves, successfully pushed it to the degree that modern English judges are said to stick to formal rules and leave policy and reform to Parliament. The English judiciary is to find the law in its sources and to formally construe any relevant legislation; whereas modern American judges apply formal rules with one eye on the substantive reasons on which a precedent is based.[268]

Returning now to the development of promissory estoppel in the United States subsequent to the 1932 publication of Section 90, an important issue argued over the next quarter century was whether the doctrine should apply to commercial transactions. Many questioned the propriety of extending a doctrine developed to avoid hardship under gratuitous promises made in the community interest, which were no longer enforceable under seal, to offers made in exchange for consideration. The story of the course taken can be told by looking at three cases all having the similar facts of a subcontractor submitting a bid to a general contractor, who then relied on that bid in calculating and submitting his own binding bid on a government construction project. Could the subcontractor be estopped from revoking his bid relied upon by the general contractor? In the first case of *James Baird Co. v. Gimbel Bros.* (1933), Hand, J. saw promissory estoppel's chief role being in the enforcement of a "donative promise" which was unfortunately no longer covered by the seal; he cited Holmes in denying that it applied to offers that "propose bargains" and were "not meant to become a promise until a consideration has been received."[269] Hand wanted to preserve the freedom of the offeror to bargain and not be bound by reliance unless it was specified as a way of accepting.[270] Section 90 did not expressly limit promissory estoppel to non-commercial promises, but Hand was unwilling to compromise the inviobility of bargain consideration even for the hardship transaction not fitting the bargain paradigm of a general contractor not being able to protect his reliance by accepting the subcontractor's bid.

In the second construction case of *Northwestern Engineering Co. v. Ellerman* (1943), the South Dakota Supreme Court expressly disagreed with Hand's position that promissory estoppel should not apply to a commercial offer and said:

> we believe that reason and justice demand that the doctrine be applied to the present facts. We cannot believe that by accepting this doctrine as controlling in the state of facts before us we will abolish the requirement of a consideration in contract cases, in any different sense than an ordinary estoppel abolishes some legal requirement in its application.[271]

In the third construction case of *Drennan v. Star Paving Co.* (1958)[272] Traynor, J. followed the logic of the South Dakota court. Traynor was more conservative in that he employed the common law fiction of an implied term and retained bargain notions by analogizing the subcontractor's bid to an offer for a unilateral contract under Restatement of

Contracts Section 45; he stated that, when a bid was justifiably relied on, there was an implied "subsidiary promise" to not revoke.[273] Although the subcontractor did not bargain for the plaintiff's reliance on the bid, Traynor said he had reason to expect that his bid would be incorporated in the general contractor's bid. The application of promissory estoppel to commercial promises was not limited to construction bids and became common in other commercial cases, such as franchises and releases and even as to negotiations short of contract formation. The comments and illustrations to Restatement Second Section 90 recognize the extension of the doctrine to commercial promises.[274]

The judicial enforcement of unaccepted commercial offers in cases like *Drennan* altered traditional ideas about the doctrine of offer and acceptance. Both Hand and Traynor deferred to the demands of offer and acceptance but arrived at different conclusions. Whereas Hand was drawn to market ideas favoring freedom of the individual entrepreneur at the negotiation level, Traynor's concern was for the injustice of the injurious reliance. While Hand protected the entrepreneur and put the burden on the individual relying on a bare offer, Traynor put the burden on the instigating offeror who could reasonably foresee justifiable reliance. Traynor's finding of an impliedly irrevocable offer went further than the trend toward enforcement of an explicit firm offer relied upon. The end of the seal hamstrung firm offers until there was judicial relief for injurious reliance and statutory relief in some non-reliance cases by the mid-twentieth century.[275]

Once *Drennan* had enforced an unaccepted offer relied upon, was it possible to extend that notion to enforce a negotiation level promise which could not be raised to the level of an offer? *Hoffman v. Red Owl Stores* (1965) answered in the affirmative in a case of both a promise of a franchise too indefinite to be considered an offer and the promisee's unbargained for reliance.[276] *Hoffman v. Red Owl* further altered traditional ideas about offer and acceptance and departed from Traynor's adherence to bargain notions. Due to the common occurrence of reliance on franchisor assurances during negotiations, franchise relations do not neatly fit the discrete, one-shot sales contract model, upon which the doctrine of offer and acceptance was grafted; and so it was probably inevitable that francisor duties would be found to arise under a promise made prior to an actual offer. *Hoffman v. Red Owl* flew in the face of the two fundamental contract formation requirements of consideration and offer and acceptance, and, when all that it tries to do is taken into account, it may be more of a harbinger of what the law might become than what it is.[277] The decision seems in tune with the suggestion that one must negotiate in good faith or else pay reliance damages.[278]

Developments subsequent to the 1932 publication of Restatement Section 90, including such decisions as *Hoffman v. Red Owl* and *Drennan v.*

Star Paving Co. and published research, influenced revisions to Section 90 in the Restatement Second of Contracts published in 1981. Besides revisions to Section 90, there was a proliferation of reliance throughout the Restatement Second in areas already discussed like the Statute of Frauds and firm offers and in cases of contract modifications and guaranty contracts.[279] Section 90 was revised by allowing for partial enforcement, by not requiring reliance to necessarily be substantial, by including commercial promises, and by including foreseeable third party reliance. These revisions were responses both to decisions subsequent to 1932, in particular those allowing for promises, and to the research of Fuller and Perdue and of Boyer who showed that caselaw prior to 1932 had been overlooked by drafters of the Restatement First.[280]

The provision for partial enforcement was the principal change in Restatement Second Section 90. Fuller and Perdue and Boyer proved erroneous Williston's position that recovery should only be for expectation damages since prior caselaw adapted recovery to what justice required in the circumstances.[281] Justice might dictate partial recovery if the award of expectation damages would be an undue hardship on the promisor, as where expectation damage in the case of a breach of a gratuitous promise to procure insurance would result in a great disparity between the value of the promised service and the face of the policy.[282] The recovery of reliance damages might be more logical in the instance of a gratuitous promise than in a commercial promise where there may have been the reliance of foregoing an alternative possibility of profit. To an extent, because of the Restatement Second's adoption of the alternative of partial enforcement, the Restatement First requirement of reliance of a "definite and substantial character" was made more flexible by not mandating substantial reliance in all cases. So in charitable subscriptions and marriage settlements, two *sui generis* categories traditionally favored under promissory estoppel as a matter of policy, the mere "probability of reliance is enough", but in more bargain-based transactions more recently falling under promissory estoppel, as firm offers and guaranties, the reliance must be substantial.[283]

Before leaving promissory estoppel, a question left to discuss is how extensive the doctrine has or will become as a means of enforcing promises. Is injurious reliance an additional ground that can exist as a complement to promises enforced under bargain consideration or is it an independent remedy that could eclipse bargain consideration as the primary ground for recovery on promises? As an offshoot of the latter, there have even been a few suggestions aired that recovery under promissory estoppel may not be a contract recovery at all.[284] The last two possibilities have in part prompted the suggestion that consideration contract is dying. Under the Restatement Second, bargain is the rule, but there is the recognition that a contract may be formed under special rules such as promissory estoppel, among others. Sight should not be lost of the fact that bargains were not the only types of transactions enforced at common law. Even when reliance might not be bargained for, it was, and still is, an additional reason for enforcement of a promise; and, within the bargain context, reliance is a substitute for other elaborated contract rules besides consideration.[285]

Is there anything to Gilmore's assertion that the consideration contract is dead or dying?[286] Gilmore's argument, perhaps instigated to stimulate further analysis, was that the bargain theory of consideration is being abandoned as it is breached on the detriment side by promissory estoppel and on the benefit side by restitution. He saw the ambiguous relationship between consideration and promissory estoppel in the Restatement First being resolved in favor of promissory estoppel, which is in effect swallowing up the bargain principle. He questioned whether the contradictory doctrines could coexist in the same compartment.[287] He prophesied the refusion of contract and tort into a unified theory of civil action and that, in the process of the reabsorption of contract into tort, the contractual requirements of offer and acceptance and consideration are largely being overlooked. As individualism was bowing to the welfare state, this reemergence of tort in promissory transactions is said to be replacing consent with a duty imposed by law and based on a moral obligation. Gilmore saw other symptoms of the demise of contract in the increased judicial hostility to such contract staples as the Statute of Frauds, the parol evidence rule and expectation damages and he added that there is a greater ease of avoidance of contractual obligation due to the increased use of duress and frustration.

Gilmore chose to ignore both the pull of the long standing idea of reciprocity in the common law and the bargain behavior of contractors; as a result, his ideas reflect only to a limited degree what happened historically and what is happening today. Courts have and will continue to preserve the persisting utility of the contractual behavior of entering into consensual bargains in order to plan for the future, to place a value on goods and services and to assure that a bargainer will receive the advantage he seeks and promised to pay for.[288] Gilmore repeated the error of a monistic urge in isolating the single idea of non-bargain duties imposed by law just as Holmes and Williston had done earlier in overemphasizing bargain. As Corbin pointed out, there have always been a variety of reasons courts have recognized for enforcing promises inside and outside of agreed exchanges, no matter how the restaters defined consideration. Indeed, a study of the emergence and later development of the doctrine of consideration is testimony to the diversity of reasons for promissory enforcement despite the monistic urge.[289]

Any possibility that promissory estoppel might have done what Gilmore suggested was stifled as bargain ideas were employed to hem in promissory estoppel before the Restatement First innovation could take off. There have been some instances of disingenuous applications of such traditional bargain doctrine as bargain consideration and offer and acceptance to cases of pure reliance. Tortured logic has been used to declare there was an offer for a unilateral contract calling for acceptance by reliance, and the use of such logic to avoid promissory estoppel is not limited to feigned bargains.[290] Bargain ideas are influencing when a promise should be enforced under promissory estoppel itself since the potential breadth of actions under promissory estoppel has caused analogy to familiar bargain doctrine in groping for parameters to the action. Orthodox bargain notions are so entrenched in promissory transactions that bargain consideration is a theme of departure in most discussions of promissory estoppel, particularly in commercial transactions.[291] Traynor tied promissory estoppel to a bargain in *Drennan v. Star Paving Co.* in keeping the power to accept open.[292] He also emphasized the reciprocal benefit to the promisor-subcontractor since it was in his best interest if the general contractor was awarded the government contract. The decision is an example of the use of promissory estoppel within a bargain context in fulfilling a contract requirement. Traynor's decision in *Monarco v. Lo Greco* is similar in using promissory estoppel to overcome the Statute of Frauds; also in that case, he allowed it to replace the Statute only if there was unconscionability or unjust enrichment. Traynor's inclination to keep the discussion of promissory estoppel within the bargain setting has influenced the tendency to resist allowing promissory estoppel to stray too far from bargain ideas.[293] Furthermore, there are other factors obscuring the differences between bargain and promissory estoppel, such as, the frequent comment that promissory estoppel is a substitute for consideration, the analogies drawn to detriment consideration and the common practice of pleading contract and promissory estoppel in the alternative.[294]

The interest in promissory estoppel is arguably more academic than practical because the range of transactions covered is too narrow to take over the contract field. Promissory estoppel's primary role is in protecting justifiable reliance in the gap between a mere promise and a bargain. Even when restitution and promissory estoppel are taken together, there is one important type of contract representing a large volume of modern cases not covered by either: the executory contract.[295] Nonetheless, promissory estoppel and restitution do serve a valuable function in providing flexibility and justice and in overcoming the peculiar formalities of bargain consideration in circumstances not fitting neatly within its relatively narrow definition.[296]

Conclusion

The inability of the common law to adjust to the enormous changes since the industrial revolution prompted legislatures to intrude upon contract doctrine to an unprecedented degree. Legislation promoted clarity, uniformity, equity and the inclusion of business usage. The common law judge was being unseated as the paramount figure in the process, and thereafter there would be no turning back from the sharing of the development of doctrine between judges, legislators and restaters of the law. By the turn of the twentieth century the judiciary was out of step with social and economic realities as it began to narrow the consideration test for enforcement of promises rather than broadening it to provide the flexibility needed in an increasingly complex society. The doctrinaire clinging to objective abstraction and dated notions of freedom of contract necessitated the development of hardship relief outside the parameters of the new bargain consideration doctrine. So what courts, now of law and equity, took away with one hand, they began to remedy on the other by taking into account contractors' expectations and the unforeseeability of a more volatile future by the liberalization of excuse, the recognition of third party rights, the toleration of greater contract uncertainty and the development of new grounds of relief in incomplete contracts for reliance suffered and benefits conferred.

These new reliance and benefit grounds provided relief in hardship cases which were not infrequently caused by an increasing lack of individual equality of bargaining positions and by an increase in cases falling through the cracks due to the narrowing of the definition of consideration. The reliance and benefit grounds for recovery began as equitable relief outside the bounds of nineteenth century contract rules, but they began encroaching on classical contract rules in the twentieth century. Decisions began to call into question fundamental notions about the basic contract formation rules of consideration, offer and acceptance and the Statute of Frauds. These adjustments violated market rules when relief was given in commercial transactions despite the fact no bargain had been reached. Although the alterations of doctrine were narrower than the judicial reforms of the sixteenth century, they hark back to the earlier assault on traditional theory waged by the King's Bench against the obsolescent writ system. Suggestions began to surface that these equitable grounds might supplant bargained for consideration as the governing doctrine in promissory transactions. Due to the cross-fertilization occurring in the second half of the twentieth century between the doctrines of bargain consideration, promissory estoppel and restitution, it appears more likely that a construct of the three doctrines is evolving as ways are found for the equitable grounds to complement the overriding bargain principle.

The doctrinal adjustments discussed in this chapter to remedy the inequities brought on by the erosion of both freedom of contract and equality in individual bargaining positions still had one eye on objective, generalized principles. That is inevitably the nature of doctrine designed to handle the mass of transactions arising in the courts. There would have still been a myriad of inequitable outcomes if the reform had stopped there since there needed to be an even greater breakdown in classical abstraction in order to take into account specific inequities not falling neatly under the exceptional doctrines discussed herein. Those additional reforms were done at legislative and judicial levels contemporaneous with the reformulation of doctrine discussed in this chapter, but that is the subject of the final chapter.

Notes

1. American Bar Association was established in 1878 and made uniformity of the law a primary objective. West Publishing Co. began the regional reporter system in 1879, soon making caselaw available nationwide.

2. *See* MAX WEBER ON LAW IN ECONOMY AND SOCIETY 301–321 (M. Rheinstein ed. 1954). Not all writers have agreed with the proposition that formalism fully supplanted the instrumental style. *See* Scheiber, *Instrumentalism and Property Rights: A Reconsideration of American "Styles of Judicial Reasoning" in the 19th Century,* 1975 WIS. L. REV. 1, 3; *and* Paine, *Instrumentalism v. Formalism: Dissolving the Dichotomy,* 1978 WIS. L. REV. 997, 998.

3. *See* Reimann, *The Historical School Against Codification: Savigny, Carter, and the Defeat of the New York Civil Code,* 37 AM. J. COMP. LAW 95, 103–106, 111–112 (1989). The appearance of a Field Code in California in 1872, along with a code in India highlighted in Pollock's 1876 Contracts Treatise, and the English Bill of Exchange Act of 1882 influenced the codification push.

4. P. ATIYAH, THE RISE AND FALL OF FREEDOM OF CONTRACT 388 (Oxford: 1979) (Utiliarian influence of principles for the largest number. *Id.* at 390.).

5. *See* C. LANGDELL, A SELECTION OF CASES ON THE LAW OF CONTRACTS (Boston: 1871); *see also* C. LANGDELL, A SUMMARY OF THE LAW OF CONTRACTS (Boston: 1880). American law was becoming more, rather than less, English.

6. *See* M. HORWITZ, THE TRANSFORMATION OF AMERICAN LAW, 1780–1860, 263–264 (Cambridge, Mass. 1977) (*Swift v. Tyson* seen as inception of move toward formalism. *Id.* at 249.).

7. *See* Clark, *The Restatement of the Law of Contracts,* 42 YALE L. J. 643, 646 (1933).

8. *See* Holmes, *Path of the Law,* 10 HARV. L. REV. 457, 465–466 (1897).

9. Nelson, *The Impact of the Antislavery Movement Upon Styles of Judicial Reasoning in Nineteenth Century America,* 87 HARV. L. REV. 513, 558–565 (1974) (principles unalterable by judicial will). *See* Reimann, *supra* note 3, at 8.

10. M. HORWITZ, *supra* note 6, at 201, 266; *see* M. WEBER, *supra* note 2, at 230; *see also* Ferguson, *The Horwitz Thesis and Common Law Discourse in England,* 3 OXFORD J. LEGAL STUDIES 34, 35–36 (1983).

11. *See* P. ATIYAH and R. SUMMERS, FORM AND SUBSTANCE IN ANGLO-AMERICAN LAW 247–248 (Oxford: 1987).

12. *See* L. FRIEDMAN, A HISTORY OF AMERICAN LAW 673, 678–679

(N.Y: 2d ed. 1985) (Middle class groups organizing for their rights became a dominant theme shaping American law. *Id.* at 540.).

13. C. LANGDELL, A SELECTION OF CASES OF SALES OF PERSONAL PROPERTY (Boston: 1871) (nearly 2/3 devoted to Statute of Frauds). This was followed in the same vein in the next generation in S. WILLISTON, THE LAW GOVERNING SALES OF GOODS AT COMMON LAW AND UNDER THE UNIFORM SALES ACT (N.Y. 1909). W. Story wrote the first American treatise on sales in 1848.

14. Lickbarrow v. Mason, 2 T.R. 63, 100 Eng. Rep. 35 (K.B. 1787) (Buller called Mansfield "the founder of the commercial law".). Mansfield had begun the process of introducing mercantile usage into the common law and recognized express warranty. Stuart v. Wilkins, 1 Doug. 18, 99 Eng. Rep. 15 (K.B. 1778). *Cf.* Llewellyn, *Across Sales on Horseback,* 52 HARV. L. REV. 725, 740–743 (1939) (Mansfield didn't have chance to decide many sales cases.).

15. Llewellyn, *supra* note 14, at 736, 744–745; 2 J. SMITH, SELECTION OF LEADING CASES 645–647 (Philadelphia: 1847 ed.); Friedman, *Formative Elements in the Law of Sales: The Eighteenth Century,* 44 MINN. L. REV. 411, 435–438, 459 (1960); Gilmore, *On Statutory Obsolescence,* 39 UNIV. COLO. L. REV. 461, 470–471 (1967); Tarling v. Baxter, 6 B.& C. 360, 108 Eng. Rep. 484 (K.B. 1827) (risk of law passed when fire without haystack moving or being paid for). Third party rights in the insolvent buyer's assets were weighed in favor of the seller; it was an issue irrelevant in earlier cases brought under the common count "for goods bargained and sold".

16. Llewellyn, *supra* note 14, at 744–746.

17. Cole v. Berry, 42 N.J. Law 308 (1880); *see* L. FRIEDMAN, *supra* note 12, at 541–543. Uniform Conditional Sales Act promulgated in 1918.

18. Williston, *The Law of Sales in Proposed Uniform Commercial Code,* 63 HARV. L. REV. 561, 563–564 (1950) (Only real difference were regarding rescission and notice upon breach of warranty.). The English Sales Act was formulated in treatises by Blackburn and Benjamin. *Id.* at 564. Uniform Sales Act was enacted by 34 states (the N.I.L. by 48). These codes were a realization of J. Story's desire in 1821 to preserve the common law from its diversity in the U.S. by commercial codes.

19. Shepherd v. Kain, 5 B. & A. 240, 106 Eng. Rep. 1180 (1821); Jones v. Bright, 5 Bing. 533, 130 Eng. Rep. 1167 (1829); Nicholas v. Godts, 10 Exch. 191 (1854); Gammell v. Gunby & Co., 52 Ga. 504 (1874); Main v. Dearing, 73 Ark. 470, 84 S.W. 640 (1905).

20. J. BAKER, AN INTRODUCTION TO ENGLISH LEGAL HISTORY 295–296 (London: 2d ed. 1979); Prosser, *The Implied Warranty of Merchantable Quality,* 27 MINN. L. REV. 117, 154 (1943); K. LLEWELLYN, CASES AND MATERIALS ON THE LAW OF SALES 247–248 (Chicago: 1930).

21. *See* Jones v. Bright, 5 Bing. 533, 130 Eng. Rep. 1167 (1829) (manufactured goods different than horses); *see also* Kessler and Fine, *Culpa in Contrahendo, Bargaining in Good Faith, and Freedom of Contract: A Comparative Study,* 77 HARV. L. REV. 401, 441 (1964).

22. Hoe v. Sanborn, 21 N.Y. 552 (1860); Jones v. Just, L.R. 3 Q.B. 197 (1868); *cf.* Barnard v. Kellogg, 77 U.S. 383, 388 (1870) (*caveat emptor* of "universal acceptance"); *see* L. FRIEDMAN, *supra* note 12, at 540–541 (Middle class judges

favored consumers, farmers and small merchants over manufacturers.); *see also* M. HORWITZ, *supra* note 6, at 199. *Caveat emptor* has retained vitality in land sales. Swinton v. Whitinsville Svgs. Bank, 311 Mass. 677, 42 N.E. 2d 808 (1942).

23. AMERICAN LAW INSTITUTE, RESTATEMENT OF THE LAW OF CONTRACTS viii (St. Paul: 1932). The object of the Institute was to adapt the law to its "social needs" and to carry on "scientific legal work". *Id.* The latter impulse won out. *And see* Milsom, *A Pageant in Modern Dress,* 84 YALE L. J. 1585, 1588 (1975) (no possibility of a Restatement in a single jurisdiction like England).

24. *Cf.* M. WEBER, *supra* note 2, at 314–315, 318 (Codes threaten academics' importance and would transform position of English judges.); *see* 1 A. DE TOCQUEVILLE, DEMOCRACY IN AMERICA 281–282 (1835) (H. Reeve tr. 1899) (Common law lawyers are aristocratic interpreters of occult science.).

25. S. WILLISTON, TREATISE ON THE LAW OF CONTRACTS (New York: 1921); A. CORBIN, CORBIN ON CONTRACTS (St. Paul: 1950).

26. *See* G. GILMORE, THE DEATH OF CONTRACT 61–65 (Columbus, Ohio: 1974).

27. Whittier, *The Restatement of Contracts and Mutual Assent,* 17 CALIF. L. REV. 441, 445 (1929) (Williston's objective theory doesn't square with caselaw.); Clark, *supra* note 7, at 664–665 (Compromises hold law back.); *see* L. FRIEDMAN, CONTRACT LAW IN AMERICA 25 (Madison: 1965); *see also* G. GILMORE, THE AGES OF AMERICAN LAW 73 (New Haven: 1977) (similar to Blackstone's attempt to preserve); *cf.* Address by B. Cardozo, AMERICAN LAW INSTITUTE 3d Annual Meeting (May 1, 1925) (Existence of Institute shows laissez-faire is gone.).

28. *See* L. FRIEDMAN, *supra* note 12, at 675.

29. Braucher, *The Legislative History of the U.C.C.,* 58 COLUM. L. REV. 798, 798–800 (1958).

30. *See* Gilmore, *supra* note 15, at 472.

31. *See* RESTATEMENT OF CONTRACTS sects. 45 and 90 (1932). *See* ENGLISH LAW REVISION COMMITTEE, SIXTH INTERIM REPORT, 1937, CMND. NO. 5449, at pp. 22–23 (should adopt firm offer due to business practice and higher moral standard of civil law); *and see* F. POLLOCK, PRINCIPLES OF CONTRACT 21 (Winfield 13th ed. 1951) (Why should firm offeror expect more consideration for leaving the offer open than the consideration of setting the price?).

32. *See* U.C.C. sects. 2–206 and 2–207. Llewellyn followed Whittier in 2–206. *See* Whittier, *supra* note 27, at 453. Confusion caused by "unilateral" since it covers dissimilar contracts and not all accepted by performance. Braucher, *Offer and Acceptance in the Second Restatement,* 74 YALE L. J. 302, 304, 306–307 (1964).

33. G. GILMORE, *supra* note 27, at 82; *see* Friedman, *supra* note 15, at 460 (atavistic resurrection of market overt).

34. Williston, *supra* note 18, at 562–563 (Formerly, similar uniform sales acts in U.S., England and Commonwealth countries provided some international uniformity. *Id.* at 564.). Corbin approved of U.C.C. Corbin, *The U.C.C. - Sales; Should It Be Enacted?* 59 YALE L.J. 821 (1950).

35. Beutel, *The Proposed Uniform (?) Commercial Code Should Not Be Adopted,* 61 YALE L.J. 334, 362–363 (1952) ("sell-out" to "bank lobby").

36. L. FRIEDMAN, *supra* note 12, at 675; G. GILMORE, *supra* note 27, at 85; Gilmore, *supra* note 15, at 472–477. *Cf.* E. FARNSWORTH, CONTRACTS 29–32 (Boston: 1982) (Code has resiliency because parties may vary rules and changing trade usage read in.) and Braucher, *supra* note 29, at 807–808. Braucher and Farnsworth were both reporters of the Restatement Second.

37. Braucher, *Freedom of Contract and the Second Restatement,* 78 YALE L.J. 598 (1969) (Corbin's review a basis of much of revision.). It is perhaps surprising that Corbin would support a restatement that provides general principles without reference to particular factual circumstances.

38. Knapp, *Reliance in the Revised Restatement: The Proliferation of Promissory Estoppel,* 81 COLUM. L. REV. 52 (1981); Farnsworth, *Ingredients in the Redaction of the Restatement (2d) of Contracts,* 81 COLUM. L. REV. 1, 9–12 (1981); Speidel, *An Essay on the Reported Death and Continued Vitality of Contract,* 27 STAN. L. REV. 1161, 1165–1166 (1975) (broader test based on moral obligation).

39. Braucher, *supra* note 37, at 599, 613–614 (tension between freedom of contract and elemental fairness). These refusals to follow the U.C.C. didn't contribute to uniformity objective.

40. L. FRIEDMAN, *supra* note 12, at 675–676, G. GILMORE, *supra* note 26, at 67–69; Summers, *Collective Agreements and the Law of Contracts,* 78 YALE L.J. 525, 565–567 (1969).

41. *See* L. FRIEDMAN, *supra* note 27, at 190 (less classical in Wisconsin in 1905–1915 than in 1836–1861); *accord* Mooney, *The Rise and Fall of Classical Contract Law: A Response to Professor Gilmore* (Book Review), 55 ORE. L. REV. 155, 175 (1976) (Classical law had little influence by 1905–1915.).

42. O. HOLMES, JR., THE COMMON LAW 292–294 (Boston: 1881). The bargained "for" translation of Holmes' "reciprocal conventional inducement" appears to invoke the this "for" that of Debt's *quid pro quo* emphasized by Holmes as the origin of consideration. *See* C. FIFOOT, HISTORY AND SOURCES OF THE COMMON LAW 395–395 (London: 1949); *cf.* Baker, *Origins of the Doctrine of Consideration, 1535–1585* in ON THE LAWS AND CUSTOMS OF ENGLAND: ESSAYS IN HONOR OF S.E. THORNE 336, 354–356 (ed. M. Arnold, Chapel Hill: 1981) (only one side of bargain remediable in Debt).

43. Wisconsin & Michigan Ry. v. Powers, 191 U.S. 379, 386 (1903).

44. O. HOLMES, JR., *supra* note 42, at 295, 300, 307.

45. *See Holmes, Peirce and Legal Pragmatism,* 84 YALE L.J. 1123, 1123–1125, 1134 (1975). On the late 19th century emphasis on collective economic energies, *see* J. HURST, LAW AND THE CONDITIONS OF FREEDOM IN THE NINETEENTH CENTURY UNITED STATES 98–105 (Madison: 1956); *see* L. FRIEDMAN, *supra* note 27, at 164–166. *See* 1 A. CORBIN, *supra* note 25, at sect. 109 (St. Paul: 1950) (Finding of consideration indicates that refusal to enforce would not satisfy the community.).

46. *See* Speidel, *supra* note 38, at 1168–1171; M. HORWITZ, *supra* note 6, at 201; L. FRIEDMAN, *supra* note 27, at 89–90; Hardesty v. Smith, 3 Ind. 39, 41–43 (1851); *see* M. WEBER, *supra* note 2, at 191–192 (Bargaining and market exchanges are communal actions.).

47. *See* J. DAWSON, GIFTS AND PROMISES 203–204 (New Haven: 1980) (Holmes required more than Kent's 1827 definition of consideration of "as something given in exchange" or "which is the inducement."). *And see* Hamson,

The Reform of Consideration, 54 L.Q. REV. 233, 234 (1938) ("Consideration, offer and acceptance are an indivisible trinity, facets of one identical notion which is that of bargain.").

48. O. HOLMES, JR., *supra* note 42, at 293.

49. Dickinson v. Dodds, 2 Ch. Div. 463, 45 L.J. Ch. 777 (C.A. 1876).

50. This contravened the subjective test of Cooke v. Oxley, 3 T.R. 653, 100 Eng. Rep. 785 (K.B. 1790). *See* Adams v. Lindsell, 1 B. & Ald. 681, 106 Eng. Rep. 250 (1818).

51. O. HOLMES, JR., *supra* note 42, at 304–307. *See* E. FARNSWORTH, *supra* note 36, at 66 (Concern shifted from substance of the exchange to the bargaining process.). Once offer and acceptance and consideration, no matter how adequate, were inextricably intertwined, it was arguable that an offer and acceptance standing alone would be sufficient for enforceability.

52. *See* C. FIFOOT, LAW AND HISTORY IN THE NINETEENTH CENTURY 20 (Selden Society Lecture, London: 1956) (Common law courts enforced bargains and not promises.); *see also* J. DAWSON, *supra* note 47, at 3–5.

53. C. FIFOOT, *supra* note 42, at 395.

54. THE REPORTS OF SIR JOHN SPELMAN (VOL. II), 94 SELDEN SOCIETY 293–297 (J. Baker ed. 1978) (hereinafter cited as SPELMAN REPORTS). *See* Gouldner, *The Norm of Reciprocity: A Preliminary Statement,* 25 AMER. SOC. REV. 161 (1960) (Most social transactions can be seen as exchange transactions.).

55. Baker, *supra* note 42, at 345, 350, 357; *see* Barton, *The Early History of Consideration,* 85 L.Q. REV. 372, 386 (1969).

56. 2 J. KENT, COMMENTARIES ON AMERICAN LAW 592 (New York: 8th ed. 1854); 1 T. PARSONS, THE LAW OF CONTRACTS 6 (Boston: 1853) (Williston edited editions of Parsons in the 1890s); Hardesty v. Smith, 3 Ind. 39 (1851).

57. *See* J. DAWSON, *supra* note 47, at 204 (Consideration was never insufficient just because obtaining consideration wasn't the motive inducing promisor.).

58. O. HOLMES, JR., *supra* note 42, at 253–259, 271.

59. Baker, *supra* note 42, at 355; C. FIFOOT, *supra* note 42, at 396.

60. C. FIFOOT, *supra* note 42, at 396. *See* 1 A. CORBIN, *supra* note 45, at sect. 110 (Criticizes Restatement of Contracts for first saying consideration must be "bargained for" but then devoting 10 sections to other factors making a promise enforceable. *Id.* at sect. 111.).

61. Allegheny College v. National Chautauqua County Bank of Jamestown, 246 N.Y. 369, 159 N.E. 173 (1927).

62. *See* J. DAWSON, *supra* note 47, at 206. *Cp.* Hawkes v. Saunders, 1 Cowp. 289, 98 Eng. Rep. 1091 (K.B. 1782) (Per Mansfield: "Where a man is under a moral obligation . . . the honesty and rectitude of the thing is a consideration."). For an expansive modern view of the principle of promise as the moral basis of contract law, *see* C. FRIED, CONTRACT AS PROMISE (Cambridge, Mass. 1981).

63. 1 A. CORBIN, *supra* note 45, at sects. 110, 112, 193–195. (A promise is not binding unless accompanied by one of factors that made it binding in the past (or will in the future). Contracts are enforced to avoid disappointment of

reasonable expectations of promisee; a finding of sufficient consideration is evidence that expectations of performance was reasonable and refusal to enforce would not satisfy the community. *Id.* at sects. 110, 112.).

64. RESTATEMENT (FIRST) OF CONTRACTS sect. 75(1) and Comment (b) (1932); *see* RESTATEMENT (SECOND) OF CONTRACTS sect. 71(1) (1981) ("bargained for"). Inadequacy is irrelevant in Restatement First Sects. 81 & 84 (a), where nominal consideration is sufficient, but a trivial consideration may be insufficient if its only a simulated bargain under Restatement Second Section 79, Comment (d).

65. *See* E. FARNSWORTH, *supra* note 36, at 295; *see also* Kessler and Fine, *supra* note 21, at 426.

66. *Foakes v. Beer,* 9 App. Cas. 605 (H.L. 1884) (Creditor went back on promise not to ask for interest.). *Pinnel's Case,* 5 Co. Rep. 177a, 77 Eng. Rep. 237 (C.P. 1602).

67. Tweddle v. Atkinson, 1 B. & S. 393, 121 Eng. Rep. 762 (1861) (Consideration must flow from plaintiff.); *cf.* S. MILSOM, HISTORICAL FOUNDATIONS OF THE COMMON LAW 359 (London: 2d ed. 1981) (that consideration must flow from plaintiff influenced past consideration rule).

68. *Pinnel's Case* was a Debt action, and Debt required actual receipt of the benefit (a part performance would not discharge a duty to pay the whole), but Assumpsit was based on a promise. C. FIFOOT, *supra* note 42, at 413; *cp.* Ames, *Two Theories of Consideration,* (pt. 1) 13 HARV. L. REV. 515, 521 (1899) (misconception to think of part payment rule as corollary of consideration).

69. *See* C. FIFOOT, *supra* note 42, at 414; *and see* J.DAWSON, *supra* note 47, at 207 (Consideration has to do with formation but has been confused with discharge and irrevocable offers.).

70. Ames (pt. 1), *supra* note 68, at 523 (Cited cases finding consideration for part payment: Bagge v. Slade, 3 Bulstr. 162 (1616) and Rawlins v. Lockey, 1 Vin. Abr. 308, pl. 24 (1639). Ames deplored fact that cases not brought to court's attention in *Foakes.*).

71. Sibree v. Tripp, 15 M. & W. 22, 153 Eng. Rep. 745 (1846). *Sibree* overruled Cumber v. Wane, 1 Stra. 426, 93 Eng. Rep. 613 (1721) (Promise in *Cumber* to take 5 pound note to satisfy 15 pound debt was no satisfaction unless creditor bettered.). *See* 2 J. SMITH, *supra* note 15, at 321 (*Cumber* followed *Pinnel,* which never appears to have been questioned.). *But see* D. & C. Builders Ltd. v. Rees, 3 All Eng. Rep. (1965), 2 Q.B. 617 (1966) (Lord Denning rejected *Sibree* since check same as cash.); *cf.* U.C.C. 2–209(1).

72. Ames argued that *Foakes* could have gone the other way had the lords been aware of Rawlins v. Lockey, 1 Vin. Abr. 308, pl. 24 (1639) ("30 pounds can be no satisfaction for 60 pounds, yet to have the money in his hands without suit is a good consideration to maintain this action upon the promise."). Ames (pt. 1), *supra* note 68, at 523. *Contra Foakes v. Beer, see* Frye v. Hubbell, 74 N.H. 358, 68A. 325 (1907).

73. *See* Ames (pt. 1), *supra* note 68, at 531; *see also* P. ATIYAH, *supra* note 4, at 440 (began ebbing of freedom of contract); *and see* E. FARNSWORTH, *supra* note 36, at 280 (frustrated the justified expectations of parties). Was freedom of contract merely a weapon of business to dispense with when it didn't benefit them as creditors? *See* L. FRIEDMAN, *supra* note 27, at 189.

74. F. KESSLER AND G. GILMORE, CONTRACTS: CASES AND MATERIALS 513 (Boston: 2d ed. 1970) (Some states have abolished *Foakes*.); ENGLISH LAW REVISION COMMITTEE, SIXTH INTERIM REPORT, 1937, CMND. NO. 5449 at pp. 19–21 (recommended legislative abolition per Blackburn).

75. Central London Property Trust Ltd. v. High Trees House Ltd., 1 K.B. 130 (1947). This case is as close England has come to promissory estoppel doctrine; there it is a defense allowed for relying on the release of an obligation but it cannot replace consideration in creating an obligation.

76. Rookwood's Case, Cro. Eliz. 164 (1588); Lever v. Heys, Cro. Eliz. 619 (1599); *see also* S. STOLJAR, A HISTORY OF CONTRACT AT COMMON LAW 135 (Canberra: 1975). The 16th century statement of the problem was there was no consideration (that is, there was no showing of a *reason why* plaintiff should have an action) rather than that plaintiff wasn't the promisee; the 19th century notion of privity didn't exist. A. SIMPSON, A HISTORY OF THE COMMON LAW OF CONTRACT 479 (Oxford: 1975).

77. *Bourne v. Mason,* 1 Vent. 6 (1669) (plaintiff did "nothing of trouble to himself or benefit to the defendant"). *Cf.* A. SIMPSON, *supra* note 76, at 479 (*Bourne* turned on whether consideration not whether plaintiff was promisee.).

78. Coke had opposed assignments due to fear of maintenance. Lampet's Case, 10 Co. Rep. 47 (1612).

79. *Dutton v. Poole,* 1 Vent. 318, 83 Eng. Rep. 523 (K.B. 1677); *see* S. STOLJAR, *supra* note 76, at 138n (*Dutton* court seemed to be aware of *Bourne v. Mason.*).

80. Martyn v. Hind, 2 Cowp. 437, 443, 98 Eng. Rep. 1174, 1177 (1776).

81. *See* A. SIMPSON, *supra* note 76, at 481–482. *Dutton* can arguably be construed as based on love and affection as consideration.

82. *See* Trueman v. Fenton, 2 Cowp. 544, 98 Eng. Rep. 1232 (1777) (Creditor permitted to enforce waiver of bankruptcy against a debtor who reaped the benefit of a large purchase on the eve of bankruptcy.).

83. Tweddle v. Atkinson, 1 B. & S. 393, 397–398, 121 Eng. Rep. 762 (1861).

84. *See* A. SIMPSON, *supra* note 76, at 477–485. The modern notion of privity and that consideration must flow from the promisee was unknown before the nineteenth century.

85. Williams v. Everett, 14 East 582, 104 Eng. Rep. 725 (1811).

86. 1 J. POWELL, ESSAY UPON THE LAW OF CONTRACTS AND AGREEMENTS 334 (1790); 1 R. POTHIER, A TREATISE ON THE LAW OF OBLIGATIONS 4 (W. Evans ed., London: 1806).

87. *See* S. STOLJAR, *supra* note 76, at 134–135.

88. Price v. Easton, 4 B. & Ad. 433, 110 Eng. Rep. 518 (1833). *See* Liversidge v. Broadbent, 4 H. & N. 603 (1859) (third party must supply consideration to have contract right).

89. Furmston, *Return to Dunlop v. Selfridge?,* 23 MOD. L. REV. 373, 382–384 (1960) (identical); G. TREITEL, THE LAW OF CONTRACT 463 (London: 5th ed. 1979) (not identical but closely connected); *see* M. FURMSTON, CHESHIRE, FIFOOT AND FURMSTON'S LAW OF CONTRACT 74–75 (London: 11th ed. 1986); *see also* A. SIMPSON, *supra* note 76, at 475–479.

90. Tweddle v. Atkinson, 1 B. & S. 393, 121 Eng. Rep. 762 (Q.B. 1861); Dunlop Pneumatic Tyre Co. v. Selfridge & Co., App. Cas. 847 (H.L. 1915) ("only

a person who is a party to a contract can sue on it."); Beswick v. Beswick, App. Cas. 58 (H.L. 1968) (reaffirmed *Tweddle*). The benefit side, much supported by Mansfield, was rarely discussed in the 19th century. Was this a part of the English reaction against Mansfield?

91. *See* ENGLISH LAW REVISION COMMITTEE, SIXTH INTERIM REPORT, 1937, CMND. NO. 5449, at p. 30 (Third party should be able to sue in own name.); *see also* Beswick v. Beswick, 3 All Eng. Rep. 1 (1966) (Denning, M.R., argued *Dutton v. Poole* never overruled.).

92. *See* M. FURMSTON, *supra* note 89, at 106–107.

93. *E.g.*, Mellen V. Whipple, 67 Mass. (1 Gray) 317 (1854).

94. Lawrence v. Fox, 20 N.Y. 268 (1859) (6–2 decision).

95. *See* RESTATEMENT OF CONTRACTS sect. 75, Comment (e) (1932) ("It matters not from whom consideration moves or to whom it goes.") The Lawrence court relied on earlier donee beneficiary logic emanating from *Dutton v. Poole*.

96. Two concurring justices in *Lawrence v. Fox* saw privity requirement fulfilled because plaintiff could ratify action of his "agent" Holly.

97. Beckington and Lambert v. Vaughan, Moo. K.B. 854 (1616). *See* S. STOLJAR, *supra* note 76, at 140–143 (Had and received count influenced rule that consideration must move from promisee.).

98. In England, Chancery will, in some circumstances, treat the promisee as a trustee for the beneficiary. Tomlinson v. Gill. Amb. 330 (Ch. 1756); Lloyd's v. Harper, 16 Ch. D. 290 (1880); *see* Corbin, *Contract for the Benefit of Third Persons*, 46 L.Q. REV. 12 (1930).

99. Seaver v. Ransom, 224 N.Y. 233, 120 N.E. 639 (1918) (4–3 decision). In addition to *Dutton, Seaver* court cited Schermerhorn v. Vanderheyden, 1 Johns. 139, 3 Am. Dec. 304 (1806).

100. Massachusetts does not recognize donee beneficiaries, and New York requires a family relationship between the promisee and a donee beneficiary.

101. RESTATEMENT OF CONTRACTS sect. 133 (1932) ("creditor" and "donee" beneficiaries). Since "creditor" and "donee" didn't recognize parties power to set terms, terminology was changed to "intended" beneficiary in RESTATEMENT (SECOND) OF CONTRACTS sects. 302, 304 (1981). Promissory estoppel is expressly available for the reliance of a third person. RESTATEMENT (SECOND) OF CONTRACTS sect. 90 (1).

102. L. FRIEDMAN, *supra* note 27, at 121; L. FRIEDMAN, *supra* note 12, at 534; Braucher, *supra* note 37, at 611–612.

103. MacPherson v. Buick Motor Co., 217 N.Y. 382, 111 N.E. 1050 (1916).

104. *See* RESTATEMENT OF CONTRACTS sect. 454, Comment (b) (1932). The failure of the assumption upon which the consideration was grounded is reason for granting a discharge.

105. *See* F. POLLOCK, *supra* note 31, (In 1921 edition separate topic of "Impossibility" was dropped and put in new topic of "Conditions and Frustration."); *see also* F. KESSLER AND G. GILMORE, *supra* note 74, at 788 (Frustration is loose synonym for impossibility today.).

106. *See* Simpson, *Innovation in Nineteenth Century Contract Law*, 91 L.Q. REV. 247, 269 (1975); *see also* Newman, *The Renaissance of Good Faith in Contracting in*

Anglo-American Law, 54 CORNELL L. REV. 553, 561–562 (1969) (so long as no reliance).

107. Abott of Westminster v. Clerke, 1 Dy. 26b, 28b, 73 Eng. Rep. 59, 63 (K.B. 1536) (illegality); DOCTOR AND STUDENT, Dial. II, c.4 (1530) (Doctor said defendant not liable because no "remedy over" to sue God, but the Student said there was a theory of self-imposed strict liability.); Williams v. Hide, Palm. 548 (1624) (Bailee discharged due to act of God of death of bailed horse.); Hyde v. Dean of Windsor, Cro. Eliz. 552, 78 Eng. Rep. 798 (K.B. 1597) (Death of performer discharged executor.). In covenant to build house, temporary excuse until plague was over. H. ROLLE, ABRIDGEMENT 450, Cond.(G), pl. 10 (London: 1668). Rolle was probably the judge in Paradine v. Jane, Aleyn 26 (1647).

108. Paradine v. Jane, Aleyn 26, 82 Eng. Rep. 897 (K.B. 1647). This is one of the few Civil War decisions later cited as a leading case. It reflects the period's strict religious sense of duty, its aversion for the prerogative of Equity, and its preference for landowners.

109. *Anon,* Dyer 33a (1537).

110. The escape of express exclusion was suggested as early as 1355. Y.B. 40 Edw. III, H.f.5, pl. 11 (1355). Contract, as a risk allocation device, left little room for excuse, though there was an educational function for not calculating well. P. ATIYAH, *supra* note 4, at 436–437; *and see* Posner and Rosenfield, *Impracticability and Related Doctrines in Contract Law: An Economic Analysis,* 6 J. LEG. STUD. 83 (1977) (From economic standpoint, if promisor is risk bearer, then no discharge.).

111. Serjeant Williams' 1802 note to Walton v. Waterhouse, 2 Wms. Saund. 420, 85 Eng. Rep. 1233 (K.B. 1684). Sjt. Williams' note cited as helping in establishing *Paradine* in Hall v. Wright, 120 Eng. Rep. 688 (1858). Some suggestion that Equity gave relief, as in Brown v. Quilter, Amb. 619 (1764), but not usually. Doe v. Sandham, 1 T.R. 705 (1787). *See* G. GILMORE, *supra* note 26, at 48 (Strict liability suited objectivists who avoided questions of fact.).

112. Adams v. Nichols, 36 Mass. (19 Pick.) 275, 277 (1837) (House builder not discharged by fire before completion.). *See* School Distr. No. 1 v. Dauchy, 25 Conn. 530 (1857) (no excuse for builder when building burnt before completion due to lightning); *see also* Superintendent Pub. Sch. Trenton v. Bennett, 2 N.J.L. (3 Dutcher) 513, 72 Am. Dec. 373 (N.J. 1859) (Contractor should have provided in contract against natural events of building falling twice before completion.).

113. Taylor v. Caldwell, 3 Best & S. 826, 122 Eng. Rep. 310 (K.B. 1863). *Taylor* didn't cover construction cases when there was a fire before completion, but it did cover contracts to repair a building since the building's existence was necessary for performance. *Cf.* Butterfield v. Byron, 153 Mass. 517, 27 N.E. 667 (1891) (quantum meruit for repairs done before fire). *And see* Holmes, *supra* note 8, at 466 ("You can give any conclusion [of policy] a logical form. You can always imply a condition in a contract.").

114. *See* 1 R. POTHIER, *supra* note 86, at 81.

115. Tarling v. Baxter, 6 B. & C. 360, 108 Eng. Rep. 484 (K.B. 1827) (seller excused if goods destroyed before risk passed to buyer). This principle is followed in U.C.C. 2–613. *See* 6 A. CORBIN, *supra* note 25, at sect. 1322 (By lessee in

Paradine going on the leasehold, he thereafter bore risk of eviction just as buyer of goods bore risk of loss after delivery in the 19th century.).

116. Hall v. Wright, El. Bl. & El. 765, 120 Eng. Rep. 695 (Exch. Ch. 1859) (Pollock dissenting gave example that there was "an implied condition" that a contract performer "shall be alive to perform them." Pollock further objected to treating a marriage contract the same as a bargain for a horse.).

117. Kingston v. Preston, 2 Doug. 689, 99 Eng. Rep. 437 (1773) (dependent condition); Laing v. Fidgeon, 6 Taunt. 108, 128 Eng. Rep. 974 (1815) (implied warranty).

118. *See* S. STOLJAR, *supra* note 76, at 189 (*Paradine* not truly impossible since impossibility was due to the wrongful act of a third party, against whom lessee had an action.). Physical impossibility is objective.

119. F. KESSLER AND G. GILMORE, *supra* note 74, at 788–789; *see* G. GILMORE, *supra* note 26, at 79 (Excuse in sales law favored sellers over buyers.). In the substantial performance field, construction contractors were earlier given relief for less than full performance, but the same protection was not afforded employees. Cutler v. Close, 5 C. & P. 337, 172 Eng. Rep. 1001 (1832); Cutter v. Powell, 6 T.R. 320, 101 Eng. Rep. 573 (1795).

120. Although it was not impossible to pay in *Paradine v. Jane,* one could view it as a frustration case in that the lessee's purpose of using the land to generate a profit was frustrated by the invader.

121. *See generally* S. STOLJAR, *supra* note 76, at 192–194 *and* Simpson, *supra* note 106, at 272–273. It is a cruel irony that equitable adjustments regarding the actual exchange were being applied to charter parties but not to benefit seamen in actions for wages. *See* Cutter v. Powell, 6 T.R. 320, 101 Eng. Rep. 573 (1795).

122. Freeman v. Taylor, 8 Bing. 124, 131 Eng. Rep. 348 (1831) (Damages owed by shipowner, but 6 week delay not so unreasonable as to be condition precedent for a discharge.); Tarrabochia v. Hickie, 1 H. & N. 183 (1856) (dictum); Jackson v. Union Marine Ins. Co., L.R. 10 C.P. 125 (1874) (failure of consideration when 6 month delay); Geipel v. Smith, L.R. 7 Q.B. 404 (1872) (Due to naval blockade charterers wanted a suspension, but the shipowner was discharged.).

123. Krell v. Henry, L.R. 2 K.B. 740 (Ct. App. 1903).

124. Chandler v. Webster, L.R. 1 K.B. 493 (1904). *See* Fuller and Perdue, *The Reliance Interest in Contract Damages* (pt. 2), 46 YALE L.J. 373, 381 (1936) (Might *Krell* plaintiff have succeeded if he'd only asked for cost of fitting room rather than balance due on inflated price?). Is Fuller overlooking fact the plaintiff was able to retain 1/3 paid?

125. RESTATEMENT OF CONTRACTS sect. 468 (1932); *see* Fibrosa Spolka Akcyjna v. Fairbairn Lawson Combe Barbour, A.C. 32 (1943) (*Chandler v. Webster* overruled "as a matter of quasi contract: as money paid for a consideration that had totally failed".).

126. Swift Canadian Co. v. Banet, 224 F. 2d 36 (3d Cir. 1955) (Plan of importing good purchased under contract thwarted by import regulations, but no frustration since had "the rest of the world" as a market.). There was a backlash in reaction to the frustration doctrine discharging a payor by allowing the use

of the defense for performers. *See* F. KESSLER and G. GILMORE, *supra* note 74, at 789.

127. Lloyd v. Murphy, 25 Cal. 2d 48, 153 P. 2d 47, 51–52 (1944) (Leasehold intended for sale of new cars but wartime prohibition barred that use.).

128. RESTATEMENT OF CONTRACTS sects. 454, 288 (1932).

129. Mineral Park Land Co. v. Howard 172 Cal. 289, 156 P. 458 (1916). In an 1850 sea freight case it was possible to perform, but at an added "enormous cost"; the court said "in matters of business, a thing is said to be impossible when it is not practicable; and a thing is impracticable when it can only be done at an excessive or unreasonable cost." Moss v. Smith, 9 C.B. 94, 137 Eng. Rep. 827 (1850).

130. *Cf.* Mishara Construction Co. v. Transit-Mixed Concrete Corp., 365 Mass. 122, 310 N.E. 2d 363 (1974) (impracticability question for jury).

131. U.C.C. sect. 2–615 (Seller excused from delivery due to failure of basic assumption.). Comment 4 mainly gave catastrophic examples, as war, embargo, crop failure, or shutdown of supply source. *Cf.* Riesenfeld, *The Influence of German Legal Theory on American Law: The Heritage of Savigny and His Disciples,* 37 AM. J. COMP. LAW 4–6 F(1989) (Suggests Llewellyn's draft was influenced by German thought on basic assumption of parties.).

132. *See* Wallach, *The Excuse Defense in the Law of Contracts: Judicial Frustration of the U.C.C. Attempt to Liberalize the Law of Commercial Impracticability,* 55 NOTRE DAME LAW. 203, 214–221 (1979) (hard to decide fault, foreseeability and assumption of risk); *see also* Jennings, *Commercial Impracticability—Does It Really Exist?* 2 WHITTIER LAW REV. 241 (1980). On the difficulty of drawing the line between what's practicable and not, *see* Ocean Tramp Tankers v. V/O Sovfracht (The Eugenia), 1 All Eng. Rep. 161 (1963) *and see* 6 A. CORBIN, *supra* note 25, at sect. 1333 (Court must exercise its equity powers and pray for the wisdom of Solomon.).

133. Ocean Tramp Tankers Corp. v. V/O Sovfracht (The Eugenia), 1 All Eng. Rep. 161 (1963) ("It must be more than merely more onerous or more expensive. It must be positively unjust to hold the parties bound." Per Denning, M.R.); Glidden Co. v. Hellenic Lines, 275 F. 2d 253 (2d Cir. 1960) (Due to negotiations, the risk was in effect allocated to shipowner.); Transatlantic Financing Corp. v. United States, 363 F. 2d 312 (D.C. Cir. 1966) (less than 15% added cost to go around Cape was not enough variation in action by shipowner for added amount incurred.). *Transatlantic* is unique in using impracticability as positive action rather than as normal excuse defense. *See* U.C.C. 2–614 (When agreed manner of delivery is impracticable, reasonable substitute must be tendered.). *See* also Posner and Rosenfield, *Impossibility and Related Doctrines in Contract Law: An Economic Analysis,* 6 J. LEG. STUDIES 83, 104 (1977) (Courts found shipowners to be greater risk bearers due to expertise.). Nor was impracticability found in 1970s oil embargo cases. Eastern Air Lines, Inc. v. Gulf Oil Corp., 415 F. Supp. 429 (S.D. Fla. 1975) (Proof problems in impracticability. *Id.* at 440–441).

134. Boone v. Eyre, 1 H. Bl. 273n, 126 Eng. Rep. 160 (1777); *see* S. STOLJAR, *supra* note 76, at 197–199 (exchange based on synallagmatic principle).

135. Actually during the 19th century there had been some equitable relief from the hardship of impossibility under restitution.

136. *See* Berman, *Excuse for Nonperformance in Light of Contract Practices in*

International Trade, 63 COLUM. L. REV. 1413, 1426 (1963) (due to great upheavals of this century); *see also* Speziale, *The Turn of the Twentieth Century as the Dawn of Contract "Interpretation": Reflections in Theories of Impossibility,* 17 DUQ. L. REV. 555, 555–558, 583–584 (1979).

137. Anderson v. May, 50 Minn. 280, 52 N.W. 530 (1892) (cited Adams v. Nichols, 36 Mass. 275 (1837) as under general rule applied).

138. Pratt, *American Contract Law at the Turn of the Century,* 39 S.C. L. REV. 415, 434–435 (1988) (Long term contracts caused problems due to steep drop in late 19th century prices.); *cp.* J. HURST, LAW AND ECONOMIC GROWTH: THE LEGAL HISTORY OF THE LUMBER INDUSTRY IN WISCONSIN 1893–1915 331–332 (Madison: rev'd ed. 1984) (Long term contracts assured supplies and protected against price fluctuations.); *and see* Coase, *The Nature of the Firm,* 4 ECONOMICA 385, 391–392 (1937); *see also* Macneil, *Restatement (Second) of Contracts and Presentation,* 60 VA. L. REV. 589, 595–596 (1974).

139. *See* Pratt, *supra* note 138, at 432–434, 437 (Antebellum uncertainty usually was with money and not the market.).

140. Sawyer, Wallace, & Co. v. Taggart, 77 Ky. (14 Bush) 727 (1879); Justh v. Holliday, 13 D.C. (2 Mackey) 346, 349 (1883); Heard V. Russell & Potter, 59 GA. 25, 38 (1877); *see* Pratt, *supra* note 138, at 436–438, 451–454 (Futures began just before Civil War in grain and pork, followed by cotton in late 1860s, coffee 1882, cottonseed oil 1904, raw sugar 1914.).

141. Bailey v. Austrian, 19 Minn. 535 (Gil. 465) (1873).

142. Mutuality was said to serve the market so that a lone, bound party could not be subjected to the speculation of the other. E. FARNSWORTH, *supra* note 36, at 107; G. GILMORE, *supra* note 26, at 33–34.

143. J. DAWSON, *supra* note 47, at 213–214 (citing Parsons' 19th century treatise).

144. *See* 1 R. POTHIER, A TREATISE ON OBLIGATIONS CONSIDERED IN A MORAL AND LEGAL VIEW 33 (tr. F. Martin, Newbern, N.C. 1802) (An agreement allowing a party "to do or not to do what he promised . . . would be absolutely void, on account of the want of obligation."). *Cf.* G. GILMORE, *supra* note 26, at 33 (Mutuality was brought on by bargain consideration theory.).

145. *See* J. DAWSON, *supra* note 47, at 213–216 (Rules regarding mutuality, discharge and firm offer are superfluous overloads on consideration.).

146. *See* 1A A. CORBIN, *supra* note 25, at sect. 152 (Option holder pays cash out but makes no promise.); *see also* Northwestern Engineering Co. v. Ellerman, 69 S.D. 397, 10 N.W. 2d 879 (1943) (Mutuality causes confusion and is "an unnecessary way of stating that there must be valid consideration.").

147. 1 A. CORBIN, *supra* note 25, at sect. 156. In an 1882 requirements case, court said seller received benefit of "possibility that more or less will be needed," and other person was "bound not to buy elsewhere." Cincinnati, S. & C. R. R. v. Consolidated Coal & Mining Co., 8 Ohio Dec. Reprint 365, 367–368 (1882).

148. 1A A. CORBIN, *supra* note 25, at sect. 158; *see* S.B. Smith & Co. v. R.S. Morse & Co., 20 La. Ann. 220, 222 (1868) (requirement contract breached if bought elsewhere).

149. RESTATEMENT (SECOND) OF CONTRACTS, sect. 79 (1981); *and see Id.*, at Comment (f) (Requirement that both must be bound is inapplicable

to: (1) a promise for performance, (2) Rest. 2d, sects. 82–94 and (3) formal contracts, as negotiable instruments.).

150. Wells v. Alexandre, 130 N.Y. 642, 645, 29 N.E. 142, 143 (1891). *See* Pratt, *supra* note 138, at 443–445 (Contrasted *Bailey v. Austrian* with *Wells* finding difference to be earlier farm state case failing to recognize modern market conditions accepted in later commercial state case.).

151. Wigand v. Bachmann-Bechtel Brewing Co., 222 N.Y. 272, 118 N.E. 618 (1915) (output); Asahel Wheeler Co. v. Mendelson, 180 A.D. 9, 167 N.Y.S. 435 (1917) (requirements). *Wigand* followed 1905 use of fiduciary obligation of railroad reorganization committee toward bondholders. Industrial & General Trust v. Tod, 180 N.Y. 215, 225–226, 73 N.E. 7, 9–10 (1905).

152. Lima Locomotive & Mach. Co. v. National Steel Castings Co., 155 F. 77 (6th Cir. 1907); New York Central Iron Works Co. v. United States Radiator Co., 174 N.Y. 331, 66 N.E. 967 (1903); *see* U.C.C. 2–306(1) ("as may occur in good faith").

153. Wood v. Lady Duff-Gordon, 222 N.Y. 88, 118 N.E. 214 (1917). *See* E. FARNSWORTH, *supra* note 36, at 529 ("Best efforts" is higher duty than good faith.). In Cardozo's 1917 reading of sense of the agreement, the promisee's motive in contracting for a positive benefit was relevant. *And see* Bailey v. Austrian, 19 Minn. 535 (Gil. 465) (1873) (Mutuality indicates defendant "has the right at once to hold plaintiffs to a positive agreement."). Results have been varied on whether a party is obligated to continue in business for the duration of the agreement. Some cases say must stay in business for contract term or until minimum quantity produced. Hickey v. O'Brien, 123 Mich. 611, 82 N.W. 241 (1900); Wigand v. Bachmann-Bechtel Brewing, 222 N.Y. 272, 118 N.E. 618 (1915). Others say you need not. In re United Cigar Stores Co., 8 F. Supp. 243, 244 (S.D.N.Y. 1934); *see* U.C.C. 2–306, comment 2.

154. Kessler and Fine, *supra* note 21, at 412; L. FRIEDMAN, *supra* note 27, at 87–89.

155. A. SIMPSON, *supra* note 76, at 65–66, 532.

156. *See* Kessler and Fine, *supra* note 21, at 412–413 (Certainty relaxed to not disappoint expectation "deal is on".). *And see* Fuller and Perdue (pt. 2), *supra* note 124, at 376–377 (Reliance damages can be a surrogate for expectation interest when there is concealed behind a certainty objection problems of remote damages or disproportionateness or willful versus innocent wrongs.).

157. L. FRIEDMAN, *supra* note 27, at 88–89 ("Practical interpretation" was rejection of classical abstraction and irrelevance of subsequent behavior.); *see* 1A A. CORBIN, *supra* note 25, at sect. 156. The Uniform Commercial Code advanced the liberalization in the caselaw. *See* U.C.C. sects. 1–205, 2–204, 2–208, 2–305, & 2–311.

158. Sun Printing v. Remington Paper, 235 N.Y. 338, 139 N.E. 470 (1923). *See* Corbin, *Mr. Justice Cardozo and the Law of Contract*, 39 COLUM. L. REV. 56 (1939).

159. *See* L. FRIEDMAN, *supra* note 27, at 88; *see also* J. HURST, *supra* note 138, at 290.

160. Pound, *Consideration in Equity* in CELEBRATION LEGAL ESSAYS 435, 459 (Chicago: 1919) ("in order to maintain the general security"); Williston, *Mutual Assent in the Formation of Contracts* in CELEBRATION LEGAL ESSAYS

525, 525–527 (Chicago: 1919); F. POLLOCK, PRINCIPLES OF CONTRACT ix-xii (London: 9th ed. 1921) (Promisor's expression of intent entitles promisee to rely.); *cf.* 1 A. CORBIN, *supra* note 25, at sect. 112 (Law's chief purpose is not carrying out will of parties but rather reasonable expectation of promisee.). *And see* M. WEBER, *supra* note 2, at 313–314 (Ultimate standard is the "expectation" parties have based on average conception of the obligation of others.). As the market became more one of strangers, in contrast to the close-knit group of London and New York traders of the 18th century, the need to rely on external manifestations increased.

161. 1 T. PARSONS, THE LAW OF CONTRACTS 6 (1855). Langdell was a research assistant to Parsons in 1851–2 in the preparation of his book, and Williston edited later editions of Parsons. During the period, there was an invocation of the merits of freedom of contract for the realization of expectations.

162. Morrow v. Campbell, 30 Wis. 90, 92 (1872) (What is relevant is not what was intended but what was done.). *See* E. FARNSWORTH, *supra* note 36, at 328 (There's public interest in justified expectation of parties.). *See also* L. FRIEDMAN, *supra* note 27, at 87 (Subjectivity didn't fit goal of abstraction.). *Cf.* M. WEBER, *supra* note 2, at 307–308 (Expectation of parties oriented toward economic meaning, but lawyer's view will never totally be in conformity due to formal character of law.).

163. *See generally* Williston, *supra* note 160 and Williston, *Mutual Assent in the Formation of Contracts*, 14 ILL. L. REV. 85 (1919).

164. Williston, *supra* note 160, at 529–532; *cf.* Whittier, *supra* note 27, at 442 (Unfortunate that one who carelessly misleads another to believe there was an assent is bound even though no reliance.).

165. Williston, *supra* note 160, at 527; O. HOLMES, JR., *supra* note 42, at 306–307; Brauer v. Shaw, 168 Mass. 198, 200, 46 N.E. 617, 618 (1897) (Holmes said it would be monstrous if offeror could affect formation without notice.).

166. Hotchkiss v. National City Bank, 200 F. 287, 293 (1911); Williston, *supra* note 160, at 527. Compare Frank, J. concurrence to Hand, J. opinion in 1946. Ricketts v. Pennsylvania R.R., 153 F. 2d 757, 760 (2d Cir. 1946) (Objectivists went too far in requiring uniform answer to meaning given non-neligent words.).

167. Williston, *supra* note 160, at 532–533 (though he added that equity was objective).

168. 1 A. CORBIN, *supra* note 25, at sect. 106.

169. *Id.* at sects. 1 and 112.

170. *Id.* at sect. 106. *See generally* Farnsworth, *"Meaning" in the Law of Contracts*, 76 YALE L.J. 939 (1967).

171. Unlike Williston, Corbin did not require an ambiguity before referring to extrinsic evidence since parol evidence could not be said to vary writing until writing's meaning found by interpretation. 3 A. CORBIN, *supra* note 25, at sect. 579.

172. RESTATEMENT OF CONTRACTS sect. 233 (1932).

173. Whittier, *supra* note 27, at 441–445; *see* S. STOLJAR, MISTAKE AND MISREPRESENTATION 11–12 (London: 1968) (Objective standard completely

Shouldn't there be reliance to hold a careless offeror? *See* Whittier, *supra* note 27, at 442; *cf.* Williston, *supra* note 160, at 529–530.

174. RESTATEMENT (SECOND) OF CONTRACTS sect. 71, Comment (b) (1981).

175. RESTATEMENT (SECOND) OF CONTRACTS sect. 201 (1981); Berke Moore Co. v. Phoenix Bridge Co., 98 N.H. 261, 269, 98 A. 2d. 150, 156 (1953); *cf.* E. FARNSWORTH, *supra* note 36, at 487–488 (However, usually there is misunderstanding and then hold party with knowledge of misunderstanding under a fault theory). If no common understanding and a party doesn't know of other's misunderstanding, then use objective standard. *See* Farnsworth, *supra* note 170, at 946–947. Corbin acknowledged that a party's understanding may require use of a meaning given by reasonable man. 1 A. CORBIN, *supra* note 25, at sect. 106. A pure objectivist would say that an objective meaning should prevail even when there was an inconsistent common understanding. *See* Hand, J. in Eustis Mining Co. v. Beer, Sondheimer & Co., 239 F. 976, 984–985 (1917).

176. *See* 5 A. CORBIN, *supra* note 25, at sects. 1102–1103; *see also* Braucher, *supra* note 37, at 599 (There's tension between freedom of contract and elementary fairness based on reliance and benefit.). There had always been a reluctance to base liability in Assumpsit simply on a promise; so unjust enrichment or induced reliance sometimes looked for. A. SIMPSON, *supra* note 76, at 323–324.

177. *See* J. DAWSON, UNJUST ENRICHMENT 25–26 (Boston: 1951) (Organization of principles risks jeopardizing needed future growth of rules at-equity.).

178. Moses v. Macferlan, 2 Burr. 1005, 97 Eng. Rep. 676 (1760).

179. Marriott v. Hampton, 7 T.R. 269 (1797) (Recovery of a second payment of the same debt was refused even though the receipt for the first payment was later found.). *See* Jones v. Hoar, 22 Mass. (5 Pick) 285 (1827). *And see* R. JACKSON, THE HISTORY OF QUASI-CONTRACT IN ENGLISH LAW 121 (Cambridge: 1936) (Had Mansfield used a less ambiguous guideline, like reasonableness instead of natural justice, his proposition might not have been pruned so much.). It has been suggested that early 19th century law was less equitable and had less concern for restitution since courts expected individual to protect himself and so left parties where they found them. *See* P. ATIYAH, *supra* note 4, at 764–765. *Cf.* J. HURST, *supra* note 138, at 302 (Principle against unjust enrichment protected exchange basis of the market.).

180. *In Re* Weaver, 21 Ch. Div. 615, 620 (1882); *cf.* Hertzog v. Hertzog, 29 Pa. St. (5 Casey) 465, 467–470 (1857). Blackstone contributed to the confusion. 3 W. BLACKSTONE, COMMENTARIES* 162. Cases making correct analysis: Hertzog v. Hertzog, 38 Pa. 465 (1857); Sceva v. True, 153 N.H. 627 (1873); Rhodes v. Rhodes, 44 Ch. Div. 94, 107 (1885). *See* W. KEENER, A TREATISE ON THE LAW OF QUASI-CONTRACTS 3–5 (N.Y. 1893) (To classify implied-in-law contract as a type of contract is wrong since it is not an evidentiary classification like implied-in-fact but refers to the source of obligation.).

181. *See* J. DAWSON, *supra* note 177, at 15–21; P. ATIYAH and R. SUMMERS, *supra* note 11, at 116, 128–132, 240–244 (U.S. has higher rate of dissenting opinions.). Lord Summer said he wouldn't apply Mansfield's vague rule and that the law was divided into only contract and tort and therefore only

contractual transactions fit under Assumpsit's money had and received. Sinclair v. Brougham, A.C. 398, 452 (1914) (However, through tracing, the English judge gave relief by extending constructive trust.). *Cf.* H. MENCKEN, THE AMERICAN LANGUAGE 98–99 (N.Y. 1963, R. McDavid 1 vol. ed.) (American life has been dynamic in contrast to the stable English social order since the 17th century, which order has impressed on the English a greater respect for custom and a sense of the static nature of society.).

182. J. DAWSON, *supra* note 177, at 21–22; *see* Perillo, *Restitution in a Contractual Context*, 73 COLUM. L. REV. 1208, 1210–1215 (1973). *See* L. FRIEDMAN, *supra* note 27, at 192–194 (19th century contract concerned about freedom to form contracts but 20th century more concerned about equitable adjustments.). *See also* 5 A. CORBIN, *supra* note 25, at sect. 1103 (Modern court of law and equity should not deny restitution relief simply because not available in Assumpsit.). Quasi-contract is like tort in that it's a duty imposed by law, and it's like contract in that there's a positive duty (as opposed to duty in tort to refrain from causing harm).

183. Ames, *The History of Assumpsit—Implied Assumpsit*, 2 HARV. L. REV. 53, 63–69 (1888).

184. W. KEENER, *supra* note 180, at 1–20 (He said he took term "quasi contract" from English writers F. Pollock and W. Anson.).

185. RESTATEMENT OF THE LAW OF RESTITUTION (1937). In addition to contract-related cases, the doctrine of restitution provided relief in circumstances related to tort law and to the law of fiduciary obligations.

186. *See* Seavey and Scott, *Restitution*, 54 L.Q. REV. 29 (1938) (Restatement reporters said term "restitution" chosen because it connoted a "right to recover back something which one once had".); *see also* 1 G. PALMER, THE LAW OF RESTITUTION 3–4 (Boston: 1978). The concept of restitution was present well before Mansfield: Detinue was an action for specific restitution; Debt *sur contract* enforced a duty to disgorge the value of benefit received; in Assumpsit it could be an indicator of benefit consideration; and there was specific restitution in Equity under a bill of rescission for benefits deemed unfair to retain. *See* RESTATEMENT OF CONTRACTS (1932) which made extensive use of term restitution; Corbin was that Restatement's Reporter on remedies.

187. *See* Perillo, *supra* note 182, at 1222.

188. Varney v. Ditmars, 217 N.Y. 223, 111 N.E. 822 (1916); Hill v. Waxberg, 237 F. 2d 936 (1956) (negotiations). There is still confusion about contracts implied-in-fact and implied-in-law as exhibited in the erroneous jury instruction in *Hill v. Waxberg*.

189. RESTATEMENT OF CONTRACTS sects. 499 & 480 (1932); *and see Id.*, sect. 502(b), Comment (c).

190. RESTATEMENT OF CONTRACTS sect. 355 (1932).

191. *See* Perillo, *supra* note 182, at 1209.

192. RESTATEMENT OF CONTRACTS sects. 347 & 468 (1932). It is equitable to relieve defendant from future performance on an impossible contract, but there is a duty to return benefit received. *And see* U.C.C. sect. 2–718(2) (Breachor can recover in restitution for benefit in excess of innocent seller's damages.).

193. Bush v. Canfield, 2 Conn. 485 (1818); Nash v. Towne, 72 U.S. 689 (1866);

see 5 A. CORBIN, *supra* note 25, at sect. 1104 (as contract termination by repudiation or substantial failure to complete performance). Furthermore, a promise for a benefit received may be enforceable even though there is no right of recovery without the promise. RESTATEMENT (SECOND) OF CONTRACTS sect. 86; *see* Braucher, *supra* note 37, at 603–604 (Sect. 86 is in spirit of promise to pay moral obligation, as were earlier promises re statute of limitations and bankruptcy).

194. *See* 1 G. PALMER, *supra* note 186, at 3, 16, 20–30; Wade, *Restitution for Benefits Conferred Without Request*, 19 VAND. L. REV. 1183, 1205 (1966); 5 A. CORBIN, *supra* note 25, at sects. 1102–1103. Historically, restitution was more common in equity.

195. Thynn v. Thynn, 1 Vern. 296, 23 Eng. Rep. 459 (Ch. 1684) (constructive trust); Morgan v. Seymour, 1 Rep. Ch. 120, 21 Eng. Rep. 525 (Ch. 1637) (subrogation); Barbour, *The History of Contract in Early English Equity* in IV OXFORD STUDIES IN SOCIAL AND LEGAL HISTORY 136, 222 (P. Vinogradoff ed., Oxford, 1914) (indemnity in 15th century suretyship); Ford v. Stobridge, Nelson 24, 21 Eng. Rep. 780 (Ch. 1633) (indemnity); Fleetwood v. Charnock, Nelson 10, 21 Eng. Rep. 776 (Ch. 1629).

196. Thynn v. Thynn, 1 Vern. 296, 23 Eng. Rep. 459 (1684); Hutchins v. Lee, 1 Atk. 447, 26 Eng. Rep. 284 (1737).

197. 1 G. PALMER, *supra* note 186, at 11–16 (There's no express contract in quasi-contract and no express trust in constructive trust. *Id.* at 3.); J. DAWSON, *supra* note 177, at 27–29.

198. Newton v. Porter, 69 N.Y. 133 (1877) (larceny); Nebraska National Bank v. Johnson, 51 Neb. 546, 71 N.W. 294 (1897) (Employee purchased land with money stolen from employer.).

199. J. DAWSON, *supra* note 177, at 29–32 (We've "created a monster" as a result of its rapid growth; it needs to be fenced in.); 1 G. PALMER, *supra* note 186, at 13–15 (Some courts avoid trust by giving specific restitution, as by ordering execution of deed.). Equitable principles have become more formalized with the Restatement of Restitution.

200. *See* J. DAWSON, *supra* note 177, at 32–39.

201. *See Id*, at 21–22, 30–32, 38–39; *see also* G. GILMORE, *supra* note 26, at 74–75.

202. *See* P. ATIYAH, *supra* note 4, at 734; *and see* Boyer, *Promissory Estoppel: Requirements and Limitations of the Doctrine*, 98 U. PA. L. REV. 459, 497 (1950) (Urged trend toward reliance, which sometimes is same as restitution, since both parties often treated more justly.). *See Id.* at 485–486 (Jurisdictions that only give restitution, when there was reliance, are not fair when expectation was greater than net benefit.).

203. *See* G. GILMORE, *supra* note 26, at 89–90 (There's a blurring of edges of tort and contract into a unified theory for benefit and reliance of "contorts".).

204. *See* Fuller, *Consideration and Form*, 41 COLUM. L. REV. 799, 814–815 (1941).

205. Fuller and Perdue (pt. 1), *supra* note 124, at 54–55; *see* Childres and Garamella, *The Law of Restitution and the Reliance Interest in Contract*, 64 NW. U.L. REV. 433, 457 (1969). *See* Acme Process Equip. Co. v. United States, 347 F. 2d 509 (1965) (All acts of part performance are a benefit.). The interests of reliance

and restitution have more to do with returning the parties to their positions prior to the transaction than to creating new value under an expectation interest.

206. *See* Fuller and Perdue (pt. 1), *supra* note 124, at 56–57. Courts protect restitution interest rather than reliance interest when it is fairer. Usher's Executor v. Flood, 83 Ky 552 (1886); Carter v. Carter, 182 N.C. 186, 108 S.E. 765 (1921).

207. *See* P. ATIYAH, *supra* note 4, at 652–653.

208. *See* RESTATEMENT (SECOND) OF CONTRACTS sect. 90, Comment (d); *See* Boyer, *supra* note 202, at 487, 497 (Granting only reliance expenses rather than expectation damages sometimes avoids injustice to promisor.). *And see* Henderson, *Promissory Estoppel and Traditional Contract Doctrine*, 78 YALE L.J. 343, 387 (1969) (expectations more relevant in commercial cases of promissory estoppel).

209. Fuller and Perdue (pt. 1), *supra* note 124, at 66–67; *and see Id.* (pt. 2) at 373–376.

210. *See* RESTATEMENT (SECOND) OF CONTRACTS sect. 139 (2) (1981); *and see* Monarco v. Lo Greco, 35 Cal. 2d 621, 624–625, 220 P. 2d 737, 740–741 (1950) (benefit not calculable of son staying on farm in reliance on promise of gift).

211. *See* Fuller and Perdue (pt. 1), *supra* note 124, at 55; *and see Id.* (pt. 2) at 405; *see also* Boyer, *supra* note 202, at 485; *cf.* Griffin v. Griffin, 206 Ala. 489, 90 So. 907 (1921) (oral gift promise not enforced but allowed restitution for improvement).

212. 1 S. WILLISTON, *supra* note 25, at 308 ("the term 'promissory' estoppel or something equivalent should be used"); 4 AMERICAN LAW INSTITUTE PROCEEDINGS, Appendix 85–114 (1926); AMERICAN LAW INSTITUTE, OFFICIAL DRAFT OF RESTATEMENT OF CONTRACTS 245–249 (St. Paul: 1928).

213. Barbour, *supra* note 195, at 166–167 (gratuitous bailment and marriage contract examples given). There was a pious "cause" in equity and in church courts for the enforcement of charitable promises.

214. J. AMES, LECTURES ON LEGAL HISTORY 142–144 (Cambridge, Mass. 1913) (common law vying for chancery's growing jurisdiction over parol promises); Milsom, *A Pageant in Modern Dress*, 84 YALE L.J. 1585, 1585–1586 (1975); SPELMAN REPORTS, *supra* note 54, at 296.

215. ST. GERMAN'S DOCTOR AND STUDENT, Dial. II, c.24 (1530), in 91 SELDEN SOCIETY 230 (J. Barton ed. 1974) (example given of a promise to pay a surgeon for healing a poor man); *see* Cleymond v. Vincent, 12 Hen. VIII, P. f.11, pl. 13 (1521); Jordan's Case, 27 Hen. VIII, M. f.24, pl. 13 (1535).

216. A. SIMPSON, *supra* note 76, at 324–325, 429–433; S. STOLJAR, *supra* note 76, at 37–38; S. MILSOM, *supra* note 67, at 357–360. The spiritual motive of fulfilling charitable promises in ecclesiastical courts was converted into a secular common law theory in DOCTOR AND STUDENT during the Reformation. *See* A. SIMPSON, *supra* note 76, at 324–325, 429–432. Detrimental reliance continued to be a basis for relief in Chancery subsequent to the sixteenth century.

217. *See* S. MILSOM, *supra* note 67, at 356–357. *And see* Hand, J. in James Baird Co. v. Gimbel Bros., 64 F. 2d 344 (2d Cir. 1933) (unfortunate that gift promise no longer enforceable under seal). The proof problem in gift promises, formerly solved by the seal, was later solved by the evidence of injurious reliance.

Furthermore, love and affection and moral consideration, were no longer available to support a gratuitous promise. An abortive attempt at a rough replacement for a sealed donative promise was the Uniform Written Obligations Act (1925), adopted only by Pennsylvania.

218. AMERICAN LAW INSTITUTE, OFFICIAL DRAFT OF RESTATEMENT OF CONTRACTS 246–249 (St. Paul: 1928) (The law is clear in reliance cases on land contracts, mortgage foreclosures, charitable subscriptions, waivers and marriage contracts.); 1 WILLISTON, *supra* note 25, at 307–308; Boyer, *Promissory Estoppel; Principle From Precedents*, 50 MICH. L. REV. 639, 644 (1952).

219. Kirksey v. Kirksey, 8 Ala. 131 (1845) (Majority saw a "mere gratuity", though one justice thought there was sufficient consideration.).

220. Trustees of Methodist Episcopal Church v. Garvey, 53 Ill. 401 (1870); *and see* 20th century cases: Wilson v. Spry, 145 Ark. 21, 233 S.W. 564 (1920) (Costly examination of land was consideration to make option binding.); Kirby v. Brown, 241 N.Y.S. 255 (1930) (Reliance on agent was detriment consideration.); Bassic Mfg. Co. v. Riley, 9 F. 2d 138 (1925 Pa.) (Reliance made license irrevocable.).

221. Holmes admitted that in cases of reliance, "courts have gone very great lengths to discover" that it was bargained for. Martin v. Meles, 60 N.E. 397, 179 Mass. 114 (1901). *See* 1A A. CORBIN, *supra* note 25, at sects. 193–195.

222. King v. Thompson, 9 Pet. 204 (U.S. 1835); Haines v. Haines, 4 Md. Ch. 133 (1853); Freeman v. Freeman, 43 N.Y. 34, 39 (1870) (Improvement "constitutes in equity a consideration for the promise" to give land.); Bright v. Bright, 41 Ill. 97 (1866) (dictum); Seavey v. Drake, 62 N.H. 393, 394 (1882) ("There is no important distinction in this respect between a promise to give and a promise to sell." The improvements "constitutes in equity a consideration."); Roe v. Fleming, 122 Pac. 496 (Okla. 1912) (Improvements made in reliance on promise to not foreclose were sufficient consideration for promise.).

223. Bright v. Bright, 41 Ill. 97 (1866) (Taking possession wasn't found to be part performance to take outside Statute of Frauds but improvements would make "promise resting upon a valuable consideration."); Seavey v. Drake, 62 N.H. 383 (1882); *see* Note, *Promissory Estoppel in Virginia*, 43 VA. L. REV. 132, 134–135 (1957).

224. Barbour, *supra* note 195, at 166–167 (example of "A" entrusting a letter to "B" upon "B's" promise to deliver it).

225. Coggs v. Bernard, 2 Ld. Raym. 909, 919–920, 92 Eng. Rep. 107 (1703).

226. More recent cases used equitable notions of good faith in pure reliance rationales. Pryor v. Cain, 25 Ill. 292 (1861); Fried v. Fisher, 328 Pa. 497, 196 A. 39 (1938).

227. Prince v. Alabama State Fair, 106 Ala. 340, 17 So. 449 (1895) (Reliance of bailing property was said to be detriment consideration.); Siegel v. Spear & Co. 234 N.Y. 479, 138 N.E. 414 (1923) (consideration found when furniture delivered to gratuitous bailee who failed to fulfill promise to insure before fire); Kirby v. Brown, 241 N.Y.S. 255 (1930) (consideration found when gratuitous agent failed to make promised bid at auction); *see* Boyer, *supra* note 218, at 666–674 (but reliance not bargained for in these cases).

228. *E.g.*, Pryor v. Cain, 25 Ill. 292 (1861); Thompson v. Bd. of Supervisors

of Mercer County, 40 Ill. 379 (1866). *See* Boyer, *supra* note 218, at 652 *and* 1 S. WILLISTON, *supra* note 25, at sect. 139.

229. Thompson v. Bd. of Supervisors of Mercer County, 40 Ill. 379 (1866) (The public had to elect the site, and the court suggested as reliance "the expense of an election and other liabilities consequent thereon."). Consideration was also found but this was not the reliance acting as detriment consideration but rather the additional factor of a benefit to defendant's property which was coincidentally adjacent to new courthouse site. *See* Faxton v. Faxon, 28 Mich. 158, 161 (1873) (Uncle's liability was not based on gain to promisor but on inducement to injurious reliance.).

230. Pryor v. Cain, 25 Ill. 292 (1861). The twist here was that the plaintiff was the defendant's fellow subscribing church members and not the promisee charity.

231. Irwin v. Dyke, 114 Ill. 302, 1 N.E. 913 (1885) (Dissent said action was not based on a contract and that payments on note undoubtedly came from farm receipts. Majority refused Statute of Frauds objections since Statute not properly pleaded.). *See* Faxton v. Faxon, 28 Mich. 158 (1873) (Uncle promised deceased half-brother's son to not foreclose if son worked farm and cared for younger children. Court said no agreement needed to allow defense of estoppel to foreclosure because of good faith and promise induced labor.).

232. 1 S. WILLISTON, *supra* note 25, at sect. 139, p. 308. *See* Kessler and Fine, *supra* note 21, at 426 (Under subjective will theory, legitimate expectations protected by *culpa* theory of equitable estoppel.).

233. *Cf.* Low v. Bouverie, 3 Ch. 82, 109 (1891) ("doctrine of estoppel seems scarcely applicable. The representation relied on . . . was more like a contract or promise than the statement of an existing fact."); *and see* Williston, *Liability for Honest Misrepresentation*, 24 HARV L. REV. 415, 425 (1911) (Estoppel was once rule of evidence on pleading but substantive rule now since goes to merits.); *see also* RESTATEMENT (SECOND) OF CONTRACTS sect. 90, Comment (a) (1981). *See* L. FRIEDMAN, *supra* note 27, at 122 (Estoppel and waiver used to avoid rigors of abstraction of classical rules.).

234. Beatty v. Western College of Toledo, 52 N.E. 432 (1898) (Court said there was an "executed gift".). Since the College agreed to pay a lifetime annuity, this could have been a way of showing consideration.

235. Ricketts v. Scothorn, 57 Neb. 51, 77 N.W. 365 (1898) (cited charitable subscription cases as precedents). It is arguable that the granddaughter waived the right to further claims by returning to work after one year. In 1909 a court applied equitable estoppel to promise to put agreement under Statute of Frauds in writing when the court was actually enforcing a promise and estopping evidence contrary to misrepresentation. *See* Seymour v. Oelrichs, 156 Cal. 782, 106 P. 88 (1909).

236. Equitable estoppel and promissory estoppel would sometimes converge. When a note is executed to a bank to make it appear there were assets to deceive a bank examiner, a receiver of the bank can recover on the note, even though the bank gave no consideration to the maker, due to the misrepresentation of fact to a third person and the reliance. *See* 1 S. WILLISTON, *supra* note 25, at sect. 139. A misrepresentation in true promissory estoppel can only be found

by stretching it to say that there was a representation that the promise would be carried out. *Id.*

237. Henderson, *supra* note 208, at 343, 382 (in discussing exception to Statute of Frauds). *And see Id.* at 378–379 (Equitable estoppel has the tortious notion of misrepresentation which could obscure Rest. sect. 90 and result in limiting recoveries to reliance damages.).

238. Dovenmuehle, Inc. v. K-Way Associates, 388 F. 2d 940, 947 (7th Cir. 1968); Meredith v. John Deere Plow Co., 261 F. 2d 121, 124 (8th Cir. 1958); Swift v. Peterson, 240 Ia. 715, 719, 37 N.W. 2d 258, 259 (1949).

239. Seymour v. Oelrichs, 156 Cal. 782, 106 P. 88 (1909); RESTATEMENT OF CONTRACTS sect. 178, Comment (f) (1932) (either estoppel from averting misrepresentation relied on that Statute satisfied or promissory estoppel for promise to make writing).

240. Tanenbaum v. Biscayne Osteopathic Hosp., 190 So. 2d 777, 779 (Fla. 1966) (Legislature must make changes.); Cox v. Cox, 292 Ala. 106, 289 So. 2d 609, 613 (1974) (otherwise Statute destroyed); C.G. Campbell & Sons, Inc. v. Comdeq Corp. 586 S.W. 2d 40 (Ky. Ct. App. 1979) (U.C.C. 2–201 exceptions as far as legislature would go); Liege Dickson Co. v. Union Oil Co., 96 Wash. 2d 291, 635 P. 2d 103 (1981) (Exceptions in U.C.C. 2–201 displaced doctrine per U.C.C. 1–103.); *contra* Jenkins v. Schmidt, 344 N.E. 2d 275, 278 (Ill. App. 1976) (substitute for compliance with Statute); Warder and Lee Elevator v. Britten, 274 N.W. 2d 339 (Iowa 1979) (not displaced by U.C.C. per 1–103); R.S. Bennett & Co. v. Economy Mechanical Ind., 606 F. 2d 182, 188 (7th Cir. 1979) (not barred by Statute).

241. Monarco v. Lo Greco, 35 Cal. 2d 621, 220 P. 2d 737 (1950); *see* Alaska Airlines v. Stephenson, 217 F. 2d 295 (9th Cir. 1954) (Sect. 90 cited in reliance on promise of 2 year written contract).

242. RESTATEMENT (SECOND) OF CONTRACTS sect. 139 (1981). Suits against farmers breaching oral grain contracts after market price increase went both ways: applying Restatement Second were Warder and Lee Elevator v. Britten, 274 N.W. 2d 339 (Iowa 1979) and Decatur Coop. Assn. v. Urban, 219 Kan. 171, 547 P. 2d 323 (1976); others opposing infringement on Statute were Farmland Service Coop. v. Klein, 196 Neb. 538, 244 N.W. 2d 86 (1976) and Farmers Coop. Assn. v. Cole, 239 N.W. 2d 808 (N.D. 1976). There is a strain of modern cases holding that the Statute of Frauds is not germane since there is no contractual basis to promissory estoppel. N. Litterio v. Glassman Constr. Co., 319 F. 2d 736 (1963); Janke v. Vulcan, 386 F. Supp. 687 (1974); R.S. Bennett & Co. v. Economy Mechanical Ind., 606 F. 2d 182 (7th Cir. 1979).

243. *See* Barbour, *supra* note 195, at 166–167 ("It is desirable in the interests of the community at large" that promises inducing reliance create a "moral duty to fulfill" gratuitous promises, including marriage contracts.); *see also* 1 S. WILLISTON, *supra* note 25, at sect. 139, p. 312 (Marriage contracts are a solemn promise which the policy of the law favors under promissory estoppel.).

244. Allegheny College v. National Chautauqua County Bank of Jamestown, 246 N.Y. 369, 159 N.E. 173 (1927). Cardozo could find maneuvering room to provide relief under either promissory estoppel or consideration, in part because Cardozo's New York did not recognize Holmesian bargain consideration.

245. Trustees of Methodist Episcopal Church v. Garvey, 53 Ill. 401 (1870);

see also First M.E. Church v. Howard's Estate, 133 Misc. 723, 233 N.Y.S. 451 (1929). Charitable subscription cases employed purer reliance logic than cases like bailments or land gifts where courts would often manipulate consideration logic.

246. Charitable tort immunity was another example of judicial support for charities. It is hardly laissez-faire for a government's judiciary to grant immunity and enforce charitable gifts.

247. *See* AMERICAN LAW INSTITUTE, OFFICIAL DRAFT OF RESTATEMENT OF CONTRACTS 247 (St. Paul: 1928).

248. *See* Milsom, *supra* note 214, at 1589; *see also* S. MILSOM, *supra* note 67, at 3353. *See* Milsom, *Reason in the Development of the Common Law*, 81 L.Q. REV. 496, 498–499 (1965) (change is possible when two lines of reasoning, developed in different compartments, come close enough for a fact situation traditionally falling in one to be represented as within the other.). *Cf.* Commonwealth v. Scituate Savings Bank, 137 Mass. 301, 302 (1884) ("It would cut up the doctrine of consideration by the roots if a promisee could make a gratuitous promise binding by subsequently acting in reliance on it." per Holmes, J.).

249. The entrustment point was most relevant in cases involving land gifts and gratuitous bailments and agencies. The misfeasance versus nonfeasance distinction appeared again later in bailment and agency cases. Coggs v. Bernard, 2 Ld. Raym. 909, 92 Eng. Rep. 107 (1703); Thorne v. Deas, 4 Johns. 84 (N.Y. 1809); *see* Boyer, *supra* note 218, at 669–670 (Distinction between liability in *Coggs* but not in *Thorne* may be because there was merely the nonfeasance of no entrustment in *Thorne*.).

250. RESTATEMENT (SECOND) OF CONTRACTS sect. 90, Comment (d) (1981) ("A promise binding under this section is a contract."); Milsom, *supra* note 214, at 1586–1587 (Promissory estoppel may push consideration contract into a separate compartment rather than swallowing it up as Gilmore suggests.). Assumpsit supplanted Covenant and Debt, and Gilmore suggests that promissory estoppel is replacing the consideration contract. G. GILMORE, *supra* note 26, at 71–72, 87–90.

251. Boyer, *supra* note 218, at 662; Pound, *supra* note 160, at 459 (Law restive under both individual will and consideration due to feeling that promises ought to be enforced and estoppel is one solution.); F. POLLOCK, *supra* note 160, at 1 (Emphasis shifting from promisor's will to promisee's reasonable reliance.); P. ATIYAH, *supra* note 4, at 771; Rehbinder, *Status, Contract and the Welfare State*, 23, STAN. L. REV. 941, 946–952 (1971) (Division of labor and mass transactions reduce individual will in favor of protection of reliance.); *and see* 1A A. CORBIN, *supra* note 25, at sect. 193 (A.L.I. definition of consideration so narrow that it was necessary to construct additional rules, such as promissory estoppel, where promise enforceable without consideration.).

252. Allegheny College v. National Chautauqua County Bank of Jamestown, 246 N.Y. 369, 159 N.E. 173 (1927). *See* 1A A. CORBIN, *supra* note 25, at sect. 112 (The chief purpose of contract is not to carry out the will of the promissor. Contracts are enforced to avoid disappointment of the reasonable expectation of the promisee, and a finding of sufficient consideration is evidence that the expectation of performance was reasonable.).

253. *See* RESTATEMENT (SECOND) OF CONTRACTS sect 90, Comment (b) (1981).

254. Henderson, *supra* note 208, at 377–379; Speidel, *supra* note 38, at 1179 (could have conditioned promise with more careful language). *See* R. POSNER, ECONOMIC ANALYSIS OF LAW 45 (Boston: 1972) (Breach of promise foreseeably inducing reliance is a form of negligence.).

255. Pryor v. Cain, 25 Ill. 292 (1861) ("is bound in good faith"); Faxton v. Faxon, 28 Mich. 159, 161 (1873); Fried v. Fisher, 328 Pa. 497, 196 A. 39 (1938); *see* Knapp, *supra* note 38, at 79 (Promissory estoppel is not doctrine to shield overreaching by stronger party, as in good faith or unconscionability, but, like a fiduciary duty or equitable estoppel, is abuse of relation of trust.). On the minority position that there is no right to trial by jury in promissory estoppel, *see* C. & K. Engr. Contractors v. Amber Steel Co., 23 Cal. 3d 1, 587 P. 2d 1136 (1978); *contra* F. KESSLER and G. GILMORE, CONTRACTS 225 (3d ed. 1986).

256. AMERICAN LAW INSTITUTE, OFFICIAL DRAFT OF RESTATEMENT OF CONTRACTS 245 (St. Paul: 1928) ("it is believed that the provisions of Section 90 do not go beyond existing law, in many jurisdictions at least."); *cf.* 1 S. WILLISTON, *supra* note 25, at sect. 139 ("would extend liability on promises" and is against great weight of authority.).

257. *See* Pound, *supra* note 160, at 459; F. POLLOCK, *supra* note 160, at 1; 1A A. CORBIN, *supra* note 25, at sect. 112. *See* L. FRIEDMAN, *supra* note 27, at 122 (Estoppel is antithetical to classical contract's abstraction.).

258. *See* Mansfield on moral obligation as a ground in Trueman v. Fenton, 2 Cowp. 544, 98 Eng. Rep. 1232 (K.B. 1777) *and* Hawkes v. Saunders, 1 Cowp. 289, 98 Eng. Rep. 1091 (K.B. 1782). *Cf.* Oldham, *Reinterpretations of 18th-Century English Contract Theory: The View from Lord Mansfield's Trial Notes*, 76 GEO. L. J. 1981–1983 (1988) (Mansfield's embrace of quasi-contract alongside consensual expectations is analoguous to uneasy existence today of promissory estoppel and consideration.). *See also* Kellogg, J. dissent in *Allegheny College v. National Chautauqua Bank* where he adopted misapprehension that Mansfield's Pillans v. Van Mierop, 3 Burr. 1663 (1765) was an early example of promissory estoppel. *And see* SPELMAN REPORTS, *supra* note 54, at 295–296 (age-old principle of morality that a promise detrimentally relied on is enforceable).

259. *Cp.* Pound, *supra* note 160, at 459 ("The feeling that a deliberate promise ought to be enforced simply as a promise will not down."). Denning, J. said that promissory reliance was a natural result of the fusion of law and equity—that a party would not be allowed to go back on his promise in a court of equity. Central London Property Trust Ltd. v. High Trees Ltd., K.B. 130, 134, 135 (1947).

260. Freeman v. Freeman, 43 N.Y. 34, 39 (1870).

261. *See* Boyer, *supra* note 202, at 459 (Sect. 90 cited at least 74 times 1932–1948).

262. *See* Currie v. Misa, L.R. 10 Exch. 162 (1875) (Consideration includes something suffered by promisee in respect of the promise.); *see also* 1A A. CORBIN, *supra* note 25, at sect. 195 (Surely reliance on a promise is acting in respect of the promise.).

263. Central London Property Trust Ltd. v. High Trees House Ltd., K.B. 130 (1947) (Holding returned rent to original contract rate for period after war.). Denning extended the rule in Hughes v. Metropolitan Ry., 2 App. Cas.

439 (1877), where a promise by a contracting party (but not a creditor) to not enforce his legal rights had a limited effect in equity without consideration. *Cf.* S. STOLJAR, *supra* note 76, at 132 (Not until *High Trees* was *Pinnel's Case* assumed to prevent rent reductions.).

264. Traditional reliance was not required in *High Trees* past the tenant making a partial rent payment on rent owed in reliance on the creditor's promise, which then made it inequitable for the creditor to claim the full amount for that period.

265. Denning stated he wasn't basing his decision on (equitable) estoppel because of Jorden v. Money, 5 H.L.C. 185 (1854) (Representation as to future must be in a contract or it's unenforceable.).

266. Combe v. Combe, 2 K.B. 215 (1951), All Eng. Rep. 767 (1951). *See* ENGLISH LAW REVISION COMMITTEE, SIXTH INTERIM REPORT, 1937, CMND. No. 5449, at pp. 24–25 (Promise should be enforced without consideration if detrimental reliance.).

267. *See* Milsom, *supra* note 214, at 1587–1588.

268. *See* P. ATIYAH and R. SUMMERS, *supra* note 11, at 88–90, 222–223, 229, 240–241, 408–409.

269. James Baird Co. v. Gimbel Bros., 64 F. 2d 344, 346 (2d Cir. 1933), citing Holmes in Wisconsin, etc. Ry. v. Powers, 191 U.S. 379, 386, 387 (1903).

270. *See* Henderson, *supra* note 208, at 355.

271. Northwestern Engineering Co. v. Ellerman, 69 S.D. 397, 408, 10 N.W. 2d 879, 884 (1943). *And see* Robert Gordon, Inc. v. Ingersoll-Rand Co., 117 F. 2d 654, 661 (7th Cir. 1941) (dictum).

272. Drennan v. Star Paving Co., 51 Cal. 2d 409, 333 P. 2d 757 (1958) (Expectation damages recovered of difference between subcontractor's bid and the amount paid another subcontractor to do the work.).

273. A Tennessee court employed a similar fiction 12 years before. Hutchison v. Dobson-Bainbridge Realty Co., 31 Tenn. App. 490, 217 S.W. 2d 6 (1946) ("binding subsidiary promise not to revoke offer"). *See* RESTATEMENT OF CONTRACTS, sect 45, Comment (b) (1932), which references Sect. 90. In cases of offers for unilateral contracts, option contracts, firm offer and promissory estoppel, only the offeror is bound.

274. Hoffman v. Red Owl Stores, Inc., 26 Wis. 2d 683, 13 N.W. 2d 267 (1965); Terre Haute Brewing Co. v. Dugan, 102 F. 2d 425 (8th Cir. 1939); Goodman v. Dicker, 169 F. 2d 684 (D.C. Cir. 1948). Although franchises are often terminable at will, protection of franchisees' reliance interest have allowed operation to continue long enough to recoup his investment or to obtain reimbursement of losses. Clausen & Sons, Inc. v. Theo, Hamm Brewing Co., 395 F. 2d 388 (8th Cir. 1968); Hardin v. Eska Co., 256 Ia. 371, 127 N.W. 2d 595 (1964). Sect. 90 used to overcome past consideration problem in releases. Fried v. Fisher, 328 Pa. 497, 196 A. 39 (1938); Brewer v. Universal Credit Co., 191 Miss. 183, 192 So. 902 (1940). 6 of 12 illustrations in the Restatement Second Sect. 90 are commercial. Nevertheless there is still some support for Hand's view in *Baird*. *See* Tatsch v. Hamilton-Erichson Mfg. Co., 76 N.M. 729, 418 P. 2d 187 (1966) (Promissory estoppel has no vitality in promises offering a bargain.).

275. Abbott v. Stephany Poultry Co., 5 Terry 513, 62 A. 2d 243 (Del. Super. Ct. 1948) (reliance); RESTATEMENT (SECOND) OF CONTRACTS sect. 87

(1981) (Option contract formed by offeree's substantial reliance. Subsect. 2. If writing recites "purported consideration" or statute makes irrevocable. Subsect. 1.). The U.C.C. enforces merchant's expressly intended firm offer without need for reliance and has effect similar to a seal. U.C.C. sect. 2–205. An attempt to in effect resurrect the sealed promise to make a gift failed when only Pennsylvania passed the Uniform Written Obligations Act (1925).

276. Hoffman v. Red Owl Stores, Inc., 26 Wis. 2d 683, 133 N.W. 2d 267 (1965). *See* Wheeler v. White, 398 S.W. 2d 93 (Texas Sup. Ct. 1965) (indefinite financing agreement enforced under promissory estoppel). Definiteness more of a problem when expectation damages are granted than when, as in *Hoffman v. Red Owl,* damages are for reliance.

277. *Hoffman v. Red Owl's* use of promissory estoppel was a multiple assault on contract doctrine by: finding liability at the negotiation level, indirectly suggesting the requirement of good faith in negotiating, allowing only reliance damages, not requiring that a promise be definite or supported by consideration, and stating that promissory estoppel wasn't the equivalent of a contract action.

278. Kessler and Fine, *supra* note 21, at 401, 412–413 (The further negotiations go, the less safe it is to withdraw.); Goodman v. Dicker, 169 F. 2d 684 (D.C. Cir. 1948) (Franchisor held liable for reliance damages in preparation for franchise even though franchise not granted.). There was no suggestion in *Goodman* that the promise was not an offer, unlike *Hoffman v. Red Owl*; the court simply said franchisor estopped from denying existence of contract due to reliance. *See* E. FARNSWORTH, *supra* note 36, at 192 (Since a contrary provision in an offer couldn't have avoided liability in *Hoffman,* the liability for misconduct might better be called a tort.).

279. RESTATEMENT (SECOND) OF CONTRACTS sects. 87, 88, 89, 139 (1981); *see* Knapp, *supra* note 38, at 60–70.

280. Fuller and Perdue (pt. 2), *supra* note 124, at 401–405 (cases of partial enforcement); Boyer, *supra* note 218, at 651, 663–665 (cases of partial enforcement and little reliance often for charitable subscriptions); Boyer, *Promissory Estoppel: Requirements and Limitations of the Doctrine,* 98 U. PA. L. REV. 459, 485–490, 492, 496 (1950) (partial enforcement when injustice to promisor and commercial promises being covered). The Restatement Second did not follow Boyer's view that third parties should not be able to recover under sect. 90 because of cases like Burgess v. California Mut. Bldg. & Loan Assn., 210 Cal. 180, 290 P. 1029 (1930) (Second mortgagee loaned money in reliance on first mortgagee's promise to debtor of part release.).

281. Thayer v. Meeker, 86 Ill. 470 (1877); Clark v. Glidden, 60 Vt. 702, 15 Atl. 358 (1888); Grimshaw v. Belcher, 88 Cal. 217, 26 Pac. 84 (1891); Scheersschmidt v. Smith, 74 Minn. 224, 77 N.W. 34 (1898); Pryor v. Cain, 25 Ill. 292 (1861) (may either grant reliance costs or enforce promise); *see* Fuller and Perdue (pt. 2), *supra* note 124, at 401–405 (Courts have adapted remedy by protecting restitution, reliance and expectation interests depending on situation.); *see also* Boyer, *supra* note 202, at 485–487 (Some jurisdictions only give restitution.). *And see* 1A A. CORBIN, *supra* note 25, at sect. 200 (Factors relevant in deciding on remedy and recovery include economic needs and capacity of parties.).

282. Northern Commercial Co. v. United Airmotive, 101 F. Supp. 169 (Alaska 1951) (promisor not liable when property owner made no effort to insure); *see*

Boyer, *supra* note 202, at 488–489 (Outcome of cases vary.); *and see* RESTATEMENT (SECOND) OF CONTRACTS) sect. 90, Comment (e) (1981) (Promise could be construed only to use reasonable efforts to insure. Clear proof of promise and reliance removes difficulties.).

283. Bright v. Bright, 41 Ill 97 (1866) (Taking possession of land given wasn't enough reliance.); Salsbury v. Northwestern Bell Tell, Co., 221 N.W. 2d 609 (Iowa 1974); *see* RESTATEMENT (SECOND) OF CONTRACTS sect. 90, Comments (b) and (f) and Reporter's Note thereto.

284. N. Litterio v. Glassman Constr. Co., 319 F. 2d 736 (1963) (Statute of Frauds not germane since no contract found to exist); Hoffman v. Red Owl Stores, Inc., 26 Wis. 2d 683, 133 N.W. 2d 267 (1965) (not equivalent of contract action); Janke v. Vulcan, 386 F. Supp. 687, 697 (1974) (Statute of Frauds concerns contracts but promissory estoppel concerns promises with no contractual basis.); R.S. Bennett & Co. v. Economy Mechanical Ind., 606 F. 2d 182, 188 (7th Cir. 1979) (Promissory estoppel claim isn't barred by Statute of Frauds because not contractually based.).

285. RESTATEMENT (SECOND) OF CONTRACTS sect. 17 (1981); *Id.* at sect. 90, Comment (d) ("A promise binding under this section is a contract."); 1A A. CORBIN, *supra* note 25, at sect. 193–196 (Before the Restatements, courts didn't acknowledge they were enforcing without consideration but were flexible enough to do it anyway.). Restatement Second sect. 17 (1) and (2) treat recovery under sections 82–94 to be exceptions to the usual bargain requirement.

286. G. GILMORE, *supra* note 26, at 69–90.

287. Rather than promissory estoppel swallowing up consideration, it might be pushed into a different compartment, as earlier Assumpsit separated from Trespass; Assumpsit and Covenant were separated from the start. *See* Milsom, *supra* note 214, at 1587.

288. J. DAWSON, *supra* note 47, at 3–4, 207; Kessler, *Contracts of Adhesion—Some Thoughts About Freedom of Contract*, 43 COLUM. L. REV. 629, 639 (1943) (Courts have emotional desire to preserve freedom of contract.); Speidel, *supra* note 38, at 1172, 1177. Contractual rather than tortious ideas are emphasized in Restatement Second Sect. 90, Comment (d) and in cases like Huhtala v. Travelers Ins. Co., 401 Mich. 118, 257 N.W. 2d 640 (1977) (contract and not tort statute of limitations applicable).

289. 1A A. CORBIN, *supra* note 25, at sects. 193–194. The error of monism in seeking a single test for enforcement of promises can be seen arising as early as the sixteenth century. *See* A. SIMPSON, *supra* note 76, at 325.

290. Promissory estoppel has been avoided by invoking public policy reasons for enforcing both charitable and marriage gifts, and sometimes executed gifts are declared. In I. & I. Holding Corp. v. Gainsburg, 276 N.Y. 427, 12 N.E. 2d 532 (1938) court found offer for unilateral contract and acceptance was charity's reliance. *See* Henderson, *supra* note 208, at 346–348; *see also* K. SUTTON, CONSIDERATION RECONSIDERED 153–155 (Queensland, Australia: 1974).

291. Henderson, *supra* note 208, at 348–353, 387.

292. And yet *Baird v. Gimbel* is still alive in some cases saying that promissory estoppel is inapplicable to promises offering bargains. Tatsch v. Hamilton-Erickson Mfg. Co., 76 N.M. 729, 418 P. 2d 187 (1966).

293. *See* Henderson, *supra* note 208, at 355–357.

294. *See Id.* at 352–353. Confusion with equitable estoppel further obscures the differences. *Id.* at 376–379.

295. *See* Boyer, *supra* note 202, at 497–498; *and see* Braucher, *supra* note 37, at 601, 604; *see also* Fuller and Perdue (pt. 1), *supra* note 124, at 61–62 (In order to protect the preferred reliance interest, protection of loss of expectations is necessary, independent of reliance, in order to encourage business reliance on a promise.); *cf.* G. GILMORE, *supra* note 26, at 72 ("Probability of reliance" may be enough for enforcement of wholly executory exchange without inquiring into consideration.). Gilmore must be referring to Restatement Second sect. 90, Comment (f), but this only covers donative promises, but, as emphasized by Comment (b), substantial reliance is required for more bargain-oriented promises.

296. *See* Boyer, *supra* note 202, at 498; (applies only to promises inducing reasonable reliance and only when need to avoid injustice); Henderson, *supra* note 208, at 353, 367.

CHAPTER 8

CORPORATE STATE AND THE UNDERDOG (1875 onward, II)

Concurrent with the reformulation of classical doctrine discussed in the preceding chapter, there was an unprecedented legislative intrusion upon the way business firms contracted with others. This intervention was precipitated by the reaction of the democratic majority against the overreaching of some corporate giants in taking undue advantage of their newly acquired superior position in the market. Formerly legislatures had largely left the regulation of market exchanges to the courts, but legislatures began penetrating the formalism of contract doctrine and in the process usurped the court's central role in administering economic transactions. Later, in the wake of the emerging welfare state, courts would haltingly begin to aid those oppressed by market imbalances by borrowing ideas from equity and tort to develop novel common law relief. The equitable developments of the past century are approached by the legal historian with some trepidation since aspects of the analysis are as much about tendencies in the law as they are about legal history.

Rise of Corporate State

The modern form of general corporation did not take shape until the middle third of the nineteenth century. American corporation law grew from colonial use of the corporate device for religious congregations, charities, schools, local government units and large business enterprises providing such public services as wharves and mills.[1] During the first half century after independence, state legislatives granted veritable monopolies through special charters to businesses to provide public services for building the infrastructure of the young republic. A model for colonial charters was the Tudor royal charters granting monopolies in business activities of public interest. Early business corporate charters were mainly in transportation, as turnpikes and canals, and finance, as banking and insurance. These special charters, which dominated until the mid-nineteenth century, were a form of legislative regulation of business through "legislative contract."[2]

There was a fear of the economic influence of these corporations, and measures were taken to control them;[3] nevertheless, they were becoming viewed as a necessary evil because of the important quasi-public functions they performed in the place of inert governmental units. During the Jacksonian period there was a heated debate over the 1830s practice of issuing special charters. Was it to be a special privilege available to a few or a standard right available to all? Was it to be part of a mercantile policy for building the infrastructure or a general instrument of private enterprise? There was a concern for a healthy democratic dispersion of power. The outcome was that the corporate form became generally available to commercial interests in the 1840s, though the widespread use of special charters continued until the 1870s, and perpetual life and limited liability were not established until after the Civil War.[4]

The increased availability of the corporate form by the 1840s allowed popular participation in the exploitation of markets and of advanced technology, e.g., steam power for both railroads and factories. The mid-nineteenth century transition from special consensual associations between the state and private interests for public service projects to a more generally available business device, providing limited liability and continuity, raised a conflict in the minds of businessmen, who on the one hand wanted to be left alone but on the other hand wanted to be protected in their accumulation of capital.[5] The corporate form grew in importance in the 1860s and became the dominating business form in the 1880s and 1890s, by which time there was such a prevalence of general incorporation acts as to suggest a policy akin to a constitutional privilege.[6] Before the Civil War most special charters were in transportation, and less than 10% were in manufacturing, but by 1900 two-thirds of all goods would be manufactured by corporations.

The emergence of the corporate state in the last quarter of the nineteenth century brought with it a fundamental modification of the notion of freedom of contract. The most creative area of contract-making now concerned the powerful instrument of the business corporation which legislatures placed in the hands of business planners enabling expansion of the scale and longevity of their market operations.[7] The right to make corporate resolutions placed a state sanctioned form of private law-making in the hands of the majority of shareholders. The corporate structure itself had in fact looked more contractual earlier when the nature of the enterprise had been negotiated between incorporators and the state issuing a special charter; once general corporation acts were passed, incorporators still agreed to form a business, but their resulting relationships was now dictated by a uniform corporation act spelling out their status and the relationship between shareholders, managers and employees.[8]

The new general business corporate form aided industrialists in amassing unprecedented private wealth and power in the last quarter of the nineteenth century. The earlier ideal of equality in forming a corporation was not realized since only the propertied class had the ability to take advantage of the privilege. The consolidation of business power in a few hands was the most important factor in the destruction of both market balance and equal economic opportunity.[9] The imbalance in distribution of wealth was aggravated by instrumental governmental policies protecting the strong through governmental franchises, public utilities and trusts.[10] Business organizations grew larger when inefficiencies of transacting business over great distances were cured by inventions in communications and transport, e.g., the telephone, telegraph and railroads.[11]

The concentration of power in a few brought on a drift toward monopoly and a diminution of individual freedom to contract. Liberalism's former presumption that most contractors negotiated on an equal bargaining level was no longer applicable. Consent was gone when a person's whole livelihood was in the market but he had no choice about the terms and often didn't even have the right to contract with a person with an individual identity.[12] A former system of market exchanges based on freedom of equal contracting parties was replaced by a neo-feudal corporate system of relations based on superiors and inferiors.[13] Courts of the last quarter of the nineteenth century, emotionally wed to the rhetoric of freedom of contract, did not interfere with private legislation by stronger contracting parties and so refused to interfere with the one-sided exercise of power since all contracts made in proper form were seen as enforceable. When objections were raised to the unfairness of limited liability for veritable corporate shells, the accepted response was that the other party freely contracted with a corporation which he knew had limited liability. Freedom of contract protected the unequal distribution of property but didn't protect weaker parties from coercion by these owners of the means of production. At least in a feudal state, the overlord had the obligation to provide protection. The courts were slow in admitting that there was only freedom of contract for the strong and that the market could be destroyed, and so they did nothing to remedy the inequities.[14] This was the scenario of corporate dealings outside the firm when dealing with non-equals. Now a look at the dynamics inside the corporate structure.

Inside the corporation, corporate administrative procedures were supplanting contract as the organizing principle for many former market transactions since the greater the vertical integration of the factors of production, the less the organization needed to contract with outsiders in the market. Contractual bargains with suppliers, middlemen and retailers were eliminated through the vertical absorption and franchising of these functions done in order to control the manufacturing and distribution processes. Franchisees had no choice but to cave in to franchisors' economic demands for fear of franchise non-renewal, and courts protected franchisors' freedom to refuse to renew. As firms merged and holding companies took control, contracts between subsidiaries were formed in the interest of the group rather than that of each unit, and litigation was eliminated because there was no suit if a subsidiary failed to perform.[15]

An authoritarian discipline dictated the systematic internal workings of the firm, and these corporate procedures were substituted for contract in administering the steps in production. The very existence of the firm depended upon the formality of hierarchical procedures providing norms and settlement procedures. The required cooperation and acceptance of near autocratic authority by the divisions of labor within the firm left no room for rugged individualism.[16] Individual minority owners of corporate shares could be subjected to contracts they didn't consent to since decisions were made by majority rule and later purchasers of shares would be impacted likewise; earlier, these businesses under the partnership form needed unanimity at least for fundamental policy changes. And, the single-minded objectives of the firm caused promises made to outsiders to no longer have the same moral strength as one manager replaced another and obligations to shareholders could make management feel obligated to breach.[17]

In exchange transactions outside the firm, the free market price generated by supply and demand, and administered by contract law, determined the allocation of resources, but within the firm the managing entrepreneur directed the allocation. Why was it preferable for large business organizations to emerge for the coordination of production in place of the price mechanism and classical contract rules? The answer seems to be that corporate procedures could better manage capital needed for new technology and that the firm, an alternative form of contracting to the market, could provide cost savings; marketing costs could be reduced both by reducing the number of exchange transactions and by helping to overcome the uncertainties of now longer term transactions. There could be reductions in the number and cost of total transactions needed by integrating the series of contracts for goods and services in the production and distribution process in-house and in their place substitute ongoing employment contracts for these formerly discrete transactions.[18]

The uncertainty inherent in by long-term contracts required the forecasting of experts, now employed by the firm, and the long range planning provided by the managing entrepreneur, who was willing to take the risk of uncertainty and guarantee a wage to those who were not so inclined. Once mutuality and indefiniteness objections were overcome in the courts, open-ended, long-term contracts were used in the planning process to solve forecasting problems of the amount of supplies required in the future, while assuring a supply, and to assure a market for the uncertain output of new technology. It seems improbable that large business organizations would have emerged during the last quarter of the nineteenth century without the need for centralized long-term planning of complex business activities, which was possible within a corporation with perpetual life, to overcome uncertainties about the future in a rapidly changing and complex industrial age.[19]

The new paradigmatic transaction was becoming the highly relational, long-term contract, e.g., long-term leases, franchises, output and requirement contracts, relations with shareholders and employees, and collective employment agreements. There were difficulties in transferring the rules applicable to the historic paradigm of the single, discrete market transaction to long-term, relational contracts. The traditional rules did not readily accommodate transactions lacking definiteness and mutuality and failing to follow traditional mercantile practices and modes of dispute settlement. In long-term contractual relations, parties have expectations that terms will be left open, that there will be cooperation and that goodwill will be kept. These ongoing relational agreements only set the general framework with periodic renegotiation of terms in a continuing relationship, and in the event of a dispute, built-in alternative grievance procedures were becoming common.[20]

New grievance procedures evolved during the last quarter of the nineteenth century as these corporate giants perceived of their agreements with other large corporations as treaties or joint ventures. Equal bargaining and freedom of contract were still present in bargains at this level. Disputes between these large business organizations didn't often appear in the courts because of concern for goodwill in a continuing relationship and because preventive measures were often taken at the planning stage to avoid the costs of litigation and the unpredictability of trial by jury. At this level, there were high quality negotiations, provisions for arbitration, mediation and other structured grievance procedures, risk allocation, and adjustments according to business usage. These corporate practices were usurping the courts' traditional central role of overseeing market transactions. Smaller operators had no choice but to seek judicial relief, no doubt partially because their contracts were not as well negotiated and goodwill was not as much of a factor since their relations didn't tend to be ongoing, but also because they had fewer resources and options to fall back on and so being paid or not could be a matter of survival.[21]

Relationships of large corporations with their suppliers, distributors, and other middlemen, and customers were becoming standardized during the last quarter of the nineteenth century. Corporations themselves could now be formed under standardized procedures and were being formed in wholesale lots. The net result was a general standardizing of legal relationships. The standardized contract was perfected earlier between merchants on an equal footing in insurance, transportation and banking transactions and spread to mass transactions during the industrial revolution continuing up to the present.[22] The mass distribution of goods and services required mass produced stereotyped contract forms to handle these new high volume impersonal transactions. Private legislation by standardized agreements was similar to an organizing statute which contains broad provisions covering activities of individuals who had no role in the negotiating or drafting. Legislative enactments governing contracts also contributed to standardizing by setting general business requirements and compulsory clauses and contracts.[23]

Business favored standardized contracts because of the cost of individualized handling of mass transactions and because of the control it gave over its agents and the factors of production. Standardization facilitated better planning and security by encouraging certainty and making risks more calculable under agreements drafted with the needs of commercial interests in mind.[24] Standardized forms included provisions for avoiding the irrational litigation factors of court procedures and trial by jury, which compromised business planning; this hostility to the irrational factors in the judicial process is a part of the same category that codes and restatements fit into.[25] Nonetheless, the formality of contract law itself was consistent with standardization, and courts were in fact instrumental in supporting standardization by enforcement of the letter of the contract and thereby encouraged uniform conduct through literal interpretation of forms. Once the formalities of contract law were complied with, under the objective theory of bargain consideration it was immaterial whether the standardized contract, drafted in favor of the seller, was read or understood.

The strict application of traditional contract rules, like objectivity, adequacy and the parol evidence rule, reflected courts' emotional attachment to "freedom of contract".[26] However, freedom of contract was a hostile theory for parties who lacked leverage but were forced into market transactions administered by standardized contracts which they did not have the option to bargain for or sometimes the capacity to understand. During the industrial revolution, non-commercial parties were forced into the market to obtain employment and the necessities of life.[27] Large industrial and commercial monopolies had the unilateral power to dictate terms, harsh or otherwise, through standardized mass produced contracts of adhesion offered on a take it or leave it basis. Individuality seriously eroded when there was no room to negotiate protection against unfair deals.[28] There was a decline in consent when legal rights and duties were determined by standardized rules rather than by the particular intention of the parties. These standardized relations dictated by the combination of large corporations, government regulation and collective bargaining units suggested a "veering back to status". Some saw the weapon of "freedom of contract" facilitating the imposition of a new feudal order by industrial and commercial overlords through the private legislation of standardized contracts by *fin de siecle*.[29]

Welfare State and the Underdog

There was little concern for social policy prior to the industrial revolution since the nineteenth century belief was that free competition secured community justice among individuals serving their own interests in developing the continent's resources.[30] A reappraisal was necessary during the last quarter of the nineteenth century, however, as excesses of the market tore at the fabric of society; these excesses included disparity of wealth and opportunity, monopoly, abuse of marketing strategy and wasteful allocation of scarce resources. There were dire social costs of unemployment on an unprecedented scale and acute housing and health problems.[31] The realization was growing that only the wealthy had a chance to freely negotiate and that the slogan of freedom of contract protected vested interests against the forces of industrial society.[32] There was a loss of faith in free choice and individualism, as free competition declined due to the trend toward monopoly. A legal order with few mandates can actually allow an increase of coercion to be exerted by the powerful. There was no freedom to contract when terms were dictated on a take it or leave it basis by the economically stronger party. Freedom to contract was available to a few who were supported by the pattern of distribution of property guaranteed by law. Americans had a traditional hostility to the destruction of opportunities by monopolization, and the consolidation of business in a few did the most to raise concern about legal formation and the relationship of the state to the economic order.[33]

It became an illusion that the law protected the public interest against the abuses of freedom of contract when freedom depended on one's position on the economic ladder. The earlier use of contract as the nineteenth century technique for organization of the market was too limited in these new circumstances since market values did not necessarily equate either with human conditions, such as housing, sanitation and health, or with concern for the future, like the environment.[34] There was an anti-fraternal ethic in market transactions which depersonalized the contractual relationship by focusing on the commodity rather than the human on the other side of the contract. Amid the modern emergence of class problems, there was a demand for a social law based on justice and dignity and directed against the dominance of a mere business morality.[35]

Late nineteenth century social scientists provided the intellectual foundations for change both by preaching the Social Gospel and by the Progressive Movement's challenge of Social Darwinism. Christian ethics were translated into a new school of economic thought which denied that man was solely absorbed in gain and now conceived of economic rules not as immutable but as developing in the context of time and place. Thus Adam Smith could be seen as correct in protesting against eighteenth century paternalistic mercantile restrictions, but it was now argued that state intervention was necessary to provide positive assistance for the furtherance of human progress.[36] A view emerged by the late nineteenth century that the democratic state should be an instrument to further common interests and to ameliorate social conditions within the context of the traditional American value of equality under law in a culture of general opportunity. There was a pragmatic sense that a democracy of wealth was a necessity and that industrial organizations, which were permitted by law, must include a social function.[37] This democratization of wealth was attempted through regulation of business enterprise.

Although the creation of the Interstate Commerce Commission in 1887 is often given as the genesis of broad, modern business regulation, there was in fact a great deal of state legislative intrusion into contractual abstraction in the nineteenth century and much of it was solicitous of business.[38] Modern social regulation of business began once legislatures recognized the community-wide effect of seemingly private contracts, as between utility company and customer, insurer and insured and railroad and farmer. By the 1880s there was a real gulf between the accepted abstraction of laissez-faire theory and actual state regulation of public utilities, labor relations, insurance, banking, health and social welfare. From 1887 onward federal regulation expanded with the need for interstate regulation of railroads, trusts, food and drugs, and labor. Objections to this process were raised by vested property interests and by business planners and formalists who criticized the undermining of contractual certainty and stability.[39]

This expanding regulatory environment was in response to the demands of the collective middle income majority of small entrepreneurs, farmers and laborers who wanted their share of power and of resources now perceived to be finite. The modern theme of group pressure shaping American law was in full swing by 1900 as the net welfare and freedom of society was beginning to be placed above the individual.[40] The Progressive proposal for a "general welfare state" was not merely an attack on formalistic laissez-faire government but was a constructive program for curing social problems. The Progressives' positive program was not meant to overthrow private enterprise but instead was a middle ground between socialism and individualism. The American welfare state did not concentrate on the allocation of resources but instead focused on improving the quality of procedures in order to cure inequalities in contractual bargaining positions in such areas as antitrust, insurance, labor law, transport and banking.[41]

Administrative procedures of governmental, corporate and labor institutions and the public ownership of such enterprises as utilities and transportation caused an increasing preemption of private bargaining. Government regulation was beginning to replace private contract as the regulator of the market as government agencies and controls overrode private intent. Regulation moved many economic transactions partially or entirely out of the realm of contract principles, and private agreements remaining were often read in light of relevant statutory policy. Common law contract principles were increasingly relegated to adjustments after breakdown and to the residue of transactions left untouched by the administrative process. The role of courts and legislatures were becoming reversed by the first decades of the twentieth century as legislatures stepped in to fill the policy void created when courts were found incapable of coping with the contextual complexity of the industrial age. A legislative democratization of wealth brought a recognition of a social content in a law of contracts formerly governed by first principles.[42]

The demands for a general welfare state were finally realized during the New Deal when there was a wholesale intrusion to obtain balance in the economy. There was a centralization of regulation as federal agency regulation replaced former piecemeal state regulation. After about 1940, the general welfare state would not have a significant challenge until quite recently when the emergence of neo-classical economic thought spawned a movement known as Law and Economics. This school of thought holds that the market utility of a business activity should be compared with the harm it produces and that government should not regulate when the net gain of the activity to everyone exceeds the loss suffered by regulation.[43]

What was the constitutional view of this unparalleled governmental intrusion upon the freedom of individuals to enter into voluntary agreements? The constitutional law decisions from the industrial revolution to the late 1930s reflect the tension between individualism and the collective pressure for an egalitarian general welfare state. Until the latter part of the nineteenth century, corporations were not afforded the degree of constitutional protection given individuals because corporations were not deemed "Citizens" entitled to "Privileges and Immunities" under Article IV of the Constitution. But, in a political climate more supportive of corporations in the late 1880s, this was altered when a corporation was found to be a "person" under the Fourteenth Amendment "due process" clause.[44] For the next half century the U.S. Supreme Court was generally sympathetic to commercial interests' substantive due process arguments that their "liberty" to contract and their right to hold private "property" should not be intruded upon by government regulation. The abstract principle of freedom of contract was elevated to a fundamental constitutional property right by the turn of the century,[45] subject to the policy exceptions of public interest and police power.

Public interest and police power were principles opposing the broad due process protection from government regulation given private agreements irrespective of social costs. In *Munn v. Illinois* (1876) the United States Supreme Court upholding of an Illinois statute setting grain storage rates was a victory for Granger regulation of railroads, grain elevators and warehouses. The Supreme Court cited as authority English Chief Justice Hale's seventeenth century support for regulation of business activities "clothed with a public interest."[46] State regulation of railroads might have sufficed had a state statute not been barred from application to railroad activities running outside state boundaries in 1886.[47] As a consequence, the Interstate Commerce Act was passed the next year. This regulation of railroads did not meet the constitutional opposition directed against other regulations because of the traditional common law regulation of both common callings and monopolistic practices.

The expansive police power argument was applied unevenly during the half century before the late 1930s. Much of the constitutional caselaw concerned state regulation of employment standards for maximum hours and minimum wages of the burgeoning urban workforce which was unable to bargain on an equal basis with industrialists. Maximum hours were allowed in 1908 for women, who a half century before were contractually disabled, to protect them from the greed of employers, but maximum hour provisions for men were struck down in 1905 for intruding on male individual liberty,[48] though it was allowed for railway workers due to public safety. A minimum wage law for women did not fare as well in the face of the freedom of contract slogan in *Adkins v. Children's Hospital* (1923)[49] because police power was inapplicable to an employee subsistence provision when there was no relation between the employee's minimum wage and the value of the employee's service to the employer. The court adhered to an amoral abstraction, seeing no difference between selling labor and selling goods; but, ironically courts invoked a kind of just price theory on behalf of employers, who had usually benefited from the adequacy rule, in suggesting a moral requirement of equivalence between services and wages. *Adkins* was reaffirmed as late as 1936, but the uncertainty about the permissibility of legislative adjustment of contracts was soon resolved in favor of the opposing view.

Realist supporters of the New Deal resurrected Holmes' dissents in *Lochner v. New York* (1905) and *Adkins v. Children's Hospital* (1923) in attacking conservative justices' atavistic clinging to freedom of contract in the face of the social costs. In *Lochner* Holmes suggested that the Fourteenth Amendment did not enact Social Darwinism nor did the Constitution embody a particular economic theory. He said that "liberty" was perverted if dominant opinion reflected in legislation could not prevail, subject to legislation not containing an unreasonable infringement. In *West Coast Hotel Co. v. Parrish* (1937)[50] a 5 to 4 majority was mustered to expressly overrule *Adkins* in a contest of a State of Washington minimum wage law. Chief Justice Hughes, writing for the majority, took judicial notice of the deprivation of the depression in declaring that "liberty" to contract has a connotation in each phase of history. He continued that liberty in a social organization is subject to the restraints of due process adopted by the community in the public interest under the police power to assist in meeting the "very necessities of existence" of workers with less bargaining power than employers. Hughes turned freedom of contract rhetoric against "overreaching" employers by quoting from Holmes' dissent in *Adkins* that the law did not compel them to hire anyone. *West Coast Hotel Co. v. Parrish* was a watershed decision recognizing the social content in contract law. The slim majority in *Parrish* soon grew, and the permissibility of reasonable legislative regulation of contractual relations has been accepted since that period as courts thereafter tended to defer to legislative public policy judgments.

The state and federal regulation of contractual relations since the late nineteenth century has had a pervasive effect on the freedom of entering into various categories of contracts no longer fitting neatly under Langdell's general principles. The scope of the present work does not permit a study of all of the effects, but a representative sampling is in order to provide a glimpse of the impact of legislative regulation. The areas selected here for discussion are antitrust, labor contracts, insurance contracts and compulsory contracts generally.

The first area of analysis will be antitrust regulation, a long standing concern of the common law. In the early seventeenth century, Coke had opposed the lingering restrictions on free trade of the declining guild system, though partial restraints were permitted. A century later a balance was found between the conflicting ideas of freedom of contract and free competition by distinguishing acceptable from unacceptable restraints under a reasonableness test—the precursor of modern antitrust law's rule of reason test.[51] By the 1830s the American practice of chartering monopolies to build the states' infrastructure was no longer needed and free competition was encouraged. However, by the 1880s, there was a grave concern about the extent of industrial monopolization, but there was no coordinated program to police the problem. Prior to 1890 the use of common law doctrine to oppose restraints of trade consisted of scattered private civil actions wherein the relief was judicial refusal to enforce the illegal contract.[52] There was a realization that abuses of freedom of contract were leading to a destruction of a free competitive market, e.g., fixing prices and production, allocations of territory, tying arrangements, restrictive franchises, etc. For an unscrupulous operator with enough leverage, freedom of contract could mean freedom to monopolize. The erosion of freedom of contract and equality of opportunity for weaker parties in the market sparked a legislative intrusion into the abstraction of freedom of contract in order to bust the trusts. When the Sherman Act[53] of 1890 declared contracts in restraint of trade and monopolization illegal, it was consistent with traditional common law doctrine; the difference was that it socialized the process by providing a nationally coordinated policy and the criminal sanctions lacking at common law. It was a consistent extension of the anti-monopolistic policy in the recent Interstate Commerce Act, but Sherman lacked an enforcement agency and its provisions were much vaguer. The Act's vagueness required judicial development of a federal antitrust common law to reflect the felt needs of the times.

The second selected category of contract regulation for analysis is the labor contract. The nineteenth century urge for the parties' consent to replace older status-based rules resulted in contract doctrine eclipsing older, relational master and servant principles. Under contract abstraction, the selling of labor was just another unit of production, not to be distinguished from the selling of goods. In the industrial setting employment was stripped of its traditional personal sentimental relationship. The right of employees to bargain freely was declared to exist when the reality for laborers not owning the means of production was one of an unequal bargaining position resulting in exceedingly low wages, 10 to 12 hour workdays, unsafe working conditions and child labor.[54] By the mid–1880's collective labor pressure on state legislatures began to cause an erosion of laissez-faire adherence to freedom of contract. This legislation on behalf of the interest of the group was detrimental to individual freedom, but it was determined that the resort to status was the only way to force employers to a realization of their social duties of providing better working conditions.[55]

One significant improvement in working conditions around the turn of the century was the advent of employers' modern social responsibility for employee injuries. During the last quarter of the nineteenth century, a contractual framework had been employed in these tort cases because industrial injuries differed from other injuries in that a contractual relation existed between the injured employee and the employer; employees' contract waivers of negligence claims were upheld under sanctity of contract, but Progressive legislation soon barred their enforcement. There was a forced legislative standardization with the abolition both of contract waivers and of the tort defenses of contributory negligence, assumption of risk and the fellow servant doctrine. The labor victory was completed with no-fault liability under workers compensation statutes.[56] This statutory relief for ill-informed workers, who were forced into the market for employment, is an important example of modern status-based protection of expectations of fairness which is divorced from consent.[57]

State legislatures were also sympathetic to the right of labor to organize by prohibiting such practices as yellow dog contracts and discrimination against union leaders; however, state and federal courts abused their equitable powers in restricting strikes and boycotts by issuing *ex parte* injunctions.[58] Federal legislation supporting the right of labor to organize and setting fair labor standards were not passed until laissez-faire contract abstraction was rejected in the mid–1930s. Taken together, the Wagner Act (1935) and the Taft-Hartley Act (1947) recognized collective bargaining agreements as enforceable contracts and required employers and unions to bargain together in good faith.[59] There was a loss of freedom of contract to employers and to any minority of employees not in agreement with the majority. The contractual nature of labor contracts was retained, however, since legislation forced neither an agreement nor its contents. More recent developments on the good faith front include the prohibition of discrimination against protected classes in employment matters under the 1964 Civil Rights Act and an emerging notion of good faith in dismissal of employees governed by the employment-at-will doctrine.

There has been a judicial recognition of the unique nature of collective bargaining agreements. The United States Supreme Court declared that "a collective agreement is not an ordinary contract" governed principally by general contract doctrine because of the need to look first to statutory policy.[60] Other differences between the common law of contract and collective agreements include the three-sided relationship of union, employer and employee; adjustments to the doctrine of offer and acceptance to accommodate union procedures for ratification by the membership; modifications in liability of successors and assigns when there is a corporate merger; deliberate ambiguity on certain issues to avoid disagreement; and the predominant use of arbitration.[61] The parties have more confidence in arbitration than in an inexpert judiciary, and the courts themselves acknowledge a national labor policy presumption in favor of arbitration.[62]

Insurance contracts and compulsory contracts are the final areas of contract regulation for discussion. Most of the insurance-related caselaw prior to the industrial revolution concerned marine insurance. Marine insurance law was English in origin and reflected eighteenth century mercantile usage among bargainers on a relatively equal footing, but equality was atypical in fire, life and casualty insurance sold to the flood of consumers entering the market during the second half of the nineteenth century. The standardized nature of insurance contracts provided better calculation of risks and generally lent predictability to transactions between merchants, but standardization could be employed to facilitate overreaching in contracts with ill-informed consumers lacking bargaining power.[63] As an example, insurers converted applicants' representations into warranties and then invoked any trivial deviation, which would have been inadequate to raise a fraud defense, to deny recovery;[64] some sympathetic courts began to restrict the freedom of insurers by narrowly construing these warranties as mere representations in the interest of protecting expectations. Other equitable devices employed against insurer defenses included waiver, estoppel, notions of fair dealing and the requirement of insurer disclosures. One of the most effective means of judicial relief was to construe harsh insurance contracts of adhesion, whether ambiguous or not, in favor of the weaker consumer. Also good faith was in effect required at the negotiation level, under a general tort duty, when expectations were raised and an insurer failed to act promptly on an offer.[65] Resort to judicial relief was an inadequate solution, however, since most nineteenth century courts were disinclined to intervene, and those that did were not well equipped to determine whether overreaching had occurred. Furthermore, the public policy approach undermined legal certainty. As a consequence of judicial ineffectualness, there were democratic demands for legislative solutions.[66]

During the third quarter of the nineteenth century, insurance became the most regulated industry. New York created a Department of Insurance in 1859, and by 1873 there were a dozen states with insurance regulations. Massachusetts prescribed that insurers use a standard fire insurance policy in 1873. The established insurers did not necessarily oppose legislatively standardized provisions because they encouraged stability, uniformity and certainty, and it enhanced public faith in insurance. Notwithstanding this regulation beneficial to consumers, twentieth century courts still find it necessary to employ the ameliorating tools of public policy, unconscionability and disclosure to protect reasonable expectations of purchasers of insurance contracts filled with technical language. In cases of unfairness, ambiguities are read according to the understanding of the consumer rather than that of the insurance law expert.[67]

The contractual nature of an insurance policy was made subject to the realization that there were compulsory social obligations owed by a state chartered insurance company in an industrial society when selling such an emotionally charged product. The modern legal relationship of insurer and insured, based on status as much as consent, violated Maine's dictum about the movement of progressive societies.[68] Insurers' obligations now resembled the traditional compulsion applicable to such public service providers as common carriers and innkeepers. Indeed, some insurance contracts became as compulsory in nature as an innkeeper's obligation to take in a traveller or a common carrier's obligation to accept a shipment, e.g., insurers of motor vehicles and of workers compensation were compelled to accept their share of government assigned risks.

The reaction against unfair business contracts of adhesion prompted the appearance of compulsory features in other contracts, besides insurance, that were deemed to contain a public interest, e.g., public utilities, employment contracts, antitrust and transportation.[69] Public utilities supplying electricity, gas and water, in a less than competitive environment, were compelled to provide services to all third party members of the public in their service area on terms set by government bodies. Government regulation of public utilities, insurance, labor, transportation and antitrust restricted the right to refuse to contract with, or to discriminate against, selected individuals. Corporations engaged in matters of a public interest, such as public utilities, collective bargaining and insurance, were compelled to bargain in good faith. Compulsory provisions reduced the freedom and bargaining power of these public purveyors and became so widespread that the contents of many everyday contracts are determined by government regulation. So continues the twentieth century process of standardizing legal relations.[70]

Judicial Innovation for Underdog

Thus far the focus on relief for the economic underdog has primarily centered on legislative intervention to fill the vacuum created by judicial resistance and ineffectiveness in devising needed remedial innovations in the common law. Modern courts of law and equity did succeed, however, in several instances in acting in their equitable capacity to provide case-by-case hardship relief for the economic underdog through such doctrines as economic duress and good faith and consumer relief under unconscionability and strict liability. An analysis of the development of these instances of hardship relief follows.

The confused doctrine of economic duress, emanating from a variety of influences at law and in equity, is clearly recognized in the United States but not in England.[71] A starting point is the common law origins of duress. Bracton, in the mid-thirteenth century, kept a strict focus on the means of the threat, and only fear of loss of life or limb or imprisonment were sufficient for duress. Fear of damage to property, and even fear of battery, was insufficient since "he may have satisfaction in damages". Coke and Blackstone followed Bracton's lead.[72] The first clear step away from the strict rule and toward a common law doctrine of economic duress came in the famous "duress of goods" case *Astley v. Reynolds* (1732).[73] The plaintiff paid 10 pounds interest, 6 pounds in excess of the legal limit, in order to recover pawned goods and then brought a money had and received count for the 6 pounds. The Kings Bench held that trover was inadequate, that the plaintiff paid under the compulsion of wrongful detention of his property and that he paid the extorted amount in reliance on his restitutionary right to get back the excess. Roughly contemporaneous with this decision, Chancery was intervening to cancel contracts when there was a shocking inadequacy of consideration accompanied by unequal bargaining positions or oppression in cases of sales of inheritance expectancies by improvident young aristocrats, sales of equities of redemption and refusals to grant specific performance. Chancery's jurisdiction over duress was broader than the common law, partly due to the added availability of its related doctrine of constructive fraud, and it was quite willing to look at lack of equivalence in a bargain under loose notions of unconscionability, fraud, undue influence and duress. Chancery's ease in mixing these ideas in arriving at a fair result in cases of economic duress would make for a confused translation into the common law in the United States.[74] A third source in the development of economic duress, in addition to the above duress of goods and equitable notions, was the granting of restitution in the 1840s for payment of overcharges to such public utilities as railroads, turnpikes, and gas and water companies when the utility threatened to refuse service unless an excess payment was made.[75] Utilities were of course being held to a strict standard, and the inequality of bargaining power was relevant.

These first harbingers of economic duress took into account the lack of equivalencies, and common law duress cases before the 1800s generally looked to objective indicators like physical detention of property or the threat of severe bodily harm. Under mid-nineteenth century will theory and economic individualism, however, equivalency was shoved into the background and a subjective standard prevailed. An inquiry into free will centered on the presence of consent rather than on the consequences of the exchange.[76] In the English case of *Skeate v. Beale* (1840)[77] it was seemingly irrelevant that there was an excessive distraint of goods causing the defendant to agree to pay the amount of rent due. The court declared that duress of goods would not destroy the free will of an individual of ordinary firmness and that *Astley v. Reynolds* should be limited to its facts of when a wrongful detention of goods forced an agreement in excess of what was lawfully allowed. This restrictive emphasis on individual consent slowed the emergence of economic duress in the United States and stopped it dead in its tracks in England. Although the English common law courts distinguished to death the earlier suggestions of an economic duress theory, these root ideas never completely lost their hold in the United States in cases where there was no suitable alternative remedy. Recognition of forms of economic duress can be seen after the fusion of law and equity, at least by the early 1860s, and have continued through the present century.[78] Nevertheless, obeisance to freedom of contract and individualism did cause an American reaction to the use of notions of economic duress when there was a threat to breach an existing contract, as exhibited in two Michigan decisions of the early 1880s authored by Justice Cooley.

In the first Michigan case of *Hackley v. Headley* (1881)[79] the defendant would only pay two-thirds the amount due on a contract for logging services, and the plaintiff accepted the lesser amount because he was near insolvency. The Michigan Supreme Court did much the same thing that the English court had done in *Skeate v. Beale* by containing *Astley v. Reynolds* to its facts. The court said that the defendant threatened "nothing which he has not a legal right to perform" and further that there would have been no basis for the duress argument if the plaintiff had not been in financial straits and so thought it "a most dangerous, as well as a most unequal doctrine." Whereas *Hackley v. Headley* involved a threat to not pay money due under a contract, the Michigan case of *Goebel v. Linn*[80] the next year involved an ice company's threat to not deliver ice contracted for delivery in the spring unless a higher price was paid by a brewer. The preceding mild winter had caused a low ice crop, and the buyer, fearful that a large quantity of beer would spoil if he didn't obtain ice soon, agreed to the increase. Justice Cooley cited his opinion in *Hackley v. Headley* as authority for the absence of duress in a "refusal to keep previous engagements." Cooley said that, even if there was duress initially, there was a waiver when the buyer in effect "freely" opted "to abide by" the higher price by continuing to pay it and not contesting until after the warm months of the year had passed.

During the decades following the two Michigan decisions, a minority position developed,[81] but *Hackley* and *Goebel* were not seriously challenged until the 1950s. Arguably the *Goebel*-type case of refusal to deliver property sold presented an easier instance for judicial departure from the strict rule because, if there was an immediate need for a particular good and there was no reasonable alternative, a lack of free choice was more obvious than in the *Hackley*-type case of refusal to pay the amount due when the seller could turn elsewhere for money until he prevailed in a contract breach action. In *Austin Instrument, Inc. v. Loral Corp.* (1971)[82] a subcontractor threatened to withhold specialized goods, unless paid more than the contract price, from a general contractor who needed the goods on time to fulfill a contract with a key governmental customer. The New York Supreme Court concluded that the threat deprived the victim of "its free will". The normal remedy of damages was inadequate; it was reasonable for the victim to feel it had "no choice" and to consider itself in an "emergency duress situation". Unlike *Goebel,* a waiver defense was rejected when the facts showed the victim went along with the modification until the threat had ceased. The decision is a logical extension of the concept of duress of goods in that there was a threat to withhold goods, which the victim had a property interest in by way of the contract right to receive the goods. The erosion of the *Hackley* rule for a threat of refusal to pay money owed has been slower due to the ready availability of money, but there have been some recent inroads, especially where an intentional withholding occurred with little benefit to the threatener and with knowledge of the victim's financial exigency.[83] The evolution of the modern law of economic duress from an assortment of legal and equitable ideas contributed to its lack of coherence. There is still judicial unease about how far the doctrine should stretch past a shockingly wrongful threat to a less grave threat causing an unfair contract modification in circumstances where there is an absence of a reasonable alternative for the victim and disparate bargaining power.[84]

The completion of the analysis of economic duress brings the discussion of judicial concern for the underdog to consideration of the sometimes related notion that parties should contract with each other in good faith. Before analyzing the development of the obligation of good faith, it will be helpful to first define this elusive concept. Good faith is opposed to notions of freedom of contract, individualism and *caveat emptor.* There is no good faith obligation in the arm's length of the market, but there is a modern sense that the arm's length dissolves and quasi-fiduciary duties arise once there is either a contract formed or foreseeable reliance. Once the contract is formed or reasonable expectations are raised, the parties trust that their defenses may be lowered on the faith of an implied agreement to act honestly and faithfully in carrying out their common purpose. Instances of a breach of this implied duty to not interfere with the right of the other party to receive the fruits of the contract would include failing to cooperate for their mutual benefit, preventing the other party from performing, making an overreaching interpretation of the contract or pressuring a modification of the terms. Indeed, the meaning of good faith is often best understood in the context of judicial findings of bad faith.[85] When it is openly articulated by the courts, it is stated as an implied promise, but at other times good faith is hidden behind such technical contract doctrine as rules of construction, offer and acceptance, trade usage and lack of consideration or it is an aspect of supplementary rules like fraud, estoppel and tort. There are several stages of contractual relations where good faith obligations may arise: during contract performance and enforcement and the two emerging areas of recognition of good faith duties during negotiations and at termination. Good faith should be distinguished from the related idea of unconscionability, which is applicable at contract formation.

For centuries the common law courts would not go beyond the express bargain and rigorously applied *caveat emptor*, adequacy, literal dependency and the absolute contracts rule. The duty owed by contracting parties was to refrain from misconduct bordering on criminality, e.g., fraud and duress. Vague abstractions like good faith were adverse to predictability and the security of the transaction. A softening of this harsh common law stance began, albeit unevenly, during the second half of the eighteenth century and then in earnest during the last quarter of the nineteenth century. Good faith notions were discussed earlier primarily in a commercial setting; it is not the intent here to rehash the good faith aspects of the earlier discussed topics of open-ended contracts, frustration and impracticability, substantial performance and compulsory contract provisions. The focus here is on the judicial creation of an independent obligation of good faith to act as a restraint on a contracting party who is in a position to take advantage.

The obligation of good faith has been primarily applied to the performance and enforcement of contracts. In the seventeenth century, Chancery held contracting parties to a higher standard of conduct during performance than at common law; witness the Chancery view in 1679 that specific performance might be denied for improper conduct which would not bar a recovery of damages at common law, e.g., a sharp practice, inadequacy or negligent misrepresentation. Kent and Story acknowledged the higher standard of fairness in equity in the nineteenth century.[86] There were, however, some instances of common law courts requiring a higher standard of conduct by the early 1800s, though that emphasis tapered off by the mid-nineteenth century. Although there would be retrogression in the nineteenth century, Mansfield instituted the process of absorbing equitable standards of good faith into the common law by: the inclusion of mercantile practices of fair dealing, a more just application of dependency rules, protection of good faith purchasers of promissory notes, the suggestion that unusual facts ought to be disclosed, and, at least in spirit, the recognition of moral consideration.[87] In the generation following Mansfield, the common law recognition of an implied warranty of quality would be a signpost on the way to a full fledged obligation of good faith for two reasons: the chief reason was that it opened up what was formerly perceived to be a single obligation supported by the all encompassing doctrine of consideration to the possibility of implying warranties and other contract terms, and, secondly, it was the first real chink in the cold armour of *caveat emptor*.

Mansfield's ideas were not extended during the apogee of individualism of the first three quarters of the nineteenth century. The alarming disparity in wealth during the final quarter of the nineteenth century, however, increased the incidence of one-sided agreements where advantage was taken and prompted the now-fused courts of law and equity to pick up where Mansfield left off. During the ensuing forty or so years, judicial invocation of a duty of good faith became common in the case reports and culminated before 1920 in judicial declarations of an implied duty of good faith and fair dealing in all contracts. The cases of this period can be loosely grouped under the categories of a failure to cooperate in a common purpose, abuse of leverage in forcing a contract modification and bad faith contract enforcement.

In the failure to cooperate cases, judges found an implied duty of good faith when a party's justified expectations were dashed by the other party's selfish actions depriving the victim of the expected contract benefit. A lack of good faith was found when: a builder willfully failed to fully perform in 1909, an insurer refused a reasonable settlement offer resulting in great expense to the insured in 1914, a producer shut down operations in the middle of an output contract in 1918 and a broker was hired but prevented from performing in 1919.[88] In the integrated economy and division of labor of the industrial era, the expectations of the other contracting party's cooperation, and the right to rely on it, were beginning to be protected by the courts.

In discussing the forced contract modification cases, attention is returned to the remanded economic duress case of *Hackley v. Headley* (1881) which ended up before the Michigan Supreme Court a second time in 1883 on an appeal from the remand hearing.[89] The plaintiff argued it was "bad faith" for the defendant to set up unfounded claims to avoid full contract payment for the logging services when it was obvious that the plaintiff needed his money. This time the court overturned the "oppressively" obtained compromise agreement because the defendant had "acted unfairly". Under nineteenth century will theory, the defendant's conduct had not been deemed egregious enough to apply economic duress in the first appeal, but the dishonesty was sufficient for a finding of bad faith. In duress, courts look to the consent of the victim, but, under the stricter standard of good faith, they look at the improper conduct of the party acting in bad faith. Eight years later the Missouri Supreme Court heard a case involving an architect, who abused the advantage he had because of the defendant landowner's timetable, by refusing to proceed without a price increase. The court found that the architect "took advantage of [defendant's] necessities, and extorted the promise" and that "to permit plaintiff to recover under such circumstances would be to offer a premium upon bad faith".[90]

A third grouping of good faith cases involved lack of good faith in contract enforcement. In an 1873 estoppel case, where there was reliance on a mortgagee's promise to not foreclose, the court said, "There is no rule more necessary to enforce good faith than that which compels a person to abstain from enforcing claims which he has induced others to suppose he would not rely on." In a similar vein, to demand full performance in cases of frustration or impracticability suggested a lack of good faith and fair dealing. Likewise a knowing failure to mitigate damages was found to violate good faith.[91]

These various case-specific findings of an implied obligation of good faith set the foundation for a declaration that there was a general duty of good faith in all contracts. New York was a leader in stating the general proposition by around 1915. In that year the New York Supreme Court heard the case of *Simon v. Etgen,* wherein a debtor had delayed for eight years in not carrying out his promise to sell certain property in order to generate funds to pay off the debt. Although there was no time deadline set in the contract, the court looked past the letter of the contract and found a presumed intent in the inner logic of the contract that the discretion in deciding when to sell would be exercised in good faith. The court went past the specifics of the case and declared: "Every contract implies good faith and fair dealing between the parties to it."[92]

The New York position set the stage for the drafters of the Uniform Commercial Code to include a general duty of good faith in the performance or enforcement of all sales contracts. What was the meaning of good faith given by the drafters? The 1949 draft of the U.C.C. defined good faith as "honesty in fact in the conduct or transaction concerned" and for merchants the observance of "reasonable commercial standards".[93] Llewellyn's definition was influenced by traditional common law good faith purchase notions, particularly those concerning negotiable instruments. In the good faith purchase context, honesty in fact for non-merchants was a subjective standard of personal ignorance of any defense; this mirrored Williston's diluted good faith definition, making negligence irrelevant, which he included in the uniform statutes he drafted at the turn of the century. There was an objective standard, however, for merchants under the requirement of observance of reasonable commercial standards, which entailed a duty of care to refrain from negligent failure to ascertain third party rights. The final draft of the Uniform Commercial Code in 1952 narrowed the merchant's obligation from the more open "reasonable commercial standards" to the more specific "reasonable commercial standards of fair dealing".[94]

Now attention is turned to the obligation of good faith during the negotiation and bargaining phase, a process which may or may not result in contract formation. The traditional rule is that bargainers who are at arm's length owe no duty of disclosure and may terminate negotiations arbitrarily, but there is a modern tendency in support of bargainers' duties to act in good faith once reasonable expectations are raised, even if a contract doesn't come into being.[95] Short of contract formation, a negotiating party might cause reasonable reliance or might try to obtain some advantage, as to tie up a party to keep him from competing elsewhere, and then arbitrarily withdraw claiming the freedom to break off negotiations at any time. In such a case, modern notions of good faith call into question traditional doctrines of offer and acceptance, consideration, *caveat emptor* and freedom of contract. The related modern developments for discussion hereafter are duties of disclosure, compulsory provisions and the effect of reliance estoppel ideas; in some aspects, the discussion following is as much about tendencies in the law as about legal history.

Regarding the duty of disclosure, absent obligations based on reasonable expectations or status, there is still vitality in the traditional denial of a good faith duty of disclosure. The traditional and modern viewpoints were discussed in *Laidlaw v. Organ* (U.S. 1817), where Marshall, C.J. held the buyer had no duty to disclose information which he had special access to about a peace treaty. However, the seller's attorney "proposed" a duty of disclosure "not [as] a romantic, but a practical and legal rule of equality and good faith." In support, the seller's attorney cited the civilian Pothier's view that there was a good faith obligation of disclosure because justice consisted of equality which was lacking when one party had better knowledge. Pothier added that under good faith a seller should also disclose defects that don't fall under implied warranty.[96] Under *caveat emptor* there was no good faith obligation to disclose defects nor was there an obligation to correct mistaken impressions; there was no liability unless there was active concealment. Nevertheless, underlying notions of good faith made inroads in this market ethic late in the nineteenth century due to the prevalence of mass produced contracts made with distant strangers. The enforcement of a stricter implied warranty of quality and insurance company disclosure obligations are examples already discussed. Failure to disclose a material fact became inconsistent with honest dealing when it was calculated to induce a false impression, and knowledge of the other party's mistake regarding a basic assumption required disclosure. More recently good faith disclosures of liability disclaimers were required over a duty to read fine print standardized contracts.[97]

It is perhaps appropriate to return to compulsory contracts to survey the imposition of a duty of good faith bargaining on corporations involved in an activity within the public interest. A new model of good faith consent developed here based on status and relational duties. Public utilities have a duty to bargain in good faith with all requesting service, and employers and unions are compelled to bargain in good faith with each other. Insurers have a good faith obligation in processing applications, which is implemented under a disguised negligence theory, in order to protect expectations and reliance caused by unreasonable delay.[98]

The last topic under good faith bargaining at the negotiation level is the use of estoppel and reliance in enforcing the obligation. Ideas under estoppel and tort crop up in decisions where in effect good faith duties are being enforced. Reliance damages may be owed for mistakes in offers caused by an offeror's negligence. Fault may be presumed in carelessly making statements that could foreseeably be relied on. Equitable estoppel may bar an insurance company from denying the fact of a premium payment, which may constitute an offer, if the insurer's receipt acknowledged payment. Promissory estoppel may arguably be portrayed as the enforcement of a good faith obligation to comply with a promise inducing foreseeable injurious reliance. Promissory estoppel has been applied to protect reliance upon offers stated to be irrevocable but lacking consideration or, more recently, to achieve compliance with the U.C.C. firm offer rule.[99] But can promissory estoppel enforce good faith negotiation duties when a promise does not qualify as an offer, as because of indefiniteness? It has been argued that a franchise negotiation case like *Hoffman. v. Red Owl Stores* (1965) points in that direction. Promissory estoppel was employed there to enforce good faith bargaining to overcome the technical doctrines of offer and acceptance and consideration. It is still an open question whether this idea is grounded in contract law or in an independent tort theory of withdrawing from negotiations after inducing reliance.[100] Alternative contract theories include either a notion of breach of an implied promise to negotiate in good faith or an abrogation of the will theory of offer and acceptance in favor of realization of reasonable expectations when there is reliance.

As a postscript to the discussion of an emerging duty of good faith bargaining, mention should be made of *Heyer Products Co. v. United States* (1956) where the U.S. Army awarded a contract to a higher bidder than the plaintiff, allegedly in retaliation for the plaintiff's testimony adverse to the Army before a Senate panel. The court held that the government had an implied duty to invite and consider bids "honestly" and in "good faith". There was no reliance in *Heyer* and yet there was liability; however, *Heyer* has not been extended and probably must be read in the context of government bids where bidders usually can't revoke.[101]

In summary, judicial recognition of a good faith duty to bargain has come a long way over the last century. Despite skeptics,[102] good faith bargaining has been required in instances of disclosure obligations and in the realm of contracts with a public interest, as public utilities, insurance, collective bargaining and government bids, and in cases of the reliance common during franchise negotiations. But how far good faith bargaining will stretch past that is for later legal historians to analyze.

Lastly, after having covered good faith duties in performance and in bargaining, a brief look will be given to an emerging obligation of good faith termination in franchise and employment relationships. The American adoption of the employment-at-will doctrine in the last quarter of the nineteenth century was a rejection of the English tradition of annual employment renewal on the grounds that the English rule failed both to comply with the definiteness requirement and to give mutuality to employers since employees could quit at any time. The trend toward recognition of good faith termination began by the 1930s in franchise relationships, an industrial hybrid of employment contracts. Courts began to recognize the equitable right of a franchisee to recoup his start-up investment before a termination would be permitted, and in a 1954 decision, reminiscent of the traditional English rule, a court said that a reasonable time was one year and that a reasonable notice should also be given. Because of the uneven application of this notion nationally, there has been state and federal legislation requiring forms of good faith termination on behalf of some franchisees.[103] In regard to employment-at-will, a few courts have followed the lead in franchise cases and in cases of good faith under insurance contracts in finding an implied covenant of good faith and that a termination "motivated by bad faith or malice or based on retaliation" was a breach of the employment contract.[104] The more widespread recognition of a good faith duty in franchises than in employment contracts calls to mind the parallel of the more flexible equity accorded independent contractors than that afforded employees in the development of the doctrine of substantial performance in the early nineteenth century.

In conclusion, the idea of an obligation of good faith in contractual relations, which began its slow accretion from equity into the common law in the eighteenth century, has seen its flowering in the twentieth century. In contrast to England, a strong majority of American jurisdictions today recognize that every contract imposes upon each party a duty of good faith and fair dealing in its performance and enforcement,[105] and a majority recognize a duty to bargain in good faith within the limits discussed above. From a macro level, it is difficult to say how much good faith duties have filtered into the crannies of the common law by the second half of the twentieth century; there are indications, though, that equity's refusal to grant a decree, when there was bad faith, has so influenced common law thinking that most judges will not grant money damages today if bad faith precludes specific performance.[106]

Likewise, the Uniform Commercial Code makes no distinction between good faith duties at law or equity.

The remaining instances of modern judicial concern for fair treatment of the economic underdog for discussion here relate to hardship relief specifically designed for consumers. Classical contract abstraction presumed sophisticated contractors on an equal footing, but this equality was absent in mass distribution on a standardized basis to consumers. Consumers were ill-informed about the market and new technology; yet they were forced into the market on a take it or leave it basis to obtain living essentials formerly often self-produced. The entrepreneur had the freedom to dictate terms in the standardized contract, and consumers seldom had a chance to dicker over the often incomprehensible prescribed terms which they adhered to and seldom even read. Merchants had expectations based on understood trade usage incorporated in their contracts and in contract doctrine itself, but consumer expectations were tied to the everyday economic meaning of a transaction, which was not necessarily in conformity with formal doctrine. Nevertheless, under the objective bargain theory, it was irrelevant to contract formation whether a party had actual intent or understanding of the contract terms.

By the late nineteenth century, there was a societal, and slowly a judicial, backlash against the inevitable harsh results for individuals lacking information and bargaining power. The objective concurrence of intention was found to not control in hardship cases as public policy dictated a breakdown in abstraction by making the status of contractors a relevant consideration. Duties were recognized according to the entrepreneur's "calling" in order to not subvert legitimate expectations of consumers.[107] Earlier, *caveat emptor* and the presumption of equality left no room for analysis of the quality of the bargaining process, absent such extremes as fraud or duress; however, the issue of meaningful consumer consent to standardized contracts became a relevant concern when there were oppressive terms and gross inequality.

Middle class American pressure groups formed during the decades after the Civil War to protect the ultimate consumer, who was a laborer, farmer or small merchant and a voter. The early consumer legislation concentrated on basic concerns for pure food and drugs and safety. Corporate sellers objected that this intrusion violated traditional law, but in fact public regulation of sales was not the novelty that formalists claimed since municipal regulation of quality and common callings had been extensive prior to the nineteenth century in England and in colonial America. The welfare state diluted *caveat emptor* in protecting consumer expectations and reliance on fair dealing. There was a pragmatic preference for legislative and administrative solutions because the judicial process was too cumbersome and less sympathetic to consumers. The

Statute of Frauds and the contemporaneous 1906 Uniform Sales Act were insignificant when compared with this unprecedented legislative intrusion on the common law of contracts, a process that still goes on unabated. The reforms meant a diminution in the applicability of common law doctrine to consumer transactions. Legislatures counteracted the imbalance between corporate sellers and the consuming public by improving the quality of the bargaining process through the techniques of mandated disclosure and control of both contract terms and unfair trade practices. There was a preference for disclosure over control of terms due to the continuing pull of market ideas and self reliance.[108]

As a means of comparison, what was happening in England in regard to consumer relief? In 1977 Parliament passed an expansive consumer contract act which is more extensive in protecting consumers than the consumer legislation found in most American jurisdictions. This is explained in part because English judges have been less solicitous of consumers than American courts, as evidenced by the English judicial resistance to the doctrines of good faith, unconscionability and strict liability. The English judiciary has not developed a result-oriented mode of analysis based on fairness like that practised by American legal realists. Instead it has been left to Parliament to make reforms. One reason given for the English scheme of judges being responsible for applying formal rules and Parliament focussing on policy and reform is the Benthamite legacy of a positivist preference for legislative over judge-made law.[109]

On the American judicial front, the origins of protection for the consumer are in equity's doctrines of constructive fraud and unconscionability and in common law implied warranties of quality and public policy. In cases of hardship, twentieth century judges have granted relief on the basis of public policy, tort notions, implied term fictions, interpretation of contracts of adhesion against the drafter and the refusal to mechanically enforce fine print exculpatory clauses. Regarding the fine print in consumer contracts, there are suggestions in the caselaw that the objective duty to read standardized contracts is being modified in hardship cases and that strict enforcement of the parole evidence rule discriminates against the economic underdog.[110] The innovative judicial use of public policy and ideas from equity and tort, as a means of departure from traditional principles favoring producers and sellers, are perhaps most dramatically exhibited by the doctrines of unconscionability and strict liability, a discussion of which follows.

Equity introduced the doctrine of unconscionability two centuries before the Uniform Commercial Code made the doctrine available for overt use at-law. There were harbingers of this new doctrine by at least the fifteenth century when Chancery entertained petitions for relief by weak parties dominated by a powerful man of the region, and, by at least the seventeenth century, there was consistent equitable relief from the penalty on a conditioned bond. The chancellor had the discretion to refuse to grant equitable relief when there was bad faith, undue advantage and when inadequacy shocked the conscience. Cancellations were given for undue advantage, as when a contract was usurious, and a mortgagor's equity of redemption was protected despite contrary contract language.[111] One fertile line of decisions for the development of unconscionability involved sales of inheritance expectancies by improvident young heirs even though there was an absence of duress. The fountainhead case was the oft-cited *Earl of Chesterfield v. Janssen* (1750)[112] wherein there was a suit to enforce a 20,000 pound bond given by an expectant heir to secure a promise to pay the lender 10,000 pounds upon the death of his grandmother in exchange for an immediate 5,000 pound loan at execution of the bond. The heir's estate prayed for relief on the bond past the 5,000 pound loan. Chancellor Hardwicke was cognizant of the importance of the contested issues since he requested that two common law chief justices and the master of the rolls join in the deliberations. Hardwicke stated that Chancery could "relieve against every species of fraud" including, in expectant heir agreements, "an appearance of fraud... from the intrinsic unconscionableness of the bargain". Hardwicke generalized that relief could be granted from "unequitable and unconscientious bargains" which "no man in his senses and not under delusion would make on the one hand, and as no honest and fair man would accept on the other." He added that a contract could be "presumed from the circumstances and conditions of the parties contracting" to be "contrary to conscience", despite the strict proof required at common law, "to prevent taking surreptitious advantage of the weakness or necessity" or "ignorance" of a party. Hardwicke's statements were dicta, however, because he found in favor of the lender, though he did follow the practice of giving relief from the penalty on the bond, resulting in 10,000 pounds being collectible.

Chancery's jurisdiction for relief from "fraud" because of unconscionability, as summarized by Hardwicke, was extended from sales of heirship expectancies in the late eighteenth century and on into the nineteenth century to non-heirship cases when there was an inadequacy coupled with a sharp practice directed against parties weakened by infirmity, old age, ignorance, need or naivete, who were considered "at least in as favorable a light as a young heir."[113] Equity did what was anathema to the common law in looking to subject matter, parties' economic standing and fairness. By the 1830s Kent and Story declared that "sharp" practices and "hard and unconscionable bargains," sometimes ambiguously characterized as "constructive frauds", would be aided by chancery,[114] making cancellation a possibility.

In the early nineteenth century the question arose whether equity could withhold relief for inadequacy of consideration alone. In 1804 the

English Chancellor Eldon denied that inadequacy was a ground for refusing specific performance but made an exception when "the inadequacy of price is such as shocks the conscience, and amounts in itself to conclusive and decisive evidence of fraud." Story's support furthered this view so that Eldon's dictum was widely invoked by the mid-nineteenth century, but shocking inadequacy alone did not appear to be the sole ground for relief in the cases since oppression or a sharp practice was usually present.[115] Nevertheless, it did expand the spectrum of cases short of actual fraud qualifying for relief and aided in opening juridical thought to further extensions.

As has been discussed, the open use of unconscionability notions was almost entirely restricted to equity until the twentieth century. There was some protection against undue advantage built into the common law, but, with a few exceptions, there was a resistance to this amorphous equitable doctrine. Having said that, it should be pointed out that since the sixteenth century the common law had shown at least a modicum of concern at the contract formation level for a party failing to receive at least some value by the bargain idea in consideration, by the past consideration rule, by *Pinnel's* compromise rule, and by protection from fraud, duress and later undue influence. The common law had followed equity's lead in providing relief against contract penalties and in requiring a fair exchange and disclosure when fiduciaries made contracts with beneficiaries. The Statute of Frauds and the parole evidence rule performed a role similar to unconscionability in protecting against fraud without requiring actual proof of it. And there is some evidence that seventeenth century colonial American Assumpsit decisions restricted parties in a superior position to an equivalent exchange when dealing with the poor or the ignorant.[116]

There was a smattering of common law decisions, however, overtly invoking unconscionability notions. In *James v. Morgan* (1675)[117] the court gave relief to a hapless horse buyer, who did not understand the seller's mathematical trick making the price astronomical, by directing the verdict at the market value of the horse. Indeed, in *Earl of Chesterfield v. Janssen* Chancellor Hardwicke cited *James v. Morgan* for the proposition that the common law would give relief against unconscionability. In a case of a mistake in a form contract making the price exorbitant in *U.S. v. Hume* (1889),[118] the trial court cited *James v. Morgan* as authority for the common law use of unconscionability, without the aid of equity, to adjust a contract to a reasonable price. The dictum in the United States Supreme Court opinion in *Hume* likewise cited *James v. Morgan* and *Earl of Chesterfield v. Janssen* with approval. Taken together, the decisions in *James* and *Hume* suggested that a gross misunderstanding or mistake regarding the price was a case for using unconscionability at common law. The foregoing cases were exceptional, however, since most hardship relief given at-law before the twentieth century was provided by manipulation of traditional doctrine.

During the first half of the twentieth century, common law decisions on hardship facts continued to reflect the proclivity of judges to operate within the confines of the system they were trained in. There was a rash of cases policing contracts from the 1920s through the 1950s, which were in-effect unconscionability cases, but were covertly rationalized under traditional doctrine: by flexible use of fraud, duress and undue influence; by inventive contract construction; by manipulation of offer and acceptance; and by public policy.[119] The covert manipulation of doctrine in the interest of fairness could be stymied, however, by the clever drafter. The exclusion of personal injury liability clauses introduced by railroads and enforced in the courts by the mid-nineteenth century presents an example. As late as 1958, in a case of an injured tenant suing a landlord for negligence, the Illinois Supreme Court refused to employ artful construction in the face of an unambiguous exculpatory clause. Similar cases in the sales area were forceful examples for Llewellyn to use in opposing formalistic preference for manipulation of doctrine; Llewellyn argued instead for legislative creation of an overt tool for common law judges to use when oppressive terms were dictated in standardized contracts.[120]

U.C.C. Reporter Llewellyn had a concern about the lack of assent to boiler plate clauses and saw the consumer assenting only to a few dickered terms in a standardized contract. His first published draft of a proposed unconscionability section in 1941 suggested that only terms lacking particularized bargaining were subject to judicial intervention. The first several drafts prior to 1948 limited the applicability of unconscionability to standardized contracts, and, although it was not ultimately so limited, it is safe to say that the impetus for the Code's unconscionability doctrine came from the impact of the mass standardized transaction.[121] Equity's unconscionability doctrine had been an individualized tool created before the upsurge of standardized contracts; equity's approach was transferred to the common law by the Code drafters with a resulting individualization of unfair standardized transactions.[122] Furthermore, following equity practices, the Code provided no right to damages and the judge, not the jury, made the determination.

The Official Comments to the final 1952 version of Section 2–302 provided a vague definition of unconscionability as clauses "so one-sided as to be unconscionable under the circumstances existing at the time of the making of the contract.... The principle is one of prevention of oppression and unfair surprise." The Comments included a late addition of a 1948 case refusing specific performance because of unconscionability, and it also included 10 common law actions from the 1920s and 1930s, 3 of which were English, whose "results" "illustrated" the "underlying basis of this section". None of the 10 cases used unconscionability logic, nor was there emphasis on the weakness of one party or the egregiousness of the other. Almost all of the cases involved boiler plate limitations on the drafters' liability through disclaimers of warranties and other limitations on the right to sue, and all of the cases involved commercial forms, with more than half of the transactions being between merchants. Formalists and business planners opposed the uncertainty of such a vague discretionary doctrine, defined in terms of itself. Supporters of the vague standard argued that its flexibility counteracted the inherent tendency of common law doctrine to become logically closed and that it encouraged common law judges to perform an interstitial role of providing a safety net for consumers falling through the cracks left between specific consumer statutes.[123] Judicial analogies to U.C.C. Section 2–302 in non-sales cases became so common that in 1981 the Restatement Second of Contracts stated that the unconscionability doctrine was applicable to all contracts.[124]

A controversy since 1952 has been whether the Code's unconscionability rule applies only to a lack of consent or whether it can also apply to significant inadequacy of consideration alone. Many courts have thus far been more reluctant to find unconscionability based on unfairness of price alone than when there is an absence of consent to unfair clauses like waiver of defense or "add-ons". Legal history sheds some light on the matter. Consideration and its attendant adequacy rule became an integral test at Assumpsit's genesis and defeated all challengers for four centuries. Although formation of a contract requires both consideration and consent, the more entrenched doctrine of consideration is less vulnerable than the johnny-come-lately will theory's concurrence of intention, which was grafted onto the formation process only in the nineteenth century. Those cases that do find unconscionability on the sole ground of gross inadequacy seem descendants of equity's exception for inadequacy shocking to the conscience or perhaps its a loose adoption of the formerly shunned *laesio enormis* theory. The drafters of the Restatement Second are of the view that inadequacy alone does not invalidate a contract, but gross inadequacy would be a factor in corroborating a defect in the bargaining process.[125]

The second instance for discussion of judicial use of public policy in response to consumer needs is the dramatic innovation of strict liability. The emergence of this new doctrine was the culmination of a century-long evolution of the liability of producers and middlemen, who were operating in modern channels of distribution of mass produced goods, for injuries caused by defective products to third parties they did not contract with. The injection of middlemen in the nineteenth century ended face-to-face transactions between producer and buyer and raised privity problems for those suing in warranty; this obstruction left the possibility of bringing an action under the new independent tort of negligence for the plaintiff's injuries caused by a defective product, but negligence was fenced in almost immediately during the second quarter of the nineteenth century. The process of limiting the negligence liability of sellers can be traced back to *Winterbottom v. Wright* (1842).[126] In that case the plaintiff was a coachman permanently disabled by a latent defect in a mail-coach sold by the defendant to the postmaster. The defendant had promised the postmaster to keep the coach in safe condition during its operation, and the plaintiff's complaint alleged that the defendant negligently failed to perform his duty to keep the coach safe. Chief Baron Abinger, a supporter of limiting entrepreneurial liability, said "the action is brought simply because" of the contract but there was "no privity of contract between these parties." He added that the court must hold for the defendant or "every passenger, or even any person passing along the road who was injured by the upsetting of the coach, might bring a similar action."

Actually, the *Winterbottom v. Wright* decision only held that the plaintiff could not bring an action on the promise from the defendant to the postmaster to maintain the coach in a safe condition, but the decision and dictum were misconstrued to mean that there could be no negligence action against the defendant for performing a sales contract badly unless the plaintiff was in privity with the defendant.[127] So, privity, a contract notion applied for several centuries on account of a concern about fomenting groundless contract actions, was manipulated to apply to tort injuries suffered because of contract misfeasance. This instrumental privity of contract fallacy effectively insulated emerging industries from liability to consumers and others who were injured but were not in privity. By the mid nineteenth century, instead of the medieval duty owed to the community to produce quality goods, a producer owed a duty of care only to the immediate buyer he had contracted with.

The subsidization of entrepreneurial activity through limitations on recovery for injuries caused by defectively manufactured goods began to undergo a reevaluation by the turn of the century on the grounds of social justice and in reaction against the formerly perceived need to protect emerging industries in light of the vast wealth accumulated by now well established enterprises. The privity requirement was dropped for plaintiffs injured on railroad property and for the sale of inherently dangerous products, e.g., selling a gun or a ladder known to be unsafe or selling a drug but negligently delivering poison. On the legislative side, no-fault liability was included in workers compensation acts, and a strengthened implied warranty of quality was incorporated in the Uniform Sales Act of 1906. Then, on the heels of the Federal Food and

Drug Act of 1906, there was the first judicial imposition of strict liability without privity in 1913 for cases of sales of impure food and drink.[128] Three years later the harsh caselaw interpretation of *Winterbottom v. Wright* was upset by Cardozo in *MacPherson v. Buick Motor Co.* (1916).[129]

Cardozo ruled that, when a manufacturer placed an automobile in the market, it assumed an obligation, imposed in law rather than in contract, to safeguard the ultimate consumer from injury. He said, "The needs of life in a developing civilization" cannot be answered by the incidental fact of the existence of a sales contract; that fact did not negate the seller's responsibility to subsequent buyers when it was foreseeable they would be affected by negligent manufacture. Cardozo added a swipe at *Winterbottom v. Wright:* "Precedents drawn from the days of travel by stagecoach do not fit the conditions of travel to-day."

In cases of sales of defective products causing injury, tort law was beginning to supplant contract law. Tort's residual capacity to cover new wrongs has been employed since the Middle Ages to provide relief for matters not yet covered under contract law. The trespassory action on the case was used by 1400 to cover misfeasance in contract performance, e.g., action allowed against a carpenter building badly. More directly here, the action on the case for deceit was the action for a false warranty in sales of goods from the fourteenth to eighteenth centuries. Then Mansfield turned express warranty into a contract action, and the implied contract term of a warranty of quality followed early in the next century. Warranty thus had an ambiguous nature due to its tort and contract origins; and, because warranty had never fully lost its tort flavor, it was possible to recross the fine line between its tort and contract character by urging recognition of an obligation imposed by law.[130] Consistent with the bimodal nature of warranty, the modern implied warranty of quality case of *Henningsen v. Bloomfield Motors* (1960)[131] would indirectly contribute to tort eclipsing contract in this area.

The *Henningsen v. Bloomfield Motors* decision contributed several important ideas to the progressive recognition of manufacturers' social obligations to consumers irregardless of the impediments of contract doctrine. Due to the "demands of social justice," the New Jersey Supreme Court did not hold consumers to the traditional duty to read standardized fine print warranty disclaimers nor did the court require buyers and users to show privity since both rules were developed during an era of face-to-face dealings between equals prior to the onset of modern marketing and technology. This line of thought was a devastating blow to the privity rule already weakened in contract law over the prior century as a result of assignment, third party beneficiary and tort actions for contract misfeasance. Since breach of warranty is a form of no-fault liability, this abandonment of privity in implied warranty actions was a turning point for strict liability in non-food cases.[132]

The idea of strict tort liability without privity for food and drink was extended to external bodily use in cases of detergents, soap and hair dye by the early 1950s, and then all sales were opened up to the possibility of strict liability when defective construction materials were covered in 1958.[133] The no-fault feature drew on several sources: one, defective manufacture was analogous to an ultrahazardous activity, like dynamiting under absolute liability; two, workers compensation created social duties attendant to production irrespective of fault; three, strict liability for food and drink; and, four, liability for breach of the implied warranty of merchantability was not conditioned on negligence. Traynor lent his stature and persuasive analysis to this new social remedy in *Greenman v. Yuba Power Products* (1963).[134] He reasoned: "The remedies of injured consumers ought not to be made to depend upon the intricacies of the law of sales." Warranties were developed to meet the needs of commercial transactions, but in consumer transactions the rules ought to provide, as a matter of public policy, that manufacturers placing products on the market bear the costs to injured consumers "powerless to protect themselves." This new strict liability in tort theory, independent of warranty and yet no-fault like warranty, caught on rapidly during the next decade and spread to cases of property damage[135] and in some jurisdictions to economic loss.

The emergence of strict liability in tort is a continuation of the process of branches of contract law being pushed out into independent categories when traditional contract doctrine is found incapable of accommodating modern economic and social realities. Manufacturers are treated like a "common calling," as once producers were regulated by municipalities during the Middle Ages; seller's liability had come full circle back to a societal obligation to provide quality goods. There was a borrowing of the ideas of welfare economy in concluding that losses caused by defective products are a social, and not just a private cost.[136] Legislatures had created similar protection for workers under workers compensation, but consumers were without the effective lobby that labor enjoyed, and so a solution was belatedly fashioned by activist judges.

Modern Characteristics and Tendencies

Classical contract doctrine was developed for cases of discrete, one-shot transactions, but it was found a poor fit for complex, long-term contracts, some of which were standardized and adhesive. These formal principles in place at the turn of the twentieth century gave no consideration to undue advantage taken of a weaker party nor to the business realities of a particular case. Llewellyn, a leader of the Legal Realism movement, pointed out the contrast between formal doctrine and the realities of everyday life and argued for adjustments to human conditions in order to achieve just results. In urging changes in the law as the context of society's values change, he promoted grouping of cases and facts into narrower categories than under the classical rules; this was a marked departure from static Legal Formalism's first principles and its refusal to look at the particular realities behind the rule applied to a case.[137] As judges noted the adverse effects of industrialization and then of the Great Depression, Realism took hold. Jumping forward in time, since the 1960s there have appeared two new schools of legal analysis which have followed Legal Realism's lead in integrating the social sciences with law. Critical Legal Studies is closer to Legal Realism in its interest in just results, but it also can have a neo-Marxist flair for "demystifying" the system to show its class bias; they see doctrine as evidence of ideology and recommend reform on the basis of altruism.[138] Law and Economics tries to solve the Realist's problem of separating right from wrong by looking back to the economic formula of the market for a solution; they fit historical doctrine into the rules of market efficiency and recommend modification when doctrine fails to fit the market construct.[139]

The Realist concern about particular facts in a case meant a diminution of the importance of classical doctrine. Generalist judges, who had formerly hidden behind abstract formal principles, were not as well equipped as legislative commissions in studying overall social and economic problems and in making hard public policy choices. Nineteenth century judges, often businessmen themselves, had a thorough personal knowledge of market transactions, but their twentieth century counterparts did not have the first-hand knowledge about the complex industrial environment to make confident policy decisions. As an example, judicial vacillation in dealing with the policy problems in unfair, but well drafted, standardized contracts of adhesion brought legislative intrusion.[140] There was a trend toward an administrative rather than a judicial process for providing public rather than private relief for the underdog. In the same vein, alternative grievance procedures, like arbitration and corporate procedures, were coming into favor. Courts had lost their position of primary arbiter of market procedures to legislative and administrative functions and had to work out their new role in a policy-charged legal environment. The judicial absorption of legislative policy has resulted in policy invading the subject matter of contracts to such an extent that there is the view that to a significant degree the law of contract has been relegated to the residue of transactions left unregulated by the legislature,[141] and, as to the residue, Traynor wrote that when it is necessary for courts to revise old rules or formulate new ones, "policy may be an appropriate and even a basic consideration."[142]

One important instance of the attention given to the particular facts of a case in order to achieve a just result was the relevancy afforded the status of contracting parties. There are a set of expectations about behavior based on role when there is a division of labor in an integrated economy, but expectations can be subverted when a dominant party forces an exclusion of his social obligations. In order to curtail this abuse, legislatures, and later courts, imposed duties based on the relation of the superior to the inferior party; this contributed to a decline of the stated will of the parties and an increase of emphasis on the status of the parties. Superior parties were treated like common callings, as compulsory duties were imposed on insurers to insureds, utilities to customers, employers to employees, franchisors to franchisees, manufacturers to consumers and lenders to borrowers. Status was the *sine qua non* of feudal relations, and the same was true of standardized contracts, whether drafted by a seller or a legislature. In feudalism there is a denial of the distinction between public and private law, and in the welfare state there is regulation of private transactions according to one's position in the social system. In this century there has been more of a standardizing of relations than a return to feudal status.[143] The end result is a decline in the applicability of the common law of contract, especially for the non-merchant, as it is replaced by statutes on antitrust, insurance, employment, consumers, etc.

All of this legislative intrusion into market transactions by the end of the Great Depression prompted the question of whether a unified law of contract could continue after the creation of a multiple system of specialized contracts.[144] Realists were not fazed by the fact that many modern contracts, such as labor and insurance contracts, differed greatly from the classical sales contract paradigm since they did not see contract law as a single set of first principles but as a number of particularized groupings brought together under the head of contract. It has been suggested that, though many modern commercial contracts are unique, there are sufficient commonalities to say there is a "family of relationships" constituting a modern law of contract. This approach suggests that there is a kinship of characteristics between modern contracts in their tendencies toward being: complex, specialized, long term, open-ended, standardized, adhesive, status-based, relational, behavioral and not uncommonly for multiple parties. Thus, instead of viewing the law of contract as a body of unified first principles, it could be seen as a "comparative law of contractual transactions" so that rules reduced in one area can be borrowed if suitable to another area's economic and social conditions.[145] A close analysis shows that modern contracts have a variety of shared characteristics and that there are some broad common principles running through them, though there is by no means the universality of doctrine to permit a restatement fully integrating modern specialized contracts with the traditional sales contract model. Despite the efforts of the drafters of the Restatement Second of Contracts, modern society is too complex to design all encompassing general rules, as Langdell once did, applicable to all aspects of modern contractual transactions. The complexity of modern contract law mirrors the complexity of modern society. There are important commonalities holding the diversity of contractual transactions together, however, and those include that each agreement plans for an uncertain future and that each is potentially enforceable in court.

The relationship between contracts exhibiting modern characteristics and traditional general rules is still in the process of being defined. The mechanical application of general principles to specialized contracts can cause injustices; however, modern courts of law and equity have at their disposal a broad range of ideas, which includes traditional rules, so long as policy and the result are kept in mind. Corbin wrote that contract law rules "are merely tentative 'working rules'" that are flexible enough to absorb the usage and policy of a complex society.[146] The incorporation of usage can aid in responding to the criticism that judicial decisions are too often out-of-step with the realities of modern life; but, notwithstanding the views of Mansfield, Cardozo and Corbin that commercial law should conform to business practices, field studies in 1957 and 1963 have shown inconsistencies between the behavior of commercial interests and contract doctrine.[147]

While common law contract doctrine should not be applied mechanically to either modern contractual behavior or to specialized modern contracts, that does not mean that it has no place in modern business planning or judicial reasoning. General contract principles apply naturally to those discrete transactions traditionally covered as well as to any unregulated residue of transactions. Past that, it may be true that a restatement cannot integrate all modern contract characteristics; nevertheless, the principles in the Restatement Second can be drawn on where useful in fulfilling the policy of a particular field. Common law contract doctrine can be viewed as a starting point for the parties' development of an agreement and for a court's analysis of a problem; it can be a common point of reference, which is based on tested foundations, to draw ideas from. Traditional principles are likewise appropriate for filling gaps in complex contracts, when consistent with policy and the sense of the transaction, and they can be useful in new contexts created by innovations in technology or business techniques. Contract doctrine bestows both a legitimacy on principles chosen and a greater confidence in their application by parties and courts.[148] Of course, if the democratic majority does not approve of these uses or of the courts' handling thereof, legislation may intrude. Similarly parties may, subject to policy considerations, modify doctrine or legislation passed in their agreements, when legislation reserves the parties' freedom to "otherwise provide".[149]

The common law of contracts reflects a set of values that continue to enjoy wide acceptance, e.g., reciprocity of bargain, self reliance, consent and the capability of planning for the future. Legislation is more effective at abolishing doctrine and making order of the past than it is in covering the future. Private entrepreneurial autonomy and planning still have strong support in this era of governmental intervention.[150] Indeed, in a broader sense, there is a current drift toward a lack of faith in governmental controls. Notwithstanding the triple-barrelled encroachment of legislative policy, equitable ideas and new forms of civil liability based on benefit, reliance and tort, the consensual freedom of contracting parties to make choices is still very much a part of Anglo-American law.

Conclusion

The rise of the corporate state precipitated a drastic reappraisal of the notion of freedom of contract and of the roles of courts and legislatures in administering market exchanges. Inside the corporation, corporate vertical integration of the steps in production erased arm's length bargaining between these formerly separated and independent units, and the uncertainties of judicial resolution of disputes were replaced with corporate procedures. In corporate dealings with outsiders, who were in weaker positions, the unfair results produced by the replacement of equality of bargaining with standardized transactions dictated by these industrial titans presented courts and legislatures with the foremost market problem of the past century. These corporations' insistence on freedom to inflict weaker parties with unfair bargains would ultimately spell the demise of freedom of contract, but the curtailment of the abuses of that right did not occur until society acted to usurp the authority of common law judges, who were seemingly unwilling or incapable of fashioning broad equitable solutions. The welfare state would significantly supplant judicial obeisance to private consent with the democratic majority's notions of fairness in dealing with market problems.

Besides the fact that courts were not temperamentally disposed to disturb vested commercial interests, they were mired within the confines of the formalistic common law construct. In the 300 years that common law courts had exercised primary authority over economic exchanges prior to the industrial revolution, there had never before been the ineluctable need for revolutionary changes in the common law. The tradition-bound common law system was simply not structured to fashion comprehensive reforms to accommodate cataclysmic change. Occasionally a Coke or a Mansfield caused abrupt departures but they were always the exception, and even a Mansfield could not have designed the solutions that legislators would formulate in concert with social scientists in responding to the needs of a society in crisis.

In the wake of legislative reform, twentieth century courts began, on a piecemeal basis, to act like the courts of law and equity they had officially been since the third quarter of the nineteenth century. There has been a resultant case by case accretion of modern decisions inching toward limited reform by innovative borrowing of ideas from equity and tort. The innovations on behalf of the economic underdog of economic duress, good faith, unconscionability and strict liability are instances of relief from the hardship caused by standardized relations with impersonal, removed profit makers.

Due to the sheer breadth of legislative intervention in the market, common law courts were relegated to the contract work of adjustment after breakdown and of hardship relief for cases falling through the cracks. Although common law contract doctrine was no longer the blueprint for all market transactions, that did not mean common law contract principles were merely for the residue where legislatures had not acted. Planners of complex business transactions employ common law contract principles in every contract they draft, and courts must pick and choose between contractual doctrine, intent and legislative policy in performing their duties as courts of law and equity. Contract principles are essential to most bargain exchanges, but they must be applied imaginatively to avoid potentially unfair results caused by their indiscriminate application to specialized, policy-charged contracts.

Notes

1. R. SEAVOY, THE ORIGINS OF THE AMERICAN BUSINESS CORPORATION, 1784–1855, 2–5 (Westport, Conn. 1982); *cf.* S. LIVERMORE, EARLY AMERICAN LAND COMPANIES 216 (1939) (Before 1800 unincorporated land companies had complexities of modern entity and were progenitor of modern business corporation.).

2. Dorfman, *Chancellor Kent and the Developing American Economy,* 61 COLUM. L. REV. 1290, 1308 (1961) (In 1814 Kent thought corporate form should be limited to public service function.); L. FRIEDMAN, A HISTORY OF AMERICAN LAW 188–196 (2d ed. N.Y. 1985) (First general business corporation act was in New York for manufacture of cloth, glass and iron products.).

3. New York required 2/3 vote to incorporate. N.Y. CONSTITUTION, Art. 7, Sect. 9 (1821). In reaction to the *Dartmouth College* case, many states reserved power to amend or repeal corporate charter, per Story's dictum.

4. *See* J. HURST, LAW AND THE CONDITIONS OF FREEDOM IN THE NINETEENTH CENTURY UNITED STATES 15–16 (Madison: 1956).

5. R. SEAVOY, *supra* note 1, at 4–5; M. HORWITZ, THE TRANSFORMATION OF AMERICAN LAW, 1780–1860, 109–110, 136 (Cambridge, Mass. 1977) (*Charles River Bridge* case shows shift from franchise monopolies to competition.); Dorfman, *supra* note 2, at 1308–1309 (Kent accepted growth of corporation for all kinds of pursuits in 1838.); J. HURST, *supra* note 4, at 16–17.

6. J. HURST, LAW AND ECONOMIC GROWTH: THE LEGAL HISTORY OF THE LUMBER INDUSTRY IN WISCONSIN 1836–1915, 327 (Mad-

ison: rev. ed. 1984); J. HURST, *supra* note 4, at 86–87 (Cultural value of freedom of association aided push for flexible incorporation.).

7. J. HURST, *supra* note 6, at 15; J. HURST, *supra* note 4, at 327–328.

8. Isaacs, *The Standardizing of Contracts*, 27 YALE L.J. 34, 45 (1917) (More or less contractual partnerships replaced by uniform corporations.); *cp.* Macneil, *Restatement (Second) of Contracts and Presentation,* 60 VA. L. REV. 589, 597–598 (1974).

9. S. FINE, LAISSEZ FAIRE AND THE GENERAL WELFARE STATE (A STUDY OF CONFLICT IN AMERICAN THOUGHT 1865–1901) 335 (Ann Arbor: 1956) (questions raised about the relationship of state to economic order); 1 R. ELY, PROPERTY AND CONTRACT IN THEIR RELATIONS TO THE DISTRIBUTION OF WEALTH 86–88 (1914) (immense increase in wealth of a few persons from 1855 to 1892); J. HURST, *supra* note 4, at 78; L. FRIEDMAN, CONTRACT LAW IN AMERICA 159 (Madison: 1965) (tension as large corporations cornering wealth).

10. 1. R. ELY, *supra* note 9, at 86–88 (Private wealth owned railroads in U.S. but they were publicly owned in Europe at time.); Goetsch, *The Future of Legal Formalism,* 24 AM. J. LEG. HIST. 221, 229–230, 243 (1980) (Due process clause protected corporate property from unfriendly state legislation.); L. FRIEDMAN, *supra* note 9, at 85–86 (Judicial finding of ultra vires infrequent in order to not hobble growth.); *see* MAX WEBER ON LAW IN ECONOMY AND SOCIETY 189, 146 (M. Rheinstein ed. 1954) (Coercion exercised by private owners of means of production and acquisition and to whom law guaranteed property and whose power was felt in market.).

11. Coase, *The Nature of the Firm,* 4 ECONOMICA 386, 397 (1937) (Improved managerial techniques tend to increase size of firm.); J. HURST, *supra* note 4, at 90. The proliferation of computerization in 1980s is having a similar effect.

12. Kessler, *Contracts of Adhesion—Some Thoughts About Freedom of Contract,* 43 COLUM. L. REV. 629, 640 (1943) ("innate trend of competitive capitalism toward monopoly"); J. HURST, *supra* note 4, at 75, 88; L. FRIEDMAN, *supra* note 9, at 191–192 (Progressives focused on unfairness in inequality of bargaining positions of different classes.); P. ATIYAH, THE RISE AND FALL OF FREEDOM OF CONTRACT 738–739 (Oxford: 1979) (Corporate agents change.). It is an open question what effect today's post-industrial era will have on equality of bargaining as small scale enterprises have experienced significant growth in business and employment opportunities.

13. A. BERLE, Jr. and G. MEANS, THE MODERN CORPORATION AND PRIVATE PROPERTY 1 (N.Y., rev. ed. 1967); *see* Fuller and Perdue, *The Reliance Interest in Contract Damages,* 46 YALE L.J. 52, 63 (1936).

14. Kessler, *supra* note 12, at 640; M. WEBER, *supra* note 10, at 188–189; J. HURST, *supra* note 4, at 90–91; P. ATIYAH, *supra* note 12, at 564–567 (*Caveat emptor* applied to purchase of shares.).

15. Coase, *supra* note 11, at 388, 391; P. ATIYAH, *supra* note 12, at 600–601, 723–724; Gilmore, *On Statutory Obsolescence,* 39 UNIV. COLO. L. REV. 461, 470–471 (1967).

16. M. WEBER, *supra* note 10, at 190–191 (The larger the firm, the more relentless can authoritarian constraint be exercised.); A. BERLE and G. MEANS, *supra* note 13, at 306–307; P. ATIYAH, *supra* note 12, at 723–724, 729, 738–

740. The corporate structure is formalistic in its statutory scope, charter, procedures and hierarchy.

17. *See* P. ATIYAH, *supra* note 12, at 656 ("irresponsible wealth").

18. Coase, *supra* note 11, at 387–391 (Firm avoids taxes on the taxable transactions eliminated. *Id.* at 393.). A modern alternative view inspired by Coase is that the firm is a legal fiction serving as a nexus for contracting relations. Bratton, *The New Economic Theory of the Firm: Critical Perspectives from History,* 41 STAN. L. REV. 1471, 1478–80, 1489 (1989) (Coase's modern view is critical supplement to earlier managerialist's theory. *Id.* at 1482–94, 1526–7.)

19. *See Id.* at 391–392; *see also* J. HURST, *supra* note 6, at 331–332 (could protect against risk of price fluctuation). In order to close deal, potential disagreement over details in complex agreements are often pushed aside in hope that issues won't arise or will be resolved amicably in future, and so only general rules of conducting relationship are settled. Macaulay, *Non-Contractual Relations in Business: A Preliminary Study,* 28 AM. SOC. REV. 55, 64–66 (1963); Summers, *Collective Agreement and the Law of Contracts,* 78 YALE L. J. 525, 528 (1969).

20. *See* Macneil, *supra* note 8, 595–596; *see also* Summers, *supra* note 19, at 528, 534; *and see* Gilmore, *supra* note 15, at 470–471.

21. J. HURST, *supra* note 6, 332–333; L. FRIEDMAN, *supra* note 2, at 534; *see* Macaulay, *supra* note 19, at 61.

22. Isaacs, *supra* note 8, at 34, 38–39, 45; Kessler, *supra* note 12, at 631; *see* Macaulay, *supra* note 19, at 58.

23. Kessler, *supra* note 12, at 631; J. HURST, *supra* note 6, at 307 (Legislative inclusion of trade usage standardizes.); Isaacs, *supra* note 8, at 38–39.

24. L. FRIEDMAN, *supra* note 2, at 548–549 (e.g., insurance); Cohen, *The Basis of Contract,* 46 HARV. L. REV. 587–589 (1933) (Judicial interpretation of forms aided in security necessary for initiative and assumption of risk.); Macaulay, *Private Legislation and the Duty to Read—Business Run by IBM Machine, The Law of Contracts and Credit Cards,* 19 VAND. L. REV. 1051, 1059 (1966) (Otherwise agents might "give away the company."); *see* Coase, *supra* note 11, at 390–391, 403–405.

25. Kessler, *supra* note 12, at 631–632 (e.g., arbitration and limits on both warranties and damages).

26. Sanger v. Dun, 47 Wis. 615, 3 N.W. 388, 389 (1879) (failure to read no defense); Secoulsky v. Oceanic Steam Navigation Co. 223 Mass. 465, 112 N.E. 151 (1916) (standard clause); Cohen, *supra* note 24, at 589; Kessler, *supra* note 12, at 639; *see* P. ATIYAH, *supra* note 12, at 732–734 (To avoid jury favoritism for consumer on questions of consent and fairness, courts turned it into question of law based on form.).

27. Non-agricultural labor was 28% in 1820, 36% in 1850, 47% in 1870 and 62% in 1900. J. HURST, *supra* note 4, at 71.

28. Kessler, *supra* note 12, at 629–633; *see* Schroeder Music Publishing Co. v. Macaulay, 3 All Eng. Rep. 616 (1974), 1 W.L.R. 1308 (1974) (dictum); *see also* Leff, *Unconscionability and the Crowd—Consumers and the Common Law Tradition,* 31 U. PITT. L. REV. 349, 350 (1970). *See* Goldberg, *Institutional Change and the Quasi-Invisible Hand,* 17 J. LAW AND ECON. 461, 461–463 (1974) (Economists overlook fact there is self interest in economically strong to change law in their favor.). But contrast that with economist's view that, pursuant to the price mech-

anism, form contracts are not used to concentrate power but instead are for benefit of consumers since lower prices are possible due to reduction of transaction costs. Coase, *The Choice of the Institutional Framework: A Comment,* 17 J. LAW & ECON. 493 (1974) (If clause is onerous to consumers, reducing value more than costs, producer won't use clause.); Trebilcock, *Doctrine of Inequality of Bargaining Power: Post-Benthamite Economics in House of Lords,* 26 U. TORONTO L. J. 359 (1976).

29. Issacs, *supra* note 8, at 39–40, 45; Kessler, *supra* note 12, at 640–641. There has been a movement from private contract to corporate administration and public law. *See* P. ATIYAH, *supra* note 12, at 725–726. It has been argued that there should only be deemed assent to the dickered terms but not a blanket assent to the whole form. K. LLEWELLYN, THE COMMON LAW TRADITION: DECIDING APPEALS 370 (Boston: 1960); *see* 1 A. CORBIN, CORBIN ON CONTRACTS sect. 107 (St. Paul: 1963) (When ill-informed presented with form contract to accept or get nothing, court might use "meeting of minds" rule against superior party.); *cp.* Goldberg, *supra* note 28, at 490 (Need government agent to provide standard terms for consumer.).

30. J. HURST, *supra* note 4, at 82–85; Kessler, *supra* note 12 at 640; *cp.* M. HORWITZ, *supra* note 5, at xiii–xiv, 140–159, 253 (alliance of commerce and bar for distribution of wealth and power in their favor).

31. S. FINE, *supra* note 9, at 289–290; *see* J. HURST, *supra* note 4, at 71–72 (By 1900 3/4 industrial power by steam and 600% increase in railroad mileage since 1865).

32. Kessler, *supra* note 12, at 639; Rehbinder, *Status, Contract and the Welfare State,* 23 STAN. L. REV. 941, 946–947 (1971).

33. M. WEBER, *supra* note 10, at 188–191, 309; J. HURST, *supra* note 4, at 82 (Industry assisted by tax policy and corporate financing device.); S. FINE, *supra* note 9, at 335; *see* 1 R. ELY, *supra* note 9, at 79, 86–88 (Law influenced distribution of property.).

34. Kessler, *supra* note 12, at 640–641; J. HURST, *supra* note 4, at 75–77; J. HURST, *supra* note 6, at 410.

35. M. WEBER, *supra* note 10, at 192–194, 308 (Before the market economy, exchanges related to family and duty.). *See* Holmes, *The Path of the Law,* 10 HARV. L. REV. 457, 466 (1897) ("We do not realize how large a part of our law is open to reconsideration upon a slight change in the habit of the public mind.").

36. S. FINE, *supra* note 9, at 177, 198–203, 252, 278–280, 373–375, 381.

37. *Id.* at 209, 284–287, L. FRIEDMAN, *supra* note 2, at 664–665.

38. L. FRIEDMAN, *supra* note 2, at 439; S. FINE, *supra* note 9, at 362–364 (federal support by land transfers to railroads and high tariffs); J. HURST, *supra* note 6, at 290–295 (lien law strengthened); L. FRIEDMAN, *supra* note 9, at 163–164 (Occupational licensing and standardized methods kept marginal businesses out.). To the extent laissez-faire existed in 19th century, along with a complementary formalism, it has been emphasized that it was an aberration from the pattern of regulation before and since. M. HORWITZ, *supra* note 5, at xiii–xv; *see* G. GILMORE, THE AGES OF AMERICAN LAW 12–13 (New Haven: 1977).

39. S. FINE, *supra* note 9, at 352–355; Kessler, *supra* note 12, at 635 (insurance); *see* Swentusky v. Prudential Ins. Co., 116 Conn. 526, 532, 165 A. 686,

688 (1933) (Public interest greater in stability of insurance, banking and utilities than in regulation thereof.).

40. J. HURST, *supra* note 4, at 73–75, 83–88, 98 (Political organization of power more important than at any time since 1776–1800.); S. FINE, *supra* note 9, at 210, 383; L. FRIEDMAN, *supra* note 9, at 164–165, 186. *See* W. NELSON, AMERICANIZATION OF THE COMMON LAW 8 (Cambridge, Mass. 1975) (By 1830s American pattern was appearing of interest groups competing in legislature for advantage.). *Cp.* J. BAKER, AN INTRODUCTION TO ENGLISH LEGAL HISTORY 187–188 (London: 2d ed. 1979) (Likewise in England, 1865 to early 1900s was period of collectivism, especially as to labor law.).

41. S. FINE, *supra* note 9, at 373–395 (Middle class movement for fairness had desire to return to conditions of a "golden age" before industrialization and corporate state.); *see also* Speidel, *An Essay on the Reported Death and Continued Vitality of Contract,* 27 STAN. L. REV. 1161, 1172, 1176–1179, 1181 (1975).

42. Pound, *Liberty of Contract,* 18 YALE L. J. 454, 464 (1909) (Sociological Jurisprudence); 1 R. ELY, *supra* note 9, at 80–83 (Public ownership cuts down on use of private control.); L. FRIEDMAN, *supra* note 9, at 154–157, 170–183, 191–199; Speidel, *supra* note 41, at 1172–1175; P. ATIYAH, *supra* note 12, at 713–762.

43. *See generally* Coase, *The Problem of Social Cost,* 3 J. LAW and ECON. 1 (1960); *and see* R. POSNER, ECONOMIC ANALYSIS OF LAW 343–363 (Boston: 3d ed. 1986); *contra* Goldberg, *supra* note 28, at 461–463.

44. Santa Clara County v. Southern Pacific RR Co., 118 U.S. 394, 396 (1886); Minneapolis & St. Louis Ry. v. Beckwith, 129 U.S. 26 (1888). *See generally* J. HURST, THE LEGITIMACY OF THE BUSINESS CORPORATION IN THE LAW OF THE UNITED STATES 1780–1970, 64–70 (Charlottesville: 1970); Goetsch, *supra* note 10, at 221, 221–223, 243–245; Maidment, *Law and Economic Policy in the United States: The Judicial Response to Governmental Regulation of the Economy,* 7 J. LEG. HIST. 196, 197–200 (1986).

45. Lochner v. New York, 198 U.S. 45 (1905); Standard Oil of New Jersey v. United States, 221 U.S. 1, 62 (1910); Coopage v. Kansas, 236 U.S. 1 (1914).

46. Munn v. Illinois, 94 U.S. 113 (1876). Hale wrote that when a private party owns the only wharf at a port, his charges must be "reasonable" since it is "affected with a public interest and [it] cease[s] to be *juris privati* only." M. HALE, DE PORTIBUS MARIS, 1 Hargrave Law Tracts 78 (d. 1676).

47. Wabash Railway v. Illinois, 118 U.S. 557 (1886).

48. Muller v. Oregon, 208 U.S. 412 (1908); Lochner v. New York, 198 U.S. 45 (1905) (Holmes dissented). *See* Holmes, *supra* note 35, at 466. The overturning of statutes by state courts was uncommon in 1850 but was a regular occurrence by 1900 as judges fell behind the zeitgeist, but state courts did accept social legislation a generation before the U.S. Supreme Court. *See* L. FRIEDMAN, *supra* note 2, at 355–362; *see also* G. GILMORE, *supra* note 38, at 63–64, 130.

49. Adkins v. Children's Hospital, 261 U.S. 525 (1923) (Holmes and Taft dissented). *Accord* Morehead v. New York ex rel. Tipaldo, 198 U.S. 587 (1936).

50. West Coast Hotel Co. v. Parrish, 300 U.S. 379 (1937). *And see* Phelps Dodge Corp. v. N.L.R.B., 313 U.S. 177 (1941). *See also* Schechter v. U.S., 295 U.S. 495 (1935).

51. Ipswich Tailor's Case, 11 Co. Rep. 53a, 77 Eng. Rep. 1218 (1614); Rogers

v. Parrey, 2 Bulstr. 136, Cro. Jac. 326 (1614); Mitchel v. Reynolds, 1 P. Wms. 181, 24 Eng. Rep. 647 (1711).

52. Charles River Bridge v. Warren Bridge, 36 U.S. (11 Pet.) 420 (1837); Richardson v. Buhl & Alger, 77 Mich. 632 (1889) (monopoly destructive); *see* J. HURST, *supra* note 4, at 90–92.

53. Sherman Act, 15 U.S.C. sects. 1–2 (1890). There were exemptions for public utilities and for middle class interest groups who won power struggle against big business, e.g., "unfair trade" laws continued and unions and farm organizations exempted. L. FRIEDMAN, *supra* note 9, at 161–162, 181–182.

54. *See* M. WEBER, *supra* note 10, at 189–191; *and see* Adkins v. Children's Hospital, 261 U.S. 525 (1923).

55. S. FINE, *supra* note 9, at 352; Isaacs, *supra* note 8, at 47 (In 1300's status used to drive laborers; now it forces employers to realize their social duties.).

56. L. FRIEDMAN, *supra* note 9, at 124, 160 (By 1911 21 states barred employment waivers.); S. FINE, *supra* note 9, at 383–385 (40 states had workers compensation by 1917). The Occupational Safety and Health Act, 29 U.S.C. sect. 651 (1970) created general duty to provide workplace free of hazards causing serious harm.

57. *See* P. ATIYAH, *supra* note 12, at 576–577, 703–704, 762–763.

58. J. HURST, *supra* note 4, at 86–88; L. FRIEDMAN, *supra* note 2, at 554–558 (Courts sided with own class.); *In re* Debs, 158 U.S. 564 (1895). Yet courts were supportive of the freedom of association of corporations.

59. Wagner Act, 29 U.S.C. Sects. 151 et seq. (1935); Taft-Hartley Act, 29 U.S.C. sects. 141 et seq. (1947). Freedom of contract has still been preserved to an extent. Mastro Plastics Corp. v. N.L.R.B., 350 U.S. 270 (1956); Teamsters Local 174 v. Lucas Flour Co. 369 U.S. 95 (1962).

60. John Wiley & Sons v. Livingston, 376 U.S. 543, 550 (1964); Textile Workers Union v. Lincoln Mills, 353 U.S. 448, 456 (1957). *See* Summers, *supra* note 19, at 525, 527, 548, 562, 574–575 (Contract rules of interpretation provided tested foundations for filling gaps in collective agreements.); but *cf.* 6A A. CORBIN, *supra* note 29, at sect. 1420.

61. *See* Summers, *supra* note 19, at 528–530, 564.

62. United Steelworkers v. Warrior & Gulf Navigation Co., 363 U.S. 574, 582 (1960); Teamsters Local 174 v. Lucas Flour Co., 369 U.S. 95, 105 (1962).

63. L. FRIEDMAN, *supra* note 2, at 545–549; M. HORWITZ, *supra* note 5, at 264–265.

64. *See* DeHahn v. Hartley, 1 T.R. 343, 99 Eng. Rep. 1130 (1786) (marine insurance).

65. Kessler and Fine, *Culpa in Contrahendo, Bargaining in Good Faith, and Freedom of Contract: A Comparative Study,* 77 HARV. L. REV. 401, 419, 441–442, 447–448 (1964); Kessler, *supra* note 12, at 632–637; J. HURST, *supra* note 4, at 98, Duffie v. Bankers' Life Ass'n., 160 Ia. 19, 139, N.W. 1087 (1913) (tort duty to act without delay). Judicial interventionism occurs whether a formalist judge declares the language clear or a realist judge declares it ambiguous.

66. Swentusky v. Prudential Ins. Co., 116 Conn. 526, 532, 165A. 686, 688 (1933) (Public interest is greater in certainty in insurance, banking and utilities.); L. FRIEDMAN, *supra* note 9, at 106 (Judicial vacillation on business forms brought in legislature.).

67. Prudential Ins. Co. v. Lumme, 83 Nev. 146, 425 P.2d 346 (1967); Gaunt v. John Hancock Mutual Life Ins. Co., 169 F.2d 599, *cert. denied* 333 U.S. 849 (1947). State "plain English" statutes typically include consumer insurance contracts.

68. Isaacs, *supra* note 8, at 34–35, 47–48 (citing Pound's Sociological Jurisprudence).

69. L. FRIEDMAN, *supra* note 9, at 160–161; *see* RESTATEMENT OF TORTS sect. 763.

70. Kessler and Fine, *supra* note 65, at 408–412; Isaacs, *supra* note 8, at 39.

71. RESTATEMENT (SECOND) OF CONTRACTS sect. 176 (1981); G. CHESHIRE, C. FIFOOT, M. FURMSTON, LAW OF CONTRACT 299 (London: 11th ed. 1986).

72. H. BRACTON, DE LEGIBUS, fo. 16b–17 (d. 1268); E. COKE, SECOND INSTITUTE 482–483 (1642); *accord* 1 W. BLACKSTONE, COMMENTARIES* at 131 ("but no suitable atonement can be made for loss of life or limb"); *but cf.* Y.B. 20 Edw. III (Lib. Ass.) 72, pl. 14 (1346) (release ineffective since made under pressure of seizure of signer's livestock).

73. Astley v. Reynolds, 2 Stra. 915, 93 Eng. Rep. 939 (K.B. 1732). *See* Summer v. Ferryman, 11 Mod. 201, 88 Eng. Rep. 989 (K.B. 1709), where defense lawyer alleged duress of goods had been upheld in an earlier case, but Holt, C.J. rejected it.

74. *See* Dawson, *Economic Duress—An Essay in Perspective*, 45 MICH. L. REV. 253, 268–282 (1947).

75. Ashmole v. Wainwright, 2 Q.B. 837, 114 Eng. Rep. 325 (1842); Parker v. Great Western Ry., 7 Man. & G. 253, 135 Eng. Rep. 107 (C.P. 1844); Newland v. Buncombe Turnpike Co., 26 N.C. 372 (1844).

76. *See* M. HORWITZ, *supra* note 5, at 261–263; *cf.* Dawson, *supra* note 74, at 277–278, 287–288 (Equitable concern for equivalency sometimes made analysis of free will incidental.).

77. Skeate v. Beale, 11 Ad. & El. 983, 113 Eng. Rep. 688 (1840). There was an alternative remedy here of suing on the excessive distraint. It is also arguable that *Skeate* differs from cases of duress of goods and utilities exacting overcharges in that they were restitutional actions but *Skeate* involved a defense to a common law damages action.

78. Cobb v. Charter, 32 Conn. 358 (1865) (duress of goods); Brumagin v. Tillinghast, 18 Cal. 265, 272 (1861) (Dictum that it was duress to exert power over person or property to exact payment when no alternative for victim.); *accord* Radich v. Hutchins, 95 U.S. 210, 213 (1877) (Per Field, J., who also wrote *Brumagin* opinion.); *see* RESTATEMENT OF CONTRACTS sect. 493(d) (1932).

79. Hackley v. Headley, 45 Mich. 569, 8 N.W. 11 (1881). An appeal of the remand of this case upheld trial verdict that the debtor's claim was not in good faith and that the release lacked consideration. Headley v. Hackley, 20 Mich. 43, 14 N.W. 693 (1883). But this later decision did not have the influence of the first appeal. In Alexander v. S.A. Truffant Commission Co., 34 S.W. 182, 183 (Tex. Civ. App. 1895) a buyer used fraud to justify a higher payment, and, despite the fact the seller couldn't continue business unless he agreed, the court said the seller "was a free man, with the courts of his country open to him."

80. Goebel v. Linn, 47 Mich. 489, 11 N.W. 284 (1882). *See* Mandel v. National

Ice and Coal Co., 180 N.Y. Supp. 429 (1920) (Claim of duress by buyer of ice rejected since proof of alternative source.).

81. *See* two construction cases where duress found under facts similar to *Hackley:* Fitzgerald v. Fitzgerald & Mallory Constr. Co., 44 Neb. 463, 491, 62 N.W. 899, 909 (1895) and Thomas v. Brown, 116 Va. 233, 81 S.E. 56 (1914). *And see* Illinois Merchants Trust Co. v. Harvey, 335 Ill. 284, 291, 167 N.E. 69, 72 (1929) (dictum where lessor threatened lessee). *See also* Dalzell, *Duress By Economic Pressure,* 20 N.C. L. REV. 237, 238–239, 263 (1942) (The talk of "consent" and of the reasonable alternative of a breach action ignores the business realities forcing acquiescence.).

82. Austin Instrument, Inc. v. Loral Corp. 29 N.Y. 2d 124, 272 N.E. 2d 533 (1971). *Accord* Thompson Crane & Trucking Co. v. Eyman, 123 Cal. App. 2d 904, 267 P.2d 1043 (1954); Ross Systems v. Linden Dari-Delite, 35 N.J. 329, 173 A.2d 258 (1961); King Constr. Co. v. W.M. Smith Elec. Co., 350 S.W. 2d 940 (Tex. Civ. App. 1961). There is no duress if there is a reasonable alternative source. Tri-State Roofing Co. v. Simon, 187 Pa. Super. 17, 142 A.2d 333 (1958). The division of labor under industrialization creates a greater dependency; thus a general contractor is vulnerable if a subcontractor refuses to perform.

83. *See* Totem Marine Tug & Barge v. Alyeska Pipeline Serv. Co., 584 P.2d 15 (Alaska 1978); *and see* Aircraft Assoc. & Mfg. Co. v. United States, 357 F.2d 373 (Ct. Cl. 1966); *see also* RESTATEMENT (SECOND) OF CONTRACTS sect. 176(2)(a) (1981). The rule in *Pinnel's Case* and *Foakes v. Beer* indirectly protected against economic duress in modification of the amount due; however, the U.C.C. drafters urged flexible enforcement of modifications short of impracticability if there is a "legitimate commercial reason" and its done in "good faith". U.C.C. sect. 2–209, Comment 2. Economic duress and impracticability both blossomed in the 20th century on the grounds of social policy and the realities of modern commerce; both mark a shift from absolutist demands of individualism and objective proof of physical harm to more malleable principles of fairness and good faith.

84. *See* Dawson, *supra* note 74, at 280–282, 290; *and see* E. FARNSWORTH, CONTRACTS 262 (Boston: 1982).

85. Kirke La Shelle Co. v. Paul Armstrong Co., 263 N.Y. 79, 188 N.E. 163 (1933); Summers, *"Good Faith" in General Contract Law and the Sales Provisions of the Uniform Commercial Code,* 54 VA. L. REV. 195, 200–206 (1968) (Good faith is an "excluder".); RESTATEMENT (SECOND) OF CONTRACTS sect. 205, Comment (a) (1981).

86. *Anon,* 2 Ch. Cas. 17, 22 Eng. Rep. 825 (1679); Day v. Newman, 2 Cox. Eq. 77, 30 Eng. Rep. 36 (Ch. 1788); 2 J. KENT, COMMENTARIES ON AMERICAN LAW 490 (N.Y. 12th ed. 1873); 2 J. STORY, COMMENTARIES ON EQUITY JURISPRUDENCE sect. 769 at 90 (13th ed. 1886).

87. Pelly v. Royal Exchange Assurance, 1 Burr. 341, 97 Eng. Rep. 342 (1757) (usage); Kingston v. Preston, 2 Doug. 689, 99 Eng. Rep. 437 (1773); Boone v. Eyre, 1 H. Bl. 273, 126 Eng. Rep. 160 (1777); Miller v. Race, 1 Burr. 452, 97 Eng. Rep. 398 (1758); Carter v. Boehm, 3 Burr. 1905, 97 Eng. Rep. 1162 (1766) (disclosure); Hawkes v. Saunders, 1 Cowp. 289, 98 Eng. Rep. 1091 (1782) ("promise is only to do what an honest man ought to do").

88. Dodge v. Kimball, 203 Mass. 364, 89 N.E. 542 (1909) (no substantial

performance); Brassil v. Maryland Cas. Co., 210 N.Y. 235, 104 N.E. 622 (1914); Wigand v. Bachman-Bechtel Brewing Co., 222 N.Y. 272, 118 N.E. 618 (1918); Carns v. Bassick, 187 App. Div. 280, 175 N.Y. Supp. 670 (1st Dept. 1919).

89. Headley v. Hackley, 50 Mich. 43, 15 N.W. 693 (1883).

90. Lingenfelder v. Wainwright Brewery Co., 103 Mo. 578, 15 S.W. 844 (1891). Architect appeared to be punishing the owner for hiring a competitor. This case resembled the "ice" case of *Goebel v. Linn* where the economic duress argument was refused.

91. Faxton v. Faxon, 28 Mich. 159, 161 (1873); 3 A. CORBIN, *supra* note 29, at sect. 541; Obrecht v. Crawford, 175 Md. 385, 395, 2 A. 2d 1, 6 (1938).

92. Simon v. Etgen, 213 N.Y. 589, 107 N.E. 1066, 1067–1068 (1915). Earlier N.Y. courts broadly applied good faith to open-ended long-term arrangements like requirements contracts. New York Cent. Iron Works Co. v. United States Radiator Co., 174 N.Y. 331, 66 N.E. 967 (1903). *And see* Wigand v. Bachmann-Bechtel Brewing Co., 222 N.Y. 272, 118 N.E. 618 (1918) (Output contract where court again declared general duty of good faith in all contracts.); *cf.* Pratt, *American Contract Law at the Turn of the Century,* 39 S.C. L. REV. 415, 458 (1988) (*Wigand* was first to declare good faith in all contracts.). *See also* Kirke La Shelle Co. v. Paul Armstrong, 263 N.Y. 79, 188 N.E. 163 (1933).

93. U.C.C. sect. 1–201 (18) (May, 1949 Draft).

94. U.C.C. sect. 10, Comment (1948 Draft); Summers, *supra* note 85, at 208–210 (Courts had disagreed over whether a subjective or objective test applied to purchasers of negotiable instruments.); UNIFORM SALES ACT sect. 76(2); UNIFORM WAREHOUSE RECEIPTS ACT sect. 58(2); UNIFORM BILLS OF LADING ACT sect. 53(2); U.C.C. 2–103(1)(b) (1952).

95. *See* Kessler and Fine, *supra* note 65, at 401–412.

96. Laidlaw v. Organ, 15 U.S. (2 Wheat.) 178 (1817) (Tobacco prices skyrocketed once harbor opened.); R. POTHIER, CONTRACT OF SALE Art. II, No. 233–241 (1762) (Under good faith party obliged to tell all he knows.).

97. Smith v. Hughes, L.R. 6 Q.B. 597, 607 (1871) (need not inform of mistake); Steward v. Wyoming Cattle Ranche Co. 128 U.S. 383, 388 (1888) (false representation to conceal "material fact which he is in good faith bound to disclose"); Donovan v. Aeolian Co., 170 N.Y. 267, 271, 200 N.E. 815, 816 (1936) (Failure to disclose may be fraudulent.); RESTATEMENT (SECOND) CONTRACTS sect. 161(b) (1981) (must correct known mistake); Henningsen v. Bloomfield Motors, Inc., 32 N.J. 358, 161 A.2d 69 (1960); *see* Levy v. C. Young Constr. Co., 46 N.J. Super. 293, 296, 134 A. 2d 717, 719 (App. Div. 1957) (*Caveat emptor* "is very nearly abolished" for personal, but not for real, property.).

98. *See* Kessler, *supra* note 12, at 634–639; *see also* Kessler and Fine, *supra* note 65, at 419, 442.

99. Drennan v. Star Paving Co., 51 Cal. 2d 409, 333 P. 2d 757 (1958); Pryor v. Cain, 25 Ill. 292 (1861) (Promisor "is bound in good faith" because of reliance.); Kessler and Fine, *supra* note 65, at 401–406, 420–424 (*culpa* liability for blameworthy negotiating); *see* U.C.C. sect. 2–205, Comment 5 (safeguard of good faith for mistaken signing of firm offer).

100. Hoffman v. Red Owl Stores, 26 Wis. 2d 683, 133 N.W. 2d 267 (1965); Summers, *supra* note 85, at 223–225; Henderson, *Promissory Estoppel and Traditional Contract Doctrine,* 78 YALE L.J. 343, 357–365 (1969); RESTATEMENT

(SECOND) CONTRACTS sect. 90 (Illustration 10 is *Hoffman v. Red Owl* facts with damages based on reliance rather than expectation since no agreement made.). It's unclear whether *Red Owl* court would've held the same if bargaining positions had been equal. Goodman v. Dicker, 169 F. 2d 684 (D.C. Cir. 1948) is a similar case, but the court did not address whether the promise of a franchise was an offer.

101. Heyer Products Co. v. United States, 140 F. Supp. 409 (Ct. Cl. 1956); *see* Summers, *supra* note 85, at 221–223.

102. Some courts still take the formalist position that good faith should not apply prior to formation except in fiduciary relationships or where there is legislation, as regarding collective bargaining. United States v. Braunstein, 75 F. Supp. 137 (S.D.N.Y. 1947); A.B.C. Packard, Inc. v. General Motors Corp. 275 F. 2d 63, 69 (9th Cir. 1960); Ruebsamen v. Maddocks, 340 A. 2d 31 (Maine 1975).

103. Perry v. Wheeler, 75 Ky. 541 (1877); J.R. Watkins Co. v. Rich, 254 Mich. 82, 235 N.W. 845 (1931) (When the termination at will "relationship is commercial . . . the option may be exercised only in good faith."); Millett Co. v. Park & Tilford Distillers Corp. 123 F. Supp. 484 (N.D. Cal. 1954); Clausen & Sons v. Theo. Hamm Brewing Co., 395 F. 2d 388 (8th Cir. 1968); "Automobile Dealers Day in Court Act," 15 U.S.C.A. sect. 1221 (1956); Petroleum Marketing Practices Act of 1978, 15 U.S.C.A. sect. 2801 (gasoline distributors); *see* The New Jersey Franchise Practices Act, N.J. Stat. Ann. 56:10–5, 56: 10–7 (West Supp. 1983); *see also* Massachusetts Fair Dealing Act, M.G.L.A. ch. 93A, 93B (1971) (amended 1977) (Prohibits termination or refusal to extend franchise unless notice and good cause.).

104. Monge v. Beebe Rubber Co., 114 N.H. 130, 133, 316 A. 2d 549, 551 (1974) (Up to jury to determine bad faith of boss whose one sexual advance rebuffed by employee.); Fortune v. National Cash Register Co., 373 Mass. 96, 364 N.E. 2d 1251 (1977). The New Hampshire court recognized a good faith obligation and the right to tort damages; a California appellate court seemed to agree, but the California Supreme Court denied that damages view and held that only contract damages were recoverable. Cleary v. American Airlines, 111 Cal. App. 3d 443, 168 Cal. Rptr. 722 (1988); Foley v. Interactive Data Corp., 765 P. 2d 373 (Cal. S. Ct. 1988) (Unlike public function of insurance contracts, duties in employment contract aren't owed to society as a whole.). *Cf.* Seaman's Direct Buying Service, Inc. v. Standard Oil of Cal., 36 Cal. 3d 752, 686 P. 2d 1158 (1984).

105. RESTATEMENT (SECOND) OF CONTRACTS sect. 205 (1981); Burton, *Breach of Contract and the Common Law Duty to Perform in Good Faith*, 94 HARV. L. REV. 369, 404 (1980); contra English v. Fischer, 660 S.W. 2d 521 (Tex. 1983) (dissent, however, sees good faith duty in all contracts).

106. *See* Newman, *The Renaissance of Good Faith Contracting in Anglo-American Law*, 54 CORNELL L. REV. 553, 559n. (1969) (1968 survey of 176 judges from 44 states showed near unanimity in refusing damages if bad faith.); *but cf.* Barr v. Dieter, 190 Pa. Super. 454, 459, 154 A. 2d 290, 293 (1959). The continuing law and equity dichotomy is still apparent in comparing real and personal property sales. A real property sale, a common case for specific performance, is often

the most valuable contract a consumer will ever enter into, and yet, *caveat emptor* retains a stronger grip than in personal property sales.

107. M. WEBER, *supra* note 10, at 307–309; L. FRIEDMAN, *supra* note 9, at 101; Kessler, *supra* note 12, at 637; Henningsen v. Bloomfield Motors, 32 N.J. 358, 403, 161 A. 2d 69, 94 (1960) (status of consumer and manufacturer relevant in mass standardized transaction).

108. *See* Bailey, *Congressional Opposition to Pure Food Legislation, 1879–1906,* 36 AM. J. SOC. 52 (1930) (190 food and drug bills introduced in U.S. Congress from 1879 until first pure food and drug act passed in 1906.); *see also* Speidel, *Unconscionability, Assent and Consumer Protection,* 31 U. PITT. L. REV. 359, 375 (1970) (Disclosure is not a solution for lower income groups.). The British Parliament recently enacted a product liability act to fill the judicial void. Consumer Protection Act 1987, 36 Eliz. II, c. 43.

109. (British) Unfair Contract Terms Act, c.50 (1977); P. ATIYAH and R. SUMMERS, FORM AND SUBSTANCE IN ANGLO-AMERICAN LAW 241–243 (Oxford: 1987) (English elitist distrust of jury. *Id.* at 38.).

110. Sanger v. Dun, 47 Wis. 615, 3 N.W. 388, 389 (1879) (failure to read no defense); Henningsen v. Bloomfield Motors, 32 N.J. 358, 161 A. 2d 69 (1960) (Fine print disclaimer on back of form contract not enforced.); Weaver v. American Oil Co., 257 Ind. 458, 276 N.E. 2d 144, 148 (1971) (Objective standard discarded when weaker party didn't know of hardship provision.); Masterson v. Sine, 68 Cal. 2d 222, 436 P. 2d 561 (1968) (Per Traynor: "the party urging the spoken as against the written word is most often the economic underdog, threatened by severe hardship if the writing is enforced."); *see* Macaulay, *supra* note 24, at 1057, 1063–1064 (Only most suspicious consumer reads forms and then doesn't understand.).

111. Barbour, *The History of Contract in Early English Equity* in IV OXFORD STUDIES IN SOCIAL AND LEGAL HISTORY 78–80 (P. Vinogradoff ed., Oxford, 1914); Dawson, *supra* note 74, at 278.

112. Earl of Chesterfield v. Janssen, 2 Ves. Sen. 125, 28 Eng. Rep. 82 (1750); *see also* Clitherall v. Ogilvie, 1 Desaussure Ch. 250, 261 (S.C. 1792).

113. Evans v. Llewellin, 1 Cox. 333, 29 Eng. Rep 1191 (1787) (infirmity); Blackwilder v. Loveless, 21 Ala. 371 (1852) (old age and in need); Fish v. Leser, 69 Ill. 394 (1873) (ignorance); Smedes v. Wild, 1 Livingston's Law Mag. 155 (N.Y. Sup. Ct. 1852) (contract between businessman and inexperienced woman); Pickett v. Loggon, 14 Ves. Jun. 215, 33 Eng. Rep. 503 (1815) (in distress); How v. Weldon, 2 Ves. Sr. 516, 518, 28 Eng. Rep. 330, 331 (ch. 1754) (Sailor's assignment set aside since sailors are "a race of men, loose and unthinking" considered "at least in as favourable a light as a young heir.").

114. 1 J. STORY, COMMENTARIES ON EQUITY JURISPRUDENCE sect. 258 (1836); 2 J. STORY, COMMENTARIES ON EQUITY JURISPRUDENCE sect. 769 (13th ed. 1886); 2 J. KENT, COMMENTARIES ON AMERICAN LAW 490 (N.Y. 12th ed. 1873) (Purchase made with "reservation of superior knowledge, would be of too sharp a character.").

115. Coles v. Trecothick, 9 Ves. Jr. 234, 236, 32 Eng. Rep. 592, 597 (1804); Lester v. Mahan, 25 Ala. 445 (1854); Marshall v. Billingsley, 7 Ind. 250 (1855); Birdsong v. Birdsong, 39 Tenn. 289 (1859); *see* Dawson, *supra* note 74, at 276–282.

116. *See* W. NELSON, *supra* note 40, at 55–56.

117. James v. Morgan, 1 Lev. 111, 83 Eng. Rep. 323 (1675) (Assumpsit).

118. U.S. v. Hume, 132 U.S. 406 (1889). Other authority for unconscionability at common law cited by the Court of Claims and the Supreme Court included: Leland v. Stone, 10 Mass. 459 (1813); Baxter v. Wales, 12 Mass. 365 (1815); Scott v. U.S., 12 Wall 443, 79 U.S. 438 (1871). *And see* Beckwith v. Guy Frisbe & Sons, 32 Vt. 559 (1860) ("unconscionable to press such advantage" by demanding excessive freight charge).

119. *See* cases cited in U.C.C. 2–302, Comment 1. The great common law thinker Corbin thought flexible use of traditional doctrine could relieve against unconscionability. 1 A. CORBIN, *supra* note 29, at sect. 128.

120. Carr v. Lancashire & Y. Ry., 7 Ex. 707 (1852); O'Callaghan v. Walleer & Beckwith Realty Co., 15 Ill. 2d 436, 155 N.E. 2d 545 (1958); K. LLEWELLYN, *supra* note 29, at 370; Llewellyn, Book Review, 52 HARV. L. REV. 700, 702 (1939).

121. K. LLEWELLYN, *supra* note 29, at 370; Leff, *Unconscionability and the Code—The Emporer's New Clause,* 115 U. PA. L. REV. 485, 489–495 (1967) (Comment A(3) to 1941 Draft: "principle of freedom of bargain" preserved for dickered terms. *Id.* at 490.).

122. *Cf.* Leff, *supra* note 121, at 537 (Code has differences with historic equity doctrine. *Id.* at 528–541.).

123. U.C.C. sect. 2–302, Comment 1; Leff, *supra* note 121, at 499–503; Ellinghaus, *In Defense of Unconscionability,* 78 YALE L.J. 757 (1969); *see* Gee v. Pritchard, 2 Swanst. 402, 414, 36 Eng. Rep. 670, 679 (Ch. 1818) (Different Chancellors' consciences might vary with the length of their feet!).

124. RESTATEMENT (SECOND) OF CONTRACTS sect. 208 (1981). *See* Sinkoff Beverage Co. v. J. Schlitz Brewing Co., 51 Misc. 2d 446, 273 N.Y.S. 2d 364 (1966) (applied to franchise termination procedure). Unconscionability was not included in Restatement First.

125. Jones v. Star Credit Corp., 59 Misc. 2d 189, 298 N.Y.S. 2d 264 (1969); RESTATEMENT (SECOND) OF CONTRACTS sect. 208, Comment (c) (1981); *see* U.C.C. sect. 2–302, Comment 1 (For "prevention of oppression . . . and not disturbance of allocation of risks because of superior bargaining power.").

126. Winterbottom v. Wright, 10 M. & W. 109, 152 Eng. Rep. 402 (Exch. 1842).

127. Langridge v. Levy, 2 M. & W. 519, 150 Eng. Rep. 863 (1837); Boulton v. Jones, 2 H. & N. 564, 157 Eng. Rep. 232 (1857); Boston Ice Co. v. Potter, 123 Mass. 28 (1877).

128. Mazetti v. Armour & Co., 75 Wash. 622, 135 P. 633 (1913); Jackson Coca Cola Bottling Co. v. Chapman, 106 Miss. 864, 64 So. 791 (1914); Parks v. C.C. Yost Pie Co., 93 Kans. 334, 144 P. 202 (1914). Express warranty hadn't been needed for the sale of food since the 15th century.

129. MacPherson v. Buick Motor Co., 217 N.Y. 382, 111 N.E. 1050 (1916).

130. *See* Kessler, *Products Liability,* 76 YALE L. J. 887, 900 (1967); *see also* J. BAKER, *supra* note 40, at 293–295.

131. Henningsen v. Bloomfield Motors, Inc., 32 N.J. 358, 161 A. 2d 69 (1960). This approach was adopted by U.C.C. 2–318 Alternatives A and B.

132. *See* Kessler, *supra* note 12, at 630 (Lessening of privity showed awareness

of growing impersonality of market and of social functions of contract.); *see also* Kessler, *supra* note 130, at 898–899. The recognition of implied warranty of quality was a harbinger of strict liability in tort.

133. Worley v. Procter & Gamble Mfg. Co., 241 Mo. App. 1114, 253 S.W. 2d 532 (1952); Kruper v. Procter & Gamble Co., 113 N.E. 2d 605 (Ohio App. 1953); Graham v. Bottenfield's, Inc., 176 Kans. 68, 269 P. 2d 413 (1954); Spence v. Three Rivers Bldg. & Mason. Supp., Inc., 353 Mich. 120, 90 N.W. 2d 873 (1958).

134. Greenman v. Yuba Power Products, Inc., 59 Cal. 2d 57, 377 P. 2d 897 (1963) (Manufacturer raised technical notice requirement under warranty rules.).

135. *See* RESTATEMENT (SECOND) OF TORTS sect. 402A (Liability may not be disclaimed per Comment m.).

136. *See* Kessler, *supra* note 130, at 925. Strict liability marked a further erosion of both *caveat emptor* and sanctity of contract's allocation of risks between buyers and sellers. There is a protection of consumers' expectations of and reliance on merchants providing safe products.

137. Llewellyn, *Some Realism About Realism—Responding to Dean Pound,* 44 HARV. L. REV. 1222 (1931); *see* 3A A. CORBIN, *supra* note 29, at sect. 624 (emphasized analysis of "operative facts"). *See* Simpson, *Contract: The Twitching Corpse,* 1 OXFORD J. LEG. STUD. 265, 270 (1981) (Iconoclastic attack on legal science of legal realism did not occur in England.).

138. Kennedy, *Form and Substance in Private Law Adjudication,* 89 HARV. L. REV. 1685 (1976); Unger, *The Critical Legal Studies Movement,* 96 HARV. L. REV. 561 (1983). Some are post-modernists rather than neo-Marxists.

139. A. KRONMAN and R. POSNER, THE ECONOMICS OF CONTRACT LAW (Boston: 1979); R. POSNER, ECONOMIC ANALYSIS OF LAW 79–126 (3d ed. Boston: 1986).

140. Kessler, *supra* note 12, at 636; L. FRIEDMAN, *supra* note 9, at 107, 122–124, 191–204; *see* M. WEBER, *supra* note 10, at 315–321. *See* RESTATEMENT OF CONTRACTS sect. 512 (1932) (Bargain is illegal if opposed to public policy.). A tradition-bound judge finds it difficult to obtain a just result with an implied term if there is a clear express term to the contrary, no matter how unjust.

141. L. FRIEDMAN, *supra* note 9, at 23–25. On the basis of Friedman's narrow reading of contract law as "pure" classical doctrine, his book would not support the broader view of modern contract law taken in this section.

142. Traynor, *Reasoning in a Circle of Law,* 56 VA. L. REV. 739, 749 (1970); *see* 6A A. CORBIN, *supra* note 29, at sect. 1375, n.9 ("Public policy is an unruly horse" but "it is not possible for courts to refuse to ride him.").

143. Isaacs, *supra* note 8, at 34–40, 47; M. WEBER, *supra* note 10, at 147 (2 kinds of contract rules apply: those valid in the group and those individually created.); Kessler, *supra* note 12, at 640–641; Rehbinder, *supra* note 32, at 946–952; 1 F. POLLOCK and F. MAITLAND, THE HISTORY OF ENGLISH LAW (BEFORE THE TIME OF EDWARD I) 230–231 (Cambridge: 2d ed. 1898).

144. Kessler, *supra* note 12, at 636 (Is unity possible with increasing use of contracts of adhesion?).

145. Summers, *supra* note 19, at 527–528, 536–537, 567–568 (Modern contracts have common problems of choosing between: subjective/objective tests, arms length/fiduciary and freedom of contract/social control.).

146. 1 A. CORBIN, *supra* note 29, at sect. 3.

147. *The Statute of Frauds and the Business Community: A Re-appraisal in Light of Prevailing Practices,* 66 YALE L. J. 1038 (1957) (Survey of 92 manufacturers showed Statute often ignored.); Macaulay, *Non-Contractual Relations in Business: A Preliminary Study,* 28 AM. SOC. REV. 55 (1963) (Interviews with 68 businessmen showed cancellations often settled for only expenses without reference to contract.); *see* M. WEBER, *supra* note 10, at 307; *cf.* P. ATIYAH, *supra* note 12, at 713–715.

148. Summers, *supra* note 19, at 547, 551, 555, 562–566.

149. Both the U.C.C. and the Restatement Second allow parties to otherwise provide. *See generally* Braucher, *Freedom of Contract and the Second Restatement,* 78 YALE L. J. 598 (1969). Disclosure statutes and other statutes concerned about contract procedure rarely mandate terms.

150. Speidel, *supra* note 41, at 1176–1183 (Jurisprudential issue of the day is whether consent or new forms of civil liability should control.); Gilmore, *supra* note 15, at 476–477.

INDEX OF CASES AND STATUTES

Anonymous Cases Cited Chronologically

Statutes Cited Chronologically

SUBJECT INDEX

About the Author

KEVIN M. TEEVEN is a Professor at Bradley University in Peoria, Illinois, and J.D. (University of Illinois, 1971). He formerly practiced law in Illinois and has published articles on development of common law contract in *Osgoode Hall Journal, Cambrian Law Review, Adelaide Law Review, Commercial Law Journal*, and other journals.

Lightning Source UK Ltd.
Milton Keynes UK
UKHW041446110521
383515UK00001B/2

9 780313 261510